NETWORKING WINDOWS NT™

John D. Ruley
David Dix
David W. Methvin
Martin Heller
Arthur H. Germain III
James E. Powell
Jeffrey Sloman
Eric Hall

John Wiley & Sons, Inc.

New York • Chichester • Brisbane • Toronto • Singapore

Publisher: Katherine Schowalter
Editor: Diane Cerra
Managing Editor: Elizabeth Austin
Composition: Kevin Shafer & Associates

This text is printed on acid-free paper.

Library of Congress Cataloging-in-Publication Data:

Networking Windows NT/John D. Ruley . . . (et al.).
p. cm.
Includes bibliographical references and index.
ISBN 0-471-31072-7 (paper: acid-free paper)
1. Operating systems (Computers). 2. Windows NT. 3. Computer networks.
QA76.76.063N473 1994
005.4'469--dc20 93-33267
CIP

Printed in the United States of America
10 9 8 7 6 5 4 3 2 1

Dedication

This book is dedicated to our fathers:

David D. Dix
Arthur H. Germain, Jr.
William T. Hall
Aaron Heller
Arthur G. Methvin
Charles B. Powell
Arnold Sloman

-and-

MSgt Joseph A. Ruley, USAF (deceased)—who would have particularly appreciated Chapter 5.

About the Authors

David Dix, formerly senior editor at *WINDOWS Magazine*, and now editor of *Marketing Computers* magazine, is the co-originator of the idea for this book. Dave provided valuable assistance to the overall organization and editing of the manuscript, and wrote Appendix 4. Dave changed jobs while this book was being prepared, yet managed short-turnaround copy-edits whenever he was asked.

Arthur H. Germain III is technical director at *WINDOWS Magazine*. Arthur's broad experience in small-, medium-, and large-scale network systems design and management made him invaluable in creating Chapters 2 and 3, and his advice was useful for the book as a whole. While working on this book, Arthur completely redid *WINDOWS Magazine*'s production network (among other things installing a Windows NT Advanced Server for testing), while buying and rebuilding a new house with his wife Patty.

Eric Hall is labs director for *Network Computing* magazine. There's very little about networks that Eric doesn't know in detail. If you want to know the specifics of how a particular driver architecture works, Eric can tell you at length, as he does in Appendix 2 and in parts of Chapters 6 and 7. Eric moved from New York to California just as his appendices were going to press, and we wondered for a while if we'd ever hear from him again. . .

Dr. Martin Heller is the author of several best-selling books on Windows programming and writes the "Programming Windows" column for *WINDOWS Magazine*. Martin is an expert on Windows programming—he knows at least as much as Microsoft does on the subject (and on more than one occasion has, in fact, identified problems for them). Martin took sole responsibility for Appendix 1, which tells programmers all they need to know to write network-aware Windows NT programs. Dr. Heller delivered two other babies almost simultaneously with this book—*Advanced Windows NT Programming*, also from John Wiley, and Eden Francesca of Martin Heller & Co.

David Methvin is the senior technical editor at *WINDOWS Magazine*. Dave's been an editor at *PC Tech Journal* and at *PC Week*, and has installed several large networks as a consultant. He wrote Chapter 10 and Appendix 3, and co-wrote Chapter 8. Dave moved while this book was being written, yet managed to turn around technical edits in jig time.

James E. Powell is Northwest Bureau Editor for *WINDOWS Magazine*. He is "our man in Seattle" and his beat is Microsoft. Jim had just come off writing an introductory book on Windows NT (*Windows NT Instant Reference*, Sybex Books, 1993) and was instrumental both in the initial organization of this book, and in the creation of Chapters 2, 3, and 4. Jim actually turned in the last of his material on his way to the hospital for an emergency operation. We're all glad to see him back in good shape for the book's debut!

Jeffrey Sloman is the Networking Windows columnist for *WINDOWS Magazine* and author of *The CD-ROM Book* (Que, 1993). Jeff co-wrote Chapter 6 and advised on Chapter 9. Jeff designed the network that Arthur installed at *WINDOWS Magazine* as this book was being written.

John D. Ruley is editor-at-large and *eNTerprise Windows* columnist at *WINDOWS Magazine*. For the last year and a half his beat has been Windows NT, OS/2, and other Windows-related advanced technologies. John is principal author of *Networking Windows NT*—which, among other things, means that he's ultimately responsible for the technical accuracy of this book, and assumes the blame for any and all errors, omissions and goof-ups. John's fiancee (Dr. Kate Bolton) moved to New York shortly before this project began—just in time to find him disappearing into the labs for days at a stretch. She has shown remarkable forbearance, and (amazingly) they're still speaking.

Contents

Foreword

Today's network professionals deal with change every working day. Corporate mainframe applications of the seventies are being *downsized* to local area network (LAN)-based client/server application suites, while departmental single-user PC applications of the eighties are *upsized* into multi-user on-line solutions. As a result, the simple local area networks of yesterday are rapidly becoming business-critical, enterprise-wide, *electronic highways*. Can this rapid evolution in information systems technology succeed? Can the distributed client/server networks of today provide the same level of reliability that yesterday's centralized mainframe systems delivered? Ultimately, will this next generation of computing systems improve our own personal productivity—and thus make a *real* contribution to your company's bottom line?

Microsoft clearly feels that the answer to all three of these questions is *yes*—and with the release of their most complex operating system to date, Windows NT, they've bet their corporate future on delivering this promise. For you and me, as networking professionals, this means we will soon be asked (or in my case, have already been asked) to take the client/server *promises* of Windows NT and create a business *reality*. That's no small challenge, considering the complexity of today's enterprise networks and the mission-critical, moment-by-moment role they play in today's corporate world.

Are you nervous? Take heart: In *Networking Windows NT* you will find something no business-critical network of today can afford to be without, a business-critical *attitude*. It's an attitude that comes from years of experience in dealing with the day-to-day issues involved in the support of business-critical information systems. With the publication of this book, John Ruley and his associates at *WINDOWS Magazine* and *Network Computing* have done something I find unique: They've truly understood what George Santayana meant in 1905, when he wrote:

[1] *Life of Reason*, Volume 1, Chapter 10.

> "Progress, far from consisting in change, depends on retentiveness... Those who cannot remember the past are condemned to repeat it."[1]

This is not just another book describing the marvels contained within the first operating system that doesn't treat the network as an add-on. *Networking Windows NT* shows you how to not only make it work but *keep it working*, day-in, day-out, and month-after-month. The book covers the full spectrum of what you need to know—and do—as we move from the host-centric world of raw data to the information-centric world of distributed objects.

Networking Windows NT takes you step-by-step from simple NT-based LANs all the way to optimized enterprise-wide electronic networks that communicate with everyone and everything. First it covers the fundamentals of an operating system designed around the client/server model (Chapter 1, "An Operating System Designed to Connect"), then what you will need to do today (Chapter 2, "Preparing to Connect"), what you will need to do tomorrow (Chapter 3, "Administrative Connections"), and what you will need to do to link your back-end, the server, to your front-end, your clients (Chapter 4, "Using NT Networking Features").

Now the fun really begins; keeping your Windows NT network running so smoothly and flawlessly that you'll reach that loftiest goal of any networking professional, managing the network *invisibly*. Chapter 5 ("Keeping Connected") along with its associated appendix (Appendix 6: "Maintenance Theory") were my two favorite sections. Within this chapter and appendix you will learn how to *proactively* put the sophisticated administrative tools included with Windows NT to work—not only keeping your network at its peak of performance but also ensuring that you get *mission-critical* reliability. I've used this information myself at Chevron Canada's data center—and I can assure you the advice given is *well* worthwhile.

The hard lessons learned during the days of the mainframes and minicomputers are retold in the context of Windows NT. The advice is fundamental and pragmatic, something one would expect when learning about troubleshooting computer systems. Appendix 6 also explains *precisely* why following a program of preventative maintenance is so important. Yet, like the rest of the book, it has been written with a humorous style that delivers a refreshing feeling of confidence and long-term optimism. It's obvious that the authors really enjoy what they're writing about, and you will find this grain of enthusiasm throughout the book. Where else would you find the Configuration Registry included with Windows NT compared to a nuclear reactor?

As your Windows NT Advanced Server network grows it will expand beyond the comfortable confines of your data center. In Chapter 7 ("Enterprise Connections") you'll find information on file replication, Wide Area Networking and remote network access. No doubt you will also start bumping into different operating environments such as the world of UNIX (Chapter 6, "UNIX Connections"), other network operating systems such as NetWare (Chapter 9, "Novell Connections"), and a veritable host of hosts, the legacy systems (Chapter 10, "Other Connections").

Finally, what about the future (Chapter 11, "Connecting to the Future")? Some feel we are about to enter the true second generation of information systems—an electronic environment that creates a fully distributed world of objects and (as a result) blurs the lines between information and the systems that process it. An environment that delivers something more than just raw data or static information, tommorow's distributed systems will deliver real-time *knowledge* to the new tenants at the top of the information systems model: you and me. The final chapter of *Networking Windows NT* examines the precursors of this next generation of operating systems, both already in alpha form, *Chicago* (Windows 4.0) and *Cairo* (Windows NT 4.0). As we approach the twenty-first century, what you and I do today as networking professionals will be a cornerstone of this technological revolution. *We* are the *invisible facilitators of change* in today's businesses—and I honestly believe that what we do today and tomorrow can make a valuable and essential contribution to the quality of life on this planet.

It's something worth doing well.

Doug Farmer,
Lead—Network Operations
Chevron Canada Ltd.
Vancouver, BC
November 1993

Preface

In the modern world an advanced PC or workstation is almost never used by itself. It's nearly always *connected* to a server, a mainframe host, or other workstations, so *connections* is the theme of this book. We examine Microsoft's Windows NT strategy in the largest sense, and the details of the Windows NT (and Windows NT Advanced Server) network implementation in the smallest sense. Along the way, we learn how to design a Windows NT local-area network (LAN), how to install it, how to maintain it, how to connect it to other LAN systems (including Novell NetWare), where it fits in an overall enterprisewide network strategy, how to implement client/server systems with it, and we explore where the future may lead.

We examine the low-level details of how connections are made, looking closely into the protocols used, as well as the device drivers, application programming interfaces (APIs), and other low-level mechanisms that make connections possible. We walk you step-by-step through the creation of connections both within Windows NT systems and from Windows NT to all different kinds of systems, management of those connections, and maintenance of the systems so that the connections can stay up. Then we cover advanced topics: wide-area networking (WANs), application services, electronic mail, details of the Windows NT Advanced Server, and all the other topics that exploit the connected operating system environment to create the modern, inextricably interconnected world in which we live.

How to Use This Book

Networking Windows NT is organized as eleven independent chapters and six appendices. We have attempted to make each chapter stand alone. You can feel free to browse through the book and pick an interesting topic, with confidence that it will be completely exposed in the chapter you are reading. You may find, if you start in the middle of the book, that you'll wish you'd read some of the earlier chapters first. But we will steer you in the right direction and you can always make use of the index and glossary, which we have attempted to make as comprehensive as possible.

While *Networking Windows NT* is organized for browsing, it's also possible to design a structured study program that may be useful in your particular situation. Here are some suggestions:

Readers unfamiliar with either Windows NT or networking should start at the beginning and read Chapters 1 through 4. Pick one of Chapters 6, 8, 9, and 10 as appropriate—if (like most people) you're going to work in an environment that has more than just Windows NT machines. For example, if you are in a NetWare environment, read Chapter 9.

If you are in a TCP/IP environment, read Chapter 6. Look through Appendices 3 and 4, and read Chapter 7. Once you've done that, you can look over the rest of the book for any special topic that interests you.

If you are familiar with Windows NT, but not with networks, then skim Chapter 1, skip to Chapter 3, and read Appendix 4. Again, pick from Chapters 6, 8, 9, and 10 as appropriate (but definitely read Chapters 6 and 7 if you're going to work in an enterprise environment). Finally, read Chapter 11, and any of the appendix material that appears to be useful.

If you're a support professional, you'll want to read the whole book—with special emphasis on Chapters 2 and 5.

If you are familiar with networks in a NetWare or TCP/IP environment, but not familiar with Windows NT, then read Chapters 1 through 4 and 7, Appendix 3, and pick from Chapters 6, 8, 9, and 10 as appropriate. Read or skim Chapter 11.

Programmers should read Chapters 1 and 11, then Appendix 1, and refer back to appropriate chapters when you run into a concept that doesn't seem to make sense. Just go to the index, look up the first definition, turn to that page and read all about it.

Management Information Systems people and decision makers—those trying to decide where Windows NT fits into a heterogeneous network environment—should read Chapters 1 through 3, 6, 7, and then pick from 8, 9 and 10 to match the particular system you have (you may need to read them all if you run a complex network). Then read Chapter 11 and Appendix 5. That's a pretty comprehensive set, so if you're in a hurry, a short form that may be useful is to read Chapters 1, 3, 7, and 11—referring to other information if you find it necessary.

How *Networking Windows NT* Is Organized

Direct your attention particularly to the "After reading this chapter you should understand..." section at the head of each chapter. We've included this specifically to help you decide, first of all, whether a particular chapter is interesting enough to invest your time reading, and to help you get the most out of the chapter. We encourage you to read the statement, read the chapter, go back and read the statement again, and as you go through the bullet-points, if you see something that you don't remember or don't understand, you'll probably want to look through that part of the chapter again.

We've also included a "For More Information" section at the end of each chapter, with reference materials—magazine articles, books, whatever. If you find that a particular topic has not been sufficiently covered to meet your needs, take a look through the list at the end of the chapter and see if one of the other references covers the material you're looking for. We've included a comprehensive index and we encourage you to use it.

Finally, we hope you will want to try things out for yourself! By that we mean to *apply* what you've learned in a *real* environment. We realize that many people are likely to read this book for information without having access to a Windows NT system—that's fine. It's our fondest hope that the book will be helpful to people in exactly that situation who need to make decisions about what equipment to purchase, what version of the system to purchase, or indeed whether Windows NT fits their situation at all.

But we've also designed this book to be a useful reference to people who are doing real-world work on Windows NT networks. If you fit that description, then we cannot emphasize enough that aside from all the fine writing we can do, all the graphs and charts we can provide you, all the further reading we can recommend to you; nothing can compare with the learning reinforcement that comes by actually getting your hands dirty and trying things out for yourself. Many people are uncomfortable experimenting with networked computers (especially servers). That's unfortunate because networked computers are not fundamentally much more difficult to deal with than individual PCs. If you're expecting to maintain a Windows NT system and to fix it when something goes wrong, you'd better get some experience manipulating it when it is working correctly!

The Chapters

Networking Windows NT is organized as a set of more or less independent chapters, each of which attempts to cover a particular topic in some depth.

Chapter 1, "An Operating System Designed to Connect," is an overall introduction to Windows NT and to basic networking concepts. It includes a detailed discussion of the differences between Windows NT and Windows NT Advanced Server, as well as concepts like portability, scalability, virtual memory, and network redirection.

Chapter 2, "Preparing to Connect," covers installation and setup of Windows NT systems, including Windows NT Advanced Servers. It includes a discussion of how to conduct a *network needs analysis* for your organization, how to select the right hardware for your Windows NT system, and all four Windows NT installation mechanisms: diskette, CD-ROM, over-the-network, and computer profile install. Six pages of troubleshooting information guide you in solving problems as they arise.

Chapter 3, "Administrative Connections," examines Windows NT administration issues for LANs. It includes the duties of the *network administrator*, and the tools used for NT net administration (user manager, disk administrator, performance monitor, backup, event viewer, the NET command-line interface and batch files), covers user profiles and login scripts, and discusses in detail the differences between Windows NT *workgroups* and Windows NT Advanced Server *domains.*

Chapter 4, "Using NT Networking Features," covers the use of Windows NT's built-in networking features, including shared file access, shared printer access, shared clipboards, and use of the Windows NT network utilities. It also provides a complete introduction to the command-line NET interface that can be used to write batch files in Windows NT.

Chapter 5, "Keeping Connected," is one of *Networking Windows NT*'s strongest chapters. It provides detailed coverage on maintaining and troubleshooting Windows NT and Advanced Server systems—including use of Performance Monitor, Event Viewer and the

Configuration Registry Editor. Fourteen pages of troubleshooting information in this chapter are tinted for quick reference. There's also coverage of the undocumented support tools and message database supplied on CD-ROM versions of Windows NT.

Chapter 6, "Connecting to the World with TCP/IP," covers TCP/IP, UNIX networking, the Internet, and the use of TCP/IP as a routable protocol for Windows NT on internetworks and WANs. It's an essential precursor to Chapter 7. Windows NT's built-in TCP/IP utilities and TCP/IP routing capability are also discussed in detail.

Chapter 7, "Enterprise Connections," examines enterprisewide network issues, including Windows NT Advanced Server domain administration, wide-area networking (including both Microsoft's *Remote Access Services* and third-party alternatives), electronic mail (including detailed instructions for upgrading the *workgroup-level* version of MS-Mail bundled with Windows NT for multi-postoffice connectivity), WANs, and Macintosh support.

Chapter 8, "Microsoft Connections," covers interoperability with LAN Manager, Windows for Workgroups, and other networks based on the Server Message Block (SMB) protocol used by Microsoft. Detailed instructions are included for upgrading LAN Manager networks to Window NT Advanced Server, as are instructions on interoperating in mixed LAN Manager/NT/Windows for Workgroups environments.

Chapter 9, "Novell Connections," covers interoperation with Novell NetWare, including Novell's NetWare Client for Windows NT, Microsoft's NWLink protocol and NetWare-compatible Client Workstation Service (NWCS), Beame and Whiteside's Multiconnect IPX—and the "back door" NFS/FTP method of NetWare access pioneered at *WINDOWS Magazine*. This chapter shows you how to connect Windows NT systems as both *clients* and *servers* in NetWare LANs.

Chapter 10, "Other Connections," looks into using Windows NT with other networks—including IBM LAN Server and Systems Network Architecture (SNA) mainframe networks, DEC Pathworks, and Banyan VINES.

Chapter 11, "Client/Server, Distributed Computing, and the Future of Windows NT," discusses client/server issues, including the use of Windows NT as a *network application server*—using Microsoft's SQL Server database for Windows NT as an example—as well as the distributed future of network computing and how Windows NT (and its follow-on version, codenamed *Cairo*) fits into it.

Appendices

Appendix 1 is a short, succinct and yet (we devoutly hope) complete introduction to the network application programming interfaces (APIs) of Windows NT. Of course, programmers cannot expect to get all the information they need from one chapter and this appendix should be used in conjunction with a good book on Windows NT programming, such as *Advanced 32-Bit Windows Programming*, by Martin Heller (Wiley, 1993). However, we hope that this appendix, used in conjunction with the rest of this book, will serve as a good introduction and give programmers some idea of where to begin.

Appendix 2 looks at drivers, low-level protocols, and other definitional issues that cause a great deal of confusion, even among those experienced with networking.

Appendix 3 covers compatibility issues. Windows NT is capable of running the Win32 programs designed for it. But it also provides compatibility with Windows 3.0 and 3.1 programs, OS/2 1.x programs, and many DOS and POSIX programs. This appendix discusses compatibility for each of these systems, outlines what will and will not work, and specifically in the case of DOS programs, explains how you can make adjustments to the systems so your programs *will* work.

Appendix 4 covers the OSI seven-layer stack model that everyone in networking eventually learns to use. This is essential reading for anyone not already familiar with the OSI model, and it won't hurt to skim and review this material periodically if you are familiar with the model.

Appendix 5, on exotic hardware, looks into the new classes of systems on which Windows NT runs. Uniquely among modern desktop operating systems Windows NT was designed to be platform independent and it is capable of exploiting very radically different processor designs. We discuss the DEC Alpha RISC CPU, the MIPS R4000/R4400 CPU and machines constructed using symmetric multiprocessor (SMP) architectures.

Appendix 6 covers the theory behind preventative maintenance, which is the foundation for the maintenance and troubleshooting information we provide in Chapter 5.

Late-Breaking Developments

Writing a book on such a broad and rapidly changing topic turned out to be a real challenge. Chapter 9, "Novell Connections," on NetWare, was rewritten six times—every time we thought we had the whole story, either Microsoft or Novell would present us with a new version requiring at least some modification of the manuscript. In fact, this is happening as we write: Novell has just refreshed their requester, and in the process invalidated at least part of what we've written: Now there *are* NetWare requesters from Novell for the MIPS and DEC Alpha versions of Windows NT.

In Chapter 7, we discuss the capabilities and limits of Windows NT's built-in wide-area networking system, Remote Access Services (RAS). Among other things, we wind up saying that you'll need a separate hardware router in order to bridge LANs together. Well, that turns out to be *partly* true—as we go to press, an agreement between Microsoft and Cisco systems has been reached that means you'll probably be able to buy a complete router *on a single accessory card* for Windows NT not long after this book goes to print.

In Chapter 11, we speculate about the next major revision of Windows NT—Windows NT 4.0, codenamed *Cairo*—and we go so far as to show a notional view of a Cairo desktop. By the time this book is printed, you may be able to get more than just a "notional" view—Microsoft's second 32-bit Windows development conference, scheduled to be held in mid-December 1993, will definitely see the release of a Windows 4.0 (codename *Chicago)* beta development kit, and is likely to be the place where Microsoft will start taking the wraps off Cairo as well.

But the biggest whopper of all has to be the Windows NT Resource Kit.

Windows NT Resource Kit

Throughout this book, in the "For More Information" section at the end of each chapter, we've referred to prerelease versions of the Windows NT Resource Kit. As we finished our last chapter, the full final Resource Kit arrived in print—an extremely frustrating situation for us. The Resource Kit contains a three-volume set of books, a CD, and several diskettes (which duplicate the information on the CD), at a list price of $109. That may seem high—it isn't. The programs and other information on the CD *alone* are easily worth the price. They include: Helpfiles that completely document all variables set using the configuration registry editor (REGENTRY.HLP), give technical specs of all NT-compatible network cards (NTCARD.HLP), list all Windows NT-compatible hardware (JUL93HCL.HLP), and help troubleshoot systems (TROUBLE.HLP); a graphical interface for the *at* command-line function (WINAT.EXE) that lists all scheduled batch jobs, a graphical monitor for domain servers (DOMMON.EXE), and a graphical monitor of domain browser activity (BROWMON.EXE); the Server Manager for Domains, User Manager for Domains, and User Profile Editor tools from Windows NT Advanced Server—along with administrative tools for use with Services for Macintosh in Advanced Server environments; a complete suite of POSIX command-line utilities including ar, cat, cc, chmod, chown, cp, devsrv, find, grep, ld, ln, ls, make, mkdir, mv, rm, rmdir, sh, touch, vi, and wc; an editor for creating your own animated cursors, and many more utilities.

The nearest and dearest of the Resource Kit programs for us, though, are the Computer and Network Administrative Tools, which include a mechanism for getting user input in batch files (CHOICE.EXE), a tool for dumping event logs as text files (DUMPEL.EXE), a tool for disabling floppy disks in high-security environments (FLOPLOCK.EXE), an SNMP MIB compiler (MIBCC.EXE), tools for operating a network-based modem pool (NET2COM.EXE and WINVTP.EXE), a command-line interface to services (NTSVC.EXE), a per-user file permissions command-line utility (PERMS.EXE), and—something our principal author swore would never be written—a *secure* (relatively speaking) remote command-line for Windows NT (REMOTE.EXE).

In conjunction with the "unsupported" tools provided on the Windows NT installation CD (discussed in the *In Extremis* section of Chapter 5), the Resource Kit utilities make a very powerful bag of tricks for Windows NT system administrators. It's now possible, for instance, to set up a complete locked-closet server, and control it from a remote system using a combination of RAS, the Advanced Server tools, and REMOTE.EXE (the latter is *very* important—there are some tasks that can't be done any other way from a remote station). Similarly, the powerful scripting capability covered in Chapters 3 and 4 is significantly augmented by the Resource Kit and "unsupported" tools—among other things, we think that the skeleton script for converting a NetWare user database to a Windows NT user database in Chapter 3 is probably doable now, using a combination of the command-line registry tool (REGINI.EXE), and PERMS.EXE. Of course, you'd need a way to dump the user information from the NetWare bindery, but a variety of tools are available for that. (In a pinch, you could run NetWare's own SYSCON tool from a Windows NT system using Microsoft's NetWare Workstation-Compatible Services (NWCS)—covered in Chapter 9—and dump the information by hand; then write a fairly straightforward script to take that information and build a Windows NT user account base. Actually implementing this script is left as an exercise for the reader!

Companion CD-ROM

We are planning to produce a companion CD-ROM to *Networking Windows NT*, but the details haven't been finalized as we go to press. Some of the features we've discussed include:

- Full Text of Networking Windows NT converted to a fully-searchable Windows Help format.
- Additional material, including example scripts and utility programs.
- Network-aware installation (install the CD on a server and access it from any station on the net).
- Possibly some multimedia surprises!

Price and availability are not set as we go to press, but you can get further information by contacting the product manager:

Robert Ipsen
John Wiley & Sons
605 Third Avenue
New York, NY 10158

email: bipsen@jwiley.com
fax: (212) 850-6088, attention: Bob Ipsen

Bob will be happy to hear from you.

Acknowledgments

Any project of this magnitude involves the assistance of many people—and this is no exception. We hope that those who don't find their names here won't be offended too much—there were so many that it's hard to remember them all. But some we managed not to forget include: Mike Abrash, Sheila Ambrose, Kate Bolton, M.D., Jean Goddin, Doug Hamilton, Dave Hart, Lee Hart, Johnny Haskins, Erin Holland, Tom Johnston, Liz Misch, Mike Nash, Carole Parrot-Joppe, Ruth Rizzuto, Blanche M. Ruley, Linda Stephenson and David Thacher.

Special thanks go to Fred Langa, editorial director, and Jake Kirchner, executive editor of *WINDOWS Magazine*, who made the *WINDOWS* lab available for us to use while working on this book; and to Scott Wolf, *WINDOWS Magazine*'s publisher, who gave us permission to reproduce original artwork from *WINDOWS* without charge.

Many thanks also to Diane Cerra, our harried-yet-patient (and always encouraging!) editor at John Wiley, and to Tammy Boyd, her ever-helpful assistant, and to Elizabeth Austin, also at Wiley, who managed the book's production. Very special thanks to Kevin Shafer and his team, who did the actual book production and layout work.

We all want to thank our families for putting up with the time we spent bringing this project together—lots of late nights in the lab instead of at home.

Finally, of course, we want to acknowledge Dave Cutler and the entire Windows NT development team, who gave us so much to write about!

1

An Operating System Designed to Connect

After reading this chapter, you should understand the basic features of Windows NT—especially those related to networking. You should also understand basic concepts to be used in the rest of the book, including: microkernel architecture, portability, object model, layered device drivers, installable file systems, networks, and network redirectors. Finally, you should understand the differences between the basic Windows NT product, which is suitable for use as a network client or standalone peer server, and the Windows NT Advanced Server, which is better suited for server use.

Windows NT is uniquely well suited to a wide variety of networking applications. To understand why this is so we must examine a number of features of the basic operating system design. The first and most pervasive of these is Windows NT's microkernel architecture.

Scalability and the Microkernel Architecture

Windows NT is designed to be scalable. It overcomes the inherent limitations of conventional PC operating systems as network servers. Although you can extend the capacity of a conventional PC network server by buying bigger hard disk drives, faster network cards, and more expensive network cabling, at some point the growing number of users will overtax a network driven by a single PC—the system will slow down, and users will complain about slow network access. This happens because conventional PCs running operating systems like DOS or Novell NetWare are only capable of utilizing a single central processing unit (CPU). Windows NT overcomes this limitation through *scalability:* if one CPU isn't enough, then several can be

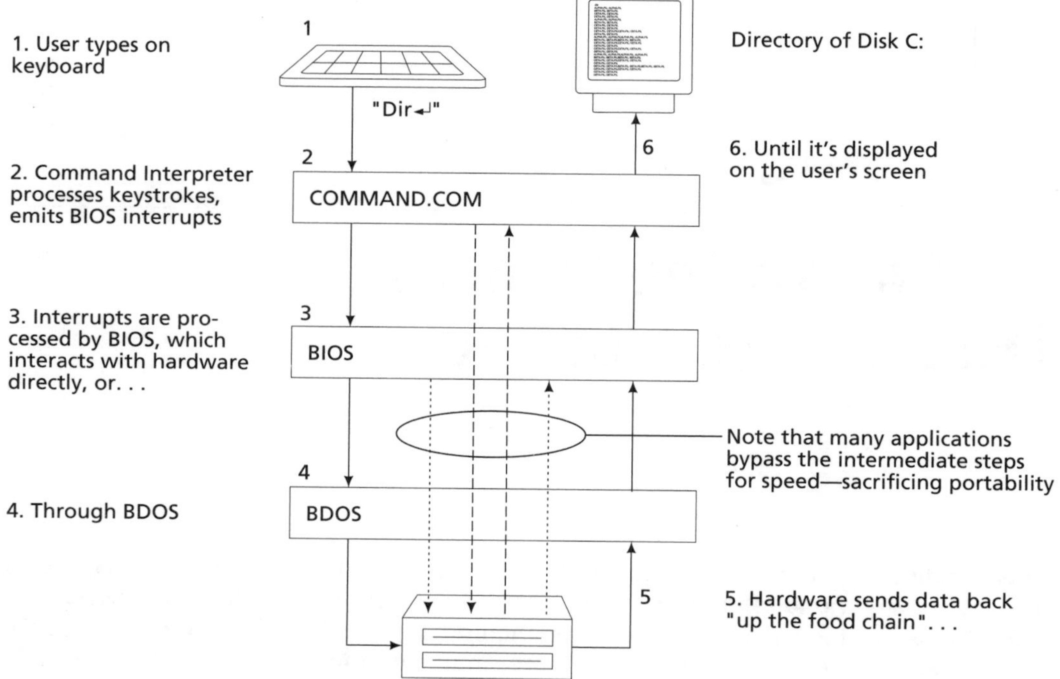
1. User types on keyboard
1
"Dir↵"
Directory of Disk C:
2. Command Interpreter processes keystrokes, emits BIOS interrupts
2
COMMAND.COM
6
6. Until it's displayed on the user's screen
3. Interrupts are processed by BIOS, which interacts with hardware directly, or. . .
3
BIOS
Note that many applications bypass the intermediate steps for speed—sacrificing portability
4
4. Through BDOS
BDOS
5
5. Hardware sends data back "up the food chain". . .

Figure 1.1 Classical OS operation.

Conventional operating system (DOS, NetWare) operation—both applications and operating system components interact directly with low-level device drivers and the hardware, limiting portability and security.

employed in a *symmetric multiprocessor* (SMP) system. Windows NT's *microkernel architecture* is a critical element in this scalability.

All operating systems have a *kernel*—it's the minimum set of functions that must be kept in memory. In the DOS operating system, the kernel consists largely of the basic input/output system (BIOS), the basic disk operating system (BDOS), and a number of essential glue functions that bring these pieces together. The other parts of DOS, which are not always needed, are stored on disk and loaded into memory only when required. As illustrated in Figure 1.1, when you type DIR on a DOS machine you're actually employing an external component: the COMMAND.COM file typically found in the root of the C: drive. COMMAND.COM provides DOS with its user interface. It monitors the keyboard, looking for certain combinations of characters—of which DIR is one—interprets this as a request for a directory, and issues the necessary BIOS commands to retrieve the directory information. Another set of BIOS commands are then called to display the directory on screen. The BIOS calls for retrieving the directory information, in turn, access the equivalent BDOS functions to access the disk drives and retrieve that information from the disk. Since both BIOS and BDOS functions are used by almost all DOS programs, they are kept resident in memory—and thus are part of the DOS kernel.

In Windows NT neither the equivalent of the BIOS (the Hardware Abstraction Layer or HAL), nor the equivalent of the BDOS (one of the many installable file systems), is a part of the kernel. The kernel in Windows NT is, for various reasons, designed to be as small as possible. It functions much as a traffic light does, directing the flow of information.

When you type DIR on an NT system, your keystrokes are intercepted by CMD.EXE, which provides a text-based user interface, monitors the keystrokes, and determines what you've typed. CMD.EXE interfaces to a layer analogous to the BIOS layer, in this case, a subsection of the Win32 Application Programming Interface (API). However, it does not talk to that interface directly (as COMMAND.COM talks to the BIOS). No application program in Windows NT is ever permitted to talk directly to the HAL or to any device drivers—instead, all such interactions occur with the Windows NT kernel.

The kernel takes the requests issued by the applications program, validates those requests according to a security object model, and—if it finds the request valid—the kernel then issues those requests on the applications program's behalf. The requests may pass to a transitional layer such as some form of API. This may be implemented as a dynamic-link library, for example, so that it's only loaded into the system when it's required. The library will wish to issue commands in much the same way the BIOS issues commands to the BDOS in DOS—but, again, this is not permitted in Windows NT. Instead, requests are issued through the kernel and—if the kernel determines that those requests are reasonable—it issues those requests on the subsystem's behalf.

This mechanism is called a *client/server* approach: any subsystem that "services" other programs is a server, and any program requesting those services is a client. All Windows NT functions are handled through server processes. Servers can function as clients although they do not necessarily have to. All interactions between clients and servers are controlled by the kernel. In addition to providing the basics for the security approach that will be discussed later, this has one tremendous benefit: It makes it possible for Windows NT to employ a very small, tight "micro" kernel. The microkernel is so small that on a multiprocessor implementation, one copy is executed on *each* CPU. This provides Windows NT with truly *symmetric* multiprocessing (each CPU can handle tasks in exactly the same manner as any other processor).

Very few operating systems behave this way, the principal one being the Carnegie-Mellon *Mach* variant of the UNIX operating system. Virtually all other multiprocessor operating systems are asymmetric in some manner—each processor can do certain things but in general only one processor can execute the operating system kernel. By breaking down this barrier, Windows NT provides tremendous flexibility and scalability. Up to *thirty* processors may be employed in current versions of Windows NT, providing computing power that was, up to now, only available in mainframe-class systems. The implications for network servers are revolutionary: there is, for all intents and purposes, no upper limit on the power of a Windows NT-based network server.

Of course, that statement is not strictly true. There is actually a very definite upper limit on the power of even an SMP-based NT server. That upper limit is dictated by a phenomenon

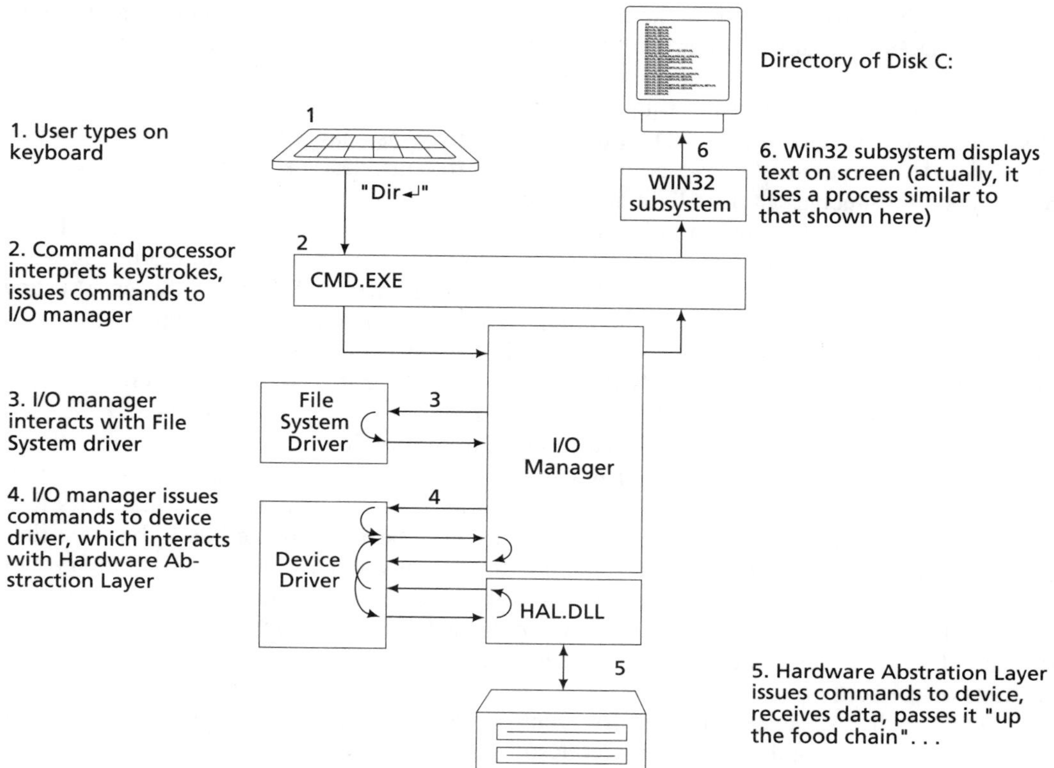
Directory of Disk C:
1. User types on keyboard
1
"Dir↵"
6
WIN32 subsystem
6. Win32 subsystem displays text on screen (actually, it uses a process similar to that shown here)
2. Command processor interprets keystrokes, issues commands to I/O manager
2
CMD.EXE
3. I/O manager interacts with File System driver
File System Driver
3
I/O Manager
4. I/O manager issues commands to device driver, which interacts with Hardware Abstraction Layer
4
Device Driver
HAL.DLL
5
5. Hardware Abstration Layer issues commands to device, receives data, passes it "up the food chain". . .

Figure 1.2 Microkernel operation.

Windows NT employs a *microkernel* architecture—applications cannot access low-level drivers or hardware services without the intervention of the operating system. Hardware dependencies are isolated in the drivers (and the Hardware Abstraction Layer), assuring portability. Security is provided when the application and operating system interact.

called contention, which is discussed in more detail in Appendix 5. Still, SMP in PC class machines significantly boosts the available power.

There is a price to pay for the scalability, security, and flexibility that the microkernel architecture confers. If you look back at our comparative descriptions of a DOS response to a DIR command and an NT response to a DIR command, you'll realize that in the DOS example there was only one call to the kernel. In DOS, when you type the command DIR, the characters are monitored by COMMAND.COM and a single call is issued to the DOS kernel's BIOS functions, which causes a number of events to happen—in the process of which the directory information is generated and presented. When you type DIR on a Windows NT system, NT requires *one kernel call for each interaction between subsystems*, as illustrated in Figure 1.2.

Every time that CMD.EXE makes a call to its API layer there must be a kernel operation mediating the interaction between CMD.EXE and the API layer. Similarly, when the API layer interacts with the HAL or with the file system, the kernel is involved. To simplify discussion of these processes, we will usually refer to the combination of the kernel and other low-level system programs as the *Executive*.

To save time and speed up common operations, the Windows NT kernel is designed to be as small as possible and to execute as quickly as possible—but there is some overhead involved. In practice, comparison testing at *WINDOWS Magazine* has indicated that the overhead is negligible. It may well be that the age and complexity of other operating systems makes them so inefficient that Windows NT's kernel competes well with them. But it's also possible that some competitor will build an operating system that provides an efficient interface between subsystems, thus bettering Windows NT's performance. Of course, one can simply execute Windows NT on an SMP system and try to make up the difference that way. But we digress. . . .

Portable Design

Windows NT provides a second major innovation: it's designed to be independent of any particular hardware. This breaks a tradition that began with IBM's introduction of the first IBM PC in 1981. Beginning with the PC, the world of desktop computing underwent a dramatic change. Prior to that time a variety of operating systems vendors had competed (along with a variety of hardware systems vendors). Many desktop computers were completely proprietary, combining a unique operating system with unique hardware—but a majority of pre-PC desktop computers used one implementation or another of the CP/M operating system. CP/M could be made to work efficiently on a variety of different computers by making changes to its BIOS layer (which described the behavior of the hardware to the operating system and vice versa). Programmers, instead of writing code for specific pieces of hardware, such as the disk controller, would execute BIOS functions that would access the disk controllers for them. The advantage of this approach was that it made programs *portable*—instead of writing a whole new word processor for each CP/M computer, the programmer could write just one CP/M-compatible program, and it would run on any of them. The only disadvantage was that BIOS-based programs tended to be slower than those optimized for a particular system.

The IBM PC killed this concept stone dead. Since the PC provided a standard hardware design, programmers could bypass BIOS and access the low-level hardware directly, gaining significantly in performance. Since the hardware was standardized, programs would still run on "PC-clones" from many vendors. In effect, by providing a uniform standard for the design of desktop hardware, IBM inadvertently created the world where commodity pricing would be introduced. Cloners soon came into play, and so it's possible today to buy IBM PC-compatible computers from almost anyone, except IBM.[1]

Windows NT attempts to reverse this history, by reverting to the concept of the CP/M BIOS. In Windows NT the equivalent to BIOS is the Hardware Abstraction Layer (HAL). To

[1]Well, PC compatibles; IBM stopped making those in the mid-1980s.

make Windows NT available on a particular architecture, the manufacturer must write a machine-specific HAL, provide a Microsoft-compatible C compiler, and then obtain the Windows NT sources from Microsoft and recompile them to the architecture. Most vendors will probably also try tuning the operating system specifically for their hardware. By writing parts of the NT kernel in a machine-specific language that best fits their specific architecture they can hope to achieve speed gains. The point is that it's relatively easy to make NT work on virtually *any* type of machine—no need to stay PC-compatible.

As this is written, Windows NT currently operates on at least four different CPU architectures: the Intel x86 architecture used by PC-compatibles, the MIPS R4x00 architecture, the DEC Alpha AXP architecture, and the Intergraph (formerly Fairchild) Clipper architecture. Before it became public, Windows NT also operated on the Intel *i*860 architecture (this was the first architecture on which the NT kernel became operational) and it's widely rumored that versions of Windows NT are being prepared for the IBM/Apple/Motorola Power-PC architecture, HP's PA-RISC architecture, and future versions of the Sun SPARC. It undoubtedly will be made available on more architectures over time.

Why So Many Architectures?

While the Intel x86 series microprocessors have been extraordinarily successful (their installed base exceeds 100,000,000 as this is written), they do not represent the upper limit of computer performance in the 1990s. There are performance limitations in the Intel designs because, like the PCs in which they execute, successive generations of Intel CPUs have been forced to carry forward design limitations in order to stay compatible with their predecessors. An entirely different kind of processor design, Reduced Instruction Set Computer (RISC), has for many years been popular in high-end UNIX workstations. However, while these workstations have been theoretically capable of much higher performance than their Intel counterparts, it has not generally been possible to run conventional DOS- and Windows-based applications programs on them.

Making Windows NT portable to RISC systems makes it possible to bring the richness and depth of applications support we have in the DOS and Windows world onto these advanced (some would say exotic) architectures. The implication of this to a computer user, and particularly to a network user, is that for the first time there is someplace to go when the current top-of-the-line Intel CPU isn't fast enough. In 1993 the latest, fastest Intel processor is the *Pentium* or P5 chip. In its current 60 MHz incarnation it's capable of achieving close to 120 million instructions per second of integer performance and is a very high performance processor by any standard. However, it's capable of only half the floating point performance of equivalent RISC CPUs from other manufacturers. If you were running a floating-point-intensive application like Computer Aided Design (CAD)/Computer Aided Engineering (CAE), there was, until now, no place else to go; the Pentium was the fastest Intel CPU, and changing to another CPU meant changing all of your software.

With Windows NT the game has fundamentally changed. If you are unsatisfied with the performance of a Pentium-based workstation for CAD work, you can carry it to any of the other architectures mentioned and possibly achieve substantially better performance.

From a networking point of view, the implication of making Windows NT portable to different architectures is astounding flexibility. NT runs on many different platforms, yet behaves nearly identically on all of them. It's possible for a Window NT network to consist of a symmetric multiprocessor functioning as a server and an arbitrary combination of single-processor (or even multiple-processor) workstation machines, some using Intel CPUs, and some RISC. You can put together the precise hardware required to do a particular job while providing a consistent user interface, uniform networking protocols, and generally identical behavior throughout the system.

Of course, all of this flexibility comes at a price—portability has three negative implications.

First, for any architecture other than Intel x86, there is a significant performance hit when executing 16-bit "legacy" applications—DOS and 16-bit Windows programs—which weren't developed specifically for that particular version of Windows NT. These applications weren't designed to run on RISC processors, and the steps NT must take to execute them involve a substantial execution overhead (see Appendix 5 for details).

The second great limitation of portability is the need to compile applications for the specific platform on which they will be executed. Applications written directly for Windows NT, generally using the 32-bit Windows (Win32) API, have to be compiled on the processor on which they will be executed. You cannot take an Intel version of a Windows NT application and expect to run it on a RISC platform, nor can you take a version of a Windows NT application developed on one RISC platform and run it on another.

Here's a specific example illustrating this second limitation: Intergraph Corporation is employing Windows NT as the operating system for its Clipper series of microcomputers used for Computer Aided Design and Computer Aided Engineering (CAD/CAE) applications. Intergraph has therefore compiled versions of their programs for both the Clipper and Intel CPUs. Intergraph has not, however, compiled versions for the MIPS R4000/4400 chips and has no announced plans regarding the IBM Power PC chip or the DEC Alpha chip. As we write this, then, it's possible to run Intergraph's application software on two of the currently supported Windows NT implementations but not on the other implementations. This can be a critical problem for network administrators faced with decisions about which specific hardware to acquire. The fact that Windows NT is portable does not necessarily mean that Windows NT *applications* are. Worse, this situation extends to some parts of the network services—for instance, a RISC-based print server with Intel clients must provide Intel-compatible printer drivers.

The final limitation of portability is similar to the limitation of the microkernel architecture defined earlier. There is an overhead associated with the fact that the Windows NT code is designed to be portable. The bulk of Windows NT is written in C—which makes it portable. Design a C compiler for a particular environment, design a HAL for that environment, recompile the Windows NT sources, and you have a version of Windows NT for the new environment. Unfortunately, C code is not optimized for a variety of performance-intensive tasks. As of this writing, tests indicate no related performance impact on Windows NT. Whether this shows that the tests are inadequate, or that Windows NT is better optimized than anyone had any right to expect, or that Windows NT's competitors are so poorly optimized that Windows NT doesn't come off badly by comparison is hard to say.

Object Model and the Security Subsystem

The subject of object-orientation, and the broader subject of objects generally, are among the most pervasive and controversial topics in modern computer science. The idea of object-orientation is to deal abstractly with data, code, and instructions as objects, without being concerned about whether the object referred to is a data file, text, a picture, a program, or whatever. The concept is not uniformly seen as effective. Windows NT does not claim to be an object-oriented operating system. It does, however, employ the concept of objects to a high degree in one subsystem—the security subsystem.

Security is an important point in Windows NT—Microsoft is positioning the security features of Windows NT as a major advantage in commercial applications such as banking. While there is undoubtedly some truth to this, it's also interesting to speculate. Helen Custer's excellent book, *Inside Windows NT*, makes it clear that the genesis of the concept that would lead to Windows NT began in 1988. This was at the very height of the Reagan/Bush defense buildup. Could it be that Windows NT is something of a Cold War operating system? It's certain Windows NT was designed with the needs of the United States government and the defense industry in mind, for Windows NT is unique among desktop operating systems in having been designed to be certifiable at the federal government's C2 and B security levels.[2]

To understand the implications of security requirements for an operating system, let's consider a hypothetical example. Suppose that you're an employee of the Central Intelligence Agency and are cleared for Top Secret information. You work with an employee who is cleared only for Secret information. As a Top Secret-cleared employee you have the clearance necessary to see any of the documents that are used by the Secret-cleared employee. The reverse, however, is not true. Suppose further that you have a need periodically to print documents. Clearly Top Secret documents cannot be printed on just any laser printer anywhere in the building. Your Top Secret documents can be printed only on a Top Secret paper laser printer (probably located behind armed guards, a vault door, and with whatever other security requirements the CIA may feel a need to enforce). The documents from the Secret-cleared employee can be printed on your Top Secret printer (although the Secret-cleared employee may have some difficulty getting past the armed guards and through the vault door to retrieve his documents). However, should you attempt to print a document on a printer "owned" by that Secret-cleared employee, whether or not your document prints will depend upon whether the document itself is cleared Secret or Top Secret.

If you're confused upon reading these last couple of sentences, I've made my point!

The issue of security is extremely complex. To provide a truly "secure" operating system, every file and every device in the system has to have an *owner*. There is a security access level (in this case Secret or Top Secret) associated with each of those files and devices. The designers of Windows NT were very aware of this requirement and they decided that this was the one place where objects made sense.

Windows NT provides an object-based security model. A security object can represent any resource in the system—files, devices, processes, programs, users; you name it and there

[2]See "Trusted Network Interpretation," a publication of National Computer Security Conference (NCSC), tel: (202) 783-3238.

is a security object associated with it. A security object carries information about what the object is permitted or not permitted to do. These permissions are carried forward with the security objects associated with system resources, and a more or less sophisticated sense of inheritance will determine what is and is not permitted to be done with any such resource. Server processes that provide secure access employ a technique called *impersonation:* the process takes on the security identifier (SID) of its client, and performs operations in the client's security context. All of this is transparent to both programmers and end-users, and (provided the security system is properly configured) interferes minimally with normal system operations.

The situation isn't really quite as complex as I've described because a computer security system designed to deal with Secret and Top Secret information would have to be certifiable to the government's B security level. Windows NT is not secured at that level (because it would be all but unusable to mere civilians). In such a system all resources are totally secured by default and it's necessary to take specific steps to apply permissions to them so that they can be used by the great unwashed.

Windows NT enforces a less restrictive standard called C2. C2 is not certifiable for the handling of Secret information. It's certifiable for the handling of Confidential information and it's well suited to banks and other facilities requiring a degree of security without making their systems virtually unusable as a side effect. The security system is theoretically capable of being upgraded to the B standard. Moreover, the security system is implemented as a privileged subsystem (a concept that we will examine shortly), and it can be replaced by another security system if desired. As this is written, Microsoft has begun to publicly discuss their intent to replace the entire security system with the Kerberos distributed security system (implemented by the Massachusetts Institute of Technology) in a future version[3] of Windows NT.

What Does Security Mean to Me?

The implications of NT security are most significant for file servers. Windows NT's provision of a relatively sophisticated security system, including the concept of file ownership and specific access permissions granted on a per-file or per-directory basis, makes it possible to completely isolate each user's files from other users of the system. This is clearly of vital importance in a high security environment and may be equally important to companies that carry privileged information on their networks. The corporate nightmare in the 1990s is to have its accounting files hacked by a sixteen-year-old with a modem who has recently seen the movie *War Games*. Should such a sixteen-year-old kid hack a Windows NT server, *assuming security has been properly set up*, his opportunity to do mischief will be significantly restricted. Whether the system is therefore hacker-proof is an open question (and a somewhat controversial one).

In principle, what one programmer can invent in a piece of software another can, if sufficiently determined, sabotage. No matter how sophisticated Windows NT security may be, any

[3]Code-named *Windows Cairo.*

Windows NT system that's physically accessible (a programmer can walk up to it, and access the keyboard, screen, and disk drive) is vulnerable. If you want your server to be protected, you must lock it up. It's also worth noting that the most sophisticated system of passwords, user accounts, and security access rights in the world is worthless if it's not used. If you create a Windows NT server and provide total access to all files for everyone in the system, then you're vulnerable—NT's sophisticated security system is meaningless because you have turned it off.

Windows NT systems also provide a powerful remote access service designed to make it possible to log into those systems remotely using a modem. While we are very impressed by Windows NT security systems, there is always a risk in connecting a system to a modem. The security procedures must be enacted with great rigor. They are vulnerable.

Finally, does the provision of such security have drawbacks? As with scalability and portability, the need for security objects to be checked as they are passed from subsystem to subsystem implies a certain amount of overhead in the system. The interesting point about this, however, is that such security capabilities have already been built into many kinds of software. When Microsoft translated its SQL Server database from OS/2 to Windows NT it was able to streamline a security layer that had been built into the OS/2 version, because the OS/2 operating system did not always provide built-in security. By exploiting the system security built into Windows NT (among other things), Microsoft achieved a significant performance increase in the SQL Server database. For many server-based applications, this kind of advantage in the security system may well offset overhead increases related to multiprocessor scalability and CPU portability. Whatever overheads are involved in the security system are clearly minimal.

Privileged Subsystems

The client/server design of the Windows NT microkernel architecture involves a certain amount of overhead. Whenever one process, such as an application program, communicates with another process, the kernel is involved. But there are components of the system that require higher operating performance than is possible in such an arrangement. There are also components of the system that require access to system resources not generally made available to applications programs. These subsystems are referred to as *privileged subsystems*. And they run with essentially the same privileges as built-in components of the Windows NT system. Privileged subsystems are important to us because one obvious place where the concept of a privileged subsystem applies is in the networking interface.

If Windows NT's client/server approach was carried to its limit in all components of the networking interface, one could quite reasonably expect that network performance in Windows NT would be poor by comparison with less protected operating systems. This, however, is not the case. Major components of the networking system are implemented as privileged subsystems communicating between and among themselves with privilege levels comparable with those used by the NT kernel itself.

There is another area where privileged subsystems are employed—and it's critical in understanding NT's place in the network world on desktops. That area is in providing "programmable personalities."

Traditionally, each operating system has had a clearly defined (and unique) user interface. For example, the CP/M operating system had a user interface characterized by a certain set of user commands and this was paralleled by an application programming interface containing certain possibilities. The DOS operating system includes a similar but more sophisticated user interface and a similar but more sophisticated programming interface. The OS/2 operating system has a still more sophisticated user interface (major components of which are implemented graphically) and a still more sophisticated application programming interface.

This proliferation of user and programming interfaces eventually tends to become an overwhelming burden for an operating system to carry. Operating systems such as OS/2 have had to make a terrible choice between carrying the overhead of compatibility to earlier systems (such as DOS)—or seeing their market-share sharply reduced. Windows NT, by contrast, exploits the concepts of privileged subsystems and the client/server architecture to provide completely replaceable personalities. In effect, Windows NT can take on the characteristics of 16-bit Windows, DOS, 32-bit Windows, OS/2, or POSIX. From the point of view of the programmer and from the point of view of an applications program, it is *exactly the same* as 16-bit Windows, DOS, 32-bit Windows, OS/2, or POSIX. To the user it does appear a bit different.

Standard User Interface

While there was early discussion of providing interchangeable user interfaces so that those familiar with OS/2 would see an OS/2 Presentation Manager interface while those familiar with Windows would see a Windows-like user interface, Microsoft has wisely decided to standardize on a user interface governed by the 32-bit Windows (Win32) subsystem. Applications programs functioning within any of the subsystems can share this user interface, as illustrated in Figure 1.3. This confers tremendous advantages upon Windows NT—for both end-users and system managers. It's not necessary to develop and acquire a completely new base of software when moving to a Windows NT system. "Well-behaved"[4] DOS, Windows, and OS/2 1.x applications will run correctly in the Windows NT environment. Well-behaved UNIX applications can be recompiled using NT's POSIX compatibility libraries and will become native POSIX applications in the Windows NT environment.

Let's look at an example. A company that has standardized on SQL Server as its corporate database, and where employees use the DOS version of WordPerfect along with Windows Excel to get work done, should be able to move to Windows NT without changing any of its software. SQL Server is an application that's implemented either on OS/2 or UNIX. The OS/2 version of SQL Server executes directly under Windows NT. Windows NT incorporates TCP/IP compatible (UNIX-style) networking so that if a UNIX-based SQL Server implementation is employed it can be left in place and Windows NT will use it.[5] On the other hand, if it's preferable to move directly to Windows NT, a native version of SQL Server for NT is available from Microsoft (see Chapter 11 for details).

---

[4]See Appendix 3 for a definition of "well-behaved" in this context.

[5]See Chapter 6 for details of Windows NT's UNIX-compatible TCP/IP networking features.

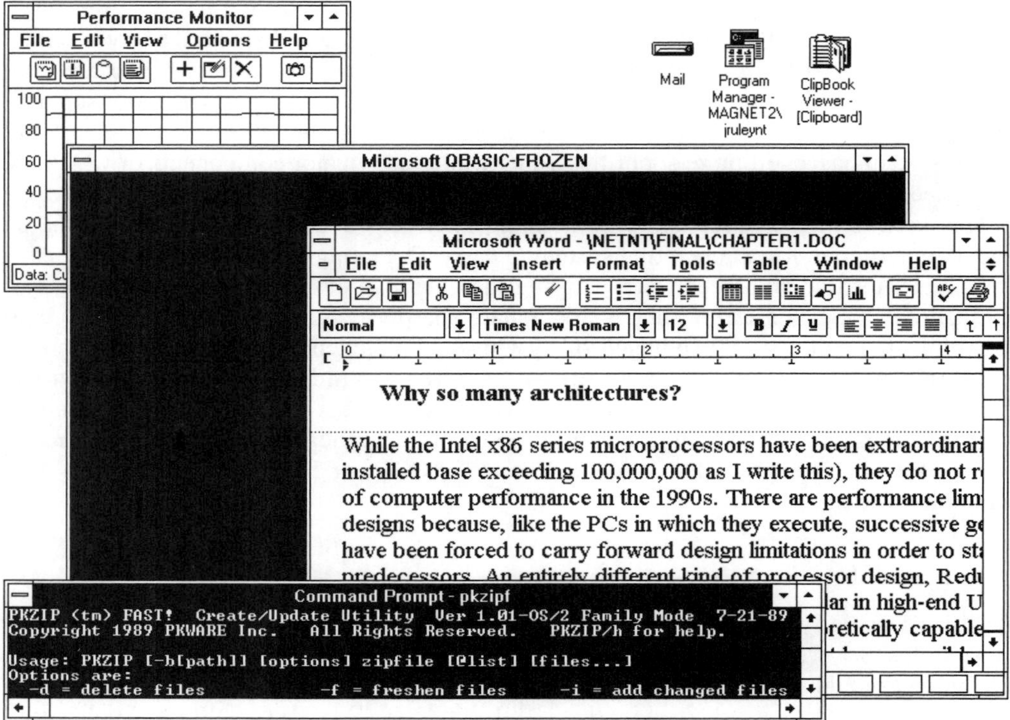

Figure 1.3 Windows NT UI with OS/2, Win16, and Win32 apps running.

The Windows NT user interface provides an integrated desktop metaphor for applications designed for 32-bit Windows, 16-bit Windows, DOS, OS/2 (16-bit character mode only), and POSIX. All but the last are shown here.

Similarly, WordPerfect for DOS and Excel for (16-bit) Windows will execute directly under Windows NT (although it may be desirable to acquire native 32-bit versions of these applications when they become available, as they will give better performance). Should the company use an in-house custom application, it will probably run in one of NT's emulation subsystems (assuming the application was developed for DOS, Windows, or OS/2). If the application was developed for the UNIX environment (where portability is normally accomplished at the source code level), then if it's a well-behaved basic character-mode UNIX application, it should be possible to recompile it for Windows NT's POSIX implementation. For that matter, if it's a graphic application, it could be possible to use it in conjunction with one of the third-party "X/Server" utilities for Windows NT—see Chapter 6.

Of course there are limitations to this approach—one is reminded of the old saw "Jack of all trades, master of none." That's not true of Windows NT. It's master of one trade—and that trade is 32-bit Windows. With respect to the other subsystems, it has greater or lesser limitations, depending on the particular subsystem. With respect to the DOS subsystem in particular, there is a significant problem introduced by Windows NT security architecture, which prevents low-level access to hardware. Software such as backup applications and utility programs that expect direct access to the hard disk controller will not work under Windows NT. Windows applications that take liberties with the Windows interface, employ undocumented system calls, attempt direct hardware access, or employ private device drivers (scanner applications and the like) will not work either.

The OS/2 support is at the OS/2 1.3 level. This is unfortunate as Windows NT is being introduced in parallel with IBM's introduction of its second major revision of the OS/2 2.x system, and the OS/2 support is character-mode only. Presentation Manager[6] applications will not work. This is sufficient for carrying forward server-based applications such as SQL Server. It's insufficient for carrying forward much of anything else. The POSIX implementation suffers similar limitations to the OS/2 implementation, and of course, requires development effort in that the application must be recompiled (this is typical of the UNIX world as a whole).

So the idea that bringing Windows NT into an organization will allow the existing software base to be carried forward without *any* change is probably naive.

Access to the World Outside: I/O

No operating system exists in isolation. People buy an operating system to run application software, and they do so in the expectation that it will work with a wide range of hardware. To make this work, Windows NT provides a very rich device-independent model for I/O services. This model takes critical advantage of a concept called a *multilayered device driver*. In DOS and other conventional operating systems device drivers are generally *monolithic*—they provide a large and complex set of services that will be understood by an intermediate layer of the operating system. In DOS this intermediate layer is the Basic Disk Operating System (BDOS). The device driver then communicates directly with the hardware—so when BDOS commands are issued, the driver provides the necessary hardware interface. BDOS commands are relatively high-level functions. They do things like open a file, read a byte from a file, close a file. The physical actions needed to fill these requests are hidden (or *encapsulated*) within the driver.

This model works, but it has some severe problems. There may be more than one type of file system. If the driver has been designed to respond to the Open File command it will, given a filename, go to a directory structure, find the file, and carry out the operations necessary to open it (this assumes the device driver knows the file system format to be used). Now in DOS this is no problem—there is only one file format to worry about, the File Allocation Table (FAT) format, so DOS device drivers assume that this is the format they'll see on the disk.

Windows NT, as we will see in the next section, is designed to use a variety of file system formats. So it's not safe for a device driver to make *any* assumptions about the underlying format. In order to get around this problem, NT uses a *multilayer* device driver approach, in

[6]OS/2's graphical user interface.

combination with a new operating system layer called the *I/O manager*. Application programs (and intermediate levels of the operating system) do not communicate directly with the device drivers. They communicate with the I/O manager, which in turn communicates with the device drivers on their behalf.

Let's consider how this works when an application program needs to access files on an NTFS (New Technology File System) disk partition. The application program issues a request to open a file. The request travels to an underlying operating system layer, perhaps the Win32 API layer. The Win32 API layer then issues an NT internal command, requesting the NT executive to open a file. The NT executive passes this request to the I/O manager, the I/O manager communicates this request to a file system driver, specifically the NTFS file system driver. The NTFS file system driver responds by issuing the NTFS specific hardware-level requests. It says "I want the information from track *x* sector *y*," which will be the location of the first tier of the directory structure, and based upon that, it issues commands to get information from other locations on the disk. The I/O manager then relays these requests to a hardware device driver, which knows that it's receiving specific requests related to getting very simple information from the device. It knows nothing about the file system. Notice that this process will work exactly the same if the NTFS driver is replaced by a FAT driver or an OS/2 High Performance File System (HPFS) driver, or a UNIX file system driver, or a Macintosh file system driver, or a CD ROM driver, *or any other driver*.

Of course, there is overhead involved with the I/O manager passing requests for information back and forth. For simple devices such as serial ports and parallel ports, Windows NT provides a single-layer device driver approach in which the I/O manager can communicate with the device driver and the device driver will return information directly. But for more complicated devices, and particularly for hard disks, tape drives, and other devices that depend on a file system (or other logical arrangement of data), a multilayered approach is superior.

Asynchronous I/O, Synchronization, and Power-Failure Recovery

Three additional device driver features are unique to Windows NT. The first is that virtually all low-level I/O operations are *asynchronous*. Rather than issue a request for information from a file and wait until the request is filled, in Windows NT you issue the request for information to the file and then go on and do something else. You're notified when the information from the file is ready.

This characteristic is masked at the programmer API level and neither programmers nor users will ever see it (other than by implication—well-designed Windows NT programs will never "lock up" waiting for I/O to complete). If you type DIR into a Windows NT command prompt, it will behave in much the same way as typing DIR on a DOS system (if you're on a POSIX subsystem, you could type "ls"). Underneath the user interface, however, very different things are going on. Windows NT is a *preemptive multitasking system*, which may be running many tasks at the same time, so it's vital that the operating system not waste time waiting for a request to be filled if it can be doing something else. The various layers in the operating system use the preemptive multitasking and multithreading characteristics of NT to enable themselves to get more work done in the same time.

Rather than waiting for a hard disk to spin up, or waiting on a request to read a directory, Windows NT continues with other tasks and deals with the directory request only when data becomes available. This feature also plays a role in NT's scalability—from our discussion of the microkernel and its application to symmetric multiprocessors you will remember that multiple instances of the Windows NT kernel execute on all CPUs simultaneously. This means that it's theoretically possible for all the CPUs in a system to attempt simultaneous device driver access, causing *contention*. To avoid this problem, device drivers, like other components of the NT Executive, make use of synchronization objects (in particular, semaphores and spin locks). The precise details of how this is done are outside the scope of this chapter. Suffice it to say that while it's possible for multiple instances of a device driver or other critical code to execute on multiple processors, they are designed in such a way that only one of those drivers at a time will have access to any critical shared resource. Just as with the asynchronous I/O, this is automatic and invisible to end-users.

The final unique feature of Windows NT device drivers is provision for power failure recovery. Windows NT is designed as, among other things, a platform for mission critical applications such as SQL Server (an Enterprise database). If a corporation has implemented its entire accounting system on SQL Server, it's absolutely critical that the system on which SQL Server is running be protected from power failure—or, should a power failure occur, it's vital that there be a graceful path to recovery. Otherwise, the entire accounting system could be corrupted—and a corrupt accounting system can cost a company millions of dollars.

Windows NT provides protection against this nightmare on several levels—the most important of which are the uninterruptible power supply service (which we will discuss later) and certain sophisticated features of the NTFS file system (ditto). There is also provision for protection from power failure *even at the device driver level*. In a power failure, even if it is very brief, the precise operating state of hardware devices becomes unstable. A disk drive, for example, which has a memory buffer for Direct Memory Access (DMA) data transfer, may be loaded with corrupt data during a power failure. Attempting to access that data will yield garbage—or worse, if that data gets written to disk, it may damage the application requesting it.

The classic way to deal with this in an operating system is to force a "cold" (power-switch) boot, lock everything out, and restart all operations from the power-off state. That takes a long time, and itself is dangerous because there may have been I/O requests outstanding. The classic example is a power failure while writing a disk file. Typically the disk file data is lost. Windows NT attempts to protect against this by designing *warm boot* code into the device drivers.[7] In other words, there is a known good state for device drivers short of the power-off state. In a power failure situation the operating system will notify all device drivers that a power failure has occurred. The device drivers then set themselves to their known good states and continue with the I/O operations that were outstanding when the power failed. If this capability works—and we've seen it demonstrated—then a power glitch on a Windows NT

[7]Note that this is an *optional* feature, and depends on battery backup for main memory power.

system need have no effect other than the brief period of time that the machine was turned off. Operations pick themselves up where they were and carry on transparently.

In fairness, this capability is very new, and it's tightly coupled to a number of new system components. To what degree it will work is still an open question. We've seen it demonstrated with SQL Server running on a Windows NT system on the NTFS file system. A power failure was created by physically disconnecting the system, unplugging it, while SQL Server was filling a query request. Power was restored. The Windows NT system came up. SQL Server came up. The disks spun for a little while to restore themselves to their own good state, and continued with the query. That was a *very* impressive performance. You probably shouldn't bet your company on it—but it's a reassuring capability to fall back on!

File Systems

Traditionally, operating systems are associated with a particular file structure that's used by that operating system for mass storage devices such as hard disks. Thus, we speak of a UNIX file system (i-nodes), a DOS file system (FAT), and a Macintosh File System (resource and data forks). While there is a native NT file system (NTFS), uniquely among modern operating systems (with the possible exception of OS/2—from which some of these capabilities were inherited) Windows NT is designed to be independent of the file system on which it operates. This capability enforces some severe requirements on Windows NT's I/O system design and device drivers, as was discussed in the last section. But it provides a very high degree of flexibility in Windows NT implementations.

By default, Windows NT supports two file systems for hard disks: the familiar File Allocation Table (FAT) system that's standard for DOS, and a New Technology File System (NTFS), which is designed to exploit Windows NT's security and fault-tolerance features. Windows NT also provides in-the-box support for OS/2's High Performance File System (HPFS)—a system with capabilities intermediate between FAT and NTFS. Windows NT also supports a CD ROM file system, eliminating the necessity for the MSCDX patch to the DOS file system that's required by all CD ROM drives used with DOS machines. The Windows NT Advanced Server also emulates the Macintosh file system using NTFS. Finally, *network services are treated as file systems in Windows NT*. Windows NT comes with LAN Manager network services which are, in effect, a file system that exists over a network. If you add Novell NetWare support you add NetWare network services—yet another file system that spans a network.

Windows NT is capable of running all of these file systems simultaneously. By far the most important is NTFS. NTFS is designed as a file system for building anything from a desktop computer to a mainframe-class enterprise server. It's designed to perform well with very large disk volumes (*up to* 2^{64} *bytes!*), a situation that is impossible for the FAT system. It's designed to never need defragmenting like a FAT drive, because it's organized in a radically different way. All of these are features it shares with OS/2's HPFS system. But Microsoft learned some things from its experience with HPFS design and development.

In contrast to HPFS, NTFS provides a unique data-logging capability that enables Windows NT to restore the state of the file system in power failure or other disk error situations, and to do so very quickly. HPFS has a similar capability but it's implemented using an HPFS version of the DOS chkdsk function and in large volumes it can literally take *hours* to execute. NTFS also, like HPFS, provides support for long filenames. You can refer to a file called *1993 Quarterly Accounts* and you can use that name for it rather than calling it something cryptic like *93QTR.ACT*. However, the use of long filenames creates compatibility problems for legacy applications. Windows NT eliminates this problem by providing automatic conversion of filenames to standard DOS style 8.3 names for DOS and Windows 16-bit applications. Thus, if you named your file 1993 Quarterly Accounts while using a 32-bit Windows application, when you go back and look for the file from a 16-bit Windows application or DOS application you will see 1993QU~1.[8]

New File System Features

Besides supporting multiple installable file systems, Windows NT provides a couple of unique features that assure high performance. The first of these is an entirely new capability called memory mapped files. Windows NT is a Virtual Memory operating system—it allows for arbitrarily large memory objects to be dealt with (if the object is too large to fit in physical memory, then only part is stored in memory, while the rest resides on disk). Memory mapped files exploit this capability by allowing a programmer to open a file of arbitrary size and treat it as a single contiguous array of memory locations. A file a hundred megabytes in size can be opened and treated as an array in a system with only twelve megabytes of memory. Of course, at any one time twelve megabytes or less (probably substantially less) of file data is physically present in memory—the rest is "paged" out to the disk. When the program requests data that's not currently stored in memory, the Virtual Memory System automatically gets it from the file. But it does so in a very efficient manner and it completely masks this operation from the programmer.

This feature could revolutionize disk-based programs (like database applications) once programmers understand how to use it. Writing applications in which large amounts of file data are manipulated in a computer is something of an art form. You must find a way to load the right data into memory at the right time and manipulate it there for speed, and then unload it and load in new data. Windows NT changes this process to one of manipulating disk-based data as you would any other array of bytes. While the entire file is never actually present in memory at any one time, Windows NT masks the deception.

Preemptive Multitasking

Computers spend most of their time doing absolutely nothing. Consider what happens when you type DIR on a DOS machine. In between your typing of the letters D, I, and R the CPU sits idle. You cannot possibly type fast enough to keep it busy. When you finish typing DIR and hit the Enter key, the CPU very quickly decides that you wanted a disk directory, issues

[8]Further details on the New Technology File System and on setting up file systems in general will be found in Chapter 2.

the necessary commands, and provides a command to the hard disk controller. It then waits while the hard disk controller goes off and gets the information, and while it waits it can accomplish no useful work.

Because of *preemptive multitasking*, this situation is very different under Windows NT. A component of the operating system called the *Task Scheduler* switches a variety of processes[9] into or out of the CPU(s), either according to a set time schedule or based upon the existence of some high-priority event, such as an interrupt. To understand how this works in practice let's consider the very same process of typing DIR—but this time on a Windows NT machine. It's all but certain that when you type DIR, that won't be the only thing you are doing with the NT machine. You will probably have a variety of other windows open, and several programs running. Yet you won't have to wait any longer for the system to respond after you type DIR than you would on the DOS machine (in fact, you may not even have to wait as long!).

The *foreground*[10] process in Windows NT gets a substantially higher priority than background processes; and real-world I/O (such as keyboard input) has the highest priority in the system. Therefore, whenever you hit a key the CPU will drop what it's doing to handle the keystroke, but in the intervening time between the keystrokes (when a DOS system would be idle) the Task Scheduler will switch among the other processes running in the system. Even if you're only running the window into which you're typing DIR, the Task Scheduler will still switch time between your processes and the processes of the Windows NT Executive. These include the processes that provide networking capability, and here we see one of the first and most important of Windows NT's advantages. Instead of being an afterthought (as they are with Novell NetWare's NetX Shell and DOS), networking functions are built into Windows NT—and the preemptive multitasking model makes for a far more effective networking implementation even for client computers.

Now, suppose you finish typing DIR and hit the Enter key. Just as in DOS, the Windows NT command interpreter determines that DIR is a command to receive a directory. It then issues the necessary commands through the NT Executive to the I/O Manager, which in turn calls the installable file system for whichever file system you're using on the relevant drive. This in turn sends a series of requests for specific information to the I/O Manager, which in turn passes those requests on to a low-level hard disk driver, which in turn gets the information from the hard disk. Now, this is a reasonably efficient process and happens very quickly, up to the point that the hard disk becomes involved. But the seek times of hard disks are measured in milliseconds whereas the operating times of microprocessors occur in nanoseconds. By comparison to a modern microprocessor, a hard disk is an extraordinarily slow device.

Rather than waiting while it receives the information from the hard disk, the Task Scheduler continues to switch other processes in and out of the CPU. When the data on the hard disk becomes available, this will interrupt other processes (because I/O has a very high priority), and information from the hard disk will be passed "up the food chain" to the process that

[9]The sum total memory space taken up by the processes constantly being switched by the task manager is called the *working set*. As we will see in Chapter 2, this has a significant impact on NT system configuration.

[10]The process running in the topmost window on the NT machine's display.

requested it. This process of having I/O and other work accomplished simultaneously is called *overlapped I/O*. Because of overlapped I/O, preemptive multitasking systems such as Windows NT are substantially faster on I/O-intensive tasks than are single-thread-of-execution systems such as DOS and NetWare.

Multithreading

What's been discussed about preemptive multitasking to this point could apply equally to a variety of other systems, particularly UNIX systems (which also run a preemptively switched, multitasking operating system kernel). Windows NT shares with OS/2 a substantial extension to this concept called *multithreading*. A thread is a low-overhead process that can be switched by the Task Scheduler (just like any other process), but it does not carry with it the overhead of starting up, ending, and managing its own resources. It inherits these from its parent process, which may have many threads.

Bearing in mind the overlapped I/O issue we discussed earlier, consider a database application. If it's written in a traditional single-threaded manner, Windows NT will benefit from overlapped I/O—but the application will not. The application cannot continue to process input for a new database record until the last record has been added—it hangs up while writing to the disk (and the user's eyes glaze at the sight of that hated Windows hourglass cursor). Windows NT can use this time to get other tasks done, but that's not terribly helpful to your end-user.

However, if the database application was written in a multithreaded manner (as a Windows NT application should be) then you might be able to get other work done within the application while it's filling that request—instead of hanging up, the application could accept input for the next record *at the very same time that the last record was being added* (see Figure 1.4). And, to abuse an accounting term, the extra productivity you achieve this way is "found money" that was otherwise going to waste (because you are paying for that end-user's time whether or not he's waiting on his computer!).

A properly written Windows NT database will *never* show the hourglass cursor. Instead, Windows NT provides a combination hourglass cursor and arrow pointer. The idea is that this shows you that work is going on—but you can get other things done at the same time. Specifically, what should happen when you enter another record into the database is that one thread will start writing the last record to the disk, while the thread in which you're entering the data remains active. Overlapped I/O now applies to the human part of the I/O equation as well as to the computer's part.

Multithreading on an SMP: *Parallel Processing*

On multiprocessing systems, Windows NT gains an additional advantage: *each thread in a program can execute on its own CPU, speeding the application up.* As we discussed in the section on the microkernel, Windows NT has a low-overhead kernel design that can simultaneously execute as many copies of the kernel as there are processors in the system. Each copy of the kernel is in fact a thread of the Windows NT Executive—which is (obviously) multithreaded.

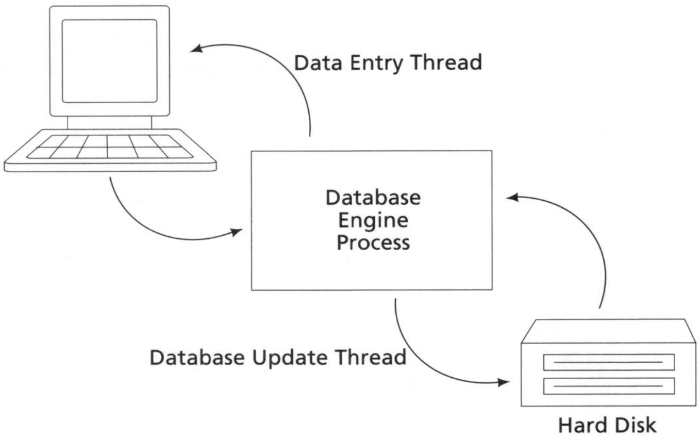

Figure 1.4 Multithread database insert.

Use of multithreading can significantly improve productivity in applications like database inserts, because the operator need not wait for one insert to complete before beginning another.

There are other multiprocessor operating systems—in particular, various forms of UNIX. Typically, these systems employ the processors to execute separate processes or programs. Thus, for instance, a database application may be executing in one processor, and another application in another processor, and so on. Because each process can execute in its own processor, each executes faster—and the system as a whole is faster. But no single process executes faster than it would if it was executing by itself.

Multithreaded processes in Windows NT can actually gain a speed benefit from executing on a multiprocessor. In the example we just gave (the database with records being entered), the thread for adding the record to the database could not only continue to execute in parallel with the execution of the thread that's taking the data from the user, *both* could execute in separate processors *at the same time*. Now, in point of fact, the advantage from multiprocessor execution of this specific example would be small. Both disk-based file I/O (the major limiting factor in updating the database), and human interface I/O (waiting on the user to enter keystrokes), are very slow processes. There is plenty of idle time in between the user's keystrokes, and while the hard disk spins Windows NT's overlapped I/O capabilities can take advantage of this even on a single processor. But consider a database *search*. . . .

As we discussed in the section on file I/O, Windows NT can provide impressive database capabilities using memory mapped files. A programmer can, in effect, load the entire file into memory (or at least *act* as if he has loaded the entire file into memory), and then search it as he would search any memory array. In a multiprocessor implementation, one could have several threads of execution searching on an array simultaneously. If each of those threads has its own CPU, this could substantially increase the speed of the database search, as illustrated in Figure 1.5.

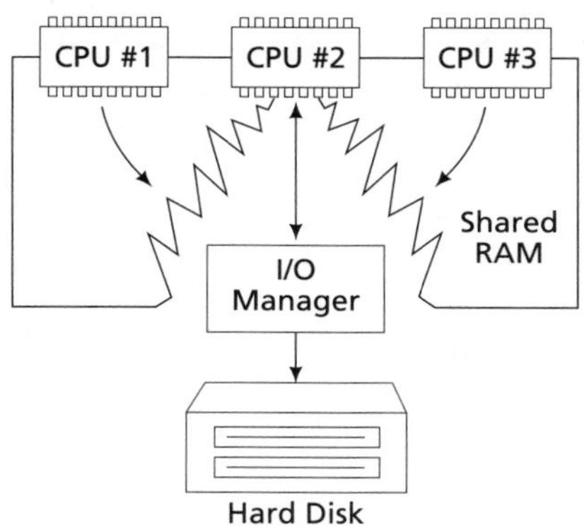

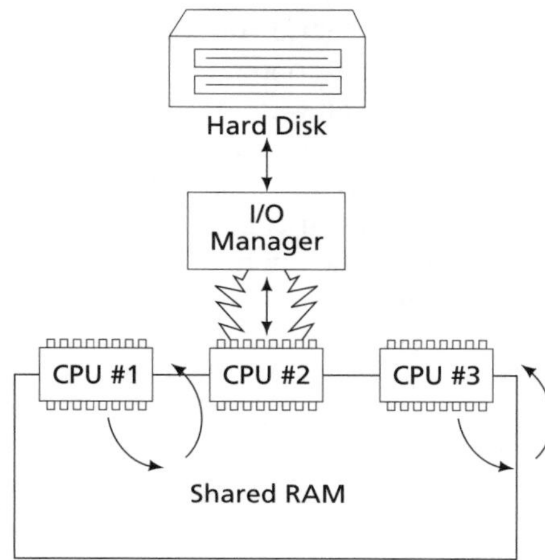

Figure 1.5 MP contention on file server.

By dividing a compute-intensive task such as a database search into multiple *threads of execution*, a Windows NT application can achieve significant performance gains when run on Symmetric Multiprocessor (SMP) hardware.

This approach has its limitations—specifically, in the example I've just given (a multiprocessor database search), contention will occur when two CPUs attempt to access the same memory address. If the programmer has done his job right, this will be minimized; but it can't be completely eliminated, and contention will slow down the system substantially. Similarly, multithreaded tasks that compete for single shared resources such as the hard disk, network cards, or the video screen are going to cause contention and performance will deteriorate.[11] But for a wide variety of applications—especially server applications—parallel processing is very, very important.

Consider the operation of a large server on a large network. It may be servicing requests from dozens, even hundreds, of users simultaneously. In a typical file and print server situation, most of what it's doing is I/O and again, just as in the earlier example, a single CPU machine will have no trouble keeping up with other information requests in its free time between filling I/O requests. The major problem is keeping all the requests straight (a hundred people can try to open files at the same time, but the hard disk can only handle them one at a time).

[11]See Appendix 5 for a more complete discussion of the contention problem on SMP systems.

The situation is different, however, if we begin to consider client/server applications—of which modern databases are a primary example. These applications tend to be compute-intensive at the server. Queries on the database are received as requests from a client computer. The actual query is conducted at the server. If five or ten people attempt to perform database queries at the same time, you not only have an *I/O* problem (getting the data into memory from disk), you also have a *compute* problem (searching the data in memory). At this point, the multiprocessor version of NT becomes a tremendous advantage. By providing additional CPU resources, it can fulfill those requests. This is the key to understanding that Windows NT is more—far more—than a simple operating system for desktop computers. Windows NT is the ideal operating system for computers that until recently we would think of as being in the mainframe class.

Memory Management

In contrast to more conventional operating systems, Windows NT runs a near-mainframe-class memory management subsystem that employs demand-paged virtual memory. In this scheme programs are presented with a contiguous (flat) address space, typically two gigabytes in size, although there will generally not be that much memory in the system. In fact, what's present in the system may not be contiguous at all.

Within the contiguous address space, memory is organized as four-kilobyte pages.[12] Pages can be freely moved between memory and a hard disk at the command of the *memory manager subsystem*. The Memory Manager does this through a mechanism called a *page fault*. Whenever a program attempts to access memory that's not physically present in the machine, a *page fault* is generated. The NT Executive then takes over and loads in the requested memory. It also unloads the least recently used memory pages from the system to make room for the memory that's being loaded in. This process is automatic and (under all but the most extreme conditions) completely transparent—and it means that programs can behave as though they have nearly unlimited memory space, when they are actually limited to memory physically present in the machine. When Windows NT runs out of memory (in the sense that programs request more memory than the machine has), response slows down because the memory manager must periodically *swap* pages between memory and the hard disk.

This is particularly important in server-based applications where, as the number of users grows, eventually the physical memory in the machine is insufficient. NT's major competitor, Novell NetWare, does not run a virtual memory system, and (as we've personal experience and scars to prove) when you add enough users and enough load to a system and do not add memory, eventually the system begins to crash regularly. This will not happen with the Windows NT system because the virtual memory subsystem can take advantage of disk space (if you run out of *both* physical memory and disk space, you may very well hit a situation in which Memory Manager does run out of available resources—see Chapter 5 for ways to avoid this problem).

[12]On x86 and MIPS-based systems. DEC AxP-based systems use an 8 KB page—and in principle, any multiple of 4 KB could be used.

Besides managing virtual memory, Memory Manager also has to provide memory protection—preventing one application from manipulating memory within another application's address space. If memory protection was not provided, it would be possible for a rogue program to take actions that would result in other programs crashing or becoming unstable (sounds like a computer virus, eh?). To prevent this, the Memory Manager checks the *page boundaries* of the application's memory space. When an application attempts to address memory outside of its page boundary, a page fault will occur and the Memory Manager will attempt to load in the missing memory page. When it sees that the page does not belong to the application, a protection *exception* is raised and the Executive shuts down the offending application (making a note of this in an audit file, if the system is so configured).

There are times when it's desirable to have two applications share memory, and thus, the memory management system has to provide a way around the memory protection. This is provided by Windows NT's *memory mapped files* mechanism, the same mechanism that can be used for high-speed access to disk file data (by treating the file as a memory array). Essentially, the reverse works as well—an array of memory addresses can be assigned a file handle.[13] Once the handle has been made available other applications can access it, provided they have the necessary permissions from the security object manager. Automatic synchronization is provided so that even on a multiprocessor system two applications will not access the same memory location at the same time. Windows NT also provides a wide range of client/server mechanisms other than shared memory for the interaction of programs.

This brings up the final issue of memory management in Windows NT: security. Windows NT treats handles to memory or memory addresses as objects in the security object monitor. Whenever memory is allocated, deallocated, or copied, the action is registered with the security database—which verifies whether the program manipulating the memory has the privileges necessary to access it.

The implications of the memory management subsystem for network applications are a substantially more reliable base upon which to run applications, particularly client/server applications. The memory mapping scheme frees Windows NT from concerns about what happens when the physical memory becomes inadequate, provides an automatic mechanism for the protection of applications from interference with one another, and provides an effective mechanism for single servers to perform multiple tasks. It also provides a powerful base upon which to build sophisticated client/server applications—and it does so with great attention to security. That's a pretty effective combination.

Built-in Networking

As we've seen, every subsystem in Windows NT has been designed with connectivity and networking in mind. This is true of other operating systems as well, particularly OS/2 (in which much of the same low-level infrastructure discussed here is provided). But Windows NT goes a step further: It provides built-in networking features that go beyond anything packaged with

[13]*Handles* are identifiers that are used to manipulate objects—including files, memory locations, devices, and the like.

any other operating system. The NEXTstep operating system comes close, but even it doesn't quite match what is provided with Windows NT. To begin with, every Windows NT machine is a *peer*—a term that seems to cause much confusion.

People see the word *peer* and associate it with *peer-to-peer networking*, as used by Lantastic, NetWare Lite or Windows for Workgroups. And it's certainly true that every Windows NT machine provides networking features—and obviously, they are all peers with each other, so you can certainly think of it as peer-to-peer in that sense.

However, there is a big difference between the peer-to-peer functionality in Windows NT and the peer-to-peer functionality you will find in "peer-to-peer" local area networking systems. *Every Windows NT system is a fully functional file server capable of supporting an* unlimited *number of network clients*. And if you will think about what we said in the preceding sections about the multitasking kernel design, virtual memory and the I/O subsystems, you will see that NT is a perfectly acceptable operating system base on which to build an effective network server. So it shouldn't surprise you that the peer-to-peer functionality of Windows NT is excellent. It provides unlimited file sharing for an unlimited number of users, unlimited printer sharing to an unlimited number of users, and electronic mail and scheduling support using Microsoft's MS-Mail 3.1 and Schedule Plus version 1.0 (although the mail and scheduling have some severe limitations—see Chapter 7 for details).

There are also a variety of ancillary programs, including network Chat, network sharing of the clipboard (using NetDDE) and Network OLE that go beyond anything provided with other operating systems at this time. You can create equivalent capabilities by mixing and matching combinations of after-market products, but you cannot buy it all in one box, and you will not get the same performance and *convenience* from the after-market products that you will get from the single box.

The Windows NT Advanced Server

The Windows NT Advanced Server provides a more sophisticated variant of the networking features that are built into Windows NT. It delivers *domainwide* administration capability—important because the one great limitation of the built-in peer networking in the Windows NT base product is that each system has to maintain its own database of user accounts. Let's say that you want to share files from your machine with one other person in your office but not with the entire office. If you want to share files with everybody in the office it's pretty simple. You open up the File Manager, click on the directory you want to share, and you will then see a display for file permissions. You select *everyone* as having *full access* and there you are.

The trouble with that approach is it really does mean *everyone*. Everyone sitting on a Windows NT, Windows for Workgroups, or LAN Manager-compatible system connected to yours can see every file in the shared directory. If that directory is the accounting database, you probably did not want to select everyone and full access rights. If you want to select limited access rights (just to provide access to one person, for example), then you must create a user account for that person on your computer. This is done using User Manager (see Chapter 4 for details). Once you've created an account for that person, you can select *everyone* as having *no access* rights but then override that by assigning full access rights to the boss.

There are also variants on the full-access and no-access privileges, You can provide *read only* access rights. This is a powerful capability that goes well beyond the security features provided with most peer-to-peer networking systems. The one problem with it is that you have to set the access rights on your computer—and we have to on our computer—and the fellow down the hall has to do it to his computer. There is no central administration and no provision for a global user account that would apply to all of the systems. That could prove to be a substantial burden if fifty different people need access to your system and all of them require separate access rights (some of the people have accounting access and some of them do not and some of them have access to your tape drive to perform backup operations and others do not). The system is technically capable of supporting that many users but you as an individual Windows NT user probably are not.

By providing *domainwide* administration, the Windows NT Advanced Server gets around this problem. In an administrative *domain* the user has an account that applies on all servers in the domain. This is a far better approach to dealing with the kind of fifty-user/fifty-different-access-rights scenario just described.

The Windows NT Advanced Server also has more sophisticated versions of some of the basic Windows NT services. For instance, the remote access service that allows a single user to dial into any Windows NT system is upgraded to a multi-user remote access service that allows many users to dial into a Windows NT Advanced Server. The Windows NT Advanced Server also provides access capabilities to Macintosh computers.[14]

The resulting combination of features—domain administration, Macintosh file system support, multi-user RAS—combined with the extremely powerful basic Windows NT feature set, makes it possible to construct very complex (and powerful) *enterprise networks* using Windows NT (see Figure 1.6). We will now briefly examine each of these features (for more details, see Chapter 7).

Domain Administration

The basic Windows NT product can function as a file server, and it does any time you use the File Manager to share a directory. It can also share printers and in principle it can share other devices, so it is a server and a very powerful one. It does, however, have one serious limitation. The user accounts created for a basic Windows NT server machine extend only to that particular machine. Suppose you have a network with two file servers, one of which is used for accounting information and the other for sales information. Obviously, salesmen have accounts only on the sales computer and accountants have accounts only on the accounting computer. But what about a corporate manager with an urgent need for access to both? In a basic Windows NT network the only way to accomplish this is to give that administrator two accounts, one for each server. Now the administrator can have the same account name and password on both servers and this will make his life simpler. But life becomes complicated for

[14]See Chapter 7 for a detailed discussion of these and other Windows NT Advanced Server issues.

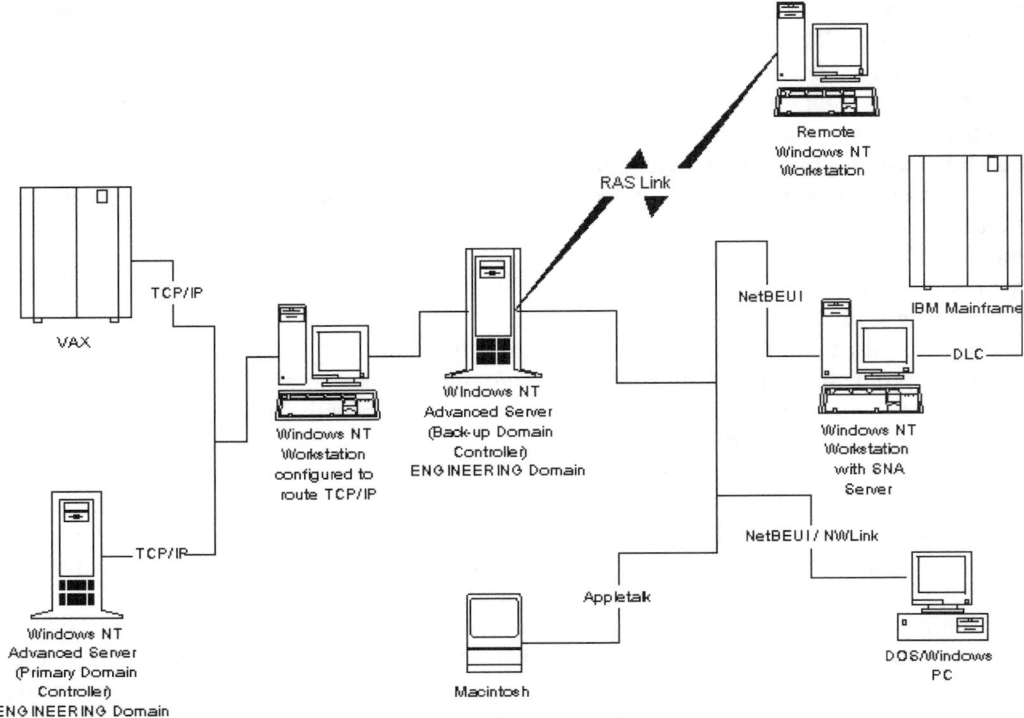

Figure 1.6 Enterprise network diagram.

Windows NT's built-in networking functions include: NetBEUI workgroup-type networking to local workstations and servers; routable TCP/IP networking for the Enterprise; Remote Access Services (RAS) for connecting remote machines over telephone, X.25, and ISDN lines; NetWare-compatible NWLink networking for application servers; and (in the Windows NT Advanced Server) Appletalk and Macintosh File System support. An add-on product (SNA Server for Windows NT) exploits the built-in Data Link Control (DLC) protocol to provide connectivity to IBM mainframes. Not shown are an array of built-in printer support functions that include print pooling, network printer support, and (in the Windows NT Advanced Server) PostScript printer emulation.

a system administrator asked to maintain such a system if, when accounts are changed, he has to change the account database information individually for each server on the network.[15]

Worse, because the Windows NT base product is not designed to be administered remotely, the system administrator has to go to each individual server to perform these

[15] This does *not*, fortunately, have to be done directly from the server console—and users can normally change their own passwords.

changes in the account database. This is the basic limitation of Windows NT networking: it cannot be centrally administered.

Windows NT Advanced Server changes this situation by introducing the concept of a domain. A domain is an arbitrary group of Windows NT servers, which may in fact be basic Windows NT servers or Advanced Servers. It doesn't matter. At least one of these servers, however, will be designated as a domain controller. There may be more than one. Domain controllers maintain a central user account database that applies to all servers within the domain. The effect of this is dramatic from the point of view of a system administrator and end-users. Each end-user needs only a single account, which can provide privileges as required to any server within the domain. Indeed, because of a unique Windows NT Advanced Server feature called *inter-domain trust,* it is possible for a single user account to have privileges spanning many domains. This concept, one of the most powerful that Windows NT has introduced, is called a *Single Enterprise Logon,* which we will return to in Chapter 7.

Administrative User Profiles

Just having the ability to create domainwide user accounts is a big advantage, of course. But the Windows NT Advanced Server goes further by allowing administrators to define *user profiles* that span all servers on the network. The user profile determines which servers a user has access to, which workstations he or she may log in from, what time(s) of day he or she may log in; it even allows an administrator to determine which Program Groups are displayed by Windows NT's Program Manager. This capability, used alone or in conjunction with Windows NT's powerful login scripts, allows tremendous administrative control, making the Advanced Server your best choice for all but the most limited Windows NT installations.

Directory Replication

Another feature the Windows NT Advanced Server adds is the ability to replicate directory tree structures from one server to another. This is useful on large networks to allow users to get logged in and access network-wide services without having to wait for a response from a particular server, and it can be a boon to administrators who need to provide copies of material (such as corporate policies, and other standard documents) that changes regularly.

Fault Tolerance

Although modern off-the-shelf PC hardware is acceptable for a broad range of applications (including basic network servers up to the departmental level), when you consider enterprise services for mission-critical applications—situations in which file servers simply *must not* go down—support for fault-tolerant hardware becomes essential. Windows NT Advanced Server provides fault tolerance by providing redundancy at the weakest point of the PC hardware—its mass data storage, generally in the hard disk. Windows NT achieves this redundancy using one or more of the following techniques: mirrored disk partitions, disk duplexing, and RAID5 mass storage.

Mirroring

The easiest of these concepts to understand is the concept of partition mirroring. In a mirrored disk environment Windows NT maintains two images of the data for a particular disk. It does this on two separate disk partitions coupled to a single controller. The first partition, called the primary, receives data just as it otherwise would. The second partition, called the mirror, receives a backup copy of the primary's data. Windows NT then performs a comparison to verify that the data written to the two partitions matches. If it does, Windows NT assumes that the data is correct. In the event that the data does not match, Windows NT can consult parity information to determine which set of data is correct. The result is a mirrored disk drive, and it is about as reliable as you can get—short of duplicating the disk controllers altogether.

Duplex Drives

This provides a level of redundancy beyond that of the mirrored disk drives and is done in the simplest possible way. Two physical disks are used and two disk controllers. Windows NT writes all information twice using the two different controllers. Again, a comparison is done every time disk information is read and this can exact a significant performance impact as two separate disk controllers have to be accessed over and above the overhead of accessing the two drives. But it does provide an additional degree of redundancy in case of extreme failure conditions. Both drive duplexing and disk mirroring are covered in Chapter 3 (and servers with dual drives can also get improved performance by using multiple swap files—see Chapter 5).

Stripe Sets and RAID5

Traditional methods of achieving redundancy in mass storage (such as drive duplexing and disk mirroring) exact a performance penalty on servers that use them. The operating system simply has to do more work, since data has to be written twice. In parallel with (and to a certain extent competing with) this has been a move to a new technology for creating very large disk spaces. This technology is called RAID, which stands for Redundant Array of Inexpensive Disks. The concept is very simple. Instead of buying a single 2GB disk drive, why not buy ten 200MB disk drives and drive them all in parallel? You achieve a number of advantages this way.

Small volume drives are often cheaper. While this economy can be lost when initially buying many small drives (a 2GB disk pack built on RAID principles is likely to cost more than a single 2GB disk drive), there is one overwhelming advantage—the hardware is *redundant.* A failure in one of the disk drives can lose, at most, one-tenth of the overall data. And the replacement cost of one small disk drive will be much less than the cost of replacing a 2GB drive. It is a very attractive proposition. It has one other great advantage: vastly increased performance.

When a RAID drive is accessed, data is *striped* across all of the disks. That is, parts of a sector are written on drive one, parts on drive two, parts on drive three, and so forth. In a RAID5 drive, data is validated by having *parity information* written to one of the disks. That parity information is vital because the one great problem with a RAID drive is: What do you do when you have a disk error? Requiring data to be written simultaneously on ten disk drives means that ten times the hardware is involved, making failures ten times as likely. So, in a RAID environment, reliability and performance trade off.

RAID5 combines the advantages of performance and data redundancy. The redundancy in this case does come with a price. In a mirrored or duplexed disk drive situation, recovering from a disk failure is simple—just remove and replace the disk mirror or the duplex disk drive at fault, and copy the data from the intact partition or disk drive (simply disabling the mirroring—"breaking the mirror"—on a mirrored partition or reverting from drive duplexing to a single drive will also let you continue to operate, but you risk losing all data because redundancy is gone). In any case, restoring data is a very quick process.

In a RAID5 drive, data restoration is a slower process because the data must be reconstructed from the parity information. However, since parity information represents total redundancy across all drives connected, short of a simultaneous failure on two drives, RAID5 data is completely redundant. This combines the ultimate in protection with very high disk performance, the penalties being expensive hardware and slow restoration of redundant data in the event a write error occurs. Because of the requirement to drive many hard disks in parallel, RAID5 support is usually achieved with a high-speed Small Computer Systems Interface (SCSI) disk controller and multiple SCSI hard disks. Windows NT Advanced Server can provide RAID5 support with from three to thirty-two disk drives or partitions. (Note that setting up a RAID drive on multiple partitions of a single physical disk will actually *reduce* performance.)

Macintosh File System Support

The Windows NT Advanced Server includes Macintosh file system support at no additional cost. That's significant because Apple's Macintosh does represent a significant proportion of the installed base of networking personal computers, and because bridging requirements in connecting Macintosh computers into conventional networks have generally been high. The form of Macintosh file system support also offers some unique advantages. This arises from the fact that providing Macintosh support in a PC-based network environment is quite challenging because the Macintosh file system is substantially different than the DOS file system or any normal PC file system. The Windows NT Advanced Server exploits the New Technology File System (NTFS) to provide Macintosh computers what amounts to a native filespace, while making that space available to DOS, Windows, OS/2 and Windows NT clients at the same time. For more details, see Chapter 7.

Remote Access Services

Remote Access Services (RAS) is a built-in feature of both Windows NT and the Advanced Server. Remote Access Services amounts to a technique for providing dial-in access (through modems and phone lines or special-purpose X.25 and ISDN interfaces) which, aside from the reduced data rate, is not visibly different from logging directly into the server over a normal network connection. RAS is well suited to copying small data files, such as text files. It is ill-suited to remote execution of networked programs or to transmission of a large data file such as Postscript bitmaps or the like.

A single-user RAS client is provided in the Windows NT base product, and Microsoft has similar software available for DOS and Windows clients. The Windows NT Advanced Server provides a more sophisticated version, capable of supporting up to sixty-four remote workstations at each server. Further details on Remote Access Services (and other forms of Wide-Area Networking) may be found in Chapter 7.

Do You Need an Advanced Server?

Many features of the Windows NT Advanced Server make it sound like an extremely attractive package. And indeed it is. But there is a price to be paid for all of these features—literally. Pricing for the Advanced Server has been set at $1,495 per server.[16] By comparison, the announced price range for Windows NT base product is under $500 and there are rumors that it will be available to corporate customers at a cost as low as $100 per station. Therefore, a decision about purchasing the Windows NT Advanced Server (NTAS) installation has to take into account the fact that NTAS costs four to ten times as much as a Windows NT base product installation—and, in terms of basic networking features, doesn't really provide anything that the Windows NT base product doesn't.

The Windows NT base product is a perfectly acceptable file, print, and device server. It simply becomes impossible to administer in a large installation. Not because of any inherent limitation of the system, but because it does not have the remote administration capabilities and the other features mentioned above. A good starting point for making a judgment about a Windows NT Advanced Server is to take a look at the unique features of the server that the Windows NT base product does *not* provide.

Windows NT Advanced Server Features:

- Single-user accounts that span multiple servers
- Administrative user profiles
- Directory replication
- Fault-tolerant disk support
- Macintosh file system support
- Multi-user remote access service

If you have need of any of the above features then you need the Windows NT Advanced Server or you need to look at a different server operating system than Windows NT.

[16] This is an introductory price. Microsoft's *list* price is $2,995. A special upgrade package is available at $695 for LAN Manager users.

System Requirements

In addition to the higher price for the Windows NT Advanced Server, you need to bear in mind that the system requirements for the Windows NT Advanced Server exceed those of the Windows NT base product. Minimum hardware requirements are a 386DX or better CPU, 16MB of RAM, and 100MB or more of hard disk. That is for the system itself; you must add hard disk space for your user files to the minimum stated here. On a RISC-based system a working minimum probably requires 32MB of memory. More memory is better, of course. And the Macintosh file system support requires additional memory above these stated minimums.

You must also take into account the additional cost of any special hardware needed to meet a server situation. In particular, an uninterruptible power supply is surely a basic necessity in an Advanced Server situation. Add the cost of tape backup, the cost of high-capacity disk drives and the additional cost of multiple disk drives if the RAID5 approach to fault tolerance is taken. Against all this, consider the costs of *not* employing an NT Advanced Server in a situation where it could be useful. It is easy, for example, to see that in a multidepartmental LAN situation involving a dozen or so servers at least one, and probably more than one of these, needs to be a Windows NT Advanced Server to function as domain controllers for the others. Likewise, in such a large-scale system there is probably a need for dial-in access and probably a need for Macintosh support, all of which the NT Advanced Server can address.

The more difficult question comes at the margins—midrange networks involving three to five servers, which could, if necessary, be managed manually. Again, start by considering the checklist. If domain administration is really needed, then the Advanced Server is required. Again, if Macintosh support is needed, or if multi-user remote access services are needed, these are available only on the Advanced Server. If these features are not required, then it may bear consideration to employ multiple Windows NT base product systems as local servers, managed on an ad hoc basis. However, in examining this pay close attention to the additional system administration time spent manually managing multiple servers. There does arise a point at which it is simply not economically justifiable in terms of person-hours.

Moreover, it is worth considering that one fully equipped Windows NT Advanced Server, taking full advantage of the RAID5 support and providing additional memory for the Macintosh support, is likely to turn out to be a 486DX2 or RISC-based machine with a gigabyte of hard disk, 32MB of memory, and an uninterruptible power supply—and is likely to cost $5,000 to $10,000 even if it is purchased on discount using no-name parts. You can look at that cost and see enough money to pay for several less powerful, less reliable, Windows NT base product servers.

But consider the implications. You achieve the advantage of redundancy by having the multiple servers, but at the cost of lower performance and higher maintenance because the probability of failure is multiplied by the number of systems. The RAID5 support, for example, while it presents an additional cost, can (in any system engineered to accommodate it) provide a significant performance improvement, and that performance boost might well compensate for the costs involved in employing such a machine. Any such decision requires an honest and straightforward cost/benefit analysis, but, in general, the centralized account management features of the Windows NT Advanced Server render it essential in situations where more than one Windows NT system will be used to provide file services.

Other Networks

While the built-in networking features of Windows NT are quite sophisticated, they have one basic problem. They are built to Microsoft's LAN Manager specifications—and therefore, while they will interact beautifully with other LAN Manager systems and with Windows for Workgroups systems (as well as other Windows NT systems, of course), they aren't designed to interoperate with Novell NetWare or other networks. Microsoft has, however, provided a mechanism that makes it relatively easy to provide additional networking services in Windows NT. While Microsoft would certainly not object to dominating the PC Local Area Networking business, they realize that they do not (nor are they likely to in the foreseeable future), so a powerful mechanism has been provided in Windows NT for after-market networking products compatible with other networking systems.

This compatibility depends, first of all, upon the layered device driver model and the treatment of networks as a file system that we described earlier. It also depends upon two new levels of interface that are built into Windows NT at the device driver level: the network device interface specification (NDIS), which defines the way that network device drivers for Windows NT are built, and above that, the Transport Driver Interface (TDI), which provides a direct link between all redirectors or network file systems and the network transport drivers.

A network provider who wishes to provide a redirector for Windows NT need only write an installable file system to provide services on that network and a transport driver for the type of networking protocol that's in use (such as IPX/SPX on NetWare, or NetBEUI for native NT networks, or TCP/IP on UNIX systems[17]). There is no necessity to write drivers for the specific network cards as NDIS can provide this. It's necessary only to write the other components. There is an option to write conventional monolithic network card drivers, and there is evidence that some network manufacturers are going to do so; in particular, as this is being written the Beta versions of the Novell NetWare director include Open Datalink Interface (ODI) drivers.

By doing this, Novell has bypassed the various layers of the NT subsystem below the redirector. Instead of the redirector behaving like a file system, communicating with the I/O manager, then communicating with a transport driver through the transport driver interface and, in turn, to a network card via NDIS, in the NetWare system the NetWare redirector communicates directly with the ODI subsystem, which communicates with an ODI driver. There are a couple of theoretical advantages to this monolithic approach. First of all, it's faster. The overhead involved in the multilayered interface used by the Windows NT native networking is eliminated. There are reports that the ODI-based Windows NT redirector is significantly faster than the built-in NT networking on the same network hardware. It's also true that this kind of approach simplifies matters for a company like Novell, which has a lot of internal expertise

[17]See Appendix 2 for details on protocols and device drivers.

built up in a system like ODI and can leverage this to quickly provide services for systems like Windows NT if they move the entire system over.

Unfortunately, this creates a situation in which Windows NT users who require NetWare support now have to deal with two completely different types of network drivers—and it's also causing some problems in debugging the NetWare support for Windows NT. Its behavior is not quite what you might expect in certain situations. Nevertheless, it can be done (see Chapter 9), and it's reasonable to expect that it will be done for other systems as well.

TCP/IP Services

In addition to the native LAN Manager-compatible networking built into Windows NT, a second kind of networking is built in: Transport Connect Protocol/Internet Protocol (TCP/IP) services of the type used by UNIX systems. Now this gets a little complicated because one can refer to a couple of different things when one refers to TCP/IP. On one hand TCP/IP is a transport. And there is a TCP/IP transport driver that is fully compatible with the built-in networking system. If you wish, you can run TCP/IP networking instead of NetBEUI-based networking—and, if you're running a large network, you'll want to.[18]

UNIX systems also use TCP/IP, but most do not use the Universal Naming Convention (UNC) interfaces that are used by Windows NT. So simply installing the TCP/IP transport to Windows NT will not immediately give you connectivity to UNIX systems. What will give you connectivity to UNIX systems are the low-level TCP/IP utilities (ping.exe, ftp.exe, etc.), which provide essentially native UNIX-style TCP/IP services. Windows NT lacks a Name File Service (NFS) file system and other facilities that would make this a complete end-to-end system. Effectively, the services that are provided are sufficient to make Windows NT an effective client to UNIX-based TCP/IP systems but not an effective server to UNIX clients (although this situation is changing and it now appears that NT will ship with, among other things, ftp and telnet "demon" servers allowing UNIX clients to log into NT servers—see Chapter 6 for details).

Summing Up

The basic system features of Windows NT have been developed with connectivity in mind. From a kernel design that supports symmetric multiprocessing for very large servers to built-in networking and a file system designed to support very large volumes, virtually every element of Windows NT incorporates some feature that makes networking easier. Truly, this is an operating system *designed* to connect.

---

[18]Actually, you'll want to run a *mixed* environment, using TCP/IP for internetworking, and another protocol for local connections. See Chapter 6 and Appendix 2 for details.

For More Information

Custer, Helen (1993), *Inside Windows NT.* Redmond, WA: Microsoft Press, ISBN: 1-55615-481-X. Outstanding (and detailed) general coverage of the Windows NT architecture. Chapter 6 (on NT's networking features) is especially valuable.

Feldman, Len (1993), *Windows NT: The Next Generation.* Carmel, IN: Sams Publishing, ISBN: 0-672-30298-5. Generally a less technically rigorous treatment than Custer's book, but makes up for it by giving a balanced comparison of NT and its competitors. Curiously enough, the networking coverage is in Chapter 6, just as in Custer's book.

Korzeniowski, Paul (1993), "Windows NT: How will it fit into your LAN environment?" *Info World,* p. 56, June 14, 1993. Good summary of current NT network status, especially with respect to foreign networks.

Letwin, Gordon (1988), *Inside OS/2.* Redmond, WA: Microsoft Press, ISBN: 1-55615-117-9. Comparable in structure to Custer's book, but more programmer-oriented. Worth a look for those wishing to cut through the IBM-vs-Microsoft propaganda; this book gives a snapshot of the situation that eventually led to Windows NT.

Ruley, John (1991), "OS/2 is Alive and Well..: The 32-bit Windows Controversy," *Windows and OS/2 Magazine*, p. 122, March 1991. This article presented coverage of the "Strategy Seminar" at which Microsoft first publicly revealed plans for Windows NT, then known as OS/2 version 3.0.

Clark, Glen (1993), "Under the Bonnet," *NET News*, p. 2, May/June 1993. Excellent low-level coverage of NT's network architecture, by Microsoft's TechNet corporate support group.

Preparing to Connect

When you have finished reading this chapter, you should understand:

- **How to conduct a network needs analysis**
- **How to select and organize components for a Windows NT network**
- **The Windows NT installation process**
- **Major installation options, including disk versus CD-ROM-based installation**
- **How to install Windows NT over a network**
- **What the most common installation problems are, and how to work around them**

You should feel comfortable installing and configuring Windows NT workstations and standalone servers. You should *not* feel "comfortable" about assuming responsibility for the planning of a network on your own, but you should understand how to go about *becoming* comfortable with your particular network needs.

Before installing Windows NT—before you even purchase the software—you must first create a plan for your network. You should think of this plan as a network blueprint which, like an architect's blueprint for a building, must contain the information necessary to create a sturdy structure for many people to use on a regular basis.

The plan will be based on the data that you provide through a *network needs analysis* for your particular business. The needs analysis is really a series of questions that you must answer to provide yourself with the information you'll require when you create your network plan and set up your server. A network needs analysis checklist follows. Use this as a guide when creating your network.

Your blueprint should be considered as seriously as the plan for a multistory office building. Just like an office complex, your server and network will store mission-critical information for your business, allow users to work together on projects, and exchange information and (electronic) interoffice mail. Just like in an office building, you'll need to provide for quick, unimpeded access to various parts of the structure.

In addition to providing access, you'll need to consider security. It may be permissible for various groups in a building to have access to the shipping and receiving department or the sales offices, but it may not be acceptable for those same people to have access to the office where personnel records are kept. Your server is no different. You'll want to provide access for groups of users to various parts of the server's file structure, but restrict them from others. This applies to access to networked resources like printers, as well as data.

Your network blueprint will provide for more than just the access of the users; you'll also need to include information about the number of users and type of work they'll be performing, the amount of storage space they'll require, and their hours of operation. This information will help you plan for the type of hardware that you'll need and the amount of RAM and server storage, in addition to the reliability of the equipment you'll use for your server and network.

Conducting a Network Needs Analysis

Network Needs Analysis Checklist

- Goal statement
- Number of initial users
- Maximum number of expected users
- Type of work to be conducted
- Application requirements
- Estimated minimum storage requirements
- Hours of operation
- Building power
- Uninterruptable power supply (UPS) required
- Level of reliability required
- Level of security required

Let's begin by looking at what you intend on doing with your network and server in the first place. To start with, you should be able to define the goal of your network in a couple of sentences. Your goal doesn't need to be complex, but it should be concrete and specific. For instance, "a way for my users all over the building to store their data," is not only vague, but, if it were truly all you wanted in a network, you'd be wasting a lot of time installing such a powerful network operating system when all you really wanted was some common data storage.

Your goal statement should be more specific to your particular business requirements, such as:

Goal: A method for the twelve-person accounting department to store and share billing and payable information, including a system of electronic mail and shared printers for printing checks, invoices, and correspondence, keeping in mind the demonstrated 20% annual increase in staffing of this department.

This goal is concrete and finite; it defines the purpose of the network and server and outlines the specific functions that the network must provide. It also reminds us that the department will have increased needs in the future.

While conducting your network needs analysis you should plan for expansion and flexibility. It's often difficult to plan for the things you are sure about, and planning for the future may seem impossible; but you do have certain facts available to assist you. For example, you can look at the growth rate for your department and the amount of work you will be performing. You also need to take into account the cyclical nature of the department and business. All of this information is important when creating your plan.

From this information, you can begin to assess the requirements of your network. While you conduct your network needs analysis, it's also important to include comments from your users. If you refer again to the network needs analysis checklist, you'll see the general nature of the questions to ask.

This is the relatively simple part of creating your plan, asking and answering questions, but people often skip this part entirely. Sometimes they forget to include those who will be using the network or they neglect to plan for future growth. Either mistake will create a problem later when the network has been purchased and installed. Better to spend a couple of days planning now than to spend many weeks later on, debating the need to purchase more hard drive storage. Enough lecture—don't neglect your plan.

Planning the Physical Layout

Once you have collected the information you need, you can begin to blueprint your physical network. The physical location of all the equipment necessary for your network should be drafted on a layer over the building blueprint. For example, on the accompanying diagram consider the accounting department's cubicles, offices and storage areas. When planning the physical layout be as accurate as possible so the correct amount of cabling will be purchased and network connections will be convenient for each workstation.

Blueprinting your network in a logical order (e.g., from the server out to the desktops and peripherals) will help you take into account all needed hardware. It will also highlight any problem areas that you need to be aware of while having cabling installed.

Server Location

The server needs to be located in a spot that is at once accessible to the network administrator and inaccessible to daily office traffic. A well-ventilated storage closet that can be locked would serve the purpose. If your building is not air-conditioned, you may elect to purchase and install an air-conditioner for your server closet. You need to be sure that the server receives power from a different electrical circuit than the air-conditioner.

Speaking of power, you *must* have an uninterruptible power supply (UPS) for your server. Power failures are especially common during the summer months, when severe electrical storms and heavy electrical usage for building air-conditioning combine to create an atmosphere conducive to brownouts or blackouts. An unexpected power failure can wreak disaster on an unprotected server.

UPSes vary in their power ratings and features, but all provide the same basic functionality. A UPS is a DC battery source that sits between your server (or workstation) and your building's AC power and uses building power to sustain its charge—usually enough to keep your server running through a proper shutdown cycle. Windows NT Advanced Server's built-in UPS device management monitors the power to your server and, in case of power failure, uses the UPS battery power to automatically, and gracefully, shut down server operations.

The Windows NT UPS control panel option lets you configure your server to work with UPS data received via one of the serial ports. When it receives data indicating the UPS has activated, an automated shutdown procedure executes. You can specify that a custom command file run prior to shutting down the system if your server has special requirements. Chapter 3 will give you more details about the UPS services for Windows NT.

Concentrator Location

As you plan your network hardware, working your way out from the server, you encounter a box called a LAN Concentrator. A concentrator provides a method for connecting all of your workstations, servers, and peripherals. The accompanying diagram shows a scheme for providing LAN connectivity via UTP (unshielded twisted pair) or standard telephone wiring. This is referred to as 10BaseT cabling.

10BaseT cabling connects your desktop systems in a star configuration to a concentrator, which can handle between eight and sixteen devices. Most concentrators can be connected to other concentrators, via 10Base2 cabling or proprietary connectors, so you can expand your network. Ethernet has a practical limit of 1,024 devices, including servers, that you can connect in this fashion. Don't try to exceed it! Plan for subnets, a series of smaller networks within your LAN connected via bridges or routers.

Typically, 10BaseT concentrators are located in the telephone service closets where the wiring can be punched down onto a block and then wired to the concentrator. Your concentrator should be mounted in a rack for stability and placed in a ventilated area. It should also be protected by a UPS, unless it has some type of on-board power management. Again, the location of these devices should be away from high-traffic areas in a place that can be locked.

Hardware Requirements and Considerations

Chapter 1 provided an overview of the advanced features and functionality of Windows NT. Before installing Windows NT on every workstation in an enterprise, it's wise to step back and evaluate just who does and who does not need NT.

Do You Really Need Windows NT on Your Workstations?

The most important consideration is the hardware you'll need to run NT. Workstations need a minimum of 12MB, and servers need a minimum of 16MB. Note the word *minimum*—systems that will make heavy use of multitasking or act as special-purpose servers will require more (as you will see in the next section). Further, if you are running on the Intel platform, do not consider NT unless you are running on 486 machines. A simple rule of thumb: If you are considering replacing older or lower-end machines with 486s equipped with large amounts of memory, Windows NT is a much clearer, more obvious choice. However, you also need to evaluate which features you will definitely use, and those you might use, before making your decision.

For example, if you are working in a secure environment (such as a financial institution), NT's file sharing security, file access audit trails, and C2 security features might justify a move to NT. If security is not a high priority, a suitable workstation solution may be Windows for Workgroups, since systems running WFW can easily be connected as clients to a Windows NT server.

Another consideration is the applications you will run on NT. Multithreaded 32-bit applications were just starting to become available at the time this book was written. If you plan to run your current suite of 16-bit Windows word processing and spreadsheet applications, there is no need to move to Windows NT.

Furthermore, not all 16-bit applications run under Windows NT. Applications that directly access hardware (such as some backup programs) cannot be run in NT because that behavior violates NT's security model.

Another consideration when making the jump to NT is the availability of drivers for your current hardware. Driver support in the initial release of NT is limited in the area of peripherals, and developers have noted that writing drivers is much more difficult under NT. Thus, you may wish to consider which drivers are available and match them to your current hardware devices to ensure that you can in fact run your applications.

Having said all that, if you've decided certain people need to run Windows NT, then here's a guide to the hardware they'll need:

Windows NT Hardware Requirements

The following is a consolidated list of requirements and recommendations that will allow you to select and configure an appropriate computer for operation as either a Windows NT workstation or server. The recommended configurations are based on personal experience and the information published so far by Microsoft. We recommend that you consult the current published Windows NT specifications for further information.

The particular system configuration that you will use will be some combination of a central processor unit, RAM (including CPU cache RAM), hard disk capacity (or other mass storage space), backup device, CD-ROM, floppy disk, network card, and printer. There are also a variety of special devices such as modems, multiport cards, and X.25 cards that may be appropriate in special circumstances.

CPU

The basic Windows NT requirement published by Microsoft is a 25MHz 386 (series B2 or later) or better Intel-compatible CPU, or an ARC[1] system-compliant RISC computer (MIPS R4000 or better). The situation for RISC computers in particular is in a state of flux as of this writing; it is recommended that if you're investigating purchase of a RISC system (such as one of the DEC AXP series systems) you consult with the manufacturer for current specifications. Anyway, that's what Microsoft recommends. Now let's say a few words about what *we* recommend.

To understand why we will *not* recommend that you purchase a 386 system of *any* configuration for use with Windows NT, it's necessary to explain a bit about cache memory. All advanced CPUs (Intel 486SX or better, and all RISC) employ a CPU cache. It's simply a small amount of static RAM (SRAM) that is closely coupled to the central processing unit and which can exchange data with the central processor at speeds much higher than that of the normal Dynamic Random Access Memory (DRAM) used in most microcomputers. The reason for the use of the SRAM cache is *speed*. In order to operate at CPU speeds SRAM caches have to have very high memory access speeds—for instance, a 50MHz CPU will require 20-nanosecond static RAM. However, if you call around to electronics suppliers you will find that 20-nanosecond static RAM is extremely expensive. On the other hand, conventional DRAM, with access speeds on the order of 70 nanoseconds, is relatively cheap. Therefore, a two-tier approach, in which a small amount of very fast memory (SRAM) is connected directly to the processor, and then that fast *cache* memory is in turn refreshed from a main memory (DRAM) that runs more slowly, tends to provide the most economical system construction while retaining high performance.

The problem with this approach is that Windows NT as a multithreaded preemptive multitasking system has much larger cache requirements than a conventional single thread operating system such as DOS or Novell NetWare. If you remember the discussion of preemptive multitasking in Chapter 1, one concept introduced was called the *working set*. That is the sum total of system processes that have to be continuously switched in and out of memory. The working set expands as you do more with the computer. A server computer will have a working set that includes the necessary threads to maintain each of its current connections. A workstation that is undertaking a number of graphical paths simultaneously will have multiple threads continuously switched in and out of the CPU for each of the tasks that it is performing. In order for a Windows NT system to operate at full efficiency you must equip it with enough cache RAM *to maintain the entire working set in memory.*

Microsoft has published no specifications on this subject, but experiments conducted by our team indicate that providing up to 256KB of cache RAM will provide a substantial gain in performance and a nearly linear gain as the cache RAM is increased. The Intel 486 series processors have an 8KB on-chip cache; the Pentium processor has a 16KB on-chip cache.

[1]Advanced Resouce Computer (ARC)—part of the Advanced Computing Environment (ACE) initiative sponsored by Microsoft, MIPS, and others.

Neither even begins to approach the kind of cache sizes that give a real benefit in Windows NT—they're too small by a factor of ten! Providing 32KB of cache RAM will improve matters, 64KB will improve it even more, 128KB gives an enormous improvement, and providing 256KB seems to be approximately the point at which the benefit tops out. Going upward from that to 512KB or even a megabyte will still provide an incremental improvement, but the improvement probably will not match the additional cost.

An exception to this situation might occur in technical workstations that are principally intended for compute-intensive tasks such as computer-aided design, computer-aided engineering, or scientific computation—tasks generally performed by RISC workstations. In these situations, going up to 512KB or even one megabyte of cache can provide a substantial benefit and, for this reason, we recommend that *all* RISC workstations be equipped with a minimum of 512KB external cache, preferably a megabyte if it's available.

Since cache is critical to system performance, and 386 processors do not include *any* internal cache memory (and because the processors themselves are less efficient than their 486 counterparts), *we do not recommend that anyone purchase a 386 system to run Windows NT.* If you have an installed base of 386-based systems in your organization, you can use them as Windows NT workstations (and perhaps as print servers), but you will not see high performance. Speed will benefit if you can upgrade the system to add CPU cache. However, the nature of most 386 motherboards is such that you probably won't be able to do this—so it's probably best to think about recycling 386 systems as DOS workstations or print servers, or for other applications that don't require high performance.

Memory

Windows NT is a memory hog by DOS standards. It requires a stated minimum, according to Microsoft, of 12MB RAM. However, based upon experience in this and other configurations, we recommend that *all* Windows NT workstations have a minimum of 16MB RAM (over and above the CPU cache). The small additional cost of the RAM more than pays off in improved performance.

These requirements seem excessive to people used to DOS systems that would require a megabyte or two, but it's worth noting that for Windows NT, strange as it may seem, 12 or 16 megabytes is just a starting point. That's significant because, as many users are beginning to find out, 16 megabytes or more in a DOS/Windows environment may present a practical upper limit. While it's perfectly possible to expand the memory in many current systems up to 32 megabytes, there are basic, fundamental operational limits in both DOS and Windows that cannot be expanded upon simply by adding more memory.

A good example is Windows 3.1 system resources—128KB, no more, no less, of system space is reserved for two system memory heaps that contain common resource information used by Windows applications. If you run many applications together and exhaust that 128KB of resource space then your system will crash. It will not matter whether the system has 16MB of memory, 32MB of memory, or 100MB of memory; the system will crash. Windows NT, on the other hand, has *no fundamental upper limits.*[2] Beyond the basic 16MB recommendation, various Windows NT options may require additional memory.

Print Server Memory Requirements

If a Windows NT workstation or server is used to provide shared print services for other Windows NT workstations it will need an additional four or more megabytes of RAM space to efficiently process remote print requests. This is needed because Windows NT employs a powerful new concept in that you need not install the print device driver for a particular printer on all workstations. Instead, when a Windows NT workstation wishes to print, it gets a copy of the necessary driver from the print server, renders the image, and transmits the resulting byte stream to the print server, which then prints the image. This is a more efficient approach. It's much easier to administer but it does mean that the print server has to carry out significant print operations itself. And for this reason, and in order not to cause a significant performance hit, the additional memory is required in the print servers. Based upon examination of Microsoft documentation it would appear that 4MB of memory will be sufficient to support up to about six printers. If more printers are to be supported in a print pool it may be necessary to add additional memory, or perhaps it would bear consideration to move the additional printers onto another machine since every Windows NT workstation can also function as a print server.

Advanced Server Memory Requirements

For Windows NT Advanced Servers additional memory will be required for a variety of services. The fault tolerance driver will require approximately 2MB additional memory (consult the Microsoft documentation or your hardware supplier for details). If, in addition to fault tolerance, you employ RAID level-5 support (stripe sets with parity) then an additional 4MB of memory will be necessary to support the overhead involved (three times the regular memory requirement for disk writes in order to provide space for the necessary parity computations). Employing the Windows NT Advanced Server's multi-user Remote Access Services or Macintosh file system support will also incur an additional memory requirement (again, consult the latest Microsoft documentation for minimum requirements). Our own experience with operation of Windows NT Advanced Server on a 32MB RISC-based platform has been completely satisfactory; so we suspect that a 32MB configuration (probably 24MB would be sufficient on Intel platforms) will be sufficient for most small-to-medium network operations. Larger networks will require more memory.

[2] The practical limit set by the 32-bit address range employed by Windows NT is four *gigabytes*—4,096MB of system memory. We believe that this limit will not be exceeded until at least until the end of this century, which as we write is only seven years away!

Hard Disk Space

The official Microsoft disk space requirement is 70MB of hard disk space, of which 20MB will be used for a paging file. Now we begin to reach one of the most complex parts of the overall Windows NT equation—because that paging file can grow and the efficiency of the paging file will be higher if its initial size is set near to the size it will eventually expand to. This is something that can be found only by experiment (and is discussed in more detail in Chapter 5). However, as a practical consideration, given that the operating system itself takes about 50MB of hard disk space, another 20MB is a bare minimum requirement for the paging file; so the stated 70MB disk requirement leaves *no* space for applications.

We recommend a bare minimum of 100MB for Windows NT workstations. Note that we say *workstations*, and it's important to be very clear about this. If you are running Windows NT stations that are connected to a network and these stations get all of their applications support over the network and store little or nothing locally, then 100MB is probably sufficient. If you wish to use *any* local applications, if you need local storage space, or if you wish to operate the Windows NT system as a standalone workstation, then we think that the disk requirement should be more like 200MB. Server requirements, of course, are higher. The basic requirement for the server is no higher than that for the workstation, but you must provide additional space for the user files, and undoubtedly (over time) for a growing paging file.

A 200MB hard disk represents a practical minimum for a small-to-medium-size server. You should add approximately 20MB for each user who will be logged into the system (less if you make little use of server resources in your configuration). In general, if the workstations are constrained in hard disk space then you will need more server hard disk space or vice versa. An example of a reasonable working minimum is about one gigabyte (1,024MB) which, based on our experience, appears to be sufficient space for a server that will service twenty to thirty users.

Besides the basic storage space requirements, there is another consideration that should be borne in mind when selecting a hard disk for a Windows NT system, and that is the type of disk controller employed. Windows NT's preemptive multitasking, as discussed in Chapter 1, provides for a very powerful feature to improve performance: overlapped I/O. That is, the central processor can initiate an I/O request, for instance, a request to read information from a disk file, and continue to work on other tasks while it waits for the hard disk controller to inform it that the request is complete. However, this applies only if a hard disk controller is used that will allow the central processor to go on and perform its work. The very inexpensive, low-end hard disk controllers that employ programmed logic or use the more primitive forms of direct memory access (DMA) don't work this way. In general, for these controllers, the CPU will have to perform the actual transfer of information into the controller, and while it's doing that, it can't do anything else. Therefore, performance of both Windows NT workstations and servers will be significantly enhanced if you select a better disk controller.

For servers, if either disk striping or RAID Level-5 (disk striping with parity) support is desired, then the only practical choice is a SCSI disk controller, as they support chaining of multiple disk drives. As a practical matter in this day and age, for server operations with large hard disks, SCSI seems to us the only practical choice. Choices for workstations will vary depending on the expense. For high-performance workstations we recommend that SCSI be looked at closely, especially given the requirement that SCSI be used for CD-ROMs and tape drives, which will be discussed later in this section. In servers, the best performance will be achieved using intelligent disk controllers, which can carry out operations independently of the system's CPU. Investigate the Windows NT hardware compatibility list and talk to the manufacturers of the systems that you're investigating as to what specific configurations are available. You probably won't want to risk selecting a hard disk controller (or *any* component) not listed on the NT hardware compatibility list unless you have actually seen this component demonstrated with a non-Beta driver. Otherwise, you are asking for trouble.

Bus Architectures

As you might imagine from the foregoing discussion of CPU, memory, and hard disk capacities required for Windows NT, the system bus architecture becomes extremely significant with Windows NT, especially in a high-performance configuration. There are currently three popular bus architectures, each with its own advantages and disadvantages. Here's a brief discussion of each.

ISA Bus

The most popular of today's bus architectures remains the Industry Standard Architecture (ISA) bus—that is, the original IBM AT bus as updated by today's cloners (curiously enough, not generally available from IBM!). The ISA bus in today's incarnation is a 16-bit bus architecture generally operating at a bus data rate of 8MHz. Memory is generally not available on the bus but instead is connected locally to the CPU and will operate at significantly higher speeds, typically 25MHz. There may or may not be a local bus connection between the CPU and the video card operating at higher speeds. If this is available, it should be investigated—particularly on workstations as it can provide a significant performance enhancement.

The major advantage of the ISA bus architecture is that it is cheap. The ISA bus machines are the popular "PC clones" that have made modern business computers a commodity item. The major disadvantage is the combination of 16-bit bus bandwidth with an 8MHz data rate, which gives a functional maximum throughput of 16MB per second. Modern CPUs operate at 32-bit data widths and speeds up to 66MHz, producing overall throughput on the order of sixteen times the ISA bus throughput. As you might imagine, this can present something of a performance bottleneck, emphatically for high-performance servers or for diskless workstations that are transmitting most of their information over the network. No matter how fast your network interface card is, you can't access it any faster than the bus rate. Therefore, we do not recommend the ISA bus for use in any but the *smallest* Windows NT server installations. It makes a great deal of sense in low-cost workstations, but should never be used where high performance is required.

EISA Bus

The Extended Industry Standard Architecture (EISA) bus was developed by a consortium of PC clone manufacturers led by Compaq, and is functionally a 32-bit extension of the 16-bit

ISA bus architecture. It has two great advantages, the first of which is that by doubling the number of bits it effectively doubles the system throughput. It also provides features that allow *bus mastering* of certain devices, meaning that a hard disk controller or network interface card (or other peripheral) can effectively take the place of the CPU for some operations and operate independently of the CPU. This is a decided advantage, especially in servers where the bottleneck introduced by shoving data across the bus and waiting for it to be processed by a peripheral can be significant. A further advantage is compatibility: 32-bit EISA bus systems will accept 8- or 16-bit ISA bus cards, although the introduction of such cards will introduce a significant performance hit into the system and, therefore, should be avoided.

The major disadvantage of EISA bus systems is cost, both for the system itself and for the peripheral cards. You should, again, bear in mind that the introduction of *any* ISA bus cards into an EISA bus system will degrade the performance of the EISA bus system to ISA bus standards. Therefore, don't buy an EISA bus system if you are going to put an ISA bus disk controller card (or network interface card) in it as you will never see the EISA bus performance advantage. EISA bus systems are good choices for high-performance workstations and for servers under Windows NT.

MCA Bus

This Micro Channel Architecture (MCA) was IBM's answer to the EISA bus development and also IBM's major attempt to replace the ISA bus that they had originated with the AT computer. The MCA bus is a from-the-ground-up redesign of the computer bus with many advantages, the principal ones being a significantly higher system bus data rate (25MHz) as well as provisions for bus mastering and for burst data transmission at high speeds. The MCA bus is a good choice for both workstations and servers, but it has one great limitation—cost and availability of components. If you are buying IBM equipment it's an outstanding choice, and IBM has a wide range of computers and peripherals that use the MCA bus. If you wish to be able to buy from third parties, however, you are going to find less availability of peripherals—and virtually everything costs more for MCA (a problem shared with EISA). However, again, MCA will provide a significant performance advantage (comparable to that provided with EISA).

Other Choices

There are a variety of other options, especially in the more exotic computers, such as the Symmetric Multiprocessor (SMP) and Reduced Instruction Set Computer (RISC) machines discussed in Appendix 5. A variety of approaches have been used, including multiple parallel memory bus architectures and proprietary local bus architectures. If you are considering any computer using such a proprietary bus architecture there are two things you should examine with great care. One is availability of peripherals on this bus architecture. The other is the provision that has been made for using an auxiliary bus, generally an MCA or an EISA bus, to install additional interface cards.

Almost invariably in a proprietary bus architecture there will be some peripherals you need that won't be available for the proprietary bus. For example, you may not be able to install the necessary interface card to accommodate a tape drive. Therefore, general practice in proprietary bus architecture systems is to employ a secondary bus—in today's environment, either an MCA or an EISA bus—for such peripherals. But you want to be very careful when you look at the system configuration. As with using ISA bus interface cards in an EISA bus computer, any EISA or MCA bus cards in a proprietary bus computer will impact performance.

How noticeable that performance impact is will depend on the devices in use. A tape drive, for example, or CD-ROM drive, might slow performance *while you are using that device*. On the other hand, in a network server, if the network interface card is sitting on the EISA bus this means that every time a network request is transmitted the system has to operate at the lower bus speeds. This can have a significant impact and it should be investigated closely.

Backup

All Windows NT servers and some Windows NT workstations will, in all probability, require backup devices. Let's repeat that statement in the strongest possible terms: *Every Windows NT server* requires *a backup device*. This is not an option. Can you configure a Windows NT Advanced Server without a backup device? Yes, and you will pay for that choice. You do not even want to consider configuring a server system without providing backup.

Windows NT has a simple but effective backup program built into it, which is covered in more detail in Chapter 3. The system's basic limitation is that it supports only tape drive devices with SCSI interfaces. Therefore, you'll need a compatible SCSI controller to support the tape backup and a tape device from the Windows NT hardware compatibility list. It is possible (indeed likely) that other options will become available from manufacturers over time. It remains to be seen whether this will show up in the form of device drivers that will permit the built-in tape backup software to support other types of backup devices or (as with other operating systems) proprietary software to drive the device. It should be noted that the latter is a much less desirable solution.

The advantage of the built-in tape backup software (aside from its inclusion with the operating system) is that it supports a variety of devices—should you someday experience difficulty with your tape backup hardware, you'll be able to substitute any other device for which a driver is available. You can't do that if you buy a tape drive with a proprietary piece of software. Unfortunately, as of this writing, Windows NT does not support compression on tape devices and, therefore, will require higher-capacity tape devices than you might be able to get away with in other environments. In general, you should buy a tape device with a capacity equal to (or for growth, greater than) the total hard disk capacity of your system.

UPS

Much as with the backup device, an uninterruptible power supply is *mandatory* on all Windows NT Servers (and desirable on workstations). Specifics of setting up the UPS service are covered in detail in Chapter 3.

CD-ROM

As with backup, CD-ROM should be considered essential for all Windows NT servers and it is highly desirable on workstations. Microsoft distributes Windows NT on both CD-ROM and floppy disks. However, the server installation consists of some twenty-four floppy diskettes—not an installation that anyone will undertake lightly. The CD-ROM installation is much simpler, consisting of one CD ROM and two floppy diskettes.

Having a CD-ROM available on the server also provides a variety of other interesting options—such as the availability of Microsoft-TechNet on CD-ROM, components of the Microsoft knowledge base on CD-ROM, and third-party products on CD-ROM. It should also be noted that placing the CD-ROM on the server and then sharing it over the network will permit you to carry out efficient over-the-network installations that cannot be easily done using floppy disks. Therefore, a CD-ROM should be considered a necessity on Windows NT servers, not an option.

As with the tape drive, the major limitation here is that Windows NT supports, as of this writing, only SCSI-compatible CD-ROMs. So, again, you're going to have to have a SCSI controller and a CD-ROM from the Windows NT hardware compatibility list. As you may imagine, given that SCSI is required for both the CD-ROM and the tape drive, for an Advanced Server, SCSI makes sense as the primary transport mechanism for your hard disks as well, allowing you to have just one disk controller for the entire system. Since SCSI also supports use of the various disk array options supported by the Windows NT Advanced Server we recommend SCSI as the standard disk controller type for all NT server installations.

Floppy Disks

Although an over-the-network installation from CD-ROM is available, works beautifully, and is much simpler and easier to maintain than handing around floppy disks on each workstation, we should point out one rather serious issue. Once you have used this approach, you are unable to provide driver updates from floppy—the files on the CD are incompatible with the diskette-based setup program, and vice-versa.[3] So in an environment where you might otherwise specify diskless workstations, you must still consider driver updates and stations that must sometimes operate independently of the network.

Therefore, machines that will sometimes have to operate independently from the network (such as portables, see below) should be set up from the first from floppy disk—even though this involves sticking some twenty or more diskettes into the computer.

Where some workstations are dedicated network-only systems, you could configure these as diskless systems. However, should the system's registry ever become corrupted, you will find it inconvenient to employ the standard Windows NT Emergency Diskette approach—the maintenance team will first have to open up the workstation and physically connect a

[3] A workaround to this problem is available. From the command-line prompt, change directories to \WINDOWS\SYSTEM32 and rename all *.inf files to *.inc. Then copy all the *.in_ files from *all* floppy disks to the directory. Then expand *.in_ to *.inf. To switch back to the CD-based install, rename *.inf to *.ind and *.inc to *.inf.

floppy disk in order to boot the recovery diskette. For fully secure operations this may be the only choice (short of physically locking the floppy disk drive, assuming that such a mechanism can be fabricated or purchased). But for anything other than an ultra-secure network installation, providing one 3.5-inch 1.44-megabyte capacity floppy diskette on each workstation will save a great deal of trouble.

Miscellaneous Devices

The use of Windows NT Remote Access Services (RAS) to provide Wide Area Networking connections between isolated Windows NT machines and the network will require compatible modems to be employed at both ends (for maximum efficiency, the server will require either an X.25 or multiport card). These issues are discussed further in Chapter 7. Likewise, Chapter 7 is the place to look for information on the necessary hardware to support the Macintosh file system, which may require either an AppleTalk card installed in the server or (preferably, for performance reasons) an Ethernet card in the server coupled to EtherTalk hardware on the Macintosh machines. The selection of appropriate UPS hardware is discussed elsewhere in this chapter. Remember that the first place to look when considering the selection of a particular hardware device is the current Windows NT Hardware Compatibility List.[4]

Portables

It may seem ridiculous after talking about 16MB RAM and 100MB hard disk requirements to even consider running Windows NT on a portable. Yet it can be done, and it has some interesting advantages. Windows NT will run reasonably well on a 486SX25 or better CPU portable with 12MB of RAM (it works better with 16MB) and 100MB of hard disk (it works better with more), basically the same requirements as a Windows NT workstation.

The most convenient approach to configuring such a portable, unfortunately, is to set it up from floppy disks from the outset. It is possible, of course, to employ a Xircom Pocket LAN adapter (or equivalent) to give the portable access to a shared CD-ROM for an over-the-network install using the WINNT.EXE file. Unfortunately, while this does get the portable up, if you then have to go back and add any drivers you will find that you cannot use the floppy disks, since the format of the information on the floppy is completely different from that on CD.[5]

You can save time and trouble when installing and configuring a Windows NT portable system by installing Remote Access Services on the first pass. This will allow you, using null-modem serial cable connections (or a compatible modem), to communicate with the server computer, and is an effective alternative to installing from floppy disks. Given an RAS connection and access to a phone line or null-modem cable, it is always possible to update drivers and so forth from the CD-ROM at the central site.

---

[4]Available on CompuServe (in download area 1 of the WINNT forum) or by calling Microsoft.

[5]See footnote 3 for a workaround.

Printers

The printing situation in Windows NT is good news indeed. Windows NT supports every printer that is supported by Windows 3.1 and also, using the built-in DLC (Data Link Control) driver, supports network printers such as the LaserJet IIIsi. The latter can be extremely convenient since it can be plugged into the network at any convenient location without requiring a direct physical connection to the print server.

All Windows NT machines can function as print servers. You need not dedicate a machine to this task, nor do you need to necessarily connect all the printers to the file server. In general, you have as wide a choice of printers as you could ask for. Selecting a printer will largely be a matter of speed, reliability, and cost. For desktop publishing and other graphics work, PostScript printers remain desirable because of the tremendous infrastructure of PostScript compatible software. For most other applications, any laser printer that supports True Type fonts will provide a perfectly acceptable result.

One issue that does bear some consideration is the implication of mixing RISC and x86 computers in a Windows NT network. The over-the-network printer driver approach used by Windows NT has the great advantage that each workstation does not have to have its own print driver. It does have the slight disadvantage that the print server has to have all types of printer drivers that might be requested of it. Therefore, if you are running a network that includes x86-based workstations, MIPS R4000-based workstations, and DEC Alpha AXP workstations; any print server that is made available to all of the above will require all three types of print drivers.

This is not difficult to do. It is merely necessary to first install the native print driver for the print server CPU on the print server, then select "other" from the list of print drivers and designate the directory from which to obtain the print drivers for the foreign types (the \MIPS directory on the installation CD-ROM, for instance). The Windows NT Print Manager will determine whether the request is coming from a RISC workstation as opposed to an x86 system and will employ the proper print driver at that time.

Simultaneous use of multiple print driver types on a high-capacity print server may require additional memory. As noted earlier, 4MB of memory should be sufficient for a Windows NT print server that services up to six printers. In an extreme case, that could turn out to be 4MB for each type so that, for instance, mixing Alpha, R4000, and x86 systems might require as much as 12MB of memory over and above the 12MB of basic memory for Windows NT in the print server. The probable requirement is less (it is unlikely that the print server will ever have to service *simultaneous* print jobs from all three types of systems), but expanding the memory is not a bad thing to do and will probably produce some performance benefit.

Limitations

Note that Windows NT cannot be run on all systems. Specifically excluded are those that use the DoubleSpace compression algorithm from DOS 6, as well as competing products, such as Stacker (Stac Electronics) or SuperStor (AddStor). This is a pity, as the disk space requirements for Windows NT are such that it could undoubtedly benefit from a compatible compressor. Hopefully some third party will fill this need in the near future.

Hardware

The major problem with hardware support on Windows NT occurs when you want to upgrade existing equipment to run Windows NT, at which point you will discover every piece of proprietary or otherwise incompatible hardware in your inventory. A useful first step is to examine the hardware requirements section earlier in this chapter as this will give you a good working understanding of what to watch out for. In the meantime, here are a few situations that we *know* will cause problems.

CD-ROMs

A variety of manufacturers (notably Creative Labs in the Sound Blaster series of add-on cards) have produced multimedia upgrade kits in which a sound board is provided with a proprietary CD-ROM interface. Generally this is a partial SCSI interface. Windows NT is not compatible with such boards and the CD-ROM drives associated with them will not work. An alternative to provide reuse of this hardware within a Windows NT network is to install these boards into systems that will run Windows for Workgroups. The drives can then be shared from Windows for Workgroups using the /s parameter on the MSCDX CD-ROM support software provided from Microsoft, and the drives can then be accessed over the network by Windows NT machines. But there is no way that you can install and use them within Windows NT workstations or servers. This is a pity, as Windows NT does support the Sound Blaster for audio output.

Tape Drives

Again, the major problem is the provision of proprietary interfaces by manufacturers, generally some form of slightly modified disk interface. It's not uncommon to find tape drives that expect to be connected either as disk B or disk D connected to a standard AT-bus disk controller. Neither will work with Windows NT, although it is possible that a hardware manufacturer might be able to get around this by providing a Virtual Device Driver (VDD)[6] that would patch their DOS software to talk to Windows NT. You should consult your hardware manufacturer for details. In general, however (as noted earlier), the use of a proprietary tape backup scheme will negate the greatest advantage of Windows NT's built-in tape backup, which is that the same tape backup software works with a variety of devices and makes it possible for you to substitute one device for another, pretty much at will. Approach this situation with caution, even if the manufacturer does provide a patch.

[6] This approach is documented in the *Windows NT Device Driver Development Guide*.

Motherboards

This can be one of the most serious limitations with Windows NT—and any organization embarking on a Windows NT pilot project (more so, on a wholesale conversion to Windows NT) should examine this with care. Many early 386 motherboards are expandable only up to a maximum of 8MB RAM and will not run Windows NT properly. (It is *possible* to run Windows NT in an 8MB configuration. It is not recommended by Microsoft, and we discourage it. The performance is, frankly, terrible and it is, in general, not worth the effort.) Machines that cannot be upgraded beyond 8MB should be used with Windows for Workgroups or other software rather than attempting to run Windows NT on them in a crippled state.

Some motherboards can be upgraded only to 16MB. Some, in particular earlier 486 motherboards from Dell, will operate slowly if more than 16MB is introduced. Another issue is the availability of cache RAM, as many early 386 and 486 motherboards not only didn't ship with cache RAM but made no provision for adding it. As noted earlier, Windows NT does not reach its full performance capability until significant amounts of cache RAM are introduced into the system. The only way to deal with this situation is to inspect the manufacturer's information for the motherboards for each computer in the organization.

Obviously, when buying new equipment, avoid any system that has these kinds of problems. Make sure the system is expandable to at least 32MB of RAM (64MB for servers), and that it will accommodate at least 256KB of on-chip SRAM cache. You can save yourself significant time and trouble if you are investigating the potential for upgrades within your organization by spending time in CompuServe's Microsoft Knowledge Base,[7] checking to see what motherboards have been reported as having problems with Windows NT. Finally, a useful reference that will save time by identifying systems that you don't need to worry about is to download the current Windows NT Hardware Compatibility List.[8]

Planning Your Installation

Before you install Windows NT, there are several decisions you need to make and pieces of information you need to gather. In this section we'll look at what you need to know before you begin.

File Systems

The primary decision you need to make is which file system to use. Windows NT introduces a completely new file system, NTFS (New Technology File System). If you select NTFS, filenames can be 256 characters long, Windows NT can fully recover in the case of problems (you

[7]Go to the CompuServe MSKB (Microsoft Knowlege Base) area. This contains up-to-date technical notes on Windows NT issues, including installation. A periodic search of this area using the keywords "Windows NT" and "motherboard" will provide you with a wealth of valuable information, and may save you from making a serious mistake.

[8]Available in download area 1 of the CompuServe WINNT forum.

no longer have to run CHKDSK), and auditing and security features found in Windows NT can be enabled.

If your C drive is currently formatted as an MS-DOS drive and uses a file allocation table (FAT) file system (the kind normally used by DOS), Windows NT refers to this as a FAT drive. If you select this drive as the destination drive, Windows NT can be installed directly on this drive, or the installation program can convert the drive to an NTFS file system drive, then install the system. Windows NT can do the same with drives formatted to the OS/2 1.x High Performance File System (HPFS) 286 specification. Here's what you need to consider when selecting a file system.

Security

Only NTFS drives can be made secure according to the C2 security specifications. You can create access control lists locally and remotely with NTFS, but only remotely for other file systems. Auditing on NTFS drives lets you monitor which users access which files. Furthermore, you can set a variety of file permissions on NTFS drives, such as restricting which users can rename files or directories. By comparison, files and directories on FAT drives can be shared or not shared, but you cannot restrict a local user to read-only access as you could if the file were located on an NTFS drive (though you can do so for *remote* users—see Chapter 3 for details).

Access by DOS Applications

During installation you can also select the dual-boot option, which allows you to choose which operating system you want to use at boot time—the one originally installed or Windows NT. You cannot convert your C (boot) drive to an NTFS drive if you still plan to use the original operating system (such as MS-DOS), as it will not be able to boot from an NTFS drive. Furthermore, if you choose to install NT on a drive other than your boot drive, such as the D drive, and select the NTFS file system for that drive, all files will be invisible to DOS applications.

Filenames

NTFS allows you to create filenames with up to 256 characters, including spaces but excluding special characters (such as question or quotation marks, forward and backward slashes, less than and greater than symbols, and so on). The file extension is separated from the filename by a period (.). To maintain DOS compatibility, NT also creates a DOS-compatible filename. The algorithm for this is given in Appendix 3.

OS/2 HPFS File System

In addition to the FAT and NTFS file systems, Windows NT supports the OS/2 High Performance File System (HPFS) 286 specification used by OS/2 versions 1.1 through 1.3. HPFS has many features in common with NTFS, including long filenames, but is generally less sophisticated and reliable. The only reason to retain HPFS partitions is if they already exist on a system being converted from OS/2; and it will probably pay to bite the bullet and convert those partitions to NTFS at some point.

Apple Macintosh File System

The Windows NT Advanced Server supports a Macintosh-accessible directory format on NTFS partitions. You'll find this subject covered in more detail in Chapter 7, but for now you should be aware that you'll need at least one NTFS partition on an Advanced Server if you intend to support Macintosh computers on your network.

Network Information

Before you begin installing Windows NT, you also need to have network information and settings you'll use for your computer.

You must know the name of your computer and the name of the workgroup or domain the computer will be part of. If the computer is already part of a Windows for Workgroups group, you may use the same name.

You must also know the type of network adapter card installed as well as the card's interrupt number (IRQ) and its base address. While the installation program will do its best to automatically sense these settings, it is best to have the information ready in case the derived settings are incorrect.

You can install NT without network settings, then add or change the settings through the Control Panel's Network icon—but it's generally much simpler to set up the network when the system starts. In particular, systems being added to a Windows NT Advanced Server domain cannot be logged in and used as domain members until a network card has been installed and configured.

Network Protocols

By default, Windows NT will be installed with the Microsoft NetBEUI (NetBIOS Extended User Interface) protocol that is standard on all Microsoft (Windows NT, Windows for Workgroups, and LAN Manager) networks. Other options include TCP/IP and NWLink protocols, as well as add-in networking from third parties. This entire subject is extremely complex, and we will not attempt to cover it here. See Appendix 2 for detailed information on Windows NT protocols and drivers, Chapters 6 and 7 for information on using TCP/IP for internetworking, Chapter 8 for information on interoperating with other Microsoft network products, Chapter 9 for information about using Windows NT with Novell NetWare, and Chapter 10 for information on using Windows NT with other types of networks.

If that seems like too much reading, stick to installing NetBEUI on the first pass, and add another protocol later if your situation requires it.

Printer Information

Unlike Windows 3.1 and Windows for Workgroups, you need install a printer driver only on the server machine in Windows NT—you do not need to define a printer on any computer that does not have a printer directly attached. In NT, you change the printer configuration using the Print Manager, *not* the Control Panel, and you can add a printer at a later time. If you want to install a printer during the NT installation process, you need to know the printer make and model as well as the communications port (LPT1, etc.) used.

Passwords

You will need to know the name of the user you want assigned to this copy of Windows NT, and you will be asked for a password. You can press the Enter key to bypass setting up a password, though this defeats a major security feature. Passwords are case sensitive, and they can be changed later. An administrator can also force the expiration of passwords at regular intervals, such as every thirty days (see Chapter 3 for more information).

Updating Your Current Windows Installation

The NT installation program will look for an existing Windows or Windows NT installation, and offer to update the version of Windows. If you select this option, NT will maintain your program groups and other settings. However, if you use the Dual Boot option, you will be unable to run NT from DOS, for example. Thus, if you are evaluating NT, it is probably wise to install NT in a separate directory until your evaluation is complete, then reinstall over your Windows 3.1 or Windows for Workgroups program.

Installation Overview

As with Windows and Windows for Workgroups, the installation of Windows NT occurs in two phases. The first phase is a text-based application, asking you for the basic parameters and settings NT needs in order to be installed on your hard disk. In the second phase, the installation process turns graphical as Windows NT copies additional files and actually sets up and displays new program groups.

The installation process also varies by your response to the questions asked by the setup program. As all machines and environments vary, there is no foolproof description we can offer to all users.

As with most Microsoft application setup programs, there are two installation options at the outset. The first, Express Setup, makes most of the decisions for you, and substitutes defaults (such as the destination directory name) for you. If you select Custom Setup, you will have more control over the exact details of the installation. Because of the complex nature of Windows NT, novice users will probably prefer, and we recommend, the Express Setup option.

The Installation Process

By far the easiest way to install Windows NT is by using a CD-ROM drive that is directly attached to the computer. However, there are other methods that also allow NT to be installed if you do not have a CD-ROM drive, and they will be described here. You should allow at least thirty minutes for a Windows NT installation, a period that varies according to the speed of your hard disk and CD-ROM (assuming there are no problems during the installation process). If you are installing from floppy diskettes, allow at least seventy-five minutes for the installation.

Before doing anything else, check the boot floppy, CD, or first installation diskette for SETUP.TXT and README.WRI files. These files will contain last-minute information that's not included in the documentation, and may save you time by helping you to anticipate installation problems *before* they occur.

Windows NT begins by requiring you to boot from a special floppy. During this boot process, the installation program examines your system for compatible equipment. For example, the installation program will review its list of CD-ROM adapters, searching for one on your system that it can work with.

Installing from CD-ROM

If your CD-ROM drive is supported by Windows NT, the installation process proceeds by reading data from the CD-ROM.

If your CD-ROM drive is recognized by DOS but not by Windows NT, you can use the WINNT installation program. Make the drive letter assigned to the CD-ROM the current drive, then move to the i386 subdirectory. Insert a blank, formatted high-density floppy in the A: drive, and type WINNT. The program asks you for the location of the WINNT program (see Figure 2.1), which is the drive and directory you're currently running from. Enter the installation destination drive and path.

If your CD-ROM drive is supported by neither DOS nor Windows NT you may be able to employ the *over-the-network installation* described below. That is, share the CD-ROM drive on a Microsoft-compatible network machine from a Windows NT machine (a Windows for Workgroups machine, for instance), set up the temporary networking stuff that's necessary on that drive, and then use the WINNT.EXE file to perform the setup.

Over-the-Network Installation

In a large organization, of course, it isn't practical to carry the CD-ROMs (much less the twenty-four individual floppy disks) from computer to computer conducting an individual installation on all the workstations. It's generally a much better practice to provide a single central point for installations across the network. Microsoft has done this in a way that also provides a mechanism for employing a CD-ROM-based installation on computers that do not have a CD-ROM physically attached. This mechanism uses a DOS executable program called WINNT.EXE that will copy all the files onto the local hard disk until a sufficient point is

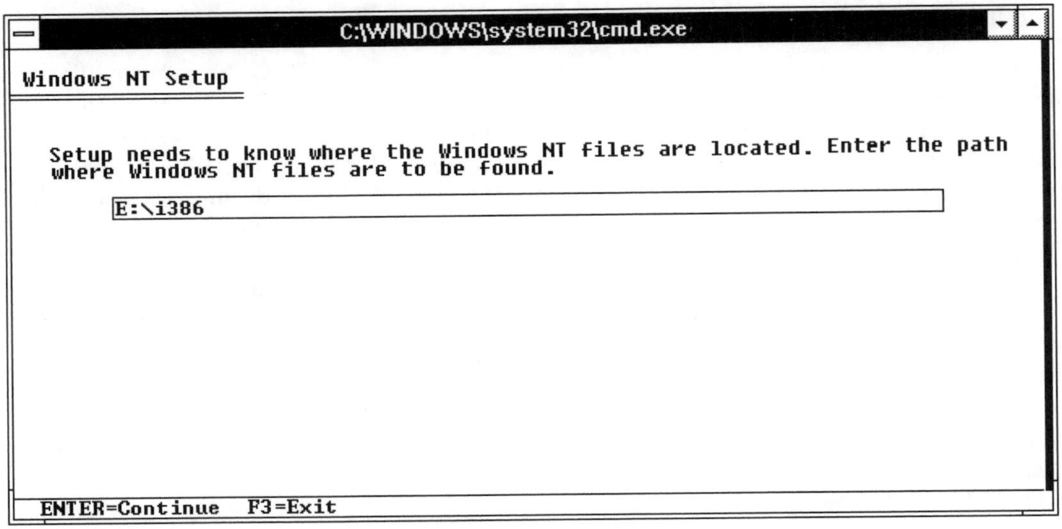

```
C:\WINDOWS\system32\cmd.exe

Windows NT Setup

  Setup needs to know where the Windows NT files are located. Enter the path
  where Windows NT files are to be found.

      E:\i386

ENTER=Continue  F3=Exit
```

Figure 2.1 Windows NT setup.

Starting the WINNT.EXE over-the-network installation program, which requires that you type in the path to the Windows NT installation files.

reached at which Windows NT can be booted, and then will boot Windows NT and complete the installation using the built-in Windows NT-based setup.

To accomplish this, it is first necessary to share the CD-ROM (or for better performance, copy the contents of the CD-ROM to a hard disk directory and share that) on the network. Then install the necessary network access software on the machine to be configured as a Windows NT workstation. There are two possibilities here: If you have an existing network in place you can use that network software. As an example, we have successfully installed Windows NT over a NetWare network, sharing a copy of the NT CD-ROM distribution files from a NetWare server and accessing the software over IPX/SPX. If you are starting a new Windows NT network, the appropriate way to do this is to share the CD-ROM from a Windows NT server or workstation and then go to the target workstation and install Microsoft's Windows Network Connection, which is supplied with Windows for Workgroups or can be purchased as a Workgroup Connection five-pack (available from Microsoft, at additional cost).

Next, carry out the appropriate configuration steps to gain access to the network, and you can then run the DOS WINNT.EXE program. This program can be run directly. It will present a series of questions, the principal one being a request for the location of the distribution files; at that point you'll have to provide an appropriate share name. A more convenient approach for a system installation that will be carried out many times is to use the following command line arguments:

```
/s:source path
```

This switch specifies the source location of all of the Windows NT distribution files—basically the image of the appropriate directory from the Windows NT CD-ROM. The source path can either be a conventional source path for a shared disk drive or, if you are using Microsoft networking, it can actually be an UNC name. So, for example,

```
winnt /s:x
```

will work if x is the local name for a shared directory on a Novell, Windows for Workgroups, or Windows NT network. If you're using Microsoft networking (Windows NT, Windows for Workgroups or LAN Manager) you could, as an alternative, type

```
winnt /s: \\mips-lab-server\d\i386
```

which would direct WINNT to get the files from the i386 subdirectory on disk D: (the CD-ROM drive) of the mips-lab-server machine. This will work only if disk D has been shared on the network, but it does not require that any special operations be carried out on the workstation, and, therefore, is superior as part of a standardized corporation-wide batch installation procedure.

```
winnt /t:temporary-drive
```

specifies a drive for temporary file storage. During the setup, WINNT.EXE will have to create a number of temporary files. Using /t: you can specify where this is to happen. Alternatively, it will look for available disk space.

The /i: switch followed by the name of an information file will specify the DOS file path for a standard information file. By default this will be DOSNET.INF on the disk from which WINNT.EXE is run. If you wish to employ a customized information file to standardize your information settings you can provide a path to this—it's great for configuring generic clients. Once the client install is standardized for an environment (apps are chosen, etc.), editing the .INF is a quick and painless way to install any new nodes quickly and effortlessly. (If you are examining that possibility we also encourage you to look at the next section on computer profile install, which was designed specifically to meet your needs.)

A /x switch will not create the setup boot floppy disk that is normally created as part of the installation process. The /f switch will not verify files as they are copied to the setup boot floppy disk. This will slightly speed up installation at the expense of running the small risk that the boot floppy will then turn out to have an error on it. And a /c will skip the free space check on the boot floppy disk.

Thus, for example, a typical command line that would carry out a complete installation over the network (assuming that the Windows NT installation CD-ROM is installed on disk D: of \\mips-lab-server) would be:

```
WINNT /s:\\mips-lab-server\d\i386 /t:c /i:\\mips-lab-server\install\dosnet.inf
/x /f /c
```

This would carry out a complete installation using the files in the i386 directory of the D: device on MIPS lab server, with temporary file storage on the local C: drive, getting the DOSNET.INF file from the install share on MIPS lab server. It will not create, verify, or perform free space check on a boot floppy (which would assume that you are carrying a boot floppy with you). This is probably the fastest way to do an installation for small-to-medium-size networks. For larger networks you should see the section on *computer profile installation*.

Installing from Floppy Disks

If your computer is not equipped with a CD-ROM, you can still proceed by using the set of high-density diskettes supplied with NT. When you boot the system, the installation program provides the directions you need.

Computer Profile Install

For departmental network installations, where a large number of machines with a common configuration will need to be set up for Windows NT, Microsoft has provided a fourth installation option: computer profile install. We're somewhat hamstrung on this subject at the moment since we've had no opportunity to see the computer profile installation. According to the information we have, it will be included in the Windows NT Resource Kit published by Microsoft Press, and you'll find a reference to that at the end of the chapter. We'll discuss the general characteristics of the installation but we can't provide any specifics—we'll refer you to the Resource Kit for further information.

In general, the computer profile install has two parts. First is the computer profile creation which is carried out by a system administrator working on a Windows NT server. The administrator creates a computer profile for the standard workstation configuration used in his or her organization using a *computer profile editor* provided in the Resource Kit. This provides the administrator with a way to specify the standard configuration of the workstations that will be set up for Windows NT, including what the network card is, what disk arrangements to set up, what file system to install, and so forth. The administrator then goes to the workstation to be set up and performs a computer profile installation using a special *computer profile installer* that, again, is supplied with the Resource Kit. This will perform a custom over-the-network install using the information provided by the computer profile editor.

The advantage of this approach, as opposed to the over-the-network installation already discussed, is that it provides what effectively amounts to a customized batch mode installation, in that all of the configurable parameters—such as the device drivers, the video type, the file system, and so forth—have been preselected by the administrator and will therefore always come up in a standardized manner. This is clearly advantageous for a large organization. It is probably possible to do something similar using a custom .INF file in conjunction with the over-the-network installation discussed earlier, but given the availability of this approach, we strongly recommend that administrators responsible for larger sites investigate the Windows NT Resource Kit and computer profile installation.

Installing Windows NT, Step by Step

Although every environment is different, here is the typical sequence of events that occur during installation.

1. After placing the special boot disk in the A: drive and booting your machine, the installation program determines if it can run from a CD-ROM. If not, you can choose to run WINNT.EXE from a network drive (or shared CD-ROM) provided by your administrator, or you can use the floppy diskette installation. In any case...
2. When the installation program begins, it asks for your Name and Company. When the next dialog box displays your entry, press Continue if all information is correct.
3. The installation program asks for your computer name. Enter the name of the computer as used in an existing workgroup or on an existing network, or enter a new computer name if this is a new node.
4. Select the language/locale from the pulldown box. The language/locale selection affects the formatting of some text, such as date, time, and currency. This setting can later be changed using the International option from the Control Panel.
5. Windows NT asks for the type of installation you want to perform. For most purposes, the Express Installation is preferable, as it's standardized and fast. Alternatively, you can set up the specific Windows components you select (such as accessories, games, screen savers, and wallpaper bitmaps), set up a network, set up locally connected printers, and set up applications NT will find on your hard disk. Check the box for each task you want NT to perform. With these options, such as installing Accessories, NT provides you with another dialog box and asks you to make further selections, such as which accessories you want to install.
6. You must next select the location of the Virtual Memory Paging file. Select an appropriate drive from the pulldown list. The installation program updates the display with the space available, the minimum size, and the recommended size. You are asked to enter a value in the Size Chosen box. The value in the Recommended Size text box is already entered. In general, follow the recommendation unless you have a good reason to do otherwise, and *never* set the paging file size to less than the size of physical memory in the computer—otherwise Windows NT will not run properly.
7. If you asked to set up a printer in step 5, NT asks you to enter a printer name. This name is displayed in the Printer Manager window and is displayed for all users that share the printer. Select the printer make and model from the pulldown list, and choose a port in the Print To list.
8. If you asked to configure the network settings in step 5, the install program finds and displays the network adapter card on your computer. Press Continue to move to the IRQ level and I/O port addresses. The installation program prefills these text boxes with the values it has determined are correct. You may change them, and they can also be changed by using the Network Settings Control Panel (see Figure 2.2). The installation program may also ask you which additional protocols it should install, which will depend on the specifics of your network setup.
9. The installation program begins to copy the necessary files to your hard disk.
10. If you are setting network parameters, the Network Settings dialog box shows the installed network software and installed adapter cards. You may add software or adapters at this time, or configure the settings (use the Bindings button to see or change the configuration). On portables, this is the time to add Remote Access

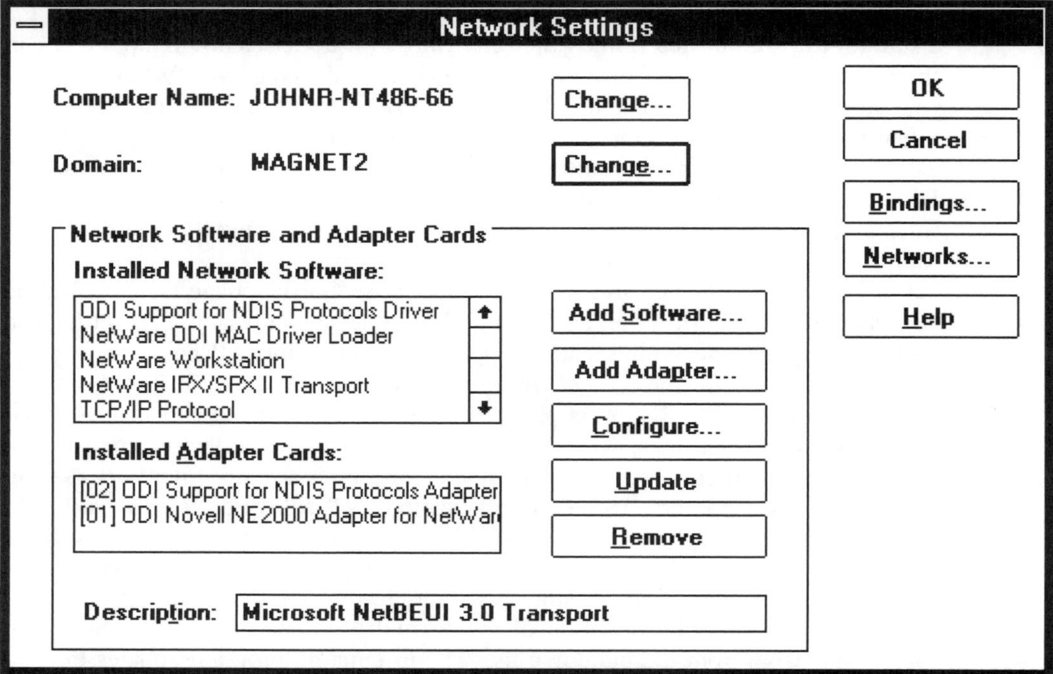

Figure 2.2 Windows NT network control panel.

Once Windows NT is installed, it is necessary to confirm the network card and software choices, using the Network Control Panel interface.

Services (RAS) to enable serial-port or modem-based connections later on. This may also be the proper time to add support for an additional network protocol or third-party networking, if needed.

11. The Domain/Workgroup Settings dialog box appears (see Figure 2.3). You are asked to select whether the computer is a member of a workgroup or a domain (Windows NT Advanced Servers will ask whether they are to be configured as the Primary Domain Controller—see Chapters 3 and 7 for more information). Generally, you should select "Domain" if you are adding the machine to a Windows NT Advanced Server Domain, or "Workgroup" otherwise. If you select domain, the dialog box expands to ask if you want to create a computer account in a domain; the dialog box also provides room for the domain administrator's user name and password. The administrator, by filling this information in, will cause a computer account to be added at the primary domain controller, automatically adding the system to the domain's database. This will save time, as this step will otherwise have to be completed manually.

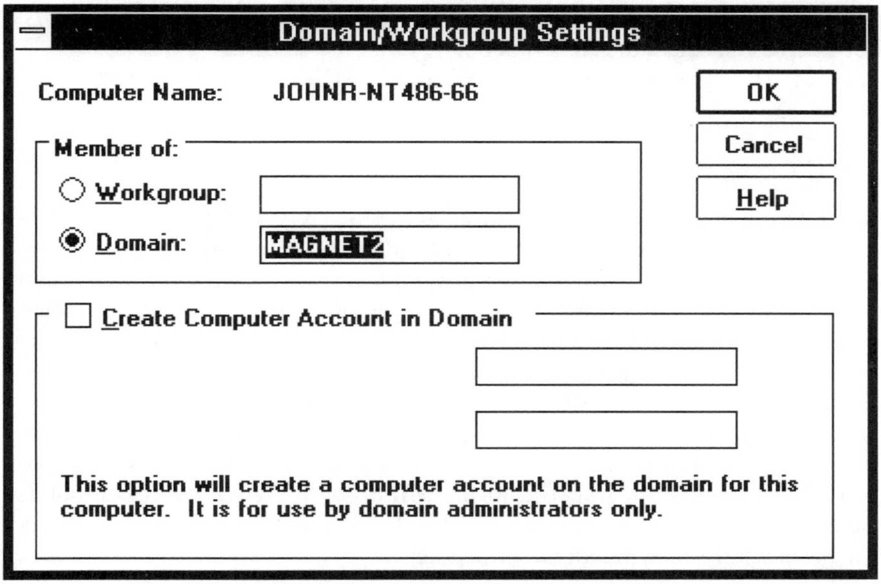

Figure 2.3 Domain/Workgroup settings dialog.

You can set Windows NT up to log into a Domain or Workgroup as appropriate. If a Domain is selected, time can be saved by creating a computer account in the Primary Domain Controller during installation.

12. The installation program builds the program groups.
13. The installation program assumes that you are an administrator, at least for your own computer. The user name is filled in (Administrator) and is not changeable. Enter a password of no more than fourteen characters, and do not include spaces in the password. Passwords are case sensitive.
14. The Local Account Setup dialog box appears. Enter a user name of no more than fifteen characters. As with the previous step, the password must be no more than fourteen characters, cannot include spaces, and is case sensitive.
15. The installation program asks you to insert a blank disk in the A: drive marked Emergency Repair Disk. This disk will be formatted with the default configuration settings. All existing data on the diskette is lost. Once this disk has been created, it should be kept someplace safe, but ready to hand: in the event that there is a problem with the system's configuration, the emergency disk provides the *only* way to recover short of installing NT again from scratch (see Chapter 5 for details)!
16. The Date/Time dialog box appears, asking you to correct the system date and time and to select a time zone. Check the box Automatically Adjust for Daylight Savings Time if you are located in an area that observes Daylight Savings Time.

17. The installation program is now complete. Remove the Emergency Repair Disk from the A drive and select the Reboot icon.
18. The Windows NT Logon prompt appears. Windows NT is now ready for use.

Installation on RISC Computers

The only installation mechanism currently supported for RISC-type computers is the CD-ROM-based installation, which is similar to that employed for x86 computers. The floppy-based installation and the WINNT.EXE installations are supported only for x86-based computers and, according to the early documentation available to us, it would appear that computer profile installation is x86 only as well. So RISC-based computers that will install Windows NT must have a local CD-ROM drive and then you complete an installation that is fundamentally similar to that for the x86 based CD-ROM installation. The only substantial difference is that you cannot boot the computer from a boot floppy, since most RISC-based computers cannot be booted from a floppy disk. Instead you will need to run a system-specific startup program. The instructions that follow are specific to the MIPS R4000/4400 series computers. Instructions for other RISC-based systems (DEC Alpha, Intergraph Clipper, etc.) may vary. See the hardware manufacturer's specifications for details.

MIPS Installation

Note: These instructions are for the March 1993 Windows NT Beta. Final install may differ. See the NT documentation.

Step 1: If necessary, contact MIPS Systems or your hardware manufacturer to upgrade the CPU hardware to R4000 version 2.0 or later. Most currently available systems (and all systems explicitly sold for Windows NT use) are version 2.0 or later.

Step 2: Configure the system for "little-endian" mode. If it displays the ARC boot loader when you start or cold-boot the system, then it's already configured for little-endian mode. If not, you need to get the boot floppy that came with the machine, insert it in the floppy disk drive, reboot the computer, and answer yes when the boot floppy executes and asks if you want to configure a Windows NT PROM. It will then make the necessary changes in the system's Programmable Read Only Memory (PROM) and on a reboot the system will display an ARC boot loader prompt with a number of options, the most important of which from our point of view is Run A Program.

Step 3: Reset the system defaults. From the ARC boot loader select the Run A Program option and enter the path for the JZSETUP program. This is normally located at the root of the Windows NT CD-ROM. You can access this with the ARC system pathname SCSI()CD-ROM(either 0 or 1 depending on your system configuration)fdisk()\jzsetup.exe. When the JZSETUP program runs, select Load Default Configuration, then select Load Default Environment, and set Autoboot to no. Then reboot the computer.

Step 4: If necessary, format a system partition. MIPS and other RISC systems require a system partition to hold the OSLOADER.EXE and HAL.DLL files. This partition must be a FAT (File Allocation Table) partition, even if you don't want to store anything else that way and you want to run a fully configured system using NTFS. In the latter case, the system partition need be no larger than 2MB. Alternatively, you can make that partition the size of the hard disk and use it as the single drive partition for the system or you can do any variation in between that suits your particular needs.

In general, using a small system partition just for those files and formatting the rest of the disk as NTFS will be beneficial. There's little advantage to providing a FAT partition on RISC-based systems since they are incapable of running DOS anyway. In any case, to partition the disk select Run A Program from the ARC boot loader menu and enter

```
SCSI()CDROM(0 or 1 as appropriate)fdisk()\mips\arcinst.exe
```

This will run the ARC system installation program and ask if you would like to create a partition. Answer yes and you can create a system partition of any desired size (minimum of 2MB) to store the necessary files.

Step 5: Start setup. Again, from the ARC boot loader select Run A Program and then enter the pathname

```
SCSI()CD-ROM(0 or 1)fdisk\setupldr.
```

This will start the setup loader, which performs the same function as the boot sector on the Windows NT CD-ROM boot disk for x86-based systems. This in turn will start the Windows NT setup program from the CD-ROM and the installation will proceed exactly as it proceeds for CD-ROM installation on x86-based computers.

Required Files

For Intel-based systems, the installation program adds BOOT.INI, NTLDR (NT Loader), and NTDETECT.COM to the root directory of your boot drive. If you chose the dual-boot option (to select among operating systems at boot time), you will also have a BOOTSECT.DOS file in the root directory of your boot drive, which is used to boot the previous operating system.

If you install NT on a SCSI disk drive, the installation program will also copy NTBOOTDD.SYS to the root directory of your boot drive. RISC-based systems will find HALL.DLL and OSLOADER.EXE on the \OS\NT directory of the boot drive.

The above files are all *required* for NT. If any one of them is missing, NT cannot be loaded.

Of course the files in the \WINNT or \WINDOWS\SYSTEM32 directories (depending on whether you've installed Windows NT from scratch or added it in an installation to an existing Windows system) are also required. A particular point to note: During the Beta process, Microsoft drastically changed the directory path structure for different versions of Windows NT and it is likely that this will happen in the future. Therefore, when upgrading from one version of Windows NT to the next, it is critically important that you examine the documentation that comes with the new version to determine whether or not it is necessary to remove the previous installation before carrying out the new installation. *Do not assume that simply installing the new one over the old one will necessarily give you a working installation.* If you have any doubts on the matter, it may be better to back the old installation off onto a tape drive, delete it, delete all files, and start the new installation from scratch.

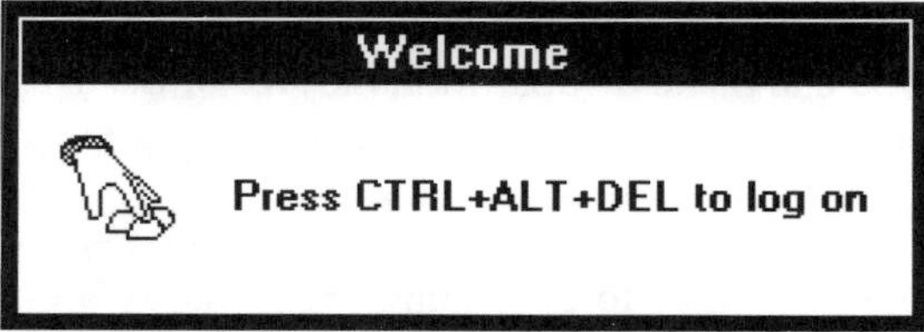

Figure 2.4 Windows NT logon.

The Windows NT logon dialog is the most visible sign of operating system security. The CTRL+ALT+DEL sequence is required in order to assure that no "password stealer" program is running in the foreground.

Starting Windows NT

After the installation process is completed, the installation program will ask you to boot the system. The Boot Loader program appears and asks you to select which operating system you want to use. Windows NT will be listed first, and your previous operating system (if any) will be listed next. Press Enter. The Windows NT logon dialog then appears (Figure 2.4) and asks you to press CTRL+ALT+DEL to begin NT. You'll be prompted for a password (which is case sensitive).

Installation Troubleshooting

The typical installation problems encountered with Windows NT will fall into one of two categories: Those in which the system succeeds in booting but doesn't operate properly and those in which the system refuses to boot.

The first category is by far the simpler. If the system boots and Windows NT starts but other things don't seem to work properly for you, then log in using the administrator account, run the Event Manager, and examine the system Event Log. The odds are quite good that this will show error messages referring to specific devices. For example, if you are coming up but failing to log-on to the network, you are likely to see an Event Log with a series of network error messages indicating that your driver has failed to bind. This indicates that either the wrong network card driver has been used or the settings on the network card do not match the settings provided to the network in the Control Panel's Networks Settings dialog.

If the system fails to boot then the situation is generally more complex and either indicates that the system as configured is incompatible with Windows NT or that inappropriate information has been provided to Windows NT during the setup process. The following is a list that describes some of the most common errors. No such list can be all inclusive; it is recommended that you examine the release notes for your version of Windows NT as well. If you are unable to resolve the problem using the release notes, the Windows NT manuals, and this list, then consult the hardware manuals that came with your system. Finally, you may wish to call the system vendor or Microsoft for more assistance.

Common Installation Errors

- **RAM:**

  If the setup program indicates that memory is insufficient to load the system when you know, in fact, that there *is* enough memory to load the system, then the odds are quite good that the system configuration has not been reset since the memory was upgraded. This is particularly true on EISA and MCA systems. It can also happen with certain ISA systems. Run the system configuration utility supplied by your hardware manufacturer. If you are attempting to install Windows NT on a system that does not have sufficient memory (12MB) to run the graphical install program that comes with the Windows NT CD-ROM, then you may be able to accomplish an installation using the WINNT.EXE MS-DOS-based CD installation. However, it should be noted that Windows NT in its present configuration, while it will run in 8MB, will perform poorly in less than 12MB. This is why Microsoft does not recommend this configuration. If, regardless of these facts, you decide to do an installation in an 8MB system, consult the section earlier in this chapter on over-the-network installation using WINNT.EXE.

  If the BIOS is unable to recognize RAM above 16MB (a problem known to happen on some early model Dell 486 systems, among others), then it will be necessary to upgrade the BIOS on the particular system. Contact your hardware manufacturer for further information.

  If you have any memory parity errors, Windows NT will refuse to run (it may error out with an F002 Parity Error). The best approach, unfortunately, is to try swapping RAM chips or Single In-line Memory Modules (SIMMs) until the system starts, at which point you throw away the offending RAM chip or SIMM because it has a hard error on it and is useless. This error is not a bug in Windows NT—you've had a hardware error all along. If you have had unpredictable system crashes that you have been attributing to Windows, it is entirely likely that after changing the offending RAM chip you will find that your 16-bit DOS and Windows system has become more reliable!

  Finally, you should disable any "shadow RAM" on the system—it has no effect on Windows NT since the BIOS is never employed in Windows NT after

Continued

the initial system start. Whatever memory is used for shadowing either the BIOS or video BIOS is not available to the system and is therefore completely wasted when Windows NT is running.

- **Network Interface Card (NIC):**

The most common NIC problems are related to the I/O address, interrupt (IRQ), and jumper settings. Interrupt conflicts are likely to cause the system to crash with an error number 0x000000A—IRQ expected to be less than or equal. Windows NT is extremely sensitive to interrupts and it will fail to load in situations that would be perfectly tolerable in the same hardware for DOS or Windows 3.1. In particular, Windows NT will not allow two hardware devices to share the same interrupt.

This typically is a problem in systems where a network interface card or other device has been configured to use IRQ 3, which is used by COM2. In such a situation, it will be necessary to disable COM2, either using the CMOS setup built into your machine-manufacturer's utility programs, or by physically removing the COM2 port card. Alternatively (and much more easily) you may wish to consider using a different IRQ setting on your network card. Similar problems can be seen with I/O address and card jumper settings, either in a situation where the I/O address duplicates an I/O address for another device or where the jumper settings on the card do not match the settings that were provided to Windows NT during the installation.

These problems will usually allow the system to boot, in which case you will observe the problems in the Event Manager. The best solution at that point is to shut down Windows NT, turn the system off, remove the card that is suspected to be the problem, inspect the jumper settings and inspect the hardware documentation that came with the card to see what settings, in fact, are set. A number of cards that are supposed to be software configurable may not work properly with Windows NT when using a software setting for which the cards have never been programmed, and it may be necessary to run a DOS-based configuration utility to reconfigure the card, and then run Windows NT.

One helpful approach is to examine the NETWORK.HLP file supplied with the Windows for Workgroups Resource Kit.[9] It may seem a little strange to recommend the Windows for Workgroups Resource Kit to Windows NT users. However, this Resource Kit's help files include a complete description of a large selection of network cards, including online diagrams showing the jumper settings, relating these to the IRQ, and jumper addresses. This can be an enormous time saver in debugging network card problems. Note that other common IRQ

[9]Available from Microsoft Inside Sales at (800) 426-9400 or (206) 882-8080.

conflicts include COM2, as described above, and printer ports. Again, Windows NT absolutely will *not* permit you to share interrupts.

If the system is starting and the Event Manager indicates that there are no hardware errors in the driver, then check to make sure that there is no duplicate computer name on your network and also to make sure that the computer name is different from the workgroup or domain name that has been set on your system. The workgroup name cannot be the same as the computer name or you'll get no network connection.

- **Video:**

If a video card refuses to operate at the specified video resolution, you may want to check and ensure that the video card has sufficient video RAM for the specification. Also check to see that any hardware switch settings on the card match the settings that were provided to Windows NT during installation. Normally, if Windows NT cannot otherwise determine how to control the video card, it will default to 640×480×16 color VGA, which works with most modern video cards. And, in general, on a system where the video has been set to an incorrect resolution, you can solve the problem by using the emergency repair disk.

Unfortunately, there is one major exception. The JZSETUP program used on MIPS RISC systems has a series of settings allowing you to set a variety of video resolutions. The experience of the authors is that on MIPS R4000 workstations, setting any resolution other than the system default will have the effect of producing a totally screwed up video display. We are sorry to say that there is no solution to this other than complete reprogramming of the system PROM on the R4000 systems. Should this happen to you, call MIPS technical support. You won't believe what they tell you to do but, amazingly enough, it will work.[10]

- **CD-ROM:**

If Windows NT loads from the CD but fails to recognize the CD-ROM after the graphical install has started, or if Windows NT goes through the installation correctly but refuses to recognize the CD-ROM after installation is complete, then you may want to see if the SCSI ID has been set to 0 or 1. If so, check to see if the system's configuration is such that 0 and 1 are reserved for hard disk addresses, in which case you will need to set another CD-ROM ID. Most CD-ROMs will come from the factory configured for ID = 6. If Windows NT fails to detect this, try setting it to 0 or 1.

You may also need to check to see whether your CD-ROM is terminated—that in the chain of SCSI devices the last device connected has a termination plug attached or has a termination switch thrown. Consult your hardware

Continued

[10]Do we know something? Yes. Do we believe it? Well,we take the Fifth on that...

manufacturer's specifications for details. On some SCSI controllers, you will need to check to see that an interrupt is specified. There are controllers that have a "no interrupt" specification that's incompatible with Windows NT.

- **Boot Failure:**

  Check to make sure there is enough space on the boot device for the paging file. That is a minimum of 20MB and it may be larger depending on what you specify during the Windows NT installation. Windows NT will not start if the paging file cannot be created. Make sure that BOOT.ANY points to the correct path. BOOT.ANY is a hidden file that will normally be in the root of the boot device. You can unhide this using the DOS attrib command and then examine the file, which is in text format. It will list the path using ARC-system-style addressing. You will need to check to make sure that the path it is pointing to indeed exists on your system.

- **Multiple Operating Systems:**

  In a multiple operating system environment, NT should always be the *last* operating system installed on the system. The reason for this is that some operating system boot loaders, such as OS/2 multiboot, will interfere with the operation of the Windows NT boot system. The Windows NT Boot Manager, on the other hand, will generally permit other boot options to be executed. From the Windows NT Boot Manager menu, you select the option for Previous Operating System on drive C: and the system will reboot—then you will be presented with whatever boot loader subsystem had previously been installed. This is known to work with the OS/2 Boot Manager approach, for example, and it provides a high degree of compatibility and flexibility in multiple boot situations such as those used by system developers.

- **Hard Disk Controller:**

  If the system is unable to recognize your hard disk after installation then it is entirely possible that the disk is not recognized by the BIOS, which makes it impossible for the NT loader to determine that it's there and functioning. In that case you will have to manually edit the BOOT.INI file and replace the pathname with the fully qualified ARC name path. There is a special tool (NTDETECT.COM) in the SUPPORT\SUPTOOLS directory of the CD version of Windows NT that may be of some help in diagnosing this sort of problem—see Chapter 5 for details.

- **1024 Cylinder Limit:**

  Windows NT uses the BIOS to determine the hard disk geometry on AT-compatible disk controllers. In some cases this information is limited to ten bits and cylinder sizes larger than 1,024 cannot be addressed. You may be able to use part of the disk by setting a custom configuration employing only the first 1,024 cylinders. (One of us[11] has been using this approach for years with a 1,280-cylinder, 80MB disk that is recognized as a 60MB disk using a custom configuration.) Or you may be able to use an approach called "head doubling," in which you state that the hard disk has twice the number of heads physically present and half the number of cylinders (the geometry table information in the hard disk controller translates this to the actual physical dimensions of the drive). Finally, you may need a BIOS upgrade or a different hard disk controller.

- **Common Error Numbers:**

Error 0x0000000A—IRQ expected to be less than or equal: This indicates an interrupt conflict. See the section on network interface card, COM port, and other interrupt conflicts already described in this list.

Error 0x00000032, 0x00000069-71—Initialization errors: These generally indicate a problem with the hard disk controller, or other problems in the first phase of NT startup. On AT controllers try running at a lower DMA transfer rate. This generally will require a jumper switch change. On SCSI systems check to verify that the SCSI chain is terminated. On any system check for IRQ or memory address conflicts, and check to see that the NTDETECT.COM file is in the root of the boot device. Absence of other NT files can also cause these errors, and if you find that a significant group of files is missing from the hard disk this probably indicates a sector error on the hard disk. You will need to clean up the hard disk using a DOS-based disk maintenance utility, such as the Norton Disk Doctor, and reinstall Windows NT from scratch.

System Error F002: This generally indicates a hardware problem, typically parity error on the RAM. It could also indicate a hardware problem with the math coprocessor. It might conceivably be caused by a machine check exception on a Pentium-based system, indicating an overheat. It may also be caused by hardware problems with the accessory cards. You will need to use whatever hardware diagnostics are supplied by your system's manufacturer.

Uninstalling NT

Should you wish to completely remove NT from your system and return to a DOS-based system, create a bootable disk that also contains SYS.COM. Place the diskette in your A: drive and boot your system. Type SYS and press Enter to transfer the system to your hard disk. Delete NTLDR, BOOT.INI, BOOTSECT.DOS, NTBOOTDP.SYS (if present), and NTDETECT.COM from the root directory. (Note that these files are both hidden. You

Continued

[11]John D. Ruley

may need to change the files' attribute or use a third-party utility program to delete the files.) Also delete PAGEFILE.SYS (the paging file), then all files in the \WINNT subdirectory. If you installed NT in the \WINDOWS directory, delete only \WINDOWS\SYSTEM32 and any subdirectories.

If you formatted an NTFS partition on the system, you will have to use the DOS fdisk utility to deactivate the partition, reassign it, and reformat it as a FAT partition. An alternative way to do this is to use the Windows NT setup program, select custom installation, refuse the setup suggested path, select the NTFS partition, select P to delete the partition and then recreate the partition as a FAT partition and either continue on with the Windows NT setup or exit. Use the DOS fdisk and format commands to replace the partition with a DOS recognized FAT partition.

Summary

You've learned how to carry out a Network Needs Analysis, how to select appropriate hardware for your needs, where to locate that hardware, and how to install and configure Windows NT on it. The next step is to establish the user accounts database, security policies, and access rights that will make the network useful to your end-users—which will be covered in Chapter 3.

For More Information

Microsoft Staff (1993), *Windows NT Advanced Server Concepts and Planning Guide (Beta, March 1993)*. Redmond, WA: Microsoft Corp. This guide, which comes with all Advanced Server systems, is invaluable—it's the best place to start (other than right here, of course!).

Microsoft Staff (1993), *Windows NT System Guide (Beta, March 1993)*. Redmond, WA: Microsoft Corp. The specifics you'll need to get set up.

Microsoft Staff (1993), *Windows NT Resource Kit, Volumes 1-3*. Redmond, WA: Microsoft Press. Volume 1, which includes setup information, should be especially helpful.

Microsoft Staff (1993), *TechNet CD (July 1993)*. Redmond, WA: Microsoft Product Support Services (PSS). TechNet is a monthly publication on CD-ROM containing a digest of topics from the Microsoft Knowlege Base, the Net News publication, Resource Kits and other information. This particular issue included a pre-release version of the Windows NT Resource Kit, which proved extremely helpful to us in writing this chapter (especially with respect to the then-unavailable computer profile install). TechNet is available from Microsoft sales —a one-year subscription (12 CDs) costs $295 and is worth every penny.

Microsoft Staff (1993), *Windows NT Device Driver Kit*. Redmond, WA: Microsoft Corp. The low-level information hardware vendors need to make their products work with NT.

Administrative Connections

When you have read this chapter, you will understand the basic concepts of system administration, user accounts, and system security including:

- **Why and how to create administrative user groups**
- **How to create and manage user accounts**
- **How to assign user access rights**
- **Formatting and management of system volumes (including spanned volumes)**
- **Administrative monitoring using the built-in performance monitor, event viewer, and alert tools**

You should feel comfortable carrying out the basic tasks of system administration on a Windows NT network, and be prepared to set up and use a small single-workgroup (or domain) network on your own.

System Management and the Network Administrator

All Windows NT systems are servers, and as such there are administrative tasks that have to be carried out on them. As a secure operating system, Windows NT requires *all* users—even local users logged in on the system console—to have a valid user account and password. The user's account, in turn, will determine what *user rights* and *resource access privileges* the user will have on the system—in effect, controlling what the user is allowed to do. Setting up, maintaining, and controlling these accounts is the job of the network administrator—you.

The Network Administrator

The role of *network administrator* is part systems technician, part shop foreman, part traffic cop, and more. It is the responsibility of the network administrator to provide access to the server and networked services on the LAN that is always available and—this is very important—*invisible* to the users.

A network that is always available is easy to understand, if not easy to provide. It means that the server and networked services on the LAN must be ready for users whenever they need to work. Of course, hardware will need to come down for maintenance and software must be upgraded, but it is the network administrator's job to manage these activities around users' peak production periods.

Providing a network that is *invisible* to the users is more difficult. This means that users must have access to the server and peripherals, like printers and network modems, without having to be aware of the way in which they are provided. In the movie *Running Scared*[1] two policemen ask their vehicle maintenance officer for a car that is fast, powerful, and invisible. He gives them a cab. This is perfect—the car is quick, the engine powerful, and in Chicago, nothing is more invisible than another yellow cab.

Your network should be a lot like that cab. It should be quick—users should be configured to have access to the things they need without resorting to searching through endless directories. It should be powerful—users must be able to print and store files on the server with confidence that their printouts will be processed quickly and their data will be backed up daily. But most of all, using the network should be *familiar*—users should work on the network the way they do on their own systems. Understanding the few network facilities they use should be as easy as pointing and clicking.

This is where Windows NT lends a hand to the network administrator. Since Windows NT is based on the familiar look and feel of Windows 3.1 and Windows for Workgroups, your users will be in familiar territory when they log into your server and access data from it. But configuring and managing users is the responsibility of the network administrator.

There are many items that go into a properly configured network to ensure that it is both available and invisible.

First is *network reliability*. This takes into account server performance monitoring, fault tolerance of the system, UPSes and proper backup and recovery systems. Windows NT provides you with many of the tools that you'll require. For example, using the Performance Monitor you can get a quick overview of the server's current performance and even set up particular items that you want to view plotted as charts. You can also set alerts to warn you when various thresholds are exceeded.

Second is *user management*. This means installation and configuration of desktop equipment, creation and maintenance of user accounts and account groups, monitoring the performance of desktop systems, user training, providing user backups, and properly preparing and anticipating for user growth. It also means providing for an automated method of user and

[1]Metro-Goldwyn-Mayer, 1986.

group creation via templates. This will help you save time and avoid making simple errors when granting access privileges.

Third is *establishing procedures*. Once procedures for providing both network reliability and user management are in place, it becomes easier to provide a stable and usable network environment. Setting up or terminating user accounts, performing daily backups and maintaining printers should all become documented and repeatable procedures.

Performing a function one day without the ability to duplicate the steps the next day is like cold fusion in a bottle—it may work great once, but it's not at all useful. You need to have documentation in order to provide a full-time network. Who knows? You may find yourself on the phone trying to explain to a user how to retrieve a file from a backup tape. It's a lot easier for both of you if he or she has a document to refer to, rather than trying to remember a series of dialog boxes in the correct order.

Fourth is *looking toward the future*. This covers many items. A properly planned network allows the network administrator to easily add additional users and additional storage to the server.

Don't think that the job is over when you have provided your group with the network they requested. To misquote a line from the movie *Field of Dreams*, "if you build it, *they will not only come, they will want more.*" More nodes, more user directory space, more remote connectivity. The list is never-ending. It's actually simple: your users have needs and desires, related to your network, that will help them be more productive. Your task is also simple: you must be prepared to provide for their requests.

Fifth, and perhaps most important of all, is *proper documentation*. Network documentation is often considered an oxymoron. But its usefulness can't be overstated. It is imperative that you document every stage of your LAN for future reference. *Network Computing* magazine lists six excellent suggestions for network documentation that you can follow *now* to avoid headaches in the future:[2]

Cross-reference users with node addresses. This is especially useful if you are assigning IP (internet protocol) addresses to your users. Otherwise, put together a list showing your users' logins with their computer names.

Network diagrams are worth a thousand words. You can get as fancy as you have time and patience for here. The items that you must include in your diagram are approximate locations of shared network resources (servers, concentrators, printers, network faxes, etc.), approximate locations of desktop PCs, basic cabling and the location of any bridges, routers, or WAN (wide area network) services to which your network is connected. This diagram should be documented as fully as possible to include items like disk capacities and amount of installed RAM for your servers and desktop systems, user names and titles, user phone numbers and modem numbers if applicable, and NIC (network interface card) MAC (media access code) addresses for servers and desktop systems. In addition, include the concentrator patch

---

[2]Franks, Mike, "Documenting Your Network (When You Don't Have Time)," *Network Computing*, August 1992, pp. 128-130.

number for each node next to the node location. This will help solve many of the endless mysteries usually associated with the phone wiring closet.

Document user and security information. Your list should contain the groups that each user belongs to, including global and local groups. Any special access should be noted here.

Document software on servers. When you install software document the title, version, and publisher, give a description, show the directory location, and list the groups and users who have access to this software. Also, add a few lines that include the serial number, physical location of the disks, and the technical support phone number for the product.

Document software information online. Take this a few steps further and organize all of the information into a simple database. This will help you to locate that single item you need to know in an emergency. In fact, if you create your network diagram using your computer, you should be able to incorporate it into your database as well. That way you can also put together all of your physical location data with your user information in one place.

Document network policies and procedures online. With proper planning, the database you created in the previous step can contain all of the information you need to run your network, including your policies and procedures.

The Network Administrator's Responsibilities

The network administrator has a series of responsibilities that fall into nine categories. These categories may be thought of as a pyramid. The bottom-most responsibilities are tasks that consume most of the network administrator's time, but are continuous activities, spaced out over time. The topmost tasks are not as frequent, but they can consume an entire day in one shot.

Network Administrator's Pyramid of Responsibilities

Putting out fires
Training users
User account management
Group account management
User desktop configuration and maintenance
Backups, performance monitoring, network security
Server and network hardware and software maintenance
--------------- Backup and recovery ---------------
------------------ Disaster planning ------------------
------------------- Growth planning -------------------

For example, growth planning consists of listening to users and anticipating their future network and server requirements. Realistically, this occurs all the time; as the network administrator you are constantly planning for future growth of your network. Windows NT provides you with many ways to monitor performance, and it's your job to put these things together and draw conclusions about them that will assist you when making future acquisitions of hardware and software.

Putting out fires, on the other hand, is a shorter, more concentrated task that has immediate consequences. When a fire occurs, such as a failed NIC (network interface card) in your server, you aren't just storing away data for later use. You are going into action *now!* You'll have to down your server, replace the card, bring the server back up, test the new card, and make the server available to users. If you've built your server with fault tolerance and failsafes in mind, and if your budget permits, you may have installed two NICs. In that case, you may only have to migrate users to the functioning NIC and replace the other when your users have met their deadlines.

The items in the pyramid fall into daily, weekly, and monthly tasks. This isn't a strict rule, but for an established network, most of the work that you do can be planned along these lines. New user creation, for example, might occur only twice a year with our original accounting department example. When it does, this task becomes a daily item, but we'll leave it under the monthly tasks due to its frequency.

Whether the network administrator is you, or someone you hire, here are a few guidelines that you can refer to when managing your server and LAN.

Daily Tasks

- *Check Error Logs*—All error logs should be checked for new entries. This should include those from *both* the Windows NT Event Viewer and Performance Monitor (covered later in this chapter). All warnings should be followed up—see Chapter 4 for troubleshooting and performance tuning information.
- *Check Help Desk E-Mail*—Read and prioritize user help requests.
- *Check Volume Free Space*—Look for anomalous disk space loss and potential space shortages (you may want to consider automating this process using Performance Monitor *alerts*, a procedure covered later in this chapter).
- *Perform Daily Backups* (if used)—If you are performing daily backups (and you must back up either daily or weekly or both), remember to check that a new tape, or the correct tape, is ready in your tape drive. Periodically, check and tension the tape drive mechanism.
- *Confirm Overnight Backups* (if made)—If daily backups are performed overnight, insure that they were successful. Do this by retrieving a sample set of files. Don't always try to retrieve the same set of files. Remove and store the tapes. *Do not* store your only set of backup tapes in the same room as your only server—doing so *risks losing all of your data* in a single event, such as a fire.

Weekly Tasks

- *Clear Errant Temporary Files*—Remove dead temporary files from user and mail directories. (You might wish to automate this task using the Windows NT *at* script command covered at the end of this chapter).
- *Create and Distribute User Space Lists*—Look for excessive disk space use, and distribute memos to responsible users requesting that they either delete or archive the files.
- *Check Mail System Status*—Look for excessive mail message archiving such as dead backup files and other temp files that should be deleted.
- *Perform Week-end Backups* (if used)—If you are performing weekly backups (and you must back up either daily or weekly or both), remember to check that a new tape, or

the correct tape, is ready in your tape drive. Periodically, check the tape drive mechanism. Be sure to confirm the backup, as specified in ***Daily Tasks*** above.

Monthly Tasks

- *Archive and Delete Dead Files*—Check files for activity and delete or archive files that have not had any activity for more than a month.
- *Perform Disaster Drill*—During off time (yes, we know, "ha ha, very funny"), perform *disaster drills* to test your disaster recovery plan and backup strategy. This is *very* important and can mean the difference between being able to recover from a problem during peak periods and not being able to recover at all.
- *Perform Month-end (or Cycle-end) Backups* (if used)—These are different from both daily and weekly backups and should be performed for use as an archive if your data is cyclical in nature. For example, you might perform backups in the middle of every other month if that is when your production cycle ends. The data that you archive will contain the final report from each of your cycles. This data should be archived off-site as a disaster recovery tool.

Creating Groups and Users

The name of this section is "Creating Groups and Users," rather than the other way around, for a reason. It is possible to collect your users into similar groups who share the same access and security requirements. For example, you may have a directory that contains network applications. Not all of the users in your network will require access to all of these subdirectories containing applications. The directory containing a CAD/CAM application should be accessed only by the engineers who use the program. The directory that contains a word processing application is probably required by everyone on your network. You should build groups according to these access requirements.

Domains and Workgroups

Before looking into the details of user account and group management, we need to understand the concept of *domains* and *workgroups*. In a Windows NT network, a workgroup is a collection of computers that are grouped together for convenience when browsing network services. The network administrator designates a workgroup for each Windows NT system and this name appears to other systems on the local area network.

The major limitation of a workgroup is that each server in the workgroup must maintain its own database of user accounts, independently of other servers in the workgroup. This means that users with a need to access more than one server will require separate accounts on each—a situation that can quickly become an administrative nightmare on a large network.

The Windows NT Advanced Server expands on this with the concept of a *domain*. Like workgroups, domains appear in the browse list, and they group servers and workstations together logically. However, domains expand on this by maintaining a single account database that applies to all servers in the domain. All account information is maintained in a single database on the *primary domain controller*. Other servers on the network (which can include Windows NT Advanced Servers and LAN Manager 2.0 or higher servers) maintain a copy of this central database, in which changes are updated every five minutes (a process called *replication*, which will be covered in more detail in Chapter 7). Any server can validate a logon request.

The great advantage of a domain over a workgroup is that users need only one account to access any system in the network. Indeed, through a process called *inter-domain trust* (see Chapter 7 for details) this approach can be applied between domains, so that a user with an account in one domain can access servers in other domains.

As a practical matter, however, you need not worry too much about the division between workgroups and domains—if your network includes a Windows NT Advanced Server then you are using domains. If not (even if you are joining a Windows NT workstation to an existing LAN Manager Domain) then you are dealing with a workgroup. In situations where the difference between these is more than just semantics, we will point it out; for now, just assume that the workgroup is a light-weight domain and you'll get the gist of it.

You should choose your domain (or workgroup) name to reflect its primary function. TIM1 is not a good choice for the accounting department, even if the vice president of accounting is named Tim. ACCT_DEPT is a better choice. It is easy to understand what department this server belongs to and it takes into account the possibility of growth to ACCT_DEPT_2. Another possibility, which may make sense in very large networks, is the use of geographical domain names. (Microsoft uses this approach itself.)

Working with Groups

The process of creating and managing user accounts and account groups is basically the same, whether you are operating a standalone Windows NT server for a workgroup, or an enterprisewide multiserver network. It is perfectly allowable for one user to belong to more than one group—in fact, it is essential to planning your network. Windows NT provides for the creation of two types of groups.

Local groups are groups of users and global groups that have access to servers from their own domain. *Global groups* (Advanced Server only) are groups of users that have access to servers and workstations from their own domain or other domains that "trust" their home domain.

Predefined groups in the basic Windows NT product include Administrators, Users, Power Users, Backup Operators, and Guests. Windows NT Advanced Server adds Domain Admins, Domain Users, Account Operators, Print Operators, Server Operators, and Replicator—and eliminates the Power Users group. Some of these groups, as you can see from their names, involve special functions and rights that you may assign to particular users. Not every one of these groups is a standalone group. Some of them are, by default, members of other groups.

You use the User Manager application (User Manager for Domains in Windows NT Advanced Server) from the Administrative Tools group to create and modify both local and global groups. Once these groups have been created you will use the File Manager to grant directory permissions to members of these groups.

User Manager

The User Manager application helps you add, change, and delete accounts for individuals and groups. User Manager is also used to control auditing compliance.

Individual users are assigned a user type that corresponds to security levels. For example, users who are part of the Administrators group may perform all User Manager tasks, and have the most control over a network. Users who are part of the Users group can create groups, then modify or delete them, and can give user accounts memberships in the groups created.

To start User Manager, click on the icon in the Administrative Tools program group, or select File/Run and type MUSRMGR.EXE in the Command Line text box and click on OK. The main window of User Manager is shown in Figure 3.1. To exit User Manager, select User/Exit.

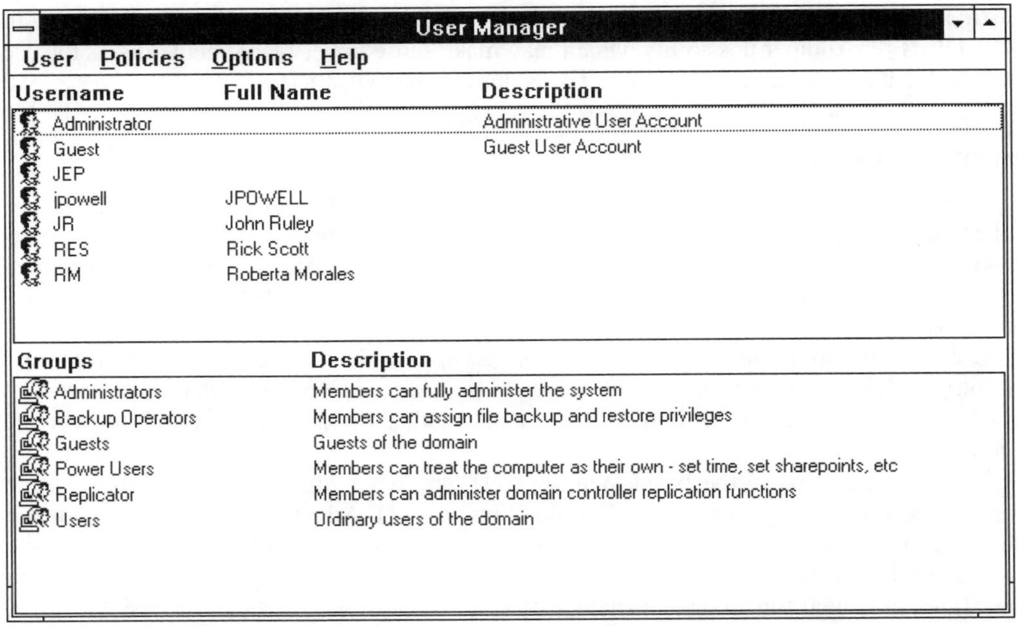

User Manager

User Policies Options Help

Username	Full Name	Description
Administrator		Administrative User Account
Guest		Guest User Account
JEP		
jpowell	JPOWELL	
JR	John Ruley	
RES	Rick Scott	
RM	Roberta Morales	

Groups	Description
Administrators	Members can fully administer the system
Backup Operators	Members can assign file backup and restore privileges
Guests	Guests of the domain
Power Users	Members can treat the computer as their own - set time, set sharepoints, etc
Replicator	Members can administer domain controller replication functions
Users	Ordinary users of the domain

Figure 3.1 User Manager screen shot.

The Windows NT User Manager (and User Manager for Domains, in the Windows NT Advanced Server) is the primary administrative tool for controlling user accounts, groups, access permissions and user rights.

Adding a Group

You can create your own local groups (Domain Administrators in Windows NT Advanced Server domains can also create global groups). To do so:

1. Select the user accounts you want added to a group, or select a user group so that no user accounts are selected. Choose User/New Local Group. The Local Group Properties dialog box shown in Figure 3.2 appears.
2. Type in the name of the group and its description at the top of the New Local Group dialog box.
3. If you want to see the complete names of the users you chose in the first step, click on Show Full Names.
4. Select Add to add members to the group. Click on OK when all users are added.
5. Select OK to exit the dialog box.

Deleting a Group

If you want to delete a local group, select the group from the User Manager window. Select User/Delete. If User Manager displays a confirmation message, click on OK. Click on Yes to delete the group.

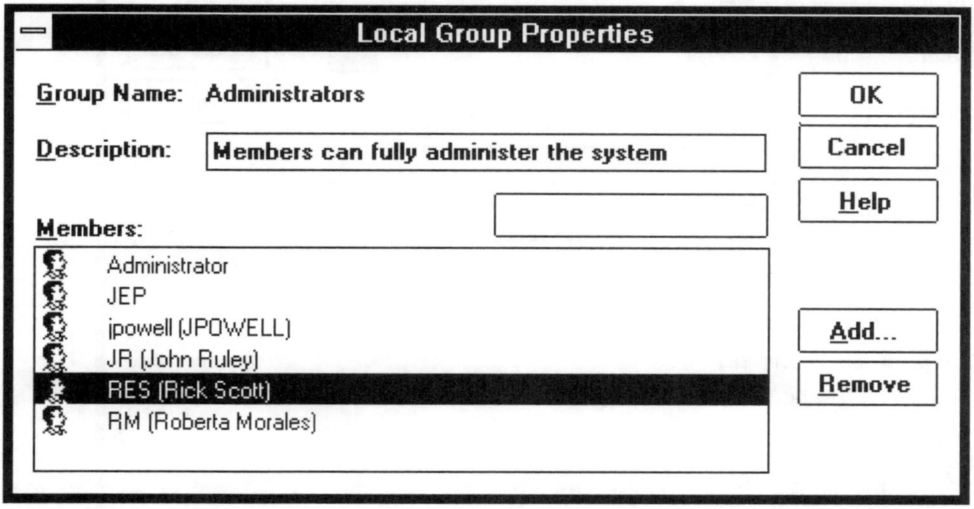

Figure 3.2 Local group properties.

Administration of Windows NT (and Windows NT Advanced Server) networks can be greatly simplified by exploiting the local and global groups. Assigning access permissions and user rights to groups automatically allocates the same permissions and rights to users within the group.

Adding a User Account

A user account is a set of information about a user, including rights and membership in groups. Several user accounts come predefined within Windows NT, and are arranged in a hierarchy by default. To add a user account to the system:

1. Select User/New User. The dialog box shown in Figure 3.3 is displayed.
2. Enter the user name in the Username box. User names must be unique, cannot exceed twenty characters, and can contain any characters except: " / \ ; : [ ] < > | = + , * ?
3. You can optionally enter the full name (first, middle initial, and last name) of the user in the Full Name box.
4. Optionally enter a text description in the Description box.
5. Enter the same password in the Password and Confirm Password text boxes. Passwords must not exceed fourteen characters and are case sensitive.
6. To require a user to enter a new password when he or she logs on for the next session, check the User Must Change Password at Next Logon check box. If selected, be sure the User Cannot Change Password check box is *not* checked.

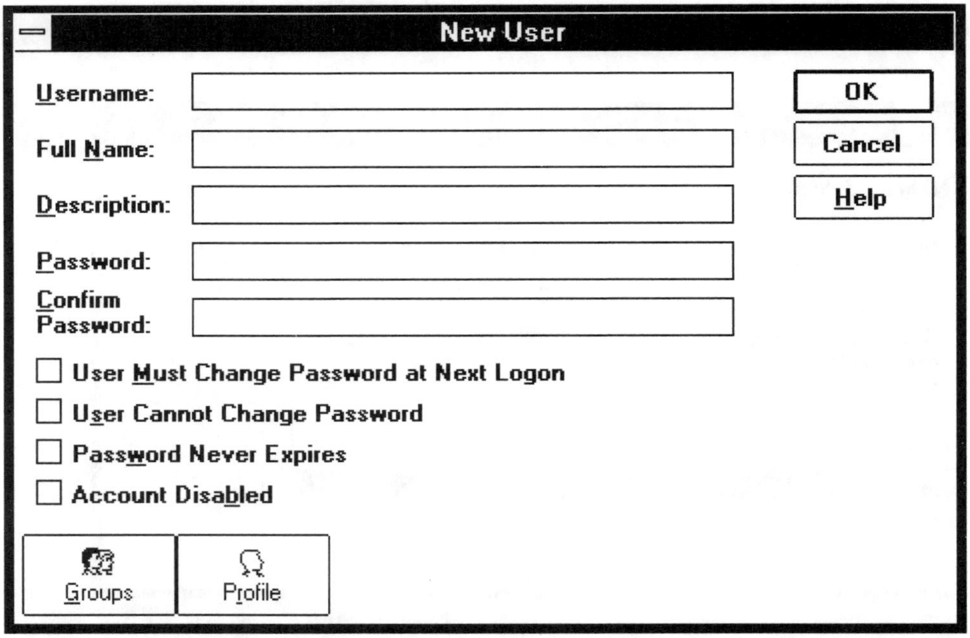

Figure 3.3 New user dialog.

You add a new user to your network using the New User dialog from the Windows NT User Manager.

7. If you want to prevent the user from changing the password you assign, check the User Cannot Change Password check box.
8. To override the Maximum Password Age in the Account policy setup (see Managing Security Policies below), check the Password Never Expires box.
9. Select Account Disabled to temporarily disable an account, a useful option for setting up multiple users in advance of their use of the system (users can be activated individually when they actually join the workgroup).
10. To administer a group or profile, select the option from the bottom of the dialog box and fill in the information as necessary.
11. Click on OK.

Note that sometimes it is actually faster to copy an existing user account and make changes as necessary. To copy a user account, select the user name from the list in the User Manager window, then choose User/Copy. The Copy Of dialog box requests information similar to that asked for new users. Complete it and click on OK.

Changing User Accounts

When a user forgets his or her password, or when conditions change within your organization, you may need to change information about a user account. To change the information in a single user account, choose the user account from the list in User Manager, then select User/Properties (alternatively, double-click on the user account name). Make the necessary corrections.

You can change more than one account simultaneously in a similar fashion. Select the user accounts from the list in User Manager by clicking on each one, then select User/Properties. If the users you selected share a common description, the description is displayed in the Description text box. You can enter a new description or edit the description if you wish. Next, set the Users Cannot Change Password, Passwords Never Expire, and Accounts Disabled check boxes as needed, and select the Groups or Profile options if desired. Finally, select OK.

To Rename a User Account:

1. Select the user account.
2. Select User/Rename.
3. In the Change To text box enter the new user name. The same naming conventions used for creating new accounts are in effect here.
4. Click on OK.

To Remove One or More User Accounts:

1. Select the user account(s) from the User Manager window.
2. Select User/Delete.
3. If you are asked to confirm the delete, click on OK.
4. Select Yes to delete the account name displayed in the dialog box. Select Yes to All to delete all user accounts (if multiple accounts were selected in step 1).

An alternative to deleting accounts is inactivating them. Such inactivation keeps the underlying user information, but temporarily disables the user account.

To Disable an Account:

1. Select the user account.
2. Select User/Properties.
3. Check the Account Disabled box, and click on OK.

Connecting Users to Groups

Once you have established user(s) and group(s), you need to attach (connect) a user to a group. Maintaining user and group connections is simple. To perform the update:

1. Select the user, then click on the Groups button at the bottom of the dialog box. The Group Membership dialog box, shown in Figure 3.4, is displayed.
2. The groups to which the selected user belongs are displayed in the Member of list box. The groups to which the user is excluded (does not belong) are displayed in the Not member of list box.
3. To add a user to a group, select one or more groups from the Not member of list, then click on Add.
4. To remove a selected user from one or more groups, select the group(s) from the Member Of list, then click on Remove.

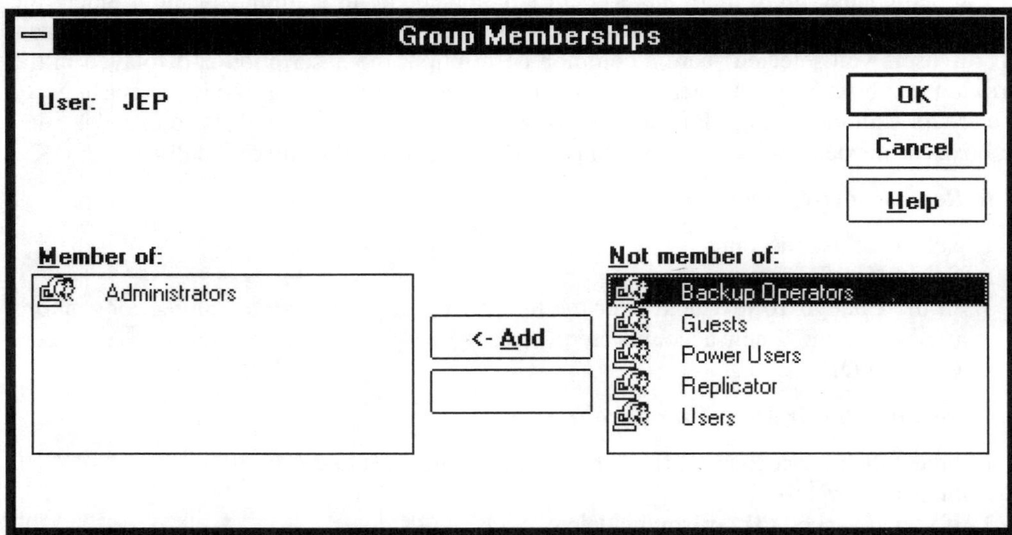

Figure 3.4 Groups.

Once the user is added, designate the groups to which he or she belongs. By doing so, you automatically assign all necessary access privileges and rights.

5. Select OK to exit the dialog box.

Adding, changing, and removing multiple users simultaneously is very similar:

1. Select the user accounts from the User Manager window.
2. Select User/Properties.
3. Click on Groups.
4. The groups to which all users belong (the common groups) are displayed in the All Are Members Of list box. The groups of which one or more members *may* be a part are shown in the Not All Are Members Of list box.
5. To add *all* selected users to one or more groups, select the group(s) from the Not All Are Members Of list, then click on Add.
6. To remove *all* users from one or more groups, select the group(s) from the All Are Members Of list, then click on Remove.
7. Select OK to exit the dialog box.

Managing Security Policies

User Manager allows you to define and configure policies that control user rights, how events are audited, and the method of password use.

Setting Account Policies

To manage the way passwords are used:

1. Select the User Account.
2. Select Policy/Account. The Policy/Account dialog box shown in Figure 3.5 appears.
3. Select the password policy or policies that are required. Select a maximum password period (up to 999 days), minimum password age (up to 999 days minimum), minimum password length, and password history options.
4. Click on OK.

Setting Audit Policies

To manage the events that are added to the audit log:

1. Select Policy/Audit.
2. To turn off all auditing, click on Do Not Audit. To audit one or more events, select Audit These Events, then select the event you want to audit. Check whether you want to log a successful event, a failed event, or both.
3. To stop Windows NT when the audit log is full, check the Halt System when Security Event Log is Full check box.
4. Select OK.

The following table describes the events that can be audited and what they mean.

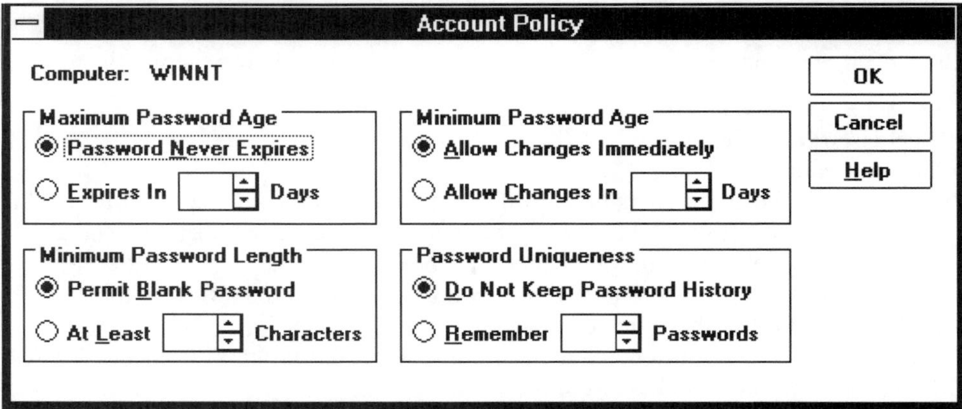

Figure 3.5 Policy/account.

You can enforce an appropriate security policy on your Windows NT network by setting appropriate policy settings on your system or domain. The Windows NT Advanced Server adds a capability to force disconnection of users who operate outside their designated logon periods.

Events:	*Triggered By:*
File and Object Access	Access a directory, printer, or file set for auditing (see File Manager for details)
Logon and Logoff	Log into or log off a computer system or connect to a network
Process Tracking	Covers a wide variety of events, including starting a program
Restart, Shutdown, and System	Restart or shut down a computer, or trigger an event that impacts the security log or security of the system
Security Policy Changes	Changes to rights of users or to audit policies
Use of User Rights	Using a user right
User and Group Management	Add, modify, or delete a user account or group account; rename, disable, or enable a user account; or change a password

Setting User Rights

To manage the authorization for a task:

1. Select Policy/User Rights. The User Rights Policy dialog box shown in Figure 3.6 appears.
2. Select the right from the Right pulldown list box. The users and groups granted the right are listed in the Grant To box. To display the advanced user rights, check the

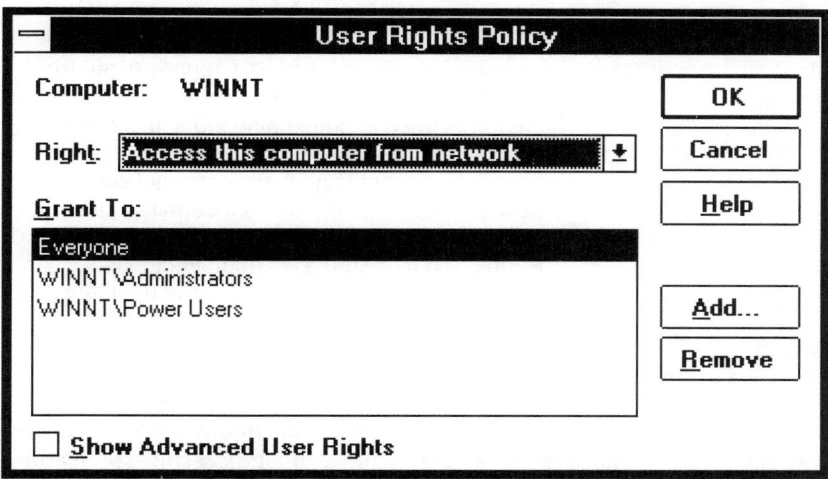

Figure 3.6 User rights.

Security is further assured by allowing the administrator to selectively assign user rights to particular groups of Windows NT users. This assures that only users who have a need to carry out sensitive operations (such as account maintenance, backup and restoration, or shutting down the system) can do so.

Show Advanced User Rights box at the bottom of the dialog box. Rights are detailed below. For a more detailed explanation, see the User Manager chapter of the Windows NT System Guide.

3. To remove a user or group from the list of the right, select it and click on Remove.
4. To add a user or group to the list, select Add. Complete the Add Users And Groups dialog box and click on OK.
5. Select OK.

User Right	*Permissions Granted*
Access this computer from network	Connect to the computer (via a network)
Back up files and directories	Permission to back up files and directories (this overrides file and directory permissions)
Bypass traverse checking	An advanced right that allows user to change directories and move through a tree regardless of any existing directory permissions
Change the system time	Set internal clock of the computer
Force shutdown from a remote system	Reserved for future use by Microsoft

Continued

User Right	Permissions Granted
Log on as a service	Register with the system as a service (used for Replicator local group's Replicator service)
Log on locally	Log on to the computer using the active computer's keyboard
Manage auditing and security log	Specify the events and file access that can be audited; furthermore, this right permits a user to view and clear a security log
Restore files and directories	Permission to restore files and directories; note that this right overrides file and directory permissions
Shut down the system	Shut down Windows NT
Take ownership of files and other objects	Assume ownership of files and directories

In our earlier example we looked at two groups, one that needed access to the CAD/CAM application and another that needed access to the word processing application. Using the File Manager, you can highlight the directory you need to work with and choose Permissions from the Security menu (or choose the Permissions button on the toolbar). In the Directory Permissions dialog box you can allow particular access to the selected directory. First you highlight a group or user, then choose Special Directory Access from the Type of Access pulldown menu. You'll open the Special Directory Access dialog box, where you can either grant full control or choose a combination of six access rights.

Managing User Profiles

A profile associates a logon script name and home directory with a user account. This can speed up the login process or help you as an administrator control the login process of your users. To set a profile for a user account:

1. When adding, copying, or changing a user account, select the Profile button at the bottom of the dialog box.
2. Optionally enter the logon script name in the Logon Script Name box.
3. If you want to use a local path as the home directory, enter the local directory in the Local Path text box. Use *%username%* to substitute the username for a subdirectory name.
4. To use a network directory as the home directory, click on Connect. Enter a drive letter (or select one from the pulldown list), then enter the network path in the To text box.
5. Select OK.

Monitoring Performance

As we noted earlier in our discussion of the network administrator's responsibilities, day-to-day performance monitoring is critical. Windows NT provides a powerful set of tools for this that include *Performance Monitor* and *Event Viewer.*

Performance Monitor

The Performance Monitor utility of Windows NT lets you observe the performance of your current system, viewing information as charts or reports. You can also create charts and log files, and set warnings about activity levels on your system. While Performance Monitor provides data on the current performance, it does not offer suggestions for improving performance (but *we* do—see the section on performance tuning in Chapter 5).

You can create up to four simultaneous views, one each for charts, alerts, logs, and reports. Each of these views can be customized, and each view's settings can be saved and recalled for future sessions. Setting and working with each of these views is quite similar. You can save the performance statistics from any of these views and use the data at a later time.

To start Performance Monitor, select its icon from the Administrative Tasks program group. To exit the utility, select File/Exit.

Views

There are four views in Performance Monitor:

- *Alert View* provides information about events that exceed user-defined limits. You can monitor more than one condition at a time, and when an event occurs Windows NT can run a program to take corrective or preventive action or alert you to the existence of the condition.
- *Chart View* allows you to display information graphically, which helps you spot system problems immediately. A sample chart view is displayed in Figure 3.7.
- *Log View* sends key information to a separate disk file for later analysis.
- *Report View* displays a simple report of event values you select to display.

To switch between alert, chart, log, and report view, select View, then select:
Alert to see the alert view. Shortcut: press Ctrl+A.
Chart to see the chart view. Shortcut: press Ctrl+C.
Log to see the log view. Shortcut: press Ctrl+L.
Report to see the log view. Shortcut: press Ctrl+R.
To clear a view, select Edit/Clear Display.

Working with Performance Monitor

The toolbar at the top of the Performance Monitor is shared by the four views. The buttons are all used in essentially the same way; only the information changed within each view is different. For example, to remove an element from a display, select the event being monitored, then select Edit/Delete, or click the Delete button from the toolbar.

On the toolbar, the plus sign button lets you add items to be monitored (charted, logged, reported, and so on). The next button (a pencil eraser moving across a screen) lets you edit values of parameters already set. The third button (an x) is used by all views to delete an element from the monitor.

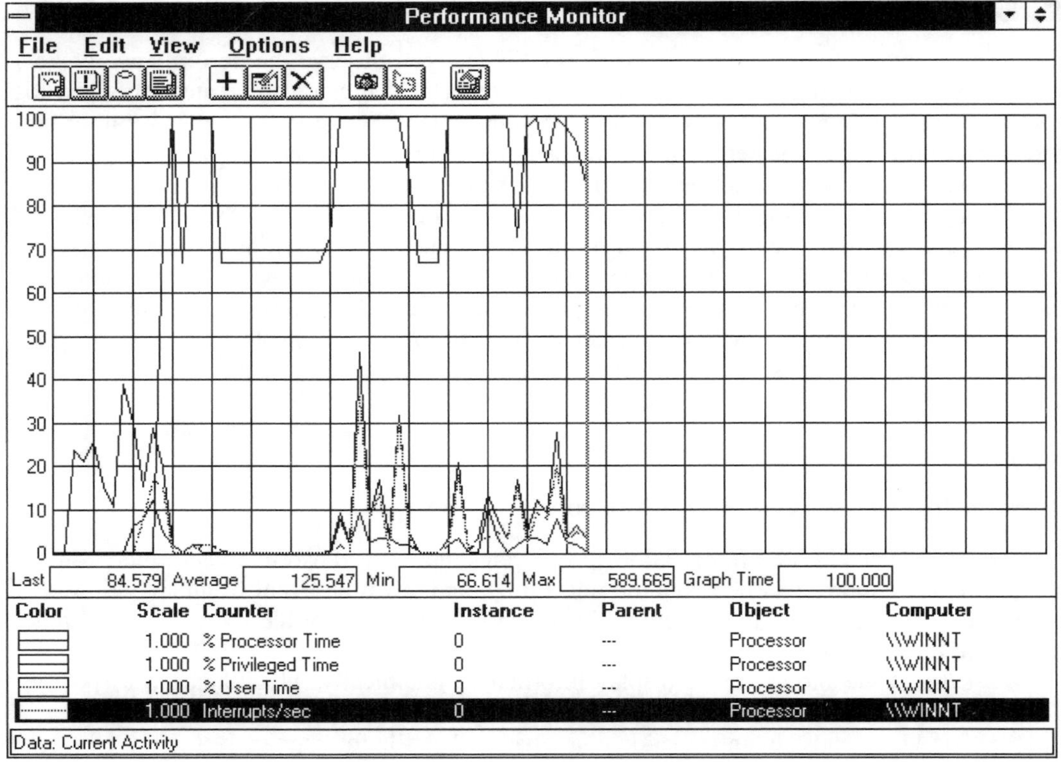

Figure 3.7 Performance Monitor chart.

The Windows NT Performance Monitor application provides a powerful capability to monitor system operations. You can observe system performance and display it graphically, set alerts when variable limits are exceeded, and log data to a file for later analysis or historical use.

The next button on the toolbar, a camera, is used to tell Windows NT to take measurements immediately. This is the Update Now button. You can also select Options/Update Now to update the display. To change the method of updating the display, select Options, then choose either periodic or manual updating. If you select periodic updating, enter a value for the frequency for periodic updates in the Interval text box. Finally, click on OK.

The button with the open book picture on it tells Windows NT to place a bookmark at the current measurement. The last button on the toolbar provides quick access to the monitor's options. Specific instructions for each view are provided below.

Alert View

To add items to be monitored to the alert view, switch to the alert view, then:

1. Select Edit/Add To View or select the Add To View button from the toolbar. The Add to Alert dialog box, shown in Figure 3.8, appears.
2. Select an object type from the Object pulldown list.
3. The Counter list box changes to display the elements of the selected object type that can be measured. Select one or more items from this list. (To read more about a counter, click on the Explain button. Performance Monitor displays a text box that provides more information about the selected counter.)
4. Select an Instance if this is appropriate to the object type you have selected.
5. The Color box is automatically updated with the next available color. To change the color, choose one from the pulldown list.
6. Enter the alert condition in the Alert If box. Enter a value that sets the minimum or maximum condition that will trigger an alert.

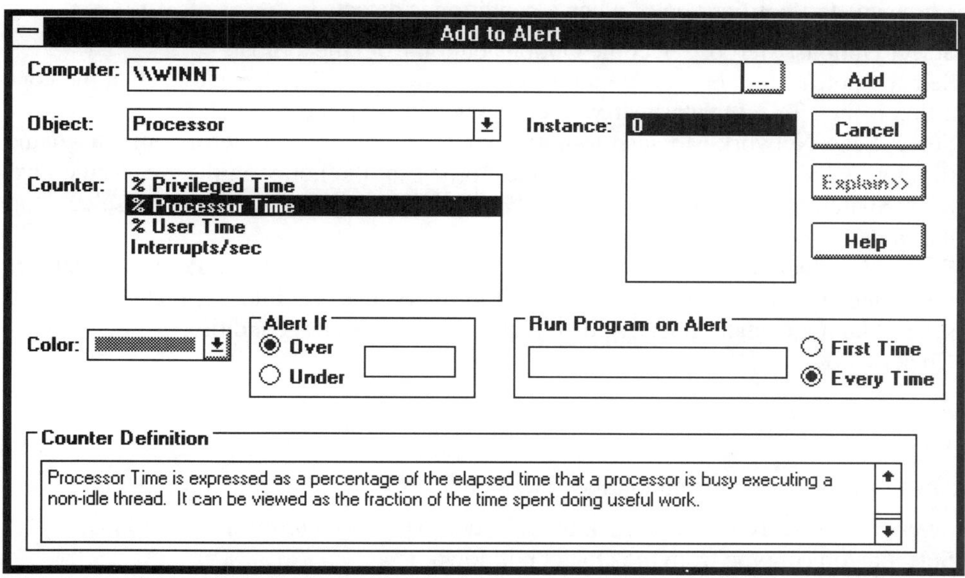

Figure 3.8 Performance Monitor Alert/Add.

Setting alerts on selected performance variables can give an early warning of system problems or security issues.

7. Windows NT can run a program when the alert condition is detected. To trigger this, type the full pathname to the program in the Run Program on Alert text box. Select First Time to run the program once, or select Every Time to run the program each time the condition is detected.
8. Select Add.
9. Repeat steps 2 through 8 until all alert conditions have been added, then click on Done.
10. To save these settings, select File/Save Alert Settings. To create a new settings file, select File/Save Alert Settings As. Enter a filename, then select OK.

To change any alert conditions:

1. Double-click the element in the legend, select Edit/Edit Alert Entry, or select the Edit Alert Entry button from the toolbar.
2. Change the desired values: color, Alert If, and/or Run Program on Alert.
3. Click on OK.

Changing Alert Notifications

To change how an alert notifies you of when a condition is detected:

1. Select Options/Alert or select the Options button from the toolbar.
2. Select a notification option. Windows NT can switch to the alert view when the condition is met. To set this property, select Switch to Alert View.
3. Select Send Network Message to notify you of a condition. Enter a computer name (do not include backslashes in the name) to be sent the notice in the Net Name box. Both Switch to Alert View and Send Network Message options may be selected at the same time.
4. Select the Update Time option: choose either Manual Update or Period Update. If you select Periodic Update, enter the time interval in the Interval text box. If you select Manual Update, select Update Now to check for alert conditions.
5. Click on OK.

Chart View

To add items to a chart view, switch to this view, then:

1. Select Edit/Add To Chart or click on the Add To Chart button from the toolbar.
2. Select an object type from the Object pulldown list.
3. The Counter list box changes to display the elements of the selected object type that can be measured. Select one or more items from this list.
4. Select an Instance if appropriate to the object type you have selected.
5. The Color box is automatically updated with the next available color. To override the selection, choose a color from the pulldown list. Likewise select a line scale, width, and style.
6. Select Add.

7. Repeat steps 2 through 6 until all items have been added. Select Done.
8. To save these settings, select File/Save Chart Settings. To create a new settings file, select File/Save Chart Settings As. Enter a filename, then select OK.

To change a chart's characteristics:

1. Select Options/Chart or click on the Options button from the toolbar.
2. Select the option you want to display from the Chart options dialog box.
3. Update the values desired, then click on OK.

Changing Items in a Chart

To change the options of an item in the chart:

1. Select the element you want to change from the legend.
2. Double-click on the element, select Edit/Edit Chart Line, or click on the Edit Chart Line button from the toolbar.
3. Make your selection of color, scale, width, or style, then click on OK.

Log View

The log file lets you record information on specific objects, then view these events later. The log file keeps an informational record, and sends this information to a separate disk file for analysis by other programs. In addition, log files can be used as input to the other views, which can then display the values captured in the log file.

To select which events are recorded in a log file, switch to Log View, then:

1. Select File/Open and enter the name of the file (log setting files have the extension .PML). To create a new log file, select File/New Log Settings.
2. Select Edit/Add To Log or click on the Add To Log button from the toolbar to add items to an existing log file. The Add to Log dialog box, shown in Figure 3.9, appears.
3. Select the type of object you want to add to the log from the Objects box, then click on Add. Repeat this step until all items are added.
4. Click on Done.

To change how events are recorded in the log file:

1. Select Options/Log or click on the Options button from the toolbar.
2. Enter the name of the log file in the Log File text box.
3. Enter the new values as appropriate.
4. Click on OK to record the options but not start the logging process. Otherwise, select Start Log to begin immediate logging of the selected events.
5. To stop logging events to the log file, select Options/Log and select Stop Log.

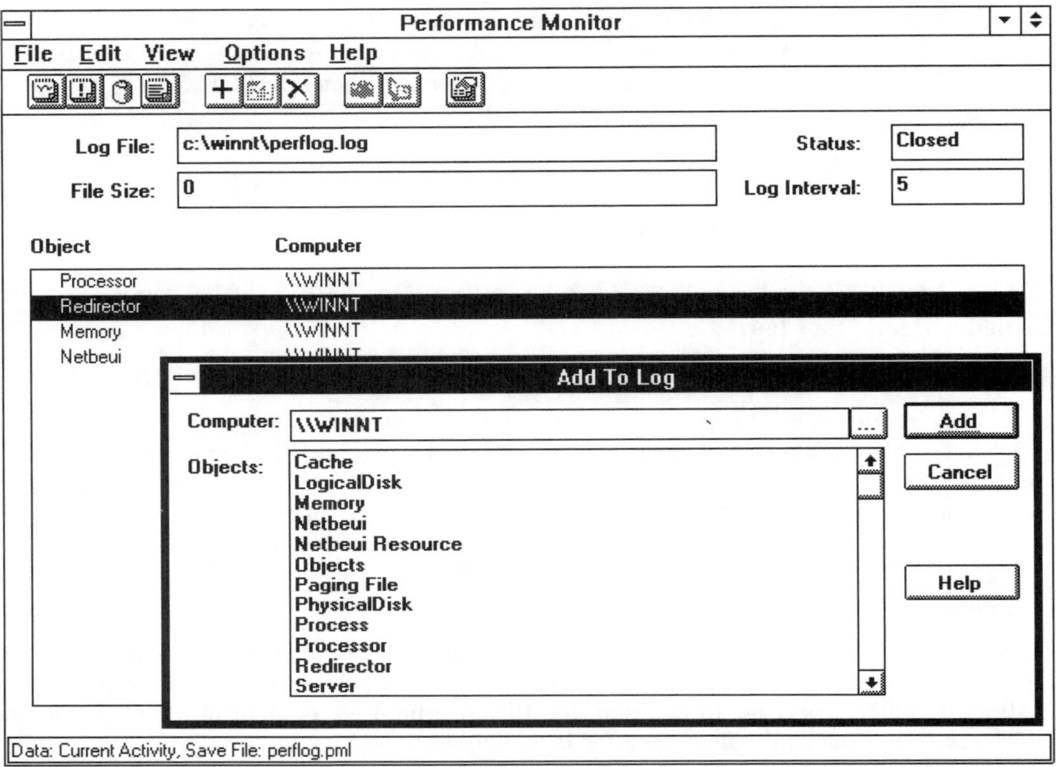

Figure 3.9 Performance Monitor Log/Add.

Writing data to a permanent log file allows you to analyze it off line and retain it for maintenance histories and auditing.

Sub-Log Files

You can create a log file that contains only *some* of the information of a full log file, thus allowing you to analyze a limited number of events using a smaller file. To create a smaller log file, the process is called relogging a log file:

1. Select Log View.
2. Select Options/Data From.
3. Enter the name of the full log file.
4. Select Edit/Add To Log (to select which objects should be relogged), Edit/Delete From Log (to prevent an object from being relogged), and/or Edit/Time Window (to change the starting and stopping time points of the selected activity).

5. Select Options/Log and type the name of the new log file. Select a new log interval, if desired, then select Start Logging.

Bookmarks in a Log File

Bookmarks, available in all views, are probably most useful in a log file. Bookmarks allow you to find key locations within the file; bookmarks are freeform text you can place anywhere within the log. Bookmarks are useful for noting the beginning and ending points of a log file when the file is used as input to a chart, alert, or report view.

To add a bookmark to a log file, select Options/Bookmark or click on the Bookmark button from the toolbar (the icon that looks like an open book). Type the text of your bookmark in the Bookmark Comment text box, then click on Add.

Viewing the Contents of Log Files in Other Views

To use the log file as input to Alert, Chart, and Report views:

1. Switch to the view you want to use.
2. Select Options/Data From.
3. In the Data Values Displayed From box select Log File.
4. Enter the log filename and select OK.

Use the options within the view to limit what events are displayed. Unless otherwise specified, an alert, chart, or report view will use the entire log file. To limit the analysis to specific beginning or ending points, select the view you want to use, then follow steps similar to the following, which explain how to control the values within a specified starting and stopping point.

1. Select Edit/Time Window.
2. Drag the beginning or ending point of the timeframe to a new location. As you move it, the dialog box displays the new time.
3. To use a bookmark as a starting or ending point, select the bookmark, then select Set As Start (to use the bookmark as the beginning point for analysis), or select Set As Stop (to use the bookmark as the end point).
4. Click on OK.

Use the Edit Menu and other editing tools for each of the appropriate views to analyze data from the log file. The steps are identical to those used for analyzing live performance data.

Report View

To add items to a report view:

1. Select Edit/Add To Report or click on the Add To Report button from the toolbar.
2. Select an object type from the Object pulldown list.

3. The Counter list box changes to display the elements of the selected object type that can be measured. Select one or more items from this list.
4. Select an Instance if appropriate to the object type you have selected.
5. Select Add.
6. Repeat steps 2 through 5 until all items have been added, then click on Done.
7. To save these settings, select File/Save Report Settings. To create a new report file, select File/Save Report Settings As. Enter a filename, then select OK.

The most common change you will make to a report is to change the frequency with which the report is updated. To change the frequency, select Options/Report or click on the Options button from the toolbar. Select Manual Update or Periodic Update from the Update Time section. Note that if you select Periodic Update, you *must* enter an time interval in the Interval text box. Click on OK.

Reusing Settings

In each view you can save the events being monitored (and critical values, if any). These settings are created using the File/Save or File/Save As settings. To use one of these settings for future monitoring:

1. Select the view you want to use.
2. Select File/Open.
3. Select the existing activity file. Alert files use the .PMA file extension, chart files use .PMC., log files use .PML, and report files use .PMR. You can select a workspace file (.PMW) that contains settings for all four views.
4. You may change any settings at this point and use File/Save to update the settings if you wish, or use File/Save As to create another settings file.

Analyzing Performance Data

To export performance data for analysis by another program, such as a spreadsheet:

1. Select the view whose data you want to export.
2. Select File/Export.
3. Select either the tab or the comma-delimited format for separating data in fields in a record, according to the format your analysis tool can import.
4. Enter the full pathname of the export file.
5. Click on OK.

Event Viewer

An *event* is any significant occurrence in the computer system or from an application that requires notification of a user, either by using a pop-up alert message or by writing a message to a log file for later review by an administrator. Windows NT makes a record of these events in an *event log*. There are three types of event logs:

1. The *System Log* tracks events triggered by the Windows NT system components, such as when a component doesn't load during startup. Another common message in the System Log is a power fluctuation involving the Uninterruptible Power Supply (UPS). A sample system log appears in Figure 3.10.
2. The *Security Log* tracks events triggered by security violations, such as illegal logons to the system or unauthorized file reads. It also records events specified by *auditing* as defined earlier in this chapter.
3. The *Application Log* tracks events that are written by an application program. These vary by the application.

You specify the type of events that are logged to the file by selecting the Audit option from the Policies menu in User Manager (see User Manager for details). You can control the file and directory events logged in File Manager by using the Auditing command from the Security menu. The event log shows the following information:

Computer	The name of the computer on which the event occurred.
Category	A classification of the event; this varies by the event source.
Date	Date of the event.
Event ID	A unique number that identifies the event.

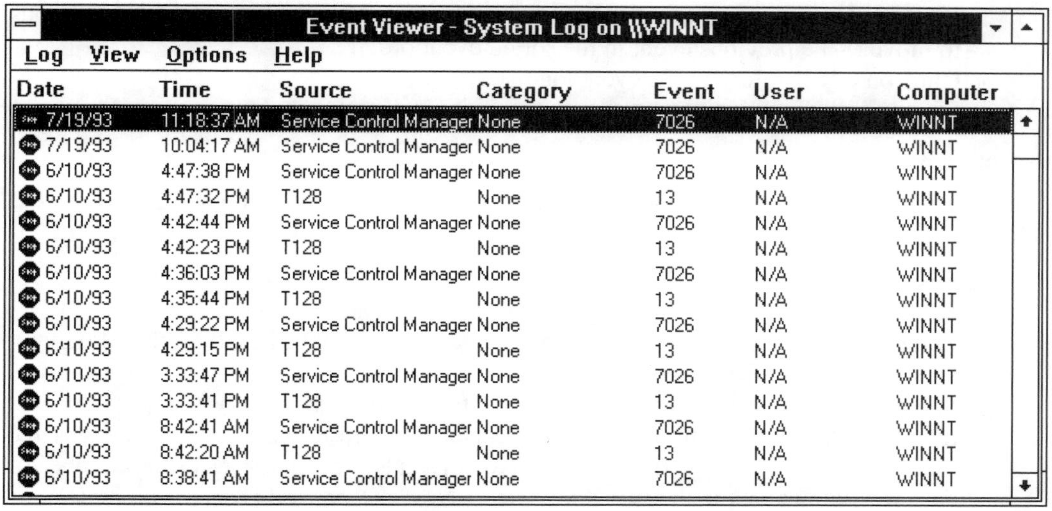

Event Viewer - System Log on \\WINNT

Log View Options Help

Date	Time	Source	Category	Event	User	Computer
7/19/93	11:18:37 AM	Service Control Manager	None	7026	N/A	WINNT
7/19/93	10:04:17 AM	Service Control Manager	None	7026	N/A	WINNT
6/10/93	4:47:38 PM	Service Control Manager	None	7026	N/A	WINNT
6/10/93	4:47:32 PM	T128	None	13	N/A	WINNT
6/10/93	4:42:44 PM	Service Control Manager	None	7026	N/A	WINNT
6/10/93	4:42:23 PM	T128	None	13	N/A	WINNT
6/10/93	4:36:03 PM	Service Control Manager	None	7026	N/A	WINNT
6/10/93	4:35:44 PM	T128	None	13	N/A	WINNT
6/10/93	4:29:22 PM	Service Control Manager	None	7026	N/A	WINNT
6/10/93	4:29:15 PM	T128	None	13	N/A	WINNT
6/10/93	3:33:47 PM	Service Control Manager	None	7026	N/A	WINNT
6/10/93	3:33:41 PM	T128	None	13	N/A	WINNT
6/10/93	8:42:41 AM	Service Control Manager	None	7026	N/A	WINNT
6/10/93	8:42:20 AM	T128	None	13	N/A	WINNT
6/10/93	8:38:41 AM	Service Control Manager	None	7026	N/A	WINNT

Figure 3.10 System log.

Windows NT provides automatic logging of significant system events, including errors.

Source	The application or system resource that triggered the event.
Time	Time of the event.
Type	Windows NT classifies the event as: error, warning, information, success audit, or failure audit.
User	The username that was logged onto the computer when the event occurred. If this column contains ***, the event triggering the log record did not capture the username (as may be the case with application programs).

To open the log file for viewing, select the Event Viewer application in the Administrator program group.

Viewing a Log File

To select which log file you want to view, select Log from the main menu. Select System, Security, or Application to display the type of log file you want to view.

By default, the event log displayed when you start Event Viewer is that of your own computer. Administrators can view events for another computer. To select another computer, Select Log/Select Computer. Type the name of the computer in the Computername text box or select one from the list provided. Click on OK.

In addition to the date, time, source, type, category, event ID, user, and computer name of each event, you can also view a description and the binary data logged by the event, usually created by an application. To view detailed information about an event:

1. Double-click on the event in the event list, or select the event and select View/Detail.
2. Click on Next to move to the next event in the sorted event order. Click on Previous to move to the previous event in the sorted event order.
3. Click on OK to return to the event log list.

Managing a Log File

You can change the amount of space allocated for each type of log and settings for event retention:

1. Select Log/Settings.
2. Select the log file from the Change Settings for Log pulldown list.
3. Enter the maximum space (in number of kilobytes) for the log file in the Maximum log size box. The default is 512KB.
4. Select an Event Retention Period option to specify how or how long events are retained in the log. Select Overwrite Events as Needed to write new events over the oldest entries in the log. If you select Keep Events, you must select the number of days to retain events in the log. If you select Never Overwrite Events, you must clear the log manually.
5. As an alternative to steps 3 and 4, select Default and all settings will be restored to the system-defined default.

6. Click on OK.

To erase the log file and begin with a new, empty file, select the type of log file you want to clear. Select Log/Clear All Events. You are asked if you want to save the current log file. Select Yes and you will see the Save As dialog box. Enter the filename and click on OK.

Managing Events

You can display only a desired type of event (called filtering), search for a specific event, or sort the list of events.

Filtering Events

The log file records all events according to other settings in the Windows NT system, but you can view only the desired events by setting a filter. To view a subset of the events in the event log:

1. Select View/Filter Events. The Filter dialog box is shown in Figure 3.11.

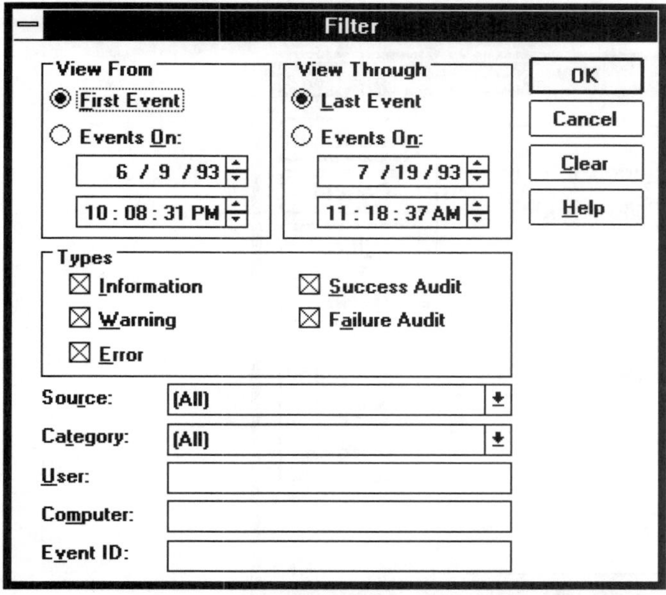

Figure 3.11 Filter dialog.

Inspection of a complex log file can be greatly simplified by filtering—selecting only the events you're immediately interested in.

2. In the Filter dialog box enter the options you want. Events that meet these specifications will be displayed. A complete description of events can be found in the Event Viewer chapter of the Windows NT System Guide.
3. Click on OK.

To remove the filters, select View/All Events.

Searching for Events

To locate specific events, use the Find feature of Event Log. To search for a specific event or range of events:

1. Select View/Find. The Find dialog box shown in Figure 3.12 appears.
2. Select the options you want to use in the search in the Find dialog box. Select the direction (Up or Down) to search from the current event forward (Down) or backward to the beginning of the log (Up). Other options are detailed in the Event Viewer chapter of the Windows NT System Guide. (Most are self-explanatory.) If multiple Types are selected, the search will look for any event that meets *any* of the criteria.
3. Select Find Next to find the event that meets your criteria.

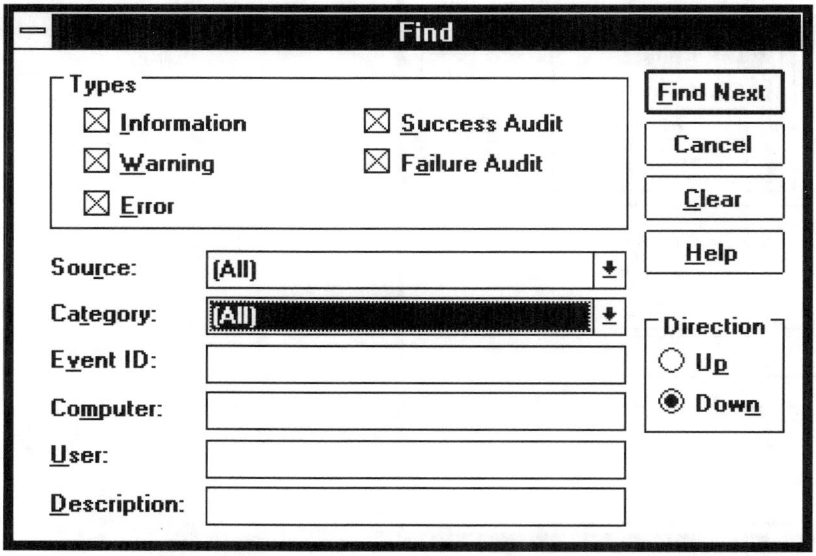

Figure 3.12 Find dialog.

Beyond filtering, a straight search capability is provided—giving you the tools to get the information you need from the log quickly.

4. Press F3 to find the next event using the same criteria.

Sorting Events

To sort the order of events in the log file, select View/Newest First to see the most recent events at the top of the list, or select View/Oldest First to see the oldest events at the top of the list.

Archiving a Log File

As log files grow, you may wish to save the event log to another file. You may also wish to perform this function as part of regular maintenance, such as every week or once each month. Archiving a log file is also useful if you want to export the data to another application, such as a database or spreadsheet, for further analysis.

When you archive a log file, the complete contents are archived and the filter options are ignored. The archived file does retain the sort order based on the export file format you select.

You can archive a log file in one of three file formats:

The standard log file format allows you to use the Event Viewer to view the contents of the archived file. The sort order of the events is ignored.

With an ASCII text file, the sorted order of the events is used. The binary data associated with an event is not included in the new file.

A comma-delimited format may also be selected. Comma-delimited format is used most often when you are exporting the data to a database or spreadsheet. As with ASCII text files, the sorted order of the events is used but binary data associated with an event is not included in the new file.

To archive a log file:

1. Select Log/Save As.
2. Select the file format you want from the Save File As Type list.
3. Enter the filename in the File Name text box. If you select the standard log file format, the file extension assigned is .EVT. The file extension .TXT is used for text and comma-delimited files.
4. Click on OK.

To view an archived log file (for log files using the standard log file format) with the Event Viewer:

1. Select Log/Open.
2. Enter the log filename in the File Name box or select it from the list of existing files.
3. Click on OK.
4. Select the type of log file you want (Application, Security, or System) in the Open File Type box, then click on OK.

Managing Disks

Disk Administrator

Windows NT's *Disk Administrator* program provides tools for managing disks, allowing you to create partitions on hard disks, create volumes and stripe sets, read status information (such as partition size), and assign partitions to drive letters.

To start Disk Administrator, select the Disk Administrator icon from the Administrative Tools group in Program Manager, or select File/Run and enter WINDISK on the Command line. The main Disk Administrator dialog box is shown in Figure 3.13.

Many commands for disks, including labeling and formatting disks, are performed from the Command Prompt in Program Manager. Only those features found in Disk Administrator are described in this section.

Once you have requested changes to your disk partitions and then quit Disk Administrator normally, Disk Administrator will remind you of your request and note which changes cannot be reversed. At this point you can change your mind and cancel the changes. In many cases you may also want to notify all users of your changes, as some modifications, such as deleting partitions, may directly impact users on the system.

Assigning Drive Letters

In many computer systems, adding a new hard drive disrupts the order of existing drive letter assignments. In Windows NT, Disk Administrator allows you to statically assign drive letters so this does not happen. Once assigned, drive letters are maintained when another drive is added to the system. To assign a drive letter:

1. Select the partition or logical drive you want to assign to a letter.

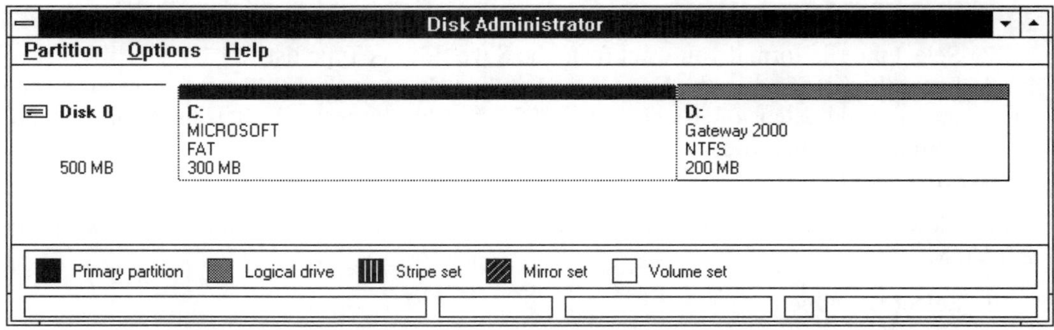

Figure 3.13 Disk Administrator.

The Windows NT Disk Administrator program provides a graphical view of disk partitions, along with central location of all disk management/maintenance functions.

2. Select Partition/Drive Letter.
3. The Assign Drive Letter dialog box appears. Select the assignment option you want.
4. Click on OK.

Primary and Extended Partitions

A primary partition is a subdivision of a physical disk; up to four primary partitions can be created per disk. A primary partition cannot be subdivided. In x86 systems, the primary partition of your C: drive is the partition from which you boot the system. Only one of the four primary partitions can be designated an extended partition (explained below).

In contrast, an extended partition is created from free space on your hard disk and can be subpartitioned into logical drives.

To create a primary partition on a hard disk:

1. Select the free space area on a disk.
2. Select Partition/Create.
3. The Create Primary Partition dialog box displays the minimum and maximum size for the partition. It also displays a text box labeled Create partition of size, in which you should enter the new partition size.
4. Click on OK.

On Intel x86-based computers, the system partition that contains the hardware-specific files needed for booting must be marked as active. In contrast, RISC-based computers do not use such markings, but are controlled by a configuration program supplied by the computer manufacturer.

To mark a partition as active for x86-based computers, select the partition that contains the necessary startup files. Select Partition/Mark Active, then click on OK.

An *extended* partition can be set up and used to create multiple logical drives, or as part of a volume set. To create an extended partition:

1. Select the free space area on a disk.
2. Select Partition/Create Extended.
3. The Create Extended Partition dialog box displays the minimum and maximum size for the partition, and displays a text box named Create partition of size. Enter the appropriate size, then click on OK.

To create logical drives *within* an extended partition, select the space in the extended partition, select Partition/Create, enter the size of the logical drive in the Create Logical Drive dialog box, and click on OK.

To delete a partition, volume, or logical drive:

1. Select the partition, volume, or logical drive you want to remove.
2. Select Partition/Delete.
3. Select Yes to confirm your delete request.

Volume Sets

A volume set is a method for allocating free space on several partitions as though the resulting set was a single partition itself. All space in the first area of a volume set is filled before space in the second area is filled; all space in the second area is used before space is used from the third area, and so on, until all areas (up to a maximum of 32) are used.

Free space from partitions can be of unequal size, and several areas can be on the same drive, in contrast to a stripe set, in which all areas must be on different drives. Volume sets also help you allocate the I/O across drives in an effort to improve overall system performance. To create a volume set:

1. Select two or more areas of free space (up to 32 areas can be selected). Select the first area, then press and hold the Ctrl key as you select the remaining area(s).
2. Select Partition/Create Volume Set.
3. Enter the size of the volume you want to create. If the size you enter is less than the total space of the selected free space, Disk Administrator attempts to divide the total space by the number of areas and allocate the same amount of space from all areas to the volume set.
4. Click on OK.

To delete a volume set, select the volume set. Select Partition/Delete. Click on Yes to confirm your delete request. All data is deleted from the selected areas.

Extending Volumes and Volume Sets

If you are using NTFS volumes or volume sets, you can expand their size by using current free space. Doing so automatically logs you off the system and then formats the new area, a process that does not affect your existing data. (Note that you cannot extend a volume if it is part of a stripe or mirror set.) To extend a volume or a volume set:

1. Select the existing volume or volume set.
2. Select one or more free space areas.
3. Select Partition/Extend Volume Set.
4. Enter the size of the new volume set that will be the result of combining the existing and new space.
5. Click on OK.

Stripe Sets

A stripe set is similar to a volume set. A key difference is that Windows NT fills one stripe of the first area, then one stripe of the second area, and so on, until one stripe from each area is filled. It then proceeds to fill the second stripe on the first area, the second stripe on the second area, and so on.

Each area of a stripe set must be on a different disk. Furthermore, Disk Administrator creates stripe sets with areas of uniform size. To create a stripe set:

1. Select two or more areas of free space (up to 32 areas can be selected). Select the first area, then press and hold the Ctrl key as you select the remaining area(s).
2. Select Partition/Create Stripe Set.
3. Enter the size of the stripe set you want to create. Disk Administrator divides this number by the total number of areas and allocates this uniform space from each selected area.
4. Click on OK.

To delete a stripe set:

1. Select the stripe set.
2. Select Partition/Delete.
3. Select Yes to confirm your delete request. All data is deleted from the selected areas.

Disk Configuration Information

You can save, restore, and search for information such as the assigned drive letters, stripe sets, and so on, using the Disk Administrator's configuration settings.

To save the current configuration settings, select Partition/Configuration. Note that changes to the configuration made during the current session are not saved. To save the changes, you must log off and log back into the system.

To save the settings, select Configuration/Save and place a floppy disk into the A: or B: drive. Click OK, and Disk Administrator will write the information to the diskette.

To restore the disk configuration information, select Partition/Configuration. Select Configuration/Restore, then insert the floppy containing the configuration information into the A: or B: drive and click on OK.

To search for disk configuration information:

1. Select Partition/Configuration.
2. Select Configuration/Search.
3. Click OK to acknowledge the warning message. *The search procedure erases your current disk configuration information, as well as any changes made during the session.*
4. Windows NT searches for other installations. When it finds one or more, it displays them in a list. Select the installation you want, then select OK.

Backup

The Windows NT *Backup* program lets you copy data from your hard disk to a tape cassette, protecting you from loss from accidental erasure, hardware failure, or damage resulting from power interruptions. Backup uses a graphical environment that is similar to the File Manager; you can select which files are backed up or restored by clicking on files, directories, and/or drive letters.

Backup works with FAT, HPFS, and NTFS file systems. You can back up files from different drives and select from several backup techniques. For example, you can back up only those files that have changed since the previous backup.

To start Backup, double-click on the Backup icon in the Administrative Tools program group, select NTBACKUP from the File Manager, or select File/Run and type NTBACKUP in the Command Line text box.

Selecting Files to Back Up

You can select all files on a drive, all files in a directory, or individual files. The technique is nearly identical to the method used for selecting files in File Manager. The major difference is that in File Manager you select files by highlighting them. In Backup a check box is used for selecting files. To select files to back up:

1. Select the drives window and double-click on the disk drive icon or letter of the drive that contains the files you want to back up. The Backup program opens a window for the selected drive, as illustrated in Figure 3.14.

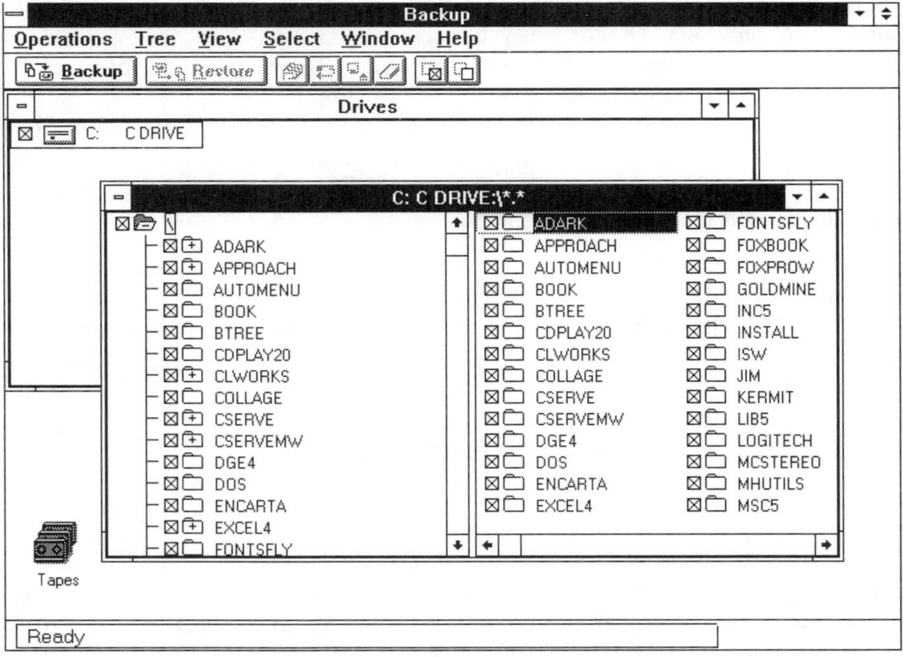

Figure 3.14 Backup program.

Windows NT includes built-in support for tape backup; a necessity for servers and highly desirable on high-performance workstations.

2. To select all files, choose Select/Check. You can also select all files by clicking on the Check button on the toolbar, or check the box for the drive from the Drives window.
3. To select a single file, select the box positioned before the file you want to select.
4. To select multiple files, press *and hold* the Ctrl key, then select each file. When all files are selected, release the Ctrl key.
5. To select a range of files that are listed contiguously, select the first file, then press *and hold* the Shift key and select the last file in the range. Choose Select/Check to select each file's check box. Alternatively, select the Check button on the toolbar.

Backing Up Files to Tape

The backup process uses three pieces of information: the files you want to back up, the type of backup you want (full, only changed files, etc.), and optionally a description of the backup, which is useful for identifying the right backup when files must be restored.

Backup graphically shows its progress and prompts you when it is time to insert tape cartridges. To back up files:

1. Select the files (see above), then click on Backup. The Backup Information dialog box appears.
2. Enter a description of the tape in the Tape Name text box, to a maximum of 31 characters.
3. Select Append to add the backup to the end of an existing tape set, or select Replace to erase the information already on the tape and replace it with the current backup. If you select Replace, Backup asks you to confirm your request.
4. To protect the tape contents from unauthorized use, check the Restrict Access To Owner Or Administrator box. Only the tape's owner or administrator with Backup rights can read, write, or erase the tape. If you restrict access and you need to restore a file to a different computer, the user performing the restore must be an Administrator or Restore Operator.
5. To add a verification step to the backup (to compare the original with the copy on tape), check the Verify After Backup box.
6. To add the Registry files to the tape backup, select the Backup Registry check box.
7. Select the type of backup you want from the table below.
8. Select an option that describes how you want to log the backup session. Choose Summary Only to log the major events (loading a tape, for example). Choose Full Detail to list all operational details, including the full pathname of the files backed up. Select Don't Log if you don't want information added to a log file.
9. Click on OK. The Backup Status dialog box appears and shows the activities as they occur. The dialog box also displays the number of directories, files, and bytes being backed up, the elapsed time, and the number of files it could not back up because of security considerations.
10. If the backup requires more than one tape, you will be prompted to insert a new tape when appropriate.
11. To stop a backup operation at any time, click on Abort.

Backup Type:	*Action:*
Normal	Back up selected files; files are marked as backed up (the archive bit is turned off)
Copy	Back up selected files, but files will not be marked as backed up (the archive bit is unchanged)
Incremental	Back up selected files modified since the last backup (the archive bit is on); files are marked as backed up (the archive bit is turned off)
Differential	Identical to incremental, but files are not marked as backed up (the archive bit is unchanged)
Daily Copy	Back up files that have been modified on the current date; files are not marked as backed up (the archive bit is unchanged)

Restoring Files from Tape

The restore operation is the converse of the backup operation. You can restore all files on a tape or just selected files:

1. Insert the tape into the tape drive unit and click on the Tapes icon.
2. Backup displays the tape information on the left side of the Tapes window. It shows the drive backed up, the backup type, and the date and time of the backup. Select the tape containing the file(s) you want to restore: Double-click the tape's icon, select Operations/Catalog, or click on the Catalog button in the toolbar.
3. Backup displays a list of the backup sets in the Tapes window. A question mark is displayed with each icon meaning the catalog (list of files) has not yet been read from the tape's directory. Select the backup set you want: Double-click on the backup set's icon, select Operations/Catalog, or click on the Catalog button in the toolbar.
4. The program displays the list of directories and files in a hierarchy in the Tape File Selection window. To restore all files, select the check box for the tape and select Select/Check or click on the Check button in the toolbar.
5. To restore an individual file, select the file's check box.
6. To restore multiple files that are not listed contiguously, press *and hold* the Ctrl key while you select each file.
7. To restore multiple files listed contiguously, press *and hold* the Shift key and select the first and last files. Choose Select/Check or click on the Check button in the toolbar.
8. Click on Restore. Restore may ask you to enter the drive to which you want to restore the file(s).
9. To force Restore to compare the data on the tape with the data restored to the hard drive, check the Verify After Restore box.
10. Select the log option you want. Choose Summary Only to log the major events (such as loading a tape or completing a backup). Choose Full Detail to list all operations and the fully qualified path and filename of all restored files. Choose Don't Log to bypass writing information to a log file.
11. To restore the Registry files, select the Restore Local Registry check box.

12. Click on OK to start the restoration. If the program needs additional tapes, you will be asked to insert a tape when necessary.
13. You may be asked to confirm replacing an existing file that has been modified since the backup with a file on the backup tape. Answer Yes to replace the file and No to restore the next selected file.
14. To stop the restore operation at any time, select Abort.

Tape Maintenance

Erasing a Tape

There are two types of tape erasure. The Quick Erase method erases only the tape header, which contains information about the name of the tape, and the Backup process considers the tape empty and rewrites over all of it. The process is usually very short (typically under one minute). However, the files backed up to the tape remain on the tape. A Secure Erase overwrites the entire tape, and hence may be a very long process.

To erase a tape, insert the tape into the tape drive unit, then select Operations/Erase Tape or click on the Erase Tape button in the toolbar. Select Quick Erase or Secure Erase, and click on Continue to begin the tape erasure.

Retensioning Tapes

Tapes need to be retensioned to reduce slippage and improve reliability. The retensioning process fast-forwards the tape to the end of the reel, then rewinds it.

To retension a tape, insert the tape in the tape drive unit and select Operations/Retension Tape, or click on the Retension Tape button in the toolbar.

Uninterruptible Power Supply

An uninterruptible power supply (UPS) is a battery-operated power supply that maintains power to a computer when the main power source is interrupted, such as during power failures. The UPS allows for the safe shutdown of the system until the main power source is restored.

Windows NT allows you to configure the UPS and how it works with the operating system. The main UPS window is shown in Figure 3.15.

Setting Up a UPS

To establish the software connection between a UPS and Windows NT, select the Control Panel icon from the Main program group. Click on the UPS icon, then check the Uninterruptible Power Supply Installed On box. Choose the port from the pulldown list box, then click on OK.

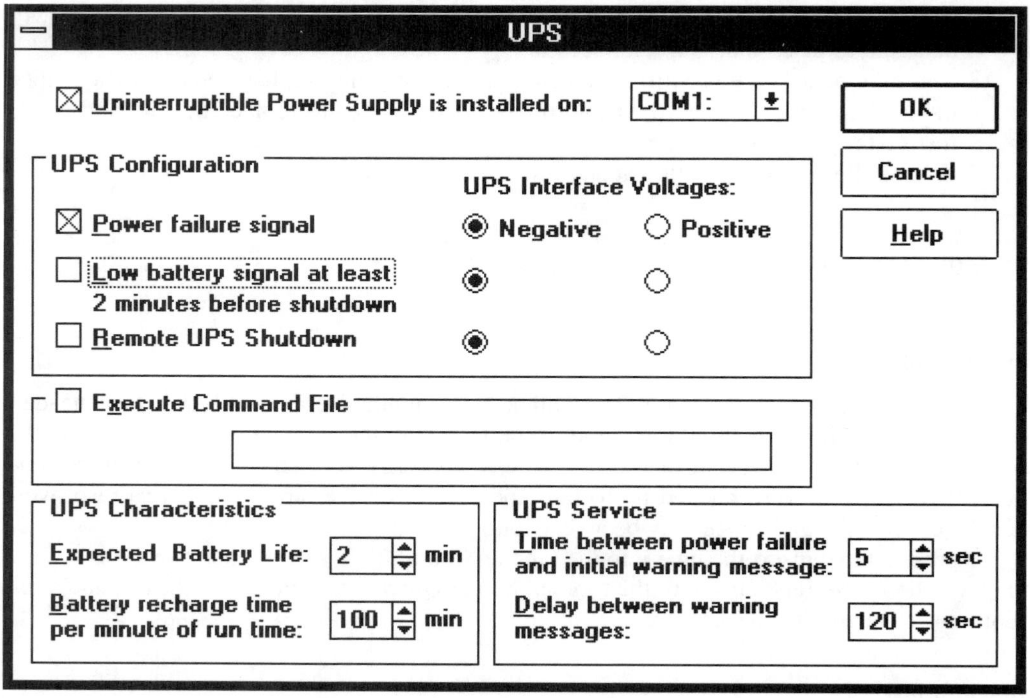

Figure 3.15 Main UPS window.

Built-in support for Uninterruptable Power Supply (UPS) assures that Windows NT servers need never experience a total power failure without the opportunity to execute a controlled system shutdown procedure.

Once set up, you need to specify how the UPS will interact with Windows NT once it is triggered. Select the UPS icon from the control panel. Then:

1. Check the Power Failure Signal box if the UPS is capable of sending a message to Windows NT when it detects a problem. Select the Negative or Positive Interface Voltage value according to your UPS hardware instructions (this varies by make and model).
2. If you checked the Power Failure Signal box in step 1, enter the value in the UPS Characteristics box. The Expected Battery Life values can range from 2 to 720 minutes (2 is the default). The setting is used in messages to notify you of the time remaining. The Battery recharge time per minute of runtime values range from 1 to 250 minutes (100 is the default).

3. Check the Low Battery Signal At Least 2 Minutes Before Shutdown box if your UPS can send a message when it detects a low battery. Select the Negative or Positive Interface Voltage value according to your UPS hardware instructions.
4. Check the Remote UPS Shutdown box if your UPS can respond to a signal to shut itself off. Select the Negative or Positive Interface Voltage value according to your UPS hardware instructions.
5. Enter the number of seconds between the moment a power failure is recognized and the display of a warning message. Enter the value in the UPS Service area in the text box labeled Time Between Power Failure And Initial Warning Message. Valid values are between 0 and 120 seconds; the default is 5 seconds.
6. Enter the number of seconds between warning messages in the Delay Between Warning Messages box. Valid values are between 5 and 300 seconds; the default value is 120 seconds (2 minutes).
7. Click on OK.

Once the settings have been established, you can test your UPS's ability to recover your system. To test the system, disconnect the power from the UPS to simulate a failure. Windows NT displays a warning or alert message. When the UPS battery reaches its low level, the system will begin its shutdown. At this point, reconnect power to the UPS. Use the Event Viewer to see that all actions were properly recorded and that none caused an error.

Administrative *Net* Commands

While most administrative functions in Windows NT are performed using one or another of the graphical applications, such as User Manager and Server Manager, there is a very powerful set of command line functions for administrative control that are essentially an extension of the basic *net* commands discussed at the end of Chapter 4. In this section we will discuss these commands and how they can be of considerable administrative use because they can be employed in batch files and login scripts. The basic net commands for control of file sharing, printer sharing, attaching two shared directories, and the like were discussed at the end of Chapter 4. In addition to those commands there is a set of commands which are intended for administrative use only. By using these commands in a batch file or login script you can generally accomplish all the same tasks that would otherwise be performed in User Manager, Server Manager, and so on.

Setting Systemwide Security Policy: *Net Accounts*

This command may be used to control the account policies for single servers or for all servers within a domain provided the command is used by a domain administrator (NT Advanced Server domains only). The syntax of the command is *net accounts* followed by any of several command switches. Issued by itself the command displays the current account policy for the server in which it is activated:

```
C:\users\default>net accounts
Force user logoff how long after time expires:      Never
Minimum password age (days):                        0
Maximum password age (days):                        42
Minimum password length:                            0
Length of password history maintained:              None
Machine role:                                       WORKSTATION
The command completed successfully.
```

Or through the use of the /domain switch it will display the domain-wide policy set by the primary domain controller. All major factors of the server account policy may be directly controlled using the following switches:

- */force logoff:* This command controls whether users will be forcibly logged off of a system when their account passwords have expired or when their allowed time on the system is exceeded. The default value is NO, which will not force a logoff. The alternative is to set a time in minutes. For example, the command *net accounts/force logoff: 10* will give users ten minutes in which to change their account passwords if they log in with an expired account or will give them ten minutes after notification that they have exceeded their permitted time on the system in which to finish up their business.
- */minpwlen:* Minimum password length. This command sets the minimum length for passwords for the server. Permitted values are in the range zero to fourteen characters where a value of zero will permit users to have a blank password. By default, Windows NT requires a six-character minimum password length. NOTE: The entire NT security system depends upon proper use of passwords. Setting /minpwlen:0 is functionally equivalent to disabling the majority of the Windows NT security system.
- */maxpwage:* Maximum password age. This command is similar in function to the force logoff function. It determines the maximum age of a password before the user will be required to change passwords. Legal values are a range of days from one to slightly over 40,000 or the keyword UNLIMITED, which allows passwords to be used indefinitely. NOTE: Again, the Windows NT security system depends upon effective use of passwords. Setting an unlimited password makes it technically possible, though perhaps not feasible, for passwords to be hacked. It is better to force passwords to be changed on a regular basis. For example, once a week would be /maxpwage7, once a month: /maxpwage30.
- */minpwage:* Minimum password age. Functionally the opposite of the /maxpwage command, /minpwage sets the minimum number of days that must pass before a user is permitted to change his or her password. This may seem like a ridiculous setting. After all, why not provide a minpwage of zero days, which is the default, and allow people to change the password at will? The reason for doing something otherwise lies in the desire and the need to maintain a record of what the user passwords *are*. If one employs, for instance, a backup system that operates on a daily basis, setting a minpwage of one or two days will prevent users from changing their passwords multiple times and having this information not be recorded. This can eliminate administrative

difficulties when an end-user forgets his or her password. Legal values are in the range of zero to slightly over 40,000. The default, again, is zero days.

- */uniquepw:* Unique password. This command requires users' passwords to be unique through a specified number of changes ranging from zero through eight. Thus, for instance, setting uniquepw:2 will require that users' passwords be unique through their last two passwords. That is, they cannot repeat an earlier password until they have used at least two new ones. This will prevent users from repeatedly entering the same password and thus functionally defeating the use of the /maxpwage command.
- */domain:* The domain switch. Use of the /domain switch in conjunction with any of the other net accounts commands will make the command refer to the entire domain rather than just to the server on which it is executed. You have to have domain-administrative privileges and be logged into a Windows NT Advanced Server Domain to use this command. The command will be remote-executed on the primary domain controller and will then affect domainwide account policies, not merely single-server account policies. For example, *net accounts /minpwage:2 /domain* will set a domainwide account policy requiring a minimum password age of two days. NOTE: This parameter has an effect only if it's executed from a Windows NT computer that is a member of an Advanced Server domain *but* is not itself running Windows NT Advanced Server, since by default Windows NT Advanced Server computers perform their account operations through the domain controller. The /domain switch has no effect if it is executed on a Windows NT Advanced Server machine.
- */sync:* User account database synchronization. This switch, usable only on a Windows NT Advanced Server, forces an update on the user accounts database to synchronize database information across the domain. It may be used only by a domain administrator and then only on a Windows NT Advanced Server. It cannot be executed remotely.

Adding Computers to a Domain: *Net Computer* (Advanced Server Only)

This command can be used to add computers to a domain database and is the primary command that needs to be executed by domain administrators in order to add new computers to an advanced server domain. The syntax of the command is net computer \\name of computer to add followed by either a /add or /del switch. The /add switch adds the computer to the domain. The /del switch deletes it. This command can be executed only on a Windows NT Advanced Server. It cannot be executed remotely. Functionally the command determines which computers will be affected by domainwide updates. The same effect as this command can be accomplished using the Network Settings section of the Windows NT Control Panel. By selecting the change button adjacent to the domain name one then is presented with a selector with a member of a workgroup or domain and create computer accounted domain. By creating a computer account in the domain you are functionally performing the same thing as a *net computer/add.*

Viewing the System Configuration: *Net Config*

This command displays information related to the operation of the server and workstation services. The command has two variants:

```
net config server
```

displays the following information:

```
C:\users\default>net config server
Server Name                          \\JOHNR-NT486-66
Server Comment

Software version                     Windows NT 3.10
Server is active on                  Nbf_ODINSUP02 (00001b48d2aa)

Server hidden                        No
Max Logged On Users                  Unlimited
Max. open files per session          256

Idle session time (min)              15
The command completed successfully.
```

or:

```
net config workstation
```

which displays the following information:

```
C:\users\default>net config workstation
Computername                         \\JOHNR-NT486-66
Username                             jruleynt

Workstation active on                Nbf_ODINSUP02 (00001B48D2AA)
Software version                     Windows NT 3.10

Workstation domain                   MAGNET2
Logon domain                         MAGNET2

COM Open Timeout (sec)               3600
COM Send Count (byte)                16
COM Send Timeout (msec)              250
The command completed successfully.
```

This command may be useful, for example, in running a periodic automatic maintenance report to a central logging facility. See the example later in this section.

Controlling Services: *Net Start, Net Stop, Net Pause, and Net Continue*

All of these commands are used to control the various services that are built into Windows NT. These services include the alerter service, the computer browser service, the directory replicator service, the event log, the rpc locator, messaging, net logon, rpc subsystem, schedule subsystem, the server service, the uninterruptible power supply service, and the workstation service—in other words, the very same services that one controls from the Services applet in the Windows NT Control Panel.

The syntax of the commands is *net start*. By itself, the net start command will list all of the services that are started in the system. *net start service* will start the service in question. For example, *net start clipbook* starts the clipbook service. *net stop service* will stop a particular service. The service may then be restarted using the net start command. *net pause service* will temporarily suspend a service or resource. This command can be used only with the net logon schedule, server, workstation, or telenet services. The suspension amounts to putting the service on hold. That is, it will not accept new requests until this command is overridden by a *net resume*. And, of course, net resume undoes what was done with the net pause. Despite what is printed in the Windows NT System Guide, at least in the Beta version, net pause does not appear to have any effect when used in association with printers or shared directories.

Controlling User Groups: *Net Group, Net LocalGroup*

These commands allow you to add and remove user account groups from a Windows NT server or Windows NT domain. User groups are among the most basic fundamental features of the Windows NT administrative account system and are covered earlier in this chapter. (See the section on the Windows NT user manager.) The *net group* and *net local group* commands allow you to add or delete user groups from the accounts system. The net local group command affects the local Windows NT server on which it is executed. Net local group group-name/add adds a group to the account database. Net local group group-name/delete removes the group. The /domain switch causes this function to be executed domainwide (it must be executed by a domain administrator). The command is actually executed on the primary domain controller. The net group command may be executed only on a Windows NT Advanced Server and sets domainwide groups. Again, net group group-name/add adds the group and net group group-name/delete deletes an entire group.

Note that the /domain switch from the net local group command has no effect when it is executed on a Windows NT Advanced Server since Windows NT Advanced Servers by default carry out their operations on the primary domain controller. However, you should not make the mistake of thinking that a net local group and a net group command are the same when executed on a Windows NT Advanced Server. NT Advanced Servers maintain separate domain groups and local groups. Domain groups are user groups that are employed for domain administration and apply to all machines within the domain whereas local groups apply to individual machines whether they are Advanced Server machines or standard Windows NT machines. You can also add or delete individual users from groups and local groups using the net group and net local group commands. For example, the command

```
net group "Domain Admins" jruleynt /add
```

adds the account jruleynt to the group of Domain Admins for a Windows NT Advanced Server domain. The command

```
net local group administrators fred /delete
```

deletes the user account fred from the local group of administrators on a local Windows NT server. If the user name is not specified, the net group and net local group commands will list the groups or the members of a particular group. For example, the command

```
net local group
```

without other arguments will list the groups within the Windows NT account database:

```
C:\users\default>net localgroup

Aliases for \\JOHNR-NT486-66

----------------------------------------
*Administrators            *Backup Operators          *Guests
*Power Users               *Replicator                *Users
The command completed successfully.
```

Then typing

```
net local group administrators
```

will list the user accounts that are members of the administrator's group:

```
C:\users\default>net localgroup administrators
Aliasname     administrators
Comment       Members can fully administer the system

Members

----------------------------------------
Administrator             MAGNET2\Domain Admins
The command completed successfully.
```

Individual user accounts can be added, deleted, or controlled using the net user command covered later in this section.

NOTE: While the net group and net local group commands allow you to add or delete administrative groups both for individual servers and for Advanced Server domains, you cannot control the permissions, the user rights granted to groups, or (for that matter) individual users from the command line. User rights can be issued only from the Windows NT User Manager (from the user-rights item of the policies menu) and then only by a Windows NT administrator or domain administrator where domain accounts are concerned. The absence of any capability to set user-rights from the command line does present a limitation from the standpoint of writing batch files, for example, to create a mass migration of accounts. This is unfortunate, but it apparently was considered a security feature by the Windows NT designers. Therefore, you can create the accounts and you can create the groups in a batch file, but when it comes to setting the permissions you have to go to the User Manager and set them manually.

Controlling Who Gets Messages: *Net Name*

As described in Chapter 3, Windows NT provides a reasonably powerful system for the issuing of systemwide messages through the *net send* command. Normally net send can be used either with individual computer names or with individual account names, or through the /broadcast or /domain switches it can send messages that will be received by all computers on a segment or by all computers within a domain. It can sometimes be desirable, however, to send to a message *alias*, that is, a name of convenience that can be used to identify a particular user or a particular computer without using the actual computer name or the actual user name. This can be accomplished by using the net name command. The syntax of the net name command is

```
net name alias /add
```

to add the name or

```
net name alias /delete
```

to delete the name. If neither the /add or /delete switch is used, a /add switch is assumed—thus the command

```
net name boss
```

is functionally equivalent to

```
net name boss/add
```

This command must be issued at a particular workstation. It is most conveniently done as part of a login script and can be convenient if one uses long, descriptive computer names. Instead, one can issue a short name or a more friendly name. For instance, as opposed to sending a command to the *jruleynt* account, one could send a message to *John*—assuming that net name John has been executed on the same workstation as jruleynt is logged into. This may seem rather pointless but a certain degree of informality is often useful. An administrative message addressed to John will appear to be much more personal than an administrative message delivered to jruleynt, for instance. Note that message aliases must be unique. You cannot add net name John on *two* workstations in the same network.

Checking Performance: *Net Statistics*

This command provides a concise report of system information for either the server or workstation service. It can be used as part of an automatic maintenance reporting system (see the example later in this section). The command has two forms:

```
net config server
```

displays statistics for the server service, for example:

```
Server Statistics for \\JOHNR-NT486-66

Statistics since 07/30/93 03:20pm

Sessions accepted              1
Sessions timed-out             1
Sessions errored-out           1
Kilobytes sent                 262
```

```
Kilobytes received           722
Mean response time (msec)    25
System errors                0
Permission violations        0
Password violations          0
Files accessed               136
Comm devices accessed        0
Print jobs spooled           0
Times buffers exhausted
  Big buffers                0
  Request buffers            0
The command completed successfully.
```

while:

```
net config workstation
```

displays statistics for the workstation service, for example:

```
Workstation Statistics for \\JOHNR-NT486-66

Statistics since 07/30/93 03:20pm

  Bytes received                                 50734
  Server Message Blocks (SMBs) received          429
  Bytes transmitted                              58320
  Server Message Blocks (SMBs) transmitted       429
  Read operations                                0
  Write operations                               8
  Raw reads denied                               0
  Raw writes denied                              0
  Network errors                                 0
  Connections made                               13
  Reconnections made                             1
  Server disconnects                             9
  Sessions started                               17
  Hung sessions                                  0
  Failed sessions                                0
  Failed operations                              429
  Use count                                      20
  Failed use count                               0
The command completed successfully.
```

Note that any Windows NT system with file sharing enabled will have both server and workstation services. The server service is necessary in providing browsing functionality to a Windows NT system so even though the system is not in fact *used* as a server, do not assume that there is no server service running. The command net statistics by itself simply lists the services for which statistics may be requested, that is, server and workstation:

```
 C:\users\default>net statistics
Statistics are available for the following running services:

Server                   Workstation
The command completed successfully.
```

Controlling User Accounts: *Net User*

This command allows user accounts to be added or deleted on a Windows NT server or domain server. It also allows control of certain features of the account, including a text comment, a descriptive comment, country code, expiration date, and home directory, as described below. As with the net group and net local group commands you can add users and assign users to existing groups. However, you cannot control other than by group assignment; you cannot control the privileges assigned to a user account from the command line. This has to be done in the Windows NT User Manager. The syntax of the net user command is

```
net user user-name password (or asterisk)
```

and one or more switches. User-name is the name of the user account to add, delete, modify, or view. Password, if present, will assign or change the password for the user account. It must satisfy the minimum length set with the /minpwlen option in the net accounts command. The asterisk character, if used, will produce a prompt for a password rather than putting the password in manually. This can be used if one wishes to set up a batch file requiring new passwords to be entered, for example, and one wishes to avoid the inherent security breach that would be represented by having the clear text password present in the file.

The */domain* switch will cause the operations employed in the net user command to be carried out on the primary domain controller in a Windows NT Advanced Server domain. As with other commands where a domain switch is used, this has no effect if it's executed on a Windows NT Advanced Server system, since by default Windows NT Advanced Servers carry out all operations on the primary domain controller. On a regular Windows NT system, not an Advanced Server, net user commands issued without the /domain switch only affect the local machine. Obviously the /domain switch can be used only by a domain administrator account.

The */add* switch will add a user account to the database. The */delete* switch eliminates a user account from the database. A variety of options may be added following the add switch. These include /active: which takes the arguments yes or no. This will activate or deactivate the account. If the account is not active the user cannot access the server using the account; however, unlike the /delete switch this does not remove the account from the database. This can be useful if a user has intermittent access to a server.

You can use */active:no* to prevent the user from having access until some formal action is taken.

The */comment:* switch followed by a text message with a maximum length of 48 characters will provide a descriptive comment about the user account. You should enclose the comment text in quotation marks. For example:

```
net user jruley /add /comment:"John D Ruley's account"
```

The */country code:* switch, which takes a number as an argument, will use the operating system country code specified by that number to set the user's help and error messages. The default is country code:0, which uses whatever the default country code is for the Windows NT server in question. This can be useful in an international system where users may be logging in who will expect to see different languages. Using this login system, you can custom configure which language base is employed once the user logs in. Unfortunately this will affect *only* the help and error messages. It will not affect the primary Windows NT language set at the workstation. This has to be controlled manually.

/expires:, which takes a date or the keyword *never*, will determine when the account expires. For example:

```
net user jim/add/expires:12/25/93
```

will create a jim account expiring on Christmas Day. The keyword *never* will create an account which never expires.

/full name: followed by a string in quotes sets a user's full name. For example:

```
net user jim/add/full name:"James M. Ruley"
```

sets my brother's full name in association with the jim account.

/home dir: followed by a pathname will set the path for a user's home directory. Note that the path must exist, so when a batch file creates and sets home directories for one or more users it will be necessary to create the directories *first* before setting the home directories. The home directory is the directory which will be set as the default directory during a remote login.

/home dir req: followed by a yes or no specifies whether a home directory is required. If so this should be used in association with a /home dir switch to set the directory.

/password chg: followed by a yes or a no specifies whether the user can change their own password. Saying /password chg:no will require administrative change in a password and can be used in systems where for whatever reason users are not trusted to set their own password.

/password req: followed by a yes or a no specifies whether a user account *must* have a password.

/profile path: followed by a path sets a path for the user's logon profile. This is functionally equivalent to the login profile information that is set using the User Manager.

/script path: followed by a pathname sets the location of a user's logon script. Again, it is functionally the same as that set in the User Manager.

/times: followed by either a time or the keyword *all* sets the hours during which the user is permitted to log on. The times are formatted as day-day,day-day,time-time,time-time where time is limited to one-hour increments. The days may be spelled out or abbreviated. Hours can be twelve- or twenty-four-hour notation. For example:

```
net user jim/times:monday-friday,8 a.m.-5 p.m.
```

will set the jim account with the permission to log in on weekdays during normal working hours. Attempts to log in at other times or on other days will fail.

/user comment: followed by a text string lets the administrator add or change the user comment for the account, a text message that is displayed when the user logs in. (This command is a hold-over from LAN Manager and has no effect in Windows NT.)

The */workstations:* command followed by computer names lists which workstation the user is permitted to log in on. If this string is absent then the user is assumed to be able to log in from any workstation.

You should realize by this time that the net user command provides a considerable, not to say enormous, degree of administrative control. You can determine the time of day a user can log in, you can determine which days the user can log in, you can force the location of a home directory, force the execution of a login script, present information to the user on login, and determine which machines he or she is permitted to log in from. As described in Chapter 1, Windows NT is a fully secure operating system. Your opportunity to effectively use this security is largely controlled by net accounts, net user, and their equivalents in the Windows NT User Manager.

Incidentally, *net user* typed by itself simply provides a list of the user names defined for a particular system:

```
User accounts for \\JOHNR-NT486-66

-------------------------------------------------------------

Administrator            Guest    Jim      Fred     Jruley          Jruleynt
The command completed successfully.
```

It's interesting to consider what it would take to write an application would first issue a net user command, then parse the results identifying each user and carrying out some operation on each user in sequence. But we digress...

Viewing, Controlling and Unlocking Shared Files: *net file*

When shared files are open on a Windows NT system it is possible to view a list of which files are in use, to see specifics on the use of the file (that is, who has the file open, whether it is locked and what permissions are in use), and if necessary, eliminate sharing on the file using the net file command. The syntax

```
net file
```

prints a list of which shared file names are in use, whether they are locked, who has them and what the file ID is:

```
C:\users\default>net file

ID         Path                                     Username            # Locks

-------------------------------------------------------------

43         d:\netnt\uuencode                        administrator         0
The command completed successfully.
```

Net file followed by an ID number prints a more specific display for the particular file:

```
C:\users\default>net file 43
File ID          43
Username         administrator
Locks            0
Path             d:\netnt\uuencode
Permissions      XA
The command completed successfully.
```

Net file ID number/close will close the file, terminating the share. This can be useful in two situations. Obviously one is if there is unauthorized use of a file, although in that situation it would probably make the most sense to kick the user off the system completely, rather than simply disconnecting the file. It can also happen that certain applications, particularly 16-bit applications, may not do a proper job of cleaning up after themselves. A file may be opened at the beginning of an application session and not closed when the application shuts down. If this happens the user will then attempt to reconnect to the file but not be permitted to do so. He or she will receive a message indicating a sharing violation or indicating that the file is otherwise in use. Under this circumstance it can be useful to issue a net file, view the list of files, identify the file in question, then issue a

```
net file IDnumber /close
```

to close the file, disable sharing, and permit the user to use the file again. Unfortunately, there is no such thing as *net close all,* which could be useful in some emergency situations. If one does wish to eliminate a user completely from a system (force them off) one can use the *net session* command, which is described next.

Controlling Login Sessions: *Net Session*

The net session command lists or disconnects login sessions connected to the server. Issued by itself the net session command presents a list of the computers that are logged into the server:

```
C:\users\default>net session

Computer                User name            Client Type       Opens Idle time

----------------------------------------------------
\\MIPS-LAB-SERVER       administrator        NT                1     00:30:28
The command completed successfully.
```

Issuing the command

```
net session \\computer name
```

for a particular computer lists statistical information about the session including what users are using the session and what shares are open:

```
C:\users\default>net session \\mips-lab-server
Username          administrator
Computer          MIPS-LAB-SERVER
Guest logon       No
Client type       NT
Sess time         23:43:28
Idle time         00:31:24

Sharename       Type      # Opens

----------------------------------------
disk-d          Disk      1
The command completed successfully.
```

The */delete* parameter will force the session to log off and will disconnect the session. For example, net session \\mips-lab-server /delete will disconnect mips-lab-server from the current session and terminate all connections. This should be used only as a measure of last resort and is functionally equivalent to employing the disconnect button from the users session's dialog in the Server portion of the Control Panel.

Time Synchronization: *Net Time*

One problem that often occurs in networking is assuring that all workstations within a domain have their system clocks synchronized. This can, for example, cause substantial problems in carrying out a distributed backup in the event that some random event such as a change to daylight saving time or hard reset on a computer has inadvertently changed the system clock. A particular machine may then carry out a backup at an unwarranted time. You can use the net time command to provide synchronization between computers and the network. The command

```
net time
```

with no arguments will print the time determined by the currently defined time server in the network, if any, while

```
net time \\computer name
```

will print the time on the selected computer. The command

```
net time /domain
```

will print the time on the current primary domain server.

```
net time /domain: domain name
```

will print that time for any specified domain server that is on the network. Any variation on this can be followed by the keyword */set,* which will set the time at the machine on which the net time command is executed to match the time on the machine from which the time was requested. Thus, for example:

```
net time /domain /set
```

will synchronize the workstation by setting the local workstation time to be the same as the time of the domain controller. This command should normally be executed as part of a login script.

Scheduling Commands for Execution: *At*

Up to now we have been concerned with the *net* series of commands that is specific to Windows NT networking. In order to understand how commands can be executed at a specified time, we now need to understand the *at* command which is a unique feature of the Windows NT Batch command set. The *at* command allows you to schedule commands for execution at a particular time. It also allows you to schedule these commands for execution on remote computers. It is a very powerful command for use by system administrators. The command has the following syntax:

```
at\\computer-name time "command-string"
```

where: \\computer-name refers to the computer at which the command is to be executed. If this is omitted then the command is assumed to refer to the local computer. Time refers to the time for execution and may be used in conjunction with the flags */every:,* which may be followed by a date of the week or month, or */next:,* which will run the command the next occurrence of the day. So, for example, the command /every:Monday will cause the command to be executed at the set time every Monday. The command /next Monday will cause the command to be executed on the next Monday.

The command-string in quotes is a string that will be executed on the machine in question. For example, the command:

```
at\\mips-lab-server 10:28a.m. "net send jruleynt the time is 10:28"
```

at 10:28 a.m. executes a net send command sending jruleynt the message "the time is 10:28." This command requires the schedule service to be started (net start schedule) on the machine on which it is to be executed. Just typing *at* on a machine will list any at jobs which are currently scheduled and their ID numbers. The */delete* keyword will delete a particular ID number (or if no ID number is set will delete all jobs on the specified computer). For example:

```
at \\mips-lab-server
```

will print

```
C:\users\default>at
Status ID   Day                     Time          Command Line
---------   --------                -------       -------------------------
        0   Tomorrow                10:30AM       net send ADMIN It's 10:30!
```

The command

```
at\\mips-lab-server 0 /delete
```

will delete this job. The command

```
at\\mips-lab-server /delete
```

without any ID number will delete all jobs. The command string can include any valid Windows NT command—including start commands to cause a separate process to start or even batch commands. Using the at command it is possible to schedule remote execution of processes such as backups, administrative maintenance reports, or whatever and to have them occur at a specified time on a specified date repetitively. This is in addition to Windows NT's basic capability to support login scripts.

Using UNC Names Directly

One point that greatly simplifies script development is that Windows NT's command-line interface accepts direct Universal Naming Convention (UNC) naming—making it unnecessary to constantly reassign network resources to local drive letters. It is completely valid, for instance, to type

```
copy \\mips-lab-server\cimspec\*.* \\johnr-nt486-66\fallback
```

Not only is this cleaner and neater than the alternative:

```
net use x: \\mips-lab-server\cimspec
net use y: \\johnr-nt486-66\fallback
copy x:\*.* y:
net use x: /DELETE
net use y: /DELETE
```

it also avoids situations in which the script fails because X: or Y: has already been used as a network drive letter (remember that Windows NT users can and will change drive assignments as and when they please).

It's interesting to think about how Microsoft might develop this technology in the future—there isn't any inherent reason, for example, why the *dir* command in Windows NT couldn't be modified to prove *net view* functionality. This might eventually lead to a situation where servers on domains appear in the directory list pretty much as disk drives and directories do now—but for the moment, that's only a tantalizing dream.

Example Scripts:

Example 1 An automatic server maintenance report sent to the administrator's workstation

```
report.cmd:
REM This is a 3 time-per-week maintenance report
REM
REM First, get to the \temp directory:
c:
cd \temp
REM
REM delete any old stuff:
REM
del a b c d
REM
REM run NET CONFIG and NET STATISTICS, piping output to files:
REM
net config server >a
net statistics server >b
net config workstation >c
net statistics workstation >d
REM
REM copy the results to the administrator's system:
REM
copy a+b+c+d R:\reports\system1\reptnew.txt
REM
REM It is the administrator's responsibility to see that REPTNEW.TXT is copied
or otherwise
```

```
REM  taken care of before the next night, so that it won't be overwritten—he
can in fact run another
REM scheduled process to do this.
```

To cause this script to be executed nightly, it is only necessary that the administrator (1) place it in the path on each server, and (2) issue the following *at* command for each server:

```
at  \\server_name 3:00am /each:monday,wednesday,friday "report.cmd"
```

(Obviously, the file should be edited slightly for each system, with the copy placing the file in reports\system2 for the second system, etc. It would be awfully nice to have this report *mailed* to the administrator, rather than copied. This is technically feasible if programmer support is available—see the section on MAPI APIs in Appendix 1.)

Example 2 A workstation login script:

```
login.cmd
REM
REM Set an informal message alias:
REM
net name Jimmy
REM
REM Synchronize time with the domain server
REM
net time /DOMAIN /SET
REM
REM Start the Schedule service (so remote at... commands will work)
REM
net start schedule
REM
REM Announce the log-in to the domain
REM
net send /DOMAIN Jimmy is logged in
```

Example 3 Porting NetWare accounts to Windows NT:
Here we can't give a simple script, but we can show *how* to write one:

```
REM Repeat this For each NetWare group:
  Net Localgroup netware_groupname /ADD
REM Repeat this For each NetWare user:
  Net User netware_username netware_password(or *) /ADD
  Net Localgroup netware_groupname netware_username /ADD
```

Once this is complete, it is only necessary to set access rights for the groups in question using the Windows NT user manager.[3] Given a list of the group names, user names, and passwords, the entire operation can be automated (except for the access rights).

[3] There's a tool in the Windows NT resource kit that allows you to set access rights from the command line. See "Late-breaking Developments" in the "Foreword" for more information.

Conclusion

In this chapter, you've learned what the responsibilities of the network administrator are, how to create user accounts and account groups, how to assign user access rights, how to monitor performance and log events, and how to write command scripts. You should be ready to get your users online, and we will look at how users can exploit the networking features of Windows NT in Chapter 4.

For More Information

Microsoft Staff (1993), *Windows NT Advanced Server Concepts and Planning Guide (Beta, March 1993).* Redmond, WA: Microsoft Corp. Excellent overall coverage of Windows NT concepts from the administrator's point of view.

Microsoft Staff (1993), *Windows NT System Guide (Beta, March 1993).* Redmond, WA: Microsoft Corp. Includes basic information on administrative tools, including User Manager, Performance Monitor, etc. Note that the similar *Windows NT Advanced Server System Guide* adds information for the domain-management tools, including User Manager for Domains, Server Manager, etc.

Microsoft Staff (1993), *Windows NT Resource Kit, Volumes 1-3.* Redmond, WA: Microsoft Press. Volume 3—*Optimizing Windows NT*—should be especially helpful.

Farris, Jeffrey L. (1988), *Saber LAN Setup Guide—A Guide to Network Planning.* Dallas, TX: Saber Software Corp., ISBN: 1-878092-69-3. While oriented toward a particular vendor's LAN Administration products, this book gives a good overall introduction to the concepts an administrator must deal with.

Using Windows NT Networking Features

After reading this chapter, you should understand the basic networking features that are included with Windows NT. You will understand how to share resources (including directories and printers) with other network users, how to use shared resources, and how to create and maintain user accounts. You will also be introduced to the utility programs that are bundled with Windows NT, including File Manager, Mail, Chat, Schedule+, Print Manager, ClipBook, and the NET Command Interface. You should feel comfortable performing basic network operations like file/device sharing, using mail, and scheduling a group meeting.

File Management

Like Windows 3.1, Windows NT contains a File Manager application that lets you manage files on floppies or on your hard drive. The File Manager application looks more like that in Windows for Workgroups: it contains a toolbar for fast access to common tasks.

Besides basic file management, NT's File Manager is responsible for setting file permissions for NTFS drives and setting the audit parameters for such files. It is also used to share directories across the network.

To start File Manager, double-click on the File Manager icon in the Main program group window. Alternatively, select File/Run from the main Program Manager menu and type WINFILE.EXE in the Command Line box, then click on OK.

The File Manager Window

The main File Manager window, shown in Figure 4.1, contains a directory panel that displays in hierarchical order the directories on the selected drive, as well as the files and subdirectories in the selected directory. If both windows are not displayed, select View/Split.

File Manager's main screen can contain several windows, each displaying a separate directory or drive. To add a window for a drive and directory, select Window from the main menu, then select New Window from the pulldown menu. Alternatively, click on the New Window button on the toolbar. To close the active directory window, double-click on the Control menu box (the minus sign in the upper-left corner).

To work with files on another drive, click on the drive icon you want. Then click on the subdirectory name. If the subdirectory icon contains a plus sign (+) inside it, you can double-click on the subdirectory and expand the tree to show all subdirectories. The icon changes to

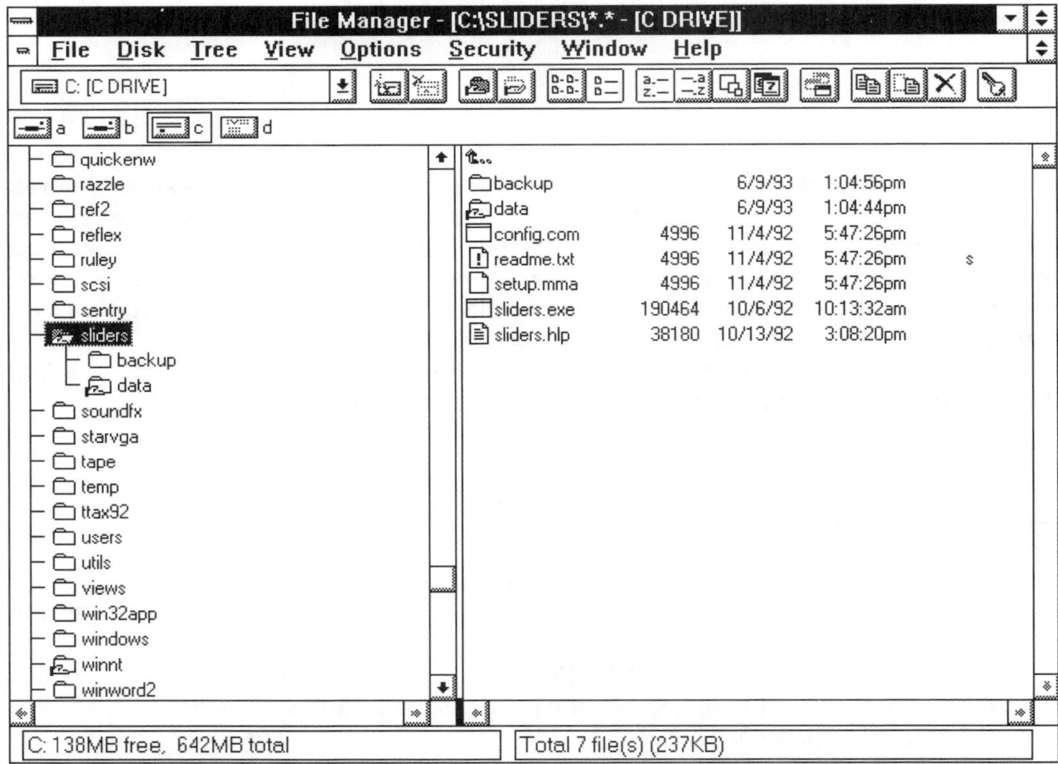

Figure 4.1 File Manager.

Windows NT file operations can be carried out using the familiar Windows 3.1-style File Manager interface. This gives users a simple, graphically illustrated, and intuitive way to manipulate files, eliminating any need to resort to the command line.

an open folder and contains a minus (-) sign inside. Double-clicking on an expanded directory listing collapses the hierarchy.

The icons that precede filenames provide information about the type of file listed:

- A folder icon indicates a directory.
- A folder held by a hand indicates the directory is shared.
- A rectangle with a small band at the top indicates a program, batch, or Program Information File (PIF) file.
- A page with lines on it indicates a document file associated with an application, such as a spreadsheet or word processing file.
- A page with an exclamation mark inside indicates a system or hidden file.
- A page that is blank is a file that does not fit into any of the above categories.

The icons are illustrated in Figure 4.1.

Sharing a Directory

Sharing a directory makes the files in the directory available to other users on your network. You must have sufficient rights to share a directory. This generally means you must be a user with Administrator or Power User rights in order to share network files. You can also share directories on your local hard disk. To share a directory on a network:

1. Select the directory you want to share. You can select the directory by clicking on it in either the directory panel or the filename panel. Select Disk/Share As or click on the Share Directory button if it is on the toolbar. File Manager displays the Share Directory dialog box shown in Figure 4.2.
2. Enter the name you want other users to see in the Share Name box. By default, File Manager displays the name of the directory. Enter the full pathname in the Path box. By default, File Manager fills this box with the full pathname you have selected. Optionally, type a comment in the Comment box. Users will see this comment when they attempt to connect to the directory.
3. Set the maximum number of users who can share this directory at any one time. Enter this number in the User Limit box or click on the up and down arrow buttons until the correct user limit is reached. If you do not want to restrict the number of users, select the Unlimited button. Setting the maximum number of users ensures that performance will not be degraded for those using the directory.
4. Click on Permissions if you want to specify permissions for the directory.
5. Click on OK.

Working with Shared Files

While a directory or file is shared, you can view which users are currently using the file(s). While anyone can see the total number of opens and locks on a file, only an Administrator or Power User can stop sharing a file.

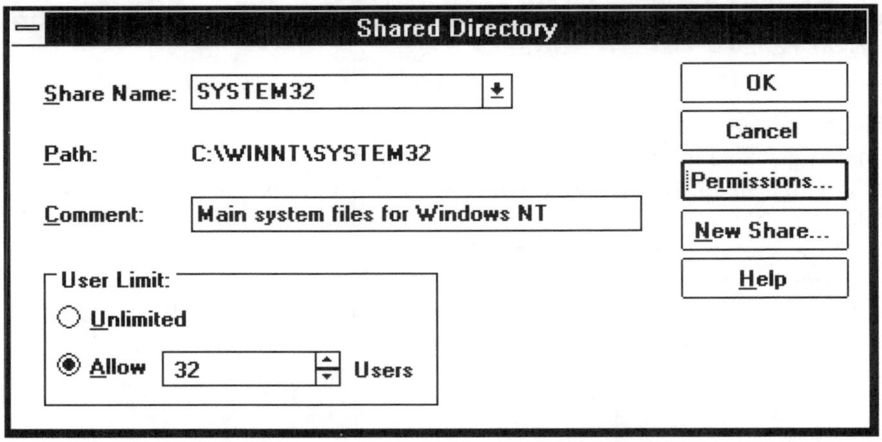

Figure 4.2 Share dialog.

Sharing directories and files is achieved by selecting the file/directory and clicking a single toolbar button. This dialog then appears, allowing definition of the Share Name, assignment of a comment, and control of who is permitted to access the share.

To view the file statistics, select the file, then select File/Properties. Click the Open By button. The filename, total number of opens and locks, and list of users using the file is displayed.

If you have proper security rights, you can stop the sharing of the file. Select the user(s) you want to remove from using the file and select Close Selected. To close the shared file for all users, click on Close All. Click on OK to return to the File Manager.

Stop Sharing a Directory

Before you stop sharing a directory, be sure that all users currently using the directory are notified and asked to stop using the directory. Otherwise, if you stop sharing a directory that is in use, those users connected to it could lose data.

To stop sharing a directory, you must be an Administrator or Power User. Select the directory you want to stop sharing. Select Disk/Stop Sharing, or click on the Stop Sharing button in the toolbar if it is present. File Manager displays the Stop Sharing dialog box. The directory you selected is already selected. Click on OK.

Connecting to a Network Drive

File Manager can connect to other drives on the network. Once connected, you can specify whether you want Windows NT to reconnect you to the drive(s) in all future sessions. To connect to a network drive:

1. Select Disk/Connect Network Drive. You may also begin by clicking on the Connect Network Drive button in the toolbar, if it is present.
2. The Connect Network Drive dialog box appears, which is shown in Figure 4.3. The Drive box contains the next available letter for your computer. To change this value, click on the down-pointing arrow key or press Alt+Down Arrow and select the drive letter you prefer.
3. If you have connected to this drive before, the path may be listed in the Path pull-down list. The Path list shows the previous ten paths you have selected. If the path you want to connect to is displayed, select it and proceed to step 5.
4. There are two options for selecting the path.

   a. If you have not connected to this drive before, or your drive is not listed in the Path list box, enter the pathname directly. Be sure to enter the network path of

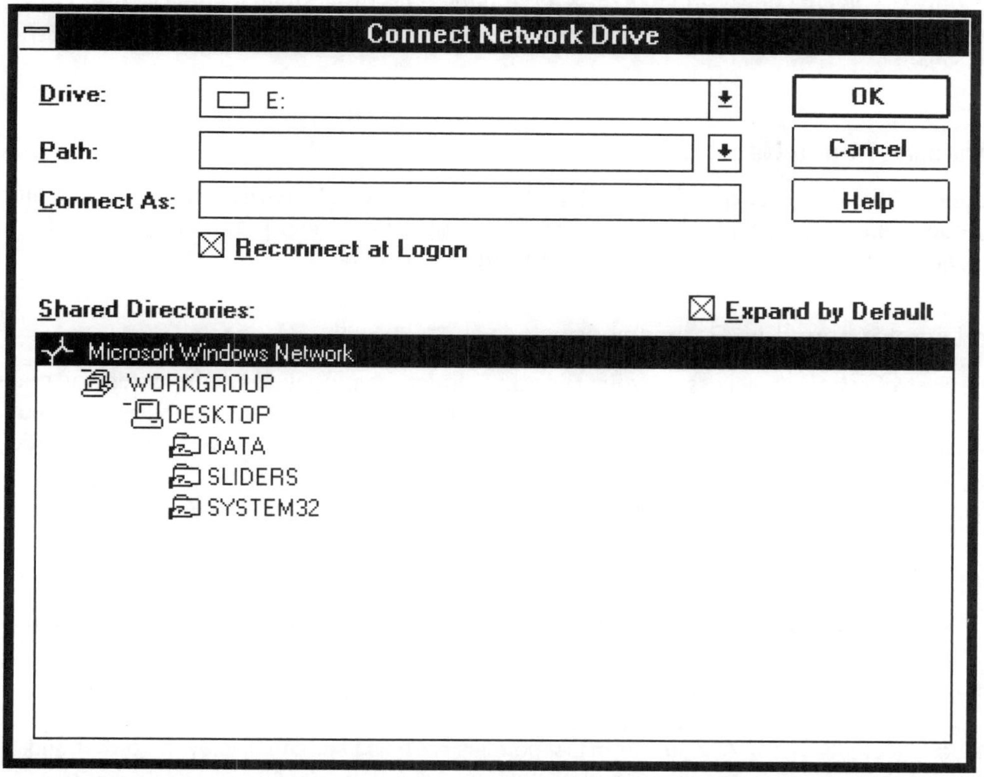

Figure 4.3 Connect net drive.

Connecting to shared directories on network servers is achieved by selecting the server and share in this browse dialog. The user can also determine what local drive letter is assigned.

the drive followed by the directory name. Network pathnames include a computer name and the name of the shared directory, such as \\MAINPC\BUDGETS.

b. Alternatively, select the shared directory from the Shared Directories box. The networks, domains, servers, user names, and shared directories are listed in a hierarchical tree structure similar to that used in the directory panel of File Manager. When you make your selection, File Manager displays the shared directories of your selection in the box at the bottom of the dialog box. Select the shared directory. File Manager displays the path in the Path box.

5. If you want to reconnect to this directory automatically when you begin Windows NT, be sure to check the Reconnect at Logon box. Caution: if the directory is on a computer that is not the server and is not certain to be running when you start Windows NT again, you will get a warning message asking if you want to proceed with connections. Therefore, we recommend that you check the Reconnect at Logon box only if you are connecting to a directory on the server for which there is a strong likelihood of availability when you log in.
6. Select OK.

Disconnecting from a Network Drive

To disconnect from a network drive, select Disk/Disconnect Network Drive. Select the drive(s) you want to disconnect from. To select more than one drive, press and hold the Ctrl key and click on each drive. Click on OK to perform the disconnect.

Setting Directory and File Permissions

You can control who has access to your files and directories, as well as the extent of that access, using what Windows NT calls *permissions*. You can limit access on any *directory*, but you can restrict access to *files* only on disks that use the Windows NT New Technology File System (NTFS).

Windows NT's set of standard permissions can be set for files and directories.

For Directories:

Standard Permission	*Access Allowed*
No Access	None.
List	Display a directory's files and a directory's attributes; user can move to any subdirectory within the directory.
Read	All rights from List permission, plus user can display the owner and permissions of a directory; this permission also allows the same Read permissions as for file permissions for all files in the directory (see below).
Add and Read	All rights from Read permissions, plus user can create subdirectories, add files to directory, and change attributes of a directory.

Standard Permission	*Access Allowed*
Change	All rights from Add and Read, plus user can delete the directory or any subdirectories below it. This permission also allows the same Change permissions as for file permissions for all files in directory.
Full Access	All rights from Add and Read and Change permissions. In addition, users can change permissions for a directory, and delete subdirectories. User can also take ownership of the directory. Full Access also allows the same Full Access permissions as for file permissions.

For Files:

Standard Permission	*Access Allowed*
No Access	None.
Read	Display the file's data; view the file's attributes.
Change	In addition to Read activities, user can launch program files, change the file's attributes, and display the file's owner and the permissions assigned to the file.
Full Access	In addition to the Read and Change activities, users can change or append data to the file.

To set permissions on a *directory*:

1. Select the directory from the directory panel. Select Security/Permissions or select the Permissions button from the toolbar (the button with the key). The Permissions dialog box shown in Figure 4.4 appears.
2. Note that the changes you make to a directory affect the directory and its files, but do not apply to subdirectories unless you check the Replace Permissions on Subdirectories check box.
3. You can change permissions, add new user permissions, or delete existing permissions.

   a. To change a permission, select the name of the user group or the individual user you want to change. Select the permission type from the Type of Access pull-down list. Then click on OK.
   b. To add a user permission, click on Add. Select the name(s) of the users or user groups you want to add and click on Add. The name(s) are added to the Add Names box. When all users have been added, click on OK.
   c. To delete a user permission, select the user, then click on Remove.

4. Click on OK to return to the File Manager window.

Setting file permissions is similar to setting directory permissions. By default, the File Permissions dialog box shows the permissions that are inherited from the directory in which it is contained. Managing file permissions is almost identical to managing directory permissions. Instead of selecting a directory, select one or more files from the file panel of the File Manager. Select Security/Permissions or select the Permissions button from the toolbar (the button

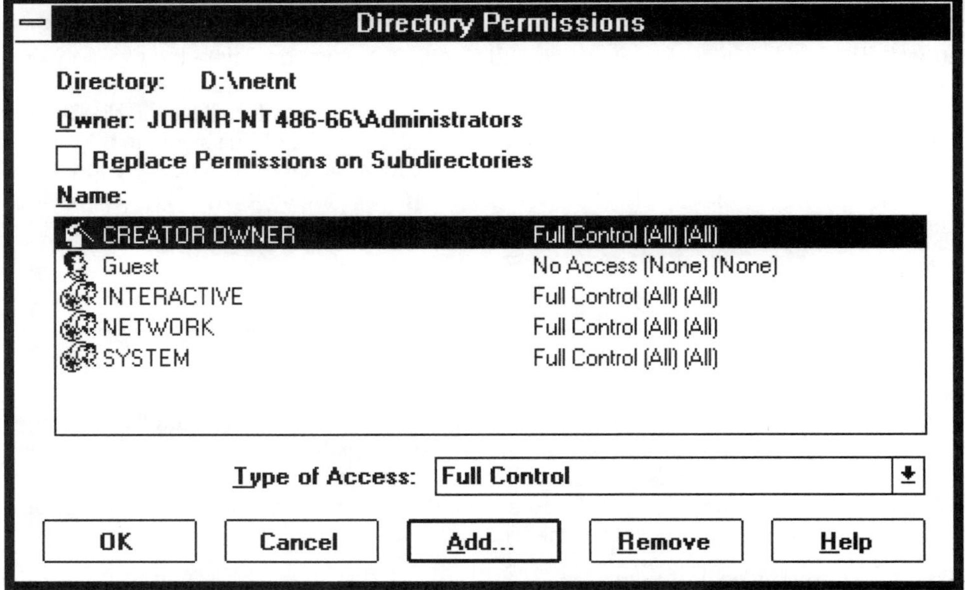

Figure 4.4 Permissions.

On New Technology File System (NTFS) partitions, total control over user access is provided for both local and network users. The security information is built directly into the directory structure, and will follow a drive if it is physically moved to another system.

with the key). Select the user(s) you want to remove or change, or click on Add to grant user(s) permission to the selected file(s).

Special Access Permissions

If the standard permissions are not sufficient to limit access to files or directories, you can use a set of special access permissions. Note that if you change the special access of a *directory* you do not automatically grant the same access to the files it contains.

The special access permissions are:

D—Delete
O—Take Ownership
P—Change Permissions
R—Read
W—Write
X—Execute

To set a *special access* permission:

1. Select the directory from the directory window to set permissions on a directory. Select the file(s) from the filename panel to set permissions on individual files.
2. Select Security/Permissions or click on the Permissions button in the toolbar (the button with the key on it).
3. Select the user or user group you want to grant special access. Then select the appropriate Special Access button. For example, to set permissions on a directory, click on Special Directory Access; for files click on Special File Access.
4. Select the check boxes for the access(es) you want to grant. Then click on OK.
5. Click on OK to return to File Manager.

Permissions on a Shared Directory

Permissions on shared directories are slightly different. You must be an Administrator or Power User to manage permissions on shared directories. Unlike NTFS volume permissions, you may set shared access permissions on *any* type of shared directory.

Permissions on a shared NTFS directory are cumulative with those set for the NTFS volume. If the permission is less extensive on the directory, the directory's permission takes precedence.

For shared directories, the standard permissions are:

Standard Permission	*Access Allowed*
No Access	Nothing.
Read	Display the files (including data) and any subdirectories, all attributes, launch programs, and move to any subdirectory of the selected directory.
Change	In addition to Read activities, create files and subdirectories, change or append data to files in the directory, change file attributes, and delete files and subdirectories.
Full Access	Same as Change.

To *add* or *change* the security permissions on a shared directory:

1. Select the shared directory from the directory panel. From the main menu select Disk/Share As, or select the Share Directory button from the toolbar.
2. Click on Permissions.
3. Select the user or name to be changed. Then select the permission from the Type of Access dialog box. When a check box contains an X, the permission is granted. When the check box is empty, the permission is not granted.
4. Click on OK.

To *remove* permissions already granted for a shared directory:

1. Select the shared directory from the directory panel.

2. Select Permissions from the Security menu, or click the Permissions button on the toolbar.
3. Select the name of the user or user group that will have the permissions removed, then click on the Remove button.
4. File Manager asks to confirm your request. Select Yes. Then click on OK to return to File Manager.

Auditing Files

Auditing provides you a view of which users or user groups are using your files or directories. The volume containing the file(s) must be an NT File System volume (NTFS volume). To audit a file or directory:

1. Turn on auditing in User Manager (Policies/Audit).
2. Select the file in the filename panel, or select the directory in either the filename or directory panel. Then select Security/Auditing. The dialog box shown in Figure 4.5 appears.
3. Check the Replace Auditing on Existing Files/Subdirectories box if you want to audit existing files. Leave the box empty (unchecked) if you want to audit only new files and subdirectories.
4. Select the user or user group you want to view.
5. Choose the events you want to audit. A check in the corresponding box means that File Manager will audit the event; an empty box means that File Manager will not audit the event.
6. Click on OK.

You can easily modify the user list. For example, to add a user to the audit list, choose Security/Auditing, click on Add, and select the user or user group you want to add. To remove a user from the audit list, select Security/Auditing, select the user and click on Remove.

Ownership of Files

When you create a file or directory, you are the designated owner of it.[1] This allows you to grant permissions. You can grant permission to another user so that he or she can act as an owner and, in turn, set permissions. When you grant another permission to take ownership of a file or directory, and that user takes ownership, you give up that ownership. If you are using an NTFS file system, you must have adequate permission to take ownership.

To take ownership of one or more files, select the file(s) from the filename panel. To take ownership of one or more directories, use the directory or filename panel. From the main menu choose Security/Take Ownership. Click on the Take Ownership button. If multiple files

[1]Unless you are an administrator—then the "administrators" *group* owns it.

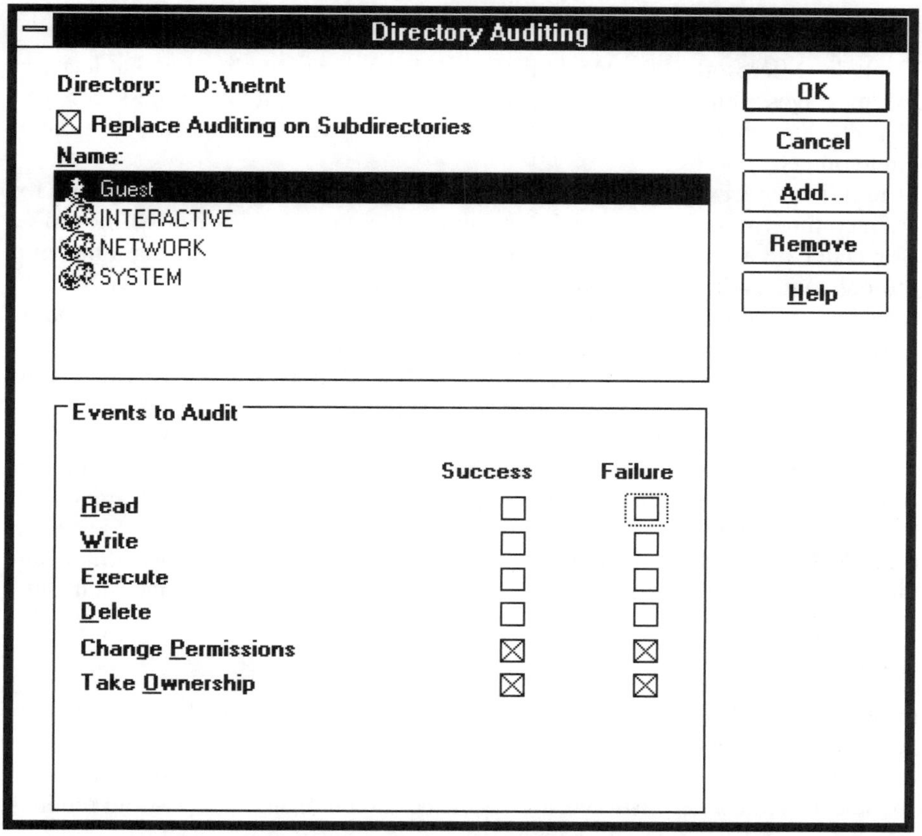

Figure 4.5 Security/Auditing.

If required, auditing may be enabled, allowing direct tracking of the use (or misuse) of system resources. Audit information is stored in the security log and may be viewed using the Event Viewer application. Auditing is also affected by the Audit Policy set using the User Manager application—for example, auditing of file events will happen only if the Administrator has auditing turned on for a given file or directory, *and* has audit policy selected for file events.

or directories were selected, File Manager asks if you want to take ownership of all selected items. Select Yes.

Leaving File Manager

To exit File Manager, select File/Exit from the Main Menu, or double-click on the Control Menu button in the upper-left corner of the File Manager window.

Microsoft Mail

Windows NT includes Microsoft Mail (MS-Mail), an electronic mail application that lets you send and receive messages with other users on your network. In addition to text messages, you can send files by attaching them to messages. You can save messages in a folder, delete them, or forward them to others.

MS-Mail uses *Postoffices*, collections of users and a storage location on hard disk for their messages. Incoming messages appear in an inbox, though messages can be moved to other folders for better organization. Each incoming message includes the sender's name, a subject, and the date and time the message was received. An icon to the left of each inbox message provides information about the message: an exclamation point indicates a high-priority message; a paper clip indicates there is an attachment to the message.

MS-Mail is also used by other applications within NT, such as Schedule+, which uses MS-Mail messages for scheduling and notification of meetings.

Start MS-Mail by selecting the MS-Mail icon from the Main program group.

Exiting the MS-Mail application can be done in one of two ways. Since MS-Mail may be in use by other applications, such as Schedule+, you may log out of the current session but keep the MS-Mail application running (so you can send meeting requests in Schedule+ via MS-Mail), or exit MS-Mail and terminate the application completely. To keep MS-Mail running, select File/Exit. To quit MS-Mail and stop the application, select File/Exit and Sign Out.

Setting Up a Postoffice[2]

When you create a new Postoffice, you are added as the administrator for the account. This allows you to add or delete users as well as change their passwords.

To create a new Postoffice and an administrator account, select MS-Mail from the Main program group. Select Create a new Workgroup Postoffice and click on OK. MS-Mail reminds you that by creating a Postoffice you will be responsible for managing it. Select Yes to create the Postoffice.

Select the directory for storing messages and user files for the Postoffice. This can be on a local hard disk, but is more usually set up on a network server. To select a network server, choose the Network button and network server and shared directory name, then click on OK. (You can create a Postoffice on a NetWare server if you grant full trustee rights to the NetWare directory in which the Postoffice is being created.) Then click on OK.

Mail will now ask you for the administration details, using the dialog box shown in Figure 4.6. An explanation of the administration data is shown in Table 4.1. When they have been entered, click on OK. Be sure to share the directory if it is not already shared.

Once you've added a Postoffice, the next step is to add users. Users can actually add themselves to a Postoffice, but you can save them the trouble by adding them during your administrative work. To add a user to a Postoffice, select Mail/Postoffice Manager. Choose

---

[2]Note: These instructions will create a local *workgroup* Postoffice. For information on creating a *full* MS-Mail Postoffice (and connecting it to other mail systems), see Chapter 7.

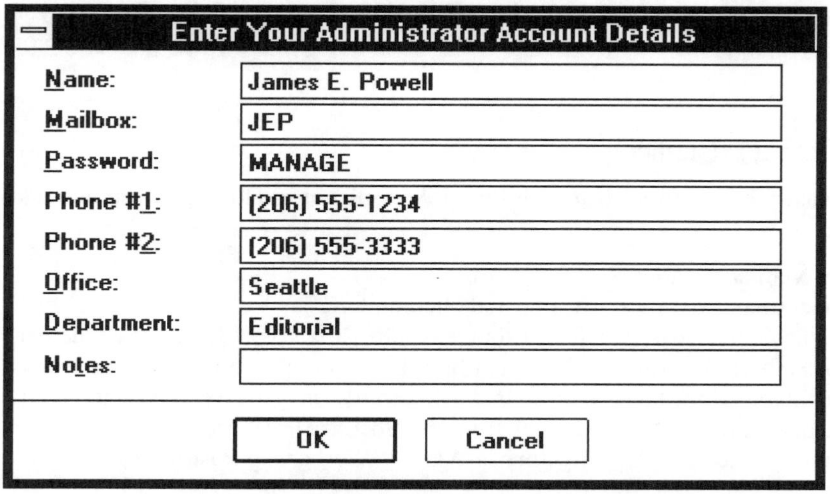

Figure 4.6 Mail Admin.

A postoffice manager can create an address list and manage users from this dialog.

Add User and enter the new user's information. (See Table 4.1 for details.) Finally, click on Close.

Table 4.1 User Information Needed by Mail

Name	Enter your full name (typically in first name-last name order).
Mailbox	A unique abbreviation for your mailbox, such as the first letter of your first name and your complete last name. The Mailbox name must be no more than 10 characters long, and will be used to log onto the mail system when you want to perform administrative duties. The name is *not* case sensitive. Enter letters or numbers only.
Password	To password-protect access to your mailbox, enter a password of no more than 8 characters, using letters and numbers only.
Optional Information:	
Phone #1	Your telephone number, up to 32 characters long.
Phone #2	An alternative telephone number, such as a cellular phone, fax, or voice mail number, up to 32 characters long.
Office	A description of your office location; 32 characters maximum.
Department	A description of your department; 32 characters maximum.
Notes	Any text you like, to a maximum of 128 characters.

To remove users from a Postoffice, select Mail/Postoffice Manager. Select the user you want to delete and click on Remove User. Select Yes to confirm your request, then click on Close.

Adding a Computer to a Postoffice

As a user, you are usually added to a Postoffice by an Administrator. However, you can add your own account this way.

1. Start the MS-Mail application.
2. Select Connect to an existing Postoffice and click on OK.
3. MS-Mail displays the Network Disk Resources dialog box. Type the name of the network path directly in the Network Path text box. If you do not know the name, select the computer name from the Show Shared Directories on list box, then choose the shared directory name on that computer from the Shared Directories on list box. The standard name for the MS-Mail directory is WGPO (Workgroup Postoffice).
4. Click on OK.
5. The next dialog box asks if you have an account. If you do, select Yes and enter your password. If not, enter your account information in the Enter Your Account Details dialog box. Enter the details as shown in Table 4.1.

Creating an Address List

Once a Postoffice has been established, you'll want to get started creating messages. MS-Mail provides an address book for you to store the most frequently used addresses. To maintain an address book, select Mail/Address Book.

To select an address book, select the Directory button (the first button in the Address Book dialog box shown in Figure 4.7). To select your personal address book, select the Personal Address Book button (the second button in the Address Book dialog box) or press Ctrl+P.

To modify an existing name, click on Details. To find a name, click on the magnifying glass button or press Ctrl+F.

To add a new address to your personal address book click on the last icon in the Address dialog box or press Ctrl+N. Enter the Name, E-Mail address, E-Mail type, and optionally a comment, then select the Personal Address Book icon. MS-Mail sets up a heading for this user. Select Cancel to return to the Address Book dialog box.

To remove a name from an address book, select the name, then click on Remove.

Creating and Sending a Message

To create and send a message to one or more users in your MS-Mail system:

1. Select Mail/Compose Note, or click on the Compose button in the toolbar. The Compose dialog box shown in Figure 4.8 appears.

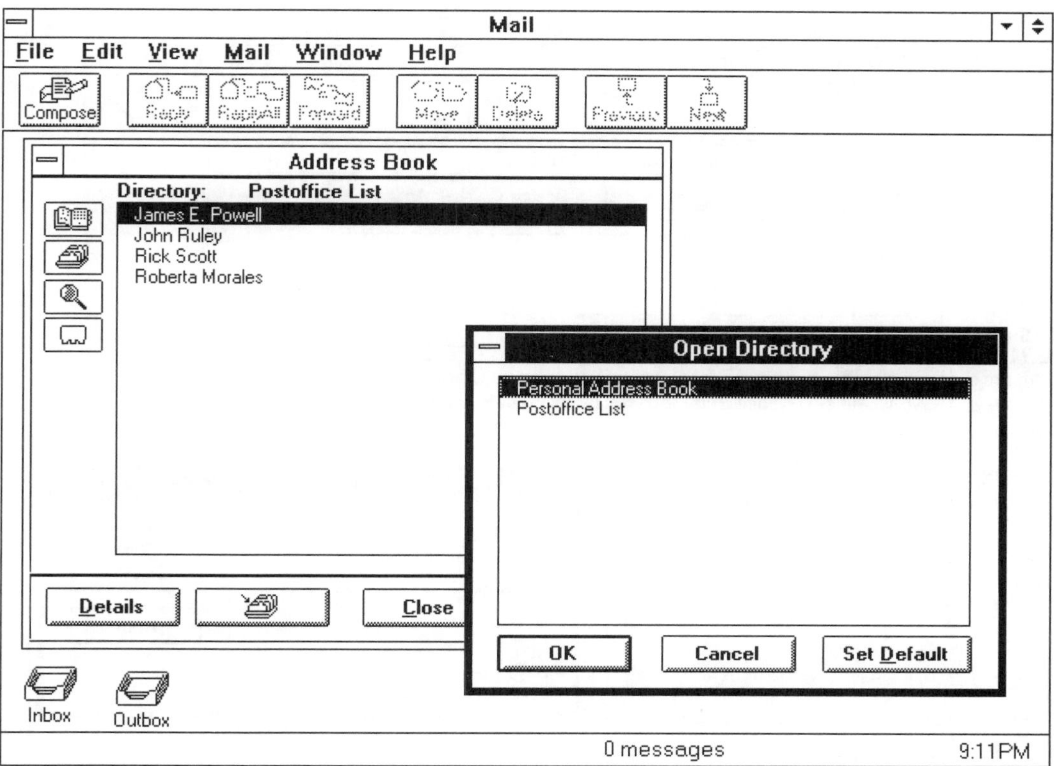

Figure 4.7 Address Book.

Every user has access to the main address list for his or her postoffice. Users can also create their own personal address books.

2. If you know the name(s) of the recipient(s), enter them in the To and Cc (carbon copy) boxes and go to step 4. If you do not know the names of the recipients, click on the Address button.
3. MS-Mail displays the Address dialog box. It contains the names of the people in your Postoffice (the users to whom you can send a message) at the top of the window. Highlight the name you want to send the message to and click on To (to add the name to the To: line) or Cc (to add the name to the list of carbon copy recipients). If you need to see the details of any user in the address list, click on Details. When all recipients have been entered, click on OK.
4. Type the subject of your message in the Subject line. This heading will appear when your message is displayed in the recipient's inbox.
5. Type the message in the area below the heading.

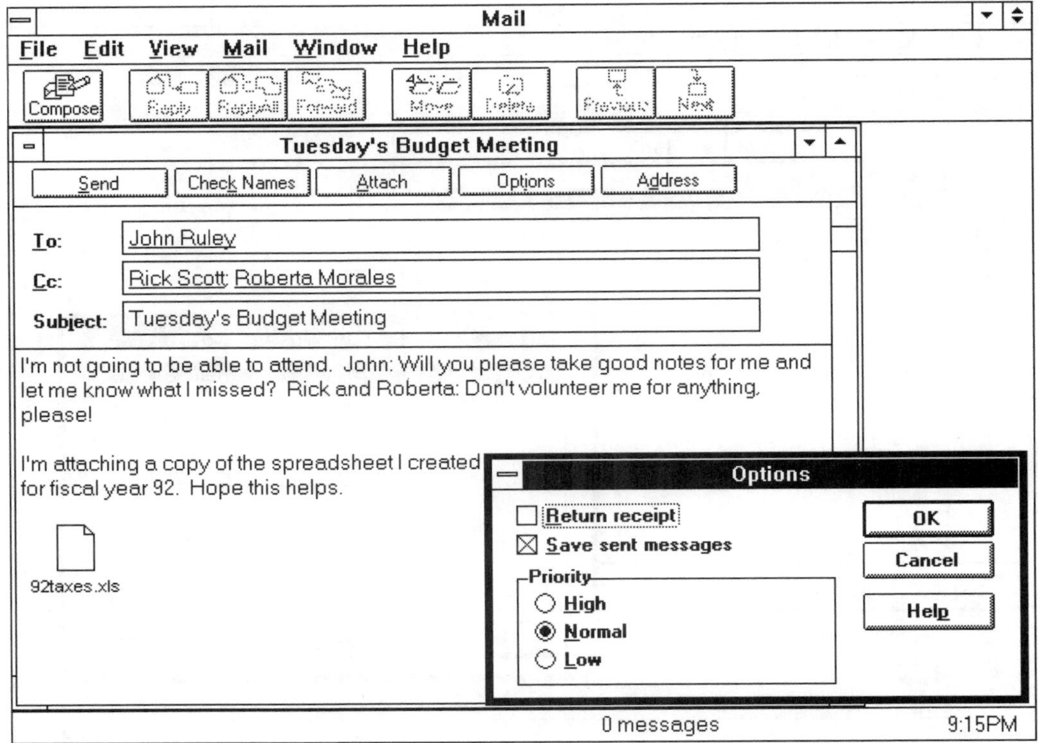

Figure 4.8 Compose Note.

Creating a message is done using MS-Mail's built-in text editor. Using OLE, a wide variety of data objects may be added, and binary files can be attached as well.

6. You can specify that MS-Mail take action when you send your message. To set optional message handling options, click on Options. Choose Return Receipt and Save sent messages if you wish MS-Mail to send you a message indicating receipt of a message or if you wish MS-Mail to save the message (for possible later resending to the same or other users). Select the priority (high-priority messages are displayed with a different icon in the recipient's Inbox). Select OK.
7. To send the message, click on Send.

Attaching a File to a Message

Besides sending plain text, you can attach one or more files to a mail message. Files can contain anything you like: sound, graphics, word processing or spreadsheet documents, and so on.

MS-Mail represents attached files by displaying an icon within the message area wherever you have positioned a file.

To attach a file to a message, compose the message text in the message area as described above. Then select Attach. Enter the name of the file you want to attach, or select it by navigating through the drive/directory listing. Select OK. MS-Mail displays an icon of the file, which you can reposition within the message area. You can also insert a reference to a network file using UNC filenames—select Insert Object from the Edit menu, select Package from the list, and use Edit/Command Line to enter a fully qualified UNC pathname (\\server\share\file).

Replying to Messages

To read a message, select the message and double-click on it to open the mail reader. After reading the message, you can send a reply to the sender or, if the message was sent to multiple users, to all of the recipients of the original message. To reply to a message, select Mail/Reply or click on the Reply button to send a message *only to the original sender*. Select Mail/Reply All or click on the Reply All button to send your message to *all recipients of the original message*. MS-Mail automatically fills in the To name with the sender's name. The original message is also displayed in the message section, which you can edit or delete if you wish.

You can *add* names to the address list (either the To or Cc areas) by entering the names directly or by selecting the Address button as you would when creating a new message. Enter your text in the message area, then click on Send to send the message.

Mail Administration

Several tasks can be handled by the administrator of a Postoffice. These tasks include changing a password, reducing disk space, and moving a Postoffice to a new location.

Changing a User Password

To change a MS-Mail user's password, select Mail/Postoffice Manager. Select the user name, then click on Details. Enter the new password in the Password box and click on OK. Then click on Close.

Managing Postoffice Space

As the number of users in your Postoffice grows, or as message volume increases, you will want to manage how much disk space is being used. You can also compress a Postoffice to recover some disk space. To manage disk space, select Mail/Postoffice Manager, then click on the Shared Folders button.

To compress disk space, notify all MS-Mail users with access to the folder, and ask each to close the folder on his or her workstation. Do not begin the compression until all users have closed their folders or loss of messages could result. Click on Compress to begin the disk compression. When MS-Mail tells you that the compress is complete, click on Close.

Moving a Postoffice

As a network changes or a Postoffice grows, you may find it necessary to move a Postoffice to a new location. To move a Postoffice to another drive or directory, notify all users of the Postoffice that they must sign out of the MS-Mail system. Failure to have all users out of the MS-Mail system could result in losing messages.

Open File Manager and select the WGPO directory of the drive where MS-Mail is installed. WGPO is the standard (default) location of MS-Mail systems. Select File/Move. Enter the new location in the To box, then click on OK.

Share the Postoffice: select the WGPO directory, select Disk/Share As, and enter the name of the Postoffice in the Share Name box. By default File Manager uses the name WGPO. Check the Re-share At Startup check box, then select Full Access in the Access Type section. If you want to password protect the directory, enter the password in the Password text box. Click on OK.

Using a text editor such as Notepad, edit MSMAIL32.INI on the server computer. Change the ServerPath= entry in the [Microsoft Mail] section to reflect the new location. Delete or edit the password entry if the directory was password protected.

Renaming a Workgroup Postoffice

To change the name of a Postoffice, you must first notify all users of the Postoffice that they must sign out of the MS-Mail system. Message loss will result if this is not done.

Select the WGPO directory from the File Manager, then select Disk/Share As. Enter the new Postoffice name in the Share Name text box and click on OK. Use the registry editor (REGEDT32.EXE) and change the ServerPath entry in the Microsoft Mail section of HKEY_CURRENT_USER/Software/Microsoft/Mail. Delete or edit the Server Password entry if the directory was password protected.

Chat

The Chat application lets you conduct an interactive conversation with another person on your network. Unlike Mail, in which users send text messages and await a reply, Chat provides two windows for immediate, real-time conversations. One window is used by you for entering text; the other window displays what the other user is typing.

To start the Chat application, click on the Chat icon in the Accessories window. The main Chat window is shown in Figure 4.9.

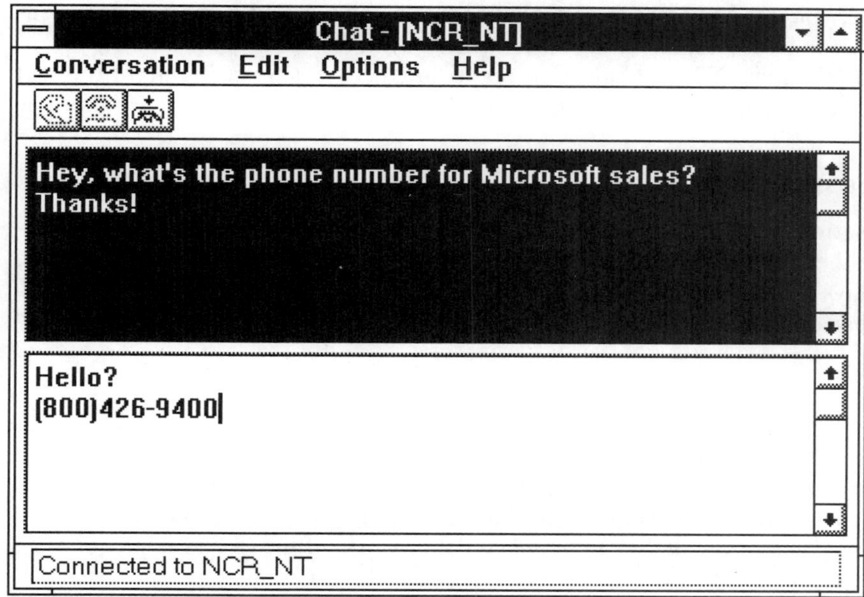

Figure 4.9 Chat.

The surprisingly useful Windows NT Chat utility provides interactive one-on-one communication between any two Windows NT or Windows for Workgroups workstations on the network. A multi-user Chat is expected to debut in later versions of Windows NT and Windows for Workgroups—probably appearing in 1994.

Starting a Chat Session

To start a chat session (conversation), click on the Dial button in the toolbar or select Conversation/Dial. Enter the computer name of the person you want to talk with in the Select Computer box. If the person answers, Chat displays a message in the status bar. You may begin typing in the top or left-most window. The response from the other user is displayed in the other window.

Answering a Call

If you are the party being called, you will hear a short sound and a message will appear in the Chat status bar. If you are not running Chat, the program begins running as an icon, indicating that someone wants to start a conversation. To answer a call, click on the Chat icon if necessary to open the application, then click on Answer in the toolbar, or select Conversation/Answer.

Both you and the person you are chatting with can enter text at the same time. As you type, your letters are visible to the other user, and vice versa. You can jump between windows—for example, you can copy text from the other user's window and paste it in your window. (To move between windows, select the other window with the mouse or press F6.)

The standard Windows NT text selection procedures (for example, highlight the text using the mouse or keyboard) are used in the Chat windows.

Ending a Chat Session

To end a conversation, click on the Hang Up button on the toolbar or select Conversation/Hang Up. Either party can end a session at any time. If the other user hangs up before you do, Chat displays an informational message in the status bar. To end the Chat application itself, select Conversation/Exit.

Schedule+

Microsoft Schedule Plus (Schedule+) is a workgroup and individual scheduling program. It can help you plan your day, find the first available meeting time for people or resources (such as meeting rooms), send meeting requests (using Mail), and help you plan tasks and to-do's.

Schedule+ lets you work with the online schedule, or work offline (for example, on your laptop), then synchronize your work.

The main Schedule+ screen contains a daily appointment calendar, a monthly calendar, and an area for notes. Four tabs run vertically down the left side of your screen. By clicking on these you can go to the current day's appointments, appointments for another day, a time planner that displays all scheduled and available time, and a list of prioritized tasks.

Another part of Schedule+ is the Messages window, which displays messages sent by others connected to your Postoffice (see the section on Mail), and is available *only* if you are connected to a Postoffice.

To begin Schedule+, select the Schedule+ icon from the Main program group. The program displays the Sign In dialog box, which asks you for your name. Enter the same name used for the MS-Mail system, and your MS-Mail password (if any), then press Enter.

Creating an Appointment

You must be viewing the Schedule window in order to add an appointment. If it is not visible, select Window from the main menu, then select your name from the pulldown menu.

Adding an Appointment with the Mouse

To add an appointment by highlighting the appointment duration in the Schedule window, select the Appts (Appointments) tab (then select the day from the calendar or select Edit/Go To Date), or the Today tab (to add an appointment for the current date). The Schedule window is shown in Figure 4.10.

Select the time of the appointment. Using the mouse, click on the beginning time and drag the mouse to the ending time. This action will highlight each block of time as the mouse

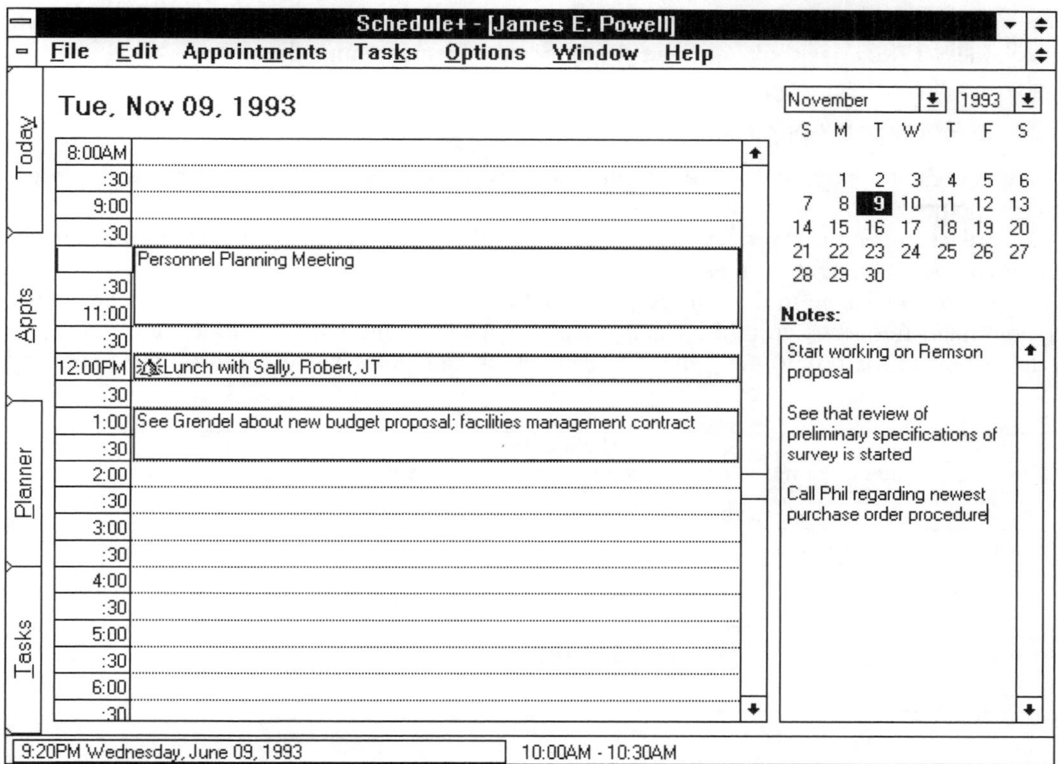

Figure 4.10 Schedule.

Like Windows for Workgroups, Windows NT includes a built-in appointment book with group scheduling capabilities.

is dragged through it. You can also use the keyboard and press Shift+Tab to move to the appointment list, press the up and down arrows until you select the beginning time, and press Shift+Down Arrow until you highlight the ending time. Enter the text for the appointment.

To set reminders (alarms) for appointments, see "Adding Reminders" below.

Using Precise Appointment Times

You can add appointments with more precise control over the starting and ending times, for example. To do this, select Appointments/New Appointment or press Ctrl+N. Type the start time and date in the When box, or click on the spin buttons (the up- and down-pointing arrow keys) to change the values that are currently displayed. Likewise, enter the end time and date in the When box, or click on the spin buttons to change the displayed values.

Enter the appointment description in the Description box. To set a reminder (alarm), check the Set Reminder box and enter the time and increment unit values.

Adding Recurring Appointments

As with regular appointments, the Schedule window must be displayed in order to add a recurring appointment.

Select either the Appts or Today tab. From the main menu select Appointments/New Recurring Appointments or press the shortcut keys, Ctrl+R.

Click on Change in the This Appointment Occurs box, shown in Figure 4.11. Select the appointment frequency from the Change Recurrence box, and choose the detailed frequency information in the box to the right. The contents of this box change based on the frequency

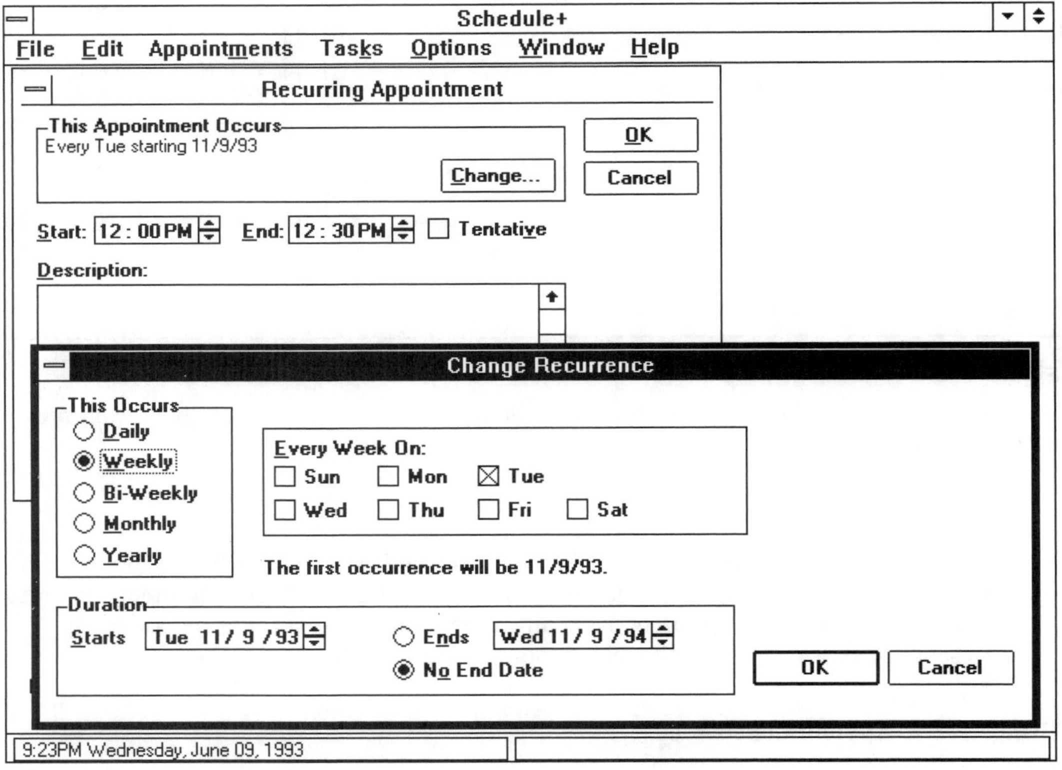

Figure 4.11 Appointment Occurs.

Designation of the time for a meeting is accomplished using this dialog.

you select. When multiple check boxes appear, be sure to check every box on which the appointment can occur.

Choose the starting and ending dates for the recurring appointment in the Duration box. By default, Schedule+ fills in an ending date that is one year from the start date. If the recurring appointment is to occur indefinitely, select the No End Date option. Click on OK.

Adding Reminders

To add a reminder to an appointment, double-click on the appointment or select the appointment and choose Edit/Edit Appt. Check the Set Reminder For box and enter the time period in the adjacent box. Click on OK. A bell icon appears to the left of the appointment, indicating that an alarm has been set.

To automatically add reminders for all *new* appointments and notes, select Options/General Options. In the Reminders box, check the Set Reminders for Notes check box to automatically set reminders when new notes are added. Check the Set Reminders Automatically box. Enter the number of time units and the time units (minutes, days, etc.) from the pulldown list. To create a noise when the alarm is triggered, check the Sound Audible Alarm box.

Managing Appointments

To *copy* an appointment, select it from the Appointment list, then select Edit/Copy Appointment or press Ctrl+Y. Select a new appointment date and time, then choose Edit/Paste or press Ctrl+V.

To *reschedule* an appointment, select it from the Appointment list, then select Edit/Move Appointment or press Ctrl+O. Enter the new appointment date and time and click on OK. If the appointment was a meeting scheduled with others, Schedule+ asks if you want to notify the other attendees of the change, so click on Yes. Optionally, add a message in the Meeting Request form. Click on Send.

To *delete* an appointment, select it from the Appointment list, then select Edit/Delete Appointment or press Ctrl+D. If the appointment is for a meeting scheduled with other attendees, Schedule+ will ask if you want to send a notice to the other attendees of the cancellation. Select Yes. Optionally, add a message in the Meeting Request form. Click on Send.

To *remove* an appointment to an archive file (which can be opened later and appointments retrieved from it), select File/Create Archive. Enter the last date of appointments—all appointments before this date will be archived. Click on OK.

Working with Tasks

A task list is simply a list of things to do. Items listed can be assigned a priority and due date; Schedule+ displays unfinished, past-due tasks in red.

Adding Tasks

To add a task, open the Task window by clicking on the Tasks tab or by pressing Alt+T. Select Tasks/New Task, and in the New Task box enter the task description. Click on Add.

Next, double-click on the task in the task list or select the task and click on the Edit button at the bottom of the task list. Schedule+ displays the Task dialog box. If the task is assigned to a project, select the project from the pulldown list or enter a new product name. By default the project name is <None>.

To enter a due date for the task, click on the By button in the Due Date box and enter the date, or use the up and down arrow buttons to choose the date. To specify the day the task should become active, enter the number of time units (1, 2, 3. . .) and select the time units (days, weeks, or months) in the Start Work text box.

You can set a reminder by clicking on the Set Reminder box and completing the reminder information.

Tasks can be assigned priorities, which are useful for viewing high-priority tasks first. Enter the priority or use the up and down arrow buttons to choose priority value. Priorities are 1 (highest) to 9, then A through Z (the lowest).

To make the task hidden from other users, check the Private box. Click on OK.

To add time to your schedule to work on the task, select Add to Schedule. Select the time you want to reserve for working on the task, and click on OK.

Deleting Tasks

To remove a single task from the task list, select the task and click on the Delete button, press Alt+L, or press the Del key. If the task is a recurring one, select Tasks/Edit Recurring Tasks, select the task to delete, click on Delete, then click on Close.

Sorting Tasks

To sort the task list, select Tasks/Sort by Priority, Tasks/Sort by Due Date, or Tasks/Sort by Description.

You can also sort tasks within a given project. Select Tasks/View by Project, or press Ctrl+Shift+V. Tasks are arranged by priority within project. Tasks with no project assigned appear at the top of the list.

Scheduling Meetings with Multiple Resources

To set up a meeting with others in your group, follow these steps:

1. You must be using the Planner window. If it is not displayed, click on the Planner tab or press Alt+P.
2. Select the date of the meeting you want to schedule, then click on Change.

3. Select the address book you want by clicking on the book icon at the top-left of the dialog box, then select the name of the person you want to invite and select Add. The name is added to the Attendees list. Repeat this step until all attendees are listed. Note that if you do not know a name, you can find it by clicking on the magnifying glass icon.
4. Click on OK.
5. Unavailable time periods are shown with colored bars. Overlapping time periods may have two colors. See Figure 4.12.
6. Select an available time slot (a time slot that has no color). Drag the mouse across the desired time segments, or use the keyboard and press the Shift+arrow keys to select a time period.
7. Choose Request Meeting. Schedule+ displays the Send Request dialog box with the date, time, and attendee list already filled in. Type in the meeting description in the

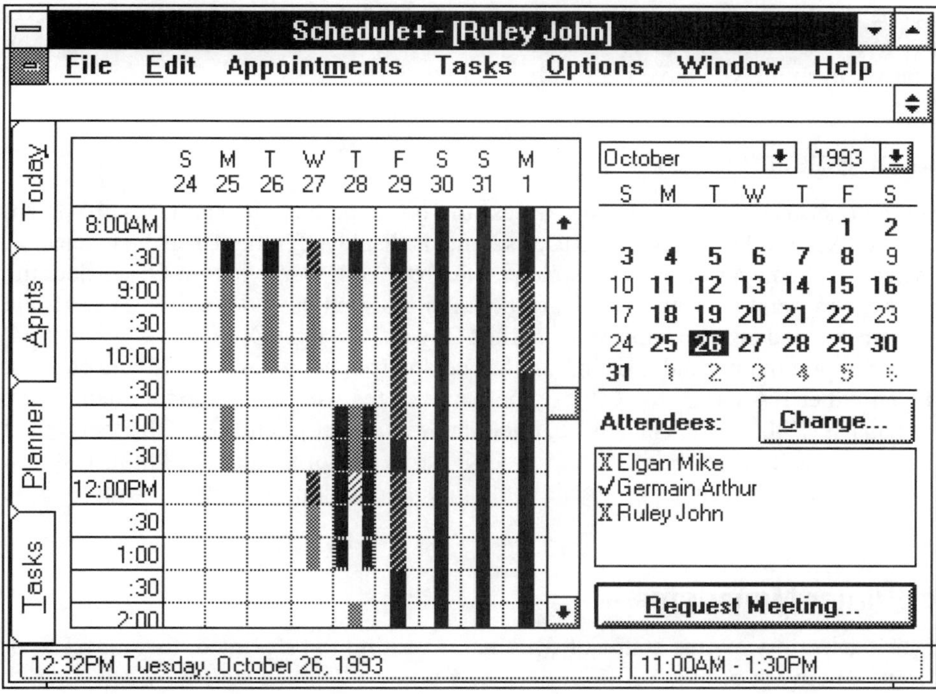

Figure 4.12 Meeting Time Conflict.

Resolution of the inevitable conflicts when scheduling meetings between several people is eased with a grapical display.

Subject box. To request attendees to reply to your meeting request, check the Ask for Responses box.

8. Click on Send. Schedule+ adds the meeting to your schedule and sends mail to the potential attendees using Windows NT's MS-Mail application.

Responding to Meeting Requests

The Messages window in Schedule+ is available if you are connected to a Postoffice. The window contains both meeting requests and meeting responses. To open the Messages window, select Window/Messages.

Messages are listed by attendee name. A check to the left of the name indicates that the person has accepted your invitation. A question mark to the left of the name indicates that the person might or might not attend. An X indicates the person will *not* attend.

When you read an invitation sent to you, you can reply in one of three ways:

1. Accept the invitation; Schedule+ will add the meeting to your schedule.
2. Decline the invitation; Schedule+ will notify the sender of your answer.
3. Tentatively accept; Schedule+ will add the meeting to your schedule but marks it as tentative, meaning you have not firmly committed to it.

Appointment and Task Security

You can grant another user on your network access to your appointments and tasks. To do so, select Options/Set Access Privileges. If the user's name is displayed in the Users box, select it. Otherwise, select Add and select the user's name, click on Add, then click on OK. Select the privilege you want to grant from the Privileges box. An assistant can add, change, and delete all your appointments and tasks except those marked Private. Click on OK.

To manage appointments and tasks of another person (one who has granted you access), select File/Open Other's Appt. Book. Choose the name of the user whose appointment book you want to manage (if the name isn't listed, click on Add, select it, click on OK, then select the user's name from the User box). Click on OK. Next, perform the scheduling tasks as needed. To work with your own appointment book, double-click on the control menu to close the window.

Print and Printer Management

Print Manager is used to view the status of documents waiting to be printed, to connect to or disconnect from a network printer, or to set up a new printer. You can start it by selecting its icon from the Main program group.

The Print Manager screen, shown in Figure 4.13, includes a window for each of the printers installed on your computer, including printers on a network. The toolbar, located at the top of the window, lets you access frequently used commands with your mouse. A status bar, displayed at the bottom of the screen, displays the name of the current printer, its status, and

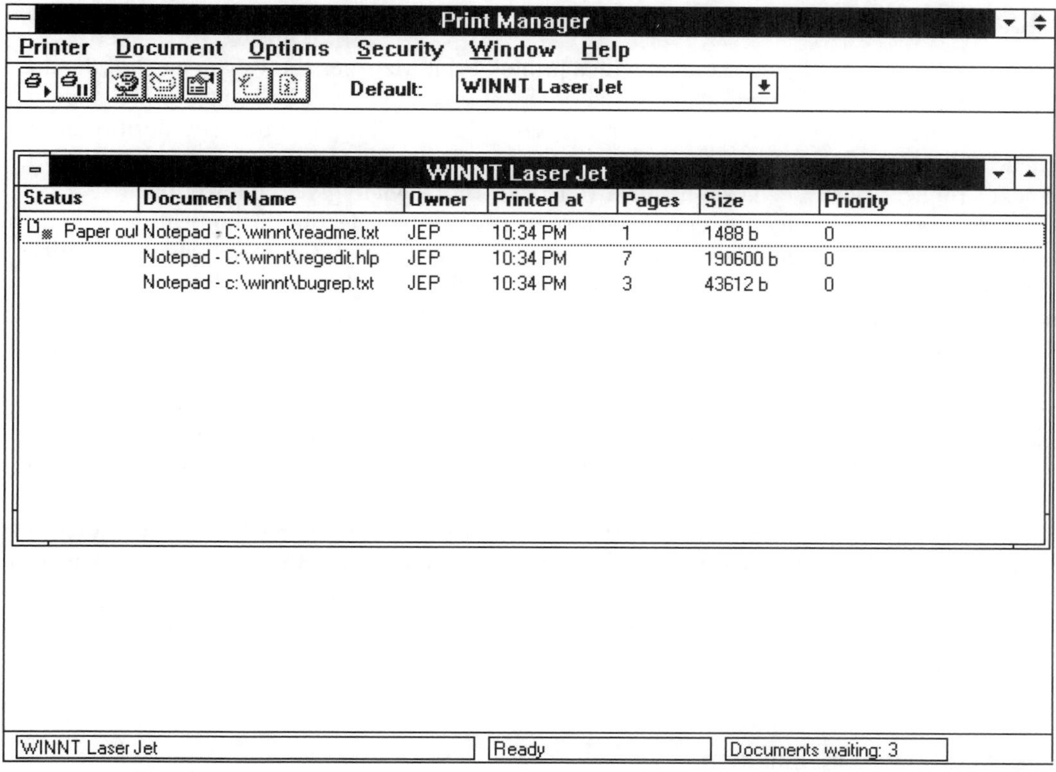

Figure 4.13 Print Manager.

Printer connections, drivers, and queues are all managed from this dialog. Even print "pools" can be handled (see Chapter 7).

the number of documents waiting to be printed. If the status bar is not displayed, select Options/Status Bar. A check mark to the left of the menu option indicates that the status bar is to be displayed.

Within each window you'll find a list of the documents being printed or in the print queue; Print Manager also lists the time the documents were generated and their size (the number of pages and the print file size in bytes).

Document Information

To see detailed information about a job waiting to be printed, select the document, then select Document/Details or click on the Details button in the toolbar.

Managing the Print Queue

When you open a window associated with a printer, Print Manager shows you a list of the documents waiting to be printed, listed in the order in which they will be printed. To change the order, and hence the priority of a document, select it, then drag it to the new position in the queue. Alternatively, use the keyboard: select Document/Move Document Up to give the document a higher priority, or Document/Move Document Down to give it a lower one.

You can also change the document's print priority by selecting Document/Details, then entering a high-priority number to print a document sooner. Select OK to set the new priority.

To stop the printing of a *single* document, select the document, then choose Document/Pause or click on the Pause button in the toolbar. Print Manager displays "Paused" after the document description. To resume printing, select Document/Resume or click on the Resume button in the toolbar.

To stop printing a document *and* remove it from the print queue, select the document, then choose Document/Remove Document, press the Delete key, or click on the Remove Document button on the toolbar. To remove *all* documents in the print queue, select Printer/Purge Printer.

You can temporarily stop printing *all jobs* by selecting the printer, then selecting Printer/Pause. Alternatively, you can select the Pause button from the toolbar. Print Manager displays "Paused" after the printer description in the Print Manager list. To resume printing, select the printer, then select Printer/Resume or click on the Resume button in the toolbar.

Note: To see the most current print information, press F5 or select View/Refresh.

Creating a Printer Definition

You cannot print a document to a printer until you have created a printer definition. This is equivalent to installing a printer driver in other versions of Windows, such as Windows 3.1. To create a new printer definition:

1. Select Printer/Create Printer. Print Manager displays the Create Printer dialog box shown in Figure 4.14.
2. Enter the name of the printer in the Printer Name text box. This name is used in the title bar of status windows. The maximum size of a printer name is 32 characters, although only 12 characters are viewed by workstations running MS-DOS.
3. Select the printer driver in the Driver pulldown list box. If the driver is not installed, select Other, then enter the complete path where the printer driver is located (usually A:\ or B:\) in the Install Driver dialog box, then click on OK.
4. Enter a printer description in the Description text box. This description is displayed to users connected on the network.
5. Select a destination in the Print to text box. The pulldown list includes the standard parallel (LPT) and serial (COM) ports. You can also specify that Windows NT send the printing to a file (Windows NT will prompt you for the filename when printing begins). Select the LPT or COM port if the printer is physically connected to your

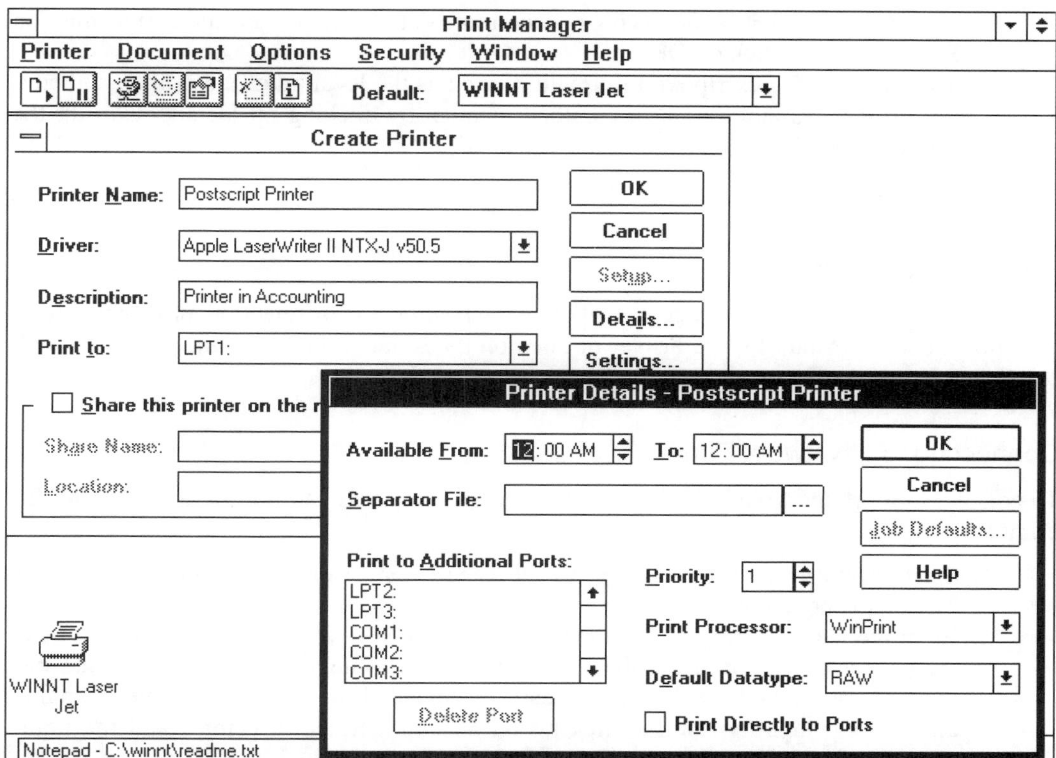

Figure 4.14 Create Printer.

Adding a new printer is done using the Create Printer command.

computer. If you are installing a printer that exists on the network, select the printer's network name or its network address. If you are creating a printer controlled by a LAN Manager 2.x or Windows for Workgroups server, select Connect To Printer, click on the shared printer you want to use, and you'll be prompted for an appropriate print driver.

6. To share the printer you are creating, check the Share this printer on the network box, then type a name for the printer in the Share Name text box. By default, the share name is the same as the printer name.
7. To set the port timeout options, click on Settings. Select the number of seconds that must pass before Windows NT recognizes that your printer is not responding. Enter the number of seconds Print Manager will wait before determining that the printer is not available in the Device Not Selected text box. Enter the number of seconds Win-

dows NT must wait before trying to send more data to the printer in the Transmission Retry text box. Click on OK.

8. You can specify descriptive information, such as the location of the printer, and control printer availability and separator filename, by clicking on Details. Consult the Windows NT System Guide for more details.
9. Click on OK.

Removing a Printer

To remove a printer from your system, *including the printer driver*, select the printer you want to remove, choose Printer/Delete Printer or click on the Remove Printer button from the toolbar. Select Yes to confirm your request.

Connecting to a Network Printer

To connect to a printer already defined on your network so you can print a document to that printer:

1. Select Printer/Connect to Printer or select the Connect Printer button on the toolbar. The dialog box shown in Figure 4.15 appears.
2. Enter the name of the printer in the Printer text box. If you do not know the name of the printer, select one from the list in the Select Printers box. The printers are displayed in a hierarchical list, which can be expanded to show the printers, domains, and workgroups by double-clicking on an entry. Select a printer and the name appears in the Printer text box. Select OK.
3. If the printer is shared by a Windows NT computer, you can now use the printer. Steps 4 and 5 should be implemented if the printer is shared by a computer *not* running Windows NT.
4. Print Manager prompts you to install a driver. Select OK, then choose the driver from the Select Driver dialog box. Enter the location (drive and directory) of the Windows NT printer drivers, then select Continue.
5. Windows NT will install the driver for you.

Disconnecting from a Network Printer

To disconnect from a printer on your network, select Printer/Remove Printer Connection, or click on the Remove Printer Connection button on the toolbar. Select Yes to confirm your request.

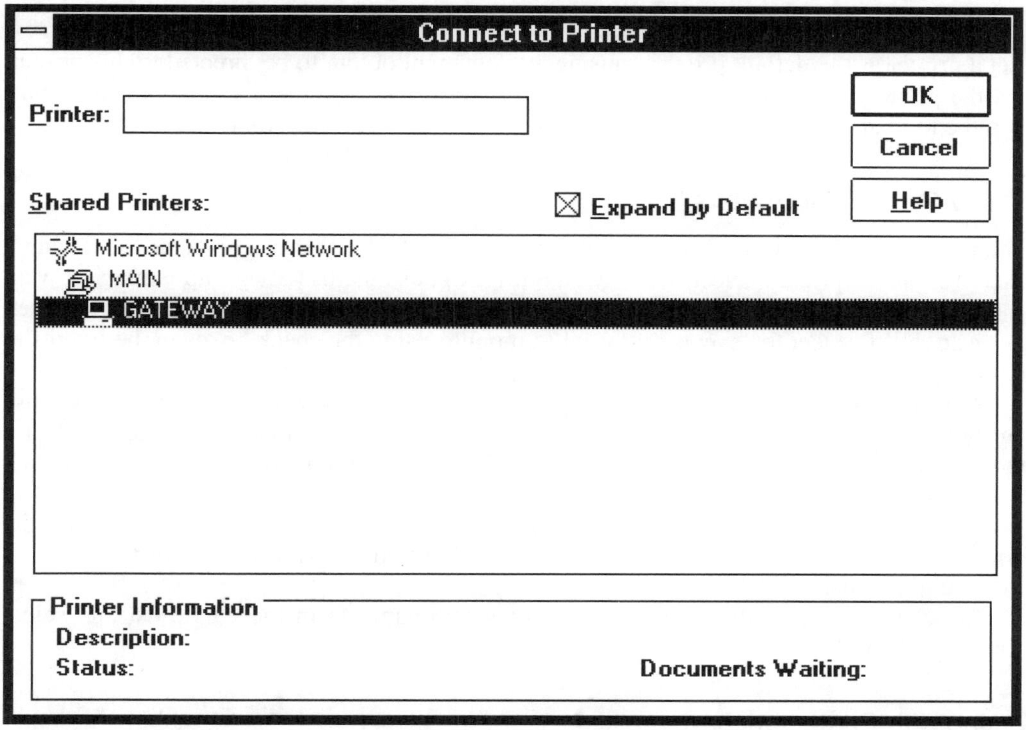

Figure 4.15 Connect Printer.

Network printers are connected using a browser similar to that used for network directory access.

Sharing a Printer

To share a printer that is connected locally on a network, select the printer you want to share, then choose Printer/Properties. Check the Share This Printer On The Network check box.

Next, enter the printer name that will appear in the list of available printers for others on the network, if different from the default name Windows NT supplies. Then type the description of the location of the printer. This name will be displayed in the Connect To Printer dialog box when other users try to connect to a network printer. Click on OK.

Setting the Default Printer

To set a printer as the default printer, causing all document output to be directed to this printer, select the printer and select Printer/Set Default Printer or click on the Set Default Printer button on the toolbar. Print Manager displays the default printer in a bold font.

Security Options for Printers

A unique feature of Windows NT is the ability to track which users or groups are accessing a printer. To *audit* a printer, select Security/Auditing. Choose the user or group name you want to monitor. If the name is not listed, select Add, select the Names and Type of Access, then select Add. Next, select the events you want to monitor using the check boxes in the Events to Audit box, then select OK.

You can also change the permissions granted to a printer. Select the printer, then choose Security/Permissions. To add a user or group name to the permissions, select Add. Select a name from the Name list, and an access from the Type of Access pulldown list box, then click on OK.

To change the permission of a user or group, select the user or group name from the Name list in the Printer Permissions dialog box. Select the permission from the Type of Access pulldown list.

To delete a permission, select the user or group name from the Name list and select Remove. Select OK.

Working with Printer Drivers

RISC-based and Intel x86-based systems use different print drivers, so you may wish to install multiple versions on your print servers.

To install a printer driver, select the icon for the printer, then choose Printer/Properties or click on the Properties button in the toolbar. Select Other in the Driver box, then enter the drive and directory where the driver is located, typically A:\ or B:\ if the driver is supplied on a diskette. Choose OK and Windows NT will load the driver.

ClipBook

Like its Windows and Windows for Workgroups cousins, Windows NT's clipboard is an intermediate area used for cutting or copying data within or between applications. Windows NT takes this further by letting you save the contents of your clipboard in a storage area called the Local ClipBook. Each item is stored in a separate ClipBook page, and pages can be arranged in several ways. In addition, you can share the contents of your Local ClipBook with those on your network, and access the contents of other shared ClipBooks.

Windows NT provides a ClipBook viewer that lets you examine what is on the clipboard and what you have saved to the Local ClipBook.

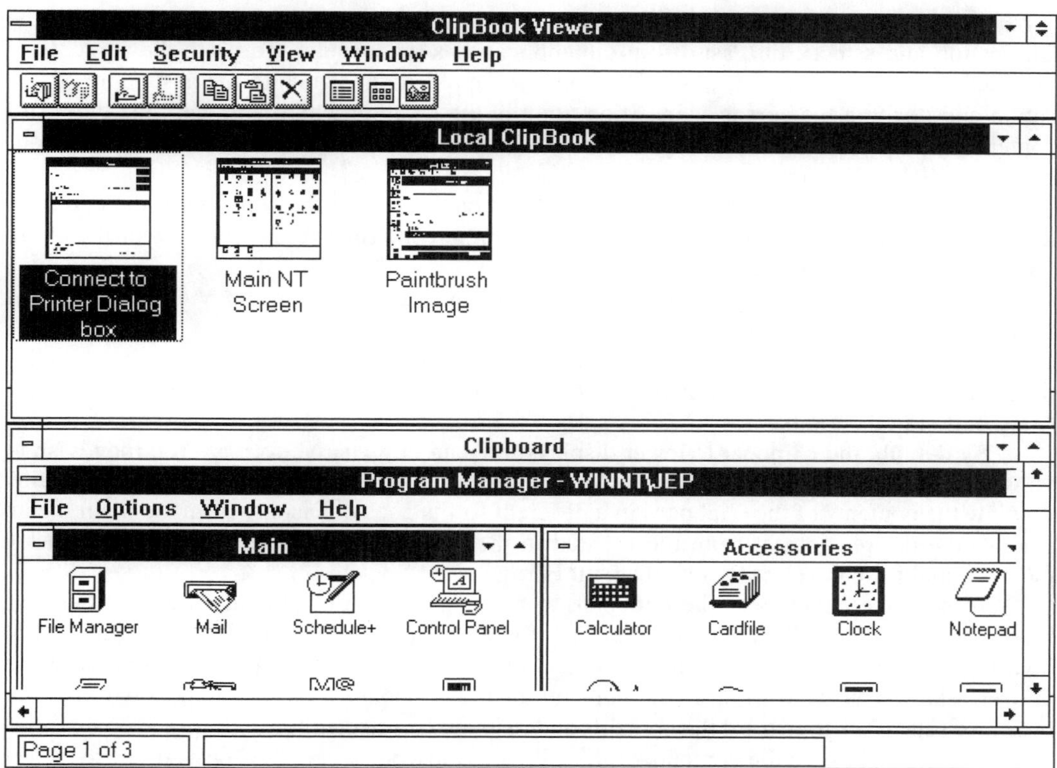

Figure 4.16 Clipbook.

Windows NT borrows the "clipbook" metaphor from Windows for Workgroups, providing a simple but powerful form of ad-hoc client/server connectivity that can be exploited by end-users.

To start the ClipBook Viewer application, click on the icon in the Main program group. When the application starts, you will see the Local ClipBook window and a Clipboard icon, as shown in Figure 4.16.

The Clipboard

Most Clipboard content is created when you select Edit/Copy from within an application. To save information from a character-based DOS or OS/2 application, open the application's control menu box (the minus sign in the upper-left corner) or press Alt+Spacebar. Select Edit/Mark and mark the data you want to copy by using the arrow keys until the selection is highlighted. Select the control menu box again and select Edit/Copy.

To copy the contents of the Clipboard into a Windows NT application, move to the application and select Edit/Paste from the application's main menu. To paste the contents of the Clipboard into a character-based DOS or OS/2 application, switch to the destination application and position the cursor or insertion point at the location where you want the clipboard contents to be placed. Press Alt+Spacebar to display the Non-Windows-NT application's control menu. Select Edit/Paste.

You can also save screen images to the Clipboard. To save the contents of the currently displayed window to the Clipboard, press Alt+PrintScreen. To save the contents of the entire screen, press PrintScreen.

To delete the current contents of the clipboard, activate the Clipboard Viewer, then select Edit/Delete (or press the Del key). Click on Yes to confirm your request.

To copy a page from a ClipBook to an application, you must first copy it to the clipboard. Select the page you want from the ClipBook, then select Edit/Copy or click on the Copy button in the toolbar.

By default, the Clipboard viewer displays the data in its native format. You may wish to view the data in another format, such as to view the embedded codes in a word processing file. To view the contents of the clipboard in a different format, select Display from the main menu. Choose the desired format from those listed in the pulldown menu. To view the contents in their original format, select Display/Default Format.

To save the contents of the clipboard to a file, select the Clipboard viewer and choose File/Save As. Enter a filename with the .CLP file extension and click on OK. To open a Clipboard file, select File/Open, select the file and click on OK. If the clipboard is *not* empty, the viewer asks if you want to clear the contents of the clipboard. Select No and save the clipboard, or select Yes to discard the contents and display the selected file.

You can also save the contents of the Clipboard to your local ClipBook. To do so, select the Local ClipBook window. Select Edit/Paste (or click on the Paste button in the toolbar) to place the image in the ClipBook. Type the name of the page in the Page Name text box. This name is used when sorting pages using the Table of Contents option. To share the page with other users, check the Share Item Now check box. Click on OK. If you opted to share the page, the Share ClipBook Page dialog box is displayed. Enter the options and select OK.

ClipBook Pages

To share a page from your ClipBook with other computers, select the ClipBook page, then select File/Share (or click on the Share button in the toolbar).

To stop sharing the page, select it and choose File/Stop Sharing (or select the Stop Sharing button in the toolbar).

To use pages from another ClipBook that is shared on another computer, select File/Connect (or click on the Connect button on the toolbar). Type the name of the computer, or select it from the Computers list, then click on OK.

To disconnect from the ClipBook, select File/Disconnect (or click on the Disconnect button on the toolbar).

In addition to sharing ClipBook pages, you can also protect them. To set the access permissions for a ClipBook page, select the page, then choose Security/Permissions. Select the user or group name whose permissions you want to change, select the permission from the Type of Access pulldown list, and select OK.

To remove all ClipBook permissions for a group, select the user or group name and select Remove. To add permissions, select Add, select the user(s) and/or group(s), and select the permission you want to grant, then click on OK.

You can also take ownership of a ClipBook page. To take ownership, select the page you want, choose Security/Owner, and select Take Ownership.

Arranging ClipBook Pages

You can arrange your ClipBook pages in three ways. To view ClipBook pages alphabetically by name, select View/Table of Contents. To view small images of each page, select View/Thumbnails. To view the entire contents of a ClipBook page, select View/Full Page.

Auditing ClipBook Pages

Auditing allows you to keep track of who is using images in *your* ClipBook. To audit a ClipBook page, select the page, then choose Security/Auditing. Select the group or user name you want to track. Choose the event(s) you want to audit, then select OK.

To add a user or group to an existing audit list, click on the Add button, select the group(s) or user name(s) you want to add, and click OK. To remove a user or group, select the user or group and click on Remove.

Note that Auditing must be turned on in User Manager (Policies/Audit).

Network Operations from the Command Line: The NET Command Interface

While it's usually easier to use the graphical utility programs like File Manager and User Manager, there are times when a command-line interface is more convenient. The Windows NT **Net** commands fill this need—essentially, every network operation that can be conducted from a graphical program can be done in this way. Aside from simple convenience, the Net interface has two major advantages: the syntax is consistent across all LAN Manager-derived networks, so users familiar with the LAN Manager, LAN Server, MS-Net, or Windows for Workgroups Net commands will immediately be comfortable in NT; and the Net commands can be employed in batch files.

Five of these commands are helpful for general use as command-line alternatives to the functions normally accomplished from File Manager, Print Manager, or the Control Panel—and one, Net Message, has no graphical equivalent. These end-user commands can be used as follows:

Listing the Available Network Commands: *Net*

Just typing **net** at the command prompt will print a list of the available commands on the display screen. This is handy when you can't remember the particular command you want, and can be used in conjunction with **net help** to quickly find the command you want. A slightly better formatted list of commands will be printed if you type **net help** without any arguments.

Getting Help for Network Functions: *Net Help* and *Net Helpmsg*

When you know you want to use a particular net command, but can't remember the command syntax, typing **net help** <command> will provide a brief description of the command and its arguments. For instance, **net help view** prints the following message:

```
net help view
The syntax of this command is:

NET VIEW [\\computername | /DOMAIN[:domainname]]

NET VIEW displays a list of resources being shared on a server. When used
without options, it displays a list of servers in the current domain.

\\computername     Is a server whose shared resources you want
                   to view.

/DOMAIN:domainname  Specifies the domain for which you want to
                    view the available servers. If domainname is
                    omitted, displays all domains in the local area
                    network.
```

Just type **net help** without arguments for a formatted list of the net commands.

Note: Many of the screens displayed by net help are quite long. If material goes by too fast for you to read, you may find the **|more** command helpful. For instance, **net help use |more** will display help on the net use command, but will do so one screen at a time.

Viewing and Browsing the Network: *Net View*

You can view lists of servers and browse shared network resources from the command line just as easily as you can from File Manager. Type **net view** without any arguments for a list of servers. To view shared resources at a server, type **net view** <server name>. In a multidomain (or multiworkgroup) network, type **net view /DOMAIN** for a list of domains, and **net view /DOMAIN:**<domain name> to see a list of servers in the specified domain.

Net view is most often used in conjunction with the **net use** command to access shared resources on other computers. A typical use begins with **net view** (no arguments) to get a list of server names, then one views the resources on a server, and finally employs **net use** to access the shared resource in question. For instance:

```
net view
Servers on MAGNET1:
\\MIPS-LAB-SERVER
```

```
\\JOHNR-NT486-66

net view \\JOHNR-NT486-66
Shared resources at \\johnr-nt486-66:

Sharename    Type      Used as   Comment

---------    ------    -------   -------
disk-d       Disk Z:
PUBLIC       Disk                Public Shared Space
```

One could then employ **net use** to access the Public share, for instance, by typing:

```
net use Q: \\johnr-nt486-66\public
```

Sharing Directories: *Net Share*

Sharing directories from the command line is done with the **net share** command. To share a directory, type **net share** <sharename>=<directory to share>. For instance, the command **net share disk-d=d:** will share the entire d: disk (and all subdirectories) with the sharename disk-d. Other users (provided they have user accounts on your system) will be able to access this directory using the **net use** command, or by appropriate actions in file manager. To designate how many users can access the share at any one time, set the **/USERS:**<number> switch—this can be useful if, for instance, you are sharing data files that only one user can safely access at a time. Or you can use the **/UNLIMITED** switch if there is no upper limit you wish to enforce (this is the default). If you want an explanatory remark to be associated with a share, you can use the **/REMARK:** "<your text here>" flag. Be sure to type the quote marks.

Sharing printers cannot be done the same way—you must use the Print Manager for this. (Windows NT's printers are tied very closely to the Win32 subsystem, so a Windows driver must be selected before a printer can be shared.)

Both shared directories and shared printers can be deleted from the command line, by typing **net use** <sharename> **/DELETE**. This will eliminate the share—and terminate any outstanding connections. (Functionally, this is the same as performing a "Stop Sharing" command in File Manager or Print Manager.)

Typing **net share** without any arguments will display information on the shares currently active (including administrative shares, if you are logged in with administrative privilege). For example:

```
net share

Sharename    Resource     Remark

---------    --------     ----------------------
ADMIN$       C:\winnt     Remote Admin
A$           A:\          Default share
C$           C:\          Default share
D$           D:\          Default share
```

```
E$            E:\          Default share
IPC$                       Remote IPC
NETLOGON      C:\winnt     Logon server share
Public        E:\Public    Advanced Server NTFS Volume Set
```

Connecting and Disconnecting Shared Directories and Printers: *Net Use*

Just as File Manager and Print Manager allow you access to shared directories and printers graphically, the **net use** command gives you this capability from the command line. Without arguments, it will display a list of whatever resources are currently connected, for example:

Displaying Currently Used Shares

```
net use
New connections will be remembered.

Status            Local name      Remote name

_____________     __________     ________________________
OK                Q:             \\johnr-nt486-66\Public
OK                Z:             \\johnr-nt486-66\disk-d
Disconnected                     \\johnr-nt486-66\IPC$
```

Terminating Shares

The keyword **/DELETE** will terminate use of a shared resource, so the command

```
net use /DELETE Q:
```

would terminate sharing on \\johnr-nt-486-66\Public, and make the Q: device name available for other use. To reuse this device name for the directory \\mips-lab-server\Public directory, for instance, one could type:

```
net use Q: \\mips-lab-server\Public
```

Persistent Shares

If a connection is meant to be retained in future sessions, you can add the **/Persistent:** keyword, which is followed by **Yes** or **No** to indicate whether sharing is to be persistent or temporary. These keywords act as a toggle, and will continue in force until changed: /Persistent: YES makes connections persistent by default, while /Persistent: No makes them temporary. For example:

```
net use Q: \\test_server\a_share /Persistent: YES
```

creates Q: as a persistent connection to the home directory defined in User Manager. All further connections in the session will be assumed to be persistent until a net use command is issued with the /Persistent:NO keyword, such as:

```
net use R: \\test_server\temp /Persistent: NO
```

which will create R: as a temporary connection to \\test_server\temp. All further connections in the session will be temporary until a /Persistent: YES is issued.

Passwords

If the device one connects to is password protected (a passworded Windows for Workgroups share, for instance) the sharename should be followed by the password—or by an asterisk placeholder, which will cause the system to prompt you for a password to be typed in. The latter is especially useful in batch .CMD files. For example, the command

```
net use Q: \\accounting\first_quarter *
```

will connect you to the accounting server's first_quarter share, if you type in the correct password when prompted to do so.

Connecting as Another User and Across Domains

In some situations, it may be desirable to establish a connection under another username—for instance, while my user name may be JRULEY on one system, it might be JDR on another. In such a case, the **/User:** keyword allows you to connect to a share using another user name. For instance, while logged in as JRULEY, I can issue the command:

```
net use Q: \\accounting\financials /USER:jdr
```

to gain access under my JDR account on the \\accounting system. If the JDR account is a domain account for the CFO domain, then the command:

```
net use Q: \\accounting\financials /USER:cfo\jruley
```

would be used.

The Home Directory

The **/Home** keyword connects a user to his home directory as defined in the User Manager. Thus, the command:

```
net use Q: \\accounting /HOME
```

would connect Q: to your home directory on the accounting server.

Sending Messages: *Net Send*

MS-Mail and Chat are the usual methods for communicating between NT users, but there are times when it's preferable to reach many users with a single command. **Net Send** meets this need—it causes a pop-up window to appear immediately on the systems to which a message is addressed, carrying your message (which must be one line of simple text).

The simplest form of the command assumes that you want to send a message to only one user, and that you know that user's name, in which case the command is, for instance:

```
net send jruley Hi There!
```

which will send "Hi There!" to the user named jruley on the network.

Sending a Message to All Members of a Workgroup

If you want to send a message to everyone in your workgroup or domain, just use an asterisk instead of the name. For instance:

```
net send * Who has my copy of Networking Windows NT?
```

would be an efficient way to see who in your workgroup has borrowed your copy of a very interesting book.

Sending a Message to All Users in a Domain

It's often necessary to send messages to users of a particular Domain or Server. In a Windows NT Advanced Server Domain, you can send a message to all other domain users by using the **/DOMAIN** keyword. For instance:

```
net send /DOMAIN Warning: Server 2 almost out of disk space
```

would let everyone in your domain know that Server 2 has a problem. You can follow the **/DOMAIN** keyword with the name of a domain if you want to send a message to users in that domain. For instance:

```
net send /DOMAIN: accounting Backup System is Down for Maintenance
```

would alert all accounting domain users to the status of the Backup System.

Sending a Message to All Users Connected to a Server

There are times when you may want to reach everyone else attached on your server—especially if you are the administrator and you know there is a problem. The **/Users** keyword meets this need, sending the message to all users of the system. Thus, the command

```
net send /USERS Server going down in 5 minutes...
```

would perform the traditional service of scaring the wits out of everyone connected to your server.

Sending a Broadcast Message

The **Net Send** command includes one form that is different from the others: when used with the **/BROADCAST** switch, it sends a low-level systemwide broadcast to all systems connected on the same physical segment. This is very different from other forms of **net send**, which send to a certain list of users; the **/BROADCAST** switch is independent of whether a system is logged in to a server. It is generally used when debugging a system, as in

```
net send /BROADCAST If you can see this message, holler!
```

The point is that if the network card is installed, the wiring is good, and the network services are running, the message should be displayed on all systems in the local network segment. This can be extremely irritating to users who are in the middle of useful work, so this command should be used with care. Its use in debugging is discussed in more detail in Chapter 5.

Conclusion

The basic networking features of Windows NT run the gamut from file and printer sharing through electronic mail, group scheduling, and ad hoc client-server links (with Network DDE). You can perform most network tasks from the File Manager, Print Manager, and Control Panel, although the ***net*** command interface gives you a character-mode alternative.

For More Information

Custer, Helen (1993), *Inside Windows NT.* Redmond, WA: Microsoft Press, ISBN: 1-55615-481-X. See Chapter 6 (on NT's networking features).

Feldman, Len (1993), *Windows NT: The Next Generation.* Carmel, IN: Sams Publishing, ISBN: 0-672-30298-5. Curiously enough, the networking coverage is in Chapter 6.

Microsoft Staff (1993), *Windows NT System Guide (Beta, March 1993).* Redmond, WA: Microsoft Corp. This is the basic reference guide to Windows NT, and comes with all Windows NT systems.

Microsoft Staff (1993), *Windows NT Resource Kit, Volumes 1-3.* Redmond, WA: Microsoft Press. Expensive ($109 for all three volumes), but the best overall coverage of Windows NT can be found in these books, especially in Volume 3.

5

Keeping Connected

When you have finished reading this chapter you should understand:

- **The principles of preventive maintenance**
- **Performance monitoring and tuning procedures**
- **Basic mechanisms of Windows NT troubleshooting**
- **Windows NT registry**
- **Special tools provided with Windows NT**

You should *not* feel comfortable facing the diagnosis of a fault in a Windows NT system on your own. No competent technician *ever* feels so confident. But you should feel comfortable taking a crack at it. You should understand the preventive maintenance techniques that will help you avoid trouble whenever you can, and you should know when to cry "uncle!" and call for professional help.

Read This First

The odds are good that if you've turned to this page you're faced with a system that is not operating as it should and you are desperately seeking help. This is the worst possible time to read about troubleshooting procedures but it's often the only time we do. *If you inspect the troubleshooting section that appears later in this chapter, you will see that the section appears in a tinted box.* These pages constitute a list of the most common errors in Windows NT, their symptoms, and the steps you need to take to correct them. So, read the rest of this paragraph and then go to the tinted pages and the best of luck to you. But when you've finished that, and your bug is fixed, come back here and read the rest of this chapter because it will tell you how to avoid having to go through this again.

The preceding sentence will strike some readers as an appallingly bad joke. It is not!

In many situations a complex piece of equipment or software (such as Windows NT or Windows NT Advanced Server) is installed by someone whose most urgent consideration is bringing the thing up as fast as possible. Once installed it will run until it breaks, at which time that same individual will be desperately looking for help—and *that's* the reason for our first paragraph. But those of us who have taken the trouble to read a chapter like this ahead of time will know that there's a much better approach. This is the approach that the United States Air Force taught me[1] at some expense in 1976. It's called *preventive maintenance* or *PM*. The principle of PM is simple: Don't wait until the system breaks—fix it *before* it breaks. Replace parts that you know will wear out before they do.

How do you find out which parts of the system are wearing out and need replacement? By applying *actuarial statistics* and *the mathematics of fault prediction* (see Appendix 6 for details). Basically, you need to keep a maintenance log for the system, recording how performance varies over time along with the date and time of any failures. By examining the log, it's generally possible to predict the overall reliability of the system, and to perform maintenance tasks in advance of an actual failure.

There's another benefit to PM: Since it forces you to undertake regularly scheduled maintenance it also gives you the foundation for *performance tuning*—keeping throughput as high as possible by "tweaking" the system to eliminate bottlenecks. Windows NT gives you some particularly sophisticated tools with which to determine system throughput. For example, it's not necessary to go through any complicated calculation to determine the Packets/Sec. the server is handling. It is necessary only to go to the Performance Monitor and *look* at it. We'll now take a look at the specifics in performance tuning and troubleshooting in Windows NT systems.

Performance Tuning in Windows NT

As discussed in Appendix 6, the overall throughput of a system is an end-to-end process, a chain in which total system throughput is no greater than the throughput of the slowest individual component. So performance tuning generally amounts to the process of determining this component, referred to as a *bottleneck* that's "bogging" the system, and increasing its throughput either by changing system settings or by replacing the component with a faster one. In individual Windows NT systems the components that can be performance tuned (aside from components that will be tuned to suit individual preferences, such as the keyboard and the mouse), include the central processor, memory, disk, video, and network.

[1]The author of this chapter is John D. Ruley, formerly a Radio Relay Equipment Repair Specialist (AFSC 30470) with the Ohio Air National Guard and Reserve Air Forces. In other words, this chapter is written from the point of view of an old-fashioned, get-your-hands-dirty technician.

General Methods of Performance Tuning

The principal tools an administrator or technician will use to perform routine performance monitoring/tuning on Windows NT systems are the Windows NT Performance Monitor (covered in Chapter 3) and the Windows NT Configuration Registry Editor (covered later in this chapter). In the sections that follow we will discuss which Performance Monitor counters to track, what threshold values to look for, and what steps you should take when a threshold value is reached. In some cases there will be little that you can do short of moving the user to a faster machine—if, for instance, you detect a CPU speed bottleneck. In other cases it may be possible to modify various Windows NT configuration values to produce a performance improvement. You will generally perform this using the Windows NT Configuration Registry Editor (a.k.a. REGEDT32.EXE), illustrated in Figure 5.1.

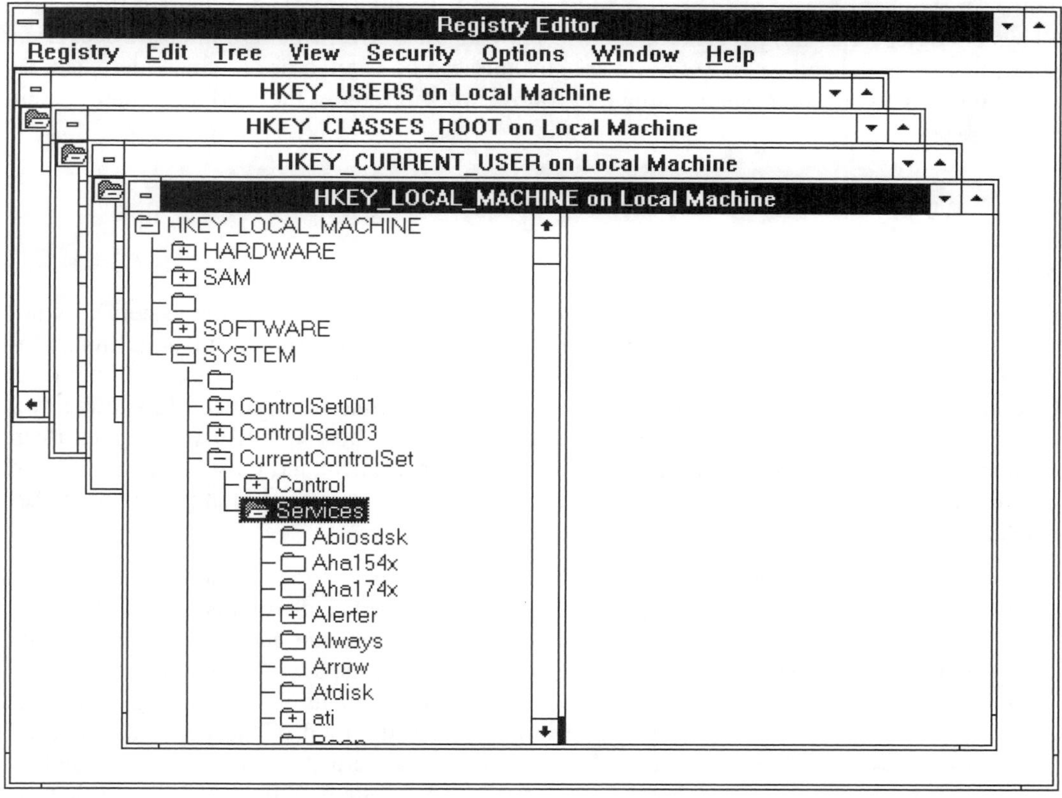

Figure 5.1 Registry editor.

Windows NT's configuration registry editor (REGEDT32.EXE) provides an interface to the *registry*—a redundant database of configuration information for the system, software, and users.

You should be forewarned that the Configuration Registry has some features in common with a nuclear reactor. It is potentially an immensely powerful tool. It is also fairly dangerous. No, it won't irradiate you and leave you with three-headed progeny—but if it's not used with care it can render a system unusable (effectively irradiating your career!). So you should always take great care when making a configuration change using the registry. And in particular, you should make sure you have the *emergency diskette* for the system you are working on close at hand. At any rate, the following section should provide a basic guide to the tuning steps administrators should take.

Performance Monitor

In what follows, we will be constantly referring to Performance Monitor *objects* (see Figure 5.2). To review (remember, Performance Monitor is covered in detail in Chapter 3), these are selections from the Objects pull-down list that appears in the Add to Chart (or Add to View) dialog after selecting Add to Chart (or Add to View) from the Edit menu. The pull-down lists all system objects that have registered themselves with the Performance Monitor service. Each object has an associated set of *counter* variables that can be charted or on which alerts can be set. In the sections on subsystem tuning that follow, we will refer to these counters and to their parent objects.

CPU Tuning

System Object

Since the central processing unit (CPU) of the system is the "brains" of the system it is not surprising that monitoring CPU performance is one of the most important functions an administrator can undertake. Windows NT provides a very high degree of capability to monitor the CPU including measuring total CPU utilization, percent of time in privileged (operating system) mode, percent of time in user (application) mode, and how frequently the system can *context switch* between tasks. All of these can be extremely useful and most can be monitored not only for the entire system but on a per-processor basis on symmetric multiprocessor (SMP) machines. The relevant counters to monitor are:

- **% Total Privileged Time**—This is the percentage of the total system time (time for all processes in the system) that is being spent in "privileged" (that is, in operating system) mode. This generally is a reflection of how much time the system is expending performing system level tasks such as disk I/O, video display operation, etc.
- **% Total Processor Time**—This indicates the percentage of time during which the processor is doing useful work and is effectively the total of the percent privileged time and the percent user time. When this percentage approaches 100% it indicates that the processor has become a bottleneck in the system. Windows NT will then be forced to suspend certain tasks in order to give others time to run and the system will slow down in much the way a time sharing system slows down when too many users are logged into it. At this point, the alternatives are (1) increase the number or speed of

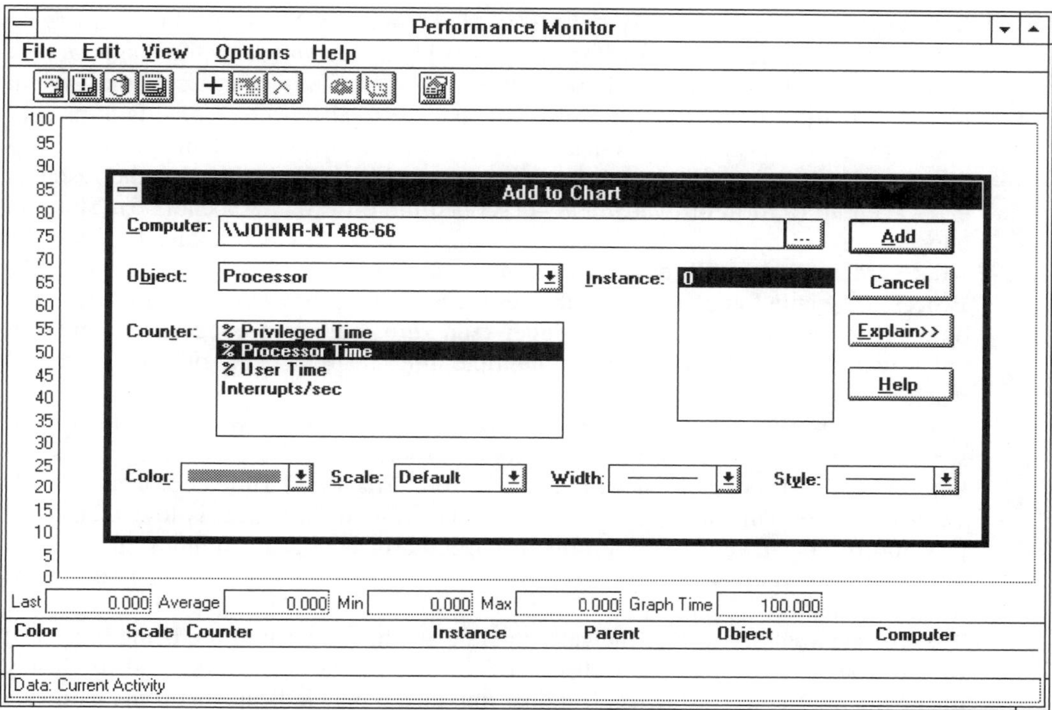

Figure 5.2 Performance Monitor.

The Windows NT Performance Monitor application gives administrators and support personnel the ability to observe, monitor and record data on a wide variety of system (and application software) components.

processors in a scalable processor system, or (2) move the user or server, as the case may be, to a faster CPU.

- **% Total User Time**—This is the percentage of a processor's time expended running user level or application code. If the system is bottlenecked at the CPU and this counter is a high percentage, then it may conceivably be possible to improve performance by changing the way applications are being used on the system. You can consider having in-house vertical applications rewritten in a more efficient way, for instance; or you may want to examine the way a user is operating on the system to see if there is any possibility that some additional efficiency can be achieved.
- **Context Switches/Sec.**—This indicates how frequently Windows NT is performing a *context switch* between one task and another task. By default, Windows NT will switch between tasks several times per second to give each task in a system a chance to run. Should this counter ever become very high, on the order of 1,000 Context

Switches/Sec., then it is likely to indicate that Windows NT is blocking on one or more shared resources in the system, quite possibly a video resource. To diagnose this, observe the % Total Privilege Time and % Total User Time counters of the System object. If both of these are at or near 50% and the total processor time is at or near 100%, then what's happening is that multiple threads within the system are contending for a single shared resource and are doing so with such frequency that the resource can't keep up (a form of *contention*—described more fully in Appendix 5). This can happen, for example, if intensive use is being made of a video application and the video card is not able to keep up with its other resources.

- **Processor Queue Length**—This indicates the number of threads queued for execution on a processor. Sustained values higher than zero indicate a congestion condition under which, as we discussed above, multiple threads are blocking on a single shared resource.
- **System Calls/Sec.**—This indicates the frequency of calls to Windows NT system service routines—not counting the graphical routines. If the preceding values are high, including Processor Queue Length, % Total Privileged Time at or near 50%, % Total Processor Time at or near 100%, but the System Calls/Sec. is low, then in all probability you have a video problem, particularly if you are running graphically intensive applications. See the section on video performance troubleshooting for more information.
- **Total Interrupts/Sec.**—This indicates the rate at which interrupts are being generated by hardware in the system for all processors. This indicator should tend to closely track with the System Calls/Sec. If it does not, then it may indicate that some hardware device is generating an excessive number of interrupts and you should then investigate and attempt to determine whether the device in question is the video card, the network interface card, the hard disk driver, or perhaps some other device, such as the mouse.

Processor Object

Like the System object, the Processor object provides indications of % Privileged Time, % Processor Time, % User Time, and Interrupts/Sec. However, this is done on a per-processor basis, rather than on a systemwide basis. This counter is generally only useful in a symmetrical multiprocessor (SMP) system and then can be used to determine to what degree the individual processors are in balance with one another. All processors in the system should tend, on average, to achieve approximately equal loadings with all processors reporting approximately equal utilization—if this isn't happening, you likely have a problem with one of your processor boards and should investigate further.

Floating Point (FPU) Performance

Unfortunately, Windows NT does not provide a direct counter for floating point operations, which would be useful in determining whether the system is being bogged by floating point

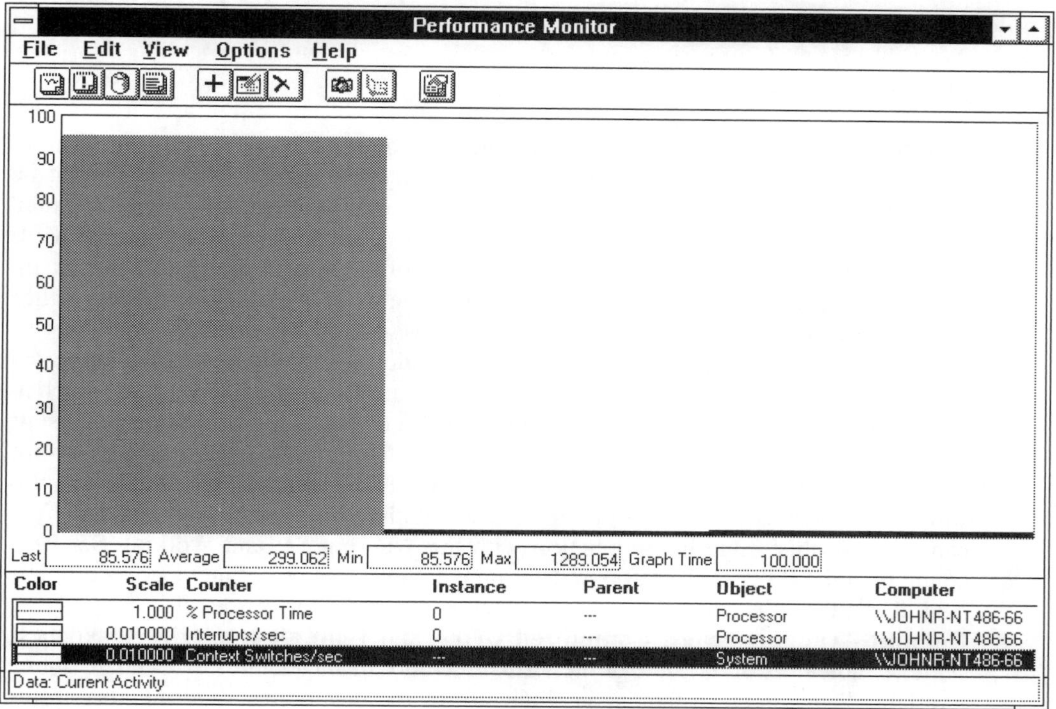

Figure 5.3 Performance Monitor, indicating FPU bogging.

This Performance Monitor display illustrates the "signature" of floating-point bogging—very high % CPU Time, with low Context Switches and Interrupts.

performance when running applications such as Computer Aided Design (CAD). However, in general, if a system is performing an application known to be floating-point intensive, and is indicating a CPU bogging condition (% Processor Time at or near 100%) with no other indication of a bogging condition (such as a high number of System Calls/Sec., high number of Interrupts/Sec., etc.), then the odds are good that the system is floating-point bogged. A typical Performance Monitor trace for such a condition is shown in Figure 5.3.

You should investigate to see whether the system in question does in fact include floating point processor hardware. No 386-based or 486SX series Intel computers have built-in floating point hardware, but all 486DX computers, all Pentium series processors, and most RISC processors will have built-in floating point hardware. If a user is experiencing a CPU bogged condition of this type and is operating on a 386 or a 486SX workstation, you may want to consider moving that user to a 486DX, Pentium, or RISC based workstation to see if the problem clears up.

Memory Tuning

Memory Object

- **Pool Nonpaged Bytes.** This counter measures the total number of bytes in the pool of nonpaged memory. Nonpaged memory is memory that is *reserved* and cannot be paged out into virtual memory (disk space) on demand. In effect, it's the total amount of memory the system is using that must at all times remain in the physical RAM. If this value rises to within 4MB of the total amount of memory in the system (for example, if it rises to over 12MB in a system that contains only 16MB of memory), then performance is compromised.

  Whenever an application is launched from Windows NT, Windows NT temporarily requires a substantial amount of space for buffers and for loading subsystems (such as the 16-bit WOW system for 16-bit applications), etc.—and in an instantaneous state where less than 4MB of nonpaged pool is available Windows NT will begin to "swap" severely in an effort to free up enough memory to get a new application started. In this situation, the best thing to do is provide the user with more memory in the system. You can also use this value in conjunction with the Working Set and Working Set Peak counters of the Process Object(s) to determine the total amount of memory required by a particular user. See the section on the Process Object for further details.
- **Commit Available Bytes**, **Committed Bytes**, and **Commit Limit.** Together these serve as indicators of the state of the virtual memory management subsystem. Commit Available Bytes is an instantaneous indicator of the *available* virtual memory in the system (i.e., virtual memory not being *used* in the system). This value fluctuates with time and is interesting to monitor but does not provide a reliable indicator of total memory available. The Committed Bytes value, on the other hand, is an instantaneous indicator of the *total* amount of virtual memory committed—reserved memory space for which there must either be backing store available within the paging file or which must have space available in the physical memory. Commit Limit is the total amount of space that is available for committing and is generally equal to slightly less than the size of physical memory plus the size of the page file (just slightly less because of memory the system reserves to itself).

  NOTE: If the Committed Bytes counter approaches the Commit Limit, then the system is running out of virtual memory and it will become necessary to expand the page file. You can use this as an indicator to expand the page file *manually*—avoiding an automatic page file expansion and the associated deterioration of system performance.
- **Pages Per Second**—This is an indicator of the total paging traffic in the system—the rate at which memory pages are being swapped between the paging file and physical memory. Systems with lots of physical memory will tend to show a zero value for Pages/Sec. Systems operating with a minimal amount of physical memory (16MB in workstations, 24MB in servers) will generally show zero Pages/Sec. in an idle state but may show paging activity (on the order of 100 Pages/Sec. or less) as applications are opened and closed in the system. Should the Pages/Sec. rise to a sustained value

above 100 Pages/Sec., this will indicate a *thrashing* condition, in which the system has reached a state where the demands made on the virtual memory manager exceed its capacity—indicating that more RAM is needed. Therefore, when the Committed Bytes indicator approaches within 10% of the Commit Limit you should begin watching the Pages/Sec. to see if the system is thrashing—in fact, this seems as good a place as any to take a bit of time out and explore the entire subject of virtual memory in a bit more detail.

Virtual Memory and Swapping

As described in Chapter 1, Windows NT is a virtual memory operating system, meaning that it can employ hard disk space as auxiliary memory to hold information that is not immediately required in RAM. The strategy that Windows NT uses to do this depends upon the operation of several sections of memory known as memory pools in conjunction with the cache manager. To begin with, there is a *nonpaged pool* that stores memory that cannot be paged out to disk—that is, memory required to be immediately on hand in order for Windows NT system components and applications to perform their functions. This memory generally appears to run in a pool of 2- to 3MB in most configurations. There is also a *paged pool* of memory that is pageable and can be swapped to disk but is kept ready to hand for immediate access. This generally will contain the memory pages most frequently requested by system components or applications. Paged pool may vary in size from a few megabytes up to the total capacity of physical memory depending upon the configuration and available free space.

Windows NT also caches disk activity within the virtual memory space, *and can employ up to one-half of the physical memory's space to store disk cache information*. That is, on a 16MB system, up to 8MB will be employed for cache, etc. When the physical memory becomes exhausted—so many applications and system components are running and requesting memory that the system cannot fulfill those requests from within the range of pages available in the Physical Page Pool—the system will begin to *page* less frequently used pages out to hard disk—freeing up these less frequently used pages to fill those requests. This process will continue until the C*ommit Limit* is reached. The Commit Limit specifies the total amount of memory that can be committed—that is, for which data space is required in either the physical memory or the virtual memory paging file—without expanding the paging file. When the Commit Limit is reached, Windows NT will attempt to expand the paging file.

Notice that we have two separate threshold situations involved here where the paging file becomes a consideration. In the first, Windows NT is paging information into the file without the Commit Limit being affected. In this situation disk I/O is *special cased*, in a manner analogous to that used by Windows 3.1 permanent swap file. That is, if you have a 16MB system with 24MB set as the initial size for your paging file, the Commit Limit for the memory system will be about 37MB (24MB plus the physical memory—16MB—less the space reserved for the Paged and Nonpaged Pools that must be retained in physical memory). Until that Commit Limit is reached, Windows NT will perform *special case* I/O—essentially raw reads and writes within the paged file space—a relatively efficient process. Paging will occur but the impact on system performance will tend to be minimal.

When the Commit Limit is reached, however, Windows NT is forced to expand the paging file—and a completely different situation occurs, analogous in many respects to the temporary swap file in Windows 3.1. It is now necessary for Windows NT's system software to carry out *create* operations in an attempt to find more room on the disk. As a result, once the Commit Limit begins to increase, performance becomes abysmal. This a situation to be avoided at all costs, particularly in file servers, because it can rapidly reach a point where the system becomes totally bogged and almost useless. But we haven't quite hit the ultimate limit. That happens when Windows NT either reaches the maximum size of the paging file (set in the Control Panel/System/Virtual Memory) or worse, if Windows NT runs out of physical disk space because application and data files on the disk partition containing the paging file don't leave enough room for the page file to grow to its maximum size.[2]

At this point it becomes impossible for Windows NT to fill the application and system requests for memory and you may expect a series of events, beginning with a "System low on virtual memory" alert, that will escalate through various error messages until the system crashes. This need not happen. When multiple pagefiles are available, Windows NT will distribute paged virtual memory more or less equally across all of them—allowing for more total paging *and* improving performance—provided that each swap file exists on a separate physical disk. Note, however, that creating multiple paging files on a *single* physical disk will slow the system down—pagefile I/O alternates between two separate locations on the same disk, keeping the disk head in constant motion.

The best performance can be achieved if the page file is on a partition or disk by itself; indeed, the ultimate performance can be achieved if a separate controller is available for the page file as this will allow page file operations to occur independently of other disk operations, which is something to consider when setting up large, multivolume file servers.

Why Not Just Add More RAM and Forget about Paging?

You might think that the solution to all these paging problems is simply to add enough RAM to the machine to prevent it from ever carrying out paging operations—on servers particularly. We know from experience that this is probably not a wise strategy where Windows NT is concerned. Windows NT has been designed to be efficient—nay, stingy—in its use of memory resources. It likes to run with just a few megabytes of RAM available as a ready reserve pool for emergency use. It does this in order to maximize disk performance, which in Windows NT is outstanding.

Essentially, the Windows NT cache manager takes over as much as possible of the free physical RAM to use for disk caching. Even on systems with what one would expect to be rather large amounts of memory, e.g., 32MB, it turns out to be relatively easy to force Windows NT to engage in some swapping behavior, particularly during application start. When applications are loaded, Windows NT attempts to load the full binary image of the application in memory and, in doing so, begins to release pages from its pageable pool (with resulting

[2]There is also a rarely encountered condition in which attempting to expand the pagefile will cause a *page fault* which cannot be handled in the cache manager, and the file will not grow *even though physical disk is available*. It is *always* preferable to expand the page file *manually*.

flush operations on the disk cache). This is one reason that first-time users of Windows NT may *think* it's slower than Windows 3.1 (or OS/2 2.1)—it really *is* slower, where application launch is concerned. Steady-state performance of applications after they're launched, however, is quite another matter.

It's not possible to configure Windows NT so it won't engage in this behavior (although it *can* be minimized, by adjusting the Control Panel/Network/Server configuration). As long as sufficient virtual memory is available to handle peak cache loads without exceeding the Commit Limit this doesn't have any significant impact on performance. In fact, it will not be noticed at all unless you have a situation in which applications are continually started and stopped. Applications that just run in a steady state for the most part will be completely unaffected—indeed, they benefit from significantly higher effective disk performance because of the large disk cache size.

The one major performance situation to watch out for is where page file limits are not sufficient and Windows NT starts raising the Commit Limit. The way to avoid this is to run Windows NT systems during a burn-in period for the first few days (or weeks) of operation and observe the Commit Limit and any change in the initial page file size. Once an initial page file size is determined that appears to work (either the page file size set automatically during Windows NT setup has not increased or there has been some increase to a steady state value), we recommend the following: If the page file size has increased over and above the preset size during the burn-in you should reset the Control Panel Initial Page File Size, and increase it by 20%. This will take care of most peak loading situations, give you a little "headroom," and minimize any performance impact due to further pagefile growth. You needn't do this if Windows NT has not expanded the page file during the burn-in period, as it's probably already big enough.

In any case, (after any expansion that may have been necessary), observe the Commit Limit using Performance Monitor. Add 10% to that value and set it as a Performance Monitor alert. This should be done on all servers, and it's advisable on workstations. As an example, if the Commit Limit is 60MB set an alert at 66MB. Make sure, of course, that the maximum page file size is *more* than 66MB, and that there is sufficient free space on the partition containing the page file to store the additional space should it become necessary.

What this will do, essentially, is set a trip wire. When the system begins to expand its paging file, as soon as that 10% threshold is crossed the alert will be transmitted and you'll likely have a chance to react to the problem. You'll want to react *quickly*, particularly if it happens on a server. Expansion of the Commit Limit doesn't indicate an imminent crash, but it does indicate a fairly severe problem that will become *very* severe if you leave it alone.

Paging on Workstations

The situation on workstations is a little different. The most common situation encountered is where a Windows NT workstation over time starts seeing a sufficient load that the page file starts to increase—and an adequately configured system starts subjecting its user to severely frustrating behavior because whenever the user does *anything* the page file grows (with associated thrashing).

Again, the way to anticipate this situation is to set an alert based on a 10% growth in the Commit Limit. This isn't a crisis situation—let's explore how this can happen. Let's say that you have a basic Windows NT workstation outfitted with what would appear up front to be plenty of memory, say 20MB—not the 12MB Microsoft recommends but the 16MB we recommend plus an additional 4MB because the system is being used as a print server or perhaps as a TCP/IP router. Initially, the system will be just fine—its users will be delighted with its performance. Users may be running a suite of applications including MS-Mail, Microsoft Schedule Plus, and two or three additional programs. Initially they are going to employ the system very much the way they would employ a Windows 3.1 or Windows for Workgroups station. That is, users will perform *task-switching* rather than *multitasking* on the system.

MS-Mail and Schedule Plus may be auto-started and minimized but for the most part users will run Word for Windows or Excel for Windows or Power Point. Over time users find that it's much more convenient to start *all* of the applications first thing in the morning, iconize the ones not immediately being used and just work away with the one on top. This works fine, of course, in Windows NT. It is a preemptive multitasking system and the intelligence built into the Virtual Memory Manager is such that the applications that are iconized (and not in use) take up a minimal amount of memory.

At some point, however, your users will find the threshold for the Commit Limit. It doesn't matter how high you set this initial threshold—believe us, they will find it! In fact, there is risk here of a more severe situation. If users *don't* find the Commit Limit, they are likely to run out of disk space on the hard disk; that situation probably deserves to be looked into with some care. Assuming that users find the Commit Limit, they are going to complain of poor performance. Even on a system with 20MB of memory and perhaps a 486/66 or Pentium processor (and heaven knows what else), which you would expect to be an excellent performer, you're going to find that System/% CPU Time is relatively low—but that System/Pages per Second is intermittently hitting a relatively high value (in the hundreds of Pages/Sec. at least) and this is happening pretty much whenever a new application is started, often when an application is closed, etc.

This happens because the *working set* for user applications totals more than the memory available in the system with the page file at its default size. Windows NT then starts expanding the page file. It does this in a very stingy manner, expanding only a little bit at a time, which means it buys just enough room to have the crisis come again ten seconds later. (It would be awfully convenient if the system were designed so that administrators could selectively control the growth of the paging file or cause an alert to be displayed suggesting to users that they might want to expand their paging file or call the administrator.)

Unlike the server situation—where this presages a crisis—for end-users it's probably not an urgent situation. Moreover, it's likely that the Commit Limit problem will grow slowly over time. Since Windows NT workstations can be inspected remotely, you can sit at any workstation, and (using administrative privileges) open a Performance Monitor session on any other user's station. The most desirable approach is probably to log Commit Limit and Working Set sizes for users on an infrequent basis—once a week or so, observe users who are approaching their Commit Limit, and (when time is convenient) expand their page file for them. In this way they will never see the problem. You can also take advantage of this situation to observe the free space availability on the disk that holds the paging file and suggest to users that they might want to move some files around if they're getting themselves into situations where there's not going to be sufficient room should the page file begin to expand. In this way you achieve that ultimate goal of administration that we talked about in Chapter 3: *invisibility*.

Video Performance

The Windows NT Performance Monitor includes no specific video object. It is nonetheless possible to get an *indirect* indication of video activity in the Windows NT system. The most convenient way to do this is with the Process Object—examine the instance called **CSRSS**, and use the **% Processor Time**, **% Privilege Time**, and **% User Time** counters:

- **CSRSS** is a subsystem of the Windows NT Executive that carries out graphical activities on behalf of applications. It contains one thread for each application that employs on-screen graphics, and is generally a reliable indicator of graphical activity. If CSRSS % Processor Time is continually absorbing a very high proportion of the overall system activity—that is, if one observes a high percent of processor time on the system and then traces this high percent processor time to CSRSS (as shown in Figure 5.4),then in all probability your system is being limited by its video bandwidth and a faster video card would improve performance.[3]

Disk Performance

Microsoft recommends monitoring two counter values when attempting to determine disk performance. The first is **Average Disk Sec./Transfer** from the **Logical Disk Object** on any logical disk. The second is **Disk Queue**. Average Disk Sec./Transfer gives a direct measure of disk access speed, although determining a transfer *rate* will also require you to look at the **Average Disk Bytes/Transfer** to estimate the size of the block being transferred. Disk Queue gives a direct indication of the number of disk transfer requests being stored temporarily because the disk is unable to respond to the request. A sustained Disk Queue above one probably indicates that the disk is becoming a bottleneck in the system.

[3] It's possible to demonstrate CSRSS tracking of video performance using an undocumented (but cute) feature of the Free Cell game that's included with all Windows NT systems. To do so, start Performance Monitor and add an entry for % Processor Time in the CSRSS instance of the Process Object. Set the Chart Scale to a maximum of 100%. If you move the mouse you'll observe a high indication on the graph. This is because the mouse is one of many graphical activities. However, you should see no more than a 10% to 20% maximum that settles to zero as mouse movement stops. Now start a Free Cell game, start a New Game, then hold down the Control and Shift keys while hitting the F10 key. A rather interesting alert message will appear. You can select either Abort or Retry and then pick any card and drag it to any empty card slot. The Free Cell game will automatically play to completion—and as it does so you will observe a very high peak in the CSRSS subsystem (because of all the graphic activity as the game automatically plays itself to completion).

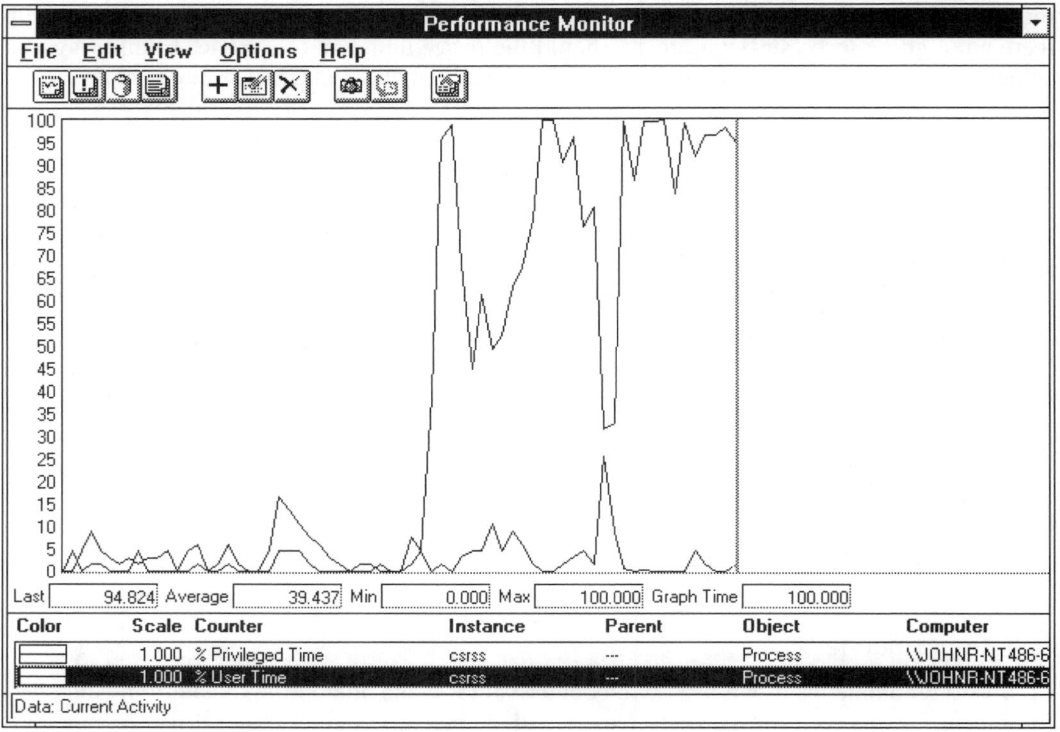

Figure 5.4 Performance Monitor, CSRSS process.

Performance Monitor does not include any counters or objects specific to video performance, but monitoring % User Time and % Privileged Time in the CSRSS process provides a workable substitute (% Privileged Time indicates time spent in the system's internal routines—in this case the low-level graphics component of Win32). This display illustrates a system that's experiencing an extremely heavy video load.

NOTE: *It is not possible to measure any of these values without turning on disk counters. These are turned off by default in Windows NT because the overhead involved in disk performance monitoring will reduce overall disk throughput by 10% to 15%. To turn them on type* **diskperf -y** *at the command line and then restart the system.*

Because disk performance monitoring incurs a 10% to 15% overhead, it should probably not be permanently turned on unless it's absolutely necessary. Disk performance monitoring is probably something that you want to do only during maintenance intervals or when problems are suspected. It might be worth considering leaving it turned on permanently on servers if, in fact, you can determine that a 10% disk performance hit will not materially affect overall responsiveness of the system. It would probably not be wise on workstations.

Logical Disk Drive Object

- The **% Free Space** and **Free Megabytes** counters indicate respectively the percentage of disk space that is not filled and the number of megabytes of disk space that are not filled. If Free Megabytes falls near to or below the space needed to hold the page file at its maximum size, then the system might be unable to grow the paging file and will start giving you "Out of Virtual Memory" indications. In general, it is probably wise to set alerts on Percent Free Space less than 5% on all drives on servers.
- **% Disk Time** indicates the activity of the disk drive including both reads and writes as a percentage of total elapsed time and is a good indicator for excessive disk activity. If this value achieves a sustained level greater than 50% it indicates that the disk is approaching a full duty cycle and may indicate a thrashing condition indicating that some corrective action needs to be taken. You may wish to examine % Free Space on all of the volumes of a server to see how load is being balanced across the disk drives and consider moving files as necessary (particularly in database server applications) to try to equalize load on the drives on the system.

The Physical Disk Drive Object

This provides a set of counters similar to those used for the Logical Disk objects. These will give you information about performance of a physical disk platter but will not give you information that can be broken down by partition and therefore are probably less useful in most circumstances. However, Microsoft does make one interesting recommendation—which is to observe Average Disk Access Time for physical disks. If you have multiple platters available, particularly in a SCSI disk system where the disks could be striped, striping will probably improve disk performance if average disk access time for the physical disk is less than average disk time divided by the number of disks available striped.

With respect to setting alerts on disk performance counters, again, bear in mind that turning disk performance counters on (using the *disperf -y* command syntax) will extract a 10% to 15% performance penalty on disks for which performance monitoring has been enabled. Having said that, on servers where you suspect that disk performance may represent a system bottleneck it might well be advisable to turn on disk performance monitoring as a debugging aid and then set an alert on the Disk Queue value in the Logical Disk Object for any disks on which you suspect that performance may be a problem. Set the alert to trip if a sustained value greater than one is achieved. This will indicate that disk transfer requests are being received faster than the disk can accommodate them. Monitoring this value might indicate when a particular disk is accessed more frequently than the physical disk hardware can sustain, in which case you should consider moving files around on the disk or replacing the existing disk setup with a stripe set.

You should also be concerned if you see a Disk Queue higher than one and cannot account for it. If the level of traffic is such that the disk ought to be able to handle it, then consider monitoring Average Disk Bytes/Transfer and Average Disk Sec./Transfer. You can use this information by dividing Average Disk Bytes/Transfer by Average Disk Sec./Transfer. You will get a *transfer rate* in Bytes/Sec. Comparing this with the specifications for the disk drive may give you an indication if a disk drive is starting to lose performance due to wear, fragmentation, and so on. Periodic monitoring of this value and historical logging of this information on a month-to-month basis may give some indication when a disk needs to be reformatted to eliminate fragmentation or when the disk hardware is beginning to have problems.

Logical Disk Object

Two counters are available for your use *without* turning the disperf-y command on. These are **Free Megabytes**, a direct indication of free space on the disk, and **% Free Space**, which is simply the ratio of free space to the size of the disk. You may wish to set alerts on either or both of these, either specifying an alert when % Free Space falls below 5% or when Free Megabytes falls below some arbitrary value. This will give you an emergency indication when the disk is running out of space and give you an opportunity to react by moving files around. These counters can be used in conjunction with the memory counters discussed above to avoid problems when an expanding paging file runs into the brick wall of absence of disk space to expand into on disks that contain page file data structures.

You definitely want to set these alerts on file servers. You may want to set these alerts on the page file drives on workstations as well, as this will give you an advance indication of when you are heading for page file trouble and allow you to take appropriate steps before system errors occur.

Network Performance

Up to now we've been concerned with monitoring other parts of the system to detect and overcome system bottlenecks, but the plain fact is that this is a book about networking and, as any network administrator knows, the odds are much higher that you will experience performance bottlenecks on your network than on almost any other component. The classic approach to this problem (other than guesswork, jiggling the network cables, and so forth—always a good idea if you're having a network problem on a workstation), is to break out the Protocol Analyzer—and this remains the preferred method of dealing with a wide variety of network problems. In a Windows NT system it is the only way to deal with performance detection involving protocols that do not use NetBIOS (such as TCP/IP except where NetBIOS on TCP/IP-NBT is in use, DLC, and NetWare IPX).

However, where NetBIOS *is* used (NetBEUI, NBT, NetBIOS on the NWLink protocol), Windows NT actually provides built-in performance tuning that will give you almost (but not quite!) the same information you'd get from a protocol analyzer. You can't get down into the wire and actually look at the bits in the packets, but you can look at data rates, and collisions—you can, in fact, perform a sophisticated level of system performance monitoring in the software itself. There are also performance counters that can be used in monitoring performance of some of the critical software components including the redirector, the LAN Manager workstation, and the LAN Manager server. We'll examine all of those in what follows.

NetBEUI Object

- The two basic counters you can monitor to determine NetBEUI throughput on a system are Bytes Total/Sec. and Packets/Sec., which represent respectively the total data transfer for all packets containing data and the total number of packets transmitted. You can work out the packet size by dividing an average of the Bytes Total/Sec. by Packets/Sec., and if that number begins to change (particularly if it begins to drop), it probably indicates a *collision* condition where you have a large number of packets that don't contain any data.
- From a performance tuning standpoint, there are two additional values you might wish to monitor, particularly if you are seeing slow traffic on a heavily loaded network. The **Piggyback Ack Time-Out** counter indicates timeouts on acknowledgments that are piggybacked onto data packets to the remote system. If this value rises to above 10% of the total number of packets sent (monitored by the Packets/Sec. counter), then you may want to consider increasing the DefaultT1Timeout value in the HKEY_LOCAL_MACHINE/SYSTEM/CurrentControlSet/Services/NBF/Parameters section of the registry.
- Similarly, you may also need to monitor **Expirations Ack,** which will indicate the number of NetBEUI acknowledgments that have expired. If this is greater than 10% of the packets transmitted you will need to decrease the DefaultT2Timeout value located in the same section of the registry mentioned above. Note that this value must always be less than T1. Finally, if you're increasing those other values, consider increasing the DefaultTiTimeout, which is the wait time before polling an inactive host. This will avoid having repeated polling packets sent before a slow host can respond to the initial packet.

Redirector Object

- As you will recall from Chapter 1, the Redirector is a software component in the Windows NT Executive that works with the I/O Manager to determine when data transfers need to be handled by local resources (such as hard disks) and when they need to be handled over the network. It is, therefore, the component that sits nearest the center of the Windows NT network and is a good place to look for network bottlenecks. Several parameters can be monitored here that may prove useful in problem detection and network tuning. The first of these is Redirector Current Commands. This indicates the number of commands queued and it should never be more than one for every network card in the system. If it rises and stays at a number greater than one for any network card in the system then there is a bottleneck either in the Redirector software, or (more probably) in the network hardware.

  The Redirector can be a bottleneck if the network is slow or if you're getting slow response to a server, in which case you may need to increase the **Maximum-**

NumberOfCommands parameter in the HKEY_LOCAL_MACHINE/SYSTEM/CurrentControlSet/Services/LanmanWorkstation/Parameters section of the registry. This defaults to a value of 50. It can be raised as high as 255 and may need to be raised (obviously) if the Current Commands counter is within 10% of 50. On the other hand, again, this invariably indicates that there is a problem somewhere in the system, otherwise the Redirector would not be queuing commands to that extent. A better solution, at this point, will be to determine *why* the commands are being queued. Either the network itself is bogged (which can be checked by a counter we'll mention shortly), or the *server* performance is extremely slow for some reason—and you will want to investigate the cause.

- The **Network Errors/Sec.** counter indicates the number of serious network errors (generally collisions) being experienced in the system. You can look for further information in the System Error Log (using Event Viewer) because there will be an entry every time a network error is generated. In any case, if Network Errors/Sec. rise above zero on a well-behaved network (or above some small background value in a heavily loaded network), you've got a problem somewhere in the subnet and you'll need to trace it down.
- The **Reads Denied/Sec.** and **Writes Denied/Sec.** counters indicate that a remote server's refusing to accommodate requests for *raw* reads or writes. Raw reads or writes are a technique that Windows NT uses to increase data rates in large data transfers. Instead of transferring packet frame information for each data packet, a *virtual circuit* connection is opened and a whole stream of raw data packets is transmitted, maximizing the throughput rate for the duration of the virtual circuit connection. If the server is running low on memory it may refuse to participate in this kind of connection because it cannot allocate the necessary local buffer space. Therefore, the Reads Denied/Sec. and Writes Denied/Sec. counters are a direct indication of memory problems at the file server.

  Obviously, the preferred solution to this problem is to increase the memory in the server (or at any rate, examine the file server and determine why it is running so low on memory that it's refusing to allocate space for raw reads and writes). If it is impossible to fix this problem promptly (i.e.: you haven't got extra RAM to put in the server, or cannot immediately take it off-line), you can set the **UseRawReads** and **UseRawWrites** parameters of the LANManWorkstation entry in the system registry to False. This will stop futile attempts to use raw I/O, thus increasing throughput. Again, however, the preferred way to deal with this is to correct the problem at the server.
- One further registry setting that might help in situations where networks are heavily used is to set the **UseNTCaching** parameter in the LanmanWorkstation registry subkey to True. This will cache I/O requests during file writes, reducing the number of requests transmitted across the network. In effect, repeated writes will be cached locally and then a single request for transfer will transmit all the information across the network. When a network is heavily loaded this may improve performance.

Server Object

All Windows NT systems are to some extent servers, irrespective of whether they are dedicated as file servers or whether they are functioning as desktop workstations. And operations in which services are provided, resources are shared, etc., are managed by the Server Object. This can be monitored from the Server Object in the Performance Monitor. Appropriate counters and indicated performance are as follows:

- **Bytes Total/Sec.** This value provides an overall indication of how busy the server is and should probably be monitored on file servers because an increase on this over time indicates a need to expand server memory (or perhaps even to consider upgrading your server hardware).
- **Errors Access Permissions, Errors Granted Access, Errors Logon**. All of these indicate security problems. These may be as innocuous as someone forgetting his password but *could* indicate that someone's attempting to "hack" your system. In particular, a high value for Errors Logon may indicate that someone is trying to hack the system using a password-cracking program. You will want to examine the system security log (using Event Viewer) and you may want to enable auditing (from User Manager) to track what's happening.
- **Errors System** will indicate the number of unexpected system errors that the server is experiencing and this will indicate that there is a problem with the server. You should probably, at this point, investigate the server to see whether it is running out of memory and the system error log to see if you have a hardware problem. If neither is indicated, then call a Microsoft-certified professional technician, or Microsoft technical support.
- The **Pool Nonpaged Bytes** and **Pool Nonpaged Failures** counters will give an indication of the physical memory situation with respect to the Server Object. Pool Nonpaged Bytes indicates the amount of nonpageable physical memory that the server is using while Pool Nonpaged Failures will indicate the number of times it attempts to allocate memory that is not available. The latter indicates that the physical memory in the system is too small. One thing you can do in an attempt to recover from this is to reset the Server Object in the Control Panel/Network settings and consider using the Minimize Memory Used optimization setting. However, this will reduce system performance. It may prove inadequate in a situation where you are attempting to establish connections with more than five systems. Increasing the physical memory is always the preferred solution to this problem.
- The **Pool Paged Bytes** and **Pool Paged Failures** parameters give a similar indication for pageable memory used by the server. In this case, the solution to the problem may be to increase the pagefile size on the system (set in Control Panel/System Virtual Memory).
- The **Sessions Errored Out** and **Sessions Timed Out** parameters give an indication of the number of times that network errors are causing a session to be disconnected or, alternatively, the number of times that an administrative auto-disconnect setting (from User Manager) is disconnecting users with idle connections. The latter may be

a useful thing to do on a system with a heavily loaded server that's experiencing memory problems.

- Finally, the **Work Item Shortages** counter indicates that you need to tune the InitWorkItems or MaxWorkItems parameters in the LANmanServer Object of the System Registry. If you are seeing a work item shortage only during system start, then probably the InitWorkItems number needs to be increased. If not, it's the MaxWorkItems number that needs to be increased.
- You can select any one of four optimization settings for Server operation (from Control Panel/Network Settings, select Server from the list of installed software, and then click on Configure, as illustrated in Figure 5.5). The four optimization settings are **Minimize Memory Used**, **Balance**, **Maximize Throughput for File Sharing**, and **Maximize Throughput for Network Applications**. The first setting is obvious; it is designed for a maximum of five network connections and is suitable only for lightly used workstations. This setting should never be selected on a file server (unless it's doing local file services on a *very* small—5 clients or less—network). The Balance setting allocates memory initially for up to ten sessions and is primarily useful for small servers or for Windows NT workstations providing local ad hoc-file sharing or functioning as print servers. Maximize Throughput for File Sharing allocates memory initially for up to 128 connections and is the basic setting for Windows NT Advanced Servers. Maximize Throughput for Network Applications detunes the Windows NT Virtual Memory System to be less aggressive in reserving physical memory to provide a buffer for application launch. This reduces swapping in systems and is a good choice for servers that primarily run network applications (such as SQL server). Indeed, this is probably the *optimal* setting for Advanced Server installations that have adequate memory (greater than 32MB).

A Final Word about Performance Tuning, Logging, and Maintenance History

The built-in tools (such as Performance Monitor and the configuration Registry Editor) in Windows NT are quite powerful and can make life much easier for a support professional who needs to maintain multiple servers and workstations. They can also, however, lead you into making a grave mistake. It's all too easy to install a Windows NT system, conduct some initial performance tuning, and then forget about it until something breaks, at which point one goes back to do the performance tuning and is left with no more information than that just described and that provided in the Microsoft documentation.

Whenever a server is put in you should carry out an initial performance tuning. You should also write down the performance results you eventually achieve in a *performance history*. This can either be a log document that is kept on the server (although if it is in electronic form you should keep a copy somewhere else, because if the server goes down you want to still be able to access the maintenance information), or it can be a separate physical record.

The point of the maintenance history is that the next time you need to conduct a performance tuning or routine check on the system, you have a *base of comparison*. That is, you know what the system performance was when you conducted the initial tuning and you know

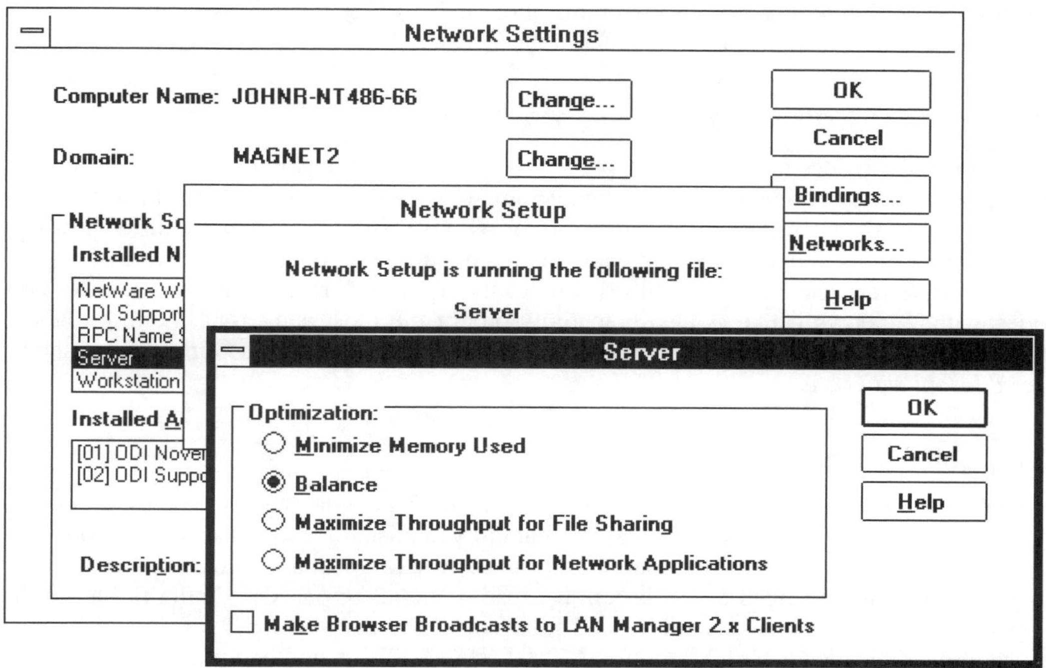

Figure 5.5 Server Object in Control Panel/Network.

The Server Configuration dialog, shown here, allows you to control the memory optimization settings of Windows NT's built-in network services. (The effects of the four settings are described in the text.) This dialog is reached from Control Panel/Network Settings, by selecting the Server Object and clicking the Configure... button.

how it differs when you look at it later. This can be enormously valuable in detecting problems. A routine performance tune-up once per month, for example, is probably a good idea. Values for basic performance criteria such as Nonpaged Pool and Paged Pool sizes from the Memory Object, Total Processor Time from the System Object, Logical Disk Available Space, Free Space, % Free Space, Average Disk Bytes/Transfer, Disk Queue and Average Disk Sec./Transfer, Netbeui Bytes Total/Sec. and Packets/Sec., etc. will make it possible when comparing these values to identify when something is going on with the system that's going to need to be corrected.

For example, if you find that the Nonpaged Pool is rising continuously you know that eventually you're going to have to increase the physical memory in the system. If you find that the Paged Pool is rising consistently, you might need to expand the size of the paging file, consider adding more virtual memory to the system, consider distributing the paging file over multiple disks to improve performance, and so on. Use your common sense. Keep a record of this information; look at it periodically, think about it. That way you will not have to resort to using the troubleshooting information later in this chapter.

Windows NT Configuration Registry

Windows NT provides an advanced approach to configuration tracking and maintenance that can be an absolute godsend to system administrators. This approach is mediated through a special tool called the Configuration Registry Editor (REGEDT32.EXE), which is a full-featured software tool for the examination and manipulation of configuration information.

WARNING: The Registry Editor is one of the most powerful administrative tools provided with Windows NT. It is also potentially one of the most dangerous. Editing registry entries and making changes to the registry blindly may render the system completely unstable. *Use this tool with care.*

The Configuration Problem

How many times have you been faced with this problem?: A Windows user comes to you and says, "My system won't work." You say, "What did you change?" Your user says, "Nothing!" You examine the system and find that it won't boot. You know that however sincere the user may be, *something* changed in the system because it booted before. On talking further to the user you find that he or she recently added some software, removed some software, and in all probability edited the CONFIG.SYS file, AUTOEXEC.BAT file, and/or any of the dozen or so *.INI files in the Windows\SYSTEM directory (or the PROTOCOL.INI file on a Windows for Workgroups or LAN Manager system). You are now faced with the nightmare of system administrators the world over—trying to correct configuration problems in the absence of any backup information at all. The odds are good that the solution of the problem will be to reinstall Windows, reinstall networking, reinstall applications, in any case to reinstall something, because there really isn't anything else you can do.

Windows NT attempts to solve this problem with a *configuration registry*—a true database organized as a multiple tree structure and maintained individually on every Windows NT server or workstation. This database contains all (well, in theory *all*, in practice *most*) of the information that is contained in the AUTOEXEC.BAT, CONFIG.SYS, and *.INI files of Windows systems or in the enormous CONFIG.SYS file of an OS/2 system, or in the PROTOCOL.INI file of a LAN Manager system. Furthermore, the data is inherently backed up—multiple copies are maintained, and a special tool is provided for manipulating the data, which, among other things, organizes the data in a logical structure and makes it possible to access the data remotely, a dream come true for many system administrators. This tool is called the Configuration Registry Editor (REGEDT32.EXE, or "Regedit").

The Bad News

The availability of a centralized configuration database and a proper tool for managing it is a dream come true for system administrators—up to a point. Unfortunately, the current implementation of the Registry Editor is less than perfect. It looks and behaves much like File

Manager—neither the best nor the worst thing that one could think of to use as a model—but its most unfortunate feature is that (much like the various *.ini files it replaces) the Registry continues the system management tradition of providing configuration information in the form of thousands of incomprehensible key values that are not documented anywhere.[4] This is extremely frustrating and potentially dangerous. It means that when you first examine the Registry you need to be very careful not to change anything—you're going to find if you do that it's almost impossible to get the initial value back because there's no place to go look it up. It also means that finding the appropriate values to modify in a system is difficult.

Configuration Registry Structure

As mentioned above, the Configuration Registry is organized as a multiple tree database. This is stored in such a manner that it is fully backed up in a system, as we will see. Changes to the Registry are made through a Registry Editor that enforces a high degree of *atomicity* in the database—you are guaranteed to see either an old or a new value for any registry key. You will never see a mixture of an old and new value even if the system crash occurs. That's the good news.

The bad news is that because of the use of a custom editor the data is stored in a binary file format. It cannot be edited using other tools;[5] you will have to use the system Registry Editor provided by Microsoft until third-party products appear that use the Win32 registry API functions. This is unfortunate because the Registry Editor provided is in no respect self-documenting.[6]

Physical Data Structure

Physically the Registry is organized as a set of files stored in the WINNT (or WINDOWS) \SYSTEM32\CONFIG directory on the boot volume of every Windows NT system. If you examine this directory you will see files named *system, software, default, system.alt, security, sam*, and *userdef*. Each of these files corresponds to a logical tree structure in the Registry Editor, as we will see in a moment. If you attempt to examine any of these files either by typing them out or by examining them in a bitwise editor, you will quickly find that they are incomprehensible because the data is stored in binary format. There is, therefore, currently no alternative to the use of the Registry Editor provided with Windows NT.

With backup of the registry information you should note that the system.alt file contains a complete alternate copy of the system file, which the system will employ automatically in the event that the System Registry file is corrupted. One could conceivably back up the Registry files manually and attempt restoration of an old Registry in the event that system

[4]Except in the Windows NT Resource Kit, Volume One, and the associated help file.

[5]Although Microsoft has also provided an unsupported command line tool, REGINI.EXE, which can be used to update the registry from a command script. REGINI.EXE is covered in more detail later in this chapter.

[6]The Windows NT Resource kit, however, includes a helpfile that fully documents all registry entries.

problems occur. This is probably a questionable procedure given that in the event that the Registry is corrupted you're not going to have a way to access the system to restore the files.

Fortunately, Windows NT goes to considerable lengths to make sure that the Registry doesn't become corrupted and it provides *last known good* configuration recovery during system start. So you will usually be able to recover at least to a previously known state in a system reboot (provided, of course, that nobody has been making dramatic Registry changes in an ill-thought-out manner).

Logical Data Structure

Because you are invariably going to access the Registry through the Registry Editor, the data structure of most importance is the logical data structure that you see when observing the Registry Editor. This is organized at the top level into four registry *keys*, that is, four entry points into the four major tree structures that contain the system Registry information. HKEY_LOCAL_MACHINE is the tree structure describing the hardware and software configuration of the machine whose Registry Editor you are running or whose Registry you are examining remotely. HKEY_CURRENT_USER is the Registry information applying to the currently logged in user of the system. HKEY_CLASSES_ROOT duplicates the OLE object class information stored in the Registry used by the Windows File Manager; which can, in fact, be more easily manipulated using the Windows File Manager Registry (REGEDIT.EXE). If that seems confusing to you, it does to me too. HKEY_USERS maintains the list of users in the local machine's local login database and the security identification number (SID) for each user along with the program groups, control panel settings, environment variables, and so forth associated with each user's login.

Of these, the most useful for system maintenance is HKEY_LOCAL_MACHINE, which contains, again, the actual description of the system and the settings that would formerly have been found in CONFIG.SYS, AUTOEXEC.BAT or *.INI files. This is the Registry key with which we are going to be most concerned in this chapter.

The HKEY_LOCAL_MACHINE Key

Starting from the HKEY_LOCAL_MACHINE entry there are five sub-keys. These are HARDWARE, Security Account Manager (SAM), SECURITY, SOFTWARE, and SYSTEM. Of these, the SAM and SECURITY sections are of interest to us only in knowing that they exist. They cannot be accessed except through the appropriate APIs (in the case of SAM; the SECURITY entry cannot be accessed at all). These registry entries contain the security information used to validate logons into the system and to validate privileges and user access rights. They cannot be edited manually—at least not with the present Registry Editor.

The HARDWARE key contains a description of the system, which is updated every time the system restarts. This is done using a *hardware recognizer*—one component of the Windows NT boot process. Examining the HARDWARE key you'll find sub-keys for DESCRIPTION, DEVICEMAP, and RESOURCEMAP. A sub-key of the DESCRIPTION will be System—and this will contain information about the central processor (or processors), the various adapters in the system, etc. The DEVICEMAP sub-key will contain a list of the I/O devices in the system, as will the RESOURCEMAP sub-key. This information is used by the various Windows NT system software components, such as the network components and the Control Panel, which will examine the HARDWARE key in the Registry to identify any or all network cards in the system and test their settings. It can be used by an administrator to examine what hardware is in the system and the status of the hardware, but obviously it can't be changed (other than by changing the hardware and restarting the computer).

The SOFTWARE sub-key contains, first of all, the sub-key called Classes, which duplicates the software class associations used by File Manager; that is, it associates a three-letter file extension with a program. This is followed by a Program Groups sub-key listing common groups that apply systemwide. There will also be sub-keys for each vendor that supplies software to the system. In Windows NT systems today you are certain to find a sub-key called Microsoft, and there is a small probability that you will see sub-keys such as Lotus and Borland in the future. (If you have the NetWare Requester for Windows NT installed, for instance, you'll see a Novell sub-key.)

In the event that a vendor employs this technique, within each vendor sub-key you will see sub-keys for particular products and within those product sub-keys, sub-sub-keys for versions of the products and within those sub-sub-keys you might find information about the product, product settings, etc. From an administrator's point of view, the value of this information lies solely in the fact that it provides a central resource for determining the versions of software currently installed in the system. You can examine the SOFTWARE entries for each vendor and if you click, for example, on the LAN Man Server entry under Microsoft you'll see a sub-key called Current Version. Clicking on that will list description and installation date, major version, minor version, etc. For instance, we know that we are looking at LAN Man Server version 3.1 with an installation date.

In any case this could be used (and over time will be used) by software such as Microsoft's forthcoming Hermes configuration maintenance tool to automatically track and update software versions across the network. The SOFTWARE key will also contain a Secure sub-key used to identify and control secure programs, and a Windows 3.1 migration sub-key. This sub-key will indicate the status of any migration information for systems providing dual boot between Windows 3.1 and Windows NT that have been upgraded from a Windows 3.1 or Windows for Workgroups installation to a Windows NT installation. After the SOFTWARE sub-key, there is only one more sub-key of HKEY_LOCAL_MACHINE, the SYSTEM sub-key. This is the one that contains practically everything of interest to a support professional.

The SYSTEM Sub-key

Opening the SYSTEM sub-key we find a number of sub-sub-keys. The most important are the *ControlSets*: CurrentControlSet, ControlSet001, and ControlSet002. A ControlSet is a tree structure containing information on all of the main services of a Windows NT system, including parameter settings. The system maintains a CurrentControlSet, which is the one currently being used in the system, and two fall-back copies representing previous configurations. During shutdown the CurrentControlSet will be copied into ControlSet001, so that always contains the ControlSet in use when the system was last shut down; that, in turn, replaces ControlSet002 during system start if the system starts correctly. In the event that the system fails to start correctly, an attempt will be made to start using the earlier configuration. You could also have the option of doing this manually using the *last known good configuration* menu, which comes up during a Windows NT system start. This feature alone is immensely valuable to system professionals because it means the system automatically protects users from themselves. If you have a system that starts to misbehave, there is a very good chance that by reverting to one of the two last known good configurations you will be able to recover.

The Select sub-key of the SYSTEM key tells you which of the Control Sets is in use. Examining this you'll see entries for Current, Default, Failed, and LastKnownGood, which (by default on a system operating normally) will have a Current value of one, Default value of one, LastKnownGood value of two, and a Failed value of zero. In the event that a configuration corruption has been detected during startup the Failed value will rise and the system will attempt to use the last known good entry as the current entry instead of using the default entry.

The Setup sub-key of the SYSTEM key contains information about the Window NT system setup that was performed when the system was installed. This includes the network card, the type of setup performed, and the setup command line employed. There is an entry for system setup in progress. If you ever examine this and it is other than zero something has gone dreadfully wrong and it will indicate the path to the system setup files. The disk sub-key to the SYSTEM key contains a basic set of information about the disks in the system. But again, the most important information from a support professional's point of view is the information contained in CurrentControlSet, which we will examine next.

The CurrentControlSet Key

CurrentControlSet contains two sub-keys, the first called control and the second called services. The services sub-key refers to particular subsystems or hardware devices within the Windows NT system, each subsystem or hardware component having a sub-key within the services key; within that sub-key the linkage of the subsystem to other parameters appears in a sub-key, and there may be a parameters sub-key that will have any user-stable parameters for the component. Some sub-keys will also have an auto-tuned parameters key associated with them, which will incorporate parameters dynamically tuned by the component itself.

The Control sub-key, on the other hand, contains information such as the load order for the device drivers and services (in the GroupOrderList and ServiceGroupOrder sub-sub-keys), much of the Control Panel and Setup data, etc. This will rarely be edited directly by an end-user or administrator, but will simply reflect the settings set for the computer using other tools. From an administrator's standpoint it is the services sub-key, finally, that contains the parts that are a matter of concern.

The Services Sub-Key

As mentioned above, the services sub-key contains, in turn, key entries (or subtrees) for each software subsystem or hardware component that is part of the Windows NT system under inspection. Each key entry, in turn, can contain sub-keys for auto-tune parameters, linkages to other subsystems, parameters, and perhaps security information. Of these the most immediately interesting is the parameter sub-key, which lets you control certain features of the system. Perhaps an example will make this clear.

If you start the Registry Editor (by typing REGEDT32 from the command line) you will see the Registry Editor display containing within it the four windows containing the four Registry keys. Select the one called HKEY_LOCAL_MACHINE and double click the HKEY_LOCAL_MACHINE key entry to list its sub-keys; double-click the SYSTEM sub-key; double-click the CurrentControlSet sub-key; double click the Services sub-key. This will give you a list of all of the services and hardware components in the system. If you now double-click on the Browser sub-key, you'll see Parameters, Linkage and Security. Double-clicking on Linkage will show a Disabled sub-key which, in turn, is empty. Double-clicking on Parameters will give you a list of parameters for the sub-key.

It should be noted that this list is not necessarily complete, and this is one of the problems with the Registry as it currently exists. It's possible for a parameters entry in a sub-key entry for a component to be empty. This does not mean that there aren't any parameters. It means that the component is using the default parameters, whatever those might be.

On the Windows NT Advanced Server system we're inspecting as we write this, the Parameters for Browser are: IsDomainMaster, which is a parameter of type REG_SZ (a string data type) set to False; and the parameter MaintainServerList, which is again of type REG_SZ and is set to Yes. Possible values for **IsDomainMaster** would be True and for **Maintain-ServerList** would be No. These settings, in fact, determine the operation of the system browser—the component that determines the response to a *net view* command or to clicking to the Connect Net Drive icon in File Manager. **ThisIsDomainMaster** determines whether the system in question stores the *browse list*—the list of systems that can be accessed on the local workgroup or domain.

In this case—despite the fact that the system in question is primary domain control for the Windows NT Advanced Server logon domain in question—it is *not* the domain browse-master.[7] In fact, one of the workstations on the system is functioning as browsemaster. However, because **MaintainServerList** is set to **Yes** the system does maintain a list of the available systems and can act as fallback to the browsemaster in the event that the Browse Master does not respond to a browse request from other workstations. (If none of this makes sense, see the section on browsing in Chapter 8.)

To edit any of these entries, for example the **IsBrowseMaster** entry, it is necessary only to double-click on it. An editor will then appear. Since these entries are of the type REG_SZ the String Editor will appear, which will allow you to type in a character string. Again, at this point we have one of the unfortunate problems with the Registry database. Obviously only certain strings will provide acceptable entries for string data types, yet there's nothing to indicate how a string should or should not be typed. In fact, the TRUE and FALSE values are uppercased, yes and no values are lowercased. You must find this kind of information by examination (for that matter, as this is written, it is not certain whether the choice of case is even significant—it may not be).

---

[7]Normally it would be—in Advanced Server domains, the Primary Domain Controller is initially set up as the Browse Master for the domain—because it is (presumably) the most reliable and available system in the domain.

Other data types are REG_DWORD, the double word data type, which contains a 32-bit binary value. Double-clicking on one of these, such as the LMAnnounce parameter in the LAN Man server sub-key, you will be presented with a Dword Editor, which will show the data in question in your choice of a binary, decimal, or hexadecimal representation. This can be of some use to you in setting a particular value because you can type it in using the most convenient form. Again, there is no explanation of what the acceptable values are. The **LMAnnounce** value, in fact, has legal values of zero or one, a one indicating that the system is to perform LAN Manager 2.x-compatible system announcements and a zero indicating that it is not. Fortunately, as with most entries in the system sub-key, it is not necessary to edit this value from the Registry Editor. You can edit the value, in fact, by using the Control Panel/Network Settings, selecting the Server from the list of installed network software, and clicking the Configure button. You will then see a screen offering a choice of four possible optimizations, and a checkbox for Make Browser Broadcasts. Checking this box and clicking OK will change the Registry value from zero to one—and if you return to the Registry Editor, you'll see, in fact, it updates itself and the **LMAnnounce** value will now be set to 0x1 as type REG_DWORD.

You will also notice a **Size** value in the LAN Man server sub-key. Size, which is a REG_DWORD, represents which of the four possible server optimization values has been selected from the Control Panel. Since the four possible values are one through four, it is obvious that a value of zero or five, for instance, would be illegal—yet there is nothing in the Registry Editor that would indicate this.

Why Go On about the Limitations of the Parameter Settings?

Why do we keep harping on this? Because it's *dangerous* to edit settings in the Registry Editor! You should *never* do this if there is an alternative. *Do not* change the LMAnnounce setting with the Registry Editor—change it from the Control Panel. *Do not* change the server size from the Registry Editor—change it from the Control Panel. Whenever you examine a setting in the Registry Editor and consider changing it, try to find an alternative way to change it first. And these ways are usually available in one or the other of the Control Panel components on a Windows NT system.

In my opinion, there really *ought* to be a button associated with the Registry Editor that would examine the LMAnnounce parameter and tell you that it can be changed in Control Panel/Network Settings. And since that way of changing it is available, the ability to edit it directly ought to be disabled. There are, of course, circumstances in which you have no choice.

The registry also allows you to configure systems *remotely.* From the Registry Menu of the Registry Editor, you can perform a Select Computer, select another Windows NT server or workstation on the network, and edit that computer's Registry. If you want to set the LMAnnounce parameter remotely, that's the only way to do it. But this is something that must be done with extreme care—when you use the Registry Editor to make a parameter change, you run the risk of typing an illegal parameter, or deleting a value and not being able to remember what it is. Possibly the worst thing that you could do would be to delete a value, then wish to reestablish it, and reestablish the wrong type.

Suppose, for example, we delete the LMAnnounce parameter. Blindly looking at the Registry Editor and thinking about the LMAnnounce parameter—remembering that it has only two possible states, on or off—we might very well tend to restore it as LMAnnounce type REG_SZ with a value of True or False. That would not work properly. Worse, it might cause the browser to malfunction, rendering the system unstable. To repeat: *Do not make parameter changes using the Registry unless you have no alternative.*

Registry Value Types

The types of entries that can be accepted in a Registry value include the following:

- **REG_DWORD** is a double word value that can be represented as a decimal, hexadecimal, or binary number. By default, when displayed in the Registry it will be in hexadecimal format.
- **REG_SZ** is a Registry string value and this will be a data string.
- **REG_EXPANDSZ** is a special string type used when you need to include environment variables within the string. For example, a legal REG_EXPANDSZ could contain the value %system root%/SYSTEM32/whatever. The %system root% environment variable will be expanded to the appropriate directory path at the time that the string is evaluated.
- **REG_MULTI_SZ** is a multiple string type. Double clicking on a REG_MULTI_SZ value will bring up a multistring editor with scroll bars, allowing you to enter multiple strings with one string on each line in the editor.
- Binary data is also supported in the Registry. This is represented as **REG_BINARY** and the Binary Editor is necessary to edit it. Binary Editor can also be used to edit other types. It provides a bit-by-bit representation of the data similar to that used by the Dword Editor with the binary type selected. You can use the Binary String Dword and Multi-string options under the Edit Menu in the Registry to select whether the Binary String Dword or Multi-string Editor is used with a particular Registry entry, and all Registry entries are, in fact, 32-bit entries. Registry Names are not case sensitive, but they do preserve case and they are unicode compatible.

Registry Limits

One limitation of the current Windows NT Registry implementation is that it does not support *quotas*. That is, users and software applications and systems are not limited on what information can be entered into the Registry. This may change in future versions of Windows NT—and one hopes so because one would not wish to exceed a system limit by adding and updating Registry information—and in fact there are some limits. Value entries in the Registry database cannot contain more than one megabyte of information and the total size of the Registry is limited to 32MB. As a practical matter, this is far beyond the size that ordinary Registry entries would see. Normal entries in a small server will be more on the order of one to two megabytes, although this will expand dramatically as the number of users is increased.

One Last Time

Finally, a reminder: The Registry is an extremely powerful tool. In a sense you can compare it to a nuclear reactor. It's tremendously powerful and tremendously useful when properly controlled. But if you get in there and meddle around blindly you are going to mess up your system beyond repair. Treat it with care.

Troubleshooting Hit List

In any system as complex as Windows NT a broad range of errors and problems can occur. As we note in Appendix 6, the potential for errors increases enormously when the system is networked. So it's impossible for us to present a comprehensive list of the errors you are likely to encounter and directions for fixing them. Having said that, there are certain errors more likely to occur than others. What we present are some of the most frequently encountered errors with suggestions about how to troubleshoot them and fix them.[8] We've arranged them by general category.

Failure to Boot

In general, when a Windows NT system that has otherwise operated correctly suddenly refuses to boot (or recover from a reboot), you have to expect that one of two things has happened. Either there was a major hardware failure or something has changed in the configuration. Major hardware failures or boot problems that occur when a system is first created are generally of the type that we covered in the Troubleshooting section of Chapter 2 and we suggest you look there.

Misconfigured System

It's worth remembering that many problems that appear to be due to boot failure can actually reflect misconfiguration—for instance, if you change the video type in Windows NT Setup to one that's not compatible with your particular hardware, you may have a completely successful boot (NT is still running) but find yourself looking at a blank screen. So the best initial step to take with *any* boot problem is to try selecting the previous configuration from the Last Known Good configuration menu, or if that doesn't work, try using the Windows NT Emergency Diskette. Get the boot diskette originally

[8] Information in this section is from a variety of sources, including the Microsoft on-line Knowlege Base (go MSKB on Compuserve), the Microsoft TechNet CD-ROM, reports from Windows NT users, and our own experience with Windows NT during the beta program. We can't claim to have personally experienced every problem (or tested every fix) reported here—but we've had quite a few!

supplied with Windows NT, insert it in drive A, reboot the computer, and when it asks whether you want to do an installation or attempt a repair, select repair and insert the emergency disk. The odds are good that this will allow the system to "heal itself"—but if that doesn't work, there are some other boot problems that may occur:

- **BOOT.INI File Not Updated.** Various versions of Windows NT have used different formats for the BOOT.INI file and in some cases the BOOT.INI file is marked *read only*. In the event that this happens, a new installation of Windows NT over an earlier version may fail to update the BOOT.INI file, in which case, Windows NT will, in fact, boot correctly but may check the wrong directories and therefore may fail to complete the boot process. Make sure that the BOOT.INI file is a read/write file before installing a new version of Windows NT. And you can also edit the BOOT.INI file to see if it refers to the correct Windows NT installation directory—C:\WINNT versus C:\WINDOWS for example, or C:\WINNT versus D:\WINNT.[9]
- **Unrecognized Partition Types.** When you install Windows NT on a system in which an unusual partitioning scheme is used or a partition type is presented that Windows NT does not recognize, it is possible for Windows NT to install but for the system partition to be incorrectly identified—the boot subsystem may assume that system files are on partition 0 when they are in fact on partition 1, for instance. As with the previous error, you should inspect the BOOT.INI file to make sure that it refers to the correct partition or logical disk drive and directory. You may also want to check and examine the arc system formatted syntax for the initial partition location. This will be in a format like this:

```
SCSI(0)DISK(0)RDISK(0)PARTITION(1)\WINDOWS "Windows NT".
```

  The PARTITION(1) is most likely to be the cause of a problem here, although, on some machines the SCSI(0) could be the cause of the problem, as noted in Chapter 2. Try changing the partition number to 0 or 2 in this case or to another partition number depending on the contents of your partition table (which can be examined using the **fdisk** program on DOS machines).
- **Boot NTLDR Not Found.** If for any reason the NTLDR file is deleted from the root of the C drive Windows NT will be unable to boot. This can be cured using the emergency diskettes, or by copying NTLDR back on the hard disk from the diskettes or from the CD.
- **NTDETECT.COM Deleted.** When Windows NT starts on x86 systems it employs the NTDETECT.COM program to detect the hardware configuration on the system—which updates the hardware information in the Configuration

Continued

[9]Note that because of fault tolerance and "sticky" drive letters, the Boot Manager drive letters may be different from those in Disk Administrator and File Manager. You're better off to use ARC-style syntax, as discussed in "Unrecognized partition types" in the next section.

Registry and begins to carry out the boot process. This insulates Windows NT from configuration errors that may occur when someone changes a hardware component. However, it also means that if NTDETECT.COM is deleted, the system will fail to boot, generally failing with a fatal general system error of 0x00000067-Configuration Initialization Failed. This can also indicate that an error has been introduced into the BOOT.INI file (an indicator for this is if an additional line appears in the BOOT.INI file besides those for NT and for any alternate operating systems that existed when NT was first installed). So this should be checked as well, but in the event that the BOOT.INI file is found to be correct you will need to restore the NTDETECT.COM file from the installation CD or floppy disks.

- **Problems in the OS Loader.** In the event that the BOOT.INI is sufficiently correct for the OS to start loading but then presents a bad path, it's possible that the OS Loader blue screen will start but then fail with one of these errors:

  ```
  Could not read from the selected boot disk.
  ```

  or

  ```
  The system did not load because it could not find the following
  file: . . .
  ```

  Again, either of these errors indicates a problem with the BOOT.INI file. A solution is to revert to an alternate operating system, boot from floppy disk, or on RISC machines use the built-in monitor program to inspect the disk directory structure and determine which directory or file has been marked incorrectly and then manually edit the BOOT.INI file and try again.
- **Failure to Boot Back to a Previous Operating System.** Windows NT uses a hidden file called BOOTSECT.DOS to store information about the physical layout of the hard disk so that the system can boot back into DOS (or other operating systems) from Windows NT. In the event that this file is inadvertently deleted or cannot be found during an attempt to boot to an alternate operating system, the boot process will fail with the message: "Couldn't open boot sector file." Unfortunately, there isn't a good solution to this problem, because the file contains very specific information about the physical disk layout, which varies from machine to machine. If you have another machine with the *exact same physical disk, partitioning,* and *directory structure*, it *may* be possible to copy the BOOTSECT.DOS file from that machine, install it on your machine, and the thing may boot back correctly. In the event that does not happen, your only solution is to revert to Windows NT, back all the files off, reformat the hard disk with the predecessor operating system, and start over (or live with the Windows NT-only installation).
- **OS/2 Boot Manager Problems.** The Boot Manager which IBM supplies with OS/2 versions 2.0 and 2.1 attempts to perform very much the same functions that

the Windows NT Flexboot performs. Unfortunately, each tends to compete with the other to a certain extent, so it's possible that a system that has been set up with the OS/2 Boot Manager will fail to operate properly after the Windows NT Flexboot has been installed. You can get around this problem by booting OS/2 from the installation disk, pressing escape at the first opportunity to get to the OS/2 command line, bringing up the OS/2 fdisk and reinstalling Boot Manager, adding entries for each of the bootable partitions in the system.

When Boot Manager is installed *after* the Windows NT Flexboot, it generally seems to operate correctly. OS/2 Boot Manager will give you the option to boot either DOS or OS/2—there won't be any mention of Windows NT, but don't fear! If you boot to DOS you will then get the Windows NT Flexboot, giving you the option to use Windows NT or DOS. Another option is to avoid the use of the OS/2 Boot Manager entirely and instead use the OS/2 Dual Boot feature in conjunction with Windows NT, although this does not give the same flexibility in terms of booting from multiple partitions on the disk.

A related common problem with the OS/2 Boot Manager is that the Boot Manager and Windows NT Flexboot may disagree on which drive letters represent which partitions in the system. The simplest solution to this is to install the OS/2 Boot Manager in the *last* partition on the drive and put Windows NT on the *primary* (first) partition at the start of the drive. If this is done then both systems will agree on the drive letter assignments for all partitions (unless, of course, the "sticky drive letter" feature of Disk Administrator has been used to modify the drive letters used with Windows NT).

CPU Problems

Generally, a problem with the Central Processor Unit in a Windows NT system will be detected during the installation process and the system will fail to install properly. Again, there are a few things to watch out for. The first, which, again, is an installation problem, is to make sure you are installing on a CPU that supports NT. Windows NT requires a 25MHz 386 or higher processor. Note that for the 386 processor it does not support version B1 and earlier 386 chips. If you have such a chip you'll need a CPU upgrade.

- **Machine Check Exception on Pentium Chips.** Windows NT machines equipped with Intel Pentium (P5) CPUs may experience a *machine check exception fault* during operation, particularly if they have been in heavy use over an extended period of time. A machine check exception on the Pentium processor chip is an indication that the processor self-test hardware has detected an internal fault. It most commonly indicates an overheat condition. This is not unknown on early model Pentium CPUs and it generally indicates a cooling problem in the system. The first solution, of course, is to turn the computer off and let it cool down. If the problem happens repeatedly, you may want to open up the case and

Continued

make sure any on-chip cooling fan is operating and make sure that there isn't any obstruction in the airflow, and consider moving the system so that the airflow holes are not being obstructed by walls, desks, or other obstructions. Finally, contact your system manufacturer to see about some kind of an upgrade.

- **Poor CPU Performance.** This is a topic that really refers back to the tuning section earlier in this chapter. If the computer is running but seems to be dead slow and the processor appears bogged with tasks that should not bog it, then you may want to check to see first if the "turbo switch" (if any) is depressed. Next, you may need to reboot the computer and examine the CMOS register settings to see if the computer is set for one or more memory wait states. A computer operating in a one wait state condition effectively is operating at half the stated CPU clock rate, because after every clock cycle involving a memory access it will idle or "wait" one cycle to give memory a chance to stabilize. In the event that your system is using one or more wait states, try resetting to a zero wait state condition. If the computer refuses to run, then your memory is physically incapable of operating at the processor full speed and the solution is to buy faster memory chips. Beyond that, refer to the section on *Performance Tuning* earlier in this chapter for suggestions on how overall system throughput may be increased.

Communication Port Problems

- **Attempting to Use One COM Port for Two Applications.** Aside from the usual problems with improperly matched baud rate, parity, stop bits, and so forth, between an application and the device attached to a COM port, Windows NT presents a new class of problems. It absolutely, positively will *not* let you assign a COM port to another application or device when one is already using it.

  You can see this by looking at the COM Port item in Control Panel. If you have a mouse installed on COM1 port for instance, then the COM1 port will not appear in the Control Panel listing even though it does exist in the system. The reason is that Windows NT has assigned the COM port permanently to the mouse and it will not allow that port to be used by any other application or service until and unless the mouse releases it.

  You can determine which COM ports are permanently assigned to physical devices in this way by inspecting the Windows NT Registry's H-key_local_machine/hardware/descriptions/SYSTEMs/multifunction adapter/0/serial controller entry (this may say EISA adapter instead of multifunction adapter on EISA machines, etc.), as illustrated in Figure 5.6. The COM port will be stored in a sub-key numbered from zero through one less than the number of COM ports; zero through three respectively, for instance, represents COM1 through COM4. The device using the COM port will appear within the numbered sub-

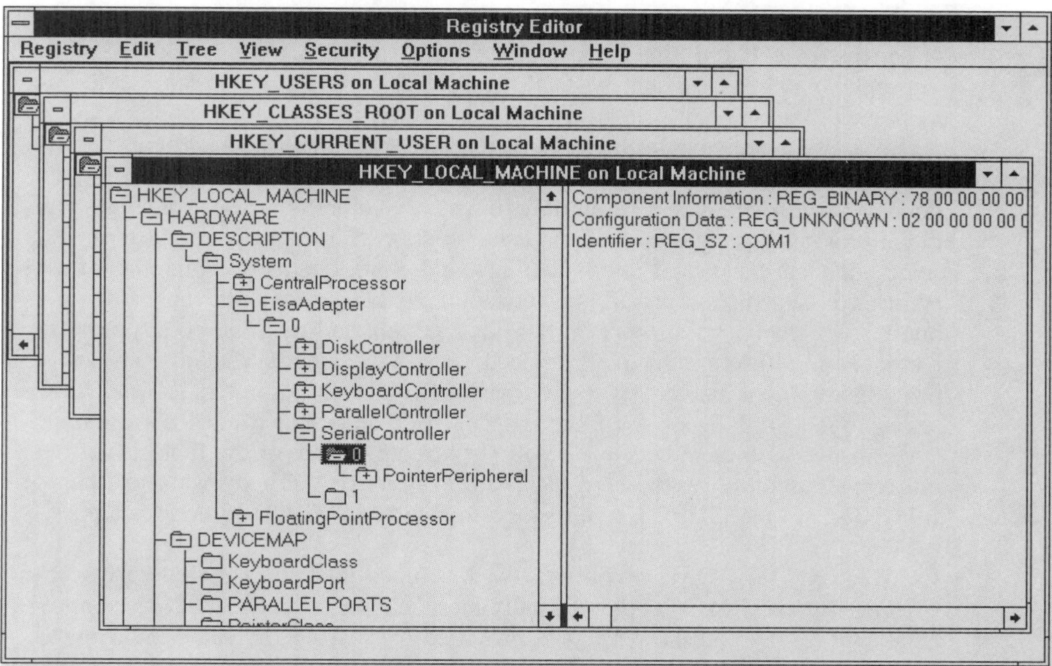

Figure 5.6 Registry entry for COM ports.

Determining which system component "owns" a communications port can be extremely confusing in Windows NT. You can find out by looking at the registry entry illustrated here, using the registry editor (REGEDT32.EXE). Note that the attachment of PointerPeripheral to the SerialController/0/ entry means that on this system a mouse is attached to the first COM port (COM1).

key for the COM port in question. If no hardware device is using the COM port, the next thing to look for is the possibility that you have some application or service using the port.

An example of this would be if COM1 is physically attached to a modem and you attempt to use COM1 from a communications program at the same time that Remote Access Services (RAS) are running bound to COM1 through the network's Control Panel—Windows NT won't let you assign the port to the communications program. The solution to this is to stop RAS (or the other service in question) using the Services applet in the Control Panel while you use the communications program, then close the communications program (or select another COM port temporarily) and start RAS again.

Continued

- **Incompatible Hardware.** Most other COM port problems will be either improper matches between the COM port settings and the external device as mentioned above, or in rare cases, you may run into a situation where a COM port is using a universal asynchronous receiver transmitter (UART) chip that is incompatible with Windows NT. The way to test for this is to attach a known good serial device (such as a dumb terminal or another computer running a terminal program) using a null modem cable to the port, run the Windows terminal, select identical baud rates, parity settings, and word lengths on both ends of the connection and then try typing on the Windows NT system's keyboard. If only one or two characters appears on the other screen, and then the port appears to hang up and refuse to transmit, you need a new UART chip. Machines known to have this problem include several models of DEC machines in the 300 and 400C series. Windows NT does support 16550 UART chips but it does not optimize performance with them because it will not take advantage of the first-in first-out buffering capability on the chip hardware[10] (although you may want to look at FIFO.CMD in the \SUPPORT directory on Windows NT CD-ROMs for a possible fix).
- **COM3, COM4,-COMn Problem.** On machines that don't include a Micro-Channel Adapter (MCA) bus—virtually all machines except IBM PS/2 computers—COM3 and COM4 support is provided by sharing the same interrupt as COM1 and COM2 with two different port addresses. That is, COM3 has the same interrupt number as COM1 but is at a different physical port address. COM4 is at the same interrupt level as COM2, but at a different port. This works fine until you try to use both COM1 and COM3 (or COM2 and COM4) at the same time. Windows NT supports interrupt sharing by the two sets of ports but it cannot and will not permit devices to use the ports at the same time. As a result you may find it impossible, for example, to attach modems to COM1 and COM3 and get two programs (for example, Remote Access Services and a terminal program or Microsoft Mail Remote) to work on both ports simultaneously. You can have one or the other, but not both.
- **Interrupt Conflicts.** Just as Windows NT is intolerant of multiple applications or devices trying to share the same COM port, it is exceedingly intolerant of devices attempting to share an interrupt. In fact, the usual indication of an interrupt problem is the refusal of Windows NT to boot (on rare occasions, it can crash *after* booting correctly, during an attempt to perform a network login). The major symptom will be the Windows NT blue screen displaying error number 0x000000A: IRQ Expected To Be Less Than Or Equal. This indicates that two hardware devices in the system are set for the same interrupt level. It most prob-

[10]Actually, the default behavior was changed to exploit FIFO buffers in the ship version of Windows NT after this was written. You *can* still use the unsupported FIFO.CMP batch file to disable FIFO buffering if it causes problems in your system.

ably will happen just after you've installed a network card or other physical device.

Remove the card that's most recently been installed and reboot the computer. Examine the hardware manufacturer's settings for the device and attempt to find an interrupt level that is not used by other devices. A common cause of this problem is interrupt cards that are predefined at IRQ3—the interrupt used by COM2 and COM4. Therefore, if you have a second COM port in your machine IRQ3 is automatically disallowed. Common interrupts in most systems include:

- IRQ0 (timer)
- IRQ1 (keyboard)
- IRQ3 (COM2 and COM4)
- IRQ4 (COM1 and COM3)
- IRQ5 (LPT2)
- IRQ6 (floppy controllers)
- IRQ7 (line printer one)
- IRQ8 (system clock)
- IRQ13 (math coprocessor)
- IRQ14 (hard disk controller)
- IRQ15 (secondary disk controller)

You will need to select an interrupt number not used by any of these devices installed in your system.

Malfunctioning Disk Drives

Most common hard disk problems are covered in Chapter 2. Aside from that, the problem that most frequently causes difficulties is failure to terminate a SCSI chain. Make sure that the last device in the chain is terminated, and that there is terminating power. Failing this, in the event that disk drives are misbehaving on Windows NT when they have been installed correctly and have been behaving themselves until now, you should check the BOOT.INI. Try reverting the configuration. Try using the emergency diskette. If none of that has any effect then you probably have a disk hardware problem and need to employ conventional hardware troubleshooting techniques. Call your hardware manufacturer for details.

CD-ROM Problems

The most frequent CD-ROM difficulty with Windows NT is adding a CD-ROM into an installation that initially did not have a CD-ROM. Making Windows NT recognize the CD-ROM is fairly straightforward: Run the Control Panel Services applet, select the SCSI CD-ROM object, and set the startup value to automatic so that the service will start

Continued

when the system boots. You may want to set the CD audio entry to automatic as well (for certain CD-ROMs, this may be required). And to avoid the necessity to restart Windows NT to get immediate benefit of the CD-ROM, you can, of course, start these services manually.

- **CD-ROM Impacting Windows NT Performance.** Certain CD-ROM players, specifically including the NEC Intersect series players, may have a dramatic impact on Windows NT performance when the CD-ROM is playing. This will occur because of the setting of a jumper switch on the CD-ROM reader that disables disconnects during read operations. Disk read operations on CD-ROMs are very slow, and if a disconnect is not available, then no other device has access to the SCSI interface card until the disk read is finished. Consult the hardware documentation for your CD-ROM reader and reset the jumper switch as necessary to enable disk connects during read operations.
- **Failure to Recognize Data on a CD.** Windows NT supports the ISO9660 CD-ROM format but does not support any format extensions. A series of extensions known as the *Rock Ridge CD-ROM format* provide additional features that are used by CD-ROMs for some systems, in particular, UNIX systems that require long filenames and a complex directory structure. Windows NT's CD file system does not recognize these extensions; such disks may be unreadable even though the CD-ROM player in use is designed to deal with these formats.
- **Use of Non-SCSI CD-ROM Devices.** This is discussed in Chapter 2. Again, it's worth pointing out that, unfortunately, drivers do not exist for proprietary CD-ROM devices under Windows NT as of this writing. This includes the Creative Labs SoundBlaster Pro card, which includes the CD-ROM interface built onto a sound card. There simply is no way to make Windows NT recognize such a CD-ROM. An alternative that may work is to install the CD-ROM in a Windows for Workgroups computer and then share the CD-ROM on the network using the /S extension from the MSCDEX.EXE program. Then Windows NT can attach to the shared CD-ROM drive as a virtual disk drive and access it over the network. But there's no way to make NT recognize such a drive *directly*.

Printing Problems

Windows NT suffers from a unique set of printing problems in common with its COM port problems, which again arises out of the fact that only one device can own an interrupt. There are a number of sound cards, including the SoundBlaster Pro card, which by default use interrupt 7, the same interrupt that is typically used by the Line Printer 1 port. If Windows NT refuses to recognize a printer attached to LPT1 start a command line prompt, and type:

```
mode LPT1:
```

If you see the message "Device Not Found" then IRQ7 is being subverted by another hardware device. You should be able to determine this using the System Registry in a manner similar to that described earlier for Communication Ports. It will be necessary to either remove the offending device, change the settings on the device, or otherwise make an adaptation so that the interrupt conflict is eliminated.

Cross-Platform Network Printing

If RISC and Intel versions of Windows NT are mixed on a network, the usual Windows NT print driver approach in which the remote printer takes advantage of the print driver installed in the print server will fail. The reason is that a MIPS RISC machine, for example, has no use for an Intel print driver. The indication will be an error message when you attempt to connect to the printer saying that the server does not have a suitable print driver installed. You then have the option to install a print driver on the local machine, or you can install print drivers for the other types on the print server.

For instance, if the print server is a RISC machine, you could install the Intel print driver. Alternatively if the print server is an Intel machine, you could install one or more RISC drivers. To do so, log into the nonnative computer (that is, if you are attempting to install Intel drivers on the MIPS machine, log in with the Intel machine; if you are attempting to install MIPS drivers in an Intel server, log in from the MIPS machine) using an administrative account. Start the Print Manager, select the Server Viewer, select the server on which you need to install drivers, select the printer for which you want to install the driver, choose Print Properties, and click the OK button. The system will then ask for the location of the printer drivers. You can designate the appropriate CD-ROM device or the print server or diskette as the case may be.[11] The drivers will then be installed on the print server and any system connecting to the print server will be presented with the driver appropriate to that system. That is, an Intel machine logging onto the print server will see the Intel print driver; a RISC machine will see the RISC driver. This can get complicated if you have multiple RISC-type machines in your operation. And as noted in Chapter 2, it may require additional memory in the unlikely event that multiple print drivers are being used simultaneously.

Network Problems

- **Disconnection.** The most common symptom of a network card problem is that the user is unable to connect to the network. The most common cause is that the network cable is not plugged into the card. So, the first thing to do if you suspect a network card error is to check the connection between the network cable and

Continued

[11]You can also do this remotely from Print Manager on any workstation, provided you have an administrative account on the server in question, and have access for the proper (RISC or Intel) print drivers.

the computer and then the connection between the network cable and the wall. If it's a 10base2 (coax) Ethernet connection check to make sure that the chain of connections isn't broken. The cable may be plugged in on the computer of the user who is reporting a problem but it may be unplugged further down the line. Of course, this will usually be easy to spot—if such a break in a 10base2 cable exists *all* of the users on the subnet will be disconnected, not just one. But that good first step is to check and be sure everything's connected. The next step to take is to run the Windows NT Event Manager and look to see if it's reporting any network errors.

- **Misconfigured Network Card**. If the network connection appears to be good and the other systems on the subnet are up, you'll need to check and see whether you have a hardware or software error. The easiest way to do this is with PING (on TCP/IP networks) or the net send /BROADCAST command (on NetBIOS networks). (Use of PING is covered below under TCP/IP Misconfiguration.).

  In either case, what you will want to do is determine whether the computer is in fact talking to the network at all, and then from this you can determine whether you have a software problem with misconfigured networking software or whether you have a hardware problem in which the network is not working at all. In our experience the net send /BROADCAST command is convenient for this because it operates at a very low level on the system. You can reliably expect a net send /BROADCAST command to tell you if the network is properly installed. If the network is installed and network communications exist, but the computer is not being logged into the network properly, the net send /BROADCAST will result in the broadcast message appearing on all the screens of all computers in the local subnet. Thus, for example, typing:

  ```
  net send /BROADCAST Can anyone hear me?
  ```

  will print the message "Can anyone hear me?" in a pop-up window on all other Windows NT workstations and/or servers on the local subnet. This can be irritating to other subnet users but it gives an immediate indication that the problem is not in the hardware. A second possibility is that net send /BROADCAST will not give an indication on other people's screens but will return with the message Broadcast message was sent to all users of the Local Area Network. In this case, the low-level Windows NT software, the driver, and the transporter are all working properly—they are getting proper indications from the card—but for some reason the transmission is not getting out on the network. This typically is an indication that the network cable is bad, and the signal is being blocked somewhere outside of the computer.
- **TCP/IP Misconfiguration**. Inability to "see" hosts on TCP/IP networks may indicate that the HOSTS or LMHOSTS database files (described in Chapter 6) contain bad information. Try accessing a local host (or router) using the TCP/IP

"ping" utility, *using the four-number IP address of the host (or router) in question.* The syntax of the command is **ping** <ip-address>:

```
ping 127.119.13.213
```

for a node with address 127.119.13.213. Do *not* use a ping to a DNS or HOSTS name (at least, not at first) because this may not be definitive; the command:

```
ping vax.cmp.com
```

will evaluate to the same command as ping 127.119.13.213 if and *only* if the vax.cmp.com DNS name properly evaluates to 127.119.12.213. In contrast, pinging "by the numbers" is an absolute—if it gives you no response, then there is a very deep configuration problem.

If a "by the numbers" ping gives a response, try a ping to the name. If that doesn't work, then check the Name Resolution settings in Control Panel/Networks TCP/IP Configuration to see whether DNS or HOSTS naming is in use, and then check the status of the DNS server (or HOSTS file) as appropriate.

If both pings work, but you still can't "see" the system in question using the built-in Windows NT networking, then check the LMHOSTS file settings, and the settings of any intervening routers. A useful diagnostic for systems that use Windows NT at each end may be to run the FTP Server Service on one end, and attempt FTP client access from the other. If that works, then the low-level linkage (and router, if any) are properly set up, and the problem *must* lie with the LMHOSTS database or Windows NT domain settings.

Unfortunately, the TCP/IP settings files (HOSTS, LMHOSTS, etc.) are *not* part of the Windows NT configuration registry, so restoring a Last Known Good configuration won't help in this situation—you'll have to figure out the problem using PING, and correct the problem by editing the files with a text editor.

Once you've done so, *save a backup copy*, so you won't have to go through the same experience the next time something changes!

- **Hardware (Interrupt) Problems.** It is quite common to experience network problems on Windows NT machines if the network card is set to interrupt level 3. Normally, Interrupt 3 is used by the COM2 port and since Windows NT does not permit interrupt sharing, if a network card is designated to use Interrupt 3, there are two possibilities: One is that you will see the infamous Blue Screen when NT boots up with "Error 0x0000000A—IRQ expected to be less than or equal." This is the most severe version. The other case is that NT starts, but the network refuses to run. In either case, take the network card out and reset it to a new IRQ setting. You'll also have to change the IRQ setting for the card in question in Control Panel/Networks.

  It's possible that the computer will boot but the network card will refuse to function. In this case, again, you need to shut down the computer, take out the

Continued

card, change the settings on the card, bring up the computer, change the settings on the Network Control Panel applet, and then shut down and restart Windows NT, and it should work. If it's not an interrupt problem and the network cables are believed to be good, then you need to begin troubleshooting procedures to determine whether you, in fact, have any connectivity to the network card and try to determine where the break is occurring. This can be done using the PING application on TCP/IP networks or the net send /BROADCAST on NetBEUI and other SMB networks.

On rare occasions, there are network cards with programmable interrupt and I/O settings in which the low-level network software can see what appears to be a perfectly good network connection, yet will not work initially. It may be worth trying the following procedure. Perform a warm boot by shutting down Windows NT and selecting the Restart when shutdown is complete switch and then try net send again. If it operates correctly after the reboot then you have a network card that requires two passes to set the software configurations. You may want to consider reconfiguring the card with a hardware configuration (if that's possible), or you may need to tell users that when they start up in the morning they're going to have to do a warm boot before they can expect to see their network.

If net send /BROADCAST reports that the network broadcast is not being sent because of a network problem, this invariably indicates that some kind of problem is occurring in the binding of the low-level network software to the network card. This should ordinarily be indicated by a problem that will show up in the System Event Log. (You did check that first didn't you?) But in any case, the problem is a low-level one. It indicates that, for whatever reason, the software is not recognizing the card. This may mean that you're using the wrong driver for the particular network card you have, or that the network card may be misconfigured. In any case, take a close look at the network card. Verify that the network settings match the settings in the Network Control Panel. Verify that you are using the correct driver, and try again.

Sound Card Problems

As with network cards, the most usual symptom for sound board problems is the user reporting that no sound comes out of the speakers and, again, as with network cards, the first thing to do is check to see that there is a speaker plugged in, that the speaker has power, that the speaker volume is turned up, and that in all other respects sound should be coming from the computer. If it is not then you may want to look at the following things:

- **Is the sound driver installed?** This may sound simpleminded, but Windows NT does not install sound drivers during installation by default, so you will very likely have to install a sound driver for each system. You do this through the Control Panel Sound Driver's applet. Check to make sure that you are using the right driver for the right sound card. In particular, with Creative Labs Sound-Blaster cards you have to be careful because there are several different versions of the SoundBlaster and the drivers are not interchangeable. For example, the driver for a SoundBlaster Pro will not work with a SoundBlaster version 1. Also note that on MIPS ARCSystem computers, you want the MIPS ARCsystem sound driver, *not* the SoundBlaster driver (even though the card in question is actually a SoundBlaster!).

- **Do you have an interrupt conflict?** Check the interrupt and port settings that are set in the driver's applet and make sure they match the settings on the audio card. (And note the fact that the SoundBlaster by default uses IRQ7. This is also the setting for LPT1 and, as noted elsewhere, Windows NT does not tolerate interrupt overloading, so it is likely that if you've installed a SoundBlaster card and it refuses to work that you'll have to change the interrupt.[12]) If you can play .WAV files (an easy way to check this is with the Control Panel Sound applet setting system sounds on and using the test button) but you can't play .MID (MIDI) files, then you may need to install the ad-lib midi driver. Because most sound boards have two independent audio chips on them, one for midi synthesis and one for wave audio, two drivers are typically required.
- As we noted in the section on CD-ROMs and SCSI, there are a number of sound card manufacturers who incorporate a **proprietary CD-ROM interface** on the sound card. Unfortunately, at the time of this writing, Windows NT does not provide drivers for any of these CDs. It requires a true SCSI compatible CD-ROM and much as it might be convenient for all of us it's not possible at this time to use a SoundBlaster or other proprietary CD-ROM interfaces with Windows NT installation. Again, a workaround is to install the card and CD-ROM in a Windows for Workgroups machine, share the CD-ROM over the network, and connect to it that way.

Video Problems

The most common video problem arises when a user changes the video settings using Windows NT Setup to try to get a higher resolution and is suddenly presented with an image that is either grossly unstable or completely blank. The solution in either case is the same: Wait until all disk activity has been stopped for at least 15 seconds, and hit the reset switch. When Windows NT starts, it will start with the character mode startup, which ordinarily will survive a change in video resolution and will present you with a

Continued

[12] Or use Control Panel/Devices and disable the parallel port driver—a convenient solution if you're using a networked printer.

"Press Escape for Last Known Good Menu" option. Immediately hit the Escape key, and select Last Known Good Configuration. Hopefully, if the user has not repeatedly modified the installation (which is almost impossible with a video problem) this will get you back to the working video.

The Messaging Database

Windows NT can produce a variety of messages during its normal operation along with a wide range of error messages. If you purchase a Windows NT Advanced Server then you will receive a Messages Guide and you can also get the same information from the Windows NT Resource Kit. If you have the base version of Windows NT then you don't get the Messages Guide, but *all* CD-ROM versions of Windows NT include the Messages Guide as a runtime Microsoft Access database (which is one of the reasons we recommend having at least one CD-ROM available on *all* Windows NT networks).

The runtime Messaging Database application is found in the SUPTOOLS\WINNTMSG directory of the CD-ROM and includes a Windows-based setup program that will automatically install the messaging database on your hard disk. By installing the database on a server, and then sharing the database directories, you can enable remote users to access the database, and this is the most convenient way to get access to the Windows NT system messages. Incidentally, the runtime Access software used with the Messaging Database is accessible not only from Windows NT systems but also from Windows 3.1 and Windows for Workgroups systems, which may be convenient for support professionals.

You need not access the database from a Windows NT workstation. To install the messaging database on your Windows NT server, insert the Windows NT distribution CD-ROM in the CD-ROM drive, start a character mode command line, and from the command line find the disk that represents the CD-ROM, for example disk D, and type the following: CD d:\suptools\winntmsg start setup. The Windows NT Messages setup program will start. It will ask whether you want to join an existing workgroup for the server installation. Answer no. It will then propose a directory for the database to be set up, which you can change to another directory if you wish, and will carry out the setup for you automatically. To make the database accessible from other systems (including Windows NT systems, Windows for Workgroups systems, and Windows systems), simply go to File Manager and select the directory in which you installed the database, and share it on the network.

To access the database from other machines, it will be necessary to set up the Access run-time query engine on the other machine. To do this, you use File Manager and the Windows for Workgroups machine where on a Windows NT machine you will use File Manager to establish a virtual disk drive connected to the directory where you shared the database and then from that directory run the setup program. This time when it asks if you want to join an existing workgroup say yes and it will go on from there. An incidental point is that you could in fact set up the database on a Windows for Workgroups machine or a LAN Manager's machine. It doesn't necessarily have to be stored on the Windows NT server.

Windows NT System Messages

As noted in the start of this section, Windows NT can produce a broad range of messages indicating system status or system errors. One of the most important functions that an administrator or support professional must carry out is determining the meaning of these messages and taking the necessary corrective action. The easiest way to do this is to use the Messaging database included on the Windows NT CD-ROM, whose installation we just discussed. Only then is it necessary to perform a database search for the particular message number or for some fragment of the message text to receive a detailed description of the message along with recommendations for corrective actions.

Alternatively, if you have the Windows NT Advanced Server, you can look the message up in the *Windows NT Advanced Server Messages* manual or if you have purchased the Windows NT Resource Kit you can look the messages up in Volume 2. In any case, the exact details of the messages and how to deal with them is beyond the scope of this book. We will present here only a brief introduction describing the types of messages you may have to deal with and giving some general suggestions for how to quickly get the information and quickly take corrective action when such a message appears.

Character Mode, Stop, and Hardware Malfunction Messages

The ultimate worst-case situation you have to deal with in Windows NT is the "blue screen crash." This happens when the Windows NT kernel encounters a completely unrecoverable error either in the kernel software or in hardware. The system will stop and display a screen similar to that illustrated in Figure 5.7.

In a "blue screen crash," the first line displayed on the screen will generally be of the form

```
*** STOP 0x000000nn DESCRIPTION
```

The 0x000...number is a unique hexadecimal identifier that identifies the STOP message number and will indicate the cause of the crash. The text immediately following it is a text description of the crash. This will be followed by a system trace including an identification of the address areas in which the crash occurred, register dump, and a system call tree indicating the various functions that are in the tree of system calls above the function in which the crash occurred. They are of value only to a system developer or hardware support engineer but if the same crash occurs repeatedly, it may be worth writing it down, in particular the first two or three lines of information on the screen, so that the information can be presented when Tech Support is called. The follow-up to a blue screen crash is generally going to involve making a change to the hardware settings in the system, removing hardware devices from the system, or other relatively drastic steps. The list of troubleshooting problems and workarounds in this chapter will give some suggestions for certain well-known errors such as the 0x0000000A IRQL problem, but this kind of crash is pretty serious.

```
*** STOP: 0xFF729E90 (0x00000000, 0x00000000, 0x00000000, 0x00000000)

eax=ffdffl3c ebx=80100000 ecx=00000003 edx=80100000 esi=ffdffl3c edi=00000000
eip=00000000 esp=00000000 ebp=00000000  p4=0300       nv up ei ng nz na po nc
cr0=00000000 cr2=00000000 cr3=00000000 cr4=ffdffl3c irql:1f DPC  efi=00000000
gdtr=80036000   gdtl=03ff idtr=80036400   idtl=07ff tr=0028  ldtr=0000

Dll Base DateStmp - Name                 Dll Base DateStmp - Name
80100000 2c51c0b2 - ntoskrnl.exe         80400000 2c3b5c01 - hal.dll
80400000 2c3b5c01 - hal.dll              80100000 2c51c0b2 - ntoskrnl.exe
80100000 2c51c0b2 - ntoskrnl.exe         80400000 2c3b5c01 - hal.dll
80100000 2c51c0b2 - ntoskrnl.exe         80400000 2c3b5c01 - hal.dll
80400000 2c3b5c01 - hal.dll              80100000 2c51c0b2 - ntoskrnl.exe
80400000 2c3b5c01 - hal.dll              80100000 2c51c0b2 - ntoskrnl.exe
80400000 2c3b5c01 - hal.dll              80100000 2c51c0b2 - ntoskrnl.exe
80100000 2c51c0b2 - ntoskrnl.exe         80400000 2c3b5c01 - hal.dll
80100000 2c51c0b2 - ntoskrnl.exe         80400000 2c3b5c01 - hal.dll
80100000 2c51c0b2 - ntoskrnl.exe         80400000 2c3b5c01 - hal.dll
80100000 2c51c0b2 - ntoskrnl.exe         80400000 2c3b5c01 - hal.dll
80400000 2c3b5c01 - hal.dll              80100000 2c51c0b2 - ntoskrnl.exe
80100000 2c51c0b2 - ntoskrnl.exe         80400000 2c3b5c01 - hal.dll
80100000 2c51c0b2 - ntoskrnl.exe         80400000 2c3b5c01 - hal.dll

Address  dword dump   Build [v1 511]                              - Name
80100000 2c51c0b2 80100000 2c51c0b2 80100000 2c51c0b2 80100000 - ntoskrnl.exe
80100000 2c51c0b2 80100000 2c51c0b2 80100000 2c51c0b2 80100000 - ntoskrnl.exe
80100000 2c51c0b2 80100000 2c51c0b2 80100000 2c51c0b2 80100000 - ntoskrnl.exe
80100000 2c51c0b2 80100000 2c51c0b2 80100000 2c51c0b2 80100000 - ntoskrnl.exe
80100000 2c51c0b2 80100000 2c51c0b2 80100000 2c51c0b2 80100000 - ntoskrnl.exe
80100000 2c51c0b2 80100000 2c51c0b2 80100000 2c51c0b2 80100000 - ntoskrnl.exe
80100000 2c51c0b2 80100000 2c51c0b2 80100000 2c51c0b2 80100000 - ntoskrnl.exe
80100000 2c51c0b2 80100000 2c51c0b2 80100000 2c51c0b2 80100000 - ntoskrnl.exe
80100000 2c51c0b2 80100000 2c51c0b2 80100000 2c51c0b2 80100000 - ntoskrnl.exe
80400000 2c3b5c01 80400000 2c3b5c01 80400000 2c3b5c01 80400000 - hal.dll
80400000 2c3b5c01 80400000 2c3b5c01 80400000 2c3b5c01 80400000 - hal.dll
80400000 2c3b5c01 80400000 2c3b5c01 80400000 2c3b5c01 80400000 - hal.dll
80400000 2c3b5c01 80400000 2c3b5c01 80400000 2c3b5c01 80400000 - hal.dll
80400000 2c3b5c01 80400000 2c3b5c01 80400000 2c3b5c01 80400000 - hal.dll
80400000 2c3b5c01 80400000 2c3b5c01 80400000 2c3b5c01 80400000 - hal.dll
80400000 2c3b5c01 80400000 2c3b5c01                           - hal.dll

Kernel Debugger Using: COM2 (Port 0x2f8, Baud Rate 19200)
Restart your computer. If this message reappears, do not restart,
Contact your system administrator or technical support group, and/or
peripheral device vendor.
```

Figure 5.7 Blue screen crash.

You should *never* see this display from Windows NT under normal circumstances. If you do, then the system has become completely unstable and will require a hardware reboot. The *** STOP 0x000000... message will identify the type of error involved, and is followed by a register dump that can be helpful in identifying what's gone wrong with the system.

Hardware Malfunctions

If a low-level hardware problem occurs on a system at such a level that Windows NT kernel cannot handle it at all, then you're likely to see a message beginning "Hardware malfunction..." and ending "...call your hardware vendor for support." And the message says it all—call the vendor.

Status and Warning Messages

These messages will appear as a Windows alert and will generally indicate some specific matter of concern for the system. They may simply indicate some piece of system information that is of general interest such as "Password too complex." They may warn of a problem with some components of the system such as a "Printer Out of Paper" message. They may indicate a more serious problem such as the "Access Denied" message that indicates that an application has tried to do something for which it doesn't have the necessary security access rights, or a basic mistake on the user's part, such as trying to write to a CD-ROM disc. In any of these messages, the appropriate step to take is to write down the text of the message and press the OK button. You hope the system will recover and you can then look the message up in the message database or one of the other manuals for corrective actions.

Network Messages

Errors that occur within the network components of Windows NT and the Windows NT Advanced Server will be identified as network errors and will have a four-digit number associated with them. In addition to the messaging database you can get a brief description of each error by typing net helpmsg and the message number, for instance:

```
C:\nwnt>net helpmsg 2102
The workstation driver is not installed.

EXPLANATION
Windows NT is not installed, or your configuration file is incorrect.
ACTION
Install Windows NT, or see your network administrator about possible problems
with your configuration file.
```

But the information in the NT messaging database will be far more complete. To get the equivalent information from the NT messaging database that you'd get from typing net helpmsg, start the messaging database (by clicking on the Microsoft Windows NT Messages icon in the Microsoft Windows NT Messages group in Program Manager) and click the Find button, enter the network error number (such as 2102) in the Find field in the Search for field, and from the pop-up list of items to look at, select Net Message ID. Once you have the Net message ID field selected and the number typed in, click the OK button. The database will conduct a search and will then give you all of the relevant database records containing information about that error number (see Figure 5.8).

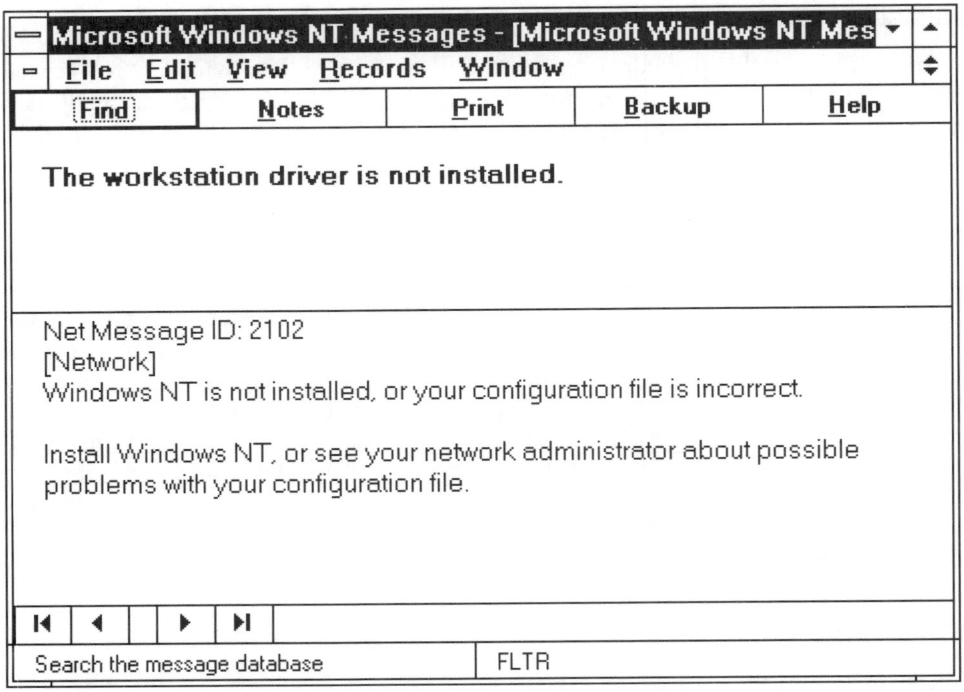

Microsoft Windows NT Messages - [Microsoft Windows NT Mes

File Edit View Records Window

Find | Notes | Print | Backup | Help

The workstation driver is not installed.

Net Message ID: 2102
[Network]
Windows NT is not installed, or your configuration file is incorrect.

Install Windows NT, or see your network administrator about possible problems with your configuration file.

Search the message database | FLTR

Figure 5.8 Messages database.

A runtime Microsoft Access database is provided on the Windows NT CD-ROM that contains definitions for all messages generated by the system. It can be run either locally or over the network—and doesn't require Windows NT as an over-the-network client.

In Extremis

There are times when any operating system will fail. Windows NT is one of the most advanced operating system designs ever produced for a personal computer and one of the most reliable. But it's also one of the most complex and that means that it's going to crash from time to time. There are crashes and there are *big-time* crashes. When a big-time crash occurs and you are "up the creek without a paddle," there is a certain set of tools that Microsoft provides on the CD-ROM versions of Windows NT that just might help. You will find these tools in the \SUPTOOLS directory of the Windows NT CD-ROM. They include the following:

- **BROWSTAT.EXE**. This is a utility that displays, sets, and resets browser status (covered in Chapter 8), which can help enormously in a situation where you find that the system is taking an appalling length of time to respond to net view commands or to react when you issue a Connect Net Drive command from the File Manager.

- **DRIVERS.EXE**. This is a program that displays information on device drivers and may help in debugging problems with access to low-level hardware devices.
- **EXETYPE.EXE.** This is a simple little command line program that displays details of the type and subsystem of an executable file. If you find that you're having problems running a particular EXE file on a particular system, try typing exetype filename.exe where filename is the name of the EXE file you're having trouble with. This will give you details on whether this is a Windows NT, OS/2, or 16-bit Windows program, what instruction set it is designed for, etc., and may help identify what's causing the problem.
- **FIFO.CMD.** This is actually a batch command file that turns on support for first in/first out (FIFO) buffering for modems that require it. There is an equivalent set of steps available that will perform the same functions through the Registry Editor.[13] Note that the FIFO.CMD file requires the use of the REGINI.EXE program described below.
- **I386KD.EXE** and **MIPSKD.EXE**—Kernel Debuggers. This may be the most unusual thing that any operating system manufacturer has ever distributed with their software. This is a fully functional debugger that will identify and display details of low-level problems in the Windows NT kernel. The use of this system is far beyond the realm of this book. There is limited on-line help available for this as part of the SUPTOOLS.HLP in the \SUPTOOLS subdirectory of the support directory on the CD-ROM. In general, using the kernel debugger will require that you connect a second computer to the computer you're trying to debug using a modem or a null modem cable and then execute the debugging kernel on the machine to be tested while running the debugger software on the second machine. This will probably not be much use to you unless you have access to a Windows System Development Kit or a Microsoft Engineer.
- **PMON.EXE**. This is the Process Resource Monitor and provides detailed information about the execution of processes including the thread count, working set size, and so forth. In general, the same functions can be achieved using the Windows NT Performance Monitor, but PMON.EXE provides an alternative user interface and may provide more detailed information. Also, because it's a character-based tool it can be executed from script files if necessary.
- **PSTAT.EXE**. This is a character-based program that displays a list of all programs running in the system along with status information and this can again be used in conjunction with the script program.
- **PVIEWER.EXE**. This is a graphical program that provides detailed information about processes comparable to that provided by the PMON.EXE program. In general, the functions here are duplicated by the Windows NT Performance Monitor but it provides an alternative user interface.
- **REGINI.EXE**. This is a command line program that allows a Registry command to be changed using a script. This is (like the Registry Editor itself) one of the most

[13]A setting for this is also available in Control Panel/Ports.

powerful and also one of the most dangerous utilities included in the Support Tools directory. Its obvious usefulness to a system administrator is that having once decided that a certain set of changes needs to be made to the Registries of a variety of systems, you can do it using a Registry script and the REGINI.EXE command executed from the command line. This means, of course, that you can execute Registry changes *simultaneously* on many systems by meddling with their login script file, but *beware. . .*

If you mess up that script file (and therefore mess up the Registry), you might not only produce the machine gun effect we mentioned earlier in describing the Registry, you can machine gun *all* of your servers (and/or workstations as the case may be), so this must be used with care.

Microsoft provides no documentation whatsoever on the Registry Script Format. However, you will find examples of the Registry Script Format in question in the FIFO_OFF and FIFO_ON INI files, located in the SUPPORT/SUPTOOLS/I386 directory of the CD, which are associated with the FIFO.CMD file. This is very much a *"use at your own risk"* situation. We *strongly* recommend that if you are for any reason considering use of the REGINI.EXE function, experiment with it on an isolated Windows NT workstation first and then make sure the system will survive a reboot after the Registry has been modified. Only after you have done that and you're satisfied that the script is safe should you attempt to do it on other systems, particularly servers.

- **SMBTRACE**. The SMBTRACE utility is potentially of great use for network professionals attempting to determine network problems. This is a server message block trace program that functionally amounts to a network sniffer implemented in software. It allows capture of SMBs from the server or redirector and allows a wide range of options for determining just how much data is captured and to what degree it does or does not impact system performance. Like PMON, NBSTAT, and so forth, it is a character-based utility.
- **NTDETECT.** This is an extremely useful item, actually implemented as a .COM file and a CMD batch file. NTDETECT is a mechanism that provides a data dump of the startup information that Windows NT detects during system startup. This could be extremely useful in debugging hardware problems that occur at startup time where a system refuses to detect a hardware component. By using NTDETECT to dump the information you may be able to determine whether the problem is in fact that the system is not seeing the component.

General Advice

The tools just described are placed in the Windows NT system with the following disclaimer from Microsoft:

> "The following tools were developed internally at Microsoft Product Support Services and are intended for use only at the direction of a Microsoft Support Engineer in troubleshooting support problems. Any other use of the tools is at your own risk. These tools

> are provided 'as is' without warranty of any kind. Microsoft disclaims any implied warrantability of merchantability, and/or fitness for a particular purpose."

Your best resource for attempting to debug the kinds of problems that you are going to run into that require these tools will be the *Microsoft Knowledge Base* either from the *Tech Net CD* or on CompuServe (go MSKB). This is likely to carry information that is of use to you. However, it is also quite likely—especially in the first six months or so of Windows NT's existence—that you will be the first person to encounter a particular bug. If this is the case, you are not going to find any reference information in the Knowledge Base—and the support information for using these tools is understandably limited. It's worth noting that the disclaimer talks about using tools at the direction of a Microsoft engineer. Don't beat your brains out trying to troubleshoot a low-level problem before you call for a support engineer!

Corrective Service Diskettes (CSDs)

As this book went to press, Microsoft released the first Windows NT CSD, set #001. This six-disk set fixes some ninety six bugs in the initial Windows NT release, many involving data corruption, and at least five causing a complete system crash. New system files provided as part of the six-disk update include: the Hardware Abstraction Layer (HAL), Operating System kernel, base service driver, mail system driver, Windows graphic device interface (GDI), DOS, OS/2 and 16-bit Windows subsystems, CD-ROM file system, New Technology File System (NTFS), most network card drivers, several hard disk and video drivers, and most system utility programs.

Obviously, as a system administrator or support person, you'll need to keep up on the CSD situation and make certain you've got the most up-to-date disks for your system. CSD files are available from the CompuServe WINNT forum's software library section 2, and will probably also be available on the *TechNet CD-ROM*s or by ftp from internet address rhino.microsoft.com. Administrators are well advised to check one of these sources regularly for CSDs and other system updates.

Summary and Conclusions

We've reviewed the basic principles of *preventive maintenance* (PM—covered in detail in Appendix 6), examined the steps necessary for performance tuning in a Windows NT system, reviewed the tools used for tuning and troubleshooting, and presented a list of the most likely problems and their solutions. Hopefully, with this information at your disposal you'll have a good idea of how to proceed when you're presented (inevitably) with your first Windows NT system crash—but we reiterate that it's *far* better to apply PM principles and avoid the crash altogether!

For More Information

Microsoft Staff (1993), *Windows NT System Guide.* Redmond, WA: Microsoft Corp. Includes a brief section on network errors and troubleshooting.

Microsoft Staff (1993), *Windows NT Messages Guide.* Redmond, WA: Microsoft Corp. Duplicates the on-line messaging database (and is included in the Windows NT Resource Kit).

Microsoft Staff (1993), *TechNet CD (July 1993).* Redmond, WA: Microsoft Product Support Services (PSS). *TechNet* is a monthly publication on CD-ROM containing a digest of topics from the Microsoft Knowledge Base, the Net News publication, Resource Kits and other information. This particular issue included a prerelease version of the Windows NT Resource Kit, which proved extremely helpful in writing this chapter (especially regarding the Configuration Registry). *TechNet* is available from Microsoft sales—a one-year subscription (12 CDs) costs $295 and is worth every penny.

Microsoft Staff (1993), *Windows NT Resource Kit, Volumes 1-3.* Redmond, WA: Microsoft Press. The *only* source (and unfortunately not yet in print as this is written) for detailed information on the Windows NT configuration registry.

Connecting to the World with TCP/IP

After reading this chapter, you should understand the basic elements of NT's TCP/IP services and how to install and configure them. You should also be able to build a Windows NT-based network using TCP/IP as the primary transport, and have a basic understanding of the TCP/IP applications provided with NT and how to use them to connect to UNIX and other TCP/IP hosts. If you're unfamiliar with TCP/IP concepts such as addressing, subnet masks, and routing, you should read the TCP/IP section of Appendix 2 before proceeding.

TCP/IP is an extremely flexible set of protocols, and Microsoft has put that to its advantage by including the basic protocol suite with NT. You can take advantage of NT's TCP/IP capabilities in many ways, or in many combinations of ways. You can:

- Run Windows NT network services over TCP/IP, either instead of or in conjunction with NetBEUI.
- Use TCP/IP-specific utilities (such as Telnet and FTP) to communicate with NT and non-NT systems alike, either instead of or in conjunction with the NetBIOS-based built-in Windows NT networking.

There are two basic areas of operations where NT's TCP/IP support can be used. The primary method will be as a routable transport protocol for Windows NT networks. If you're unable to utilize NetBEUI in complex environments, then you will naturally turn to the built-in support for TCP/IP as a way to get the most use of NT's networking capabilities. The secondary use of NT's TCP/IP support will be in heavily mixed environments (especially UNIX environments) that rely on TCP/IP-specific applications for host access. In this case you may or may not be using NT's built-in NetBIOS-based network services.

Among the sections in this chapter, "Installing and Configuring TCP/IP" covers the details of configuring NT to use TCP/IP, regardless of what upper-layer network services you plan to use with it. "Using TCP/IP with Windows NT's Built-in Networking" covers the issues specific to that environment. Finally, the section titled "Using Windows NT TCP/IP Utilities" introduces applications and services such as Telnet.

The Network Stack

In NT's modular network design, each component acts like a LEGO® block, providing stubs and sockets for interacting with other components. Figure 6.1 shows a basic overview of the networking modules of NT. Since the uppermost layer for most of the bundled applications is geared toward NetBIOS, it is the most important layer from an end-user's perspective. Applications such as Chat, NetDDE, ClipBook, and Messenger all rely on NetBIOS. If you wish to use any of these services (or the Windows NT workstation or server), then you must have the NetBIOS interface installed. If you don't need these services, or if your applications are strictly TCP/IP-based, then you do not need the NetBIOS interface. Almost everyone will use the NetBIOS services, however, since most of NT's network functionality is dependent upon then.

As shown in Figure 6.1, the NetBIOS service can be bound to the TCP/IP protocol stack, allowing these applications to run across WANs and complex LANs. The result is known as NetBIOS-on-TCP/IP, or NBT. NetBIOS is not a "routable" protocol, meaning that it can communicate only with other devices on the same network segment. TCP/IP, however, is fully routable, allowing systems to communicate across just about any medium, from serial lines to

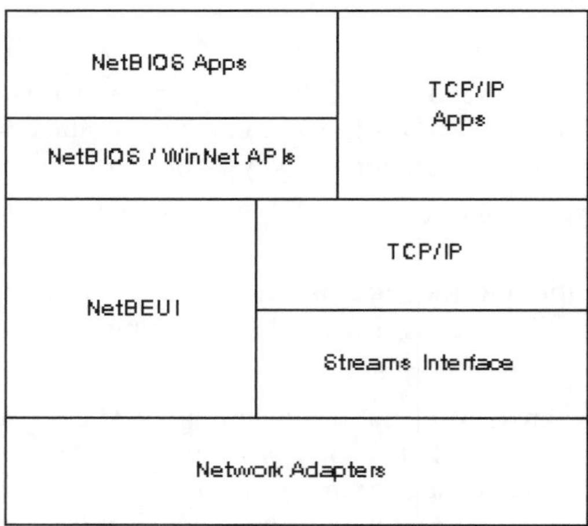

Figure 6.1 NT network architecture.

A high-level view of NT's network architecture.

satellite links. Since NBT rides on TCP/IP (technically, the NetBIOS packets are *encapsulated* within TCP/IP), NBT is routable to a limited degree.

Since NetBIOS is the protocol that applications use, there must be some way for TCP/IP to make NetBIOS act as though remote nodes were local. Likewise, there must be a facility for NetBIOS to hand TCP/IP a destination address that both can understand. NetBIOS uses workstation "names" to identify devices, an approach that works well in the small network environments for which NetBIOS was designed. TCP/IP, however, uses 32-bit binary addresses (most commonly represented by four 8-bit digits), providing a large and flexible address space for large and complex networks.

The process of converting NetBIOS names into IP addresses is managed with a text database called LMHOSTS, which we will discuss in detail later in this chapter. LMHOSTS contains a map of the network, associating workstation IP addresses with their NetBIOS pseudonyms. The TCP/IP service looks at this file whenever it gets a request from the NetBIOS service. It looks up the name, pulls out the IP address, creates a destination packet, and sends it to the network adapter.

There are, of course, limitations with this design, both inherent and man-made. We'll examine them and potential workarounds throughout this chapter. For now, let's move into installing the TCP/IP protocols.

Installing and Configuring TCP/IP

Before beginning the installation procedure, you need to know what your planned usage of TCP/IP will be. Do you simply want to use the transport for TCP/IP-specific applications such as Telnet and FTP? If so, you can eliminate much of the extra software that NT installs for you. If you need to run Windows NT's built-in network services over the TCP/IP stack, and have no need for NetBEUI, then you can also eliminate the NetBEUI protocols that NT automatically provides, freeing up more memory for other applications. Take a few moments to figure out what you plan on using TCP/IP for, and then proceed with the installation. Use the table below to help you plan:

If You Need This:	***Then Install This:***
TCP/IP	TCP/IP Protocol
Windows NT built-in networking over TCP/IP	TCP/IP Protocol TCP/IP NetBIOS(NBT—added by default) NetBIOS Interface

If You Don't Need This:	***Then Remove This:***
Windows NT built-in networking over NetBEUI	NetBEUI Protocol
Windows NT built-in networking over TCP/IP	TCP/IP NetBIOS(NBT—added by default)
Windows NT built-in networking or NetBIOS support	NetBIOS Interface

By default, when you add network components to your system, NT installs the NetBEUI and NetBIOS Interface modules, and then binds them to each adapter you've specified. Also by default, when you install TCP/IP services to your system, the protocol stack is bound to each adapter, although only one of them is used for routing, and only one can be used for NetBIOS applications (the same adapter cannot be used for *both* routing *and* NBT—therefore, to have routing support you will need *two* LAN adapters). Later in this chapter we'll examine ways to use more than one adapter with TCP/IP. However, there is no way to use NBT NetBIOS with more than one TCP/IP adapter.

The "Network" Control Panel

If you are configuring network services during installation, you will be presented with these options during the initial setup routines. If you are changing an existing installation, you need to load the "Network" control object from the Control Panels utility. Double-click "Control Panels" from the "Main" window in Program Manager, or type "CONTROL.EXE" in the <File><Run...> menu of either Program Manager or File Manager. Likewise, you can type "CONTROL.EXE" from the Command Prompt. Once the Network control object has loaded, you will be presented with the dialog box shown in Figure 6.2.

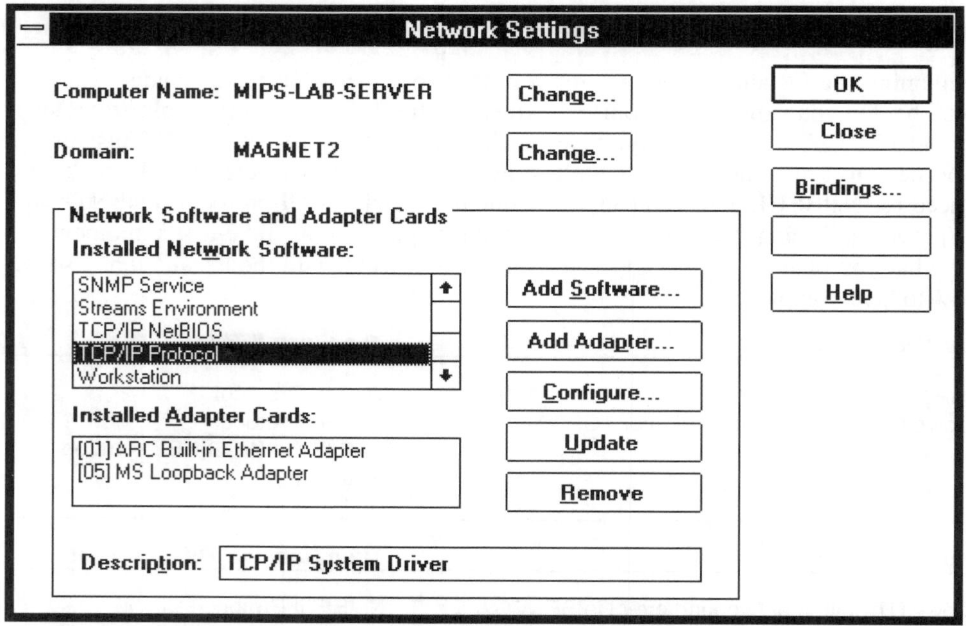

Figure 6.2 Network dialog.

The "Network" dialog box from Control Panels is the primary control point for all Windows NT network components.

By default, none of the TCP/IP services are installed, but the NetBEUI protocol is. To add the TCP/IP services, click the "Add Software..." button, and select "TCP/IP Protocol" from the drop-down list. When adding the TCP/IP protocol, NT automatically adds the NBT service as well. If you don't need the NBT service, you can remove it by selecting it in the "Installed Network Software" listbox, and clicking the "Remove" button. Likewise, if you do not need the NetBEUI protocol, you can remove it by selecting "NetBEUI Protocol" from the "Installed Network Software" listbox, and clicking the "Remove" button.

When you first add the TCP/IP protocol, you cannot configure the software immediately. Instead, you must select the "OK" button, and NT will prompt you for the configuration details. If this is a modification of an existing installation, you can select the "Configure" button to make changes to the TCP/IP protocol. Either way, NT will present you with the TCP/IP configuration dialog, illustrated in Figure 6.3.

You will mainly be concerned with three entries in this dialog: Default Gateway, IP Address, and Subnet Mask. These three parameters identify the logical location of your workstation. (For more information on IP addresses, see Appendix 2.) Your network administrator

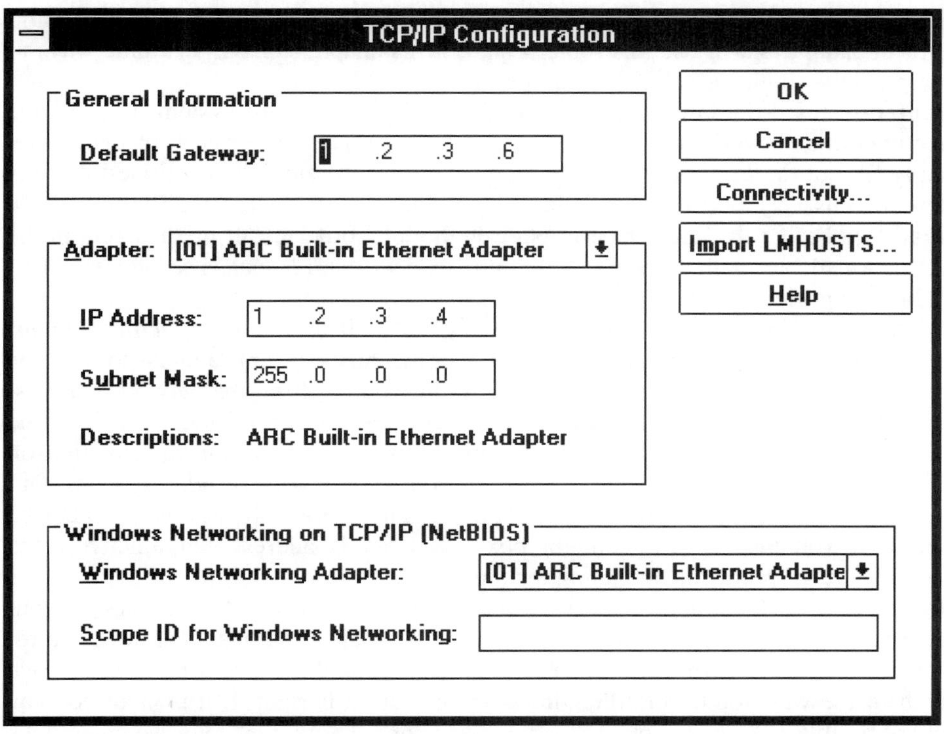

Figure 6.3 TCP/IP Configuration dialog.

The TCP/IP Configuration dialog allows you to manage all aspects of TCP/IP protocol operation.

will know the proper numbers for these boxes, but in general a TCP/IP address is a number made of four 8-bit bytes. There are several types of notation used to write IP addresses, but Microsoft chose to represent them as four decimal numbers ranging from 0 to 255, and separated by dots.

NOTE: Although assigning yourself an IP address arbitrarily will work—provided you are internally consistent on your network—it makes sense to get a registered IP address (as explained elsewhere in this chapter).

When you first add TCP/IP to a network adapter, this dialog box is empty. If you've already set these parameters in a previous install, then the dialog will show them instead. The various elements of the dialog box, and their meaning and potential values, are explained below.

- **Default Gateway—**This entry indicates where TCP/IP traffic should be sent when its address indicates that it needs to be forwarded to another logical or physical network. Although TCP/IP supports routing of protocols dynamically, NT's implementation does not. Therefore, you must provide a *default route*—tell the system where to forward packets that are not addressable on the immediate subnet. This address points to a router—either another computer, or a piece of dedicated hardware—that is responsible for this function. Get this information from your TCP/IP network administrator. All of the adapters will use this route. Later in this chapter we will examine ways to get around the single default router limitation.
- **Adapter—**This drop-down box lists all of the adapters in your system. If you have more than one network card, then you can set the parameters for each of them here. Simply fill out the information for the first adapter, then select the next one from this drop-down list. NT will remember the settings for all of the adapters. The number in parentheses before the adapter description is the load order of all the adapters in the system. An adapter with a (1) means that it is loaded first, (2) means second, etc. This will be of significance later.
- **IP Address**—This is where you put the network address for *this specific adapter*. Each adapter gets its own unique address. Other machines use this address to find you when they have network traffic to send. Get your address from the network administrator. If you *are* the network administrator, get a valid block of addresses from the Network Information Center (details for doing this, as well as more information on TCP/IP, are available in Appendix 2). When you receive your IP address from your network administrator, be sure to copy it carefully and confirm that it is correct. Do the same when you enter it into the dialog box—duplicate IP addresses on a network can cause all sorts of problems, including lockups.
- **Subnet Mask**—This number is used to mathematically "mask" IP addresses on your network. In other words, it eliminates those parts of an IP address that are alike for machines on your network. It is absolutely essential that this number be correct. Treat this the same way you do the IP address—make sure it is right. If it is incorrect, you will not be able to "see" the other machines on your network. Once you've entered the IP address, NT will automatically guess the appropriate subnet mask, based on the "class" of the address. You will need to modify this value only if you are using non-

standard subnet masks on your network. All systems using the same addressing schemes must use the same subnet mask in order to see each other (refer to Appendix 2 for more details on subnet masks and how they can be useful).

- **Windows Networking on TCP/IP**—Windows networking products (NT and Windows for Workgroups) can use their native NetBIOS transport over a TCP/IP network. This can be done either on the same network adapter used for normal TCP/IP or on a different one. The native network services in NT are derived from Microsoft's work with LAN Manager, which uses NetBIOS as the common network application interface. This NetBIOS layer can be bound to only *one* network adapter's TCP/IP stack. By default, it is bound to the first adapter, although you can change it here if you need to. **NOTE**: Be sure to remember the adapter and its IP address for inclusion in the LMHOSTS database.
- **Scope ID for Windows Networking**—The "Scope ID" allows you to set a filter on the NBT traffic you want the machine to see. By default, NT uses the system's domain name as the Scope ID. Like subnet masks, the Scope ID must be consistent across all machines for the systems to see each other.
- **Import LMHOSTS**—Since Windows NT's built-in networking uses NetBIOS for naming, in order to use the address-specific TCP/IP services you must have the LMHOSTS database to map server names and their role in the domain to their IP addresses. Pressing this button allows you to use a predefined database. If you are not using the TCP/IP services for NBT purposes, you can ignore this. However, if you are running NBT over TCP/IP, then you *must* use this file for the system to join a Windows NT workgroup or Windows NT Advanced Server (or LAN Manager) domain. Copy the LMHOSTS file from an existing system, or create a new one using a text editor (see the section on LMHOSTS later in this chapter for details), and copy it to a floppy disk. When you press this button, NT will prompt you for the file. Failing to use "Import the Database" during initial installation will result in errors, and you'll have to do it later anyway.
- **Connectivity. . .**—Pressing this button opens the dialog illustrated in Figure 6.4. The TCP/IP Connectivity Configuration dialog allows you to set the various parameters related to DNS (Domain Name Service). The DNS server on your network lets you use names, rather than numbers, to connect to other machines. The only alternative to DNS is the HOSTS file. This is a list of IP names and addresses stored in a text file similar to the LMHOSTS file used for NBT networking. The advantage of DNS over HOSTS is that central storage of names and addresses on the DNS server allows a single change or addition to be used by everyone on the network. NOTE: While Windows NT can use a DNS server, no DNS server for Windows NT is available as of this writing.
- **Host Name**—This is the name that others will use to connect to your workstation. By default, NT uses the system's workstation name (assigned during installation) as the TCP/IP hostname. If you want to change it, type in the new value here, but make sure you tell the other users so they can update their HOSTS database files.
- **TCP Domain Name**—If you are in a TCP/IP domain, type in the domain name here (this is *not* the same as your Windows NT Domain or Workgroup). Get this value from

your network administrator. (See Appendix 2 for more information on TCP/IP domain names.)

Combining the Domain Name and Host Name entries will give you a complete DNS name. For example, if your machine name is colossus and your domain name is forbin.com, your fully qualified domain name (FQDN)—equivalent through DNS to your numerical IP address—is colossus.forbin.com. Note that the ".com" part of this name indicates that this is a commercial enterprise. Other extensions are used to indicate other types of organizations; for example: .edu for educational institutions, .org for nonprofit organizations, .net for networks, .mil for military (thus *milnet* is the military section of the *internet*), etc.

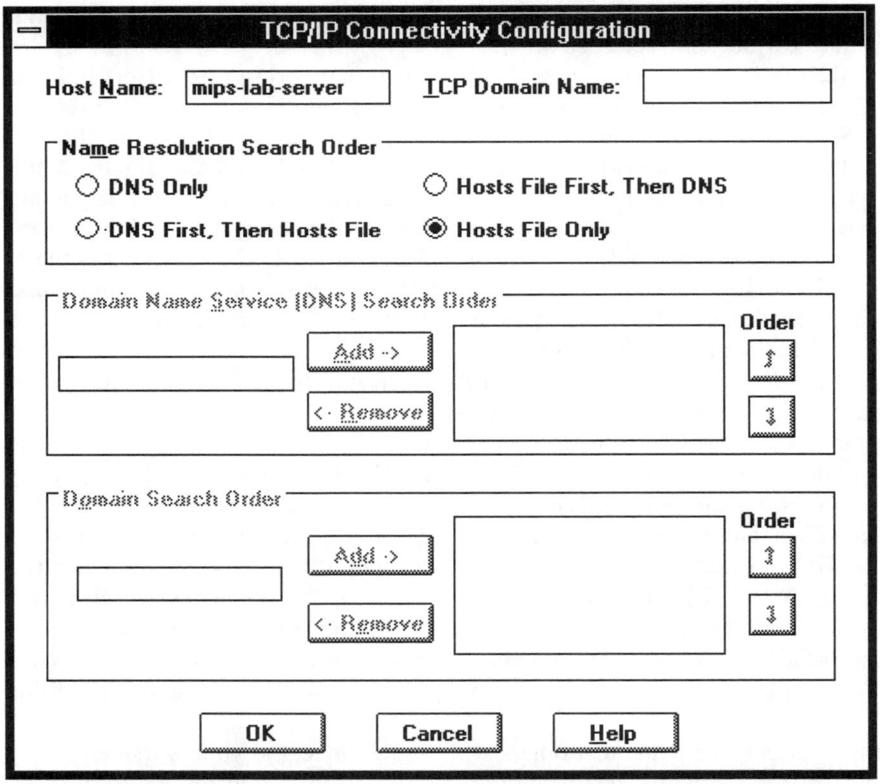

Figure 6.4 TCP/IP connectivity

The TCP/IP Connectivity Configuration dialog box determines what method Windows NT uses to resolve *names* into valid TCP/IP *addresses*.

- **Name Resolution Search Order**—Unlike NetBIOS, TCP/IP does not use hostnames to communicate with other nodes, but instead uses IP addresses. You can tell NT to use the HOSTS database file to map hostnames to IP addresses, or to use a Domain Name Service (DNS) server. You can also tell it to use both, in case one or the other fails (for more information on DNS and name resolution in general, refer to Appendix 2).
- **Domain Name Service (DNS) Search Order**—If you tell NT not to use DNS, this portion of the dialog box will be disabled. If you *are* using DNS, then you must tell NT the IP addresses of the name servers you wish to use, and their precedence. To add a DNS server to the list, type in the IP address in the edit box on the left and click the Add button. To change the search order for DNS queries, select the IP address from the listbox on the right, and click the up or down arrow buttons to move the server up or down the list as desired.
- **Domain Search Order**—If you tell NT not to use DNS, this portion of the dialog box is grayed out. If you are using DNS, then you need to tell NT the TCP/IP domains that you want to search in. By default, NT will look in the domain you specify in the TCP Domain Name field discussed above. To add other domains, type them in the edit box on the left and click the Add button. To change the search order for DNS queries, select the domain name from the listbox on the right, and click the up or down arrow buttons to move the domain name up or down the list as desired.
- **Completing Your TCP/IP Installation**—To complete TCP/IP configuration, press the OK button, which will return you to the TCP/IP configuration dialog. You will be notified that your machine needs to be restarted for the configuration to take effect. You have the option to reboot the machine at this point; choose Yes if you want to use TCP/IP right away. Otherwise, your changes will take effect next time you restart your NT system.

Routing

In the previous section you saw how to configure your NT system to use TCP/IP. This included choosing whether to use DNS (Domain Name Service). If you are on a network with a DNS server, you should use it. If your network doesn't offer DNS, though, you will have to create and maintain a local HOSTS file for name resolution.

The HOSTS, LMHOSTS, NETWORKS, PROTOCOL, and SERVICES Files

Although most of the configuration settings for the TCP/IP services are managed by the Network Control Panel object, there are a collection of files that can make life easier for your users. These files are stored in the directory specified by the HKEY_LOCAL_MACHINE\CURRENT_CONTROL_SET\Services\Tcpip\Parameters\DataBasePath entry of the Windows NT system registry (\winnt\system32\drivers\etc by default). The filenames and a description of their functions are listed below.

Filename	*Description*
HOSTS	Hostname to IP address database
NETWORKS	Network name to network number database
PROTOCOL	Protocol name to protocol number database
SERVICES	Application/service name to port number database

WARNING: *Unlike most other Windows NT configuration and settings files, the HOSTS, LMHOSTS, NETWORKS, PROTOCOL, and SERVICES files are not maintained in the Registry database, and fallback data for these files is not part of the "Last known good" data available on system restart. It is essential that administrators maintain backup copies of these files!*

HOSTS

People have a difficult time remembering 32-bit binary numbers, which is why the IP address is most commonly represented by four 8-bit numbers instead. But even then, remembering a bunch of obscure number sequences can be a mental strain. TCP/IP allows users to use hostnames for systems instead, making life easier. For example, to connect to a VAX, you could type "telnet vax" instead of "telnet 192.155.13.116.", provided your host file is properly set up as shown below.

Windows NT TCP/IP uses a file called HOSTS to map IP addresses to well-known hostnames. The file is simple in structure, containing an IP address, the hostname, and (optionally) a comment preceded by a pound (#) sign. An entry in the HOSTS database file to substitute "vax" for IP address 192.155.13.116 would look like this:

```
192.155.13.116        vax          #Mapping for local VAX mini
```

Hosts you connect with often can be added to this database at any time. TCP/IP will consult the database whenever a hostname is passed to it (provided the proper Name Resolution Search Order setting has been selected, as described above).

HOSTS File Tips

- **Back up HOSTS before making changes.** The copy can be placed in the same directory as the real HOSTS file and will protect you from inadvertent changes you might make during editing. HOSTS files can become large, with many entries, and they just won't work if the IP addresses are incorrect.
- **Keep the HOSTS file up-to-date.** Be sure to keep track of machines added to or taken from the network, and make sure your HOSTS file reflects these changes. To help automate this process, the administrator can use email to send changes and updates that can be placed in the HOSTS file through copy and paste. If you can maintain exactly the same HOSTS file on *all* machines, the process of update is even simpler. The administrator can place the updated file directly into the machines directory

with no user intervention using NT's native networking capabilities. Obviously, this is less critical if your network uses DNS—but be aware that the HOSTS file is the fall-back for DNS name resolution if the DNS server is down; so even on DNS networks, periodically updating HOSTS is a good idea.

- **Keep HOSTS entries in order.** Since HOSTS files are read in the order they're written, you should place the entries covering your most frequently used hosts at the top of the file to speed searches.
- **Editing HOSTS.** If you have a big HOSTS file, you might find it easier to maintain in a spreadsheet. To do this, update the spreadsheet, then save it as text—*not the native format*—of your spreadsheet. This way you can use the database and organizational functions of the spreadsheet on your library of IP names and addresses. Alternatively, you can create a Program Manager icon that automatically launches Notepad with the HOSTS file to make maintenance easier. To do so:

  1. Run Windows NT Program Manager, and bring the Administrative Tools group to the topmost Program Manager window.
  2. Select New from the Program Manager File menu. The New Program Object dialog appears. Select the Program Item radiobutton and click OK.
  3. The Program Item Properties dialog appears. Edit the Command Line field to read:

     ```
     notepad.exe HOSTS
     ```

  4. Edit the Working Directory field to point to the \DRIVERS\ETC subdirectory of the SYSTEM32 directory. If your system has a WINNT directory, then the Working Directory field should read:

     ```
     C:\WINNT\SYSTEM32\DRIVERS\ETC
     ```

  5. Enter "TCP/IP HOSTS File" in the Description field, and click OK.

Obviously, you can use the same approach to provide icons for the LMHOSTS, NETWORKS, PROTOCOLS, and SERVICES files, if you want—and you can substitute any other appropriate program (such as the spreadsheet mentioned above) for NOTEPAD.EXE.

LMHOSTS

This text file works just like the HOSTS file and uses the same format. The difference is that it is used to translate Windows NT names to numerical IP addresses for use by the NetBIOS-over-TCP/IP (NBT) protocol. It's covered in more detail below, in the section on "Mapping NetBIOS Names to TCP/IP Addresses."

NETWORKS

Just as you can create alias names for hosts, you can create alias names for networks. If you are in a complex environment, creating aliases helps you keep track of different networks. For example, you can type the command "netstat -r", and see that network "Lab 10baseT" is up, rather than having to remember that 192.155.12 is the IP number for that network. To do so, the NETWORKS file would need the following entry:

```
Lab10baseT                192.155.12
```

PROTOCOL and SERVICES

The remaining two TCP/IP files are not likely to require editing in normal use. PROTOCOL allows you to define the specifics of the IP, TCP, ICMP, etc., protocol levels within the overall TCP/IP suite. If you replace (or augment) Windows NT's built-in TCP/IP protocol stack with a third-party stack then you may need to edit this file. SERVICES provides a similar capability for mapping application-level communication requests to a well-known TCP/IP port number. More information on these files can be found in Appendix 2, and in the Microsoft TCP/IP documentation included with Windows NT.

Using TCP/IP with Windows NT's Built-in Networking

Since most of NT's network functionality is dependent upon the NetBIOS APIs, most users will need to incorporate the NetBIOS-over-TCP/IP (NBT) services into their configuration. Configuring NT to map NetBIOS machine names to IP addresses is a nontrivial task, although the payback can be great, especially in large networks.

An Overview of NetBIOS on TCP/IP (NBT)

NetBIOS (which, as we've seen, is used by Windows NT's built-in networking) uses *machine names* to identify nodes on the network, and for all exchanges of information between them. NetBIOS accomplishes this almost exclusively with *broadcasting*. When a new node comes on the net, it broadcasts its assigned name, and if no other node challenges the name (or claims to be using it already), it keeps the name for itself. It does not register the name anywhere, but instead each node is responsible for maintaining its own name tables. If a subsequent node comes on the net and claims the same name, it is the responsibility of the first node to challenge the new one.

Likewise, when a node needs to communicate with another node, it uses broadcasting to find the remote system. The remote system is responsible for responding to the broadcast with a directed reply. Once nodes have identified each other, they can communicate with directed messages.

An example that illustrates the broadcast-dependent nature of NetBIOS is the *net view* command. When you type "net view" from a command prompt, the Windows NT Workstation service issues a directed query to the domain browsemaster—unless it can't find the browsemaster, in which case it sends a broadcast on the subnet(s) it is attached to. After a specified amount of time, it lists the servers that responded to the broadcast. If you want to see a specific node, such as "mips-lab-server" you can issue the "net view mips-lab-server" command, and a directed query is sent to the known node.

The Windows NT NetBIOS implementation for built-in networking is *protocol independent.* NetBIOS is just an API. It does not have to use any specific low-level transport protocol to communicate with other systems. However, all of the systems that wish to *communicate* with NetBIOS must use the *same* low-level transport protocol. Otherwise, they would never see each other, and the NetBIOS API would be useless.

By default, Windows NT uses NetBEUI as the transport protocol. NetBEUI is based on the X/Open standard Server Message Block (SMB) protocols, with a NetBIOS API. It was originated by IBM in 1985, for use with small LANs. NetBEUI is very small, fast, and efficient.

However, NetBEUI is a *nonroutable* protocol, meaning that it has no mechanism for identifying different network segments. The entire network must look like one big wire in order for NetBEUI to communicate with remote segments. Unfortunately, the number of nodes a single network organized in this way can handle is fairly limited, and bridging multiple segments into one large network—especially when wide-area links are involved—is a sure way to kill performance. Likewise, since NetBIOS uses a flat, nonhierarchical database for node names, it has no mechanism for targeting broadcasts to a remote segment. Thus, NetBEUI is a poor choice for large, complex networks.

Fortunately, the NetBIOS APIs can be used with *any* low-level transport protocol—such as TCP/IP. Unlike NetBEUI, TCP/IP is completely routable. Indeed, it is predominantly a point-to-point protocol that avoids broadcasting whenever possible. Thus, using TCP/IP as a way to move NetBIOS-based data is an attractive alternative to NetBEUI, especially in large and complex environments. Although this is an improvement, it is still hindered by the need for NetBIOS broadcasts (using TCP/IP sockets instead of NetBIOS would eliminate this problem, and may be an optional course of action for Microsoft in the future).

Since NetBIOS uses *names* for addressing purposes, while TCP/IP uses *numbers*, there must be some way to map the two so that both of them see what they expect. In order for NetBIOS-based applications to run over TCP/IP networks, the NetBIOS application must see names, and the IP protocol must see numbers, yet neither can see the other. A layer between the two must map NetBIOS names to IP addresses, and convert IP addresses back to NetBIOS names. This layer is known as the NetBIOS-over-TCP/IP (or NBT) service. Figure 6.5 shows a high-level view of the various layers.

Mapping NetBIOS Names to TCP/IP Addresses

TCP/IP standards are defined by *Requests for Comment*, or RFCs. Anyone may submit an RFC for inclusion in the TCP/IP protocol suite standard (even you). Two such RFCs are 1001 and 1002, which define a standard method for running NetBIOS over TCP/IP. RFC 1001 defines a general overview, while RFC 1002 defines the detailed specifications (for more information on RFCs, refer to Appendix 2).

There are three types of NetBIOS nodes defined in the RFCs. A b-node (broadcast node) is one that uses broadcasting to find other nodes on the network. A p-node (point-to-point node) uses directed UDP and TCP calls to communicate with other nodes. The name-to-address mapping for a p-node is handled by a dedicated *nameserver*. Finally, an m-node is a mixed node, one that uses both p-node nameservers and broadcasting to find other systems.

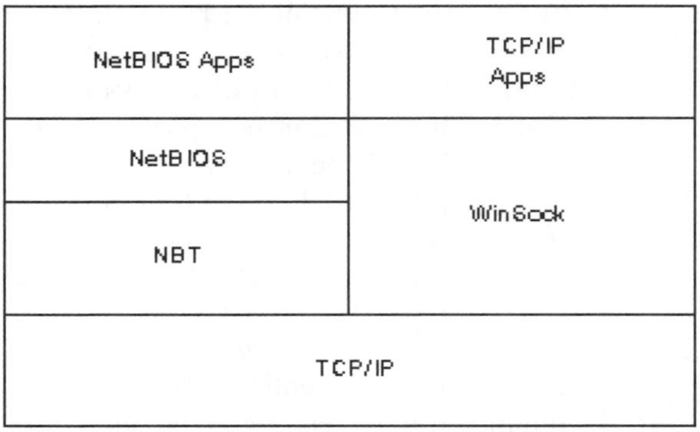

NetBIOS Apps	TCP/IP Apps
NetBIOS	WinSock
NBT	
TCP/IP	

Figure 6.5 NBT.

The NetBIOS-over-TCP/IP (NBT) layers.

Remember that the node types apply only when a node is attempting to find other systems. Once the two have discovered each other, they use directed messaging.

NT systems use a modification of the b-node specification. They are broadcast-reliant nodes. *But broadcasts can't be routed between network segments,* since IP routers don't typically forward broadcast packets (if they did, an entire network could easily be bogged down with broadcast traffic spreading from subnet to subnet like a cancer!). How do nodes on one segment find nodes on another? Simple: they are told how to using a file called LMHOSTS that contains a database of NetBIOS names and the node's "real" IP address.

The LMHOSTS format is identical to the HOSTS file described earlier, with a numerical IP address, a tab character, and a Windows NT name (and optionally, a comment); for example:

```
128.0.0.1 lm-machine
```

LMHOSTS is read by the NT system at startup and cached in memory, so any changes you make will not take effect until you either restart or execute NBSTAT -R from the command line.

Do not confuse the LMHOSTS database with the HOSTS database. Although they are similar in use and structure, they serve two entirely separate purposes. The HOSTS file is a database for *all* the systems you use, while the LMHOSTS file is strictly for Windows NT (and LAN Manager) machines. Typically, the LMHOSTS file only shows a few systems. This does *not* mean that there are only a few nodes on the network, but that there are only a few *remote* nodes that must be addressed directly. Let's look at the name resolution process in detail. As an example, we will use the **net view** command discussed in Chapter 4.

Assume that your PC is on subnet 192.155.11, and you're a member of the marketing domain (which contains the marketing1 and marketing2 servers). There are also two servers named app1 and app2, which are *not* in the marketing domain, but are listed in your

LMHOSTS file. Typing net view from your PC's command line would start the following sequence of events:

1. The NBT service will convert the NetBIOS broadcast into a UDP broadcast.
2. All of the servers on the local segment that are members of the marketing domain will respond.
3. NBT will send the query directly to the marketing1, marketing2, app1, and app2 servers.
4. marketing1 and marketing2 will respond.
5. Your system displays a list of all the servers on the local subnet that are running TCP/IP and are in the marketing domain, and also shows the marketing2 and marketing3 servers. The app servers aren't in your domain, so they don't appear.

There are many things *not* happening here as well. There may be many other servers on other subnets that are not being queried (because they are *neither* on the immediate subnet, *nor* listed in your LMHOSTS file). Therefore, b-node queries are never generated for them. Simply put, they are invisible to your system.

Servers like app1 and app2, that *are* on the local subnet but are *not* in the marketing domain, also don't show up in the net view query, because they are not in the domain. Even though b-node queries were generated for them, they are not in the marketing domain and thus would not respond to the query (unless an *inter-domain trust link* has been set up for them—see Chapter 7 for details). This is a function of Windows NT NetBIOS, and not a function of NBT.

LMHOSTS simply acts to extend the realm of the broadcast area to include hosts that would otherwise be unreachable. By using this method, NT takes advantage of both the broadcasting and point-to-point architectures, without relying on a dedicated nameserver. Since broadcasting is necessary in the dynamic environments so typical of peer-to-peer LANs (because it's impossible to predict *which* systems will be available *when*), it is the preferred vehicle for name resolution. For example, if the primary domain controller were down, then another would respond to any broadcast-based query, such as a login request. This increases network reliability tremendously, without forcing users to place servers on every segment.

More specifically, name resolution takes the following steps to find a node's IP address:

1. NBT searches its internal cache for the NetBIOS name and IP address.
2. If the address is not found in the cache, a b-node broadcast is issued.
3. Failing a response from a local node, NBT searches the LMHOSTS file.
4. If a match is not found, a name-not-found error is returned to NetBIOS.

By understanding the sequence of events, and also by knowing a few tricks that we're about to show you, you can customize your environment for both speedy responses and flexibility.

The Name Resolution Cache

Since NBT first checks the local name cache for entries, it is best to preload some names into the cache at boot time. Thus, your system won't have to wait for the local broadcasts to time out, nor go through the trouble of having to check the LMHOSTS file. Adding a name to the cache is done by adding a "#PRE" command to an entry in the file:

```
192.155.11.10      marketing1      #PRE    #Marketing Domain Controller
```

Preloading the marketing1 server into NBT's cache speeds up the name resolution process considerably. Likewise it's worth preloading the app1 and app2 servers, if they're acessed frequently. In fact, you can preload every node on the network (up to a maximum of 100). There isn't much of a need to do this, however, since successful resolutions via broadcasts and lookups are also held in the cache for a while. If you need to preload more than 100 addresses (which you might in a really large network), here's how to do so:

1. Start the Registry Editor by typing "REGEDT32.EXE" in the <FILE><RUN> menu of either Program Manager or File Manager, or from a command prompt.
2. When the Registry Editor starts, select the HKEY_LOCAL_MACHINE key, and find the SYSTEM tree.
3. Double-click the SYSTEM folder icon, and select the CurrentControlSet folder. Continue working down the tree until you get to the SYSTEM\CurrentControlSet\Services\Tcpip\Parameters folder, and then select it.
4. Under the <EDIT> menu, select <Add Value>. In the Value Name field, type the keyword MaxPreload and then select a Data Type of REG_DWORD. Click the OK button, and type the desired number of preloaded entries into the String Editor dialog box.
5. You must shut down and restart the system after making these changes in order for routing to begin.

Items stored in the cache with the #PRE command never leave the cache unless forced. Using the NBTSTAT -R command will flush the cache, and reload the first 100 #PRE entries from the LMHOSTS file.

Note that although the # symbol in the LMHOSTS file normally signifies a comment, Windows NT uses the #PRE string as a valid flag. This is for backward compatibility with LAN Manager servers that do not support selective preloading. They will ignore the #PRE command, simply because they will not see it.

Specifying Domain Controllers

Whenever a client attempts to log onto the network, broadcasting is used. Normally, a broadcast message follows the chain of events described above, but where domain controllers are involved, it is sometimes necessary to bypass normal channels. We certainly don't want domain controllers broadcasting password changes to every node on the network *and* all the nodes in the LMHOSTS file!

To signify that a system is a domain controller, put the #DOM flag in the LMHOSTS file:

```
192.155.11.10      marketing1      #PRE    #DOM    #Marketing Domain Controller
```

The #DOM keyword activates a pseudo-backchannel for communication between domain controllers. All domain controllers should have entries in their local LMHOSTS files for all of the other controllers within their domain. Also, if trust relationships have been established across separate domains, then there should be entries for the primary controllers within the trusted domains (and perhaps for backup domain controllers as well).

In fact, you might want to set #DOM for all Windows NT Advanced Servers on your network. Otherwise, if the primary domain controller fails, then a server that promotes itself to domain controller will not be able to use the backchannel for domain administration.

Sharing LMHOSTS Files

Obviously, large networks with multiple trusted relationships and many hosts will have a hard time dealing with massive LMHOSTS databases. There are a couple of tricks that can help in this situation. One is to use the #INCLUDE flag. #INCLUDE tells NBT to read not only the local LMHOSTS file, but other files as well. This would allow you to point NBT to a shared LMHOSTS file on a departmental server or domain controller. For instance:

```
#INCLUDE \\marketing1\public\lmhosts
```

In this example, the local PC will incorporate any entries in the remote LMHOSTS file whenever a lookup is needed. Although you can point to as many remote databases as needed, you should keep the remote #INCLUDE list as small as possible. If you do this, make sure to give users at least read-only access to the shared file. Also, *never* reference drive letters for remote systems, but instead use the UNC names of the share point whenever possible (remember, remote drive letters can change!). For servers that need to share master copies, you can take advantage of NT's replication features to make sure that backups are always available (see Chapter 7 for details).

There are other tricks that you can do with the #INCLUDE command. For example, suppose that marketing1 was down. You would not be able to read the remote LMHOSTS file. You would not want to put multiple #INCLUDE statements for each of the servers in the marketing domain, as that would increase your search time with no foreseeable benefit (the data in each file would be the same).

However, by enclosing a block of #INCLUDES with #BEGIN_ALTERNATE and #END_ALTERNATE commands, you can tell NBT to search the first available LMHOSTS file. Thus, if marketing1 were down, NBT would search marketing2's LMHOSTS file:

```
#BEGIN_ALTERNATE
#INCLUDE \\marketing1\public\lmhosts
#INCLUDE \\marketing2\public\lmhosts
#INCLUDE \\marketing3\public\lmhosts
#END_ALTERNATE
```

Miscellany

There are a few other issues that arise when using NT's TCP/IP protocol suite. These are things that you need to be aware of before building your NetBEUI-less networks.

- Windows NT systems that will only be using TCP/IP to connect with a domain controller on a remote subnet will not be able to join the domain unless an LMHOSTS file is preconfigured for the system. Otherwise, the b-node broadcasts would never make it to the domain controller. When you first install the software, remove NetBEUI from the bindings, add TCP/IP, and follow the directions for "Import LMHOSTS..." as described at the beginning of this chapter.
- LMHOSTS files cannot use DNS names in lieu of IP addresses. The file *must* include IP addresses for mapping to remote systems. Although technically there is no reason why it shouldn't work, it doesn't.
- NBT works over only one adapter. By default, it is the adapter numbered (0) in the Networks Control Panel. To modify this, either deactivate the first binding, or change the load order of the adapters with the "Bindings..." button within the Network Control Panel. Select the adapter you want to promote from the drop-down listbox, and click the up and down buttons to change its load order.
- To ease administration, you can name your NT domains the same as your TCP/IP domains.
- Although you cannot run pure TCP/IP applications over Windows NT Remote Access Service (RAS), systems that connect to a server via RAS will be able to see NBT resources if the RAS server has TCP/IP loaded (and NBT properly bound). See Chapter 7 for more information on RAS.

Using Windows NT TCP/IP Utilities

If you are familiar with using TCP/IP utilities on a UNIX system, you will be right at home on an NT system. The utilities provided by Microsoft are of the standard variety with little difference from any others you may have used.

The utilities included with Windows NT allow you to take advantage of UNIX systems, and others with TCP/IP server capabilities. These capabilities include:

- Connecting to a remote host for an interactive session using Telnet
- Transferring data between your workstation and the host with the UNIX-standard File Transfer Protocol (FTP)
- Executing programs on the remote host with Rexec

With the exception of the built-in FTP service, Windows NT cannot provide any of these services out of the box, although it *can* access these services as a client. This means you will probably be connecting to a UNIX system unless you purchase a third-party package that gives Windows NT additional capabilities. The behavior of remote systems contacted via IP client utilities is remarkably consistent. Whether the system is running UNIX, VMS, DOS, or even Windows, once you become familiar with connecting to any one of these systems you will find yourself quite at home with the others.

Connecting to a Remote Host

The IP utilities provided with Windows NT offer at least two different ways to interact with a remote host. First is *Telnet,* which allows you to login to the remote machine using terminal emulation. This works just as if you had a terminal hard-wired right to the remote host. The other method is through the *finger* utility. Finger offers a way to ask a remote host for information without actually logging in.

Telnet

Since a Telnet session requires a terminal emulator, Windows NT uses the 32-bit version of the standard Windows Terminal application (TERMINAL.EXE) for the job. Typing "telnet" in a command window will start the NT Telnet network service, launch Terminal and display the telnet> prompt (Figure 6.6). It is now ready for Telnet commands.

The Windows NT Telnet service supports ten commands and aliases. To begin a Telnet session, use the *open* (or *connect*) command. The syntax for this command is simple:

```
telnet> open remote_host
```

where remote_host is the name or numerical IP address of the desired host. For example, to connect to a host called colossus in the domain forbin.com, type:

```
telnet> open colossus.forbin.com
```

or

```
telnet> connect colossus.forbin.com
```

alternatively, the numerical IP address can be used in decimal dotted form:

```
telnet> open 128.0.0.1
```

(For more information on IP addresses, see Appendix 2 and the configuration section of this chapter.)

The Windows NT Telnet service will respond with:

```
Trying...
```

to indicate that it is attempting to make your connection. Assuming you don't see a "Connect failed" message (which indicates a problem), what happens next depends upon the remote system. Below is the way a typical session starts; this is a general purpose machine—a VAX, as you can see from the text:

```
telnet> open nwc.com
Trying...
Connected to nwc.com.
Escape character is '^]'.
VAX
Username:
```

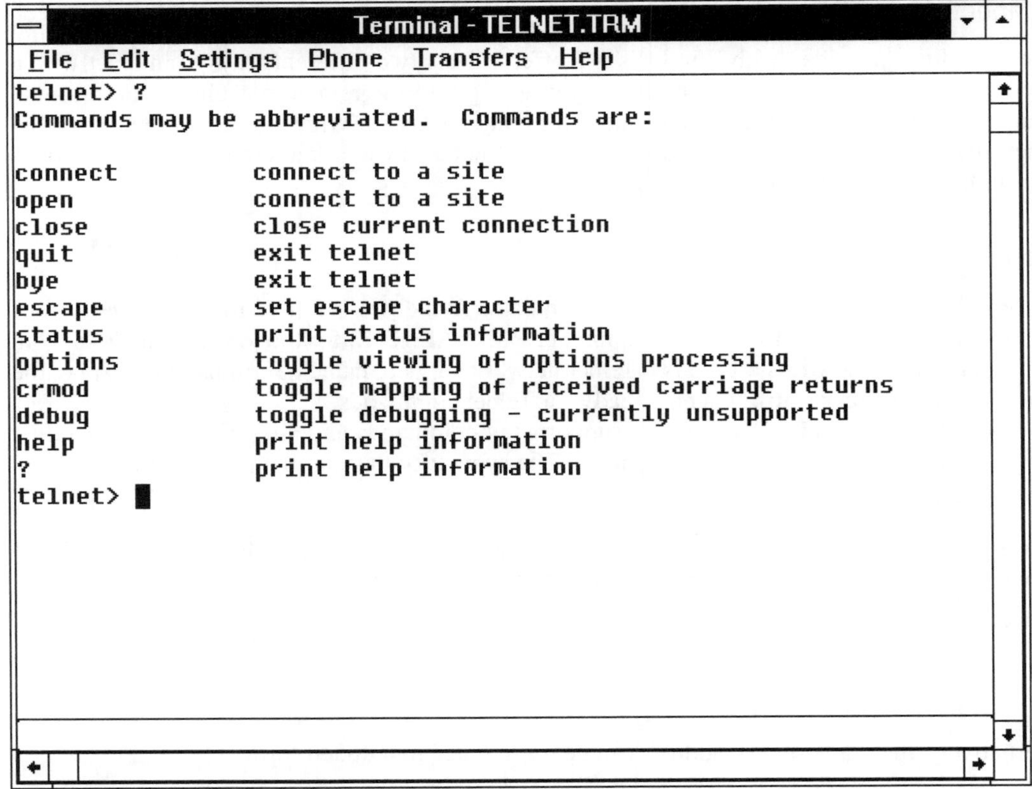

Figure 6.6 Telnet.

Telnet support is provided through the Windows Terminal Program.

Typically, the first thing the remote system sends is a description of the operating system running. This helps clue you in on the structure of the file system and, if you are familiar with the operating system, commands that will be available to you.

Next is the login prompt, which is literally:

```
login:
```

on UNIX systems. As you can see, the VAX system in our example offers a Username: prompt, which is what VAX systems do. Anything that follows your login is entirely up to what you do with your connection.

Some systems are intended to provide special services via a Telnet session. On these systems the initial screen varies dramatically. For example, here's a screen from the InterNIC gopher, a system that provides information about systems and users on the Internet:

```
telnet> open rs.internic.net
Trying...
Connected to rs.internic.net
Escape character is '^]'.

SunOS UNIX (rs) (ttyr3)
**************************************************************************
*—InterNIC Registration Services Center  —
*
* For gopher, type:                    GOPHER <return>
* For wais, type:                      WAIS <search string> <return>
* For the *original* whois type:       WHOIS [search string] <return>
* For the X.500 whois DUA, type:       X500WHOIS <return>
* For registration status:             STATUS <ticket number> <return>
*
* For user assistance call (800) 444-4345 | (619) 455-4600 or (703) 742-4777
* Please report system problems to ACTION@rs.internic.net
**************************************************************************
Please be advised that the InterNIC Registration host contains INTERNET
Domains, IP Network Numbers, ASNs, and Points of Contacts ONLY. Please
refer to rfc1400.txt for details (available via anonymous ftp at
either nic.ddn.mil [/rfc/rfc1400.txt]  or ftp.rs.internic.net
[/policy/rfc1400.txt]).
Cmdinter Ver 1.3 Fri Jul 16 16:12:16 1993 EST
[vt100] InterNIC >
```

As you can see, this looks quite different from a generic UNIX login, provides a lot of specific information on how to use the system, and does not require a login name—since it is a public service.

During your Telnet session you may need to change a local parameter from the Telnet command line. You do this by entering the *escape character* (which defaults to CTRL+]). This character was chosen because it is very unlikely to show up in text or be needed for anything else. If this conflicts with something that you need to do, you can change it using the escape command. Entering the escape command at the telnet> prompt gets the response:

```
new escape character:
```

Simply type your choice for a new escape character and hit ENTER. You choice will be confirmed with a message:

```
Escape Character is '^='.
```

where your new choice is inside the single quotes—in this case CTRL+=, with CTRL indicated by the caret (^).

Using the escape character does *not* end your Telnet session—it simply "escapes" to the prompt so that you can enter commands to change your Telnet configuration. While some Telnet clients have several options that might be useful at this point, the version supplied with NT at this time has only one option that you might use during a session: *crmod.*

The crmod command toggles Windows NT Telnet's addition of a carriage return when it sees a line feed. You need this only if you find that your display is being garbled by the remote system. To use crmod, just type it at the prompt. You will receive the confirming message:

```
Will map carriage return on output.
```

Remember, crmod toggles the state of this option. Since the default is off, typing it the first time turns it on. Typing it again turns it off.

While you are at the Telnet prompt you can get information about the session in progress with the Status command. To return to your Telnet session, hit ENTER.

Ending a Telnet Session

Ending a Telnet session is accomplished in one of two ways. First and best is to simply log out from the system to which you are connected. This will terminate your Telnet session. The other is useful if the remote system is not responding, or for some reason will not release your session; you can use the escape character to get back to your Telnet prompt and issue a *close*, *quit*, or *bye* to end the session.

RSH and REXEC

If you don't need a completely interactive session with a host, you can use the RSH and REXEC utilities to execute a single command on a remote system. These are noninteractive utilities, so you can't run a text editor or the like in this manner, but you can retrieve a directory listing, or type out a file, or execute any noninteractive commands.

RSH and REXEC are virtually identical. In fact, they both provide the exact same service, and even use the same command-line parameters. The difference between the two is based on authority. While RSH uses the concept of trust between remote hosts, REXEC does not. The latter requires a username and password to pass to the host for authentication before executing the command.

For example, assume that there are two hosts named GRUMPY and DOPEY. GRUMPY "trusts" the NT system, using either the .rhosts or /etc/hosts.equiv files. A user on the NT system could list the files in his or her home directory on GRUMPY by issuing the command "rsh grumpy ls." Since the host GRUMPY trusts the NT system, it accepts the RSH request, logs in with the user's account, executes the command "ls," and returns the results. Then it logs the user out.

DOPEY, however, doesn't trust the NT machine. When a user wants to run a program on DOPEY, the user needs to use the REXEC command. This requires the user to provide a username and password for the remote command. Thus, to list the files in the user's home directory on DOPEY, the user would type "rexec dopey -l username ls." Then NT will ask for a password to go with the username entered in the command line. The username and password are sent over to DOPEY, which verifies the account, and if accurate, logs the user in and runs the command. Note that the REXEC utility will abort if no password is given, so if the remote user ID doesn't have a password, you can't use this program. RSH, however, allows you to use usernames with no password.

In order for a host to provide remote command execution services, it must be running the appropriate remote server service programs. Currently, NT does not offer this functionality, so it can act only as a client. Furthermore, although the default action for the RSH command is to allow users to log in if no command has been passed on the command line, the RSH and REXEC utilities bundled with NT do not allow this. A command must be provided in order for the utilities to run.

For information on setting up trust between hosts, refer to the documentation provided with the system that will act as your server.

Finger

Another way to interact with a remote system is through the *finger* command. Finger is, essentially, a way to query a remote system for information in the form of text. The principal use of finger is to identify users on the remote system (hence its name), but it has gained popularity as a way of distributing any sort of information that a system administrator wants to provide. The traditional use of finger—identifying users—is simple. At the NT command prompt type:

```
finger user_name@host.domain.com
```

Depending upon how the remote system supports finger, your results will vary. For example, the Massachusetts-based public access UNIX system "world" run by Software Tool & Die takes a finger request pretty seriously:

```
finger bgaret@world.std.com
jgaret@world.std.com
[world.std.com]
world—The World—Public Access UNIX—Solbourne 5E/900 OS/MP 4.1A.3
  5:14pm  up 24 days, 15:05,  69 users,  load average: 13.33, 15.51, 17.16
bgaret . Bill Garet            Login Fri 16-Jul-93 1:11AM from std-annex.sto
  [3374,3374]  </users/bgaret>;  Group: bgaret
  Groups: hamradio bgaret
  bgaret has new mail as of Fri 16-Jul-93 4:58PM
  last read Fri 16-Jul-93 8:24AM
```

Clearly, world.std.com provides plenty of information about the user. On the other hand, some system administrators consider *finger* a security hole, and disable it.

The other way that finger is used is to provide specific text files, but from your point of view it works the same. For example:

```
finger weather@iugate.ucs.indiana.edu
```

This will provide the text for the National Weather Service forecast for central and southern Indiana.

Transferring Data between Hosts with TCP/IP

The TCP/IP client utilities included with NT offer three programs to move files between hosts. RCP, the remote copy program, is the simplest, providing the same functionality as the DOS copy command between hosts. The other two, FTP and TFTP, are the client side of the FTP server discussed later in this chapter. These two programs allow the transfer of files through the standard TCP/IP File Transfer Protocol (FTP) by interacting with the remote machine's server and creating the necessary communications channels.

RCP

RCP stands for "remote copy," which is what this command is all about. You can exchange files with remote hosts—or even copy files from one host to another—without having to log onto them explicitly. RCP uses trust between systems, via either the .rhosts or /etc/equiv.hosts files on the remote systems. You can use explicit user names on the command line, but there must still be trust between the hosts and the NT system.

RCP also supports copying files on the local system, similar to the NT (or DOS) *copy* command line utility. To copy a file named SCHEDULE.TXT to the c:\accounting directory on the remote system, type the command "rcp schedule.txt c:\accounting\schedule.txt".

To copy binary files, such as an executable program or a document with extended characters, use the "-b" option. To copy a file named PAYROLL.WKS from one directory to another, type the command "rcp -b payroll.wks c:\accounting\payroll.wks." If the -b option is left out, RCP assumes that ASCII transfer is all that's needed.

To copy the same spreadsheet to the remote host GRUMPY, use the command "rcp -b payroll.wks grumpy:payroll.wks." To copy the file from GRUMPY to the local NT system, type the command "rcp -b grumpy:payroll.wks payroll.wks."

You can copy entire directory trees from one host to another using the RCP utility as well. If you need to move a bunch of files from a remote host to the local system, or vice-versa, this is the quickest way to get the job done. To copy the entire accounting directory on GRUMPY to the NT system, type the command "rcp -b -r GRUMPY:/accounting c:\accounting". This command will create a directory called c:\payroll on the local NT system, and copy all the files in all of the subdirectories in GRUMPY's /accounting directory.

Like the RSH and REXEC services, the RCP utility is implemented as a client service only. You cannot RCP to and from the NT system from another system. Also, remember that the remote hosts you exchange files with must trust the NT machine you are using. For information on setting up trust between hosts, refer to the documentation provided by the vendor of each system that you want to use.

FTP

The FTP client software included with NT is of the simple command line variety. It lets you establish a connection to the remote machine, log in as a user, and then interact with the host to locate and transfer files. FTP can be used for upload or download, and while it has many subcommands, you need to know only a few to use FTP effectively. There are third-party FTP clients available that offer a friendlier Windows interface.[1] If you find yourself using FTP as

[1]Among others, from Beame & Whiteside, Dunda, ONT, Canada (416)765-0822, and NetManage, Cupertino CA, (408)973-7171. Both companies had announced NT versions as we went to press; but neither shipped product in time for us to describe them here.

part of your daily Windows routine, a Windows NT version of one of these products is probably a good idea. For occasional use, though, the included utility is adequate.

Establishing a Connection

The first step in using the FTP client is to establish a connection. There are two ways to accomplish this. First, if you are not yet running the FTP program, is the command line:

```
ftp <hostname>
```

where hostname is the name or numerical IP address of the host to which you wish to connect. This will execute the FTP program and initiate the connection to the named host. If the FTP program is already running, the open command will perform the same function at the FTP prompt:

```
ftp> open <hostname>
```

The prompt ftp> is displayed whenever the FTP program is running to indicate that it is active.

Logging In

Once the connection to the remote host is established, you will be prompted to log in. Frequently, FTP sessions are of the "anonymous" variety. Anonymous FTP is a way to allow users without accounts on a particular machine to access a public directory (usually called "public" or "pub") to get or send files. Anonymous FTP is prevalent on the Internet. The first message you will see upon connecting is an informational message about the FTP server:

```
220 hostname Windows FTP Server <Version 1.0>.
```

This message provides the name of the machine (hostname), and the operating system/server software. Note the number in front of the message: 220. Each message sent by the FTP server is preceded by a message number. These numbers are used by the client software to determine the meaning of the message. The numbers are standard and can be used to determine what the server is saying with no ambiguity. The text messages are there for your benefit and may vary depending upon the server.

Immediately after this informational message you will be prompted for a user name. This message comes from the client software, *not* the server. When you enter the name, the FTP program uses it as the argument for the "pass" command. For example, if you answer the login prompt:

```
User <hostname:>: anonymous
```

(where <hostname> is displayed by the client to remind you of where you are logging in, and "anonymous" is the user name that you entered). This is then translated by the FTP program and sent to the host as:

```
PASS anonymous
```

Before you saw the User prompt from the FTP program, the server sent a message asking for a login. It was intercepted before you saw it. If for some reason you want to see all the messages, you can use the *verbose* command; just enter it at the ftp> prompt, i.e.:

```
ftp> verbose
```

This will give you a full view of all the messages, which may be useful if you're debugging a system (or interesting if you're just curious). Here's what a successful login looks like:

```
C:\users\default>ftp 130.26.0.100
Connected to 130.26.0.100.
220 emsworth Windows NT FTP Server (Version 1.0).
User (130.26.0.100:): anonymous
331 Anonymous access allowed, send identity (e-mail name) as password.
Password:
230 Anonymous user logged in as ftpuser.
ftp>
```

In this example, the numerical address of the server named "emsworth" is used to connect directly from the command line. The user name anonymous is used; the password—which does not echo—is the real internet email address for the user logging in. This is traditional, since it allows administrators to contact the user should some sort of problem occur. This is not enforced by the server, since it doesn't know who you are. The message that starts with 230 tells us that the login was successful, and for information, indicates that we were logged in as ftpuser. This is the account name that the system administrator assigned to anonymous FTP logins, and determines various access permissions. Most commonly this will say guest, but it can be anything. The return of the ftp> prompt indicates that the FTP client program is ready for the next command.

Navigating on the Remote Host

Once logged in you have access to the directory structure that the remote hosts administrator has made available to FTP users. If you know DOS or UNIX commands, FTP navigation will be old hat. The first thing you are likely to want to do is get a directory of the remote drive. You can do this in more than one way. The two simple ways are with the "dir" and "ls" commands.

The dir command works the way it does in DOS. Exactly what the remote host returns, though, will depend on the file system in use there. There are FTP servers running on just about every sort of machine that can be connected to the Internet. The most common type to see, though, is UNIX. Many FTP servers will even translate their non-UNIX file system into something that looks like one for FTP users. On a NetWare FTP server, the dir command returns:

```
- [RWCEAFMS] supervisor        20319      Aug 12 06:49     vol$log.err
- [RWCEAFMS] supervisor        10423      Aug 12 06:50     tts$log.err
- [RWCEAFMS] supervisor        20480      Aug 12 09:48     backout.tts
d [RWCEAFMS] supervisor          512      Aug 13 09:49     login
d [RWCEAFMS] supervisor          512      Aug 13 10:07     system
```

```
d [RWCEAFMS] supervisor          512      Aug 13 09:49    public
d [RWCEAFMS] supervisor          512      Aug 13 09:49    mail
```

This is a variation on a standard UNIX structure (the differences lie in the way the permissions are indicated). What's important to you, as an FTP user, is the lowercase *d* that precedes the letters in square brackets. This indicates that the entry is a *directory*, instead of a *file*. The UNIX style *ls* command is a quick directory that eliminates everything except the names:

```
vol$log.err
tts$log.err
backout.tts
treeinfo.ncd
login
system
public
mail
```

In this NetWare example, there is no indication that an entry is a directory. On many UNIX systems, a directory will be followed by a forward slash:

```
file
file
directory/
```

One thing to keep in mind as you connect to remote systems is that the file system in use there may be something completely foreign to what you are used to. Some IBM mainframes, for example, use a flat system with no subdirectories, and are very hard to navigate.

Once you determine what is available in the root directory of the remote host, you'll want to switch to the directory of interest. You will almost always have to do this, since it is rare that any files will be in the root directory on an FTP server. Once again your DOS experience will help out. The cd command is used to move to other directories. Remember, though, the DOS convention of "\" as a separator is exactly the opposite of the UNIX world where "/" is used. Just type:

```
ftp> cd directory/directory
```

to switch the working directory. To find out where you are, use the *pwd* (print working directory) command:

```
ftp> pwd
257 "/sys" is the current directory.
```

Getting Files from the Remote Host

You have two choices in transferring files: one at a time or in a batch. The simple one-shot file transfer is done with the *get* command. The syntax is very simple:

```
get <remote file name> <local file name>
```

It works just the way it looks, getting the remote file and storing it in the local file you've named. For instance, the command:

```
get myfile.dat c:\temp\myfile.dat
```

will cause the remote system to send MYFILE.DAT to your system's C:\TEMP directory. The batch method is very similar, using mget (multiple get). With mget, wildcards are allowed, which simplifies batch transfers. For example, to get all the files in the current directory that start with "my" use the command:

```
mget my*
```

Note that the wildcards are UNIX style, so this will get everything that starts with my, *regardless of extension*. The FTP program will prompt you for an OK on each file it finds that matches the wildcard criteria.

Sending Files to the Remote Host

Sending files is done with get's companion command, *put*. There is also an *mput* command, which (surprise!) does a batch-style (or *m*ultiple) *put*. These commands work the same way as *get*:

```
put <local file name> <remote file name>
```

that is:

```
mput c:\temp\myfile.dat myfile.dat
```

or

```
mput my*
```

just as in the previous example.

Manipulating Directories and Files

FTP offers a set of commands to manipulate directories and files:

```
mkdir <directory name>
```

Make Directory creates a directory on the remote host. This command will fail if you do not have sufficient permissions.

```
rmdir <directory name>
```

Remove Directory removes a directory on the remote host. This command will fail if you do not have sufficient permissions.

```
delete <file name>
```

deletes a remote file. This command will fail if you do not have sufficient permissions.

```
mdelete <file spec>
```

Multiple Delete deletes a set of files specified by a wildcard. This command will fail if you do not have sufficient permissions.

```
rename <file name>
```

renames a remote file. This command will fail if you do not have sufficient permissions.

Configuration Commands

There are a few FTP commands that help to make the FTP environment more suitable to your particular use.

```
ascii
```

puts FTP into *ascii* mode for transferring text files. This mode is needed because, for historical reasons, American Standard Code for Information Interchange (ASCII) text files are stored differently on UNIX sytems than they are on other systems (including Windows NT). The UNIX convention is to follow each line of text with the ASCII *linefeed* (LF) character. Most other systems (including Windows NT) follow each line of text with a pair of characters—an ASCII *carriage return* (CR) and then an LF (a few systems use just the CR, as if matters weren't complicated enough already!). This mode does automatic CR/LF translation where appropriate, which is great for text files, but inappropriate for binary file transfer.

```
binary
```

This companion to ascii switches to binary mode, which transfers characters as a binary stream verbatim from the other system (without any CR/LF translation).

```
mode
```

displays the mode—binary or ascii.

```
bell
```

toggles the bell indicating completed operations. This is useful if you are doing long transfers and want to know when they are complete.

```
hash
```

toggles the printing of a hash mark (#) for every 512 bytes of data transferred. This is useful if you have a slow connection or are transferring large files—it lets you know that things are progressing.

Ending an FTP Session

To end a session simply type *close* at the ftp> prompt. This disconnects you from the remote machine. The *open* command can then be used to begin a new connection. To close the connection and exit the FTP program, type *bye*.

Getting Help

The help included with the FTP program is minimal, but still useful—at least as a reminder. Type *help* or *?* at the ftp> prompt for a list of available commands:

```
ftp> ?
Commands may be abbreviated. Commands are:

!             delete        literal       prompt        send
?             debug         ls            put           status
append        dir           mdelete       pwd           trace
ascii         disconnect    mdir          quit          type
bell          get           mget          quote         user
binary        glob          mkdir         recv          verbose
bye           hash          mls           remotehelp
cd            help          mput          rename
close         lcd           open          rmdir
ftp>
```

For a little information on any particular command, type help <command> at the ftp> prompt.

```
remotehelp
```

The nature of FTP is that it translates local commands into a set of standard commands. Not all FTP server software supports the entire command set. If a command does not seem to be working, typing *remotehelp* at the ftp> prompt might shed some light with a list of supported commands.

TFTP

The Trivial FTP program is a command line FTP client that allows simple transfers from the command line. It is useful for quick transfer operations, and use in batch or command files. TFTP does not allow user logins, which means that the remote file/directory must allow "world" access. The syntax for TFTP is:

```
tftp [-i] <hostname> <put|get> <source file> <destination file>
```

The -i option tells TFTP to use binary (image) mode instead of the default ASCII, which performs translations of control characters. Use binary mode to move compressed and executable files. Put or Get do just what their FTP counterparts do—transfer files to (put) or from (get) the remote host. The source and destination files are the name of the file on which the operation will occur (source) and where it will end up (destination). If no destination file is specified, the source filename will be used.

Using the NT FTP Server

FTP (File Transfer Protocol) offers an easy way to share files stored on an NT system with other systems—UNIX workstations, for example. An FTP server can be used to allow other systems (non-NT) to place files where they can be shared by NT systems through NT's native networking. One additional advantage of FTP is its prevalence on the Internet. An NT server connected to the Internet can offer "anonymous" FTP to Internet users that can connect to it. This allows general distribution of files to users who do not have a normal account on the server machine (to maintain good security, the FTP directories should reside on an NTFS partition).

FTP is a client/server-based transfer protocol. The client package translates commands to FTP-compliant syntax, and translates data between file systems where incompatibilities exist. NT comes with a command line-based FTP client, which is described earlier in this chapter.

Installing the NT FTP Server

The NT FTP Server is an optional component of NT, but installation is simple. Membership in the Administrator group is required to install and/or configure the FTP server. Because of the potential security risk the FTP server presents, be sure you understand the implications before making the FTP server available. To install the FTP server:

1. Launch Control Panel.
2. Double-click the Network icon in the Control Panel window. This invokes the Network Settings dialog box.
3. Press the Add Software button.
4. Locate the FTP Server entry in the Network Software listbox, and select it. Press Continue. A dialog box warning of the potential risk to passwords appears. This warning means that during the establishment of an FTP session, the password is sent by the client in plain text. This is a potential security risk if someone is listening to the traffic on the network. If this is an unacceptable risk, you can consider installing a separate NT machine just for FTP, and offering only anonymous FTP—that is, FTP where there are no privileged accounts. This arrangement can still be very useful.
5. Press the Yes button, unless you wish to abort the installation.
6. You will be prompted for the path to the NT distribution files; provide it in the edit field, and press the Continue button.
7. NT will now copy the required files to your system; once this operation is complete you will be given a chance to configure the server—this must be done before the server will operate.

Configuring the NT FTP Server

Like installation, configuring NT's FTP server is a simple process, but before you begin, you should have some idea of what you intend to use the server for. There are two most likely scenarios for the NT FTP server:

1. The FTP server will be used to provide connectivity to an NT machine (or network) for UNIX-based workstations. If this is your main objective, there are a couple of things to consider. First, the security of FTP is not as good as the security of NT itself. You can do some things to ensure maximum security, but it will not match

NT's native capabilities (this is probably an issue for only a small number of sites). If you must have maximum security:

- Use a separate NT machine to act as a server, and provide users with special accounts for that server *only*.
- Be sure that the passwords for these accounts are *not* the same as for the users' regular accounts.
- Make sure that the FTP server accesses *only* NTFS partitions, where the file system is secure.
- Use FTP to transfer only *nonsensitive* data; assume it is accessible.

The second consideration in this scenario is that, by the time you read this, several implementations of NFS (Network File System) will probably be available for NT. NFS is a standard developed by Sun to allow "mounting" of remote volumes as if they were local, and is well supported throughout the UNIX world. Though not identical, it is the functional equivalent of NT's native networking. If this is what you need, NFS is a much better choice.

2. The FTP server will be used to provide "anonymous" FTP access to users with no accounts in your organization, as well as to some known users. The NT machine may even reside on the Internet. This seems the most likely scenario, and the best use of the FTP server. Paradoxically, this scenario actually makes security easier. By limiting FTP logins to user "anonymous," there are no privileged accounts, and no passwords to secure.

   Yet even with this limited access, the FTP server has a great deal of utility. If a user has native NT access—through NT's built-in networking—nothing prevents privileged access to the same directories to which FTP has only minimal permissions. For example, through anonymous FTP an outside user could only upload or download files in a particular directory, while an internal user with an account on the machine could delete or edit those same files. This allows the FTP server to act as a distribution and collection point for your organization.

   It is most likely that you will wish to use FTP this way. In order to accomplish this, you must:

   - Create an account with the appropriate permissions, which will be used for every user who makes an FTP connection.
   - Limit FTP connections to *anonymous* only.
   - Create a directory structure, accessible to the *anonymous* FTP user, which facilitates the server's intended application.

Selecting Configuration Options

If you are in the process of installing the FTP server, the FTP Service dialog appears automatically at this point. If you are reconfiguring the server, or if for some reason the dialog is not on screen, you will find it in the Control Panel:

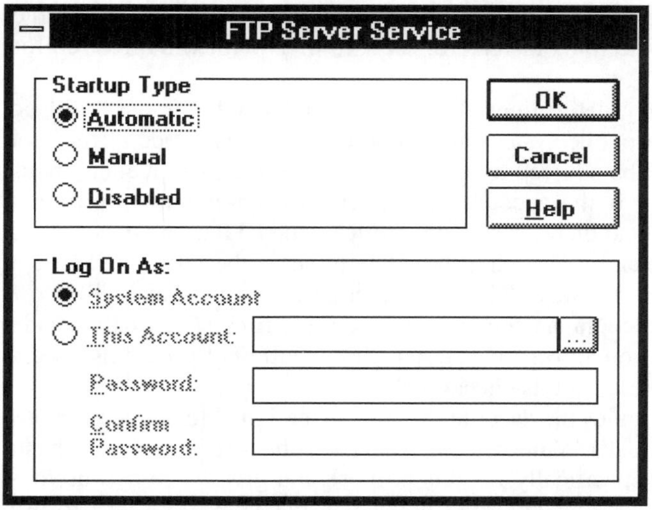

Figure 6.7 FTP Service.

The FTP Service Dialog.

1. Launch Control Panel.
2. Double click on the Network icon; this will invoke the Network Settings dialog.
3. Locate the FTP Server entry in the Installed Network Software listbox and select it.
4. Press the configure button—this will invoke the FTP Service dialog, illlustrated in Figure 6.7.

- **Maximum Connections**—This setting determines the number of FTP connections the system will allow. This setting defaults to 20, which may be too large for your site. Remember that FTP sessions are data intensive since they are purely file transfers. Determining the optimum value for your situation will take practical experience of what your particular users do with the FTP server. Watch for degradation of the machine's performance while many users are connected as a sign that the number should be reduced. On the other hand, complaints from users that they cannot connect because of the limit is a clue to increase the number, which cannot exceed 50.
- **Idle Timeout**—This setting determines the length of time (in minutes) a user can remain idle before the server will disconnect that user. This setting is somewhat interactive with the maximum connections setting—if many idle connections are tying up the server, logging them out makes the slots available for other users. The

ten-minute default time is reasonable, and should serve most purposes. If, for some reason, you need to disable the timeout feature, set it to 0. The maximum value for this setting is 60.

- **Home Directory**—This entry determines the directory in which the user will be placed once connected. For a public system, it is wise to make this directory the root of whatever area the user will be allowed to access. If you're setting up an anonymous FTP server, remember that it is the account you specify for anonymous users that determines the permissions—and therefore the directories—the FTP user can access.
- **Allow Anonymous Connections**—This checkbox determines if the server will accept connections from the user "anonymous." This is an Internet convention, and will allow users who do not have an account on the system to access files specifically made available to them (see discussion above). If you have no intention of providing access to your server to outside users, leave this checkbox blank.
- **Username**—This entry determines the account that will be assigned to the anonymous user. The default is the standard Windows NT *guest* account. It is probably best, though, to create an account specifically for this purpose and give it the permissions needed. You can name this account anything you wish, but it makes sense to use something logical like "ftpuser." Keep in mind that this account will also be accessible from any machine on your network.
- **Password**—This entry is the password for the account selected in the *username* entry defined above. Note that this is *not* required for anonymous FTP login. Instead, it is the password for the account when it is used as a normal login (the usual password for an anonymous FTP connection is the email address of the user who is connecting).
- **Allow Only Anonymous Connections**—This checkbox limits connections to the FTP server to the user *anonymous*. It is strongly suggested that you run the FTP server in this fashion. If this checkbox is selected, *no other account can be used to log into the FTP server*. This eliminates the security problem of unencrypted user passwords being passed over the network.

Completing FTP Server Configuration

Once you have filled in the various fields and checkboxes press the OK button in the dialog box. Another dialog will appear, explaining the requirement to restart NT for changes to take effect. If this is the first configuration, you do not need to restart the system. Instead, close the control panel and reopen it. You will now find an FTP Server icon in Control Panel. There is one more configuration operation that must be completed before the FTP server will operate.

1. Double click on the FTP server icon in the control panel. This will invoke the FTP User Sessions dialog (this dialog is also available from the FTP menu in the Server Manager on Windows NT Advanced Servers). Press the Security button. This invokes the FTP Server Security dialog.
2. From the Partition combo box, select the partition(s) that the FTP server will access (remember that it is best to use an NTFS partition, not a FAT one).

3. Select read and/or write access from the checkboxes provided. This determines whether the FTP server will allow upload, download, or both, to the FTP user.
4. Press the OK button when finished, or cancel to abort the operation. Changes made in this dialog are immediate, and do not require a system restart. The FTP server is now configured for operation.

FTP Server Administration and Control

Most of the administrator's job is done when the FTP server is configured; but there may be times when you'll need to take special steps. When you do, the most likely places you'll take them are in the FTP Server Configuration section of the Networks object in Control Panel, as discussed earlier, or in the separate FTP Server object in the Control Panel, illustrated in Figure 6.8.

The FTP Server Control Panel object simply lists the number of FTP sessions currently in use, and allows you to disconnect any or all of them. It also gives a limited capability to enable additional FTP security, through the Security... push-button. This will give you access to the dialog illustrated in Figure 6.9.

This Security dialog lets you determine which volumes in the system FTP users are permitted to read from and write to. Obviously, this gives you a simple way to significantly enhance FTP server security: create a separate volume (logical disk drive) for FTP users, and restrict their access to that volume.

A Separate FTP User Account?

As discussed earlier, the most convenient way to provide FTP users with access to a Windows NT system is with Anonymous access—which normally uses the system's Guest account. The only trouble with this is that you may want to use the Guest account for other purposes—letting other NT and WFWG users from outside your domain or workgroup access shared directories, for instance—that conflict with the need to restrict FTP login. You can get around this by creating a separate FTP User account that is used *only* for FTP login, and not for other purposes.

Advanced Topics—Routing and SNMP

Multiple Adapters and IP Routing

Although most TCP/IP systems support dynamic routing, the Windows NT implementation does not. You must tell each NT system explicitly how to get to other network segments. You can point all nonlocal traffic to a default router, or you can build route entries for specific remote networks. For complex networks with multiple paths to the same remote destination, you must use a non-NT system that supports dynamic routing.

NT can act as a very basic router for users who have only a few segments and do not need dynamic routing capabilities. In order to do this, you must have multiple network

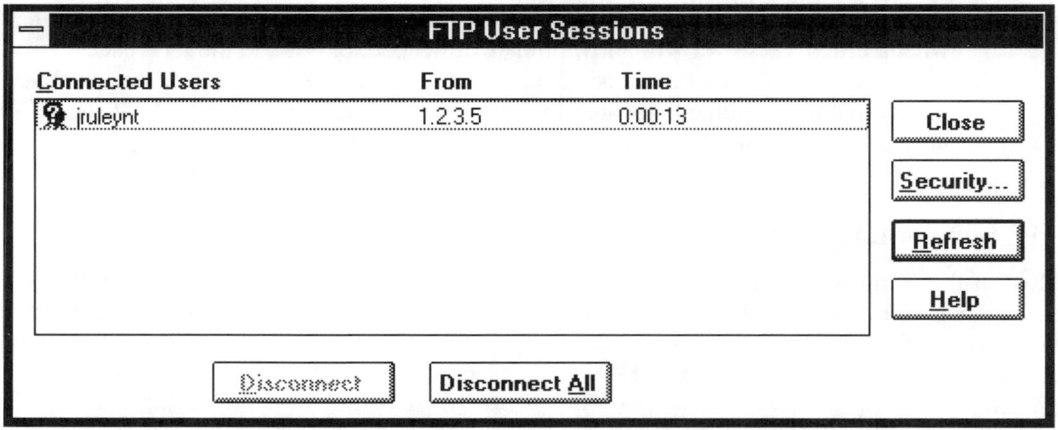

Figure 6.8 FTP Server.

The FTP Server Control Panel indicates who is connected, and allows you to control access.

adapters with TCP/IP enabled on all of the ones you want to route IP traffic between. Then use the Registry Editor utility to turn on static routing between network adapters, and then use the ROUTE.EXE utility to create the static routing maps. For information on configuring TCP/IP on multiple adapters, refer to the "Installing TCP/IP" section earlier in this chapter.

Enabling Routing

To start the Registry Editor, type "REGEDT32.EXE" in the <FILE><RUN> menu of either Program Manager or File Manager. Likewise, you can type "REGEDT32.EXE" at the command prompt. When the Registry Editor starts, select the HKEY_LOCAL_MACHINE window, and find the SYSTEM tree. Double-click the SYSTEM folder icon, and select the Cur-

Figure 6.9 FTP Security.

The FTP Server Control Panel/Security Dialog lets you designate which disk partitions may be accessed, and how.

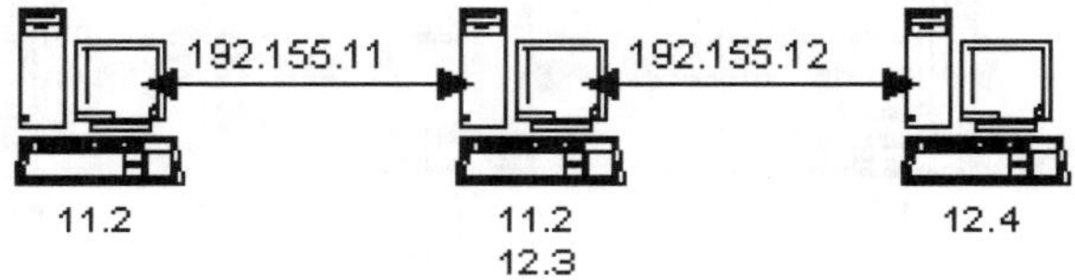

Figure 6.10 Routing-1.

Simple network layout and routing. The middle system "routes" traffic between networks 11 and 12.

rentControlSet folder icon. Continue working down the tree until you get to the SYSTEM\CurrentControlSet\Services\Tcpip\Parameters folder, and then select it.

Under the <EDIT> menu, select <Add Value>. In the "Value Name" field, type the keyword "IpEnableRouter," and then select a "Data Type" of "REG_DWORD." Click the "OK" button, and type "1" into the String Editor dialog box. The value "1" turns on the internal IP routing mechanism, and a value of "0" disables it. You must reboot the system after making these changes in order for routing to begin.

Routing on Small Networks

After you have enabled routing and rebooted the system, your system will provide local routing services to the networks it knows about. You can then point other systems' default routes to the NT system. Any network segments that the NT system is not physically connected to must be entered into the route table manually.

ROUTE.EXE is a command-line utility that lets you add or delete static routes between networks or hosts. You can define multiple routes to a destination, and if the first one fails, the second will kick in. You must define routes to all intermediate points along the way. For example, let's look at the simple network illustrated in Figure 6.10.

There are two network segments (192.155.11 and 192.155.12), and 3 nodes (x.2, x.3, and x.4). When NT was installed on nodes 192.155.11.2 and 192.155.12.4, the default router was given as node x.3, meaning that all nonlocal IP traffic will be passed to the server in the middle. However, by default, x.3 is unable to route the traffic. The network administrator must enable TCP/IP on each adapter in node x.3, and then enable IP routing using the Registry Editor as described above. At that point, the node at x.3 will be able to forward traffic from 192.155.11.2 to 192.155.12.4, and vice versa.

Routing in Mildly Complex Networks

Let's look at the more complicated setup shown in Figure 6.11. As in the example in Figure 6.10, node 192.155.11.2 points to 192.155.11.3 as the default route. However, node x.3 knows only about networks 192.155.11 and 192.155.12, since that's all it is directly connected to.

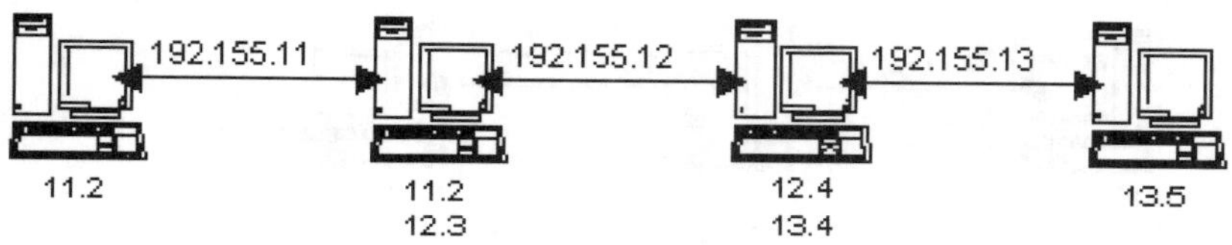

Figure 6.11 Routing-2.

Mildly complex network routing setup, with two routers handling traffic for three networks.

Likewise, node x.4 knows only about networks 192.155.12 and 192.155.13. In order for packets from network 192.155.11 to reach network 192.155.13 (and vice-versa), several things must happen.

First of all, nodes x.3 and x.4 must be configured to route, as in the example above with node x.3. Then, static routing entries must be defined for nodes x.3 and x.4, telling them about the remote networks. For node x.3, the command would look like this:

```
ROUTE ADD 192.155.13.0 192.155.12.4
```

This command adds a static route to node x.3's routing table. Then, any packet coming from subnet 192.155.11 destined for network 192.155.13 will get passed to node 12.4 for handling. In order for x.4 to return packets to network 192.155.11, it must be informed about the route as well (remember that NT doesn't support dynamic routing). Therefore, the following command must be given to node x.4:

```
ROUTE ADD 192.155.11.0 192.155.12.3
```

Now packets will make it from any node on any net to any other node on any other net. Believe it or not, this is a very simple example, and serves to illustrate the complexity inherent in multiple-segment IP networks. The more segments you add, the more systems you must manually configure. The static routing model breaks down after about five segments, at which point the administration and configuration becomes overwhelming.

Routing in Very Complex Networks

A very complex network, more typical of large corporate sites, is illustrated in Figure 6.12, where there are many departmental routers throughout a company connected over a high-speed backbone with redundant links between the routers. All of these routers have separate interfaces for multiple small networks. Workstations on each of the smaller subnets have a single adapter running TCP/IP, and they identify the nearest backbone router as their default router.

This method is the simplest to configure and maintain, as each of the routers is capable of updating the others via RIP or OSPF or some other router-to-router protocol. Since they are directly connected to each segment, the network numbers are seen automatically by the routers, and forwarded out with no maintenance or configuration required. If a node on net-

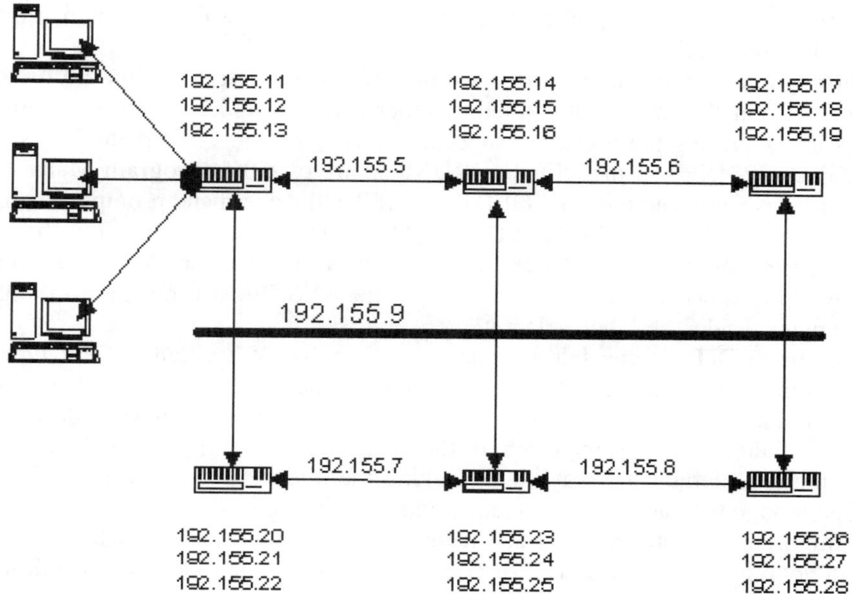

Figure 6.12 Routing-3.

A large corporate or campus network, with many dedicated routers sharing a central "backbone" for internetwork communication.

work 192.155.11 sends a request to a node on 192.155.28, the routers are capable of automatically forwarding and rejecting packets as needed. The clients simply point to the closest router as their default, and let the network hardware do its work.

Purchasing and maintaining these dedicated routers[2] is an expensive procedure however, and many companies prefer to let other devices handle the routing work instead. Almost all of the UNIX and NetWare implementations support RIP or other dynamic routing protocols, and NT would benefit from this as well, allowing customers to use departmental servers as routers. Microsoft has hinted at the possibility of providing this functionality in the future (for more information on IP routing, refer to Appendix 2).

Secondary Default Routes

In some environments, users may see multiple routers on a single segment. This is similar to the example in Figure 6.12, where each router has multiple paths in the event that one fails.

[2]See "Dedicated Multiprotocol Routers" in Chapter 7 for a list of router suppliers. There's also some news on this subject in the "Late-Breaking News" section of the Preface.

However, here we are speaking of multiple routers on the clients network, which might look something like Figure 6.13.

In this type of environment, users would need to be able to define multiple default routes. In the event that one router failed, another router would be used automatically. NT allows this by modifying the registry, using the Registry Editor. To start the Registry Editor, type “REGEDT32.EXE” in the <FILE><RUN> menu of either Program Manager or File Manager. Likewise, you can type “REGEDT32.EXE” at the command prompt. When the Registry Editor starts, select the HKEY_LOCAL_MACHINE window, and find the SYSTEM tree. Double-click the SYSTEM folder icon, and select the CurrentControlSet folder icon. Continue working down the tree until you get to the SYSTEM\CurrentControlSet\Services\Tcpip\Parameters folder, and then select it.

Under the <EDIT> menu, select <Add Value>. In the “Value Name” field, type the keyword “AdditionalGateways,” and then select a “Data Type” of “REG_MULTI_SZ.” Click the “OK” button, and type the IP addresses of the additional default gateways desired into the String Editor dialog box. You must reboot the system after making these changes. You can also add additional default gateways after making the initial changes with the “ROUTE -S” command, although they are not permanently added to the registry.

It’s important to note that you can have multiple default gateways for every network interface in your system. For example, if you have two dynamic routers on two different segments to which you are directly connected, you can have up to four default routers. In the event that one of your adapters or subnets fails, you will still have two routers on the other segment that you can use. This is an expensive and unlikely wiring scheme, but it is completely possible.

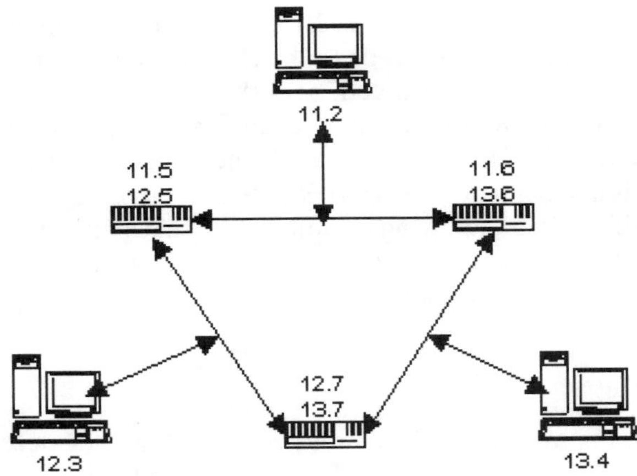

Figure 6.13 Routing-4.

TCP/IP Routing in a redundant network. Each subnet is hooked to two routers, providing multiple ways for traffic to pass.

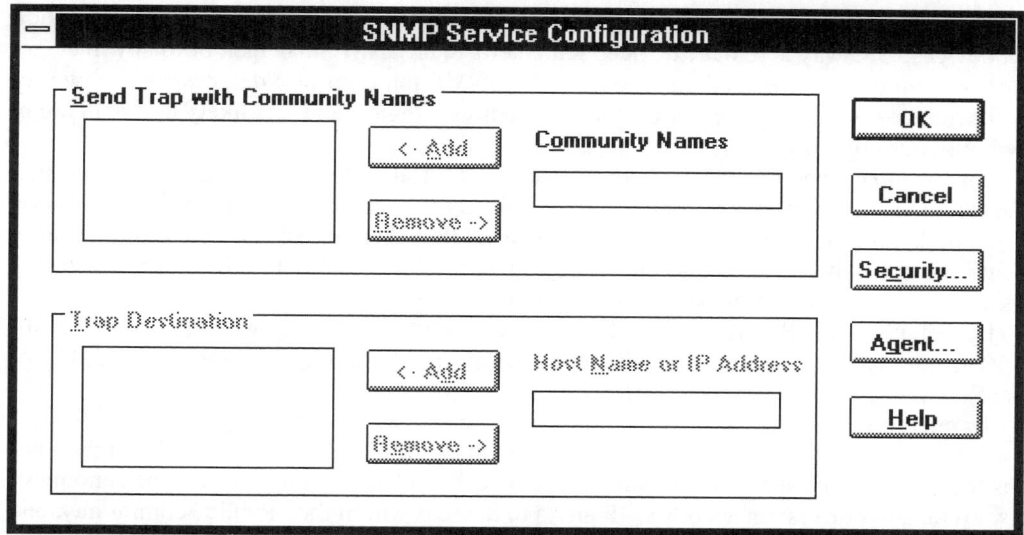

Figure 6.14 SNMP Configuration.

The SNMP Service Configuration dialog box is used to set up NT's support for Simple Network Management Protocol (SNMP).

SNMP

SNMP stands for Simple Network Management Protocol, and that's exactly what it is. It provides basic administrative information about a device so that network administrators or SNMP management software can monitor the overall health of the network (as well as individual systems). In order to take advantage of NT's SNMP services, you must have an SNMP manager that can monitor and display SNMP alerts. Several such programs are available for a wide variety of platforms.

To install the SNMP service, load the "Network" control object from the Control Panels utility. If you are configuring the SNMP services during the original system installation, you will be presented with these options during the initial setup routines. If not, you need to load the Network control object manually. Double-click "Control Panels" from the "Main" window in Program Manager, or type "CONTROL.EXE" in the <File><Run...> menu of either Program Manager or File Manager. Likewise, you can type "CONTROL.EXE" from the Command Prompt. Then double-click the Networks icon to load the Network Settings dialog box.

To add the SNMP service, click the "Add Software..." button, and select "SNMP Service" from the drop-down list. After the system copies the necessary software to the hard drive, you are presented with the SNMP Service Configuration dialog that is illustrated in Figure 6.14.

There are two methods that SNMP management software can use to collect information about devices. One way is to have devices send alerts to an SNMP manager, or to any manager in the community. Another method is to have the SNMP manager poll devices every few seconds (or minutes or hours). There are benefits to both strategies, and it is likely that both are in use within your organization.

For example, when an SNMP device can send an alert to a management station, that device can do so as soon as something starts to fail. By the time a polling management station gets to a node that has started failing, it may be dead altogether, leaving no clue as to the cause of death. Conversely, devices that are in good health clutter the network with unnecessary alerts, and it's better to let a manager poll nodes when needed.

By default, NT's SNMP service does not send alerts. It does, however, support SNMP queries from any device in the "public" community (a community is a logical grouping of devices).

To enable the SNMP service to send alerts, select the "Community Names" edit box, type in the community name you wish to add, and click the "<- Add" button. Although "Public" is the default community for inquiries, it is not the default community for the sending of alerts. To make your system send SNMP alerts to devices within the "Public" community, add it here. If you have a departmental SNMP community, add it here as well. A node can be in more than one community at a time, simply by adding additional community names as needed.

By adding the "Public" community to the alert list, any management station within the community will receive the alerts, and may also be able to make changes to your configuration. If you want to send alerts only to a specific management station, you can add it to the "Trap Destinations" listbox by selecting the "Host Name or IP Address" edit box, typing in the address or hostname of the management station, and clicking the "<- Add" button. Then only that management station will receive the alerts.

Remember that by default NT will respond to any management station request that comes from the "Public" community. To disable this feature, or to add a new community name, click the "Security" button, and you will be presented with the dialog illustrated in Figure 6.15.

If you want to remove the "Public" community from the list, select it and click the "Remove ->" button. If you want to add another community to the list, then click in the "Community Name" edit box, and click the "<- Add" button.

If you want to restrict the management stations that can query your machine for SNMP statistics, click the "Only Accept SNMP Packets from These Hosts" radio button, and add the desired management stations to the listbox below it. To add a host, click the "Host or IP Address" edit box, type in the hostname or IP address of the management station you want to add, and then click the "<- Add" button.

The "Send Authentication Trap" checkbox in the upper-left corner is for alerting managers that an unauthorized host is attempting to pull statistics from your machine. If a management station that does not belong to one of the accepted communities queries your machine, and this option is checked, then the software will send an alert to the management stations listed in the Trap Destinations from the SNMP Service Configuration dialog box.

You can customize additional information about your system for inclusion with SNMP alerts and responses. From the SNMP Service Configuration dialog box, click the "Agents"

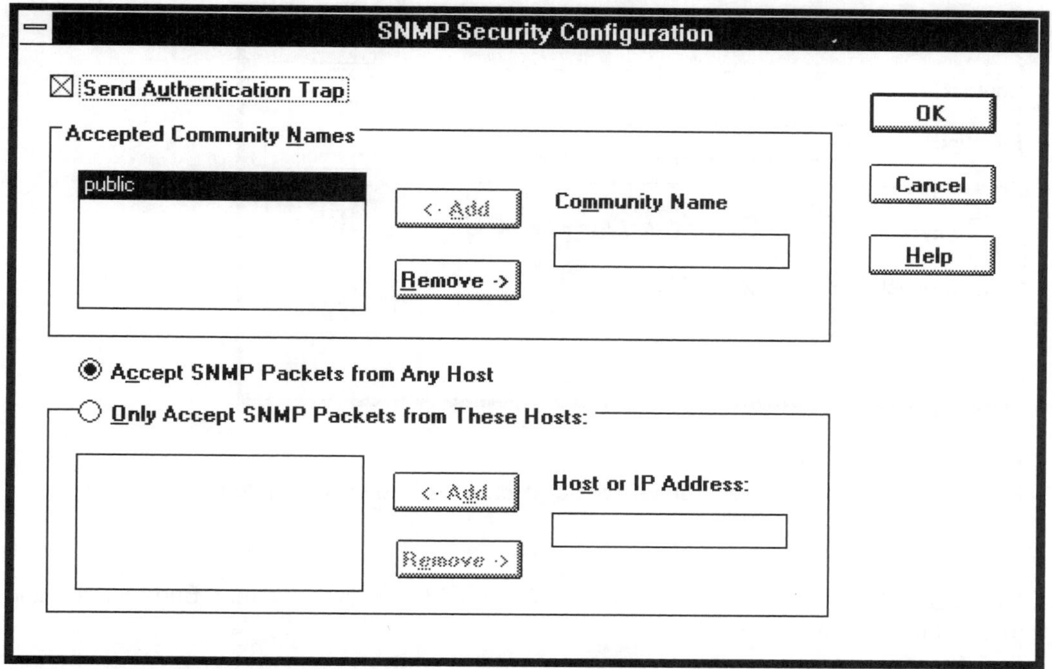

Figure 6.15 SNMP Security.

The SNMP Security Configuration dialog box, which determines who can get access to system data via SNMP.

button, and the dialog shown in Figure 6.16 will appear. Type in either your name or the name of the system administrator in the "Contact" edit box. Type in a location, such as building, floor, or room number in the "Location" edit box.

The "Service" group box consists of several checkboxes that allow you to detail various levels of specific information. The "Physical" checkbox pertains to the low-level wire and physical network statistics. If your node acts as a part of the physical network (i.e., a repeater, bridge, or router), then you should check this box.

The "Datalink / Subnetwork" checkbox applies only if you are acting as a part of a logical network, such as a bridge. The "Internet" checkbox applies only if you are acting as an IP router. Errors generated within the higher-level network software are passed to the management stations if these checkboxes are enabled.

The "End-to-End" checkbox applies to devices that act as an end-node on the network. If you're running TCP/IP, then you are acting as an end-node at least some of the time. "Application" alerts have to do with TCP/IP-based application-generated errors, such as email failures,

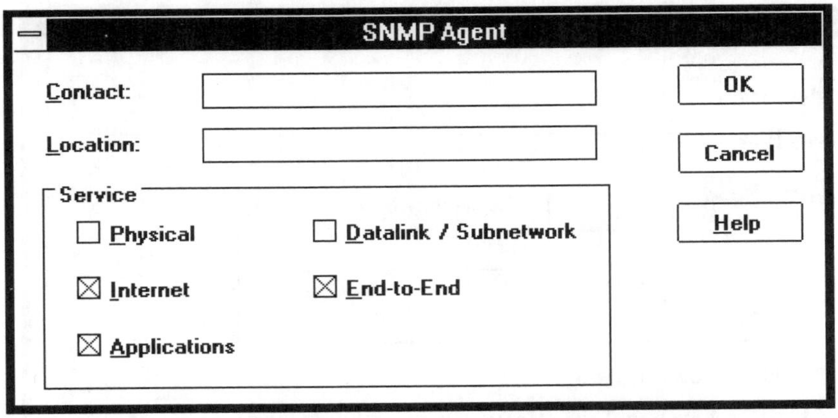

SNMP Agent

Contact:

Location:

OK

Cancel

Help

Service

☐ Physical ☐ Datalink / Subnetwork

☒ Internet ☒ End-to-End

☒ Applications

Figure 6.16 SNMP Agent.

The SNMP Agent dialog box lets you designate which errors are to be reported—and to whom.

or FTP errors. All NT systems that use SNMP should have at least the "End-to-End" and "Application" checkboxes enabled.

Conclusion

Windows NT's TCP/IP support, while not perfect, does provide a broad range of the most-needed TCP/IP features, including FTP Service, Telnet (client) support, and the usual range of TCP utilities. In addition, Windows NT TCP/IP provides a routable alternative to NetBEUI for use in large networks—and this feature is augmented by NT's built-in static router support, which allows a single computer with two network cards to functionally replace an expensive dedicated router in some TCP/IP routing applications. Now that we've examined these pieces of the Windows NT network puzzle, we can put them to use in creating multidomain *enterprise networks,* the subject of Chapter 7.

For More Information

Arick, M. (1993), *The TCP/IP Companion*. Wellesley, MA: QED Publishing Group, ISBN: 0-89435-466-3. Good end-user-oriented discussion of TCP/IP and utilities.

Comer, D. (1991), *Internetworking with TCP/IP*, Volume 1. Englewood Cliffs, NJ: Prentice Hall, ISBN: 0-13-472242-6. Mandatory desktop reference for the TCP/IP administrator.

Black, U. (1992) *TCP/IP and Related Protocols*. New York: McGraw-Hill, ISBN: 0-07-005553-X. Mandatory desktop reference for the TCP/IP administrator.

Hunt, C. (1992), *TCP/IP Network Administration*. Sebastopol, CA: O'Reilly & Associates, ISBN: 0-937175-82-X. Mandatory desktop reference for the TCP/IP administrator.

Albitz, P. and Liu, C. (1992), *DNS and BIND*. Sebastopol, CA: O'Reilly & Associates, ISBN: 1-56592-010-4. Great book for learning Domain Name Service (DNS).

Allard, J. (1993), *Advanced Internetworking with TCP/IP on Windows NT (tcpipnt.doc)*. Redmond, WA: Microsoft Corp (downloadable via anonymous ftp from rhino.microsoft.com). This is a 34-page paper on networking that explains advanced TCP/IP topics for Windows NT, including static routing, in great detail.

Microsoft Staff (1993), *Microsoft Windows NT TCP/IP*. Redmond, WA: Microsoft Corp (part of Windows NT documentation). Brief overview and reference on Windows NT TCP/IP functionality.

Enterprise Connections

After reading this chapter you'll understand:

- **Why enterprise networks are different from simpler LANs**
- **The need for administration across multiple domains**
- **Wide-area networking issues**
- **The need for routers and gateways**
- **The central importance of e-mail**
- **Multivendor issues**

You'll have a basic understanding of the principles involved in creating, operating, and maintaining networks characterized by size, complexity, and the need for communications between multivendor platforms, and you'll have a good understanding of where to go for further information.

Introduction

Enterprise networks—this term has come into general use only recently and has tended to displace more descriptive technical terms like *internetwork*. Fundamentally, the idea behind an enterprise network is the idea of making all data from any network in an enterprise (that is, a corporation) available to users on all other networks provided, of course, that they have the necessary security privileges. The idea leverages the total information resources of an enterprise by making, for example, information from the shipping and receiving department available to management, an approach that is clearly essential if you are looking at, say, just-in-time manufacturing and wish to maintain minimum inventory. These kinds of issues are becoming increasingly important as industries engage in downsizing or rightsizing operations.

From the system administrator's perspective, the central issues involved with enterprise networks are really threefold. First is the issue of *communicating across great distances,* because the odds are high that an enterprise network will not exist within a single building. Second is the issue of *complexity,* because the Enterprise Network by its nature involves many servers and users—and this is closely related to the third and most complex issue, *multivendor connectivity*.

Enterprise networks almost never comprise components from a single vendor, and it's unlikely that anyone will establish a totally Windows NT-based enterprise network (even Microsoft hasn't done this). So, there are issues of integrating the Windows NT networking components with existing networking components.

Because of the complex relationship among these facts, and the need to provide an administrative communications medium that includes them all, *we* consider that there is a fourth over-riding concern on enterprise networks—*electronic mail.* In our experience, only electronic mail can possibly be used to provide reliable connectivity throughout the enterprise.

You can provide specific connections between different points in the enterprise for specific purposes—and we'll talk about how to do that—but the bottom line is that the only reliable way to connect *every* individual within the enterprise is to use some form of *e-mail* that works across all platforms. Since Microsoft Mail is incorporated in Windows NT (and at the moment is the *only* e-mail system we can say with confidence works in Windows NT), that's the main e-mail platform we'll talk about.

Windows NT in Enterprise Networks

Microsoft clearly had enterprise networking issues in mind when the Windows NT (especially Windows NT Advanced Server) networking architecture was conceived. Windows NT incorporates some unique features for use in enterprise networks that have never before been packaged into a single networking product. Among these are Windows NT Advanced Server's domainwide administration features, and a very important additional feature, *inter-domain trust.* This allows separate administrative domains of Windows NT systems to communicate their user account databases to one another.

Windows NT also comes with Microsoft Mail workgroup clients preinstalled. This provides the essential electronic mail infrastructure just discussed. Unfortunately, even on Advanced Server systems, Windows NT does *not* provide the facilities necessary to connect multiple e-mail "post offices"—so we're going to discuss what is necessary to expand upon this. We'll also discuss the issues of providing connectivity between the MS-Mail system and other e-mail systems the company may already have installed such as IBM PROFS or the UNIX-based simple mail transfer protocol (SMTP).

Windows NT also has a limited degree of wide-area networking support built in by its support for the remote access service (RAS), which is provided in a single-user version on basic Windows NT workstations and in a multi-user version on Windows NT Advanced

Servers. This is important because the fact that enterprise networks normally span many local area networks combined within a larger geographical area makes it impractical to string wires and physically connect all the elements of an enterprise. There must be some mechanism provided for connecting across the wider area. RAS allows you to do this over dial-up phone lines, Integrated Services Digital Network (ISDN), or x.25 packet switching links.

Windows NT also provides a high degree of multiprotocol support (as discussed in Chapters 6, 8, 9, and Appendices 2 and 4). In particular, the provision of support for the Transport Connect Protocol/Internet Protocol (TCP/IP) provides the necessary foundation for creating an enterprise network. Frankly, it is not practical to even consider constructing a Windows NT-based enterprise network without TCP/IP, as we will see.

Finally, Windows NT and Windows NT Advanced Server support a very wide range of network clients, including DOS, 16-bit Windows, OS/2, Windows NT, UNIX, and Macintosh workstations. This makes Windows NT—and particularly Windows NT Advanced Server (which has Macintosh support built in)—*ideal* platforms for creating or expanding an enterprise network with a mix of client types.

The Search for Perfection

The preceding laundry list of features makes it sound like Windows NT and Windows NT Advanced Server are a one-stop shopper's dream for enterprise network problems. Don't make the mistake of believing this! Windows NT has an excellent network architecture and is based on some very advanced technology. It's a good design but the phrase "Jack of all trades, master of none" comes to mind.

In our opinion, there are major (though not fatal) flaws in the Windows NT network architecture that become glaringly apparent when you examine enterprise connections. In particular, Windows NT depends upon the TCP/IP protocol to provide a routable enterprise backbone—yet it modifies that protocol by transporting NetBIOS packets over it. As a result, the Windows NT subcomponents of an enterprise net always make up a network within an enterprise network that must be administered separately from other systems that use TCP/IP.[1] This makes it impractical to incorporate Windows NT systems into an overall enterprise network management scheme that would incorporate other kinds of networking as well (with the possible exception of using IBM NetView or SNMP tools).

Windows NT remote access services (RAS)—the wide-area networking that's included in Windows NT—is *grossly* insufficient to provide the essential connection between subnets that is the foundation for creating an enterprise network; therefore it's necessary to use other solutions (in particular, hardware gateways and routers to connect the subnets) when you create an enterprise network or add Windows NT components into an existing enterprise network. The list goes on and on.

We don't mean to say that it's impossible or outrageously difficult to incorporate Windows NT into an enterprise network. Sadly, it will present many of the same difficulties that

[1]Microsoft's NetBIOS-on-TCP/IP (NBT) system passes SMBs over the net—not much help if you want to connect to NFS, or other structured UNIX protocols.

incorporating any other proprietary networking into an enterprise network will. It's greatly to Microsoft's credit that they have provided *some* of the essential infrastructure as part of the Windows NT and Windows NT Advanced Server packages. It's to their great *discredit* that they did not take the additional steps to make Windows NT an ideal enterprise networking platform.

Enterprise Network Architectures

As we said earlier, one of the central facts of life for an enterprise networking environment is a network that commands a large geographic area, where it is not practical to string physical wiring to connect all components of the enterprise and, in all probability, the existence of myriad network hardware and software within the subnets that make up the network. To put this in perspective, let's consider a hypothetical example:

A small growing company has, up to a given point, grown its own local area network at the corporate headquarters (say in New York), and then opens a branch office (say in California). The existence of the branch office immediately creates some enterprise network issues. How are the branch office workers to be connected into the corporate headquarters? Some form of wide-area networking will be necessary. There's no realistic way to string private cable from New York to California—so dial-in support over modems will be needed. But will that be fast enough? If not, there are other possibilities extending all the way up to T-1 dedicated telephone circuits (which amount to buying the dedicated wire from New York to California from the phone company at a rather hefty price). Finding the right combination of network hardware and software to achieve this connection efficiently and economically is one of the keys to enterprise networking.

The situation is further complicated if the company grows over a period of time or—to take a modern example—gets taken over and integrated into another corporation. It's quite possible that our small company will have grown up using one networking system—for example, Novell Netware—and the acquiring corporation may have standardized on another networking system—perhaps DEC Pathworks. At this point, you are not only faced with the wide-area networking problems in connecting the new division into the corporate headquarters of the acquiring organization, but also with the problem of matching incompatible network protocols, transports, and hardware (and heaven only knows what else).

When Windows NT enters this networking picture you're presented with some immediate opportunities because Windows NT Advanced Server includes some enterprise features, in particular domainwide management, inter-domain trust, and built-in wide-area network support.

Administrative Domains

One of the essential decisions that will confront network administrators attempting to carry out an enterprise network situation, whether they are expanding an existing network to become an enterprise network incorporating new subnets that have come through acquisition, or in the creation of a branch office—or whatever—will be deciding when to use the features that have been built into Windows NT, *and* when to go outside and acquire other components, and, most of all, deciding on the overall structure for the network. This is an administrative and management issue and a very important one. It has to do with the relationships between the *administrative domains* that make up the network.

As we learned in Chapter 1, Windows NT can support two different administrative architectures. One is a *workgroup* architecture, essentially an ad hoc collection of more-or-less independent machines that happen to be linked on the same subnet. The second is an *administrative domain.* Administrative domains are characterized by the existence of a single Primary Domain Controller (PDC), which must be a Windows NT Advanced Server. All users log on to the PDC and the PDC stores account information for all computers in the domain. This greatly simplifies an administrator's responsibility because it's possible to *centrally* manage those user accounts for all users in the domain.

Of course, when one starts to consider an enterprise network this begins to present some problems. It is possible, although unlikely, that an enterprise network can, in fact, be managed as a single account domain. However, as you reach a very large number of users connecting over a very large network, you'll run into some very severe problems. The first of these is the basic bandwidth limitation of the network hardware that's currently in general use. The most common network media today is 10-base-2 or 10-base-T Ethernet, which has a bandwidth of ten million bits per second. That sounds like a lot. But let's suppose an enterprise has built its entire network at its headquarters around a single Ethernet backbone (without routers[2]).

Our hypothetical enterprise has a thousand employees. They all arrive between 8:30 and 9:00 A.M. on a Monday morning, turn on their workstations, and attempt to log into the primary domain controller. Now, assuming (for argument's sake) that the login sequence requires an exchange of ten data packets between the workstation and the server, each packet containing one kilobyte of information, the total information that needs to be transmitted through the company during this login "storm" will amount to just ten million bytes of information. Ethernet should be capable of handling this within eight seconds, and we have half an hour—so it should be perfectly adequate. It isn't.

We've neglected the fact that for each one of those user logons the primary domain controller must perform disk accesses to locate the user's records in the database, update them, etc. Since Windows NT employs a very efficient caching architecture based on its virtual memory system, it may be able to keep up with this example. At some point—if we expand the number of users to five thousand or ten thousand—we're going to saturate either the server or the network itself. Worse, as we've discussed earlier, the odds are high that not all parts of the company are going to be connecting over a ten megabit per second Ethernet. Branch offices are likely to be transmitting their login information over wide-area network channels that will have variable speeds ranging from 9600 baud telephone lines up to T-1 circuits that can approach Ethernet transmission rates.

If all of the users in a large branch office are attempting to transmit their login information over a single 9600 baud phone line, you may find yourself with a very frustrated branch manager on the telephone. You might think that the solution to this is to avoid the use of domains altogether and use the workgroup model instead. That won't work in an enterprise

[2]Nobody could be that dumb? Guess again—while this example is hypothetical, it's based on a real case!

network—the administration problems involved in supporting user accounts across myriad servers will quickly become totally unmanageable.

Fortunately, Microsoft has provided a rather elegant solution to this problem. In Windows NT Advanced Server domains, while only one server can be the primary domain controller for the user accounts, *any* server can support a login request and can *replicate* the primary domain controller's account database. For instance, our hypothetical branch office might have its own login controller (a Windows NT Advanced Server set up to replicate the database on the primary domain controller). This *login server* would then handle all of the login traffic on Monday morning on its own over the local Ethernet. It would simply receive information from the primary domain controller on a regular basis (we'll discuss how to do this shortly).

The one problem with this approach is that creating or modifying user accounts requires interaction with the primary domain controller, so the administrator will wind up bearing the burden of communication over the wide-area connection. A workaround for this situation (which also provides for more centralization and control of the network) is for all administration to be handled in the corporate headquarters and for requests for changes in user accounts to be transmitted to the administrators by electronic mail.

There are variations on this approach—and Microsoft has taken these into account in Windows NT Advanced Server, which provides *inter-domain trust*. The idea behind inter-domain trust arises from the fact that it isn't always practical for an enterprise to have a single account domain.

Suppose that the branch office in our example grows to include several hundred people. At this point, even with the account database being replicated on the branch office server, there's going to be enough administrative traffic to become a real burden traveling across whatever the wide-area networking link is between the corporate headquarters and the branch office. If e-mail is used for communicating with the central MIS group that includes all the administrators, a certain amount of frustration and friction will likely attend dealing with that distant and seemingly unresponsive MIS department.

At some point, with a large branch office you're going to wind up needing an administration group, essentially an MIS department in miniature, for the branch office. And the best solution, obviously, is to create a separate login domain and separate user accounts at the branch office. You then confront the same problem discussed when we defined the difference between workgroups and domains. A home office employee needing to access files on the branch office server will need *two* accounts, one at the branch office and one at the home office. For example, suppose the branch office handles West Coast regional sales. Then the West Coast branch office manager will probably need to have a user account at the home office—to communicate with other branch managers and the sales department chief. Similarly, the sales manager at the home office will need to have access to directories on the branch office server.

The traditional way to handle this is that the MIS heads at the branch office and the home office will communicate—and try to keep their user account databases in sync. Invariably, this results in problems. It means an increased overhead both at the branch office and at the home office and if an organization has many branch offices, the overhead at the home office can become overwhelming.

To get around this problem, Windows NT provides inter-domain trust. A *trust relationship* is created between the domain servers for two domains. The trust relationships are inherently *one-way*. Thus, the fact that the branch office trusts the home office does *not* imply that the home office trusts the branch office (although it is possible to arrange two-way trust). With two-way trust, our problem goes away—our West Coast regional sales manager has an account on the branch office domain server. The home office server trusts the branch office domain server.

Since the regional sales manager is a member of the sales managers group and sales managers have read/write access to the sales data directories, this individual *automatically* has access to the data directory on the home office server as well as on the branch server. With a trust relationship extended in the other direction the head of the sales department at the home office will have the same kind of access on the branch server, not only in California but in any other branch the company has. The account management problem is essentially eliminated. The home office MIS group only needs to maintain accounts for people who have local access to the local server. Access to the remote servers is handled automatically. Only the trust relationships need to be maintained.

The one degree of coordination that is required between the MIS director at the home office and the branch office MIS directors is, first of all, to maintain the trust relationships and second, to agree on the group names. The need to manage separate user accounts for remote individuals is eliminated. This is a tremendous assist in a complex enterprise situation and particularly for organizations with many branch offices.

The only problem with inter-domain trust is that it *only* works with Windows NT Advanced Servers, not only at the home office but at all branch offices. You cannot extend inter-domain trust privileges to a NetWare server or a UNIX server or even to a LAN Manager server (in its current incarnation). Therefore, to provide inter-domain trust capabilities, it will be necessary to install a Windows NT Advanced Server for domain control at each branch that needs to be trusted or needs to trust the central office.

Windows NT Advanced Server Domain Administration Models

Given the existence of Windows NT Advanced Servers at the home office and all branch offices, trust relationships can be arranged a number of different ways to provide one degree or another of centralized administrative control over the network. Microsoft defines four basic models for trust relationships, which we will look at next.

Single Domain Model

This is the most obvious of the models and essentially is the baseline case. There is one user domain applying to one primary domain controller, which maintains *all* accounts for the entire enterprise. This provides, obviously, the maximum degree of centralized administration and control and it can work for very large networks (up to around ten thousand user accounts) with judicious use of replication and fallback servers to provide local logon server capabilities for remote offices and divisions. The network traffic, however, will become considerable on this kind of networking scheme, particularly for organizations with branch offices that must replicate the primary database controller over a wide-area networking link and for organizations where user accounts (particularly remote user accounts) change frequently.

Master Domain Model

In this approach there may be more than one domain but there is a single domain to provide central control, probably the MIS domain at the central site. All other domains trust this master domain. This model is ideal for organizations maintaining a centralized MIS department but supporting users at many branch office sites, and it can be used with very large networks (this is basically the approach that Microsoft uses itself[3]). The central MIS department in Redmond, Washington (Microsoft's Corporate HQ) is the central master domain for all account operations throughout Microsoft's organization worldwide. Users are members of local domains. They are *not* members of the central MIS domain. All user accounts are created in the central MIS domain—but since the remote domains trust the MIS domain, users automatically have access privileges on their local servers.

The administrator can define which servers and workstations the user is permitted to use at the time the user account is created. Requests for user account modification are communicated by electronic mail to the central account operators in Redmond. Local system administrators do not have account operator privileges and cannot create or modify user accounts, but they do have the necessary permissions to administer servers and to administer groups of users.

This approach provides central MIS control over the network, and a single central authority for creating and granting user access rights (with a high degree of security), while minimizing network traffic between central MIS and the remote sites and providing administrative flexibility at the remote sites. This scheme makes sense for large organizations.

Multiple Master Domain Model

This approach, recommended for very large networks (greater than ten thousand users), employs essentially the same logic as for the master domain but allows more than one master domain. Each subdomain trusts one or more of the master domains. The master domains might or might not trust each other (it will probably be most convenient if they do). In a very large organization this would allow a distributed MIS environment in which there are central MIS groups for several divisions within the organization, and would provide the benefits of the Master Domain Model without the necessity for centralizing all user accounts.

This approach might make sense when an organization expands by acquisition. If you find it necessary to add a completely new suborganization within your network, you could consider absorbing the existing MIS infrastructure into a Multiple Master Domain Model.

---

[3]Actually, Microsoft's net has features of *both* the Master Domain and Multiple Master Domain models; but (as we understand it) all user accounts are created in Redmond, so it seems closer to the former.

Complete Trust Model

The final model that Microsoft discusses is one that, in all honesty, appears to make *no* sense for an enterprise network. This is a model in which all domains operate independently but all domains trust all other domains within an enterprise. The idea here is that there is no central MIS department. Instead, each server is separately administered, but (by the maintenance of the necessary inter-domain trust links) users who have an account on any server will be able, with appropriate privileges, to use any other server in the enterprise.

The problem with this approach is that it depends *critically* upon the diligence of the network administrators supervising each of the trusted domains in the organization. Laxness on the part of any one administrator (for example, in closing obsolete user accounts or enforcing password changes) can propagate throughout the network via the trust relationships creating a large opportunity for security breach.

Since this type of networking is inherently insecure, we do not recommend it.

A Mixed Domain Model

In addition to the four models that Microsoft recommends, it's likely (especially as Windows NT capabilities are added onto existing networks—or as subnetworks are acquired and incorporated into an enterprise running a Windows NT network) that a need to *mix* the various models will arise. In particular, a model we think makes some sense is a combination of the Single Domain and Master Domain Model. In this approach, one would have a more-or-less independent account domain with a local administrator that also trusts a central Master Domain. Account control can be accomplished either locally *or* from the Master Domain. Local user accounts can be created locally; local or remote user accounts can be created by the Master Domain (i.e., the central MIS department).

This approach may be advantageous in several situations. When Windows NT networks are initially added to an existing enterprise it's unlikely that there will, in fact, *be* a Master Domain for the local domain to trust. Therefore, it will make sense to create an independent domain. Later on, if the company accepts Windows NT as a standard, you're faced with the problem of grafting these independent subnetworks into the Master Domain Model. This can most conveniently be done by trusting the Master Domain—servers then begin life with local user databases that can be supplanted (or augmented) by a remote account database at the Master Domain. There is no need for users who only use a particular domain server to have an account in the central MIS account database, and it may simplify things initially if they do not.

Similarly, when a remote site needs to be added to an existing Windows NT Master Domain or Multiple Master Domain network, it may not be possible (initially) for that branch network to be administered using the Master Domain Model—probably because the remote domain does not, in fact, *have* a Windows NT Advanced Server available initially as domain controller. In this situation, it may be convenient to allow the domain to operate more-or-less independently, and transport the foreign accounts from the existing network onto a Windows NT Advanced Server. Again, you're faced with essentially an independent network. By having this network trust the central Master Domain you gain the opportunity for remote administration and for access by users who have accounts in the remote network.

There is a problem with this approach—synchronizing account database information between the local network administrators and the administrators in the Master Domain. It's possible in this kind of model to wind up having multiple user accounts, one presented from the MIS domain and one from the local domain. Cooperation between the administrators can prevent this from becoming a significant burden, and the overall security risks reflected by the complete trust model do not occur because the trust relationships in this approach are essentially *one-way*. A variation on this approach would be to have the remote domains not only trust the Master Domain but be trusted by the Master Domain. It's not necessarily required for each of these domains in turn to trust each other. Such a two-way trust model will present something of a security risk, but not as great a one as the Complete Trust Model discussed earlier.

Now that we've examined the basic administration models for Windows NT, let's take a look at the specific steps involved in creating the necessary inter-domain trust links.

Setting Up Inter-Domain Trust Linkage Relationships

The steps for establishing inter-domain trust links (assuming that you have administrative status on both the domain to be trusted and the trusting domain) are:

1. Start User Manager for Domains. Select Select Domain from User menu. The Select Domain dialog appears. Select the Domain to be Trusted from the list (or type it in if you can't see it).
2. Select Policies/Trust Relationships from User Manager for Domains. The Trust Relationship dialog appears (see Figure 7.1).
3. Click the Add... button on the lower (Permitted to Trust this Domain) listbox and add the Trusting domain to the list. The Permit Domain to Trust dialog appears. At this point you will also have to type in (and confirm) an Initial Password for the trust relationship. This will only be used the first time the trusting domain is attached—at that point the system automatically changes the password on both systems, and the modified password (which you cannot change) will be used for further connections. Click Close to dismiss the dialog.
4. User/ Select Domain, and select (or type) the *trusting* domain name.
5. Policies/Trust Relationships. The Trust Relationships Dialog appears again. Click the Add button on the upper (Trusted Domains) listbox. The Add Trusted Domain dialog appears. Type in the Domain name to be trusted and then the password from step 3.
6. Assuming steps 1–5 work properly, an infobox will appear with the message "Trust relationship established with domain <domain name>." If not, examine the Event Log to see if an error occurred and carefully repeat steps 1–5.

Once these steps have been accomplished, administrators in the trusting domain can assign permissions to users and groups in the trusted domain at will. Administrators cannot, however, create or delete user accounts in a domain other than their own, nor can they assign rights to resources in the other domain (unless granted the right to do so by an administrator

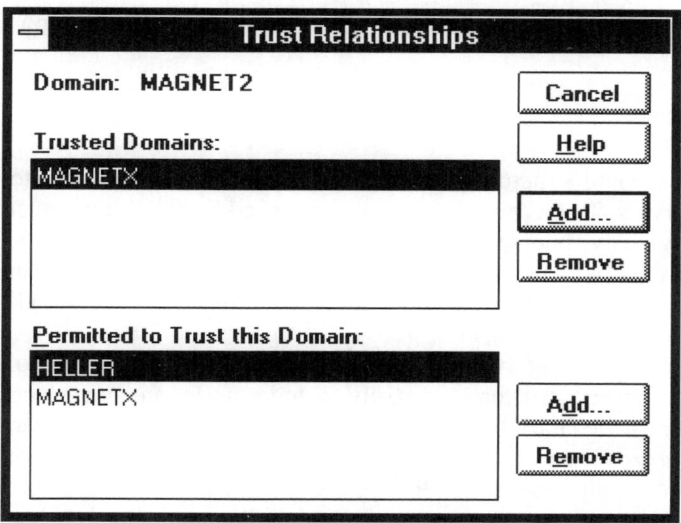

Figure 7.1 Trust Relationships dialog.

Inter-domain trust relationships in Windows NT Advanced Server are set using this dialog from User Manager.

from the trusting domain). Some coordination between administrators is necessary to make the system work; but it's still a vast improvement over separately administering each server.

Replication

The mechanism Windows NT Advanced Servers use to provide for users to log onto machines other than the primary domain controller is called *account replication*. The way this is done is actually relatively simple: every five minutes, the primary domain controller examines its account database to see if any changes have occurred. If they have, then it transmits these changes to *every other Windows NT Advanced Server in the domain*. In this way all Advanced Servers within a domain maintain account information that is within five minutes of being current across all servers. This also means that if for any reason there is a network failure that blocks out the primary domain controller, users can continue to log in using the information in their local servers (although changes to the user accounts—which have to be accomplished through the primary domain controller—won't work until the linkages are reestablished). While Windows NT workstations within the network do not replicate the account database, they *do* cache the account information for the most recently logged-on user, so (even if no logon server is available when the user next logs in) the system will identify the user based on the information stored from the last logon and will permit the user to use the computer if the information matches.

With that information under our belts, let's examine the specifics of setting up the replication service in Windows NT.

Replicating Directories

In addition to replicating the user account structure you can exploit the *replicator service* to copy other information between servers. This is necessary in an Advanced Server domain that employs *logon scripts* because (obviously) you want to have users log on to any server in the network but still use the same script that you maintain on the primary domain controller. It can also be desirable if you need to maintain centrally controlled information that has to be broadcast to all servers in the network (policy statements, etc.).

Each Windows NT Advanced Server can maintain an *export* directory structure and an *import* directory structure. These directory structures normally include the logon scripts and data. You can add additional subdirectories into the directory structure if you want. However, *only one directory tree may be exported from each server*. Windows NT workstations cannot export but can *import* through the replication system. With replication in place, changes within the directory tree will be transmitted to other systems on the network either immediately when they occur or (at the administrator's discretion) after a two-minute stabilization period.

This approach provides a transparent method for replicating the script information throughout a domain. It also can be employed to provide *automatic backup* of information. For example, one can replicate the critical data directory structures of a server, export that information, and import it on a backup server. You can use this in a variety of ways.

You should not view this replication approach as a panacea for providing automatic near line backup of user directory information. One site that attempted to do this[4] by replicating all user directories on backup servers every six minutes found that it almost immediately saturated a 100 megabit-per-second FDDI backbone. It is simply not practical to use the replication mechanism for frequently changing data at existing data rates.[5] You should use it only on data that changes *infrequently* or data so important that you can't afford to risk its loss. For user information that changes on a minute-by-minute basis, you should consider some other mechanism for critical data backup, such as a near line magneto-optical storage system.

Step-by-Step Instructions for Setting Up Replication

Given that you've decided to exploit replication for cross-server account maintenance or for some other purpose, here's how to get it running.

To set up replication export (assuming you have domain administrative privileges):

1. Start Server Manager from the Admin Tools group.

[4]See *Enterprise Connectivity in a Multivendor Environment,* paper from 1992 TechEd conference, included on Microsoft's TechNet CD.

[5]It might conceivably be possible, if data can be transmitted over a *very local area network* (VLAN)—essentially memory space in each computer that's tied together using fiber-optic cable. The memory-mapped files described in Chapter 1 might well have something to offer in this regard.

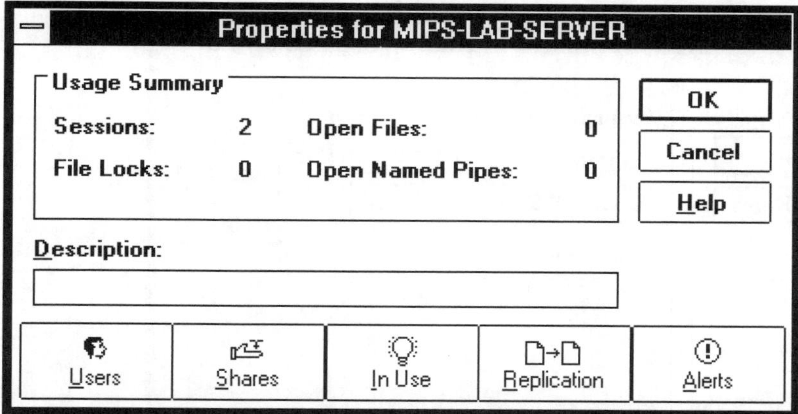

Figure 7.2 Properties dialog (from Server Manager).

The Properties dialog from Windows NT Advanced Server's Server Manager application duplicates the Server component in Control Panel—but from Server Manager, you can control servers over the network.

2. Select View/All (this will show both servers and workstations in the domain).
3. Select the server you wish to have export directories (typically the Primary Domain Controller). The Properties for <Machine Name> dialog will appear (see Figure 7.2) (functionally, this is the same as the running the Control Panel Server object locally on <Machine Name>).
4. Click the Replication button. The Directory Replication dialog (see Figure 7.3) appears.
5. Click the Export Subdirectories radio button. The default path for export (typically, the \WINNT\SYSTEM32\REPL\EXPORT path) appears in the From Path... field. You can edit the path if needed (note that you can export directories from only one directory).
6. If needed (to control replication of subdirectories and record-locking within the replication path), click the Manage... button. The Manage Exported Directories dialog appears. This allows you to add or remove subdirectories from the export list, determine whether the entire subtree or only the top-level subdirectory is exported, and control whether replication can occur while the contents of the export directories are being changed. You can also "lock out" specific directories that you do *not* want to export (the first time through, you're well advised to click the Help button for a more detailed explanation). When you're satisfied with the export management settings, click the OK button.
7. By default, the system will export replicant directory data to *all* importing systems in the *local* domain. If that's what you want, then you can click the OK button now, and skip ahead to step 9.

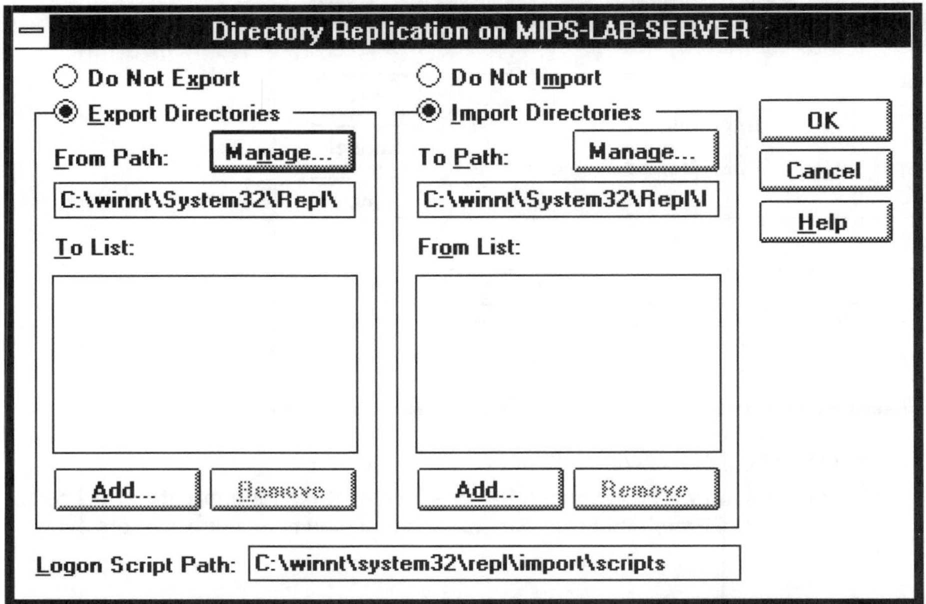

Figure 7.3 Directory replication dialog.

Directory replication is set using this dialog from Windows NT Advanced Server's Server Manager application.

8. If you want to limit which systems are permitted to import replicant data, or if you want to export data to systems outside the local domain, then you will need to add these systems explicitly in the To List. You can do so using the Add button, which will display the Select Domain dialog. You may select just a domain name to export to all systems in the domain, or you can select specific systems (NOTE: in wide-area network systems selecting the domain may not be sufficient—you may need to select each system to be exported to explicitly).
9. Click the OK button. The replicator service will be started, if it was not already running. If import has not been set up on any system(s) you will now need to set up replication import on the relevant system(s)—see the instructions that follow.

To set up replication *import* (assuming you have domain administrative privileges):

1. Start Server Manager from the Admin Tools group.
2. Select View/All (this will show both servers and workstations in the domain).
3. Select the server you wish to have import directories (typically all Backup Domain Controllers). The Properties for <Machine Name> dialog will appear.
4. Click the Replication button. The Directory Replication dialog appears.

5. Click the Import Subdirectories radio button. The default path for import (typically \WINNT\SYSTEM32\REPL\IMPORT) appears in the To Path... field. You can edit the path if needed (note that you can import to only one directory, although that directory can be loaded with information from multiple *export* servers).
6. If needed (to control replication of subdirectories and record-locking within the replication path), click the Manage... button. The Manage Imported Directories dialog appears. This allows you to add or remove subdirectories from the import list, determine whether the entire subtree or only the top-level subdirectory is imported, and whether replication can occur while the contents of the import directories are being changed, and "lock out" specific directories that you do *not* want to import (the first time through, you're well advised to click the Help button for a more detailed explanation). When you're satisfied with the import management settings, click the OK button.
7. By default, the system will import replicant directory data from *all* exporting systems in the *local* domain. If that's what you want, then you can click the OK button now, and skip ahead to step 9.
8. If you want to limit which systems the system will import from, or if you want to import data from systems outside the local domain, then you will need to add these systems explicitly in the From List. You can do so using the Add button, which will display the Select Domain dialog. You may select just a domain name to import from all, or you can select specific systems (NOTE: in wide-area network systems selecting the domain may not be sufficient—you may need to select each system to be imported from explicitly).
9. Click the OK button. The replicator service will be started, if it was not already running.

Enterprise Connectivity One—The Local Area Networks

An Enterprise Network is made up of one or more local area networks (typically many *local* area networks), connected together through a backbone system or across wide-area network (WAN) links. The structure of the individual LANs that make up the enterprise network is similar to an isolated small business local area network—but there are some differences that come into play when multiple local area networks must be connected. In particular, protocol selection (a rather arbitrary choice in an isolated LAN), becomes a critical issue when applied to large-scale enterprise networks, and this is especially true for Windows NT and other Microsoft networking products because they depend so heavily upon NetBIOS broadcasts.

TCP/IP as the Backbone Protocol

TCP/IP connectivity was discussed extensively in Chapter 6 and some readers may find it confusing that we chose to discuss TCP/IP networking *before* introducing the enterprise issues. The reason we did this is very simple: if you are doing enterprise networking with Windows NT you *must* use TCP/IP as the backbone protocol. You have no other choice.

TCP/IP is the only protocol that Windows NT can use for its native networking that is fully routable. You can connect two local area networks to each other using TCP/IP routers and traffic will be routed between the two TCP/IP networks including the NBT (NetBIOS over TCP/IP) packets necessary for Windows NT native communications involving the Network Browser (File Manager or the administration tools or so forth). The other protocols supported by Windows NT (e.g., NetBEUI and NWLink IPX) are not routable.[6] This is particularly true of NetBEUI, whose virtual circuit architecture inherently limits it to operation over a single subnet. The reason for this should be obvious: Were the NetBIOS broadcasts to be routed, a large-scale network could quickly be saturated by routed broadcasts not intended for any particular subnet; since broadcasts are inherently not addressed to a particular location, it isn't possible to route them selectively. Therefore, the broadcasts are blocked at the router—and any subsystem requiring broadcasts (in particular the browser) cannot function across the router.

TCP/IP avoids this problem because the HOSTS and LMHOSTS databases (or a Domain Name Service (DNS) server[7]) provide addresses for any and all message traffic. This eliminates the need for broadcast announcements to locate a given machine and allows Windows NT to operate effectively through quite complicated routing situations. Because of this fact, *any* Windows NT system that involves routers *must* use TCP/IP as the backbone protocol.

Does This Mean No Other Protocol Can Be Used?

The fact that TCP/IP is required as the backbone protocol does not mean that it must be the only protocol used in an enterprise network. There are significant advantages to using a multiprotocol solution. TCP/IP is quite complex (which is why we've devoted an entire chapter to it). And setting up and maintaining TCP/IP protocols is a significantly more complex task than setting up more standardized protocols like NetBEUI or IPX. The reason for this is the complicated addressing scheme that has to be manually set up and maintained using the HOSTS and LMHOSTS database files. There's also a performance implication.

The NetBEUI protocol that Windows NT uses by default is designed as a high-efficiency protocol for small networks. It provides a *virtual circuit* scheme for high data rate *raw* I/O transmissions between the server and the client. This works well on small subnets and delivers higher performance than TCP/IP (although it obviously militates—along with the broadcast issues discussed earlier—against use of NetBEUI over wide-area network links, where error handling can be a severe restriction). The IPX protocol has similar (though lesser) limitations. Again, however, it does not provide any provisions for NetBIOS broadcasts to be forwarded and thus cannot be used in a routed situation (with certain exceptions that we'll get to shortly).

---

[6]Actually, NWLink *is* routable to a limited degree—it generally will route one hop; that is, you can have machines on either side of a router that will "see" each other. If two routers are involved, however, it fails to route the essential NetBIOS broadcast messages. Hopefully, this problem will be eliminated in future versions of Windows NT.

[7]See Chapter 6 for more information.

What you *can* do is set up a mixed protocol network. Consider a network situation in which a central office local area network backbone needs to communicate with a remote office for account information. Obviously it's necessary for the central office backbone to run TCP/IP. TCP/IP will also be the preferred protocol for a wide-area network connection between the central office and the remote server. Now, does this mean that one should run TCP/IP for *all* of the clients on the remote network? The answer is probably no, both for performance reasons and for simplicity of administration. Rather than doing so, you should run *two* network stacks in the remote server. The TCP/IP stack will be used for communications with the central office (including the necessary traffic for maintaining the account databases and communicating inter-domain trust links). The second protocol should be either NetBEUI or NWLink depending on the needs of the particular site—preferably NetBEUI. This will be used for connections between the remote server and clients on the remote LAN.

The implication of this is twofold. First of all, it means that the remote clients will *only* be able to see the remote server and will not be able to establish connections across the wide-area network to the central office. If such connections are necessary, then a particular client will need to have TCP/IP protocols installed either as a replacement for, or augmentation of, NetBEUI in that client. Alternatively, a remote access services (RAS) connection could be established directly from the remote client into the central office—this may be preferable in certain situations.

Using dual network stacks in Windows NT computers presents no particular problems—it's simply a matter of loading and configuring the necessary protocols. Moreover, you can choose to manipulate the bindings using the Control Panel/Networks object and can place the most heavily used bindings first in the list. This would mean, presumably, the NetBEUI bindings for the local traffic. This will have the effect of performing what amounts to a primitive routing function. Any traffic that can be sent over the NetBEUI links will be sent that way. Traffic that cannot be sent over the NetBEUI links will automatically go to the next step in the bindings to the TCP/IP and NBT portions of the stack for transmission that way. The result is effectively a TCP/IP network extending between the remote server and the central office that overlaps a NetBEUI-based local area network between the remote server and its clients on the remote LAN.

The advantages of this approach are, first, better performance—with NetBEUI for all traffic on the LAN and TCP/IP only for remote connection when needed. Second, it makes for a much reduced administrative burden. The network administrator at the remote site only needs to maintain TCP/IP connections between the remote server and the central site. The workstations on the LAN don't require TCP/IP addresses, since they will principally use the much simpler NetBEUI stack. This makes it easier to plug and unplug computers as necessary. If a few users need connections extending into the central office, they can be provided with TCP/IP stacks—but the number of addresses needing maintenance will be minimized.

Windows NT has an additional advantage in this kind of environment. The *static routing* capability it provides for TCP/IP is suitable for use at many branch offices. Rather than installing an expensive hardware router, one of the Windows NT workstations—or even the server itself—can have two network cards installed and maintain a static routing table for connections to the central office (see Chapter 6 for details).

Unfortunately, Windows NT does not as yet provide any support for TCP/IP WAN links. The TCP/IP point-to-point protocol (PPP) and serial link interface protocol (SLIP) aren't supported, and therefore special hardware is required to connect the subnets. That's unfortunate because—again—TCP/IP is the essential backbone protocol. See Chapter 6 for more information on routing and other TCP/IP issues and Appendix 2 for more detailed information about various protocols supported by Windows NT.

Step-by-Step Instructions for Multiprotocol Binding Tuning

If you're setting up a network with TCP/IP as the backbone protocol and NetBEUI or NWLink as the local protocol, you'll need to tune the bindings appropriately. Here's how:

1. Start the Windows NT Control Panel, and select the Network Settings icon. Then click the Bindings... button to display the Network Bindings dialog (see Figure 7.4).
2. Select the Workstation Object in the Show Bindings For field.
3. Bindings at the top of the list are executed first, so in a mixed NetBEUI (or NWLink) and TCP/IP environment, make sure that the local protocol (NetBEUI or NWLink) bindings are at the top of the list. If not, select the appropriate binding and click the Up-Arrow button to "promote" the binding as necessary.

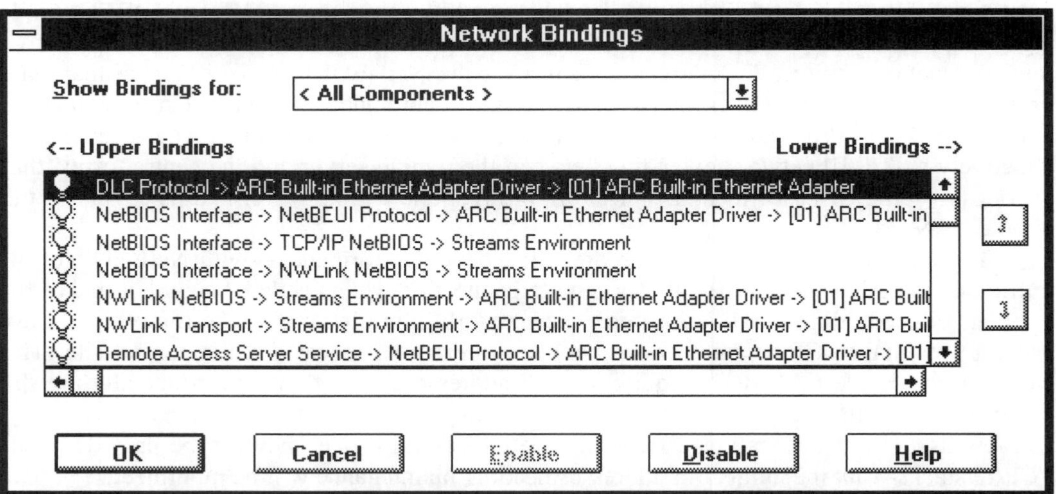

Figure 7.4 Network Bindings dialog.

In multiprotocol environments, you can control the order in which network bindings are executed using this dialog from Control Panel/Networks.

4. You can disable unused bindings (a step that may prove helpful in troubleshooting) rather than removing them. To do so, click on the binding step in question and click the Disable button. The light-bulb icon for the binding in question will be dimmed.
5. Click the OK button. You will be returned to the Network Settings dialog. Click OK again to exit to the Control Panel. You will need to exit and restart Windows NT to apply the new bindings.

Services for Macintosh

Microsoft provides another unique capability in Windows NT Advanced Server by supporting Apple Macintosh computers as network clients out-of-the-box. This is done using *Services for Macintosh* (SFM), a combination of a Windows NT server, file system driver, and network protocols that provides:

- Macintosh-compatible namespace on NTFS volumes
- Native (and fully routable!) support for Appletalk network protocols
- Postscript emulation on non-Postscript printers (allowing Macs to leverage non-Postscript printers already on the network)
- Access to Apple Laserwriter (and compatible Postscript printers on the Appletalk network) by Windows NT, Windows 3.x, DOS and OS/2 clients

SFM is included with Windows NT Advanced Server—there is nothing additional to buy (with the possible exception of a compatible Appletalk card for the server if you want to use LocalTalk[8] cabling to the Macintosh workstations). It requires no additional software on the Macintoshes (although it can provide better security if a Microsoft authentication package is used in place of the Macintosh's default authenticator—this is included with Windows NT Advanced Server). SFM does require approximately 2MB of additional disk space in the server, and directories to be made available to the Macs must exist on an NTFS drive (or CD-ROM).

Installing SFM

SFM is installed from Control Panel/Network settings, as follows:

1. Click the Add Software button, select Services for Macintosh from the list, and click Continue. You will be asked to specify the source directory for installation, which

[8]LocalTalk is the native form of networking built into all Macintosh systems since the 512KB "Fat Mac." It is less than 1/4 as fast as Ethernet; but for many users this lower performance is more than offset by its low cost. It's also possible to put Ethernet cards into most newer Macintoshes—or to use a LocalTalk/Ethernet router to bridge Macintoshes into an existing Ethernet. Windows NT is compatible with all of these solutions, although (as always) it's wise to check that any Appletalk or Ethernet cards you're thinking about buying are listed in the current *Windows NT Hardware Compatibility List*.

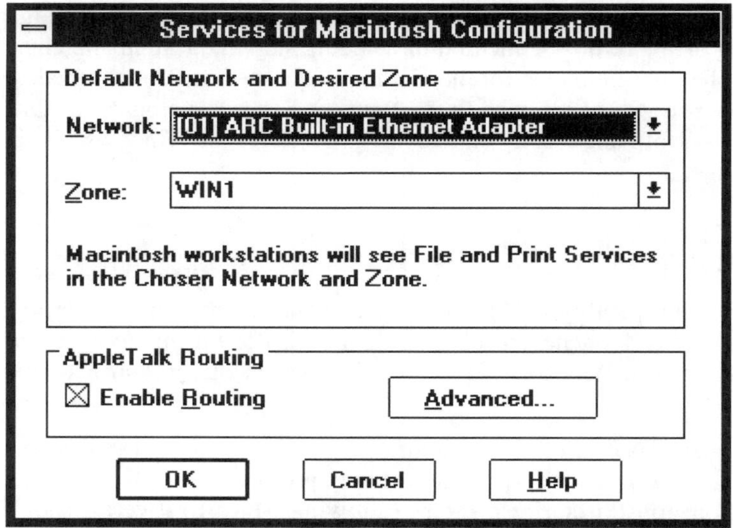

Figure 7.5 Services for Macintosh Configuration dialog.

Windows NT Advanced Server's Services for Macintosh are configured using this dialog.

may be A: or the appropriate directory on a Windows NT Advanced Server CD. The SFM files are then copied to your hard disk.

2. The Services for Macintosh Configuration dialog appears (see Figure 7.5). This is where you will designate the network card and Appletalk Zone[9] to use for SFM. You can also control Appletalk routing by checking the Enable Routing box and clicking the Advanced button.[10] When you're satisfied with the network and Zone settings, click OK.
3. Click OK again from the Network Settings dialog. You will need to reboot the computer to start Services for Macintosh.

After it's installed, SFM can be started/stopped/paused/continued from Control Panel/Services (or Server Manager/Services) like any other Windows NT service. You will also find that MacFile menus have been created in File Manager and Server Manager—and that a MacFile icon has been placed in the Windows NT Control Panel. You will use these new features to control operation of the SFM service.

[9]Appletalk *Zones* are used for routing in much the way Windows NT uses *Domains*.

[10]Details of Appletalk routing are beyond the scope of this text—see *Windows NT Advanced Server—Services for Macintosh* (listed in For More Information at the end of this chapter) for a detailed discussion of this topic.

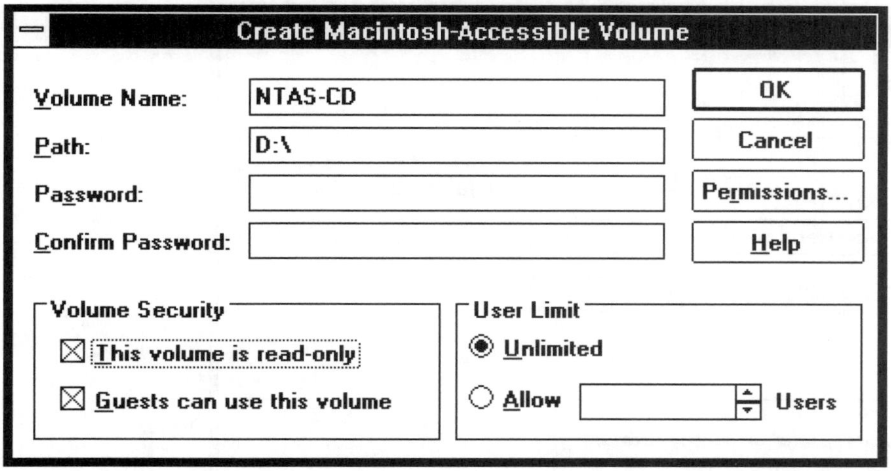

Figure 7.6 Create Macintosh-Accessible Volume dialog.

MacFile volumes are created within the filespace of an NTFS disk using this dialog, from Windows NT Advanced Server's File Manager.

Creating SFM Volumes

Once SFM is installed, it's neccessary to create an SFM-compatible "volume" that Macintosh clients can mount. This is done as follows:

1. Create the directory tree you want Macintosh systems to access using File Manager (or the equivalent command-line functions) on an NTFS disk volume. NOTE: SFM volumes include *all* subdirectories of the root directory that's made accessible to Macs, and SFM volumes cannot overlap—you cannot share only part of a directory subtree, nor can you share a directory and also share its subdirectory with a separate volume name).
2. Select the root of the directory tree you want to make accessible to Macs using File Manager, then choose MacFile/Create Volume. The Create Macintosh-Accessible Volume dialog appears (see Figure 7.6). You may now declare the volume name, edit the path, and specify a password[11] that Mac users will have to issue for access to the volume. You may also designate a maximum number of users for the volume (the default is unlimited). Note that none of this affects the status of the

[11]This *volume password* is a separate, additional, security measure for Macintosh users—it is *not* the same as the Windows NT username and password, which still must be issued in order for Mac users to access the volume.

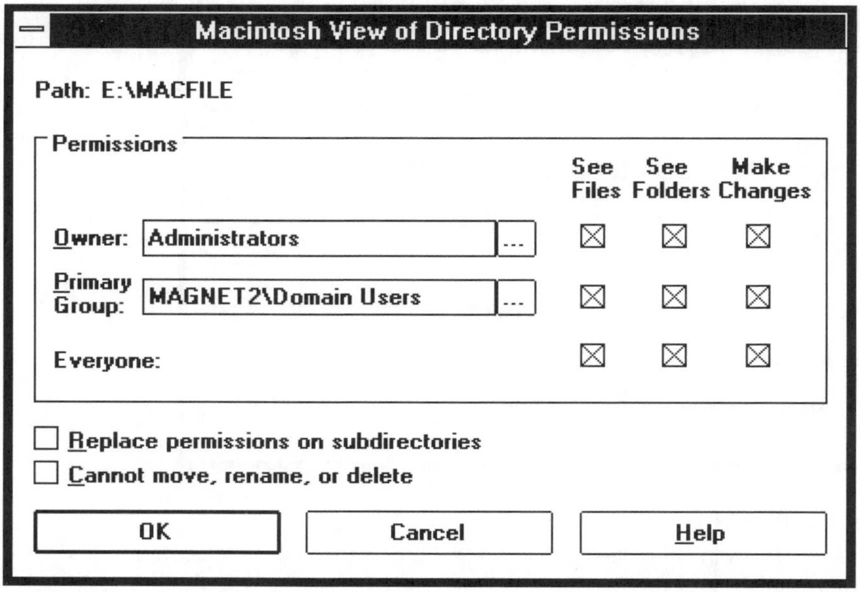

Macintosh View of Directory Permissions

Path: E:\MACFILE

Permissions

		See Files	See Folders	Make Changes
Owner:	Administrators	☒	☒	☒
Primary Group:	MAGNET2\Domain Users	☒	☒	☒
Everyone:		☒	☒	☒

☐ Replace permissions on subdirectories

☐ Cannot move, rename, or delete

OK Cancel Help

Figure 7.7 Macintosh View of Directory Permissions dialog.

MacFile directory permissions are set using this dialog, from Windows NT Advanced Server's File Manager.

NTFS directory that contains the volume—it's still a valid NTFS directory, and can be accessed by PCs in the usual way.[12]

3. Click the Permissions button. This will bring up the Macintosh View of Directory Permissions dialog (see Figure 7.7), which you will use to decide which users have permission to access the volume (this is in addition to the regular NTFS security settings—however, be aware that Macs see access controls on a directory-by-directory, rather than file-by-file basis). When you're satisfied with the permission settings, click OK to exit the MacFile Permissions dialog.
4. Click OK to exit the Create Macintosh-Accessible Volume dialog. The volume is now available for access from Macintosh clients.

[12]SFM extends the existing filename translation scheme that NTFS uses to present 8.3 names to DOS users to Macintoshes as well. Macintosh-created long names are treated as native NTFS filenames (with the exception of certain illegal characters, which are replaced). These are then translated into 8.3 DOS-compatible names for PC users. Windows NT users see the long filenames. NTFS filenames will appear exactly as created to Mac users, *provided* the names are 32 characters or shorter—if not, NTFS converts them to 8.3 names for the Mac users.

Once a MacFile volume is created, you can modify its settings by selecting it in File Manager and selecting MacFile/View-Modify Volumes. You can eliminate Macintosh access to the volume using MacFile/Remove Volumes (note that this removes the MacFile volume associated with the directory, *not* the directory itself—you do that with File Manager in the usual way).

You can use exactly the same procedure to make CD-ROM directories available to Mac clients—just skip the first step (it's usually most convenient to share the entire CD, starting from the root directory, specifying read-only access. This allows you to change discs in the CD player without having to reset the MacFile volume sharing).

SFM Printer Support

As mentioned above, SFM provides *Postscript emulation*, so that Macintosh users can take advantage of non-Postscript printers (such as the HP LaserJet), and also makes Macintosh printers accessible to PCs. SFM does this by exploiting the Windows NT Print Manager (and the associated print spooler)—along with a little trick called "capturing" the Macintosh printers.

To understand how this works, you need to be aware that Macintosh printers are usually connected to the *Appletalk Network*, rather than to any particular Macintosh[13]—they're *Network Printers* in much the same sense as HP's LaserJet IIIs (which contains its own Ethernet card).

By "capturing" LaserWriter printers, Windows NT Advanced Server assures that the administrator has control of all print jobs dispatched to that printer—it only accepts jobs from the Advanced Server (which in turn makes a *logical* printer available to both Macintosh and PC users). This has the additional benefit of avoiding the "Laserprep Wars" that can result from incompatible versions of the LaserWriter print drivers on Macintoshes attempting to access the same printer—instead, Windows NT sends its own LaserPrep code with each print job.

Of course, using PC printers with Windows NT Advanced Server doesn't involve any form of capture—the printer is connected directly to the print server (or at least controlled by it).

To set up SFM printing on your Windows NT Advanced Server:

1. Start Print Manager, and select Printer/Create Printer. This brings up the Create Printer Dialog (see Figure 7.8). Type a name for the printer in the Printer Name field, and select an appropriate printer driver (for PCs this will be the native driver for the printer, *not* Postscript—unless, of course, you're using a Postscript-compatible printer). You can also type in an optional Description.
2. Select an appropriate device for printing from the Print To list. For a printer connected directly to the server, this will be an appropriate LPT port. For a LaserWriter (or other AppleTalk printer), choose the Network Printer entry in the Print To list.

[13]We are referring here to Apple's LaserWriter (and compatible) printers—not the various dot-matrix printers made by Apple.

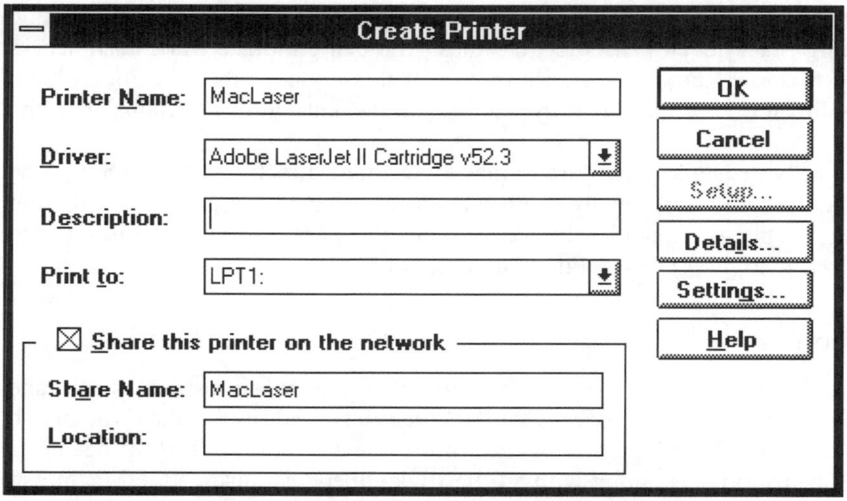

Figure 7.8 Create Printer dialog.

Administrators create logical printers using this dialog from Windows NT Advanced Server's Print Manager. Once created, the printers can be made accessible to Macintosh and/or PC clients on the network.

This will present a Print Destinations dialog (see Figure 7.9), from which you can select AppleTalk Printing Devices.

3. Assuming you are connecting to an AppleTalk printer, you're now presented with an Available AppleTalk Printing Devices dialog (see Figure 7.10). Select the Zone and printer from this list, and click OK. The printer will be captured by the Advanced

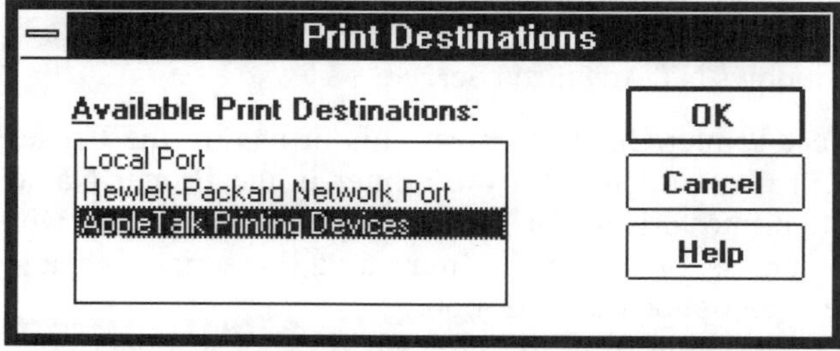

Figure 7.9 Print Destinations dialog.

This dialog, from Windows NT Advanced Server's Print Manager, allows administrators to "capture" AppleTalk (i.e.: Macintosh-compatible) printers for control by the Windows NT Advanced Server. Captured Appletalk printers can be made available to PC users as though they were connected to the server itself.

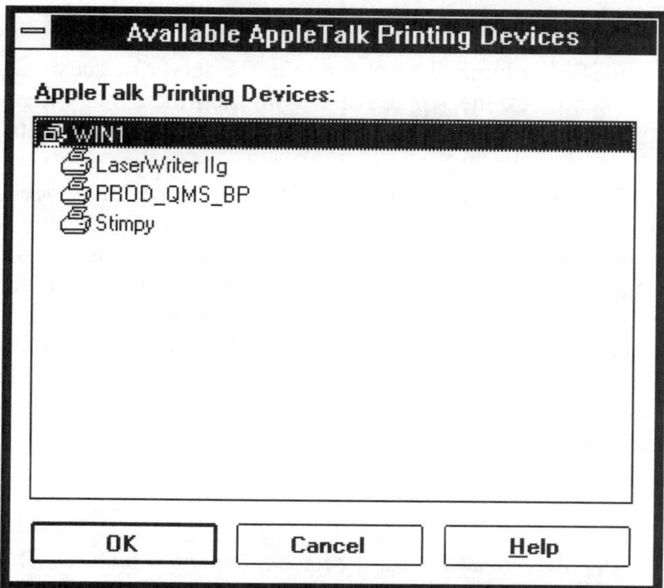

Figure 7.10 Available AppleTalk Printing Devices dialog.
This dialog lets an administrator designate an Appletalk printer to capture.

Server by default—meaning that instead of printing to it directly, Macintosh users will have to print to the logical printer you create in the next step. If you do *not* want to capture the printer (warning: not capturing the printer means you cannot control which jobs it prints in what order, and runs the risk of LaserPrep wars), you'll need to click the Settings... button, which will bring up the AppleTalk Port Configuration dialog. Un-checking the Capture this AppleTalk Printing Device box will eliminate capture of the printer.

4. To make the printer available to other (Macintosh and/or PC) users, check the Share this printer on the network box, and enter a sharename and (optionally) location.
5. The printer should now be available to PC clients in the usual way. To make it available to Mac clients, one further step is needed: a user account for Mac printers must be created. Start Control Panel/Services, select Print Server for Macintosh, and click the Startup button. A Print Server for Macintosh dialog will appear. Click the Choose This Account button, and type in a user account name (and optional password) for Mac print jobs. Then click OK. Macs should now have access to the printer just as PCs do.

Accessing SFM Volumes and Printers from Macintosh Clients

Before a Macintosh client can access an SFM volume, it must log in to the server in question. This is done using the Macintosh Chooser. Click the AppleShare icon, then the Zone where the server is located. This will present a list of file servers, from which the Mac user selects the name of the advanced server.

At this point a Connect to the file server... dialog appears. If Guest access has been enabled on the Advanced Server, then the Guest button can be clicked. Otherwise, the registered user button must be clicked, requiring the entry of a valid Windows NT username and password.[14] Once this is done, a list of available volumes is presented; the Mac user can mount one by selecting it and clicking the OK button, at which point an icon appears on the Mac desktop that represents the shared volume. The Mac user then accesses this icon in the usual way (see Figure 7.11). Macintosh workstations access Windows NT Advanced Server printers (including captured AppleTalk printers) through Chooser in exactly the way they use any other AppleTalk printer—there is no difference at all.

A Final Word about SFM

In summary, SFM is one of Windows NT Advanced Server's best-implemented features. By simply installing SFM and configuring it properly, you can provide full file-and-printer sharing to Macintosh clients, while giving Windows NT, Windows, OS/2, and DOS clients access to the very same printers and files. To the enterprise network administrator, this represents a significant advantage over other network servers, which require add-on software or bridging to connect Macs and PCs to the same directories. The Windows NT Advanced Server approach to this is completely seamless, leverages the advantages of NTFS (including excellent performance and fault tolerance), and is extremely easy to set up.

Unfortunately, there are limitations. One of the most serious is that RAS doesn't support AppleTalk, as AppleTalk doesn't use (or send) NetBIOS packets. MS-Mail can support Macintosh clients, but they are provided with neither Windows NT Advanced Server, nor the MS-Mail and Schedule Plus Upgrade kit—you'll have to buy them separately (and buy the Upgrade Kit—the Mac clients aren't compatible with Workgroup mail). Macintosh clients logged into a Windows NT Advanced Server also do not execute login scripts and cannot take advantage of User Profiles—nor can they participate in inter-domain trust relationships or "see" resources from other Windows NT systems (unless those systems also run SFM and have access to the *same* Appletalk or Appletalk/Ethernet network as the clients).

With all that said, however, SFM is by far the *cleanest* approach we've seen for giving Macs and PCs simulataneous access to the same files. We consider it one of the best reasons

[14]And here we run into a security problem—Appleshare passwords are sent in clear-text over the network, which violates Windows NT's C2 security standards. All is not lost, however—Microsoft provides an alternate Microsoft UAM sign-on with password encryption. Its installation is detailed in the *Windows NT Advanced Server—Services for Macintosh* manual that's included with Windows NT Advanced Server.

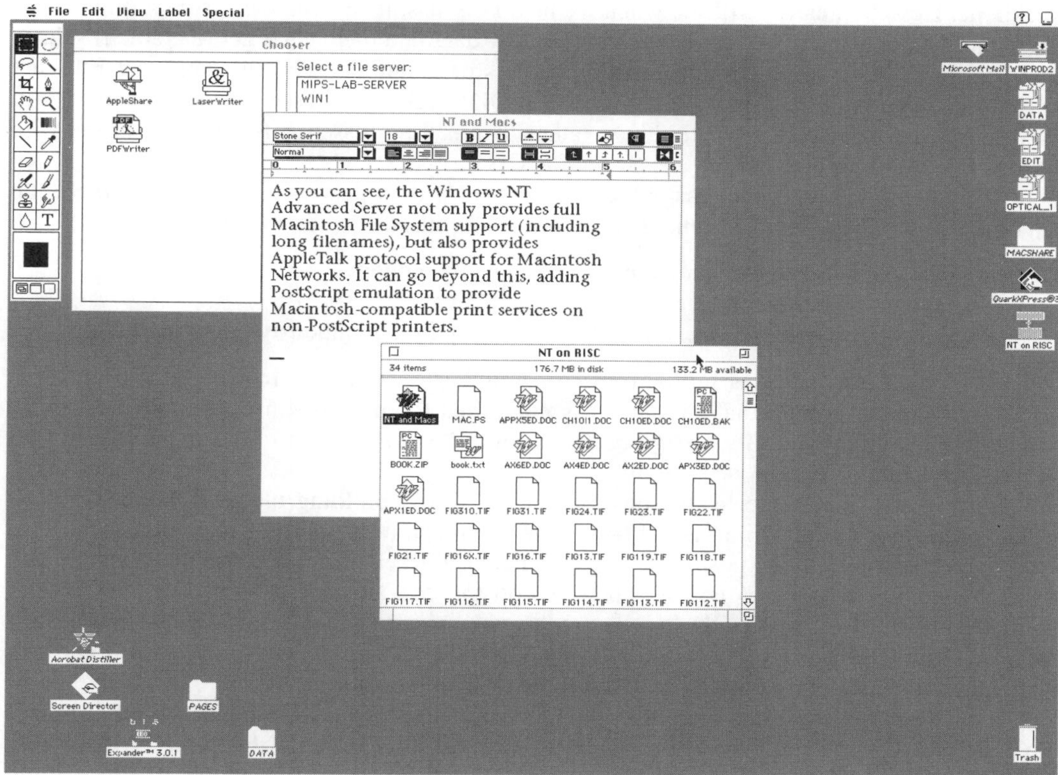

Figure 7.11 Macintosh access to Windows NT Advanced Server.

Macintosh users "see" Windows NT Advanced Server files and directories as icons and folders on the Macintosh desktop.

for buying a Windows NT Advanced Server—and hope that Microsoft will improve the support for Macintosh clients in future versions of Windows NT.[15]

Enterprise Connectivity Two—Electronic Mail

The most general method of connecting up the LANs that make up an enterprise network is to connect them via one form or another of wide-area networking link or through an enterprise

[15]We suppose it's too much to hope that Microsoft might see fit to exploit the SFM technology to give Windows NT *native* access to AppleTalk. That's a pity—it's completely routable yet avoids the incomprehensible addressing problems of TCP/IP. An optional native AppleTalk capability for *both* Windows NT *and* Advanced Server would go far toward making the dream of Mac-like plug-and-play connectivity a reality for PCs.

backbone. However, as we will see when we begin discussing WANs, the assumption that one can simply extend a network connection across low data rate media and get tolerable results is often false. Wide-area networking links are orders of magnitude slower than local Ethernet networks, slower still by comparison with, say, FDDI backbones. They're also expensive—in WANs you must pay for use of the wire, rather than having (essentially) free use of the wire once you've paid for installation, as is true of LANs.

This being the case, the least expensive and most flexible way to connect people in an enterprise system is often electronic mail (e-mail). This has the following advantages:

- Low-cost wide-area connections are possible by modem.
- Disparate systems can be connected with gateways.
- Connections are *asynchronous*—they don't require continuously operating links.

Windows NT includes built-in e-mail, which we discussed in Chapter 4. Unfortunately, the built-in e-mail that's included is not suited to enterprise use. It's a Windows for Workgroups-style *workgroup postoffice* that cannot be connected to other postoffices—the key requirement for enterprise systems.

As we saw in Chapter 4, the postoffice is the basic building block of Microsoft Mail (which is included with Windows NT)—it's the central storage point for messages, which are communicated between the postoffice and the clients. To create an enterprise mail system, you need a capability to *forward* messages between postoffices, along with some sort of *directory*, so that postoffices know what to do with messages intended for users outside the local postoffice. The workgroup postoffice built into Windows NT lacks this *store-and-forward* capability—but you can get it by upgrading to a full MS-Mail 3.0 postoffice.

MS-Mail 3.0 is a true store-and-forward system that uses a DOS-based (or OS/2-based) EXTERNAL.EXE program to copy mail between postoffices. To do this, you must set up a machine (known as a *mail server)* that runs EXTERNAL.EXE, and which can "see" both postoffices, either using a network connection or via modem. On a preset schedule, EXTERNAL.EXE copies files from one postoffice to the other. If you can't rig things so that a single copy of EXTERNAL can see both postoffices, then you use two copies of EXTERNAL—one for each postoffice—and connect them by modem. It's a simple (you might almost say crude) approach, but it does work—provided you have EXTERNAL.EXE.

To get it, you can use the *MS-Mail and Schedule Plus Extensions for Windows for Workgroups* to upgrade the workgroup postoffice. This is a $695 product that changes the postoffice directory into MS-Mail 3.0 form, and it includes that much-needed EXTERNAL.EXE program (the DOS version).

The most convenient approach to using the Extensions with Windows NT is to:

1. Create a Workgroup Postoffice on the Windows NT system in question per the procedure for "Setting up a Postoffice" from Chapter 3. This will create a Workgroup Postoffice in a directory named WGPO by default.
2. Follow the instructions for "Upgrading a Workgroup Postoffice in place" that are given in the *Microsoft Mail Administrator's Guide* (included in the Extensions). This will give you a complete MS-Mail postoffice in the same WGPO directory you created in step 1.

3. Share the WGPO directory on your network. Workstations will most conveniently access the directory if they access it as local disk M: (because the MS-Mail client and EXTERNAL.EXE expect to see mail files on disk M:).

With this done, you have a full store-and-forward postoffice that can be connected to other MS-Mail postoffices, or to other mail systems using an additional piece of software called a gateway.[16] Connecting postoffices together is a fairly simple process; one simply configures EXTERNAL.EXE to "see" both postoffices and configures it for periodic update. This is most easily done as follows:

1. Select a workstation that can function as the "mail server" (i.e., run EXTERNAL.EXE). This may be the same system that has the postoffice set up, or it may be another system.
2. Configure the mail server to "see" the postoffice directory as drive M:, for instance, by the *net use* command:

```
net use M: \\mips-lab-server\WGPO
```

3. Or the equivalent File Manager steps. Do this even if the postoffice is physically on the mail server—it expects to see mail files on drive M:.
4. Configure the mail server to "see" the other postoffice as drive N: (assuming that it is on the network), for instance:

```
net use N: \\mailhost\maildata
```

   (The MSMAIL\MAILDATA directory on MS-Mail 3.0 systems is functionally equivalent to the WGPO directory on Windows NT systems that are upgraded in place using the Extensions).
5. Run EXTERNAL.EXE on the mail server, using the -A switch to disable modem operations, and the -d switch to specify drives to search for mail files; for instance (assuming that EXTERNAL.EXE is itself on drive M:):

```
M:external -A -dMN
```

6. External will now run and will poll the two postoffices for mail needing to be moved to the other postoffice. When it finds any mail that needs to be moved, it will move it.

If your setup doesn't permit a single machine to "see" both postoffices, you'll need to run one copy of EXTERNAL.EXE on *each* postoffice, and connect the two via modem, according to the instructions given in the *Microsoft Mail Administrator's Guide.* This will also give you some alternatives; for example, the -w switch lets you specify Wide-Area Network (WAN) connections that are to be used only at a specified time. You can use this in conjunc-

[16] Gateways are beyond the scope of this book—each e-mail system requires its own MS-Mail gateway, as each has its own unique file structure. In general, gateways will be separate DOS programs that function in much the same manner as EXTERNAL.EXE. Microsoft has a catalog of MS-Mail gateway products, you can request it from Microsoft sales.

tion with remote access services (RAS) to create a low-cost forwarding scheme for low-priority mail messages—an example of which is given in the section on Wide-Area Networking later in this chapter.

A Critique of MS-Mail and Windows NT

There are a couple of problems with this approach: First, we are relying on a DOS-based program (EXTERNAL.EXE) to provide the vital forwarding of messages between postoffices. Windows NT's DOS support is quite good, of course, and running EXTERNAL.EXE this way should be generally quite reliable, but there are some issues that need to be considered.

First, as a DOS application, EXTERNAL.EXE takes no advantage of Windows NT's security, reliability, and built-in performance (and event) monitoring. Worse, as it isn't implemented as a Windows NT service, you *can't* assume that it will be automatically started on a system reboot. You can, of course, make it part of the startup group for the default user, but this won't help unless you have someone physically present to log in as default user on system restart (unless you defeat the Windows NT security system by setting up a no-password automatic login on startup [see "Running a Windows NT Server in a Locked Closet" later in this chapter], a procedure that violates system security). It's also worth noting that Microsoft didn't design MS-Mail to be operated from a Windows NT DOS prompt—it's intended to be used from a standalone DOS machine. On a heavily loaded system, it's possible that poor performance may render the DOS-based version of EXTERNAL.EXE unreliable—especially when it's used with high-speed modem connections.

As a workaround, you can substitute Microsoft's OS/2-based Multitasking Mail Transfer Agent (MTA) for the DOS-based EXTERNAL.EXE. This is essentially an OS/2 version of the DOS-based program, but it has the advantage of having been designed to run in a protected-mode multitasking environment. Unfortunately, it's expensive ($1,995 as this is written), and like the DOS-based version it is a character-mode legacy application, rather than a Windows NT service—and thus must be run from the command line, with all the security and auto-start implications that implies. It also depends upon NT's OS/2 1.3 emulation subsystem, which is only available on Intel x86-based systems, so you can't use it with RISC-based servers.

Clearly, what's needed is a Windows NT-based MTA, and curiously enough, that's precisely what Microsoft is working on.

The Enterprise Messaging Server (EMS)

Microsoft's Enterprise Messaging Server (EMS) standard will debut in mid-1994. EMS will include new clients, gateways, etc. (all MS-Mail 3.2 compatible) that will be NT-based, graphically administered, x.400/500 "standards"-based, and network-independent (which presumably means that they'll exploit the same sort of approach that SQL Server for NT uses with the NWLink protocol [as described in Chapter 11] to provide connectivity on NetWare LANs).

Since EMS will be MS-Mail 3.2-compatible, gateways built to the current MS-Mail File API (FAPI) and clients written to the Messaging API (MAPI) will work with it too—and a new Gateway API (GAPI?) will make it easier to "roll your own" solutions for special e-mail problems. It all sounds great, but it's six to nine months off as this is written. For the moment, integrating Windows NT mail beyond the local postoffice requires either a DOS or OS/2 form of EXTERNAL.EXE, per the instructions above.

This situation might well provide an opportunity for an enterprising programmer (anyone out there listening?). It might be possible to construct a "patch" or "shim" program to give character-mode DOS or OS/2 EXTERNAL.EXE a Windows NT Service hook as a front end. Indeed, if the idea is extended to other character-mode applications, such a "universal service control" might be a convenient way to provide a wide variety of legacy applications with a Windows NT Services interface.

Other Mail Systems

Of course, if you're working for a corporation that's standardized on another mail system—UNIX Simple Mail Transfer Protocol (SMTP), or cc:Mail, for instance—the preceding discussion will have struck you as weird. Couldn't we just ignore MS-Mail, and substitute another mail system instead?

In principle, the answer is *yes*—provided, of course, that the necessary client, MTA, and Gateway software runs under Windows NT. Since most such software is DOS-based and uses store-and-forward techniques similar to those used by MS-Mail, it will probably work under Windows NT (and cc:Mail, at least, is planning to support Windows NT as a client platform directly, although the software was not available as this was written).

However, you want to consider the move to a different mail system carefully. Microsoft has repeatedly stated a strategic intent to make e-mail functionality a part of the operating system, rather than an add-on product, and the Messaging API (MAPI), specifically, is a part of the Windows NT standard. Substituting a non-MAPI-compatible mail client, such as cc:Mail, runs the risk of encountering incompatibilties with software that expects this functionality to be available.

A better approach may be to go ahead and install a Windows NT-based MS-Mail postoffice, upgrade it to a full MS-Mail store-and-forward postoffice as described above, and then install a cc:Mail (or SMTP or other as appropriate) MS-Mail gateway. This will give Windows NT systems access to the corperate standard mail system without abandoning the built-in 32-bit mail cleint and associated MAPI support . . . but it's expensive.

Hopefully, other mail vendors will support NT with 32-bit mail clients, and MAPI interfaces, in their future releases—in which case the entire problem will go away.

RAS—Windows NT's Built-in WAN

LANs are fine for local connections, and e-mail can help with certain kinds of connections at any distance, but there comes a point when you're going to need direct connection and you can't find (or buy) a long enough wire. That's when you must resort to *wide-area networking*, in which LAN-style connections are extended across phone company lines and other elements of the larger telecommunications system. Uniquely among today's operating systems, Windows NT comes with a limited-use WAN built-in. It's called *remote access services* (RAS).

RAS is a *NetBIOS router* implemented as a Windows NT service. In effect, it takes the network connections of the *RAS Server* (the machine on which RAS dial-in services are running) and extends them over a WAN connection to the *RAS Client* (a machine that's connecting to the RAS server using RAS client software). Since all NetBIOS connections are routed, RAS is *protocol-independent*: NetBEUI, TCP/IP, and NWLink SPX/IPX connections can all be handled, *provided they have Windows NT NetBIOS bound to their protocol stack.*[17]

Two versions of RAS are provided, a single-user version with Windows NT, and a multi-user version with Windows NT Advanced Server. Both versions can be used as clients by a local user logged into the system console, connecting over the WAN to another RAS server. The single-user version provided with Windows NT allows one user at a time to access the Windows NT system remotely over the WAN, while the Windows NT Advanced Server version supports up to 64 users logged in at one time.

Both versions of RAS are installed from Windows NT's Control Panel/Network Settings, using a procedure that we'll examine shortly; but first, there are some things you need to know about the different kinds of WANs that RAS can support.

Modems

The first, and least expensive, option is connecting by an asynchronous MOdulator/DEModulator (MODEM). Modems are widely available today that will work at data rates up to 38,400 baud,[18] which is actually faster than most telephone systems can handle—the maximum data rate available on standard phone lines that are digitally switched (most offices) is 14,400 baud; some older systems are limited to 9,600 baud.

RAS works well with modems, although—given the limitation of the low data rate—the resulting connection is mostly useful for transferring data files or administrative information on an intermittent basis. The major issues of concern in using modems with RAS are:

- Get fully compatible modems—preferrably identical ones—at each end of the link.
- Get modems that work *symmetrically*. Some high-speed modems use a low data-rate *back channel* for receiving that can be overwhelmed by RAS traffic.
- Get modems that are compatible with Windows NT, for which the Windows NT Hardware Compatibility List[19] is indispensible.

Since modems can be used with normal telephone lines, you need only pay the usual telephone company connect charges for use of the line, which makes this approach by far the

[17]Note that *only* NetBIOS connections are routed. RAS will not route non-NetBIOS TCP/IP or IPX traffic. In particular, it cannot be used for Windows NT's built-in TCP/IP utility programs (such as FTP) or by NetWare client redirectors. The RAS design allows for routing these connections, but the current implementation is NetBIOS-only.

[18]Baud is an archaic measure of bandwidth that works out to about ten times the number of bytes per second, thus 38,400 baud is about 3,840 bytes/sec.— less than 1% of Ethernet data rate (10 MBits/sec.).

[19]This is available online in the CompuServe WINNT forum, as well as in the Microsoft Windows NT documentation.

most economical if you don't require continuous high-speed connection. If you do, then one of the other choices will probably suit you best.

RS-232 Null Modem—NT's "Zero-Slot" LAN

One interesting way to use RAS isn't really *wide*-area networking at all: If you replace the modem used for asynchronous communication with a widely available RS-232 *null-modem* cable, you get a wired connection good for speeds up to 115,000 baud (about 10% of Ethernet) that *doesn't require a network card at all!* This kind of approach can be useful in several situations—for one thing, given the fact that all Windows NT systems (not just advanced servers) can use RAS to support one user at a time, it makes a very convenient way to connect a portable computer running the DOS-based (LAN Manager) or Windows for Workgroups version of RAS. Another possible application for RAS with null modems would be to provide low-cost "zero-slot" LAN connections for up to 64 users to a Windows NT Advanced Server. Given the low cost of Ethernet cards and cable today, this probably won't be a common solution—but many sites have *miles* of serial cable left in the walls and ceilings from the Seventies and Eighties, when connecting terminals to host mainframes was common. Multi-user RAS on Windows NT Advanced Server offers an effective way to reuse that cable, where full Ethernet data rates aren't required.

Multiport RS-232 Cards

Windows NT Advanced Server can support up to 64 simultaneous remote WAN users on RAS, as mentioned earlier. Of course, it can't do this using the 1–4 communication ports[20] built into most PCs. If more ports are needed, the solution is a multiport serial communications (RS-232) board.

Multiport boards include their own coprocessors and memory, offloading the main CPU from the need to oversee all communications between the system and the outside world. You can use a multiport board to connect Windows NT RAS with modems, or (using a *null-modem cable* as mentioned above) as a zero-slot LAN for local systems.

In any case, the vital issue in selecting a multiport board for Windows NT is to get one for which a Windows NT driver is available. Check the Windows NT hardware compatibility list (availaible in the CompuServe WINNT forum, as well as packaged in the Windows NT shrinkwrap) before buying.

X.25 Links

If asynchronous modem data rates (14,400 baud) aren't sufficient—or if you're spending so much time connected that long-distance telephone bills are becoming a major expense—then

[20]Note that COM3 and COM4 on most PCs are implemented sharing the COM1 and COM2 interrupts—and Windows NT doesn't support interrupt sharing. This means that on all but IBM's PS/2 systems, Windows NT supports simultaneous use of only two built-in communication ports. If you want more than two connections, you need a multiport card!

another option to consider is use of an *X.25 packet-switching network.* X.25 is a communications standard for digital switching of customer data over long distances. It provides data rates as high as 56 KBits/sec., or can multiplex many low data-rate connections together into a single high-speed connection. There are two ways that Windows NT can use X.25—directly, through a *smart card*, or indirectly, through a *Peripheral Access Device* (PAD).

PADs are generally used for client connections, and usually connect to a standard asynchronous modem. This makes it possible for remote clients to dial into a PAD but have their data transmitted over the X.25 packet switch to the server, which can use either a PAD or a smart card. Since modem connections to PADs are limited to the usual data rates for asynchronous communication, you might think this is a waste of time, but it isn't.

To understand why, consider what's involved in connecting five remote users to an RAS server using conventional modems. Each user requires a modem and telephone line, and the server will need five modems (and a multiport serial card, described below). The total investment in equipment alone will run into the thousands of dollars, and if the phone lines get a lot of use (and remember that they're limited to just a few percent of Ethernet data rates, so things will happen slowly) the connection charges—especially if they're long-distance—will become quite a burden.

By using X.25, you can save money in this situation. The server gets a single X.25 smart card and a leased line from the local telephone company connects it to an X.25 provider (such as Tyment, Sprintnet or Telnet). Client systems connect to the server by modem, making a local telephone call to the X.25 provider's PAD in their area. The cost will be lower (*if* the system is heavily used), because the hourly charge by the X.25 provider is typically much less than that from the telephone company, and the line conditions are better (so the connection is more reliable).

For Windows NT clients, there's another advantage to X.25—by using a smart card at both ends of the connection, you can get much higher data rates (typically 56KBps) than from modems. For applications that require such data rates (and use of RAS for more than intermittent copying of small data files certainly qualifies!), these data rates can be not just convenient, but *essential.*

ISDN

The final option for using Windows NT RAS is *integrated services digital networking* (ISDN). In contrast to the X.25 and asynchronous modem options, ISDN was designed from the beginning for computer use, and provides throughput as high as 128 KBits/sec.[21] By comparison with X.25, ISDN is generally cheaper (at the maximum data rate), and gives higher throughput. It's almost certainly a better choice for remote clients who need high-speed connections. On the other hand, X.25 PADs offer great flexibility—a server with an X.25 smartcard installed can support a single high-speed client (itself connected with a smartcard) or a number

[21] ISDN normally provides a maximum of 64KBps, but can do so bidirectionally for a *total* throughput of 128KBps—however, be aware that the maximum you will see in one direction (when copying files for instance) is 64KBps.

of low-speed clients (using dial-in PADs). ISDN is also limited to the larger metropolitan areas, and is not generally available overseas.

RAS Hardware

Companies that make multiport boards, X.25 smartcards and ISDN interfaces for use with Windows NT RAS include:

Vendor	*Address*	*Telephone Number*	*Products*
Comtrol Corp.	2675 Patton Rd. St. Paul, MN 55113	(800)926-6876	Multiport Controllers
DigiBoard	6400 Flying Cloud Dr. Eden Prairie MN 55344	(800)344-4273	Multiport Controllers, ISDN cards.
Star Gate Technologies, Inc.	29300 Aurora Rd. Solon, OH 44139	(800)782-7428	Single slot serial/ parallel controllers.
Link Technology Inc.	P.O. Box L-127 Langhorne PA 19047	(215)357-3354	ISDN Basic Rate Adaptor
Eicon Technologies	14755 Preston Rd., Suite 620 Dallas TX 75240	(214)239-3270	X.25 smartcards

Installing Windows NT Remote Access Services (RAS)

Now that we've looked into the various WAN options that RAS supports, lets see how it all works out in practice. To install the RAS server:

1. Start the Windows NT Control Panel and select the Network Settings icon. The Network Settings Dialog appears.
2. Click the Add Software button. The Add Network Software dialog appears, containing a list of items you can install. Select Remote Access Service from the list, and click the Continue button. You will be asked to type a path for the installation disks (or CD). As several disks are involved, the CD is far more convenient, if available.
3. The Add Port dialog appears. You will need to select a communications port to use from this list. Once the port is selected, the Configure Port dialog appears (see Figure 7.12). You'll need to select an appropriate modem (or X.25/ISDN card) from the list. The "Hayes Compatible 9600" setting works with most 9600 baud modems, but does not take advantage of V.32 compression on advanced modems—you're better off to select the precise model of modem you have. You will also have to select one of the three possible Port Usage settings—Dial out only, Receive calls only, or Dial out and receive calls. Servers should generally be set to Receive calls only and Workstations to Dial out only. You can adjust low-level settings using the Settings...

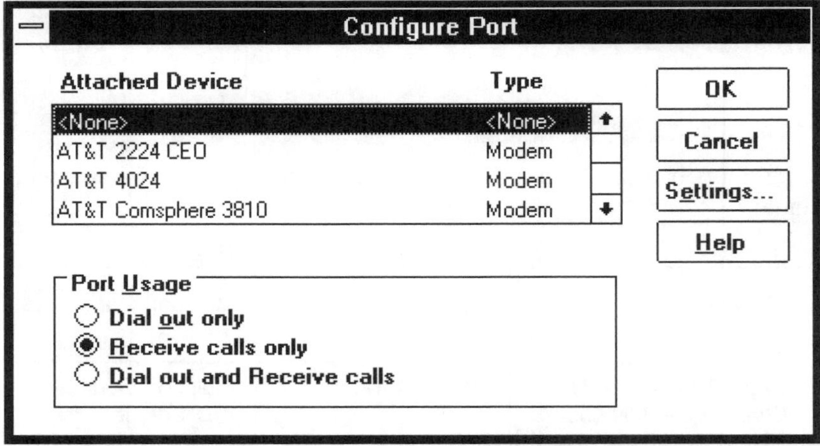

Figure 7.12 Configure Port dialog (RAS).

Windows NT Remote Access Service requires selection of a communications port for operation. This is done using this dialog.

button, but start with the default settings, as these are most likely correct (in particular, note that Enable Hardware Flow Control *must* be checked for RAS to operate properly. When the port is properly configured, click the Continue button.)

4. The Remote Access Setup dialog appears. Click the Advanced... button to bring up the Advanced Configuraton dialog (see Figure 7.13), which allows you to decide whether RAS will allow access to the entire network or only to the local computer. In the former case (the default for Windows NT Advanced Server) RAS will function as a *gateway* to the LAN for remote users, while in the latter case (the default for Windows NT), it only provides access to the resources of the local computer. When you are satisfied with the setup, click the OK button.
5. Setup creates a Remote Access Service common group in Program Manager. You will use the icons in this group to run RAS after it's installed. Setup then informs you that RAS has been installed, and suggests that you configure it using the Remote Access Administration program.

Using RAS

Once RAS is installed, it's necessary to configure it using the Remote Access Admin program (see Figure 7.14) from the Remote Access Service group. You can start RAS using the Server/Start Remote Access menu (or it can be started from Control Panel/Services).

Users/Permissions allows you to grant or revoke remote access permissions to any user of the server, and also allows you to specify whether a *call-back* option is specified for any

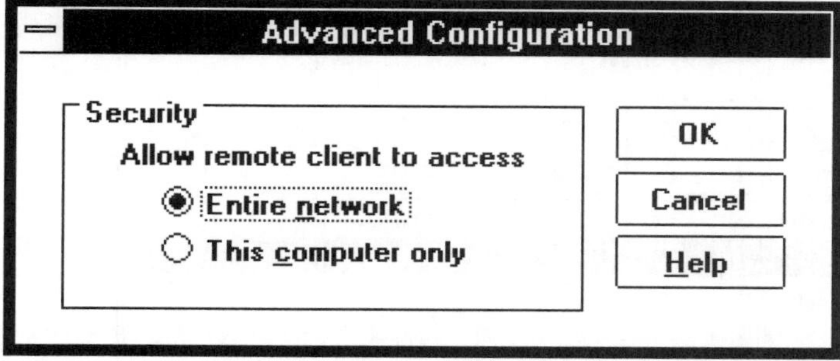

Figure 7.13 Advanced Configuration dialog.

Advanced Remote Access Services configuration settings are controlled from this dialog.

caller. Call-back is both a convenience and a security mechanism—it's convenient because the *set by caller* option lets remote users dial the RAS server, then hang up and have the RAS server call them—which puts the burden of telephone connect charges on the server rather than the client. For people who will use RAS from home or the road, this can be a great convenience.

As a security feature, the *preset to* Call-back option assures that only authorized personnel connect, by hanging up on dial-in and then calling back to a preset number. This makes it practically impossible to hack RAS (unless the hacker has physical access to a RAS client).

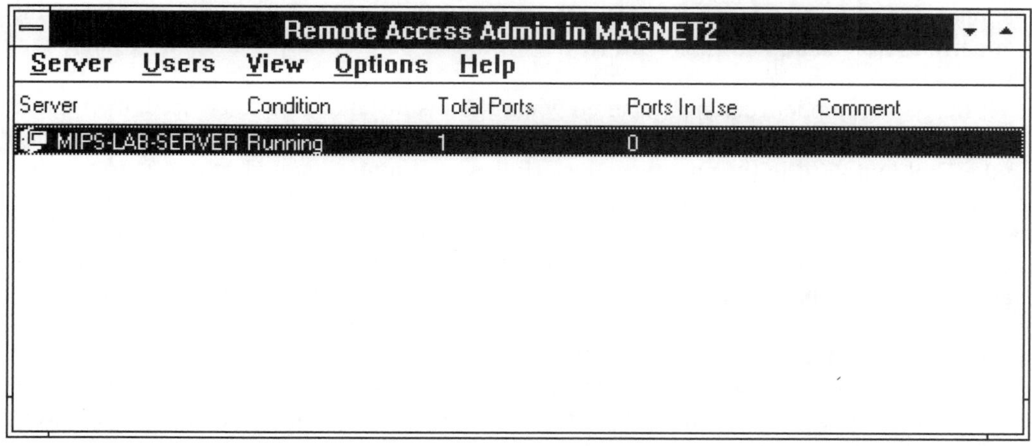

Figure 7.14 Remote Access Administration program.

Administrators control access to Remote Access Services (and settings such as dial-back), from the Windows NT Advanced Server's Remote Access Administration program.

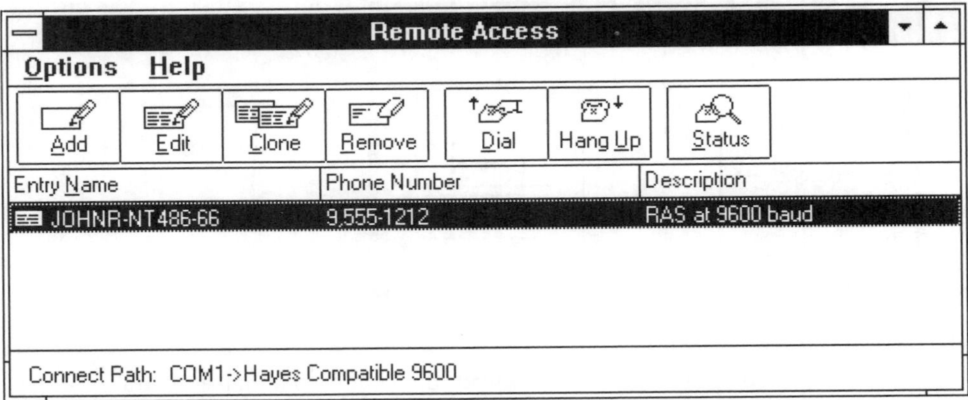

Figure 7.15 Remote Access program.

Remote users access Windows NT (or Windows NT Advanced Server) Remote Access Services through the Remote Access application.

With access permissions granted and dial-back set, you can access the system from other Windows NT, Windows, or DOS systems that support a remote-access client. To do so, install RAS on the client system, and then run the Remote Access program (called RASPHONE.EXE in earlier versions) from the Remote Access Services group (see Figure 7.15). The first time this is done, you will be prompted to add an entry, which can be done using the Add... toolbar button. This brings up an Add Phone Book Entry dialog that allows you to type in an entry name, phone number, and description, and designate whether or not RAS is to log in using the user's current user name and password (if not, you will be prompted for the user name and password when RAS makes a connection).

If the default modem settings (entered when RAS is installed) are to be used, then this is all that's required, and you can click the OK button to complete creation of the entry, and then click the Dial button to initiate a connection. However, if a nonstandard setting is to be used (modem connection on a system where ISDN is the default RAS connection type, for instance), or a different port is to be used (outgoing dial through a single modem on COM1 while incoming calls are handled by a multiport board, for instance), you'll need to click the Advanced... button. This will expand the Add Phone Book Entry dialog to show advanced feature buttons, which allow you to designate the specific type of connection you want associated with this phone book entry. Again, when the entry is complete, the OK button returns you to the main Remote Access screen, from which you can initiate a RAS connection (using the Dial button), terminate it (with the Hang Up button), Add, Edit, or Clone phone book entries, and examine the status of an entry.

When a connection is initiated (with the Dial button), the RAS client initializes the modem (or other connecting device), dials out (or performs the other steps necessary to make the connection), and waits for a response from the RAS server. The server and client then exchange username and password information (note that the password *itself* is never sent in clear-text over the wire; instead a Security Identifier derived from the password is sent, and compared at the server)—at which point, you're prompted for a username and password if the Authenticate Using Current User Name And Password checkbox was not checked. Assuming that the user name and security identifier match at both ends, the connection completes—at which point you have a complete network connection between the client and server (and a gateway to the rest of your network, if the server has been configured to permit access to the entire network).

Several things can go wrong with this process—in particular, if you haven't properly configured the RAS client or server for the modems they're using, or if the modems do not match (especially on high-speed connections), then you're likely to get a message that RAS failed to authenticate. Our experience with this situation is that you should drop both the server and client back to a known connection state (we've found the Hayes-compatible 9600 baud setting to work for most modems), and try again. If it still doesn't work, check the configuration settings for RAS at both ends, check that the user who's attempting to dial in has in fact been granted remote access permissions at the RAS server, and check for RAS-related error messages using the Windows NT Event Log (note that login errors will often show up in the *Security* log)—and refer to the RAS documentation included with Windows NT for further suggestions.

Advanced Uses of RAS

Besides providing interactive WAN connections for end-users, RAS can be invaluable to administrators. As mentioned earlier in this chapter, using Windows NT Advanced Servers at remote locations invariably requires some sort of connection between servers to exchange user account information (and other replicated data). RAS is ideal for this, provided you can live with the available data rates. RAS is also a useful adjunct to MS-Mail: Instead of having the Mail Transfer Agent (MTA) on your local postoffice dial another MTA directly (thus subsidizing your local telephone company), you can use RAS to create a WAN connection, and have the MTA use that. In fact, Microsoft's EXTERNAL.EXE MTA provides a special class of "WAN" device setting for just this purpose—and you can even configure the MTA so that it will use the WAN for routine messages while retaining the ability to use a modem connection for messages that can't wait.

The key to using RAS *economically* for administrative or mail connections is to have it connect only at preset times of the day—typically times when the telephone (or other connection) charges are low, say between midnight and 4:00 A.M. You can do this by exploiting the fact that RAS is implemented as a Windows NT *service*, which can be started and stopped using either the Service Control Manager application in the Windows NT control panel, *or* the *net start remoteaccess* command-line syntax from a command prompt or script file. Dialing from the command-line is accomplished using the *rasdial* command. Since the replicator service can also be started and stopped using net start and net stop, we have here the makings for a completely effective periodic replication script:

```
net start remoteaccess
rasdial replicant_server
net start replicator
net accounts/sync
```
[22]

The only problem with this is determining when it's safe to terminate the connection. It will be remembered that the replicator operates every five minutes, so we suggest having a separate script that reverses these steps:

```
net stop replicator
rasdial replicant_server/DISCONNECT
net stop remoteaccess
```

If the first script is named REPLISTART.CMD and the second REPLISTOP.CMD, then the commands:

```
at 12:00 am/EVERY Monday Wednesday Friday REPLISTART.CMD
at 12:15 am/EVERY Monday Wednesday Friday REPLISTOP.CMD
```

will get the job done. Similarly, you can use command-line starting (and dialing) for mail connections, using a script something like this:

```
net start remoteaccess
rasdial mail_server
net use w: \\mail_server\WGPO
m:external.exe -A -Ww
```

Again, the trick is knowing when to disconnect. Since EXTERNAL.EXE can be configured to transfer mail on one pass and then quit, it isn't necessary to have two scripts, as are needed for replication. Instead, just allow EXTERNAL.EXE to finish, and end the script with:

```
net use w: /DELETE
rasdial mail_server /DISCONNECT
net stop remoteaccess
```

As with the replication script given above, this script is most conveniently executed using a Windows NT *at* command. Since the -W option on EXTERNAL.EXE is designed for automatic transfer of low-priority mail each day at 3:00 A.M., it's probably best to start this script a bit early, and allow five to ten minutes for it to make the connection before EXTERNAL tries to send mail. Thus, if the script is named RASMAIL.CMD, you'd need to execute:

```
at 2:50 AM/Every Monday Wednesday Friday RASMAiL.CMD
```

[22]Per Chapter 3, the /sync option on net accounts (equivalent to Server Manager's Synchronize Entire Domain command) *must* be executed locally on the Domain Controller. Therefore this script must be executed on the domain controller—or there should be another *at* command that forces synchronization, e.g.:

```
at \\domain_controller 12:05 AM net accounts /sync.
```

RAS Limitations

As we've seen, RAS is an extremely flexible and powerful system for extending Windows NT's built-in networking features over wide-area links, but it has three very serious drawbacks. The first of these is that RAS is limited to routing NetBIOS traffic. This is not a serious limitation where the built-in networking is concerned, since all Windows NT built-in protocols (NetBEUI, TCP/IP and NWLink) rely on NetBIOS packets for connection information—but it means that RAS cannot be used to extend non-NetBIOS protocols, such as UNIX-style TCP/IP (e.g.: FTP and Telnet), or NetWare IPX over wide-area connections. Since these protocols do not carry NetBIOS packets, there is nothing for RAS to route.

The second limitation is the unfortunate fact that RAS is implemented as a network *service* rather than a network *driver*—which means that you can't *bind* RAS to a specific network protocol. Again, this is a consequence of the fact that RAS routes NetBIOS traffic, rather than low-level network packets. You can control which traffic is routed to a limited extent by disabling the NetBIOS interface to the protocol in question using Control Panel/Network Settings/Bindings; but this renders the protocol in question useless for all built-in Windows NT network operations, not just for RAS.

The final, and most serious, limitation is that while RAS does route NetBIOS traffic, it will not bridge it across networks—thus it isn't possible to use RAS to connect two subnets together into a single internetwork. This latter limitation renders RAS useless for most large-scale WAN operations, as these invariably require connecting subnets to one another.[23]

An example may make this point clear: Suppose we need to connect five users in a remote office to their home office. Using RAS this requires five connections—one for each user. A much more desirable solution in this situation would be to *bridge* the remote LAN into the home office LAN, which RAS will not do.

Alternatives to RAS

Fortunately, there are alternatives. First of all, a wide variety of WAN solutions for TCP/IP are available (indeed, that's why TCP/IP is so widely used in a WAN environment), so if you've followed our directions and used TCP/IP as your backbone protocol, you should be able to use one or more of these to achieve WAN connectivity.

[23]All three of these limitations could potentially be eliminated by implementing a low-level Windows NT network driver with RAS-like async communication capabilities. In particular, using such a driver with Windows NT's built-in TCP/IP router would appear to provide very nice bridging/routing capabilities. Microsoft is working on a future version of RAS with some enhanced capabilities, including non-NetBIOS routing and an ability to bridge subnets; but this is likely to be implemented as a service rather than a driver. If there's a driver developer out among our readers with an entrepreneurial turn of mind, we think that a protocol-independent asynch (ie: modem) driver implemented for NDIS would be a paying proposition—especially if it used the UNIX Point-to-Point Protocol (PPP).

Dedicated Multiprotocol Routers

The principle alternative to RAS for Windows NT wide-area networking is use of a *multiprotocol router.* This is essentially a special-purpose computer whose sole mission is to take traffic in one protocol—for instance, NetBEUI, IPX, or TCP/IP—and convert it to (or from) another protocol, such as X.25, PPP, or frame-relay. By using a pair of such routers, one can acheive a much higher degree of wide-area networking than that provided by Windows NT Remote Access Services.

Perhaps an example will help: Consider the same branch office-to-home office link that we've been using throughout this chapter. With RAS, if you need to connect five remote clients to the home office, you will need five separate connections—one per client. You can implement these as five separate modem connections (requiring a multiport serial board and multiple modems at the home office RAS server), or using X.25 (requiring the five clients to dial in to a local X.25 provider's PAD, and then requiring an X.25 card and leased line at the server), or by ISDN (requiring one ISDN connection for each client and one at the server)—or you can mix these approaches. But what you *cannot* do is link the two *subnets* (the one in the branch office and the one at the home office).

With multiprotocol routers at both ends, the situation changes—the two networks can be connected simply by linking the routers, using X.25, frame-relay, PPP, or whatever.

An optimal multiprotocol router setup for Windows NT will involve TCP/IP as the primary protocol (because, as noted earlier, this is the *only* Windows NT protocol that is fully routable), and whatever secondary protocol is best suited to your particular needs. Determining the best protocol for your situation is beyond the scope of this book; but the general rule in WANs is that you pay for speed: Low data-rate dial-up lines (up to 14,400 baud) are relatively cheap; high-speed circuits tend to be extremely expensive.

Aside from the protocols needed, selecting a router is largely a matter of features and price—you can pay from $2,000 to $25,000 for a router, depending on the features it provides. Aside from multiprotocol support, some routers provide simple network management protocol (SNMP)-compatible remote maintenance features, out-of-band (generally RS-232) console features, and varying degrees of upgradability. You would be wise to request literature from *all* the firms on the following list before selecting a router for your network:

Vendor	*Address/Phone*	*Comments*
Advanced Computer Communications	10261 Bubb Rd. Cupertino CA 95014 (408)864-0600	Routers
Cabletron Corp.	P.O. Box 5005 Rochester NH 03867 (603)332-9400	Routers, Hubs
Cisco Systems	1525 O'Brien Dr. Menlo Park, CA 94025 (415)326-1941	*De-facto standard central router for TCP/IP environments.*

Vendor	*Address/Phone*	*Comments*
Clearpoint Research Corp.	35 Parkwood Dr. Hopkinton, MA 01748 (508)435-2000	Routers
David Systems Inc.	701 East Evelyn Ave. Sunnyvale CA 94088 (408)720-8000	*Unique, Windows-based graphical management system.*
Digital Equipment Corp.	146 Main St. Maynard MA, 01754 (508)493-7161	*OSI-protocol routers for European applications.*
Hewlett Packard Co.	Roseville Networks Div. 8000 Foothills Blvd. Roseville CA 95747 (800)752-0900	Routers, NetView LAN Management system.
IBM Corp.	One Old Orchard Rd. Armonk, NY 10504 (800)772-2237	*SAA/DLC routers for mainframe connectivity*
Network Systems Corp.	2001 Gateway PL, #700 West San Jose, CA 95110 (408)452-8400	Routers
Novell Corp. Internetworking Products Division	2180 Fortune Dr. San Jose, CA 95131 (800)638-9273	*IPX/SPX routers, mainly for use in NetWare LAN environments.*
Proteon Inc.	Nine Technology Dr. Westborough MA, 01581 (508)898-2800	Routers
3Com Corp.	5400 Bayfront Plaza Santa Clara, CA 95052 (408)764-5000	Routers, network cards, and other network components
Xyplex Inc.	330 Codman Hill Rd. Boxborough, MA 01719 (508)264-9900	Routers
Welfleet Communications	15 Crosby Dr. Bedford MA 01730 (617)275-2400	Routers

Shiva Netmodem

Another alternative that may work in smaller applications is the Shiva Netmodem. This is a high-speed modem with internal hardware that enables it to function as a network bridge. Models are available for both NetWare IPX/SPX and NetBIOS networking—the former is suitable for use with Windows NT's NWLink protocol, and the latter with NetBEUI. Unfortunately, while the Netmodems will *bridge*, they do not *route*—so all network traffic is transmitted from one net to the other, regardless of whether it's intended for nonlocal recipients. This makes the Netmodem useful only for very small networks unless one can combine it with a separate router (in the IPX case—NetBIOS, of course, is not routable in this sense).

Management and Maintenance Issues

Managing and administering enterprise networks is not fundamentally different from managing LANs, although the complexity of the network tends to make the administrator's job a bit harder; troubleshooting, on the other hand, takes on its own character where enterprise networks (especially WANs) are involved.

Microsoft provides a number of advanced administration tools with Windows NT Advanced Server that can make life for the administrator easier. These include *User Manager for Domains*, *Server Manager*, *User Profile Editor*, and *Remote Access Services Admin*. There are other administration tools that are specific to third-party add-ons, such as those for SQL Server (see Chapter 11) and SNA Server (Chapter 10), but the tools included with Advanced Server—building on those included with the base Windows NT product (Disk Administrator, Backup, Event Viewer, Performance Monitor, and Registry Editor), of course—provide most of what you need to get an enterprise network up and running.

Server Manager

The most important of the Advanced Server administration tools is the Server Manager (see Figure 7.16). From this program, you can add computers to your Advanced Server domain, remove them from the domain, inspect the users, shares, replication, and alert status of any computer in the domain, synchronize user accounts accross all servers in the domain, send messages (such as the ever-popular "Server going down in 3 minutes!"), or promote a server to be the Primary Domain Controller.

All of these tasks are performed in a straightforward manner—you select a computer from the list (which may be brought up to date at any time using the View/Refresh menu item), then either select a command to execute from the Computer menu, or double-click the entry (equivalent to Computer/Properties) to bring up a Properties—it's equivalent to the Server dialog in the Control Panel, and allows you to inspect (and control) logged-in user accounts, shared resources, connections, replication, and administrative alerts in exactly the same way. Perhaps the most critical use you'll make of this is controlling administrative alerts—clicking the Alerts button brings up an Alerts dialog (see Figure 7.17) that allows you to send administrative alert information to specified computer- or user-names. This can be

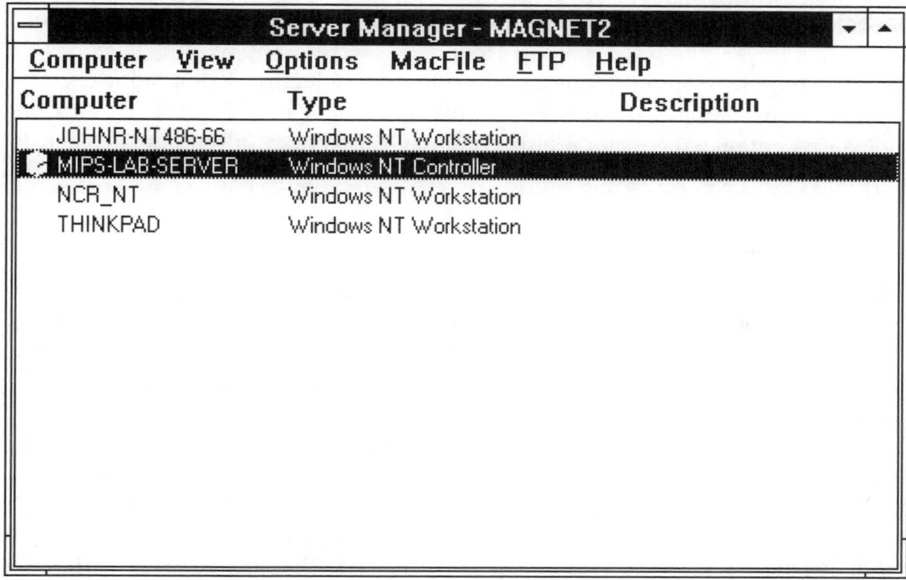

Figure 7.16 Server Manager.

Administrators can view and control all servers (and Windows NT workstations) in a Windows NT Advanced Server domain from the Server Manager.

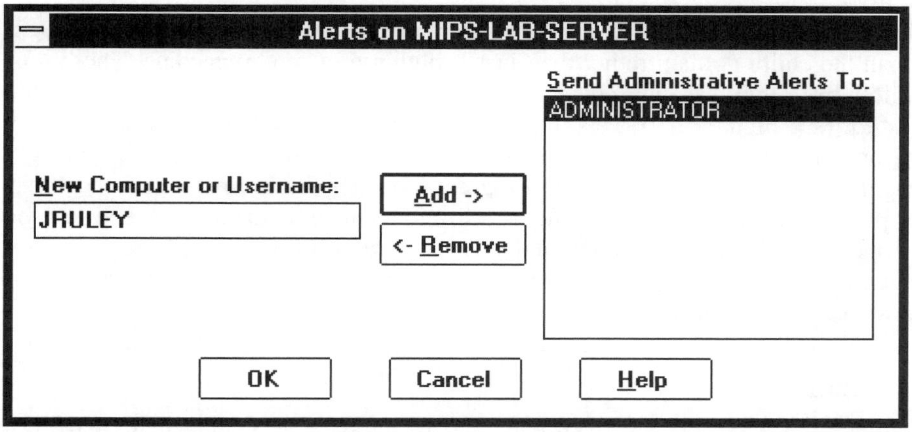

Figure 7.17 Alerts dialog (Server Manager).

The Alerts dialog, accessed from Server Manager's Computer/Properties menu, allows an administrator to determine where alert notifications are sent on the network.

particularly convenient when the server is locked up and you want alerts to show up on your workstation.

Services on the remote system(s) can be controlled by selecting Computer/Services, which brings up a Services dialog that's identical to that from the Control Panel. This allows you to start/stop/pause/continue services on any Windows NT system in the domain, and to determine the startup parameters (if any).

User Manager for Domains

As we've discussed (at some length!), the management of user accounts in Windows NT Advanced Server differs from that in the base product—especially when inter-domain trust is involved. Not surprisingly, Microsoft provides a different version of User Manager for Advanced Server administrators. User Manager for Domains looks almost identical to Windows NT's User Manager, but provides several additional features.

The first is that you can select a domain to administer, from the User/Select Domain menu item. You will need administrative access in the domain you want to administer, of course. One that's done, the list of user names in the main User Manager screen will update, showing users and groups in the selected domain. Double-clicking on a user name brings up a User Properties dialog (see Figure 7.18) that appears similar to the single-server version—except for the additional buttons on the bottom of the dialog. These buttons allow you to specify the hours during which a user may log in, the systems they're permitted to log in on, the date that the account expires (this differs from the date the account's *password* expires), and whether the account is *global* or *local.*[24] In all other respects, User Manager for Domain operates identically to the single-server version of User Manager (covered in Chapter 3).

User Profile Editor

One of Windows NT Advanced Server's nicest features is the availability of per-user login profiles that span the entire domain rather than just applying to a single machine. These profiles (which differ from the *user environment profile* set in User Manager), are set with the User Profile Editor (see Figure 7.19). This tool lets you control many features of a Windows NT user's environment, including what features are enabled (or disabled) in Program Manager and File Manager, what startup group is set in Program Manager (it need not be named "Start Up"), whether program groups are locked (the user cannot change them) or unlocked (can be changed at will), etc. Used in conjunction with the user environment profile and user rights set in User Manager, and (if necessary) a login script, this allows you a very high degree of control over the environment of your users.

Remote Administration

Although the tools just mentioned are shipped with Windows NT Advanced Server (and require one to be present on the network and configured as Primary Domain Controller), they

[24]See Chapter 3 for an explanation of *local* and *global* user accounts.

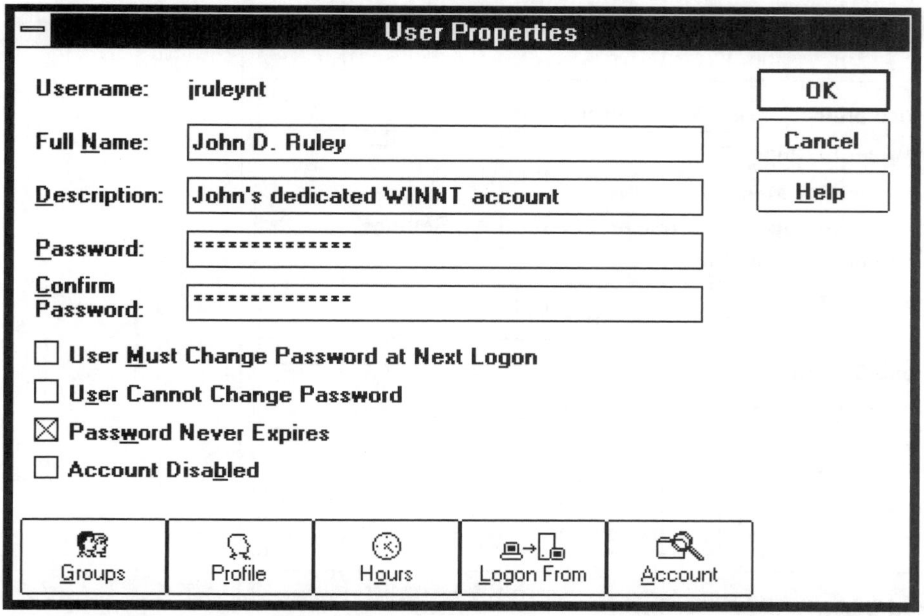

Figure 7.18 User Properties dialog.

This dialog, from Windows NT Advanced Server's User Manager for Domains, allows administrators to control most aspects of user access to Windows NT servers and workstations in the domain.

do *not* have to be run from one. Indeed, you can run them from any Windows NT workstation on the net—even remotely, using RAS.

There are two ways to do this. The obvious one is to share the domain controller's WINNT\SYSTEM32 (or WINDOWS\SYSTEM32) directory, limiting access to administrators, and then run Server Manager (SRVMGR.EXE), User Manager for Domains (USRMGR.EXE), User Profile Editor (UPEDIT.EXE), etc., remotely over the network (you could even set up a "Remote Admin" program group for this in User Profile Manager). We don't recommend this approach for two reasons: the necessary administrative share on the \SYSTEM32 directory represents an unnecessary security threat[25], and running the programs over the network isn't practical on slow WAN links (like RAS over modems). Instead, we suggest the following procedure:

1. Create an RADMIN directory on your workstation.
2. Copy SRVMGR.*, USRMGR.*, and UPEDIT.* from the domain controller's \SYSTEM32 directory to the RADMIN directory on your workstation (you can do

[25]Microsoft disagrees—the ADMIN$ hidden share on *all* NT systems shares the WINNT directory.

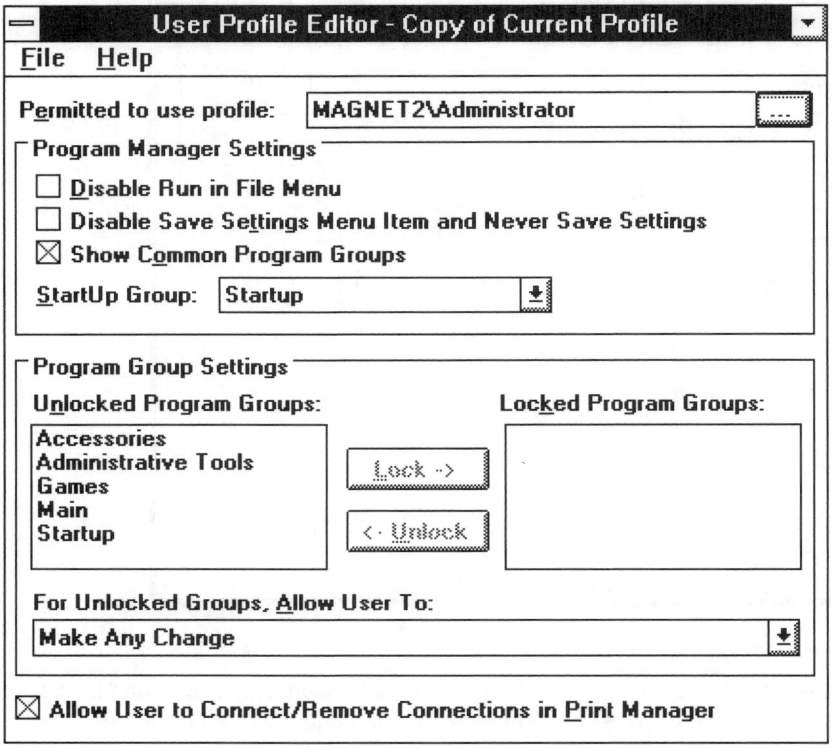

User Profile Editor - Copy of Current Profile
File Help
Permitted to use profile: MAGNET2\Administrator
Program Manager Settings
☐ Disable Run in File Menu
☐ Disable Save Settings Menu Item and Never Save Settings
☒ Show Common Program Groups
StartUp Group: Startup
Program Group Settings
Unlocked Program Groups: Locked Program Groups:
Accessories
Administrative Tools
Games
Main
Startup
Lock ->
<- Unlock
For Unlocked Groups, Allow User To:
Make Any Change
☒ Allow User to Connect/Remove Connections in Print Manager

Figure 7.19 User Profile Editor.

Windows NT Advanced Server administrators can control user access to specific Program Manager, File Manager, and Print Manager features using the User Profile Editor.

this over the network—or by “sneakernet”[26] in situations where a network copy isn’t practical).

3. Create a personal (*not* common!) “Remote Admin” program group in Program Manager on your workstation.
4. Create icons for the .EXE files you copied over from the domain controller.

With this done, you can perform all administrative tasks from your workstation, using either the “Remote Admin” group’s domainwide administration tools or those in the Workstation’s “Administrative Tools” group. Bear in mind that many of the regular administrative tools—Performance Monitor, Event Viewer, and the Registry Editor, for instance—already allow remote administration from a Select Computer menu item or dialog entry field. You may

[26] Copy the files onto floppy and carry ‘em over yourself.

also want to copy over the Advanced Server's Remote Access Administration program and any administrative programs used for network applications—SQL Administrator and SNA Administrator come to mind.

There is one more setting that will help if you administer a Windows NT domain remotely—Server Manager and User Manager for Domains both support the "Low Speed Connection" option that saves time on slow data links by not displaying the full list of servers, users, etc. This option is also available on the RAS Admin program, and on many other tools.

Running a Windows NT Server in a Locked Closet

Locked-closet servers are of interest to both domainwide and single-server administrators, of course, but the issue is such a no-brainer for domainwide administration that we decided it was best covered here.

The main problem with locking up an NT server is that it normally requires human intervention to start up—specifically, the Ctrl+Alt+Del sequence that's used to log in. Until this has been done, any command scripts or auto-started programs (from the Start Up program group) won't run.

Microsoft's recommended solution to this problem is to exploit Windows NT's *services* interface, which *does* allow for automatic startup before any user logs in. Any Windows NT service can be designated for automatic startup from the Control Panel/Services (or Server Manager/Properties) Startup... button. The resulting dialog allows you to select *Automatic* startup, which will happen immediately on system start.

The one problem with this approach is that it *only* works for Windows NT services—and as yet, there are many critical system tasks (Microsoft's own EXTERNAL.EXE mail transfer agent, for instance) that are not yet implemented as services. To get those programs started automatically on system start, it's necessary to defeat Windows NT's logon security system. To do so:[27]

1. Start the registry editor, select HKEY_LOCAL_MACHINE\Software.
2. Select Microsoft\Windows NT\CurrentVersion\Winlogon, and enter values for DefaultDomainName, DefaultUserName, and DefaultPassword.
3. Create an Auto Admin Logon value of 1 in the same ...\WinLogon subkey.

Of course, entering the username and password into the registry means that anyone with administrative access can see them (using the registry editor), but administrators have the ability to *change* the password anyway. And the fact that the system comes up automatically logged-in doesn't seem like much of a security risk if it's already locked up. We *do* recommend that you use a specially created user account—*not* the Administrator account—for such an automatic login account. This minimizes the security risk to the system, since a person who jimmies the lock to the server room will not thereby gain automatic administrative access to the server. If Administrative access is required, it can be obtained by using Registry Editor on

[27]Our thanks to Microsoft's Dave Hart for pointing out this procedure—it's documented in Microsoft Knowledge Base article Q97597.

another system to eliminate the DefaultUserName and DefaultPassword entries set in the procedure above; then log off from the server's console and log back in as the administrator, and reset the defaults when you're done (you could even write a script for this using the REGINI.EXE program provided in the \SUPTOOLS directory of the Windows NT CD).[28]

However, the most important things to do in support of a locked-up Windows NT server don't require meddling with the registry—just use Control Panel/Services (or Server Manager/Properties) to verify that the *Workstation* and *Server* services are set for automatic startup. That way, even if the system doesn't come up properly, you can control it from an administrative workstation. You may want to set the *Remote Access Server* service for automatic startup too, so that you can get into the server using dial-in. And of course, locked-up servers (like any NT servers) should have a UPS installed, and the UPS service properly configured, per Chapter 3.

Troubleshooting Enterprise Networks

As we mentioned earlier, while administration of an enterprise network is much like administering a very large LAN, troubleshooting problems in an enterprise environment is a different matter altogether. The reason for this is that enterprise networks are so much more complex than LANs—if a user can't see a server in a LAN environment, there are really only four possible causes: the server's gone down, the wiring's bad, the network card's bad (more likely, the cable *to* the network card is unplugged—always check this first), or (*most* frequently) the software in the user's workstation is having a problem. There really isn't anything else to break!

Add a couple of routers and a WAN link to the connection, however, and you greatly multiply the possible causes of trouble. The WAN link might be down, or just having line noise problems. One of the routers may have failed. A power glitch may restart a router with a bad routing table—and the list goes on and on. . .

As it happens, there's a fairly simple approach to troubleshooting these problems that we feel confident in recommending: It's used twice a year by the "network warriors" of the INTEROP shows, who accomplish the amazing feat of creating a large (over a dozen routers, an FDDI backbone, several hundred nodes) TCP/IP network, called ShowNet, *in just a few days*. That approach is to use the standard TCP/IP PING.EXE utilty—and little else.[29]

The reason the INTEROP folks do this is that the huge network they put in really represents something of a worst-case multivendor net—each node on the network terminates in a booth on the show floor, where vendors plug in whatever network hardware and software they're trying to sell. By using PING to get underneath whatever software the vendors are using, the ShowNet team isolate themselves from the details of a particular vendor's software.

---

[28]You may also find the Resource Kit REMOTE.EXE utility helpful here. See "Late-Breaking News" in the Preface.

[29]It's particularly instructive that they do this even though *most* nodes on the INTEROP ShowNet support SMTP, NetView, or any of a dozen proprietary network management schemes.

This lets them concentrate on making sure that the cabling is good and the routers are properly configured. They start looking at the software *only* after checking the hardware with PING.

We think this makes good sense for NT networks, especially since (as we discussed at some length at the start of this chapter) *all* routed NT networks *must* use TCP/IP as the backbone protocol. We do think it makes sense to leverage NT's built-in tools as well (in particular, using Performance Monitor to check on network throughput, per Chapter 5), and it's *always* a good idea to look at the event log when a problem occurs; but if the cause of the problem isn't immediately apparent, we suggest that a good place to start is to use PING from the workstation or server to the router. If PING gets through, then you know the hardware's good. If not, then you have a hardware (or router configuration) problem that's got to be solved first, before looking at any higher-level issues.

We also recommend that you look carefully at *out-of-band signaling* in enterprise networks—especially big ones. Out-of-band signaling means that you don't lock yourself into sending all administrative data and commands over the network itself—because otherwise, if there's a hardware problem, it will stop the administrative data just as it stops the network traffic. There are basically three ways to get an out-of-band capability in a Windows NT-based enterprise network:

1. Use RAS on your servers—set up a separate dial-in *only* modem and line on each server (or one server in each closet), and grant access rights *only* to administrative users. This gives you a reliable "back door" to get into that server remotely, and doesn't compete with user traffic on other RAS links you may have.
2. Configure a non-NT PC on the network to run a DOS- (or Windows-) based remote control program, such as PC Anywhere for Windows—again, with a dedicated modem line configured only for dial-in, and with access restricted to administrators. This gives you access to the local network, and can be especially useful in resetting a balky router (when you're on the wrong side of the router).
3. If you buy a multiprotocol router, get one with an RS-232 port, and (again) put a dedicated modem on that port for administrative access. This gives you direct control of the router from a remote location (if you're using Windows NT's built-in static router feature, setting up RAS on the routing machine gives you the same capability).

In any case, the point is: *give yourself a back door!* It doesn't matter whether your operation is standardized on NetView or SNMP or what-have-you; make sure there is a network-independent way to get in. This will save you from the need to go in yourself on an emergency call.

One more thing to consider: On a really large enterprise system, there may be unattended servers (and routers) in locations that aren't easily accessible. Clearly these are candidates for one of the back-door dial-in approaches we've just listed; but there's also a need for these systems to get the word out that they're in trouble.

One way to handle this is to reverse the RAS-based back-door we've just discussed: make sure that your own administrative workstation runs RAS with a modem set up for dial-in, and configure the system you're worried about with RAS and a modem set to dial-out. You can then set up alerts (in Performance Monitor) to execute a script like this one:

```
rasdial trouble_line
net send Administrator Help! Router in trouble!
rasdial trouble_line/DISCONNECT
```

This way, the router calls *you*, and you can then call it back (assuming it has a dial-in line) to find out the specifics and fix the problem.

If you're in charge of a truly mission-critical system that has to operate 24 hours a day, the ultimate way to handle this is, of course, the inevitable beeper. You may wish to investigate Fourth Wave Technology's[30] WinBEEP application, which sends a configurable beeper message on command.

Summary and Conclusion

We've examined the challenge represented by enterprise networks, and seen how the features of Windows NT—and especially Windows NT Advanced Server—can be used to ease the implementation of enterprise networks. We've explored what makes an enterprise network different from a LAN, and determined that the governing factor is *complexity*. We've noted that electronic mail is, to a large extent, the vendor-independent glue that holds an enterprise network together, and we've examined Windows NT's Microsoft Mail system in some detail—including observing its limitations—and how to get around them.

Beyond sheer complexity, enterprise networks are characterized by geographic dispersion—they extend beyond one building or office complex (often beyond even one city, state, or country), requiring WAN connectivity. We've examined RAS, Windows NT's built in WAN, and found that while it's certainly useful, it cannot substitute for a dedicated multiprotocol router.

We've also examined some issues of special interest to enterprise administrators, including Windows NT Advanced Server's built-in support for Macintosh computers; and issues involved in managing and maintaining enterprise networks, including remote administration and complex network maintenance.

By now, you should have a good feel for the features built into Windows NT. The next three chapters will extend these concepts beyond Windows NT's built-in networking, as we examine what's involved in connecting Windows NT to other Microsoft SMB networks (Chapter 8), Novell NetWare (Chapter 9), and other networks—including IBM's LAN Server and SNA systems and Banyan VINES (Chapter 10).

For More Information

Microsoft Staff (1993), *Windows NT Advanced Server—Services for Macintosh.* Redmond, WA: Microsoft Corp. The best (and only) reference on SFM.

Microsoft Staff (1993), *Windows NT Advanced Server—Remote Access Service.* Redmond, WA: Microsoft Corp. All the details of RAS, including specifics of use with modems, multiport cards, X.25 smartcards, and ISDN.

[30] 560 Kirts Blvd., Suite 105, Troy, MI 48084; (313) 362-2288.

Microsoft Staff (1993), *Windows NT Advanced Server—Concepts and Planning Guide.* Redmond, WA: Microsoft Corp. Detailed coverage of domain management, inter-domain trust, printer services, etc.

Microsoft Staff (1993), *Win32 Products and Services Catalog for Windows NT* (Spring/Summer 1993 edition). Redmond, WA: Microsoft Corp. Lists software, hardware, peripherals, and services of interest to Windows NT users and administrators.

Renaud, Paul (1993), *Introduction to Client/Server Systems.* New York: Wiley. ISBN: 0-471-57774-X. Among other things (it's no accident we've cited him elsewhere in this book), Renaud has good coverage of end-to-end system management that's as applicable to Windows NT as it is to UNIX systems.

Microsoft Connections

When you finish this chapter, you should understand how Windows NT's networking features arose from the old MS-Net/LAN Manager products, and how to achieve interoperation between NT and other products in the LAN Manager and Windows for Workgroups product family. You should feel comfortable connecting NT clients and servers into LAN Manager and Windows for Workgroups networks, understand what's involved in operating a mixture of LAN Manager and Windows NT servers, and know the difference between workgroups and domains.

Microsoft Networks

Although Windows NT and its companion Advanced Server version are the most ambitious network products that Microsoft has ever built, they are not the company's only network products. Microsoft also offers its Windows for Workgroups product as a peer-to-peer network for sites with modest networking needs. And despite Microsoft's coolness to OS/2, their OS/2 LAN Manager was Microsoft's high-end networking solution until NT arrived.

All Microsoft network products use the Server Message Block (SMB) protocol (see Appendix 2), which gives them a baseline level of interoperability. In practical terms, that means you can usually share a printer or a directory subtree between any two Microsoft-based networks. However, the differences between the products often mean that advanced features like security and system administration are not fully interoperable.

Microsoft's Early Networks

Microsoft is far from a newcomer to networking. It has been in the business since the early 1980s, when it offered its MS-Net product. Instead of selling MS-Net directly to end-users,

Microsoft licensed MS-Net to vendors, who then modified it—sometimes in incompatible ways—and resold it under many names. For example, IBM sold MS-Net as the IBM PC LAN Program, while 3Com's version was called 3Plus.

LAN Manager

When Microsoft and IBM announced OS/2 in 1987, they also announced an OS/2-based network solution compatible with MS-Net. Microsoft called the product OS/2 LAN Manager. As with MS-Net, Microsoft licensed OS/2 LAN Manager to vendors like IBM (LAN Server), 3Com (3+Open), and DEC (Pathworks), who made their own enhancements and modifications.

In 1990, Microsoft made an important change in the way it sold networking products. It began to offer OS/2 LAN Manager as a retail product under the Microsoft name, but continued the licensing agreements with vendors like IBM, 3Com, and DEC. Since then, Microsoft has moved its networking emphasis from licensing to retail sales, capitalizing on the familiar Microsoft name.

Windows for Workgroups

Today, Microsoft offers Windows for Workgroups (WfWG) as its low-end peer-to-peer network. WfWG is essentially Windows 3.1 with networking built in. In addition to having file sharing features built into File Manager, Print Manager, and common dialogs, WfWG includes versions of Microsoft Mail and Schedule+ scheduling software in the box.

Using Windows NT with LAN Manager

As you would expect, since Microsoft wrote both LAN Manager and Windows NT, and the networking features in Windows NT are derived from those in LAN Manager (one can think of Windows NT Advanced Server as LAN Manager 3.0), this all works together rather better than some of the third-party networking issues that are discussed in Chapters 6, 9, and 10. Windows NT workstations can utilize the resources of LAN Manager servers, pretty much seamlessly. LAN Manager workstations can make use of Windows NT servers, pretty much seamlessly. There are a few rough edges—particularly when one tries to mix LAN Manager and NT servers in the same domain—but there are workarounds for this. On the whole it's a very usable system.

It's All the Same. . .

The networking features in Windows NT are advanced 32-bit versions of the networking features that Microsoft has built into the LAN Manager 2.x series. Windows NT and LAN Manager share many features in common, including: being based on SMB networking, use of NetBEUI as the principal protocol (with TCP/IP as the enterprise protocol), and use of NDIS device drivers. Many of the APIs and the data structures and even the syntax of the commands are the same. The systems are generally quite compatible and the migration process moving from LAN Manager to Windows NT is not a difficult one.

Except When It's Not

The LAN Manager/NT situation is something of a good news/bad news story. The bad news is, first of all, that the structure and operation of the administrative domains differ and, as we will see, this can become a real problem when you start to mix LAN Manager (OS/2) and NT servers. There's also a difference in the way that network browsing and announcement is handled. This is easy to get around in that Microsoft has made it possible to reset Windows NT to use the LAN Manager-style browser service, but unfortunately, there are very good reasons why they changed it—so this is not a permanent solution either. There is also a difference in the way the passwords are handled in the two systems (a problem that LAN Manager and NT interoperation shares with Windows for Workgroups and NT interoperation). Finally, the directory replication mechanism differs and in large networks this can be a major issue. But having said all that, take heart—you can get there from here. Microsoft was not foolish enough to build a totally incompatible networking architecture into its new operating system.

With that as an introduction, let's begin at the beginning—in all probability, if you have an established LAN Manager system your first experience with NT will be adding workstations.

Windows NT Workstations with LAN Manager Servers

Windows NT workstations work well with LAN Manager servers. The one major issue of concern is the browsing service. That's the service that is activated when you go into the file manager and select Connect Net Drive or type *net view* from the command line.

Network Browsing in Windows NT

This is as good a place as any to discuss the browse service. To understand the Windows NT situation, we should begin by understanding some basic facts about server message block (SMB) networking and the way LAN Manager works. Network browsing in the SMB system depends on a *broadcast* mechanism that uses APIs called *mailslots.* In the broadcast situation, whenever a LAN Manager server or workstation is joined to the network it begins by sending a class-2 mailslot message to all other machines on the local network segment looking for a server. Any servers will respond with a message directed back to the workstation announcing who they are. The workstation looks for the Primary Domain Controller (PDC), which is the center of administrative control in a LAN Manager network.

There is a major problem with this approach in that *broadcast announcements cannot be routed beyond the local subnet* (otherwise, a complicated internetwork with many routers would spend most of its time doing nothing but broadcast announcements). Therefore, routers do not pass the broadcast announcements—creating a "double hop" problem. If you connect more than one LAN together, the LAN Manager-style browsing breaks down. Workstations in one subnet cannot see servers outside their subnet.

A variety of mechanisms have been attempted to get around this problem—and the cold fact of the matter is that Microsoft is still working on it. The ultimate solution appears to be use of TCP/IP as a standard internetworking protocol for multiple-hop networks (and you'll find detailed coverage of this in Appendix 2 and Chapter 6). Aside from the double-hop problem, the use of broadcasts as a method of network browsing creates two difficulties. The first is that whenever a workstation logs into the network it has to broadcast its presence on the subnet. It will then sit for up to a minute waiting for a response from the domain controller. This can be extremely annoying. On a heavily loaded network it may be necessary for the workstation to make several broadcast announcements before the server will respond—a very frustrating situation for end-users. Worse, on large LANs with many stations *race conditions* can exist where so many stations are attempting to log on at once that it's impossible for the server to keep up with them. This can actually have a significant impact on the overall network traffic.

Beginning with Windows for Workgroups and with the first Beta versions of Windows NT, Microsoft began to eliminate the use of broadcast announcements during login. Instead, Windows NT and Windows for Workgroups employ the concept of a *browsemaster*. In the browsemaster scenario one station within the subnet (the primary domain controller in a Windows NT Advanced Server domain, or an elected Windows NT or Windows for Workgroups machine in a Windows for Workgroups/Windows NT Workgroup) maintains a list of all the other servers and workstations in the workgroup or domain. During login, instead of sending a broadcast message to all systems on the subnet, a workstation needs only to communicate its presence to the browsemaster, which in turn communicates the location of other systems—including the domain controller, to whom the system sends a login message. No broadcasts are required.

Unfortunately, difficulties can still occur in this kind of networking. The whole thing comes unglued if the machine that has been selected as browsemaster is not turned on. In this condition, the machines that are turned on will attempt to contact the browsemaster, but "time out" after a preset interval and then conduct a *browsemaster election* (which involves the same broadcasts we were trying to get away from in the first place) in which they identify each other; the machine with the best performance characteristics will generally elect to be the new browsemaster.

To avoid having constant browsemaster elections, it is possible to *force* a machine to be a browsemaster. On Windows NT machines this can be accomplished using the registry editor (REGEDT32.EXE) by opening HKEY_LOCAL_MACHINE\SYSTEM\CurrentControlSet\Services\Browser\Parameters, and creating an IsDomainMaster value, defining it as type REG_SZ, and specifying the text TRUE for the value of the string. This will cause a machine to maintain the browse list irrespective of whether it is elected as a browsemaster. This is essential in a situation where a remote workgroup does not have a domain controller associated with it.

While Windows NT and Windows for Workgroups have migrated to a new manner of maintaining browse information, the existing installed base of LAN Manager 2.x systems have not. So whenever Windows NT is used in conjunction with LAN Manager computers, it is necessary to make a few adaptations. The most important of these is a parameter called Lmannounce (LAN Manager announce), which essentially forces a Windows NT (or Windows for

Workgroups) machine to engage in the same behavior that a LAN Manager machine would. This doesn't mean that you will automatically wind up waiting one minute every time you log in on a Windows NT workstation. The Windows NT machine continues to employ the browse-master principle. It just adds the periodic broadcast messages the LAN Manager machines will need in order to see the Windows NT system.

To set LAN Manager-style broadcast announcements under Windows NT, run Network Settings in the Windows NT Control Panel, select Server, press the Configure... button, and check the "Make Browser Broadcasts to LAN Manager 2.x clients" check-box at the bottom of the Server dialog. If you don't have local access to the Control Panel, then use Registry/Select Computer to open the registry on the system you want to adjust, run the Registry Editor (REGEDT32.EXE), select HKEY_LOCAL_MACHINE\SYSTEM\CurrentControlSet\Services\LanmanServer\Parameters, and create an Lmannounce keyword, defined as type REG_DWORD with a value of 0x1. Just as with the much simpler Control Panel setting, this will cause you to broadcast.

LAN Manager Domains Are Windows NT Workgroups

Here we get into a really unfortunate piece of semantics. The concept of an administrative *domain* is a simple one. This is a logical grouping of servers and workstations that are treated as a single administrative unit. In the LAN Manager environment all domain members share a centralized security account database that is controlled by the primary domain controller (PDC).

Unfortunately, in Windows NT we have a completely different type of domain controller and an incompatible domain system. As we'll see a little bit later on, in a Windows NT Advanced Server domain, LAN Manager systems are essentially second-class citizens and the PDC *must* be a Windows NT Advanced Server. Standard Windows NT workstations can participate in Windows NT Advanced Server domains only as *domain members*.

Does this mean that a standard Windows NT system cannot participate in a LAN Manager domain? No. Just as in Windows for Workgroups, the solution is to operate the Windows NT machine with a *workgroup* name but to set it to the same name that is used for the LAN Manager *domain*. At this point, everybody's happy and they can all talk. The Windows NT machine believes that it is part of a Windows NT workgroup. The LAN Manager machine sees the Windows NT machine as a workstation, not a server, in the domain. Everything works fine until the Windows NT machine tries to behave as a server by sharing files and printers.

Windows NT Systems as Servers in LAN Manager Domains

Since Windows NT machines cannot participate as domain members, they cannot share security account information with the PDC and its cohorts. Therefore, a Windows NT machine takes the role of a standalone server or *peer* in a LAN Manager environment. That is, it must maintain its own user account database. This is very similar in principle to the existence of Windows for Workgroups machines within the domain. However, it incurs a greater responsibility (and more difficulty) on the part of the Windows NT system operator in that you have to have a true account database. There must be an account name and password for every individual who is going to attempt to use the shared directories and printers on the Windows NT machine. Therefore, standalone Windows NT machines present a significant administrative problem as part of LAN Manager domains—so if you want to employ Windows NT servers, you should upgrade at least one LAN Manager server to a Windows NT Advanced Server (and as we'll see by implication, that means you will have two).

However, for light duty purposes and for things like printer sharing, you certainly can operate with the base Windows NT machine as a standalone server in a LAN Manager domain. As mentioned earlier, you must set the Lmannounce parameter to 1 using one of the two methods defined in the section above to avoid browsing problems. If you do not do this, LAN Manager users on OS/2 or DOS machines within the domain will find it impossible to locate the Windows NT server or its shared resources.[1] Again, you must think of any such standalone NT system administratively. Windows NT machines sitting within LAN Manager domains are best thought of as *peers* (version 2.0 of LAN Manager supported a special category of OS/2 machines as peers, standalone machines capable of resource sharing). This is very much the same situation that a Windows NT machine takes. It will work—albeit with some difficulty.

There are generally two approaches. One is to simulate a Windows for Workgroups environment. Windows NT does not support the Windows for Workgroups style of resource sharing, in which any user can access a shared resource assuming he or she has the necessary password; but Windows NT does support a *guest account,* which is very similar to that used by LAN Manager systems. If you set the guest account to have a null password and give the guest account privileges for a shared printer, for example, then everyone will be able to access the shared printer, irrespective of whether they have a user account on the print server (if the server does not recognize the user name at login it will log you in as a guest). This approach is fine for printers, but it's completely insecure, and therefore may not be a good idea for shared directories.

The alternative is to maintain a full user name and password list on the Windows NT machine. This represents a pretty substantial job to expect of an end-user. It is theoretically feasible to construct some kind of a batch file system that would automatically export account information from the LAN Manager server to a Windows NT system (possibly using some of the same techniques that were discussed at the end of Chapter 3, where we introduced a batch file for automatically converting NetWare accounts to Windows NT accounts). However, Microsoft does not provide any such capability in the Windows NT box—and in any case it represents a significant maintenance problem. Therefore, we do not recommend this approach.

It is possible to mix the two approaches—enable the guest account on Windows NT servers for nonsecure access, and augment this by maintaining user accounts *only* for users who require access to secure resources: but again, this quickly can become a major administrative burden, since you must maintain these user accounts separately on each NT server. If you must enforce user-level security from within Windows NT servers that are part of a LAN Manager domain, it's time to upgrade the domain to a Windows NT Advanced Server domain.

---

[1] Although resources *can* be accessed by typing in the full UNC name.

Windows NT Advanced Server and LAN Manager

Microsoft has a special version of the Windows NT Advanced Server (Windows NT Advanced Server Upgrade for LAN Manager) that not only includes additional migration tools for converting the user accounts, access controls, and even directories to work with NT, but also is priced considerably lower than the regular Windows NT Advanced Server package ($595 vs. $1,495 as this is written).

Now we begin to see the method in Microsoft's madness—it's all very straightforward if instead of thinking *NT Advanced Server* you think *LAN Manager 3.0.* As LAN Manager has migrated from version to version, it has acquired new features while retaining a certain degree of backward compatibility. Administrators have consistently been in the position of needing to upgrade the primary domain controller to the latest version. The current situation is no exception—even though the name of the product has changed.

Windows NT Advanced Server functionally is the latest version of LAN Manager—and there is a definite need in a mixed environment to upgrade the primary domain controller to a Windows NT Advanced Server system. Fortunately, you don't need to upgrade *all* the servers in the system. It is perfectly possible to apply an Advanced Server as a domain controller and have it work with OS/2 LAN Manager 2.0 machines as backup controllers.

Note, however, that a significant issue arises if only *one* Windows NT Advanced Server functions as primary domain controller in a LAN Manager domain. What happens when the domain controller fails? Although the LAN Manager machines can participate as backup controllers and can *replicate* the user account database, they cannot export it to another Windows NT system. For this reason we strongly recommend that you upgrade *two* of your OS/2-based LAN Manager 2.x servers to Windows NT Advanced Servers. The second machine should be regarded as the fall-back controller in case something goes wrong with the primary. The other LAN Manager servers can continue to participate in the domain as well (although only a Windows NT Advanced Server can authenticate login requests from Windows NT Workstations participating in the domain).

Pass-Through Permissions and Interdomain Trust

The issue of interdomain trust and multidomain administration is discussed in more detail in Chapter 7. Suffice it to say that Windows NT Advanced Server brings a new and very powerful concept to enterprise system administration—a domain can be set to "trust" the users of another domain—providing a mechanism for account management that spans many domains and (potentially) many subnets. That's the good news. The bad news is that LAN Manager does not support this capability—so when you mix LAN Manager and Windows NT servers you immediately create a problem. Of course, existing LAN Manager systems do not employ interdomain trust (since they don't support it), so converting from a LAN Manager server to a Windows NT Advanced Server as primary domain controller does not immediately create this problem.

However, when interdomain trust services are instituted from a Windows NT Advanced Server, or if an attempt is made to tie a LAN Manager domain to a Windows NT Advanced Server domain, then you'll have problems. As a workaround, since the LAN Manager machines cannot support interdomain trust, you can create *local* user accounts for the inter-domain-trusted users. Essentially this amounts to resorting to the LAN Manager style of administration (which was to maintain duplicate accounts on each primary domain controller). This is clumsy but it's better than not working at all.

As described earlier, it is also necessary to employ Lmannounce=1 on the Windows NT machines that will be talking to the LAN Manager machines. Finally, with respect to *directory replication* (duplication of critical data on more than one server to maintain an ultimate degree of fault tolerance[2]), as described earlier, LAN Manager machines can *import* replicant data but they cannot *export* it to the Windows NT machines—so it's not really practical to use LAN Manager Servers as a backup to Windows NT Advanced Servers. As a result, again, we recommend that if the primary domain controller is converted to an NT Advanced Server another machine also be converted to an Advanced Server (in effect, convert them in pairs). That way it is possible to step immediately from the Advanced Server primary to an Advanced Server fall-back and not miss a beat.

In the event that all Windows NT Advanced Server primary domain controllers fail, you *can* have the replication data on a LAN Manager server and can manually go through the necessary steps to restart the system using LAN Manager user accounts. The major issue here, of course, is that the LAN Manager user account database and the Windows NT account database are incompatible. As we will discuss a little further on, migration tools exist that will automatically convert from the OS/2 LAN Manager account database to the Windows NT Advanced Server account database. The tools do not exist, however, going in the other direction. And so, the fact that the replication data exists on an OS/2 machine does not mean that it's going to be easy (although in principle it is always possible) to reestablish the system with an OS/2 domain controller. In effect, converting from an OS/2 LAN Manager domain to a Windows NT Advanced Server domain is a one-way process.

These incompatibilities relate to another issue. Obviously, in implementing pilot programs many sites will wish to minimize the initial investment in the new technology. In these situations, it certainly makes sense to convert one LAN Manager machine to an Advanced Server, convert one more as a fall-back, and see how things work out. However, once it has been decided that Windows NT is an environment that everyone is comfortable with, the incompatibilities with the OS/2 machines will render it increasingly cumbersome to deal with them in the environment. It's also probably unlikely that Microsoft will see fit to significantly enhance the OS/2-based server products over time.[3] Administrators with large-scale systems are advised to contact Microsoft and ask about quantity pricing.

LAN Manager Workstations and Windows NT Servers

Here the situation is generally much cleaner than it is for servers. In general, LAN Manager workstations see Windows NT servers, including both base product NT machines that are sharing resources and Windows NT Advanced Server machines, just as if they were LAN

[2]See Chapter 7 for replication details.

[3]As this was written, we were told that all major OS/2-related development work had stopped at Microsoft.

Manager servers. There's little difference in the way they're handled. It is necessary to employ the Lmannounce parameter as discussed earlier so that the DOS, Windows, and OS/2 workstations will be able to see the NT systems.

Compatibility Issues

While operation of LAN Manager workstations and NT servers is generally a clean process, there are a few things to watch out for. The first of these is passwords. Windows NT systems employ a password validation mechanism that is case sensitive. That is, "PASSWORD" and "password" are not the same in a Windows NT environment and if the uppercase "PASSWORD" has been employed for a resource or a user account name, typing in the lowercase one will generate an error. To support backward compatibility with LAN Manager and Windows for Workgroups systems (which are not case sensitive), Windows NT detects, during login, the fact that it is talking to a foreign, non-Windows NT system and uses a case-insensitive validation technique.

This can lead to one unfortunate situation, if a user employs both Windows NT and LAN Manager systems to access a Windows NT server. If the user changes his password from a non-Windows NT machine NT will begin employing the case-insensitive logic and will continue to do so *even when the user logs in from a Windows NT machine*. The solution to this is to suggest that users always change their password from Windows NT.

Another item to watch out for is login scripts from Windows and Windows for Workgroups machines. When a Windows or Windows for Workgroups user logs into a Windows NT (or, for that matter, LAN Manager) system in which the administrator has defined a logon script, the Windows 3.x machine initiates a virtual DOS session in which to execute the script. However, the virtual DOS system remains "live" for only approximately thirty seconds—and this is not a configurable parameter. Therefore, if a script takes more than thirty seconds to execute, it will fail. The user will see an error message that the script has violated system integrity and will come to the system administrator ("bearing gifts," one might say).

The solution for this is to keep your scripts short—or disable script operation entirely when you have Windows users logging in. This is probably a particular issue for remote users logging in over Microsoft's remote access services (RAS) or through a remote TCP/IP gateway traveling over async modem lines—all operations are going to be slow over such a connection. The script support feature in the Windows control panel can be disabled. To do so run Control Panel, choose the Network icon, choose the Networks button, select Microsoft LAN Manager in the Other Networks In Use box, choose Settings... and clear the "Logon to LAN Manager Domain" check-box (Figure 5.2). This is not an ideal solution but it will get the job done.

Finally, watch out for DOS and Windows workstations that hang during login because multiple processes are attempting to address the network adapter card while the card is handling an MS-DOS command. Microsoft supplies a TSR program called COMNDIS.COM that solves this problem. It's on the LAN Manager 2.2 installation disks in the LANMAN.DOS/NETPROG directory. If COMNDIS.COM is used, it should be the last thing loaded in AUTOEXEC.BAT and it must start before any LAN Manager commands (except netbind).

COMNDIS.COM is not necessary with Windows for Workgroups, which uses a protected-mode protocol stack and does not have the problem (unless it's used with real mode drivers, in which case COMNDIS might be desirable). In any case, try this solution only on those workstations with a demonstrated propensity to hang when running with Windows NT (or LAN Manager) servers.

How LAN Manager Clients Access Windows NT Servers

In general, a LAN Manager client will see a Windows NT server as if it were a LAN Manager server—and the same operations that are normally used on the client (File Manager from Windows, File Manager or the *net* command-line interface from OS/2, the NET.EXE program from DOS) will be used to access the Windows NT server. All of these procedures work very much the same for Windows NT as LAN Manager—and in general you should see the LAN Manager documentation for details.

We present here a very limited subset of the commands that are portable between (so far as we know) *all* versions of LAN Manager, Windows for Workgroups, and Windows NT. It's useful for a system administrator to be able to walk up to any station and be able to carry out a minimal set of steps with a known response. However, there are better solutions for each individual environment and we encourage you to consult the documentation for the system in question. Our portable command-line subset is as follows:

1. To use a shared resource from a LAN Manager, Windows NT, or Windows for Workgroups server:

   net use *device \\server name\share name*

   Net use will permit you to redirect a network resource on a particular server and see it as a local device. Network resources include both shared directories and (LAN Manager only) printers. The syntax of this command is generally similar to the equivalent Windows NT command that is defined in Chapter 3. It works almost identically on Windows NT, Windows for Workgroups, OS/2 LAN Manager, and DOS LAN Manager systems. As an example:

   ```
   net use m: \\mips-lab-server\WGPO
   ```

   will redirect the WGPO shared directory on \\mips-lab-server to local drive m:. Just typing net use by itself, with no arguments, will list any shared resources currently in use at the local workstation.

2. To browse shared resources (directories and printers) on LAN Manager, Windows NT, and Windows for Workgroups servers:

   net view

   or

   net view *\\server name*

Without arguments, net view displays a list of servers on the default domain or workgroup. Net view \\server name displays a list of the shares on the server. Thus the process of command line browsing on any form of LAN Manager, Windows for Workgroups, or Windows NT is generally to type net view to see the list of servers, net view and the name of a server to see the list of resources at the server and net use local device name \\server name\resource to access the resource. When resource sharing is finished, you can type net use device name /delete to terminate use of a shared resource.

3. To send messages on LAN Manager and Windows NT networks:

net send *name message text*

or

net send /DOMAIN:*domain name message text*

or

net send /BROADCAST message text

Net send provides basic messaging capabilities using class-2 mail slot broadcasts, as we described in the introduction to this section. In general, the form of the command is **net send** *name text*. For example:

```
net send Administrator How do I use this blankety-blank thing?
```

will send the text "How do I use this blankety-blank thing?" which will appear in a pop-up display on the workstation that Administrator is logged into. Rather than sending to a user name it is also possible to send to an alias that is usually set using a **net name** command, to a computer name or (on all systems except Windows for Workgroups) using the keyword /BROADCAST.

The net send /BROADCAST command is a special case that should be used *only* for debugging. This sends a basic class-2 mailslot broadcast message with no defined recipient. As such it is unique among LAN Manager commands in that it is totally independent of the security logon—it works irrespective of whether a logon has been completed or indeed can be completed. It is therefore useful for debugging purposes. If you are ever faced with an SMB network of any type (other than Windows for Workgroups) that is refusing to log on, the first thing you should do is bring up a command line and type:

```
net send /BROADCAST Hello, does anyone see this?
```

If you have an effective binding between the various protocols on the network adapter card, then you will see pop-up messages on other machines carrying the text that you typed, *even though the user cannot log into the system.* If that's the case it means that the low-level portions of the network software are operating correctly but for some reason the user account database or login is corrupted and you need to look at the user name, password, and so on. If the net send /BROADCAST does not work, then something is very badly broken within the protocol stack—and you need to examine the interrupt setting of the network card, whether the adapters are loaded, the error log on the Windows NT or OS/2 system, and so on.

Try to avoid the /BROADCAST setting, other than for troubleshooting, because it is a class-2 broadcast with no specified addressee and this is exactly the kind of message that will slow down the entire network.

4. To share resources on LAN Manager, Windows for Workgroups, and Windows NT systems:

   `net share` *`sharename=local path`*

   The syntax of the net share command is net share share name = directory specification. Thus, for instance:

   ```
   net share disk-D=D:\
   ```

   will share the D:\ device (and subtrees) with the share name disk-D. This is a completely portable syntax among all versions of LAN Manager. There are various switches and flags, which will vary from version to version. On all versions of LAN Manager that support sharing, you can also type net share without any parameters to get a list of any shared devices and net share share name /DELETE to terminate sharing of a device.

Portable Administration

With these four commands an administrator can pretty reliably get things done moving from system to system in a mixed LAN Manager network. LAN Manager DOS workstations, LAN Manager DOS workstations running Windows, Windows for Workgroups systems, whether version 3.1 or 3.11, Windows NT systems, whether standalone or Advanced Server, and LAN Manager OS/2 systems, be they standalone servers, peers, or domain servers, all handle these four commands in generally the same way. It is one of the nicest, if least understood, features of the entire LAN Manager system.

Integrating WfWG with Windows NT

Although Windows for Workgroups (WfWG) and Windows NT look very similar, there are differences at almost every level. Architecturally, Windows for Workgroups is built on top of DOS and inherits many DOS limitations. That makes it less robust than NT, which is designed from the ground up as a secure and robust operating system. On the positive side, WfWG supports many more systems and peripheral devices than Windows NT, since vendors have been working with DOS for many years.

WfWG does take advantage of the 386 architecture to a great extent. For example, network drivers are implemented as 32-bit Windows device drivers, which leaves more low memory for running DOS applications. Although WfWG does offer a standard-mode implementation that can run on 286 systems, it has many differences and limitations in capabilities compared with running WfWG in 386 enhanced mode. The discussion here assumes you're running WfWG in the preferable 386 enhanced mode.

From the network standpoint, the most important difference between WfWG and NT is that WfWG always uses share-level security to share resources between stations on a network. This approach is less secure and harder to centrally manage than the user-level security primarily used by NT. If you already have a Windows for Workgroups LAN installed, you can add one or more NT systems and use Windows NT's built-in Guest account to simulate share-level security equivalent to that used in Windows for Workgroups.

Workgroup or Domain?

Taken on its own, Windows for Workgroups is a completely decentralized network that emphasizes sharing rather than security. You configure each WfWG system to be a member of a *workgroup*, which is primarily an organizational convenience. For example, when you browse the network from a File Open dialog in WfWG, you see the other users arranged in a two-level hierarchy based on the workgroup to which they belong.

Workgroups do not figure into the WfWG security scheme. In fact, the only security options you have when sharing a directory on a WfWG PC is to either make the directory read-only or to protect access (either read-only or read-write) with a password. All other WfWG, Windows NT, or LAN Manager-compatible systems can connect to the shared directory, whether they're in your workgroup or not. The only way you can control who accesses the resource is by controlling the password for it.

The casually cooperative and decentralized nature of WfWG and its workgroup scheme lets users share files and devices with a minimum of hassle. However, if you're planning to use WfWG with Windows NT Advanced Server, you may want to make WfWG users part of a *domain*.

With Windows NT Advanced Server, a *domain* is a group of servers that use the same set of user accounts. Domains, unlike workgroups, are an important contributor to security and system administration. The details of how to configure WfWG users for either workgroups or domains are presented later in this chapter.

File Sharing

To set up file sharing connections in Windows for Workgroups, you use File Manager. The WfWG File Manager is visually very close to the one in NT (see Figure 8.1). Both share the toolbar that is lacking in the Windows 3.1 version.

Sharing a Directory

When you share a directory on a WfWG system, you can access the directory from any WfWG, Windows NT, or other LAN Manager-compatible system on the network. In addition to the obvious use in sharing a hard disk directory, you can also share floppy drives, Bernoulli removable disks, or CD-ROM drives this way.

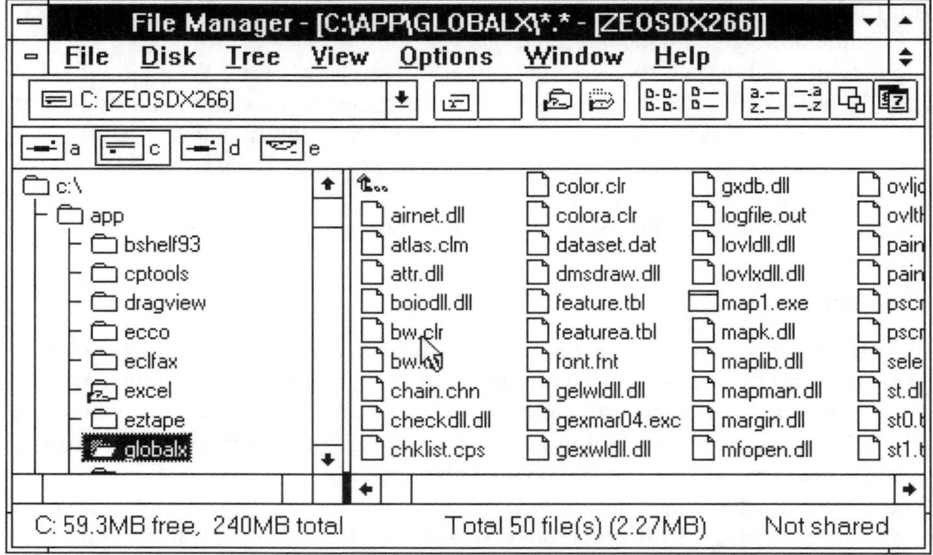

Figure 8.1 File Manager.

The Windows for Workgroups File Manager is very similar in appearance and function to the Windows NT File Manager.

From File Manager, select Disk/Share As from the menu or click on the toolbar icon of a hand holding a folder. You'll get the dialog box shown in Figure 8.2.

Enter the name of the directory you want to share. The share name must be unique for this system, but does not need to be unique network-wide. That is, other computers could share a resource with the name EXCEL, since each share name will always be associated with (and qualified by) a particular computer name.

If you want to share the directory temporarily (for example, for someone to copy a few files), then clear the Re-share at Startup check-box. If this box is checked, WfWG will automatically reshare the directory each time you restart your system.

WfWG offers only two levels of access, read-only and full. You can require that someone who wants to use the directory provide a password for either or both types of access. Remember that full access allows anyone to delete or rename files and subdirectories below the shared directory. Also, although NT lets you share a directory multiple times by different names (and different access control permissions), WfWG lets you share a particular directory only once.

Once you've shared a directory, File Manager's directory tree will give you a visual clue that the directory is shared by using the folder-in-hand icon, rather than the standard folder icon. Also, if you click on a directory that is shared, the right side of File Manager's status bar will show you the share name mapping.

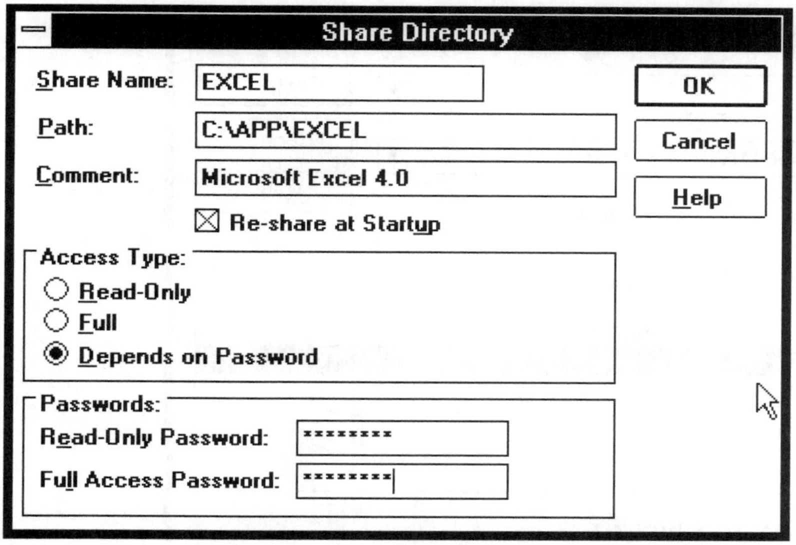

Figure 8.2 Share Directory dialog.

Directory sharing in Windows for Workgroups is controlled through this dialog, which appears when the "Share As..." menu item (or speed button) is selected in File Manager.

Stop Sharing a Directory

Before you stop sharing a directory, be sure that all users currently using the directory are notified and asked to stop using the directory. Otherwise, if you stop sharing a directory that is in use, those users connected to it could lose data. You can find out who is using files in one of your shared directories by selecting the directory, choosing File/Properties from the menu, then clicking the Open By button.

You can either select Disk/Stop Sharing from the menu or click the toolbar icon of a hand holding a grayed-out folder. Select the directory you want to stop sharing from the list in the dialog box. If other people are currently using the directory, you'll get a warning that they might lose data if you continue, and be asked for confirmation.

Using a Remote Directory

Windows for Workgroups is flexible about letting you make connections to other PCs. You can either set up these connections from File Manager ahead of time, or wait until you need a file and make the connection at that point.

To connect a remote directory from within File Manager, select Connect Network Drive from the Disk menu or click the toolbar button showing the network drive icon. You can also get to this dialog through the File Open and File Save dialogs used by most applications. If the

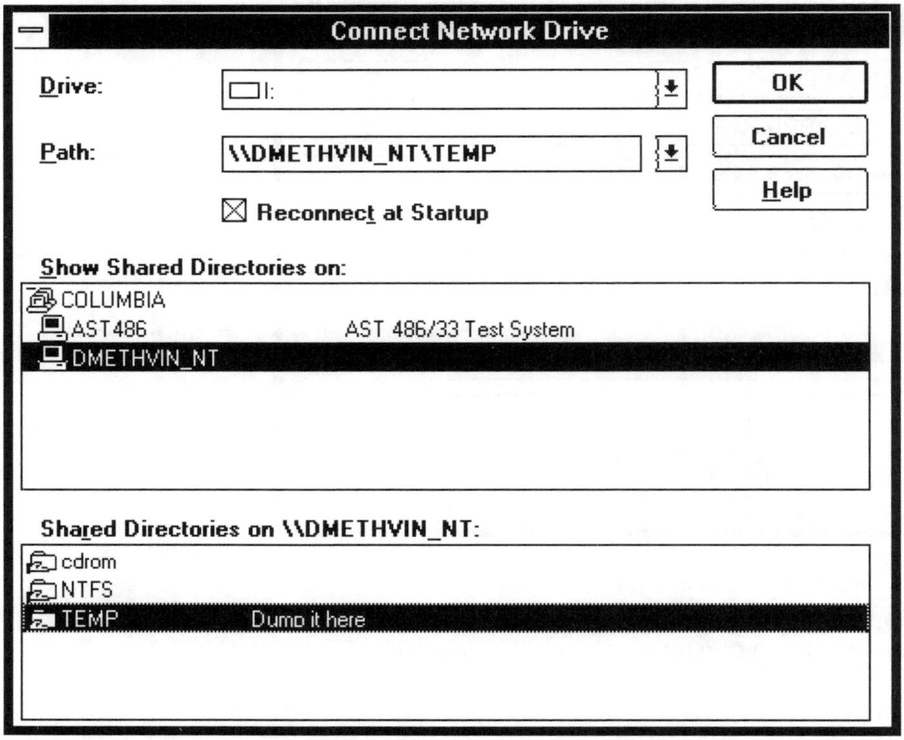

Figure 8.3 Connect Network Drive dialog.

Using a shared directory on a Windows for Workgroups system is done using this dialog, which appears when the "Connect Net Drive..." menu item (or speed button) is selected in File Manager.

application uses the standard dialog, there will be a button labeled "Network..." you can click to bring up the Connect Network Drive dialog (see Figure 8.3).

Regardless of how you get to the Connect Network Drive dialog, it works the same way. If you click on one of the system names in the upper box, the shared directories on that system are displayed in the lower box. You can double-click one of the directories to establish the connection. Before you do, though, be sure the Reconnect at Startup check-box is set the way you want it. If this box is checked, WfWG will reestablish the connection each time you restart the system. If it's not checked, the connection will end when you exit Windows and never come back to bother you.

Stop Using a Remote Directory

To stop using a remote directory, select Disk/Disconnect Network Drive from File Manager's menu or click the toolbar button that shows an X-mark over a grayed-out network drive. You'll get a list of your network connections; just double-click the one you want to disconnect. You can also select multiple connections by control-clicking on them, and then click OK to disconnect them.

When you disconnect a network drive, it's disconnected for good, even if you checked the Reconnect at Startup check-box when you were in the Connect Network Drive dialog originally. That option applies only when you exit Windows with drives connected, then restart Windows.

If you have File Manager running and then create your first connection outside of File Manager (using the net command-line interface, for example), you won't get a drive icon for that connection inside of File Manager. Also, the menu option and button to disconnect drives stay grayed out, which, of course, makes it pretty hard to disconnect anything. If you exit File Manager and restart it, or press the F5 key, you'll see all your connections and be able to pull the plug on any of them.

Printer Management

A Windows for Workgroups system can share any printers that are locally attached to it. However, each PC that wants to share a printer must install the Windows printer driver for that printer locally. It's usually easiest to install drivers for all your printers on every PC when you install WfWG, so you won't be hunting for installation disks when you'd rather be printing.

Print Manager is a vital part of the WfWG printer sharing scheme, not just for establishing connections but also for maintaining them. You must start Print Manager and keep it running to share printers. This is different from the situation with File Manager, which establishes file shares but does not need to be running for those shares to work. If you're connected to a printer that many other people use, it would be a good idea to put a Print Manager entry in your Program Manager StartUp folder. Figure 8.4 illustrates a typical Print Manager window.

Sharing a Printer

To share a printer, select File/Share Printer from Print Manager's menu, or click the toolbar icon that shows a hand holding a printer. You will then see the dialog box shown in Figure 8.5.

Select the printer you want to share, and assign it a name. You can optionally assign a password that other users must enter before they can use the printer. Select Re-share at Startup if you want the printer to be shared each time you start Print Manager. If you clear this checkbox, the printer will be shared only until the next time you exit Print Manager.

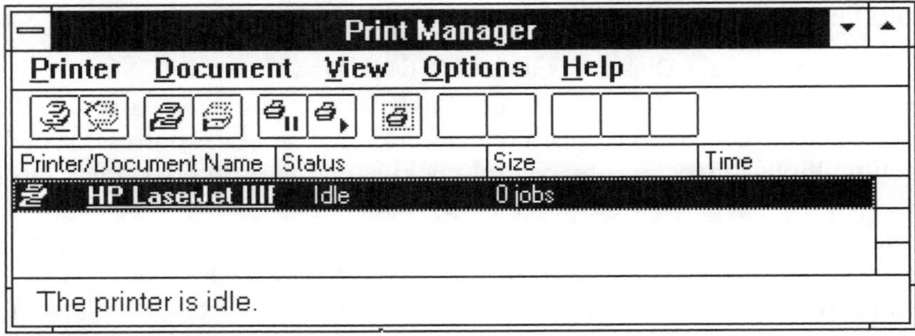

Figure 8.4 Print Manager.

The Windows for Workgroups Print Manager application controls the use of network printers in much the same manner as the Windows NT Print Manager. The two systems differ, however, in their use of printer drivers.

Stop Sharing a Printer

You can use either the menu selection Printer/Stop Sharing Printer or the toolbar button showing a hand with a grayed-out printer. Either way, you'll then get a dialog box showing all the printers you are currently sharing. Select the printer you want to stop sharing, then click OK.

Using a Remote Printer

Again, note that to use a remote printer you will need to have a driver for that printer on your local system. (This isn't true for Windows NT, which can automatically obtain the driver from the system that shares the printer.)

To make the connection, select Printer/Connect Network Printer from the menu or click on the toolbar icon showing a printer with a network wire connected to it. There might be a

Share Printer
Printer: HP LaserJet IIIP on LPT1
Share as: Dave's HPLJ
Comment: Room 117
Password: *******
OK
Cancel
Help
Re-share at Startup

Figure 8.5 Share Printer dialog.

Printer sharing in Windows for Workgroups is controlled from this dialog, which appears when the "Share As..." menu item (or speed button) is selected in Print Manager.

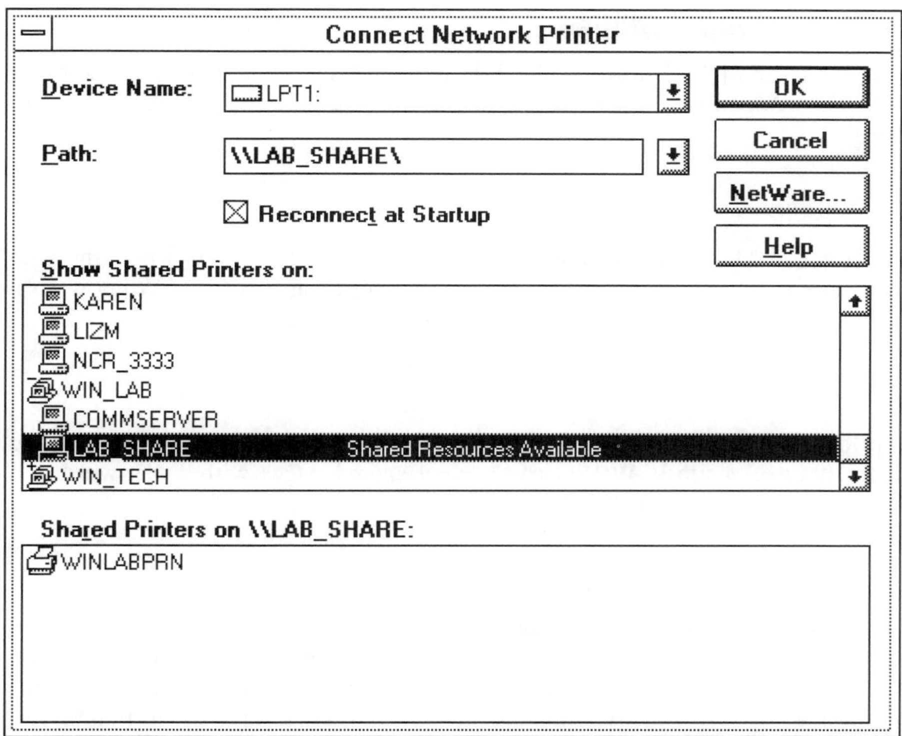

Figure 8.6 Connect Network Printer dialog.

Use of network printers by a Windows for Workgroups system is controlled from this dialog, which appears when the "Connect to Printer..." menu item (or speed button) is selected in Print Manager.

slight delay while Print Manager polls the network for available printers, then you will get the dialog box illustrated in Figure 8.6.

Many applications will also let you select a network printer from a Print dialog or Print Setup menu selection. This is the most convenient option if you use a certain network printer only occasionally. You will need to check the specific application to see if it supports network printers directly.

Stop Using a Remote Printer

To terminate a remote printer connection, select Printer/Disconnect Network Printer from the menu or use the toolbar button that depicts a network-connected printer with an X-mark next to it. You will get a dialog box with your current network printer connections. Select the printer you want to stop using, then click OK.

Windows for Workgroups Utilities

In addition to the bread-and-butter utilities like File Manager and Print Manager, there are other applications that make it easier to exchange data and messages with other users, and to diagnose problems.

MS-Mail and Schedule+

The versions of Microsoft Mail and Schedule+ that are provided with WfWG work fine with the Windows NT versions. It's usually best to set up the mail postoffice on a Windows NT system, then share the post office directory so that the WfWG systems can use it.

ClipBook Viewer

The WfWG ClipBook operates very much like its namesake utility in Windows NT. The big difference is in the area of security. WfWG can protect shared pages with a password, but doesn't offer the user-based security of Windows NT.

Chat

The WfWG Chat utility is a split-screen message utility for point-to-point conversations over the network. It interoperates with and looks identical to the Windows NT version. At present, WfWG does not come with a broadcast messaging utility that would let you receive a note such as "Main server going down in five minutes" from a Windows NT system. Future versions of Windows for Workgroups may include this capability.

NetWatcher

NetWatcher (illustrated in Figure 8.7) lets you see what connections other PCs have to your PC and when those connections were last active. You can also forcibly break connections.

WinMeter

WinMeter (illustrated in Figure 8.8) shows the CPU time use on a computer. One color is used for local applications, and another for the server component. This is a quick way to see if a PC is being bogged down by access from remote users. You can control the amount of CPU time remote users can get through the Network section of Control Panel.

User Account Management

Although Windows for Workgroups itself does not provide user name-based security, it can be integrated nicely into the Windows NT security scheme. There are essentially three options you can choose when integrating WfWG users and Windows NT or NT Advanced Server systems. Your decision in implementing user accounts should balance the need for security

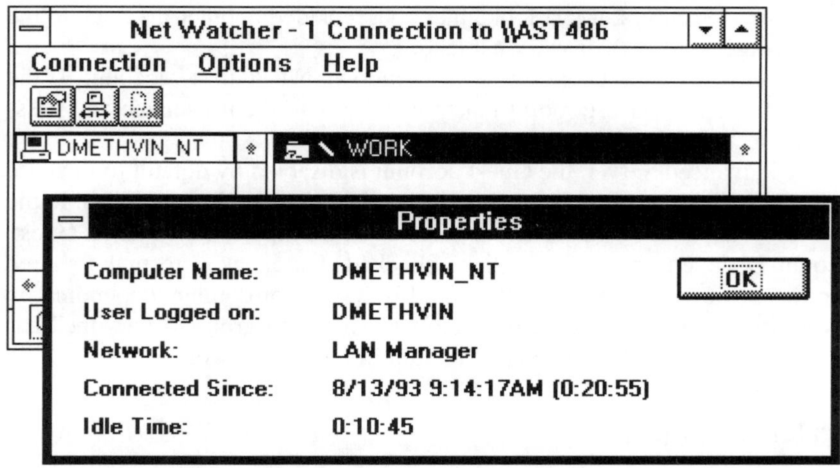

Figure 8.7 NetWatcher application.

The Windows for Workgroups NetWatcher application provides a degree of control over remote network connections similar to (but more limited than) the Server applet in the Windows NT Control Panel.

against convenience and hassle-free access to resources. Also remember that a very secure system will require someone to administer the user accounts and set permissions appropriately.

Option 1: No Accounts, Share-Level Security

If you have an established WfWG system, or if security is not a critical issue, you can add the Windows NT and NTAS servers to your network and use share-level security to make their resources available to the network. These new servers will simply show up in the browse lists

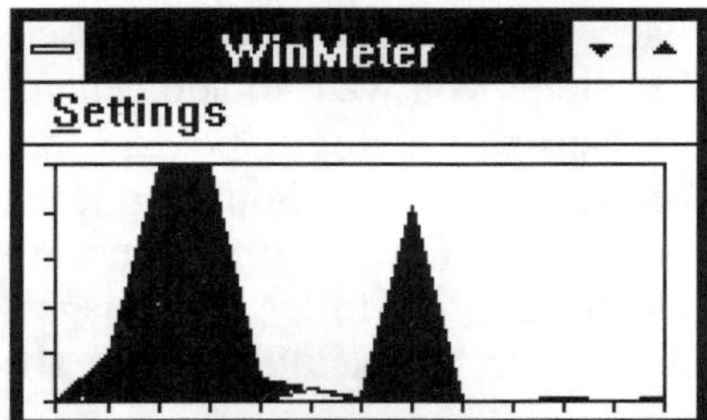

Figure 8.8 WinMeter application.

The Windows for Workgroups WinMeter application provides a visual indication of system activity similar to (but more limited than) that provided by the Windows NT Performance Monitor.

like all the WfWG computers. To users, it just looks like you've added another machine to the network but there's no change at all in their work habits.

This option works because of the behavior of the Windows NT "Guest" account. If the user name and password for a WfWG user don't match exactly with the user name and password of the NT system, you are granted Guest access anyway.

On a Windows NT Advanced Server, the Guest account is disabled by default to increase the security of the network. If you want to use this option on NTAS, you'll need to enable the Guest account. To do this, run User Manager and double-click on the account named Guest. By default, the Account Disabled check-box will be checked. Un-check it to make shared resources available to those who don't have accounts on this system (or domain, depending on how you've set up security). Now, any shared resource for which the group "Everyone" has been given access in File Manager will be accessible to all users on the network.

Option 2: Windows NT User Accounts

If you require more security than option 1 allows, you can get it by creating an account on each of your Windows NT systems for every WfWG user. The password should be the same password they use to log into their WfWG system. Whenever a WfWG user connects to a resource on a Windows NT system, it will use that user's name and password to validate security, rather than the Guest account.

You can, of course, have a hybrid between options 1 and 2 where most of the users use the Guest account permissions and you only create a few accounts for users who need more (or less) access. For example, to restrict access to certain shares, give the Everyone group the No Access permission, and override this by giving Full Access (or other) Permissions to specified groups of users. Be warned, however, that this can become unwieldy if you have many users and/or NT systems. At some point you may want to move to option 3, not for security, but for simplicity of account management.

Option 3: Domain Login

This is the most secure way to run a WfWG system with NT Advanced Server. You actually set up the WfWG system so that it logs onto your network domain when WfWG starts. To implement this, you should first create the domain and user accounts under NTAS. The user accounts should match the names of the users of the WfWG systems you want to add. Then, on each WfWG system go into Control Panel and open the Network dialog. Click on the Networks button at the bottom of the dialog; a list of installed networks should appear. Select LAN Manager from the Other Networks in Use list and click on the Settings button. The dialog illustrated in Figure 8.9 will be displayed. Check the Log On to LAN Manager Domain check-box, and enter the domain name. Wend your way out by clicking OK on all the dialog boxes.

Although option 3 is the most organized and secure approach, it does have its share of caveats. Users need to come to this dialog to change their passwords, so that the domain controller is informed of the change. (You can also use the NET PASSWORD command from a DOS prompt, discussed under the next section in this chapter. Don't depend on domain login

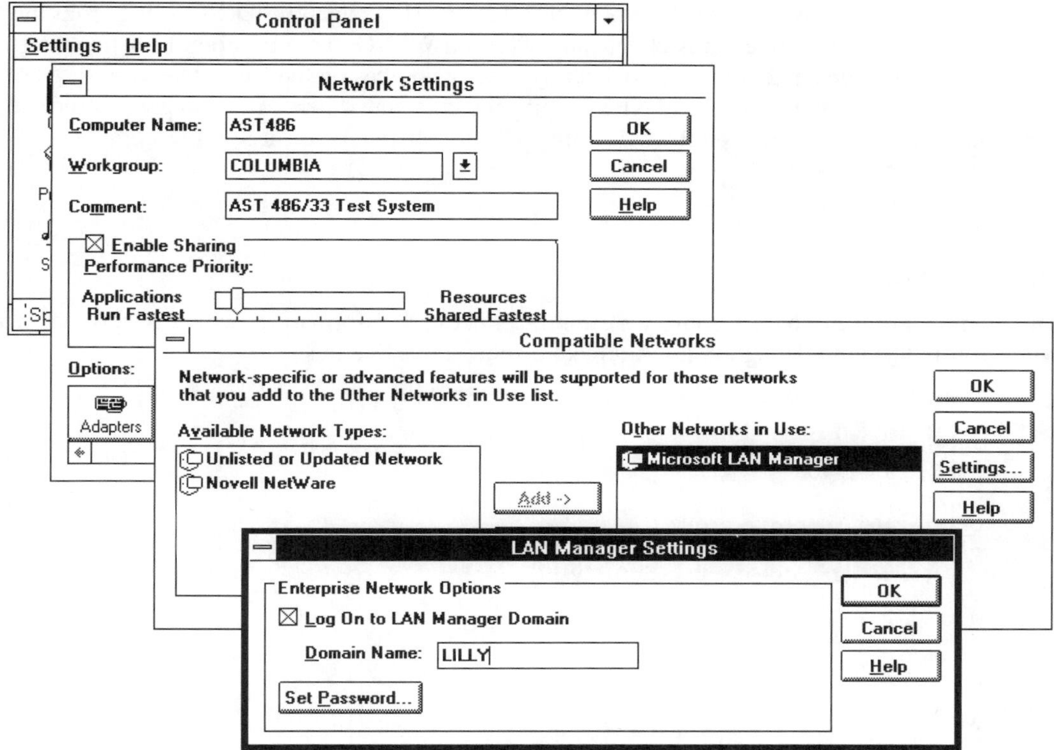

Figure 8.9 LAN Manager Settings dialog.

This dialog, accessed from the Windows for Workgroups Control Panel/Network Settings, allows the specification of a LAN Manager (or Windows NT Advanced Server) logon domain and associated password.

to keep local information on a WfWG system safe. A knowledgeable person can disable domain login and boot the system by removing the LMLogon entry in the [network] section of SYSTEM.INI. At the very least, someone could boot the system into DOS and copy sensitive files.

Command-Line Network Interface

Windows for Workgroups includes a DOS command-line interface (NET.EXE) that gives you access to many of the resource-sharing features. They are particularly useful inside automated batch files. A nearly identical NET command-line interface is also included in a product called Microsoft Workgroup Connection (MWC). MWC lets a DOS-only system use files or printers that are shared by a WfWG or Windows NT system. However, the DOS system running MWC cannot share resources; it is client-only. Even on WfWG, the NET command-line interface does not include any commands to actually share resources on the current system.

A summary of the most useful NET commands is included here. You can get a complete list of commands and their options by typing **NET /?,** or details on a specific command by typing **NET <command> /?.**

NET CONFIG

This command gives you a summary of this PC's network information, which is very useful while you're trying to debug things. A typical display looks like this:

```
C:\WFWG> NET CONFIG
Computer name                  \\AST486
User name                      DMETHVIN
Software version               3.1
Redirector version             2.50
Workstation root directory     C:\WFWG
Workgroup                      COLUMBIA
The command completed successfully.
C:\WFWG>
```

NET LOGON

This command logs this system into the workgroup. If you don't supply a username or password on the command line, you will be prompted for them. Any NET USE commands that you specified as PERSISTENT (and the ones specified as "Reconnect at Startup" inside File Manager) are reconnected at this time.

NET LOGOFF

The NET LOGOFF command logs you off the workgroup and breaks any network connections that may exist.

NET PASSWORD

This will change your logon password. If you don't enter the old or new passwords on the command line, you'll be prompted for them. You can specify computer, domain, and user names if you also want to change your password at an NT server or an NT Advanced Server domain. Otherwise, the password will be changed only in your local password file (<systemname>.PWL in the \WINDOWS directory).

NET PRINT

This command lets you display the print queues on printers you are sharing, and also lets you delete a print job that you have submitted to a printer that hasn't yet printed.

NET TIME

This will let you synchronize your computer's clock with the clock on a Windows NT system or Microsoft LAN Manager time server. This is especially handy as part of each system's AUTOEXEC.BAT file to make sure all the clocks on the network are in sync.

NET USE

The NET USE command establishes or breaks connections to network files and printers, and has numerous options that are explicitly documented in the online help. If you enter NET USE with no arguments, it will display your current connections.

You can make a connection persistent by specifying the option /PERSISTENT:YES. This means that WfWG will reestablish the connection each time the network is started. Normally, NET USE will save the password along with the persistent connection. If you prefer to reenter the password each time the computer starts, then specify /SAVEPW:NO.

Other options of NET USE let you manage your persistent connections. You can display your persistent connections that will automatically be created the next time you start this system, clear the list of persistent connections, or make all your current connections persistent. This last option is useful so that when you get your connections set up the way you want them, you can "snapshot" that for later sessions.

Migration from LAN Manager (OS/2) to Windows NT Advanced Server

If you're running LAN Manager Servers today, how do you go about moving to Windows NT? First of all, you'll notice that the heading of this section says "Migration from LAN Manager OS/2 to Windows NT *Advanced Server*." It doesn't say "Migration ... to Windows NT" because you can't do that. If you convert from LAN Manager for OS/2 to the Windows NT base product you will lose domain administration and the ability to maintain a single account database for all users in your network. To provide centralized account management it is essential to move to an Advanced Server environment.

As stated above, Windows NT servers cannot participate as members of OS/2 LAN Manager domains. They can participate only as members of a Windows NT Advanced Server domain. So you're going to have to upgrade at least one system to a Windows NT Advanced Server and as we've recommended earlier, if you upgrade one, you had better upgrade two. The first matter then is to set up a machine as a Windows NT Advanced Server. You probably won't want to do this with the machine being used as the primary domain controller in the OS/2 network, for obvious reasons. The accounts from the OS/2 LAN Manager system can be converted to Advanced Server accounts using the PORTUAS.EXE utility included with Windows NT Advanced Server software. This command has the syntax

```
portuas -l filename
```

where filename specifies the LAN Manager 2.x NET.ACC file. Of course the file name is always NET.ACC but you have to use the full network pathname. For example:

```
portuas -l \\primary_server\admin\net.acc
```

There are two flag variables that can be used: -u followed by a user name will specify a single user or group to port if you don't want to port the entire user account base. This makes sense, particularly in setting up a pilot project where only a certain group of people are initially going to be exposed to the Windows NT Advanced Server environment. The second is -v, which displays all messages and which we recommend. This will give you a notification if there are any problems.

You must have administrative privileges to run portuas. Further information on portuas can be found in the online help system for the Advanced Server and in the Advanced Server documentation.

Once the user accounts are converted, it is necessary to restore the OS/2 access control list to Windows NT access rights. At this point, of course, we have a major issue with respect to the file system, because access rights at the directory and subdirectory level require NTFS on Windows NT. Therefore, when migrating from an OS/2 LAN Manager system to a Windows NT Advanced Server it is necessary for the Advanced Server to have an NTFS volume for the administrative information. This conversion is done using the ACLCONV.EXE utility. This command has the syntax

```
aclconv /data:datafile /log:logfile
```

where *datafile* specifies the full pathname for the OS/2 LAN Manager BACCACC.ACL datafile (created using the OS/2 LAN Manager BACKACC command) and *logfile* specifies a file where aclconv will log information about failed conversions. For example, the command

```
aclconv /data:\\primary_server\admin\baccacc.acl /log:error.log /newdrive:x
```

will convert the BACCACC.ACL file in the ADMIN directory on the OS/2 LAN Manager primary server to directory permissions on the current NTFS volume and will store information about failed conversions in the ERROR.LOG file. You would then inspect the ERROR.LOG file and carry out any missing conversions manually. Note that the drive letter for the NTFS volume where the ACLs are being restored must be *the same* as the drive letter on the original machine unless you specify a different drive letter with the /NEWDRIVE switch.

In summary, the steps necessary to convert from a LAN Manager OS/2 server primary domain controller to a Windows NT Advanced Server as primary domain controller are as follows:

1. Take the primary domain controller off line. You will probably want to do this after-hours when fewer users will need to be forced off the system.

2. Back up access permissions by using the LAN Manager for OS/2 BACKACC command.
3. Share the administrative disk drives on the OS/2 system and make them accessible to the Windows NT system.
4. From the Windows NT system issue the portuas command to port the user accounts from the LAN Manager for OS/2 system.
5. Use the OS/2 LAN Manager BACKACC command to back up the permissions on the directories on the server.
6. Transfer them to the Windows NT system using the ACLCONV command.

Windows NT Advanced Server Upgrade for Microsoft LAN Manager

As we went to press, Microsoft announced that the $595 upgrade price for LAN Manager servers moving to Windows NT Advanced Server would include an additional set of tools to make upgrading even easier. These include:

- BACKENV—A tool to back up the complete LAN Manager server environment (network card, network address, shared files and printers, etc.).
- BACKAT—Copies prescheduled AT-command events.
- HCOPY—Tool to copy files from LAN Manager server across the network.
- BACKACC—Tool to back up user accounts and permissions.
- ACLLIST—Tool to list access control lists (permissions).
- BACKUP—Tool that backs up data to tape.
- CONVERT—Tool that converts FAT and HPFS partitions to NTFS.
- PORTUAS—Tool that ports the LAN Manager user account database to Windows NT.
- USERCONV—Tool that automatically converts multidomain LAN Manager user accounts and permissions into a single database for integrated cross-domain management.
- ACLCONV—Tool that converts access control lists (permissions) to Windows NT format.
- RESTENV—Tool that restores the server configuration under Windows NT.
- ACLCOMPARE—Tool that detects changes between the permissions before and after a LAN Manager-to-Windows NT conversion has been carried out.
- SMFCONV—Tool that converts Macintosh File System volumes from LAN Manager to Windows NT.
- A complete, graphically oriented, step-by-step application that guides you through the use of these utilities on both LAN Manager for OS/2 and the Windows NT Advanced Server.

Details of the LAN Manager Upgrade for Windows NT Advanced Server are beyond the scope of this book, but the combination of this impressive set of tools, step-by-step instructions, and a substantially lower price (less than half the Advanced Server introductory price) makes the Upgrade an extremely attractive package. We urge anyone considering switching from LAN Manager to Windows NT Advanced Server to call Microsoft for more information.

Application Programming Interfaces (APIs) for Microsoft Networks

NT supports only class-2 mailslots and Microsoft is trying to avoid broadcasts, so it's discouraging the use of mailslots in applications. Microsoft is increasingly pushing in the direction of the remote procedure call (RPC) as the standard API for network applications, but since Windows NT is the only system that supports it this is as yet a gleam in the eye of Bill Gates. Named pipes and NetBIOS remain the standard mechanisms for IPC between stations. They are supported to varying degrees by all systems and are completely portable. For the most part the mailslots are portable as well (since class-1 mailslots are rarely seen on LAN Manager systems). For details on the APIs supported by Windows NT see Appendix 1. Protocols supported by Windows NT include TCP/IP, NetBEUI, and NWLINK (SMB on IPX); all are discussed in Appendix 2.

Conclusion

What used to be called LAN Manager networking (and Microsoft would now like to call Windows networking) is in a state of flux—as represented by the changed names, browsing specification, mailslots and named pipes to RPC as the standard protocol, and so on. Any time there's change there's a certain amount of confusion—and no doubt we've added to that confusion here.

It's worth noting that the migration problems introduced by Windows NT are certainly no worse than those faced by people upgrading from NetWare 3.x to NetWare 4.0. And it also seems clear that LAN Manager/Windows networking has a bright future. The Windows NT Advanced Server has been embraced as a database application server by every major vendor of client/server database software. Hardware manufacturers are lining up to supply platforms for servers and for high-end workstations.

The move to TCP/IP as the standard networking protocol, which began with LAN Manager 2.1, is accelerating under Windows NT. That particular subject is so fast moving that it's evolving as we speak. As of this writing we just became definitely aware (less than a week ago) of the fact that a file transfer protocol (FTP) server for TCP/IP will ship with Windows NT—providing a significant new level of connectivity that's discussed in detail in Chapter 6. The advantages of incorporating Windows NT into LAN Manager and Windows for Workgroups networks far outweigh any disadvantage. This is a system you can migrate to with confidence.

For More Information

Microsoft Staff (1993), *Windows for Workgroups Resource Kit*. Redmond, WA: Microsoft Corp. The encyclopedic guide to every setting in every initialization file in Windows for Workgroups. Also discusses the overall WfWG architecture and the differences between real and enhanced mode operation of WfWG.

Microsoft Staff (1993), *Windows NT Advanced Server Upgrade Guide for Microsoft LAN Manager*. Redmond, WA: Microsoft Corp. This guide gives detailed planning information for administrators planning to upgrade a LAN Manager system to Windows NT Advanced Server. If you have a LAN Manager system and are looking at Windows NT, this should be your first point of reference.

Microsoft Staff (1993), *Windows NT Advanced Server Concepts and Planning Guide*. Redmond, WA: Microsoft Corp. A solid and well-written introduction to Advanced Server issues including administration, replication, fault tolerance, and user environment management. A bit weak on the details of migration from LAN Manager but essential information. If you begin an Advanced Server installation without reading this book you are making a serious mistake.

Microsoft Staff (1993), *Windows NT Advanced Server System Guide*. Redmond, WA: Microsoft Corp. All the gory details.

Microsoft Staff (1993), *Net News (May/June 1993, Volume 3, Number 2)*. Redmond, WA: Microsoft Corp. "Under the Bonnet," p. 2. This article is a good introduction to the network architecture in Windows NT and among other things discusses the details of named pipes and mailslots. Net News is a publication of the Corporate Technology Team organization within Microsoft—a tremendous resource of up-to-date information including free technical notes that can be ordered through Microsoft Outside Sales (go technet on CompuServe).

Novell Connections

After reading this chapter, you will understand the fundamental similarities and differences between Windows NT's built-in networking and the networking services provided by Novell NetWare. You will understand five approaches that may be taken to establish connectivity between Windows NT and NetWare:

- **Novell's NetWare Client for Windows NT, which lets NT clients access shared directories and printers on NetWare servers and supports *both* nonstandard (for Windows NT) *Open Datalink Interface* (ODI) drivers, *and* Windows-NT standard *Network Device Interface Specification* (NDIS) drivers.**
- **Microsoft's NetWare-compatible Client Services (NWCS) for Windows NT, which uses the NWLink IPX/SPX Protocol stack (see the next item) to provide access to shared directories and printers on NetWare servers with standard (for Windows NT) NDIS drivers. Besides shared file and printer access (like Novell's NetWare Client for Windows NT), NWCS also provides command-line access to NetWare resources through the Windows NT *net* command interface, and supports most DOS-based NetWare utilities.**
- **Microsoft's NWLink IPX/SPX Protocol, which lets NetWare clients access Windows NT *services* in exactly the same way they would normally access *NetWare Loadable Modules* (NLM)—an especially useful approach for client-server applications such as multi-user databases.**
- **UNIX services (including FTP and NFS), which allow limited connection of NT to NetWare for file sharing without using any form of NetWare IPX**

protocol—a preferred method for connecting to NetWare over *Wide Area Network* (WAN) links.

- **Beame and Whiteside's *Multiconnect IPX* add-on package for Windows NT, which provides full IPX/SPX *and NetWare Core Protocol* (NCP) capability, effectively allowing a Windows NT system to function as a NetWare *server*.**

You will see that the flexibility of Windows NT makes it possible to connect to NetWare—but as must be expected in any multivendor internetworking situation, the connection is not an easy one.

The NetWare Story

It's a fact of life, probably obvious to everyone reading this book, that the story of local area networking is very much the story of one company, namely Novell—just as the story of desktop graphical user interfaces is very much the story of one company, Microsoft.

Novell's great contribution was to eliminate the link between proprietary network hardware and software that characterized virtually all networking systems in the seventies. Instead, they introduced the notion of a Network Operating System (NOS) that could work with hardware from many vendors.

Today, Novell's *NetWare* NOS covers some 70 percent of the local area networking market. And there is no way that any desktop operating system can exist in today's commercial environment without providing some degree of NetWare connectivity. In this chapter we will examine what this means to Windows NT.

There is a school of thought that sees Windows NT and NetWare as *competitors*—and this is surely correct to some extent; but the idea that *any* other operating system will replace NetWare as the de-facto standard for file/printer sharing in the next few years is naive. Indeed, Novell and DEC recently demonstrated NetWare running on a DEC Alpha AxP RISC processor—a clear indication that NetWare can be expected to evolve even as NT gets into its stride.

So finding effective ways to exploit Windows NT in a NetWare environment is not only important *today*, we can expect it to be just as critical *tomorrow*.

And Now, a Warning

We know that if you're reading this chapter, you probably have a NetWare server and need concrete advice on how to connect a Windows NT system to it. We will do our best to help you do that. In the process, we will recommend some things that do not have the blessing of either Novell or Microsoft. This entire subject area is an extremely complex and fluid one for reasons that will become apparent. The relationship between Microsoft and Novell is complex and, as of this writing, less than amicable.

In view of this, please bear in mind that this is the one chapter of this book most likely to be overtaken by events. You are *strongly* advised to check what we have to say *for yourself*. At each stage, wherever possible, we have given you reference information to direct you to where you can get the very latest and most up-to-date information. Please treat this chapter as a starting point. It's vitally important if you are to succeed in establishing and maintaining a good NT-to-NetWare relationship that you develop and maintain your own active up-to-date sources of information.

Why Connecting Windows NT to NetWare Is Difficult

The facts of life are sometimes unpleasant. One unpleasant fact of life for Microsoft is that while Windows was becoming the dominant desktop environment, NetWare was becoming the dominant NOS. This is unfortunate from the point of view of the Windows NT user because Microsoft proceeded to make a number of rather engaging attempts in the networking field over the last few years. A whole series of products described in Chapter 8 were introduced over the last few years with little success, ending with the technically impressive—but commercially unsuccessful—LAN Manager 2.x series.

The reason for this is simple—NetWare provides a *shared resource* networking environment that in many respects is very similar to the kind of desktop operating system Microsoft has provided with DOS—while Microsoft made the mistake of trying to deliver something that might be better *technically*, but didn't work as well for the end-user.

NetWare NOS Advantages

In the formal sense of the word neither DOS or NetWare are modern operating systems. There are many features that we demand of a modern operating system (such as Windows NT) that NetWare does not provide. In particular, it lacks virtual memory, preemptive multitasking, or any kind of a memory protection scheme.[1] The cognnoscenti among programmers are often inclined to say that DOS is not an operating system, it's a monitor.[2] By the same standard, neither is NetWare. In many respects, NetWare is effectively DOS scaled up to run a network.

What NetWare *does* have is an incredibly efficient low-level I/O architecture employing special techniques such as *elevator seeks* that make it extremely efficient as a file-and-print server. In effect, NetWare exploits its own limitations—it may not provide virtual memory or preemptive multitasking, but it also doesn't have the overhead associated with such high-end features. As a result, NetWare gives good performance in memory configurations where a Windows NT Advanced Server won't run at all.

The performance of Windows NT and Novell NetWare on a given single-processor Intel-based machine is always likely to favor the NetWare machine: First, if the machine has enough memory to run Windows NT then it has *more* than enough memory to run NetWare.

---

[1]Memory protection is provided in NetWare 4.0, but as of this writing it is rarely used.

[2]Monitor: A term used by hackers in denigration of an operating system. It refers to a kind of "operating system" typically loaded into a single-board computer with less than one kilobyte of memory during the 1970s.

And second, NetWare will get better advantage from whatever disk drives and controllers are built into the machine than NT will. The fact that NT can offset this with features like symmetric multiprocessing or by abandoning the Intel processor for another line of CPUs is all well and good—but it falters on a basic fundamental fact. Windows NT's built-in *Server Message Block* (SMB) networking is inherently incompatible with Novell's *NetWare Core Protocol* (NCP).

Even though the packets Windows NT transmits can be received by a NetWare server (assuming a NetWare-compatible IPX stack is in place), the NetWare server does not understand the SMB packets or UNC-formatted requests issued by the NT machine—and even if it did respond, the NT machine would not understand the NCP formatted results.

Therefore, any approach to connecting NetWare to Windows NT has to take account of the fact that they are designed to operate with completely different protocols. At the same time, one should not stop at this point, drop the buck, and assume that Windows NT is not important because it won't talk to NetWare (or equally assume that NetWare is useless because it won't talk to Windows NT). There are, in fact, no less than *four* ways (and at least one more on the way) to connect Windows NT systems to NetWare servers. We will go through all of these approaches in the sections that follow.

NetWare Client for Windows NT

We begin with the approved approach according to Novell (which has also had statements of support from Microsoft). This is the NetWare Client for Windows NT—a redirector for Windows NT implemented as an installable file system and a collection of drivers.

Novell Network Services for Windows NT is a client redirector. It's delivered and maintained by Novell. As of this writing it's in Beta. We anticipate that it will be delivered in much the same way that Novell has delivered redirector clients for OS/2, DOS, and Windows—although for political and legal reasons it's unlikely to be packaged with Windows NT in the manner that requesters for Windows 3.0 and 3.1 have been. Still, this is the Novell-approved way of doing things and therefore it calls for a close look.

The major feature of the NetWare Client for Windows NT is primarily that it provides full file and print sharing services to the Windows NT client machine. That is, the Windows NT user, through the File Manager (operating in much the same way as when he or she uses the built-in NT connectivity) can connect to NetWare Servers, use NetWare directories and NetWare printers, and receive NetWare messages.

The Protocol Problem

In early versions of the NetWare Client for Windows NT, Novell chose to break with the NDIS standard for network drivers used by Microsoft, and introduced its own Open Datalink Interface (ODI) system. There are many arguments one could make about the relative merits of NDIS and ODI. ODI is potentially faster than NDIS, because it passes a pointer between the kernel-level network card driver and the protocol stack, essentially allowing the two layers to share memory. Unfortunately, this appears to violate the basic principles of NT's multilayer system protection, in which data is *never* shared between the kernel (in this case driver) and user (in this case, protocol stack) layers, and it can lead to severe system crashes if the shared memory address is corrupted by either component.

NDIS drivers, by contrast, do not share common memory between the driver and protocol layers—instead, data is copied between separate memory regions in the two layers. This is a slower process; but it's safer (in point of fact, *either* approach should be completely reliable once the drivers are fully debugged).

Against this, there's one major advantage to using ODI drivers, over and above the possible performance enhancement—the 32-bit revision (F) drivers in question are *the very same drivers used by NetWare 4.0 servers*. This can be extremely convenient for administrators in a NetWare 4.0 environment; because if you have NetWare 4.0 server drivers for your standard network cards, then you can use these same drivers with Windows NT systems.

However, there are two problems with using Novell's ODI drivers in a Windows NT environment: First, while NetWare 4.0 is designed to be portable (as the recent debut of a prototype NetWare 4.0 running on DEC's Alpha RISC processor demonstrates), as a practical matter, *most* revision (F) 32-bit ODI drivers are presently available only for Intel x86-based systems; so you can't reasonably expect to use them on Windows NT systems in a RISC environment. The second problem is that, while the driver .LAN files work perfectly with Windows NT, they require a customized OEMSETUP.INF file[3] in order for Windows NT setup to install them. As of this writing, OEMSETUP.INF files are available for about one hundred network cards. Novell has said that it's working on a tool to create these files automatically, but it hasn't announced whether or not this will be made available to the public. Effectively, this means that Novell's ODI drivers are useful in an NT environment *only* if the vendor also supplies the Windows NT .INF file for the driver in question.

One or Two Network Cards?

Another problem with the need to use ODI drivers is that the ODI/NDIS incompatibility causes problems if you want to run *both* the NetWare redirector *and* built-in Windows NT networking (if you want to run *only* NetWare networking on your Windows NT systems, see "Eliminating Windows NT's Built-in Networking," later in this chapter). This arises because both ODI and NDIS want to "own" the network card—something that doesn't work out very well if you only have one network card in your system.

One solution is to use two network cards in the same machine—one bound to ODI for NetWare, and the other bound to NDIS for NT. This approach works, and provides better performance and higher reliability than a single-card approach. But it's expensive, and it creates a configuration problem (you can't run both cards at the same interrupt level and I/O address, for instance).

A single network card solution has been made available by Novell. This uses a custom "shim" driver called ODINSUP, which acts as a translator layer between the ODI network card drivers and the Microsoft NDIS system. Therefore, it's possible to run one network card, ODINSUP and the proper ODI driver, and have it run with *both* the NetWare NT Client *and*

[3]Documented in the Windows NT Device Driver Development Kit.

Windows NT's built-in networking—a solution which potentially offers better performance than using a pure-NDIS approach.

Lack of NetWare Utilities

There are some problems with the NetWare NT Client as of this writing. In particular, there are no NetWare utilities. NetWare users are accustomed, for example, to employing the *slist* utility to print a list of NetWare servers on their terminal screen. The same functionality is effectively provided in File Manager when the Network Services for Windows NT is running—one sees two major network lists at the top level of the Network Browser, namely LAN Manager Services and NetWare Client. However, if you need command-line access to a list of servers, while it's possible to use the *net view* command for a list of Windows NT (or LAN Manager or Windows for Workgroups) servers, there is no equivalent command for listing the NetWare servers when running Novell NetWare Client for Windows NT (Microsoft's competing NWCS *does* have such a capability, as we will see).

Novell has announced that when they upgrade their requester to provide DOS-compatible NetBIOS services at some future date, you'll be able to run the DOS NetWare utilities. You would run the DOS version of *slist* and access it through NetBIOS. We view this solution with a somewhat jaundiced eye—users of a 32-bit operating system ought reasonably to expect 32-bit utilities rather than DOS-based ones. NetWare Client for Windows NT also currently provides no support for NetWare script or batch files. These are commonly used in a wide variety of NetWare systems to provide administrative control and management.

We've heard various statements regarding the eventual availability of some form of NetWare login script support. Obviously, when (and if) DOS BIOS-level NetWare support is added it will become possible to execute NetWare scripts using Windows NT's built-in DOS emulation system. The other story we've heard is that there won't be any need for login scripts, since the Windows NT File Manager, which is the usual mechanism for accessing NetWare files through the NetWare Client for Windows NT, supports reconnection of existing shares, and the print manager does likewise for printers. It's certainly true that this is the most common use of NetWare login scripts, but it's hardly the *only* such use.

Other NetWare Limitations

The NetWare requester also provides only a FAT-compatible DOS-style Name Space. That is, applications, whether 16-bit or 32-bit, are restricted to eight-character names and three-character extensions. This is unfortunate because NetWare is capable of supporting multiple Name Spaces, and long filename support has long been available for Macintosh clients. We hope that Novell will see fit at some point to provide an NTFS Name Space for Windows NT clients.

Finally, while versions of the NetWare Client for Windows NT exist for some RISC systems (including MIPS R4x00 and DEC Alpha AxP systems), availability of ODI drivers for these platforms remains an issue.

How to Install and Use NetWare Client for Windows NT

Installing NetWare Client for Windows NT is relatively simple. You get the NetWare Client for Windows NT installation disks from your Novell representative, the Novell Network packaging, or (in the present Beta situation) by downloading the NWNT.EXE file from the NOVFILES forum on CompuServe, and then expand it (typically it's shipped as self-extracting .EXE file) to an NWNT directory or floppy diskette.

You can install NetWare Client for Windows NT from the Control Panel/Network applet (you need to be logged in with administrative privileges to carry out this operation). Installation typically involves the following steps:

1. Run the Windows NT Control Panel/Networks applet, and click the "Add Software" button.
2. Select "<Other> Requires Disk from Manufacturer" from the pick-list, and click the "Continue" button.
3. An "Insert Diskette" dialog will appear requesting the full pathname for the updated software files. Enter the pathname for the directory or disk where you stored the expanded NWNT files, e.g.: "D:\NWNT" or "A:\", and click the "OK" button. When the list of software you can install appears, select Novell NetWare Client from the list (Figure 9.1)
4. The Novell NetWare Client for Windows NT will load, and you'll be presented with a NetWare Client Installation dialog, asking which IPX protocol stack you want to use. The default is Novell IPX/SPX II, which requires ODI drivers. Alternatively, you can select Microsoft NWLink, which will work with the NDIS drivers included with Windows NT (and installed by default). You'll find more information on NWLink in the section on "Microsoft's NWLink Protocol Stack," later in this chapter.
5. If you selected Novell's IPX stack, a set of instructions will be presented for removing the NDIS driver already installed in your system (if present). Follow the instructions that appear on the screen.

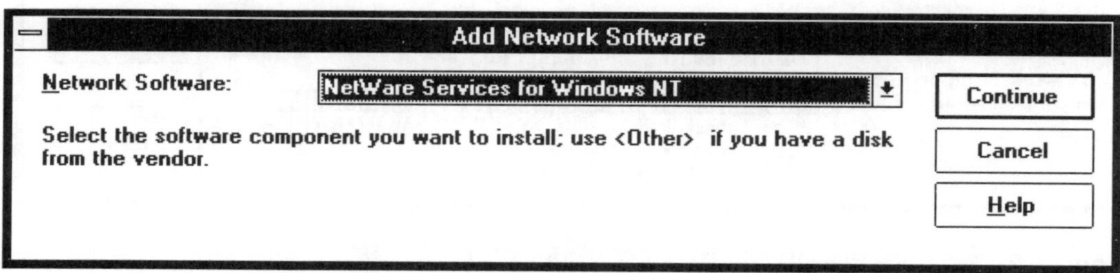

Figure 9.1 Control Panel/NetWare Services.

Loading Novell NetWare Services for Windows NT is done using Control Panel/Network Settings Add Software button.

6. If you're using ODI drivers, click the Add Adapter button. An Add Adapter dialog will appear asking you to select an ODI adapter driver. Select the ODI driver for your network card from the list (if it's not on the list, then your best move at this point is to abort the installation, find a revision (F) 32-bit ODI driver for your card, and then add it manually using the Control Panel/Networks "Add Adapter" button). Set the options (base address, IRQ, etc.) for the card and click the "Continue" button.
7. If you're using ODI drivers, an IPX Frame Type dialog appears. Select the proper Frame Type for your network from the list (the default, 802.3 Ethernet, is correct for most applications).
8. If you're using ODI drivers, at this point what happens depends on whether you need NDIS support for NT's built-in networking, and if so, whether it will be run on a separate network card or on the same network card as ODI. If you have two network cards, you will have been asked which card to bind the ODI driver to, and (provided you bound it to a card separate from NDIS—check with the "Bindings" button in Control Panel/Networks), you're done.
9. If you need to add NDIS support for NT's built-in networking on a machine that's got ODI installed (generally you will need this in any system with just one network card *unless* you want to completely disable NT's built-in networking, as mentioned above), then click the "Add Adapter" button, and select "Novell ODI support for NDIS drivers (ODINSUP)" from the list, as illustrated in Figure 9.2. This will load the "software shim" described above.
10. If you don't want *any* form of built-in networking, install the Microsoft Loopback Driver, or disable the built-in network services as described in "Eliminating Windows NT's Built-in Networking" later in this chapter.
11. With NetWare Client and either Microsoft or Novell IPX protocol stack and adapter drivers installed, click the Bindings button to bind the adapters to the cards and

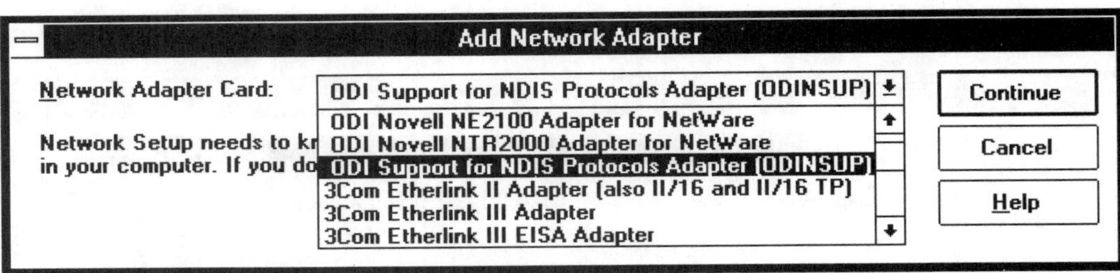

Figure 9.2 Control Panel/ODINSUP.

In environments where both Netware Services and Windows NT built-in peer networking are to be used with a single network card, it's necessary to load Novell's ODI Support for NDIS (ODINSUP) "shim" driver, using the Control Panel/Network Settings Add Driver button.

review the order of the connections. Once this is done, you can click "OK" to exit the Control Panel/Network Settings applet. You will need to restart the computer before using NetWare Client for NT.

If everything has gone right, the computer will restart normally. If the computer does not restart normally, the odds are extremely high that some error has been made in configuring the networking support for the network card.

The best solution in this case is ugly, but fairly reliable. Turn off the computer, physically remove the network card, and restart the computer. The computer typically will start up and display an error message indicating that it was unable to locate the network card and that one or more services are not complete. Start Control Panel Networks, select the network card driver, press the configure button and check to verify that the interrupt and address of the card are properly selected. Also, double-check to make sure you have, in fact, installed the driver for the right network card. Once these things have been verified and adjusted as necessary, turn the computer off, put the network card back in and reboot the computer. If it fails again, the odds are high that one of two things has happened: Either you have not successfully completed the preceding steps, or you have successfully completed the preceding steps but your particular network card and computer are not compatible with the current generation of ODI drivers—in which case, your only option is to turn the computer off, remove the network card, restart the computer, use the Remove button in Control Panel/Network Settings to eliminate the Netware Client, reinstall the NDIS drivers for Windows NT, and proceed with one of the other three options for NetWare compatibility described later in this chapter.

Eliminating Windows NT's Built-in Networking

Many NetWare administrators wish to operate Windows NT clients in a NetWare-only environment, without Microsoft's built-in peer networking. Unfortunately, this isn't possible with the current release of Windows NT (and for architectural reasons it's unlikely to be possible in future versions). Novell's NetWare Client for Windows NT is built on a number of the built-in subsystems; so attempting to eliminate it makes the NetWare Client unworkable. However, Microsoft and Novell jointly recommend one work-around, and we've found another.

First our approach: follow the instructions we've given above to install Novell's NetWare Client and the requisite ODI or NDIS driver, but do *not* install the ODINSUP binder for the built-in (NetBEUI) networking. Instead, install the MS Loopback Adapter Driver as a second network card driver, and bind NetBEUI to it. This will give you a working system with the built-in networking reflected back to itself and the NetWare networking bound to the proper ODI driver and network card—we've tried it, and it works.

The approach reccomended by Novell and Microsoft, on the other hand, is to disable the built-in network services using the Control Panel/Services applet. Set a Startup Type of *Disabled* for the Alerter, Workstation, Computer Browser, Messenger and Net Logon services. This completely disables Windows NT's built-in networking.

On the other hand, administrators may find that the built-in networking's not a bad thing. From our experience, there doesn't seem to be any great problem in running both NetBEUI and IPX traffic over the same network card, and running both networks gives you the added

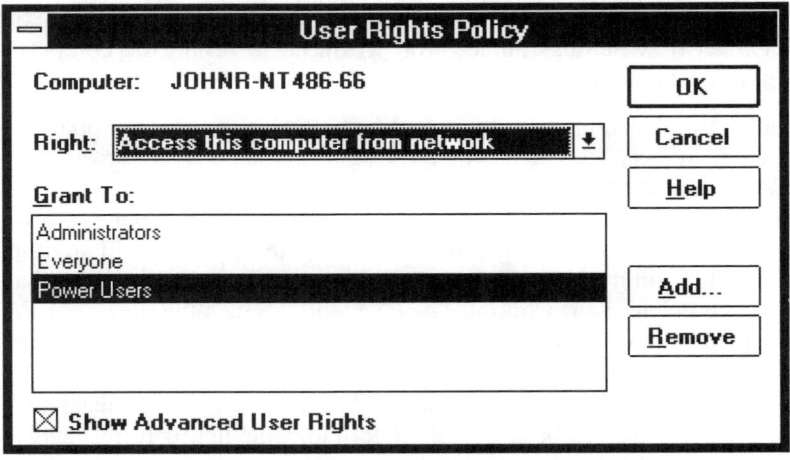

Figure 9.3 User Rights dialog.

Administrators who wish to effectively prevent users from employing Windows NT's built-in peer network services can make it impossible for anyone other than Administrators to access Windows NT systems over the network. This is done using the User Manager Policies/User Rights dialog.

flexibility of having the peer networking available for administrative purposes. Rather than eliminating it, you may want to simply make it unavailable to your end-users. You can do so with the following procedure:

1. Run User Manager from the Administrative Tools group.
2. Select the user (or group) that you don't want to use built-in network services.
3. Select User Rights from the Policies menu. When the User Rights Policy dialog (Figure 9.3) appears, make sure the Show Advanced User Rights box is checked, and select "Access this computer from network," and click the Remove button. Then select "Create permanent shared objects," and click the Remove button.

If you do this for all nonadministrative users on all of your Windows NT systems, you will render it impossible for any of them to use the peer-to-peer networking features. A user can create a temporary share in File Manager, but nobody else will be able to use it—and it will disappear when the user logs out. Administrators, however, will retain the ability to create and use shared directories (and printers) for administrative purposes.

Configuring the NetWare Client for Windows NT

Once the NetWare Client is installed, it's a simple matter to use it—as we'll see shortly. There are a couple of configuration settings you may need to set, depending on your installation (these settings are available *only* if Novell IPX/SPX and ODI drivers are used; they are *not* available with NDIS drivers): They are the *preferred server* for NetWare login, and the *frame type* for IPX/SPX traffic. Of these, the preferred server most commonly needs attention—in a multiserver environment, NetWare tends to log into the first one that responds when the client comes online; which may not be the server you want to access. Setting a preferred server eliminates this problem by forcing the redirector to log into a specific server of your choice. You'll need to be logged into the Windows NT system with administrative privilege to carry out the following steps.

To set a preferred server for NetWare log-in:

1. Start Control Panel/NetWare applet, and click the Configure button.
2. The Network Settings dialog appears. Select NetWare Workstation from the list, and click the Configure button.
3. The Netware Workstation Setup dialog appears. Select the appropriate server from the list, and click the OK button. You will have to restart the computer to make the preferred server selection take effect.

Alternatively, it's possible to set a preferred server using the Windows NT Registry Editor (REGEDT32.EXE), as shown in Figure 9.4. Edit the Preferred Server entry in KEY_LOCAL_MACHINE\SYSTEM\CurrentControlSet\Services\NetWareWorkstation\Parameters. It's usually preferable to do this from the control panel, but the registry approach can be used if you need to set a preferred server on a remote system or if you want to create a batch file for changing preferred server settings.

To change the frame type:

1. Start Control Panel/NetWare, and click the Configure button.
2. The Network Settings dialog appears. Select NetWare IPX/SPX II Transport from the list, and click the Configure button.
3. The Netware IPX bind dialog appears. Click the OK button. The IPX Frame Type dialog appears. Select the appropriate frame type from the list, and click the OK but-

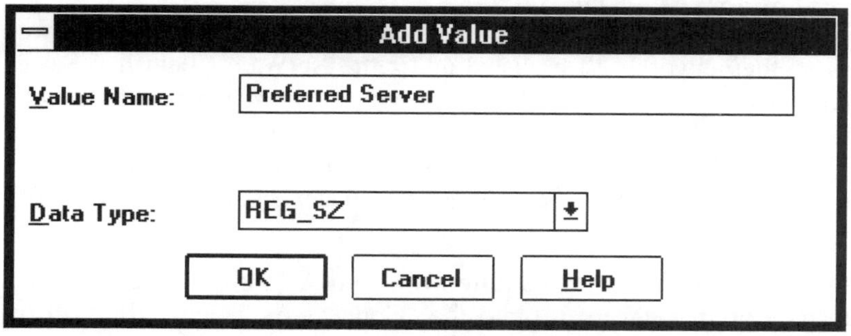

Figure 9.4 Registry/Preferred Server.

Setting a Preferred Server for Netware Services is done using the Registry Editor's (REGEDT32.EXE) String Editor, accessed from Edit/Add Value.

ton. You will have to restart the computer to make the frame type selection take effect.

Alternatively, it's possible to set the frame type using the Windows NT Registry Editor (REGEDT32.EXE). Edit the Frame Type entry in KEY_LOCAL_MACHINE\SYSTEM\CurrentControlSet\Services\IpxSpxII\Parameters. Valid values are ETHERNET_802.3, ETHERNET_802.2, ETHERNET_II, and ETHERNET_SNAP. It's usually preferable to do this from the control panel, but the registry approach can be used if you need to set a preferred server on a remote system or if you want to create a batch file for changing preferred server settings.

Using NetWare Files and Directories

Fortunately, once the vagaries of the installation process have been navigated, using NetWare Client for Windows NT is generally quite pleasant. To access shared files and directories on NetWare servers:

1. Select Disk/Connect Network Drive. You may also begin by clicking on the Connect Network Drive button in the toolbar, if it's present.
2. The Connect Network Drive dialog box appears, which is shown in Figure 9.5. The Drive box contains the next available letter for your computer. To change this value, click on the down-pointing arrow key or press Alt+Down Arrow and select the drive letter you prefer.
3. If you have connected to this drive before, the path may be listed in the Path pull-down list. The Path list shows the previous ten paths you have selected. If the path you want to connect to is displayed, select it and proceed to step 5.
4. There are two options for selecting the path:

   a. If you have not connected to this drive before, or your drive is not listed in the Path listbox, enter the pathname directly—note that Windows NT uses UNC-format names, *not* NetWare NCP format, i.e.: \\WIN1\SYS\MSMAIL is correct, while WIN1/SYS\MSMAIL is *not* correct.

   b. Alternatively, select the shared directory from the Shared Directories list. NetWare servers on the network will be listed under the NetWare Client list. Select the server you want to connect to by double-clicking on it. When you make your selection, File Manager displays the shared directories of your selection in the box at the bottom of the dialog box. Select the shared directory by single-clicking on it, or double-click to display subdirectories. File Manager displays the path in the Path box.

5. If your NetWare user ID and/or password differ from your Windows NT user ID and password, then type your NetWare ID into the "Connect As:" field. You will be prompted for your password when the connection is made.
6. If you want to reconnect to this directory automatically when you begin Windows NT, be sure to check the Reconnect at Logon box (which is checked by default). *Caution*: if the directory is on a computer that's not the server and is not certain to

be running when you start Windows NT again, you will get a warning message asking if you want to proceed with connections. Therefore, we recommend that you check the Reconnect at Logon box *only* if you are connecting to a directory on the server for which there is a strong likelihood of availability when you log in. Note that if your NetWare user ID and/or password differ from your Windows NT user ID and password, you'll be asked for the NetWare password each and every time you log in.

7. Select OK.

Matters are greatly simplified, for obvious reasons, if the NetWare user name and the user name under Windows NT are the same. If so, connections proceed identically as if they

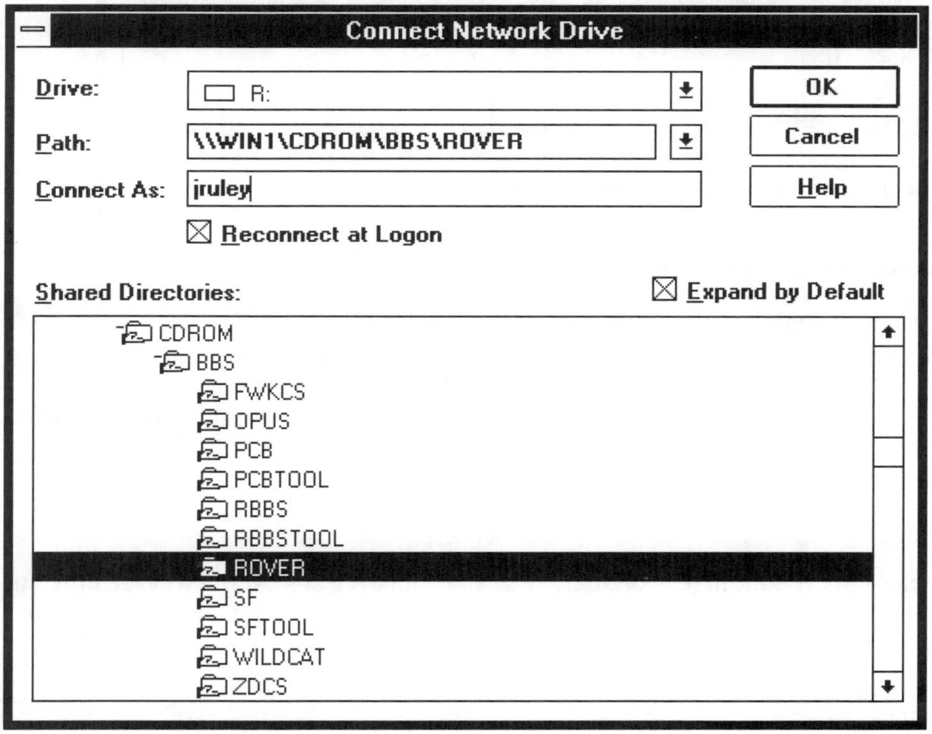

Figure 9.5 Connect Network Drive—NetWare.

Windows NT users connect to NetWare shared directories just as they do to Windows NT shared directories—using the Connect Network Drive dialog in File Manager. Note that the need to use this dialog (and the associated browser service) makes it impossible to completely eliminate Windows NT built-in networking if NetWare Services are to be used. A work-around (binding the built-in networking to a "loopback" driver) is given in the text.

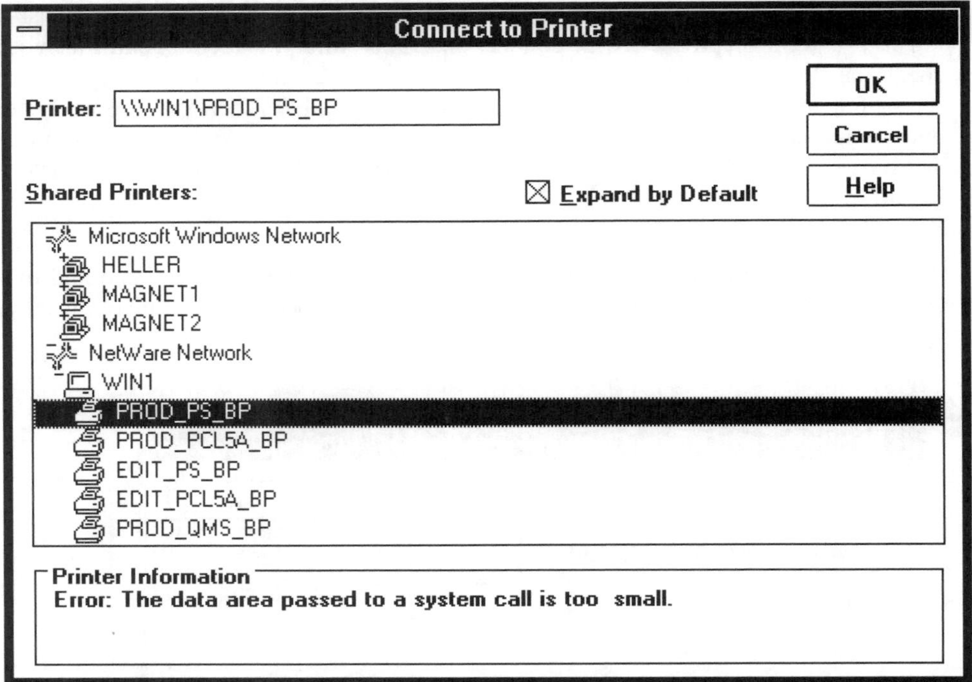

Figure 9.6 Connect Network Printer—NetWare.

NetWare printers are connected in exactly the same way as Windows NT network printers—using Print Manager's Connect Network Printer dialog. NetWare printers do require installation of local printer drivers on the client systems. It is also possible to *re-share* NetWare printers over the built-in networking for access by Windows NT (and other SMB) clients that do not have NetWare redirectors installed.

were connections to the built-in networking. When you connect to a server in which a different user name and password are employed, it's necessary to type the appropriate user name into the Connect As: field.

Using NetWare Printers

It's just as straightforward to use NetWare printers as it is to use NetWare directories:

1. Select Printer/Connect to Printer or select the Connect Printer button on the toolbar. The dialog box shown in Figure 9.6 appears.
2. Enter the name of the printer in the Printer text box. If you do not know the name of the printer, select one from the list in the Select Printers box. The printers are dis-

played in a hierarchical list, which can be expanded to show the printers, domains, and workgroups by double-clicking on an entry. Select a printer and the name appears in the Printer text box. Select OK.

3. If the printer is shared by a Windows NT computer, you can now use the printer. The steps that follow should be followed if the printer is shared by a computer *not* running Windows NT.
4. Print Manager prompts you to install a driver. Select OK, then choose the driver from the Select Driver dialog box. Enter the location (drive and directory) of the Windows NT printer drivers, then select Continue.
5. Windows NT will install the driver for you.

Re-Sharing NetWare Printers

One surprising feature of the Beta NetWare client for NT is that it permits NetWare printers that have been connected using the Windows NT Print Manager to be *re-shared* over the Windows NT (NetBIOS) network, and accessed by Windows NT workstations that don't have the NetWare redirector installed. To re-share a NetWare printer (that's already been connected using the steps listed above):

1. Open Print Manager and select the NetWare Printer you wish to re-share.
2. Select the Properties item from the Print Manager Printer menu.
3. Check the "Share this Printer on the Network" check-box, type a name into the "Share Name" field, and click the OK button.

Other systems using Microsoft SMB networking (Windows NT, Windows for Workgroups, or LAN Manager systems) will now be able to access the printer as if it was installed locally. This approach is useful, among other things, for connecting NetWare printers to machines that don't have a NetWare requester for Windows NT installed. It can also be used to make NetWare printers available to Windows NT clients logged in using Remote Access Services (RAS). Whether this feature will be maintained in future versions of the requester we cannot say—but we hope so. (As we went to press, Microsoft was providing a capability to re-share Netware *directories*, as well as printers, in beta versions of their NWCS redirector.)

NetWare Messaging

Support for NetWare Messaging has varied in the three different refreshes of the NetWare Client for Windows NT that have been presented so far. While all versions of the requester can *receive* NetWare messages, early versions provided an interesting (and useful) Connections dialog in the NetWare applet of the Windows NT Control Panel that allowed for *sending* messages. Later versions have eliminated this feature—and this leaves us somewhat confused because the NetWare Messaging feature worked perfectly from the first. We presume that this feature will be reintroduced into the NetWare client at a later date. Consult the documentation that you receive with the NetWare client for Windows NT for details.

What the NetWare Requester Does *Not* Do. . .

It's appropriate at this point to consider just what the limitations of the NetWare requester are. While it provides complete access to shared NetWare files and printers (clearly the most needed feature) as of this writing, it lacks the following features:

- Support for NetWare login scripts (expected in future versions).
- Any form of NetWare utilities (expected in future versions).
- DOS support (beyond simple redirected disks and printers—which must be set up using the Windows NT File and Print Managers—but this is expected to change, as in items 1 and 2 above).
- NetWare Message Handling Service (MHS) support—used by many NetWare-specific electronic mail programs (again, expected in future versions).
- Any means for existing NetWare clients to access resources on Windows NT servers.

The first four limitations are likely to be overcome when the requester is upgraded to provide DOS-level services (something Novell has repeatedly promised to do), and equivalent services to native Windows NT applications.

Microsoft's NWCS for Windows NT

As this book went to press, Microsoft announced that they would supply their own, NDIS-based NetWare client for Windows NT. In contrast to Novell's approach, Microsoft doesn't use nonstandard (for Windows NT) ODI network drivers, thereby avoiding at a stroke all the driver problems discussed in the previous section. Instead, Microsoft's client uses the NWLink IPX/SPX driver stack (covered in the next section of this chapter).

Besides using NDIS drivers, the Microsoft NWCS provides two major advantages over Novell's redirector: First, it allows you to use Universal Naming Convention (UNC) names to transparently refer to *both* Microsoft (Windows NT, LAN Manager, and Windows for Workgroups) servers *and* Novell NetWare servers. For example, the command:

```
net use x: \\server\sharename
```

works for both Microsoft and Novell servers, if you use Microsoft's NWCS—which makes it very convenient for writing network-independent scripts. Second, NWCS provides limited support for DOS-based NetWare command-line utilities, such as SLIST, SYSCON and SETPASS. In our opinion, this more than compensates for its lower performance.

Installing NWCS

As NWCS uses the NWLink driver stack, you first need to install NWLink (covered in the next section), and then add NWCS itself. You can install NWCS from the Control Panel/Network applet (you need to be logged in with administrative privileges to carry out this operation). Installation typically involves the following steps:

1. Run the Windows NT Control Panel/Networks applet, and click the "Add Software" button.
2. Select "<Other> Requires Disk from Manufacturer" from the pick-list, and click the "Continue" button.
3. An "Insert Diskette" dialog will appear requesting the full pathname for the updated software files. Enter the pathname for the directory or disk where you stored the expanded NWNT files, e.g.: "D:\NWNT" or "A:\", and click the "OK" button. When the list of software you can install appears, select NetWare Workstation Compatible Service from the list, and click the OK button.
4. NWCS will load. Click OK to exit Control Panel/Network Settings. You will be prompted to restart the computer—do so.
5. Windows NT restarts and presents a Select Preferred Server for Netware dialog. Select the server you use most often from the list.
6. If your Windows NT and NetWare login passwords are different you'll be prompted to enter your NetWare password (if your NetWare and NT user names are different, then you'll get a "user does not exist" error message, and you'll need to make connections manually using the Connect As field in File Manager's Connect Network Drive dialog or the /USER: switch on a NET USE command line).
7. If you don't want to use Windows NT's built-in network services, follow the instructions given in "Eliminating Windows NT's Built-in Networking" earlier in this chapter.

Configuring NWCS

Once NWCS is installed, it's very easy to use. There are a couple of configuration settings you may need to set, depending on your installation: They are the *preferred server* for NetWare login (normally set in the first login after installing NWCS), and the *print options* for NetWare printers.

To set a preferred server for NetWare login, or print options for NetWare printers:

1. Start the Control Panel/NWC applet. The NetWare Workstation Compatible Service dialog appears (Figure 9.7)
2. To set a preferred server, pick the server you most frequently use from the list in the Select Preferred Server field. You can pick <None> if you have no preference.
3. The printer options you can select include whether a form feed is added at the end of each job, whether you are notified with a NetWare message when a print job is completed, and whether a banner page is printed at the start of each job. These are controlled using the Add Form Feed, Notify when printed, and Print Banner checkboxes, respectively.
4. Click OK to exit Control Panel/NWC. Your changes will take effect immediately (if you changed your preferred server, Windows NT will immediately send your user-

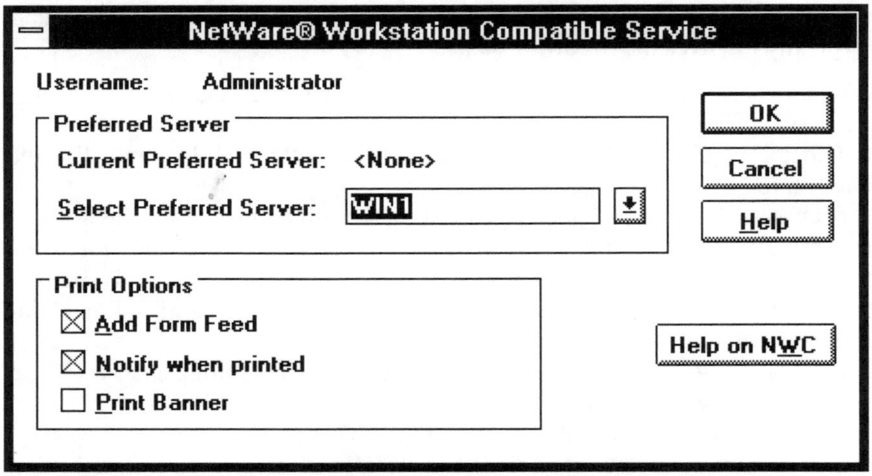

Figure 9.7 NetWare Workstation Compatible Service.

Microsoft's NWCS provides this dialog, available from Control Panel/NWC. It allows control of a preferred NetWare server and of options for printing to NetWare printers.

name and password to the selected NetWare server for authentication). There is no need to restart the system.

Using NWCS

In most respects, using NWCS is no different than using Novell's Netware Client for Windows NT—or using Windows NT's built-in networking, for that matter. You can access NetWare volumes (shared directories) or printers from File Manager or the command line, and you can access NetWare printers from Print Manager or the command line. The instructions given in "Using NetWare Files and Directories," "Using NetWare Printers" and "Re-Sharing NetWare Printers" earlier in this chapter apply to NWCS just as they do to Novell's NetWare Client for Windows NT. Where NWCS goes beyond the Novell Client is in command-line access to NetWare resources, and the ability to use DOS-based NetWare utilities.

From the command line, you can view NetWare servers using the Windows NT *net view* command with the /NETWORK:NW switch. For instance, the command:

```
net view /network:nw
```

gives the following response on our network:

```
Resources on NetWare(R) Network

------------------

\\OPTICAL1
\\WIN1
```

```
The command completed successfully.
```

Net view also lets you inspect shared resources available on a server, for example the command:

```
net view \\win1 /network:nw
```

gives this response:

```
Shared resources at \\win1
__________________________
Disk          \\win1\BOOKSHELF
Disk          \\win1\CDROM
Disk          \\win1\DATA
Disk          \\win1\SYS
The command completed successfully.
```

To access shared directories, you use the *net use* command, in much the same way as it's used with the built-in Windows NT networking (documented in Chapters 3 and 4). For example, \\win1\bookshelf can be associated with the drive letter w: with the command:

```
net use w: \\win1\bookshelf
```

If your NetWare and Windows NT accounts have different user names, then use the /user switch to set your NetWare username, i.e.:

```
net use s: \\win1\sys /user:jruley
```

See the "Network Operations from the Command Line: The NET Command Interface" section of Chapter 4 and "Administrative NET Commands" in Chapter 3 for more information on command-line network access in Windows NT.

Access to NetWare Utilities

Unlike Novell's NetWare Client for Windows NT, NWCS allows you to access DOS-based NetWare utilities from the NT command line. Utilities like SYSCON, SLIST, WHOAMI, SEND, etc. can all be run from a Windows NT command prompt with NWCS running. Here's an example of an NWCS session:

```
C:\users\default>net use z: \\win1\sys
The command completed successfully.

C:\users\default>z:
Z:\public>slist
Known NetWare File Servers             Network    Node Address Status
__________________________             _______    ____________ ______
OPTICAL1                              [      122][            1]
WIN1                                  [      112][            1]Default
Total of 2 file servers found
Z:\public>whoami
You are attached to server WIN1, connection 20, but not logged in.
Server WIN1 is running NetWare v3.11 (100 user).
```

For more information on how to use NWCS, including command-line control of NetWare print queues, see the NWCS documentation or the NWDOC.HLP file that ships with NWCS. Microsoft has not made NWCS generally available as this is written, but has announced that NWCS will be made available on CompuServe (presumably in the WINNT forum), and will be distributed free of charge.

Why Two NetWare Redirectors?

The availability of two competing approaches to connecting Windows NT to NetWare servers may appear confusing—but in our view it's an overall win for NT users. Both approaches work with Windows NT's native NDIS drivers, and Novell's Client gives you the option to use NetWare 4.0 Server drivers if they're available. Microsoft's client, by supporting command-line access to NetWare servers, gives you the capability to write network-independent scripts. In general, the competition between both clients should assure Windows NT users of excellent NetWare connectivity in the future.

Microsoft's NWLink Protocol Stack

Beyond redirecting simple shared files and printers, there's the larger matter of providing seamless client/server connectivity (in NetWare-speak, the function usually provided by an NLM). Microsoft's NWLink protocol stack takes care of this—while providing the low-level infrastructure needed by Microsoft's NWCS.

For obvious reasons, Novell does nothing to accommodate servers by other companies. Microsoft has, therefore, provided its own solution. NWLink is a NetWare-compatible protocol stack that provides full 32-bit IPX/SPX connectivity from an NT server. In effect, it lets existing NetWare DOS, Windows, and OS/2 clients access Windows NT in much the same way that they access NetWare servers—up to a point.

NWLink does not provide any file or printer sharing (unless you add the Microsoft NWCS). Instead, the full NetBIOS protocols are supported, the various levels of the Windows Network and Sockets APIs are supported, and Named Pipes are supported. Since all of the above are implemented on top of an IPX/SPX stack (mostly using NetBIOS calls) a simple NetBIOS redirector in the client machines, such as Novell's IPX/NETX combination, provides a surprisingly high level of connectivity.

This is more than sufficient for use as an *application server*—the role traditionally filled in NetWare environments by an NLM executing in the NetWare server. For example, consider a company that runs its financials or customer service database using a high-end product like Novell's SQL NLM or Microsoft SQL Server. In that sort of environment, access to shared directories is meaningless—what you want is a way to link the client software in the workstations to the host database, exactly the capability that NWLink provides.

For all practical purposes, you can think of this approach primarily as a means for Microsoft to provide NetWare users with access to *network applications* running on Windows NT servers. (Of course, having put such a server into a Novell network, it would only be necessary to change the software in the client machines to provide dual protocol networking). Aside from the lack of file and print services (unless Microsoft's own client software has been added), which renders NWLink suitable only as an application server and *not* as a general purpose server, the only limitation is that the IPX implementation supported by NWLink is not truly routable (when used to provide SMB-based file and print services to Microsoft networking clients—because it encapsulates non-routable NetBIOS broadcasts. See Appendix 2 for details). As a practical matter, this is probably insignificant since the deployment of NWLink servers is likely to be aimed only at a local segment—and in any case, even when used for file-and-print sharing, NWLink NetBIOS packets *do* route over one hop (again, see Appendix 2 for details).

Instructions

NWLink is supplied on both Windows NT and the Windows NT Advanced Server as part of the standard Network Services package. To install it's necessary to:

1. Launch Control Panel.
2. Double-click the Network icon in the control panel window. This invokes the Network Settings dialog box.
3. Press the Add Software button.
4. Locate the NWLink IPX/SPX Compatible Transport entry in the Network Software listbox, and select it. Press Continue. You will be asked to designate a source for the software (the installation disks or CD), and Windows NT will then copy the NWLink files to your local hard disk.
5. Click the OK button.
6. Windows NT will configure the network and perform a binding analysis. When it reaches the bindings for the NWLink transport, an NWLink Configuration dialog will appear, as shown in Figure 9.8. Check this to see that NWLink is bound to the proper adapter card (if more than one is installed), and that the Network number and frame type are correct (it defaults to Network 0 and an 802.3 Ethernet Frame—both correct for most installations—see "Configuring NWLink" later in this chapter for other options). Then click OK.
7. NT will prompt you to restart the system in order to start NWLink.

Connecting to an NWLink-serviced application varies from application to application, so we can't make any specific statements about that here (see Chapter 11 for a detailed example using Microsoft SQL Server for Windows NT). In general, an application that exploits NWLink will need to set itself up using a name recognized by the NetWare *bindery*. Microsoft SQL Server for Windows NT ships with a DLL that does this by sending out a Service Advertising Protocol (SAP) packet out via IPX that gets picked up by a NetWare server. The server loads the SAP information into the bindery. Client applications can then use standard NetWare APIs for a list of servers to see the NT Server.[4] As a practical matter, the only applications that support this model as we write are Microsoft's SQL Server and SNA Server for Windows NT.

[4]Programmers interested in implementing this kind of system should see the article on Windows Sockets in the July, 1993 issue of *Microsoft Systems Journal*.

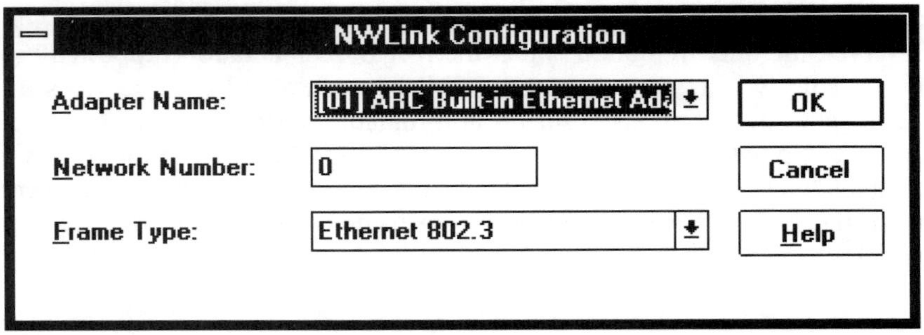

NWLink Configuration

Adapter Name: [01] ARC Built-in Ethernet Ad
Network Number: 0
Frame Type: Ethernet 802.3
OK
Cancel
Help

Figure 9.8 NWLink Configuration.

Microsoft's NWLink IPX/SPX protocol may be configured directly from Control Panel/Network Settings, by picking the protocol from the list and clicking the Configure button. This dialog is then displayed, allowing you to select the network card bound to the protocol, the network number, and the frame type. It's also possible (though not recommended) to set these parameters using the Registry Editor (REGEDT32.EXE).

Configuring NWLink

The basic NWLink configuration that's performed as part of the installation can also be performed later by running Control Panel/Network, selecting NWLink Transport from the list of installed software and clicking the Configure... button. Aside from determining which adapter the protocol is bound to (note that while Windows NT supports having multiple network cards in the system, NWLink can be bound to only one network card at a time), you can set the network number and the frame type.

The **network number** will be 0 by default—and should be left at 0 in all but the most unusual circumstances. IPX network numbers are comparable to TCP/IP subnet addresses, but are set up dynamically at runtime. Setting the network number to zero initially causes NWLink to send a RIP (Routing Information Program) broadcast message, which will be responded to by the local subnet server (which will send the network number). If no server responds, the default setting of zero will be retained, indicating that IPX packets are intended for the local subnet, which is compatible with the client software in most IPX implementations.

The only case where the network number will need to be reset to anything other than zero will be if you're trying to use NWLink to provide application services to a *different* subnet than the net it's on, and if you can't rely on RIP routing to get the job done for you. In this case you'll need to find out the 4-byte IPX network number for the subnet you're trying to send to, and set that in the control panel.

The **frame type** will be set to 802.3 Ethernet Frame by default, which is standard for most Ethernet systems. If your hardware supports Ethernet II, then you can set this frame type. If you're running a Token Ring or FDDI network card, you'll need to set either 802.2 or SNAP as the protocol type, depending on your hardware. The final selection, Arcnet, would be used only with Arcnet-type cards (Arcnet is an obsolete competitor to Ethernet), which are not supported by Windows NT at this writing.

NWLink Performance Tuning and Advanced Settings

Besides the three settings for NWLink in the Control Panel, there are a number of parameters that can be set for NWLink in the Windows NT Registry. A detailed description of these parameters (and their uses) is beyond the scope of this book, but you'll find them detailed in Microsoft's on-line Knowledge Base on CompuServe (go MSKB) and on Microsoft's TechNet CD (see "For More Information," below). Settings are available for controlling the use of NetBIOS-over-IPX traffic (used if NWLink is employed for interconnecting Windows NT systems as well as for application services to NetWare clients), controlling a variety of low-level IPX and SPX behaviors, and controlling RIP (or static) routing of NWLink traffic. NWLink also makes a variety of *performance counters* available for use with the Windows NT Performance Monitor application—including packet-level performance of IPX, SPX and NetBIOS packets transmitted over NWLink (see Figure 9.9). These can be used for performance tuning and maintenance in much the same manner as the other network parameters detailed in Chapter 5.

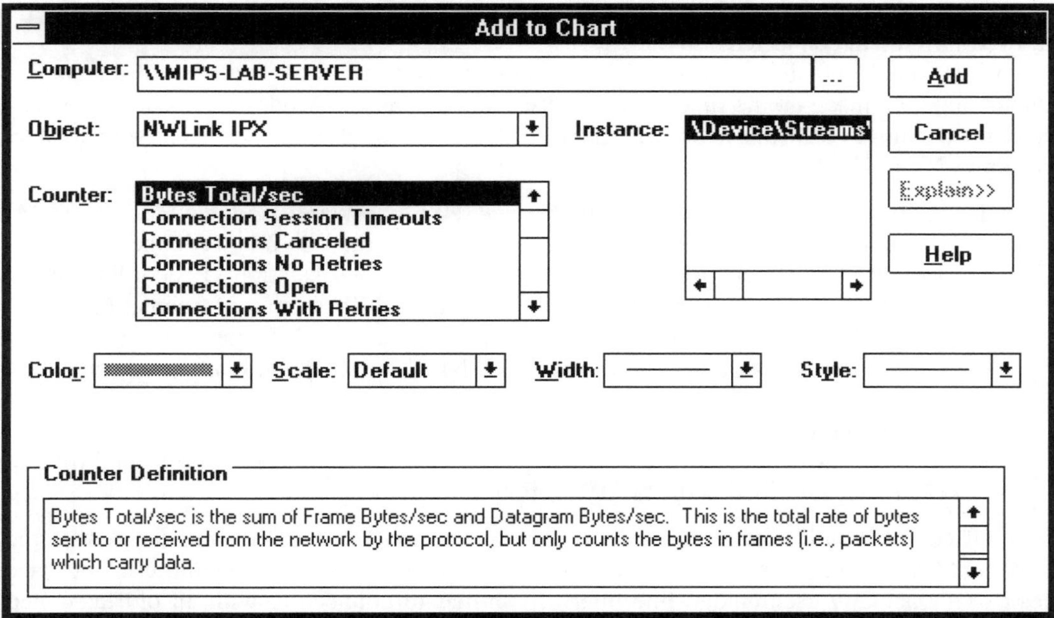

Figure 9.9 Performance Monitor NWLink object.

Microsoft's NWLink IPX/SPX protocol provides a number of useful Performance Monitor counters that can be exploited by Network Administrators in NetWare environments.

Beame and Whiteside's Multiconnect IPX

As mentioned in the section on NWLink above, neither the Novell nor the Microsoft approach to connecting Windows NT and NetWare makes it possible for NetWare clients to see shared files and printers on a Windows NT server. Doing so requires that the server not only have an IPX/SPX protocol stack, but that it also have the NetWare Core Protocol (NCP) responder. The latter is comparable to the *Server Message Block* (SMB) server used by Windows NT's built-in networking.

As we went to press, Beame and Whiteside[5] announced a product that does exactly this. Multiconnect IPX makes Windows NT into an NCP server—and by doing so, makes it possible for NetWare clients to access shared files and printers on Windows NT systems. Unfortunately, this product has just been announced as this is written. It's expected to be available early in 1994.

The Final Alternative—The FTP "Back Door" Approach

With all the limitations we've described on both the Novell and Microsoft approaches to Windows NT/NetWare connectivity, you're probably wondering if there's an alternative. There is—although, to be honest, it's not one we think most users will take seriously. Basically, it exploits Windows NT's built-in UNIX-style TCP/IP networking (detailed in Chapter 6). Since Windows NT knows how to talk to TCP/IP, all you need to do is make NetWare talk TCP/IP, and you have them connected!

This sounds too simple to work—but it does. We've tested it (in fact, four of this book's authors together made up the first team to successfully connect a Windows NT client to a NetWare host, using exactly this approach, in late 1992). So, if all else fails, here's how to connect Windows NT to NetWare via TCP/IP:

1. Acquire and install the *Name File Service* (NFS) NetWare *Loadable Module* (NLM) on your NetWare Server. Note that this cost $5,000 the last time we looked.
2. Install TCP/IP networking on your Windows NT workstation(s) according to the instructions in the "Installing and Configuring TCP/IP" section of Chapter 6.
3. Assign IP address numbers to the NetWare server and the NT workstation(s).
4. Restart the NetWare Server with the NFS NLM installed and configured (including assigning the IP address).
5. Restart the workstation(s).
6. You can now access the NetWare Server via UNIX-style File Transfer Protocol (FTP), as described in the "FTP" section in Chapter 6.

Of course, you'll spot problem #1 as soon as you look at step one—it's the cost of the NFS NLM. Problem #2 is that FTP isn't exactly an example of world-beating user interface design (it's actually a command-line interface similar to connecting with an old-fashioned

[5]Dunda, ONT, Canada—(416)765-0822.

text-mode bulletin board system). Problem #3 with this approach is that while it does give you shared access to NetWare files, it doesn't give you any access to NetWare printers.

But in spite of everything, it *does* work!

Summary and Conclusions

In this chapter, we've reviewed the history of Novell NetWare, and discovered why Windows NT is incompatible with it. We've examined several approaches—from Novell (the NetWare Client for Windows NT), Microsoft (the NWLink protocol and Microsoft NWCS), and third parties (Beame and Whiteside Multiconnect IPX). Each has unique advantages and disadvantages. Finally, we've briefly described an alternative (using NT's built-in TCP/IP File Transfer Protocol service to access a Name File Service NLM) that isn't pretty but has been proved to work.

This entire field is in a state of flux, and new developments happen on a day-to-day basis. Readers are urged to watch the trade magazines and both Novell and Microsoft's support forums on CompuServe (NDESKTOP and WINNT respectively) for more information as this volatile subject develops.

For More Information

Clarke, D.J. (1993), *The Complete NetWare Construction Kit*. New York: Wiley, ISBN: 1-471-58259-X. Clarke's information on NT is one-sided, but this book provides an invaluable practical overview of NetWare.

Custer, Helen (1993), *Inside Windows NT*. Redmond, WA: Microsoft Press, ISBN: 1-55615-481-X. Custer's description of the TDI-layer redirector is essential in understanding how the various kinds of NetWare connectivity fit into NT.

Microsoft Staff (1993), *TechNet CD (July 1993)*. Redmond, WA: Microsoft Product Support Services (PSS). TechNet is a monthly publication on CD-ROM containing a digest of topics from the Microsoft Knowledge Base, the Net News publication, Resource Kits and other information. This particular issue included a prerelease version of the Windows NT Resource Kit, with considerable information on the NWLink protocol. TechNet is available from Microsoft sales—a one-year subscription (12 CDs) costs $295 and is worth every penny.

10

Other Connections

When you finish reading this chapter, you should have a better idea of where to go for further information on connecting Windows NT to other networks. As this book is being written, many vendors have announced that they will support NT in their existing network structure, but none have delivered finished products. Among the networks for which NT-compatible products have been announced are:

- **IBM LAN Server**
- **IBM SAA Networks**
- **DEC Pathworks**
- **Banyan VINES**
- **Advanced UNIX (X/Windows and NFS) Networks**

Although Windows NT and NT Advanced Server have been shipping for a few months as this chapter is written, network vendors are still struggling to deliver their connections to these new platforms. Although we were unable to fully test any of the products listed here, we present what information we were able to acquire about each. We *strongly* recommend that you contact the vendor directly for more information.

IBM LAN Server 3.0

Back when IBM and Microsoft were on civil terms, IBM licensed Microsoft's LAN Manager product, modified it to improve performance on IBM hardware, and sold the resulting product as the IBM LAN Server. Since then, the relationship between the two firms has become somewhat complex, but LAN Server networks still share a common code base with the SMB-based networking that's built into Windows NT and other Microsoft networking products. In fact, it's quite possible to use LAN Server clients on Windows NT LANs (see Figure 10.1), and Windows NT clients on LAN Server networks.

Aside from the fact that it uses IBM's OS/2 2.1 as the base operating system, instead of Windows NT, LAN Server is actually quite similar to NT (and other Microsoft networks) in operation.

Tuning LAN Server for Windows NT Interoperation

The most critical element in getting LAN Server and Windows NT networks to interoperate is protocol selection. As it happens, IBM's OS/2 NetBIOS protocol (the LAN Server default pro-

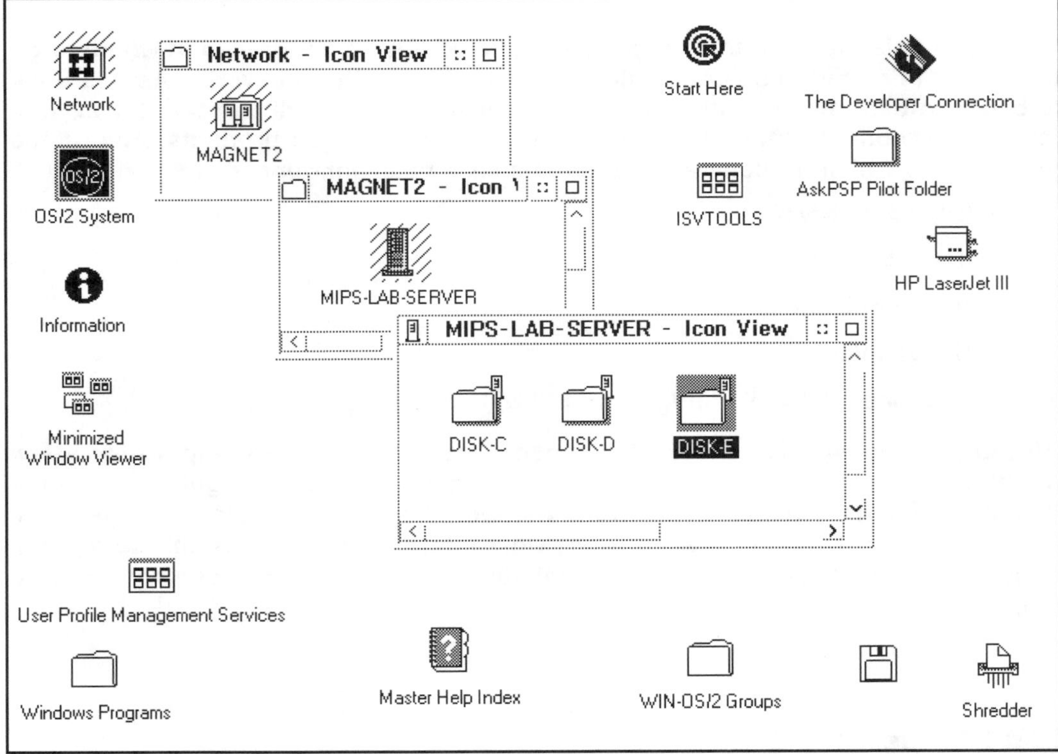

Figure 10.1 LAN Server (OS/2).

IBM LAN Server 3.0 for OS/2 provides a networking environment that's functionally equivalent to and compatible with Windows NT's built-in networking for file- and printer-sharing. Advanced management features of the two networks, however, are incompatible.

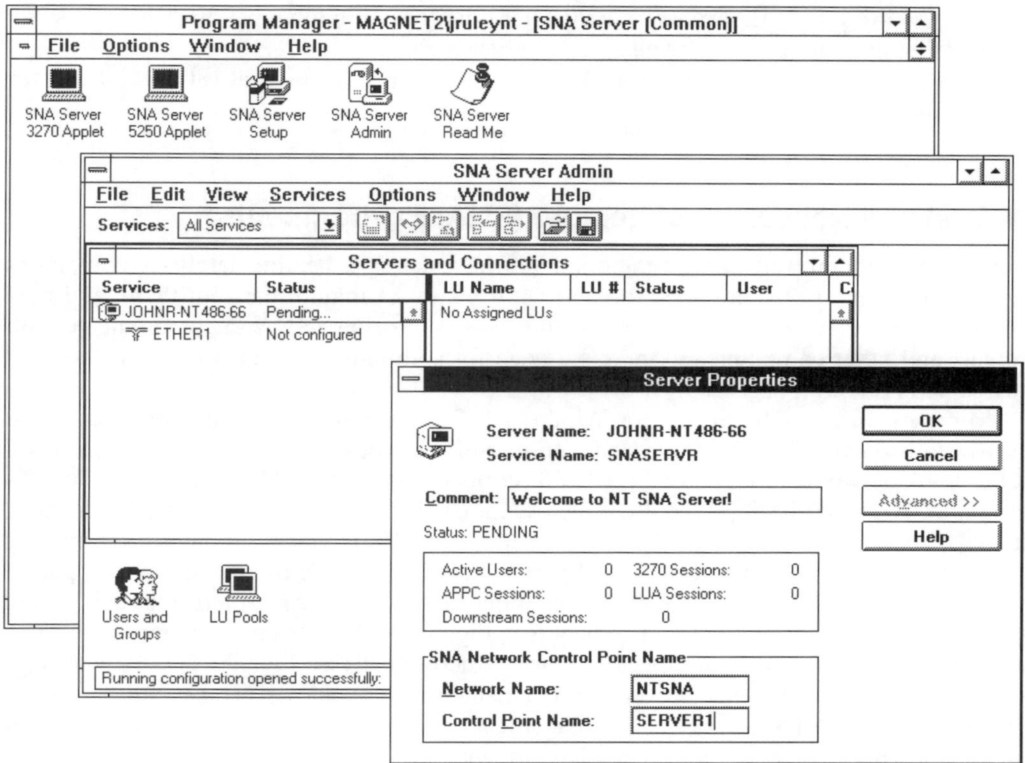

Figure 10.2 SNA Server (NT).

Microsoft SNA Server for Windows NT functions as a gateway between SNA networks and LANs. It's implemented as a Windows NT service, and takes full advantage of the Windows NT APIs to provide graphical administration, integrated security, and other advanced features. A large number of 3270 terminal emulator vendors have announced support for this product.

tocol) is functionally equivalent to NetBEUI (the Windows NT default protocol), and since both systems use SMBs, they interoperate quite well at the resource-sharing level.

The major problem with interoperating LAN Server and NT systems is synchronizing user accounts. Basically, any Windows NT user who needs to log into a LAN Server system will need a valid LAN Server user ID and password (set using LAN Server's administrative *net* command-line interface, similar to that covered in Chapter 3). Similarly, LAN Server users will need a user account on any NT server they need to access. On Windows NT Advanced Server domains, LAN Server users should be given *local* user accounts similar to those for LAN Manager users, as documented in Chapter 8.[1] It should be noted that LAN Server work-

[1]It's also possible for LAN Server users to access Windows NT resources via the NT GUEST account.

stations *must* log into a LAN Server controller—neither Windows NT nor Windows NT Advanced Server systems can validate a LAN Server login.

LAN Server 3.0 is available from IBM Corporation. Call them at (800)342-6672 for more information.

IBM Systems Network Architecture (SNA) Environments

Although IBM mainframes and minicomputers have taken a beating lately as companies move applications to PC networks, there are still plenty of mainframes out there, and they have lots of important data on them. High-end IBM systems use SNA to communicate with terminals and other computers, so there's a need for solutions to connect these SNA-based networks to NT.

Microsoft offers SNA Server for Windows NT as their solution to this problem. SNA Server installs on an NT or NTAS system and provides a protocol *gateway* between the LAN and the SNA network. It supports 3270/5250 terminal emulation, LU6.2 Advanced Peer-to-Peer connectivity, and LU0 protocols. It also supports IBM's NetView network management system. 3270/5250 terminal emulators are bundled with the product, although it offers only basic functionality; Microsoft expects third-party vendors to provide more extensive support.

SNA Server for Windows NT wasn't shipping as this book was written, although we did have a chance to experiment with a late beta (see Figure 10.2) that showed many of the same features that impressed us about SQL Server for Windows NT (see Chapter 11). As with SQL Server for Windows NT, SNA Server is implemented as a Windows NT *service*, integrates well with Windows NT's security and management systems, and provides graphical management tools. It appears to be a very impressive product.

Many vendors of terminal emulation and mainframe connectivity software have pledged support for SNA Server for Windows NT and participated in Microsoft's beta test of the product. Contacts and product names are listed in the table below.

Company and Phone	*Product Name*	*Type*	*Price*
Attachmate Corp. (800)426-6283, (206)644-4010, (206)747-9923 fax	Extra!	Terminal emulation	Not Announced
	Automation Development Kit	Mainframe application integration (HLLAPI)	$395
Digital Communications Associates (800)348-3211, (404)442-4000, (404)442-4366 fax	IRMA Workstation	Terminal emulation	Not Announced

Company and Phone	*Product Name*	*Type*	*Price*
Eicon Technology Corp .Access (514)631-2592, (514)631-3092 fax	APPC Developer's Toolkit SNA Function Mgmt Developer's Toolkit	Terminal emulation SNA protocol stack	Not Announced $1000 $1000
Microsoft Corp. (206)882-8080, (206)936-7329 fax	SNA Server for Windows NT	As described in text	Not Announced
Network Software Associates, Inc. (714)768-4013, (714)768-5049 fax	Dynacomm/Elite NT; Elite/400 NT	Terminal emulation	Not Announced
ROI Company, Inc. (800)395-6105, (404)923-6105, (404)923-0016 fax	ROI/COM/400	AS/400 serial communication	N/A
Wall Data Inc. (800)487-8622, (206)883-4777, (206)885-9250 fax	RUMBA	Terminal emulation, mainframe application integration	Not Announced

Microsoft SNA Server for Windows NT is expected to be available by the end of 1993 directly from Microsoft. Call your local dealer, or (800)426-9400.

Digital Equipment Corp. (DEC) Pathworks

Like IBM's LAN Server, DEC's Pathworks is based on Microsoft's LAN Manager technology, which simplifies the problems of interoperability with Windows NT. Pathworks clients on any platform can access Windows NT or Windows NT Advanced Server systems, as well as Pathworks servers based on the VMS, Ultrix, SCO UNIX, or OS/2 operating systems.

DEC intends to ship Pathworks for Windows NT in the fall of 1993. This product will be offered for Intel, MIPS, and DEC's own Alpha AxP processors, and will interoperate with existing Pathworks clients (Windows 3.1, DOS, OS/2, and Macintosh).

One of the most significant interoperability items in Pathworks is the support for Digital's DECnet protocol at the network transport layer. This support can coexist with TCP/IP and NetBEUI protocols on the same server or workstation. DECnet events can be viewed through the standard Windows NT Event Viewer and Performance Monitor tools. Device drivers are provided for DEC's networking cards, including Digital's FDDI (Fiber Distributed Data Interface) EISA card.

In addition to support for NT's user- and administrator-level tools, there will be a Pathworks for Windows NT Developer Kit that provides API support for Pathworks Sockets and other DEC-specific networking protocols. The Windows NT APIs for WinSock, NetBIOS, and remote procedure calls are also supported when using DECnet as the network transport protocol.

For further information, contact DEC at (508)635-8420; fax (508)635-8724.

Banyan VINES

The VINES (VIrtual NEtworking Software) network operating system from Banyan Systems has been a viable alternative to Novell and Microsoft networks, especially for large installations. Its biggest strength is the StreetTalk network name service, which lets users access resources on the network without needing to know where the services are located.

VINES server software is based on a version of AT&T UNIX, modified and supplemented by Banyan to provide a wide selection of network services. VINES can run on symmetric multiprocessor (SMP) systems with up to eight processors. Banyan sells VINES either preinstalled as part of a hardware-software bundle or as a software-only product.

Banyan is currently beta-testing VINES network support for Windows NT (see Figure 10.3) As of this writing, it is available on their Banyan Online Access BBS, (508)836-1834, as NTEAP2.ZIP (this filename is likely to change over time, so searching the BBS for "Windows NT" may be a preferable way to locate the driver files). Banyan has not yet set a final release date for the finished product.

Because VINES uses the standard Microsoft NDIS network driver model, it can coexist with NT's standard networking and use the same network card. VINES NT support includes the VINES IP transport protocol that is most commonly used by Banyan's networks. Most NT network operations are supported through VINES IP, including client-server applications such as Microsoft's SQL Server.

The Banyan VINES Toolkit, due to be released in early 1994, will provide 32-bit versions of the VINES APIs. Existing Win-16 or DOS applications that use VINES APIs are also supported. The WinSock API is supported if you use Microsoft's TCP/IP transport on NT systems and then install FTP Software's PC/TCP on DOS or Windows systems that are running VINES. Although similar, the Microsoft TCP/IP and Banyan VINES IP protocols are not interoperable.

At the user and application level, Banyan takes advantage of Windows NT's Network Provider APIs to integrate VINES networking smoothly into the environment. For example, VINES StreetTalk names show up in the browse list when you connect a network drive, along with the system and share names from NT's built-in networking. However, the first version of VINES support will not support common login, so that you will need to log in first to the NT system, then to the VINES network.

Banyan has not ported their Intelligent Messaging product to NT, but the DOS version can run using NT's DOS application support. A 16-bit Windows version is due in early 1994 that should also run under NT. Banyan plans to support MAPI in the future; when this is

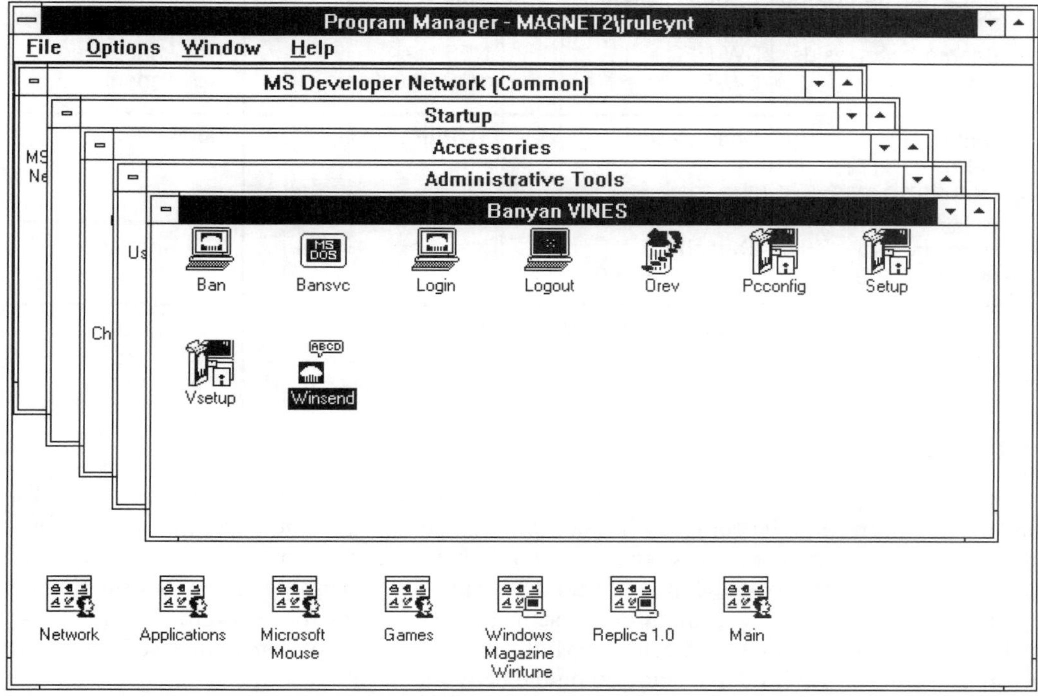

Figure 10.3 VINES (NT).

Banyan's VINES client for Windows NT is implemented as a Windows NT service and a set of Windows-based utility programs. The VINES client employs VINES/IP as the transport, and currently requires a separate login from the Windows NT security system. Banyan has announced plans for a more integrated version at a later date.

implemented you could use the 32-bit NT Mail application as the front-end software for mail sent through VINES.

For more information, call Banyan at (800)222-6926 or (508)898-1000.

UNIX Connections (NFS, TCP/IP, X Windows)

Although Windows NT supports the TCP/IP protocol and offers a simple set of TCP tools (see Chapter 6 for more information), its UNIX connections could be better. Third-party companies long-established in this field plan to offer an expanded set of utilities that include Simple Mail Transfer Protocol (SMTP), NFS client software, and X Window server software. Some of the products that have been announced include the following:

Company and Phone	*Product Name*	*Type*	*Price*
Beame & Whiteside (416)765-0822	BW-NFS BW-Services	NFS client TCP/IP utilities	Not Announced Not Announced
NetManage (408)973-7171, (408)257-6405 fax	Chameleon	TCP/IP utilities	$495
Hummingbird (415)617-4560	eXceed-NT	X server	Not Announced
SunSelect (508)442-0000	Sun PC-NFS for NT	NFS client	Not Announced

Lantastic

Artisoft's Lantastic software and network protocols are not compatible with Windows NT's built-in networking, and the company has not (yet) announced any intent to support NT. However, the Lantastic Ethernet boards are supported by NT, since they are compatible with Novell's NE2000 board. If you are willing to abandon Lantastic, you can get a network running by installing Windows NT on your high-end systems, and Windows for Workgroups on the less capable ones. DOS workstations can use Microsoft's Workgroup Connection software, but cannot act as servers (i.e., share resources) on the network.

There may be an alternative by the time we go to press—we've recently been told that Artisoft is looking into providing some sort of Lantastic-to-Windows NT bridging capability. No such capability has been shown, but we urge anyone who has a substantial investment in Lantastic to call Artisoft at (800)846-9726 and ask for more information.

11

Client/Server, Distributed Computing, and the Future of Windows NT

In this chapter, you will learn:

- **What characterizes client/server computing**
- **How Windows NT compares with other client/server platforms**
- **Why Windows NT is (currently) best suited for use in a client/server database environment**
- **Why and how Microsoft plans to migrate Windows NT (as well as Windows itself) to a distributed computing model, using OLE 2.0**

We will use Microsoft's SQL Server database for Windows NT as an example client/server application, exploring it in some detail—and in particular, examining how to leverage SQL server for Windows NT in Novell NetWare environments.

Paradigm Shifts and the Rise of Client/Server Computing

It's often said that we're now in the "Fourth Generation"[1] of computing. While deciding just what constitutes a "generation" in data processing terms is difficult, it's certainly true that

[1]Thus, 4GL for *Fourth-Generation Language* when referring to client-server development tools.

we're now into the fourth major paradigm for using computer resources. These paradigms have (so far) been as follows:

Batch Processing: The model for most computer use until the mid-1970s was that of the authors' experience[2]—queues of users waiting in line to submit "jobs"—programs and data for the computer to run (typically, a punched card deck). This model was a reflection of the sheer cost of computing—typical systems like IBM's 360/370 or Control Data's Cyber-700 cost upwards of $1 million, required dedicated support staffs numbering in the dozens, and represented a major cost center at any organization. The only way such systems could be afforded by most corporations was to have many people use the computer during the course of a single day.

Host-centric Remote Processing: Batch processing's major problem was that it required all users (or their assistants) to physically bring their jobs to the computer. In the mid-1960s, IBM developed a way around this called Remote Job Entry (RJE), which basically allowed an organization to have several card readers for batch processing in several locations—which at least made for shorter lines! However, as the cost of electronics dropped, a more sophisticated idea developed, called *time-sharing*. In this approach, many users could share a computer that would execute each user's job in a round-robin manner. Unlike the batch (or RJE) approach, however, instead of running each job to completion, a certain amount of time would be spent on your job—then it would be *suspended* while the computer worked on someone else's.

Since the computers were far faster than the terminal users (who initially communicated through teletypewriters at a speedy 11 characters per second), many people could use a single computer *at the same time*. This model persisted for years (it still exists today in many UNIX environments), but the constantly falling cost of electronics caused the teletypewriter to speed up, and evolve into a video display terminal (VDT) that could operate at much higher speeds. As more electronics became available inside the VDT, another paradigm shift occurred...

Shared Resource Servers: Eventually, several companies—notably IBM and Hewlett-Packard—added fairly sophisticated logic to their VDTs, making them into *smart terminals*. But it took someone outside the world of mainframe computing to envision the ultimate end result of this combination: Adding microprocessor-controlled logic *and* substantial local storage to the VDT made it into a completely separate unit—the *personal computer*, or PC. Initially, PCs were mainly used on a standalone basis, but the need to share expensive resources like hard disk drives and printers, not to mention sharing data, led to the idea of *resource sharing*. In this model, expensive resources are centralized on a *server*, and those resources are accessed by desktop computers (PCs) connected back to the servers over some sort of network hardware. This is the model that today is typified by Novell NetWare.

Client/Server Computing—The Fourth Generation: Inevitably, the rise of shared-resource servers provoked a reaction from the makers of classical host (i.e., mainframe) systems. The first to react was IBM, which arrived at an idea called *Connectivity* (note that capital "C"). Connectivity, in IBM-speak, meant that the PC was to be treated as a terminal that would normally be connected to the host. Since IBM was, by this time, using quite sophisti-

[2]Well, *some* of us are actually that old.

cated page-oriented VDTs in its host-centric systems, it wasn't all that much of a stretch to view the attached PC as a *client*, which would interact with a host-based *server* to accomplish the computing task at hand. The resulting *client/server* paradigm has gradually displaced the others as the mechanism of choice for high-value (especially *mission-critical*) computing tasks.

Why Is Client/Server Computing Important?

You may well ask why the client/server model has become so pervasive in high-end systems. The reason, in brief, is that it exploits the power available at *both* the client(s) *and* the server—and it does so *while keeping network traffic to a minimum.*

An example may make this clear—let's consider a typical line-of-business application, say, travel agents querying an airline database for flight availability. If this application is host-based, then every keystroke issued at every agent's terminal must be transferred over the network and handled by the host.[3] The host then must react—even if the keystroke(s) it receives are incorrect (or simply irrelevant). Even if every user of such a system *always* enters data without introducing errors (a virtual impossibility), as the usage of the system rises, the amount of network traffic rises—until, at some point, the network (which is usually the slowest component in the system) saturates. At this point the *queuing effect* comes into play (see Appendix 6), with results familiar to everyone who has ever worked on such a system—response slows down (with the side effect that impatient users make more errors, which have to be processed and slow the system down still further).

Now consider the very same application implemented using client/server principles. Instead of a VDT, the agent has a personal computer, which runs an appropriately designed client/server *front-end* application. The user never accesses the host computer directly—instead, the query on the host database is developed in an interaction between the agent and the front-end application, and only when this interaction is complete does the front-end interact with the host. Network traffic is minimized because *only* the bare minimum information needed to fulfill the query gets passed over the network (indeed, more sophisticated front-end applications have their own local data store, and fulfill some of the requests from that rather than passing all queries through to the host).

Types of Client/Server Computing

For historical reasons, the client/server model has been applied in three widely disparate environments. Windows NT can play in all of them (of course), but its unique features are most fully exploited by only one, as we will see.

---

[3]Eventually, some designers decided to offload the host by putting in sufficient electronics to handle one full screen (or *page*) of information at a time *without* host interaction, giving us *page-oriented terminals* (sometimes called *smart terminals*) of which IBM's 3270 is the prime example.

IBM SAA

Not surprisingly, as the company with the most to lose from the rise of microcomputers, it was IBM that invented a way to link them to larger systems. IBM's approach, part of their *Systems Network Architecture* (SNA) specification, basically used a PC to replace the page-oriented IBM-3270 or -5150 terminals used with mainframe-based applications. Initially, the PC just replaced the terminal (running appropriate emulation software), with little advantage gained; but the availability of computing power on the desktop gradually came to be used as a way to offload processing that didn't *have* to be done in the mainframe. This process of migrating computation to the desktop was eventually formalized in the *Application Program-to-Program Communications* (APPC) specification of SNA, and is still in use today.

The SNA/APPC networking approach basically amounts to using the old IBM-3270 page-oriented terminal protocol as a mechanism to transfer data between client and server. A front-end application, which may look totally unlike a 3270 terminal screen (in fact, it will often provide a Windows interface nowadays) will nonetheless send -3270 keystrokes to the host computer, which responds by sending information to the front-end application as if it were a -3270: one screen at a time. Windows NT brings to this environment all the features that make it a good platform for mission-critical applications; but there's little to differentiate it from other advanced operating systems for this sort of use—and in any case, the days of SNA/APPC networking are probably numbered.

Windows NT doesn't support SAA networks directly, but it's significant that one of the first applications Microsoft announced for Windows NT was SNA Server—and that it arrived with substantial third-party support from terminal emulation vendors. SNA Server for Windows NT is (briefly) covered in Chapter 10 of this book.

X/Windows

Yet another approach to distributing computer power is provided by the X/Windows system that's become popular in UNIX networks. X/Windows was originally developed by the Massachusetts Institute of Technology, and is now controlled by the X/Consortium sponsored by MIT. The X.11 standard defines X/Windows interfaces, which provide a client/server *graphics interface* for host-based applications (known as X/Clients). An X/Client is written using the X.11 APIs and protocols, and communicates through those protocols to X/Server software in the workstation computers. The workstations respond, in turn, by taking the action requested by the X/Client—drawing on the screen, in most cases. This is a powerful concept—it's as if you could execute a Windows application on someone else's computer, yet have the application draw on your screen and respond to your keyboard and mouse (more to the point, since one X/Server can access many X/Clients, X/Windows provides unique *multi-user* capabilities for graphics software).

Much like IBM's APPC/SNA approach, while X/Windows has its place, that place is primarily on the desktop—it's designed to maximize the effectiveness of host-based programs by making the workstations do all the work of drawing their own screen displays. Again, Windows NT is well suited to this kind of application in the general way that it's well suited to any high-end desktop use; but there's nothing special about it as a platform for X/Servers. While no X/Server is shipped in the Windows NT box, several are available from third parties—such as Hummingbird's eXceed/NT, covered in Chapter 10.

Client/Server Databases

The preceding two sections could make one wonder what, if anything, justifies Microsoft's incessant advertising of Windows NT as *the* operating system for client/server computing. Is it all just hype?

No!

You'll remember that IBM actually started the client/server movement by employing PCs to replace page-oriented terminals in applications like order-entry. At about the same time, a number of companies began looking at applying minicomputer technology on the other end of that connection—the host computer.

Minicomputers of the late 1970s and early 1980s approached mainframe hosts in both processing power and storage capacity. In effect, you could replace a mainframe host with a minicomputer directly (as many people did, especially using DEC's VAX series of minis). This made it possible for big corporations to *downsize*—putting applications that heretofore ran on mainframes onto minis... and *most* of these applications involved databases.

Think about virtually *any* major line-of-business application: insurance claim processing, payroll, accounts receivable, airline reservations, you name it, and a major part of the job is maintaining (and manipulating) a database. For reasons that we will get to shortly, most of these databases are described as (more or less) *relational*, and virtually all use some form of *structured query language* (SQL) as the mechanism to get data in and out (don't worry too much about the precise meaning of those buzzwords just yet—we'll get to that); so virtually all downsizing involves moving SQL databases from mainframes to minis—or at least, it *used* to.

Some years ago, Novell got the idea of putting a database on its NetWare servers. That database was Btrieve, and it was neither relational nor SQL, but it grew into a SQL NetWare Loadable Module (NLM). At around the same time, several companies—a major one being Sybase Inc.—started moving minicomputer SQL onto PCs (386s and 486s turned out to be powerful enough to run the same UNIX operating system that runs on most minis), and this turned the downsizing movement into a virtual avalanche.

You see, the same money that'll buy one mainframe—or ten minis—will buy *a whole lot of PCs.*

While all this was going on in "back room" data center operations (and making life sheer hell for MIS departments, minicomputer makers, and eventually even for IBM), another revolution was taking place on computer desktops, where Apple's Macintosh, Microsoft's Windows, and (to a lesser extent) IBM's OS/2 got users to expect a graphical interface to their applications, and forced corporations to buy really powerful systems in order to run the graphics.

Hey! Isn't a powerful desktop system *exactly* what you need for client/server? Why fiddle around with 3270 emulators or X/Windows? *Why not write a Windows- (or Mac- or OS/2-) based front-end application that sends SQL commands and has enough intelligence built in to format the database queries itself?*

Good idea, and a dozen or so companies have overturned most of the information systems doing exactly that. Now let's take a look at where Windows NT fits into all this.

SQL Server for Windows NT: A Client/Server Database

First off, we'd better explain what SQL is, and why it's important. SQL was invented—like so much else in the computer industry—by IBM, as a lingua franca for *relational databases*. Without going too deep into the theory involved,[4] basically relational databases seek to protect us from ourselves. Nonrelational databases are usually organized as some form of sequential list—an approach that works well until the list becomes very large, or very complicated (sometimes, parts of the list are *pointers* to other lists—which makes things get complicated in a hurry). Relational databases are organized in such a way that you can always be *certain* that a properly formatted query will have an answer—albeit a ridiculously huge one.

SQL is the mechanism that assures the queries are properly formatted—it's a special language for data access that makes it *impossible*[5] to issue an illegal query. Moreover, by convention modern SQL implementations include transaction-locking mechanisms that assure database integrity even if a query fails—the query isn't *committed* until all aspects of the transaction are complete.

But enough of the details. The point you need to understand is that *most* serious, large-scale databases for business use are relational, and use some form of SQL. Now where does Windows NT fit in?

A Brief History of SQL Server

As mentioned above, Sybase was one of the pioneers in bringing SQL databases first to UNIX minicomputers, and then to PCs (when they got powerful enough to run UNIX). In addition, Sybase licensed its technology to other companies who wanted to create powerful database products. One of those companies was Microsoft.

Microsoft SQL Server for OS/2 was (and is) a direct port of the UNIX-based Sybase SQL Server products to the OS/2 platform. It leverages the inherent efficiency of OS/2 to pro-

[4]If you *must* know, it's *set theory*. There—aren't you glad you asked? See *SQL Self-Teaching Guide* by Stephenson and Hartwig (in "For More Information" at the end of this chapter) for a somewhat lengthier explanation.

[5]Well—*almost* impossible—the ability of people to screw up knows few absolute limits!

vide minicomputer-class database services on 286-, 386- and 486-based PCs. It's also designed to integrate well with Microsoft's LAN Manager networking system to give good multi-user performance, and it's become something of a standard over the years.

Unfortunately, SQL Server for OS/2 has its share of problems, among which are the 16MB barrier (currently, SQL Server for OS/2 is a 16-bit OS/2 1.3 product, which can only address 16MB RAM), limiting the size of the databases (and number of users) it can support, incomplete exploitation of OS/2's multithreaded variable-priority process model (a legacy of the original Sybase design, which came from the pre-Mach, nonthreaded UNIX world), inability to scale onto more powerful platforms (like RISC or SMP), etc.—besides, given Microsoft's recent (and extended) donnybrook with IBM, how would it look for *Microsoft* to go out and push an *OS/2-based product*?

This must have been frustrating to Microsoft, because for years they've been exponents of the power available in desktop computers, and here was a virtual revolution taking place in that field, with Microsoft getting only a little piece of it. It was time for a change.

The change, of course, is the arrival of Windows NT, which makes a much better platform for SQL Server than OS/2 (or UNIX for that matter) ever did!

SQL Server for Windows NT—Specifications

Microsoft's goals with SQL Server for Windows NT are quite ambitious—they quite literally (and seriously) want to make themselves a first-class power in the downsizing arena, by providing a client/server database that's not only competitive, but breathtaking. They have two principle weapons for this: *scalability*, and *ease of use*.

Scalability draws directly on the Windows NT scaling features we first examined in Chapter 1 (and detail in Appendix 5). SQL Server for Windows NT is multithreaded, and therefore automatically takes advantage of SMP hardware. It's also portable—initial beta versions appeared simultaneously for Intel x86 and MIPS R4x00 architectures (and a version for DEC's Alpha is expected soon as this is written). It's a full 32-bit application, breaking SQL Server for OS/2's "16MB barrier" at a stroke.

As for ease of use, SQL Server for Windows NT integrates directly with Windows NT. It is implemented as a Windows NT *service*, and so takes advantage of the service control interface, Control Panel (or Server Manager) Services interface, automatic startup, and other services interface features. It exports data counters to the Windows NT Performance Monitor and so may be monitored and tuned remotely. It sends error messages to the Windows NT event viewer.

Finally, all—and we really do mean *all*—SQL Server for Windows NT functions and tools are available from graphical user interfaces. SQL Server for Windows NT installs from a CD-ROM (or diskette)-based graphical installation program, and provides graphical tools for administration, object management, configuration, and security—all of which, in addition to having a graphical user interface, are completely networkable and therefore provide for easy remote administration. The integration into Windows NT is seamless and the overall implementation bears as little resemblance to most high-end database tools as Windows NT itself does to a Seventies-era character-based OS.

Microsoft has also leveraged the built-in networking features of Windows NT to give SQL Server for Windows NT outstanding multi-user LAN-based client capabilities. SQL Server for Windows NT supports simultaneous access over multiple protocols—including both TCP/IP and Microsoft's own NetWare-compatible NWLink protocol stack. The latter allows SQL Server for Windows NT running on Windows NT to be dropped into a NetWare LAN, *and be immediately available to NetWare clients without modification*. In effect, it looks exactly like a SQL NLM—but has the advantage of running on a far more powerful application platform.

Finally, SQL Server for Windows NT exploits structured exception handling and Windows NT's fault-tolerance features to provide a very high degree of reliability. Should a query fail, it will take down the data structures and threads related to just that one query—*not* the entire SQL Server process. (OS/2 and UNIX implementations of SQL Server, by contrast, run either as a single process, or on a one-process-per-query model. In the former, crashing a query takes down the entire server; in the latter it takes down the entire query process.)

These are ambitious goals. Let's see how close Microsoft has come to achieving them.

How Well Does SQL Server for NT Work in Practice?

Let's begin with the issue that ultimately determines whether a database can be used for a given purpose—*performance*. Fortunately, the area of database performance is one where it's not necessary to wade through a lot of incompatible manufacturer's claims. There is a single, recognized standard for database performance measurement—the *Transaction Processing Council's*[6] TPC-A and -B benchmarks (mainly the -B benchmark, which simulates teller operations in a hypothetical banking application). The TPC benchmarks are well defined, and a full-disclosure report is required before any vendor is permitted to use the name TPC-A or TPC-B (as each is trademarked).

Microsoft has worked with Compaq computer to get TPC-B benchmarks on SQL Server for Windows NT (running on Compaq ProLiant 486-50 and dual-Pentium systems)—Figure 11.1 shows how it compares with other systems on which TPC-B has been performed. These are *very* impressive results—even on basic 486/50 hardware, SQL Server for Windows NT outperforms a single-CPU SPARC workstation—and at far lower cost (it's notable that the 486/50 MHz single-CPU result is *four times faster* than for OS/2 SQL Server running on the same hardware). The dual Pentium result illustrates the scalability of well-designed 32-bit software on SMP hardware—it outperforms everything except the VAX 9000 (which it approaches) at very moderate cost. Microsoft internal tests (not yet submitted to the TPC for review) show that this scaling also applies to RISC-based systems, which deliver even better performance.

The 4 : 1 difference between the OS/2 and NT versions is a direct reflection of the 32-bit design and full exploitation of threading and Windows NT security (of course, SQL Server for Windows NT also dispenses with the "16MB limit" at a stroke!), but what's really impressive

[6]c/o Shanley Public Relations, 777 N. First St., Suite 600, San Jose, CA 95112.

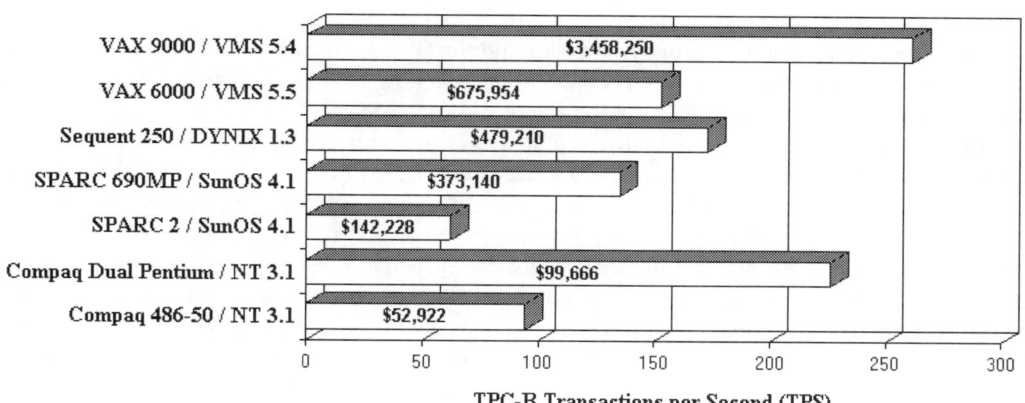

Figure 11.1 SQL Server Performance.

Tests using the Transaction Processing Council "B" benchmark (which simulates teller operations at a medium-sized bank) demonstrate that properly designed client/server applications on Windows NT can functionally replace mainframe-based equivalents.

here is the scaling of SQL Server for Windows NT on varying hardware—there is a 3 : 1 difference between the Dual MIPS performance and the single-486. If this scaling holds up for larger SMP systems—and there's no reason to believe it won't[7]—then the upper limit for SQL Server for Windows NT would *probably* be somewhere in the range of several thousand tps on a Sequent WinServer with thirty-two 486 processors. This is *more than ten times the performance of a VAX-9000!*

But what's even more impressive is that a single-CPU 486-50 system (which outperforms a single-CPU SPARC) can be configured as a completely usable single-user system for under $5,000 complete (hardware and software). This is a completely new situation where high-end SQL databases are concerned. Up to now, SQL databases have been almost exclusively used in multi-user systems. Single-user systems have remained within the purview of nonrelational databaes like dBase, Paradox, and Clipper.

Windows NT changes the rules at the low end, just as it does at the high end. Since it combines the multitasking operating system with a Windows user interface, it's entirely possible to install a single-user system based on Windows NT, running single-user SQL Server for Windows NT on it as a desktop database. The cost for such a system is slightly higher than the cost for a comparable nonrelational system (largely because Windows NT requires more expensive hardware); but the SQL Server for Windows NT solution can be upgraded to a multi-user database by purchasing a multi-user SQL Server for Windows NT license (and, if necessary, upgrading the hardware). More importantly, the SQL databases developed on such a system will scale onto much larger systems when growth is required.

[7]Over and above that nagging issue of *contention*—see Appendix 5.

This seamless scalability from low-cost single-user systems all the way up to SMP systems that deliver mainframe (or better!) performance is new to SQL Server for Windows NT; it hasn't any equivalent in any other database that we know of.

In fairness, not all SQL Server for Windows NT features are specific to a Windows NT implementation. Microsoft is working on a new, 32-bit version of SQL Server to run on OS/2 2.x systems; it will have no 16MB limit and will fully exploit OS/2's multithreading; potentially it can offer single-user capability comparable to the NT version. (Since OS/2 also provides a 16-bit Windows subsystem, front-ends developed for Windows should run equally well on OS/2 or Windows NT.) It will not, however, have the benefit of portability to non-Intel platforms, nor will it be able to run on SMP systems[8]; so it won't offer the seamless scalability that SQL Server for Windows NT has; but it will probably be a good alternative in smaller sites.

For that matter, *any* 32-bit operating system that supports multithreading (the Carnegie-Mellon MACH version of Unix, for instance) could support SQL Server for Windows NT-style SMP support, and a number of other advanced SQL Server for Windows NT features (improved optimizer design, per-extent logging, reentrant lock management, negotiated network packet size—up to 32K—in named pipe environments), are not dependent on NT features at all.

With all that said, however, SQL Server for Windows NT does offer the tremendous advantage of giving users a wide range of hardware options *without* needing to change their database or operating system—and that's important. SQL may be the "lingua franca" of high-end databases, but there are huge differences between SQL implementations by different vendors, and migrating from one vendor's SQL to another's (or even from a particular vendor's SQL on one operating system to another), can be quite difficult.

Finally, while SQL Server for Windows NT is a fine database, there are some Windows NT features that its designers chose not to exploit. SQL Server for Windows NT retains its own internal cache management scheme for the transaction log, inherited from the original Sybase product, so it does not take full advantage of Windows NT's built-in cache management (although it does get a significant benefit from NT's disk caching[9]). It also doesn't appear to significantly exploit Windows NT's memory-mapped files capability—again, probably because the Sybase code wasn't designed that way. That's a pity, because the combination of memory mapped files (which can be shared between threads in a process) and multithread-

---

[8]IBM is working on a dual-processor version of OS/2; but it is an *asymmetric* design in which only one CPU is used for general computation, while the other is dedicated to I/O operations. An advanced microkernel-based operating system called Workplace OS is also under development that will offer Windows NT-like capabilities. In any case, we don't expect Workplace OS to ship until this book has been in print for some time.

[9]As well as other high-throughput NT features, such as overlapped I/O.

ing would seem to be ideal for implementing databases. Perhaps future versions of SQL Server for Windows NT will exploit this feature.[10]

With the theory under our belts, let's take a direct look at what's involved in setting up and using SQL Server for Windows NT on our own LAN.

SQL Server for Windows NT: A Guided Tour

We call this section a Guided Tour because that's just what we mean it to be—a "high-level" overview of a client/server database that's really well optimized for Windows NT. This section is *not* meant to substitute for the the SQL Server for Windows NT manuals—it can't. SQL databases are complicated, and SQL Server for Windows NT is no exception. It's true that the author of this section[11] was able to get SQL Server for Windows NT up-and-running in less than a day from a standing start (pretty impressive considering that he'd never set up a SQL database before); but you really do need to *study* the SQL Server for Windows NT manuals if you're to have any hope of using it effectively.

You'll also need a good book on SQL—we recommend *SQL Self-Teaching Guide*, by Stephenson and Hartwig, which is referenced at the end of this chapter. While this book is written around Gupta Technologies' SQLbase product, we can say with confidence that the instructions and exercises work with SQL Server for Windows NT as well.

With that said, let's start our tour with the SQL Server for Windows NT installation program. In contrast to the installation of most high-end databases (and other back-end software generally), SQL Server for Windows NT is installed from a professionally designed Windows-based setup program (Figure 11.2). This will guide you through the step-by-step process of setting up SQL Server for Windows NT on your installation.

To install SQL Server for Windows NT on your system, you will (of course) need Windows NT or Windows NT advanced server, and you'll need at least 16MB RAM (on an Intel-based system; you'll need more on a RISC-based system). During the installation you'll be asked whether you want to operate SQL Server for Windows NT using integrated, mixed, or SQL security. Integrated security means that SQL Server for Windows NT will use the Windows NT user accounts database, which makes administering the system much easier, and has the additional advantage (especially in enterprise environments) that inter-domain trust links can be used to make SQL Server for Windows NT available to users outside the local domain. It's only available for trusted (i.e.: Windows NT named pipe) links. The standard SQL Security opton is like that used on other operating systems. The mixed security option tries to log users in with the standard Windows NT user information first, and then falls back on the standard approach if the Windows NT login doesn't authenticate properly. Later, you can also use

[10]If not, it's likely that some other vendor's NT database product(s) will!

[11]John D. Ruley.

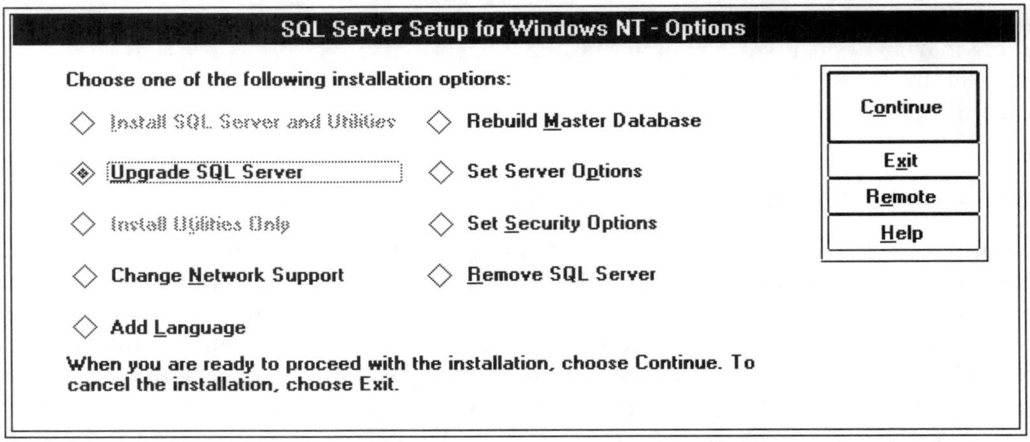

SQL Server Setup for Windows NT - Options

Choose one of the following installation options:

Install SQL Server and Utilities
Rebuild Master Database
Upgrade SQL Server
Set Server Options
Install Utilities Only
Set Security Options
Change Network Support
Remove SQL Server
Add Language

When you are ready to proceed with the installation, choose Continue. To cancel the installation, choose Exit.

Continue
Exit
Remote
Help

Figure 11.2 SQL Server Setup.

In contrast to most "back-end" line-of-business and database applications, SQL Server for Windows NT features a well-implemented graphical interface for all functions—including setup.

SQL Setup to change the security (or other optional) settings, rebuild the master database, upgrade SQL Server for Windows NT, or remove it from the server.

During the initial installation (or later, if you decide to change the settings), you'll need to specify what protocols you want SQL Server for Windows NT to support. By default, it supports a NetBIOS-based named pipes protocol that's interoperable with that used by SQL Server on OS/2 systems. It can also support a STREAMS-based protocol for use in TCP/IP environments, and an SPX sockets-based protocol in conjunction with Microsoft's NWLink IPX/SPX driver stack that makes it available to NetWare clients. You'll need to pick the system that's appropriate to your installation, bearing in mind that the TCP/IP-based approach is the only one that Windows NT systems can use for routable WAN connections in enterprise environments.

Incidentally, if you have SQL Server for OS/2, or Sybase SQL Server on UNIX systems, you can migrate your datasets, tables, etc. completely seamlessly—SQL Server for Windows NT is completely compatible with datasets and Transact-SQL scripts from SQL Server version 4.2 on other platforms. The migration process is handled automatically by the SQL Setup program—in fact, it's even possible to switch back and forth between OS/2 SQL Server and SQL Server for Windows NT, using the same database and query files with both versions (although you cannot, of course, run both at the same time!).

Once SQL Server is installed, you'll see a SQL Server for Windows NT common program group in Windows NT Program Manager (Figure 11.3). Note that *all* SQL Server for Windows NT functions are accessible from the programs in this group—even straight command-line SQL can best be issued using the ISQL/w utiltity (although you *can* run a straight character-mode ISQL session from a Windows NT command prompt, if you really insist!).

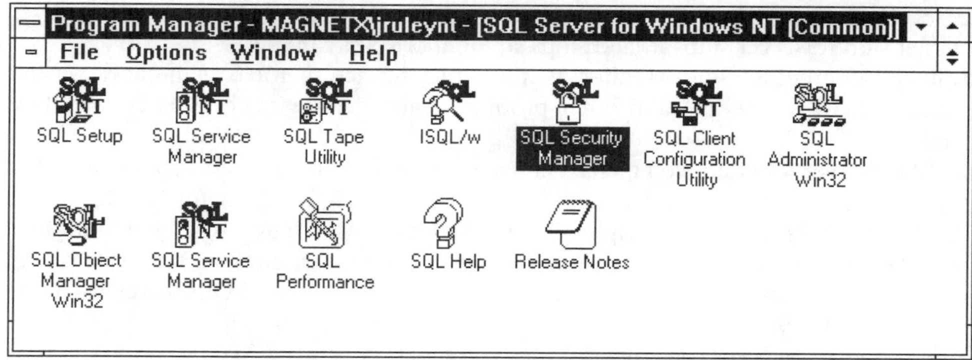

Figure 11.3 SQL Server PROGMAN group.

After installing SQL Server for Windows NT, you'll find a common group in Windows NT Program Manager containing icons for all SQL Server for Windows NT functions.

You start SQL Server for Windows NT from SQL Service Manager (Figure 11.4). This silly-looking interface is really just a custom hook into the Windows NT services database—you can start SQL Server for Windows NT just as easily from Control Panel (or Server Manager on Windows NT Advanced Servers) /Services—which gives you the additional option to have SQL Server automatically started on system boot (ideal if you keep your server locked

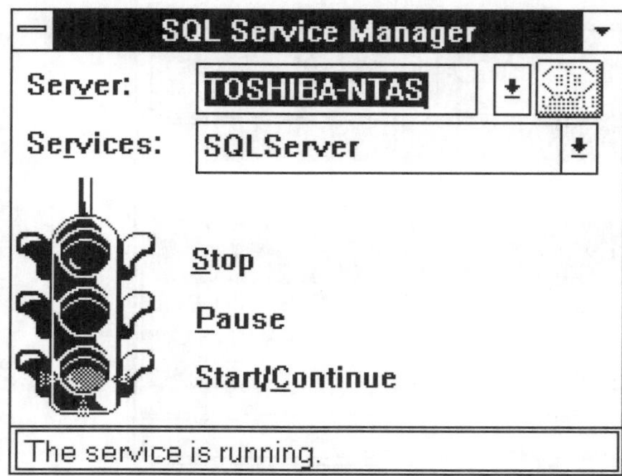

Figure 11.4 SQL Service Manager.

If there is one place in the SQL Server for Windows NT user interface where the designers went overboard, this may be it. Double-clicking on the green start/continue light starts SQL Server for Windows NT.

up). SQL Server can also be started and stopped from the command line: net start sqlserver will start it, net stop sqlserver stops it (and stops sqlmonitor if it's running).

A companion process, SQL Monitor, is a separate service that acts as a check on the first, detecting runaway queries (and other problems) and dealing with them before they become fatal.

Once SQL Server's started, you manage it using the SQL Administrator application (Figure 11.5). From here you can control virtually every aspect of SQL Server for Windows NT, determining which users have access rights for which databases, controlling a wide range of configuration settings (set using Manage/Configure SQL Server after clicking the System button in the toolbar), including the max worker threads count (by default, SQL Server for Windows NT runs each worker thread per query, which can be inefficient when handling lots of clients simultaneously on SMP systems), setting how much system RAM SQL Server is permitted to use, and determining whether the temporary database (tempdb) used for all implicit and explicit transient objects, including query optimization, is stored in RAM or on disk.

Tuning SQL Server for Windows NT for maximum performance is largely a matter of getting these settings set to their optimal values—a task that's eased by SQL Server for Windows NT's use of the Windows NT Performance Monitor as a reporting and measurement tool. A SQL Performance icon in the SQL Server for Windows NT program group launches a Program Manager session with SQL counters preselected; using this makes it easy to view the operation of SQL Server for Windows NT during queries. If you need to stress the system with

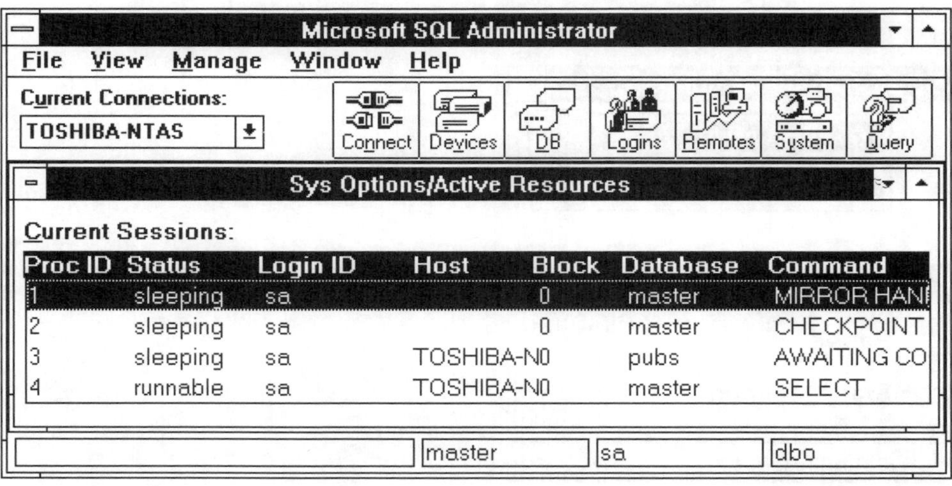

Figure 11.5 SQL Administrator.

The Administrator's interface for SQL Server for Windows NT follows Windows NT conventions, providing a completely graphical point-and-click user interface for SQL administration and management tasks.

a large number of simulated clients, the SQLSTRESS utility (available on CompuServe—go MSSQL) can do this for you.

SQL Server for Windows NT can leverage the disk-striping and RAID support built into Windows NT and Advanced Server, instead of (or in addition to) dividing up disk space into SQL Volumes, as is done in other operating systems. Using NT's disk striping generally produces better results.

But the crown jewel of the SQL Server user interface, in our opinion, is the SQL Object Manager application (Figure 11.6). This little gem lets you create, modify, back up, reproduce, import and export, and otherwise manipulate your databases *without writing a single line of SQL code!*

We can't resist giving you one example of SQL Object Manager's power: If you select a database and click the Scripts button, you'll get a Generate SQL Scripts dialog. Checking the boxes and selecting the objects as shown in Figure 11.7 will cause SQL Object Manager to automatically generate a script that completely replicates all the objects in the database—not the *data*, but the *structure*. For anyone who's ever been faced with the need to reverse-

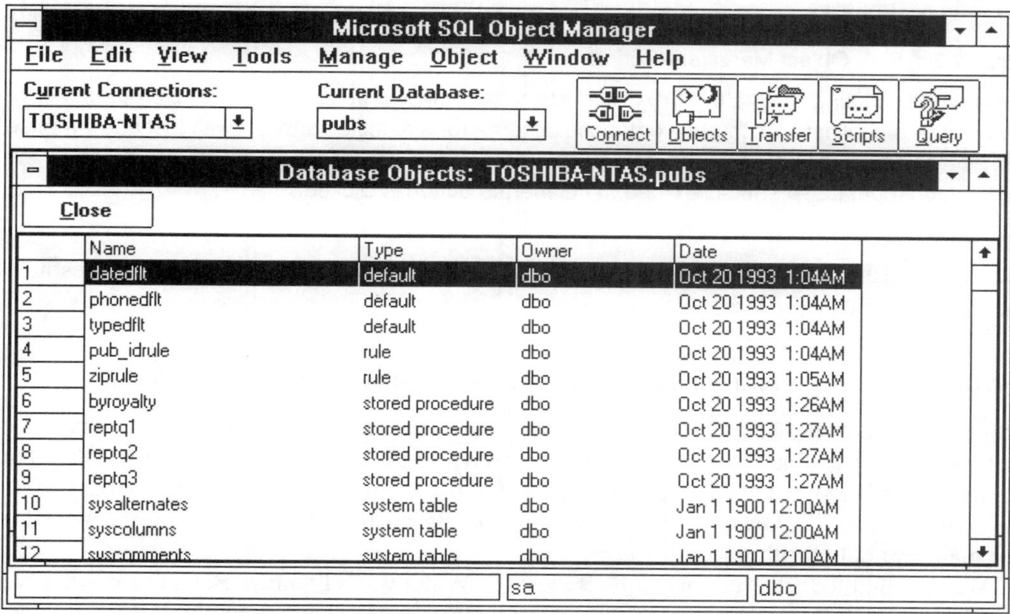

Figure 11.6 SQL Object Manager.

SQL Server for Windows NT even provides a graphical interface for managing data objects within the SQL database structure. Using this tool, tables, databases, and indices can be created, deleted or modified at will.

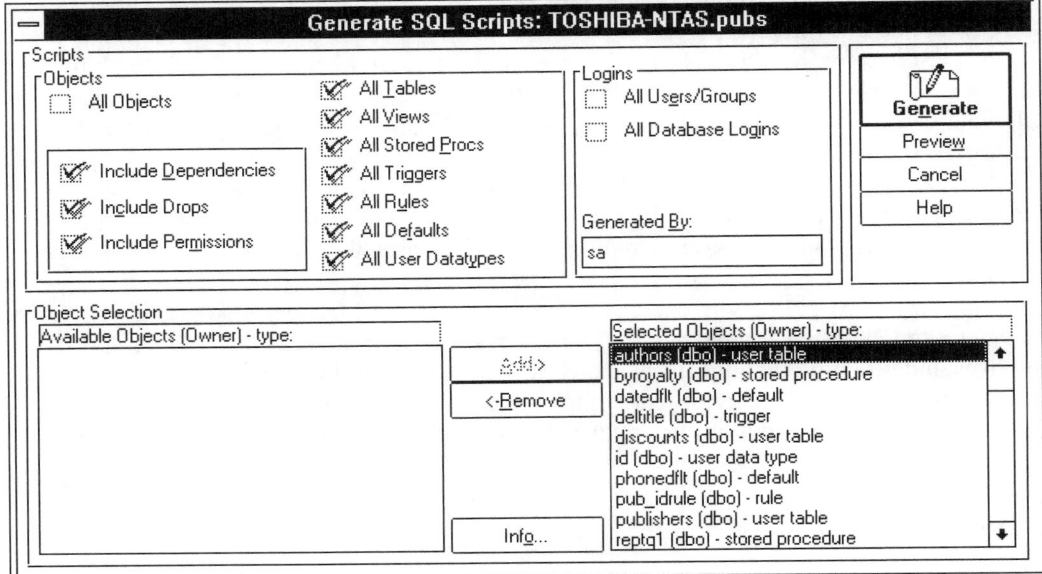

Figure 11.7 SQL Object Manager—scripts.

An automated scripting feature in SQL Object Manager makes it possible for a SQL programmer or administrator to duplicate a complete database schema (or a selected subset) with just a few mouse clicks. The settings shown here, for instance, will cause the generation of a script to recreate the standard "pubs" database structure when the Generate button is clicked.

engineer an existing database in order to apply it somewhere else, this capability comes near to magic!

Conclusion—SQL Server for Windows NT: Client/Server Comes of Age

No doubt the preceding section comes off sounding like an ad for Microsoft SQL Server for Windows NT. In part that's because we're impressed—but it's also a reflection of the fact that SQL Server for Windows NT is the first (and so far, the *only*) true client-server database to be made available for Windows NT. *That*, not any pro-Microsoft favoritism, is why we picked it as the main example for this section.

We're delighted[12] to see that SQL Server for Windows NT validates much of what we said in Chapter 1 (where we repeatedly used a client/server database example)—it really does

[12] It really goes beyond that—Chapter 1 was written months before we had any opportunity to sit down and work with a SQL Server beta. The correspondence between what we *hoped* would be true of Windows NT-based network applications, and what SQL-NT actually *does* is slightly astonishing.

take advantage of multithreading and portability to make itself scalable from standalone single-user applications all the way up to enterprise installations. We hope that other vendors will follow it with choices that are just as good—they'd have a hard time doing any better.

More choices *are* on the way. Most of the large database makers have either committed to releasing Windows NT products or at least stated an interest in doing so—rumors are even floating around that IBM may do a Windows NT version of its DB2 database (although we've not been able to confirm this). Within a year, you'll have many choices for database support in Windows NT.

Now that we've looked at the status quo—which seems pretty good from this vantage point—it's time to look into the future. Where is Windows NT headed, and *why* is Microsoft codenaming its new Operating System prototypes after cities?

Information at Your Fingertips—The Future of Windows NT?

Two years ago at Comdex, Bill Gates[13] gave a talk on a concept he called "Information at Your Fingertips" (IAYF). This was a general concept based on the following ideas:

- Ubiquity of computers
- "More personal" PCs
- Data made independent of location
- Greater use of nontraditional data types like voice and live (or animated) video

He didn't just give a slide show and make a speech—the concept was illustrated with an impressively produced multimedia video presentation to drive home his points. This showed computers being used in a much wider range of situations than just traditional desktop use—truly mobile (including pen-based) computing was a big part of the presentation. So were "multimedia" elements like videoconferencing and video memos sent by electronic mail. But at the heart of the presentation lay a very powerful concept: That end-users shouldn't need to know (or care) where and how data is stored.

If we might mix our examples a bit, the first episode of *Star Trek, The Next Generation*[14] had one character bring up a map of her ship's internal layout. She did this by saying "Tell me the location of Commander Data," *not* by saying something like "Display MAPFILE\PERSONNEL\LOCATION\DATA," as we'd have to do today—the *computer* did the locating, *not the human operator.*

In Gates' Comdex presentation, this was handled a little differently—instead of employing a File Manager-style interface to find files, he (and the actors in his IAYF show) used a query-based interface that worked a lot more like our *Star Trek* example: rather than remembering (and regurgitating) the directory path to a file, a combination of dates, subjects, media type, and creator name fields was used to create a query; and the result of that query was the

[13]William H. Gates III, CEO of Microsoft Corp.

[14]A production of Paramount Pictures.

information in question—truly Information at Your Fingertips! But that was all staged—does IAYF have any bearing on reality? And if so, where does Windows NT fit in?

Earlier in this chapter we examined the client/server computing model, and spent some time examining SQL Server for Windows NT as an example. We saw how Microsoft leveraged Windows NT's unique capabilities to provide an outstanding client/server applications platform. Now we'll look ahead a bit, examine the concept of distributed computing, and (based on what we've learned in the rest of the book—and some early information available to us about the Windows 4.0 user interfaces), we'll make some predictions about what the next major version of Windows NT, *Windows Cairo*, will be like.

Distributed Computing

Earlier in this chapter we examined the classical host-based and shared-resource models of computing and saw how client/server computing naturally grew out of a combination of those two approaches (and the need to minimize network traffic). Let's consider a *fifth* model of computing which, to a certain degree, has actually competed with client/server computing up to now. This is the *distributed computing* model.

In distributed computing, computing resources are distributed throughout the machines on the network and computation is done wherever it makes the most sense on the network. In particular, most computational models for distributed processing attempt to *equalize* resource utilization across the network. For instance, if computation work needs to be done, the system finds an idle processor and does the work there.

The beauty of distributed computing is that it can fully leverage *all* network resources in a way that is impossible for any of the other models to achieve. Even the client/server model—with all the advantages we discussed earlier in this chapter—can only leverage the resources of a *particular* client and a *particular* server to accomplish a *particular* task. It doesn't matter that there may be over a hundred CPUs on your network sitting idle—if the server's bogged, no work will get done.

A limited degree of distributed processing is possible by operating multiple servers (for example, having database functions provided by a database server, file functions provided by a file server, etc.). The limitation of this scheme is that you're still locked into the client/server model for any *particular* process—if the database server becomes overloaded with requests, the system will slow down even though the other servers are idle.

There's no way in a multiple client/server model to distribute the database server functions among other servers on the system—a single bogged server can slow down the entire network. In a Windows NT environment with properly designed server software[15] that exploits symmetric multiprocessing, we can try to throw a bigger server at the problem—but at some

[15]Such as Microsoft SQL Server for Windows NT. Are you getting the idea that we're impressed with this product?

point, even the largest SMP will run out of steam.[16]

What's needed is a way to distribute the functions of the database server among multiple servers on the network. *That's* the goal of distributed processing.

From a programmer's perspective, the key element in any distributed computing scheme is a Remote Procedure Call (RPC). Windows NT 3.1 provides a very powerful RPC implementation[17] that's partly compatible with the Open Systems Foundation Distributed Computing Environment (DCE) RPC. Using RPCs, a programmer can write a program that will call functions transparently—*without knowing whether the functions are executed on the local computer or on another computer on the network.* A good example is the distributed Mandelbrot sample program provided by Microsoft in the Windows NT Software Development Kit (SDK). Figure 11.8 illustrates this program, with the graphical console running on a Gateway 486 machine and the computational engine running on a MIPS R4000 server machine. The Performance Monitor, which is shown overlapping the Mandelbrot window, shows the actual system loads on the two systems—and you'll notice that the MIPS machine is actually undergoing a more severe CPU load than the local machine, *even though the local machine is doing all the display work.*

This is a form of client/server computing—the MIPS machine is functioning as a *compute server* for the Mandelbrot demo application. However, a programmer *could* construct a variant of this program that would have an additional intermediate step: When making the remote procedure call that will carry out computations the program could have a form of *indirection,* in which the remote procedure calls were issued to different machines based on a network task scheduler—on detection of idle time, for instance. The programmer would not know (or care) *where* the computation was being executed.

What is lacking from the present Windows NT implementation, then, is some way of assigning the RPCs such that neither the programmer nor the computer user (nor ideally the system administrator) will need to know the specifics of which machine receives the assignment. Perhaps another example will help to clear this issue up. It's common in the publishing business to run out of disk space on the production file server (or servers) as an issue is produced. This used to happen at *WINDOWS Magazine* constantly. As the production staff finished a particular issue, they created a large number of PostScript images—these take up a great deal of disk space. Several years ago one of us[18] constantly found himself frustrated with the following situation: The production server available at that time was an OS/2 LAN Manager computer (a lineal ancestor of Windows NT) with about one-half gigabyte of disk space. We would consistently overshoot that disk capacity by about 100MB, *yet we had over a dozen*

[16]Probably when the network itself is saturated with traffic—I have often wondered what sort of network card could possibly keep up with a 32-processor Sequent WinServer under full load!—JDR.

[17]Documented in Appendix 1.

[18]John D. Ruley.

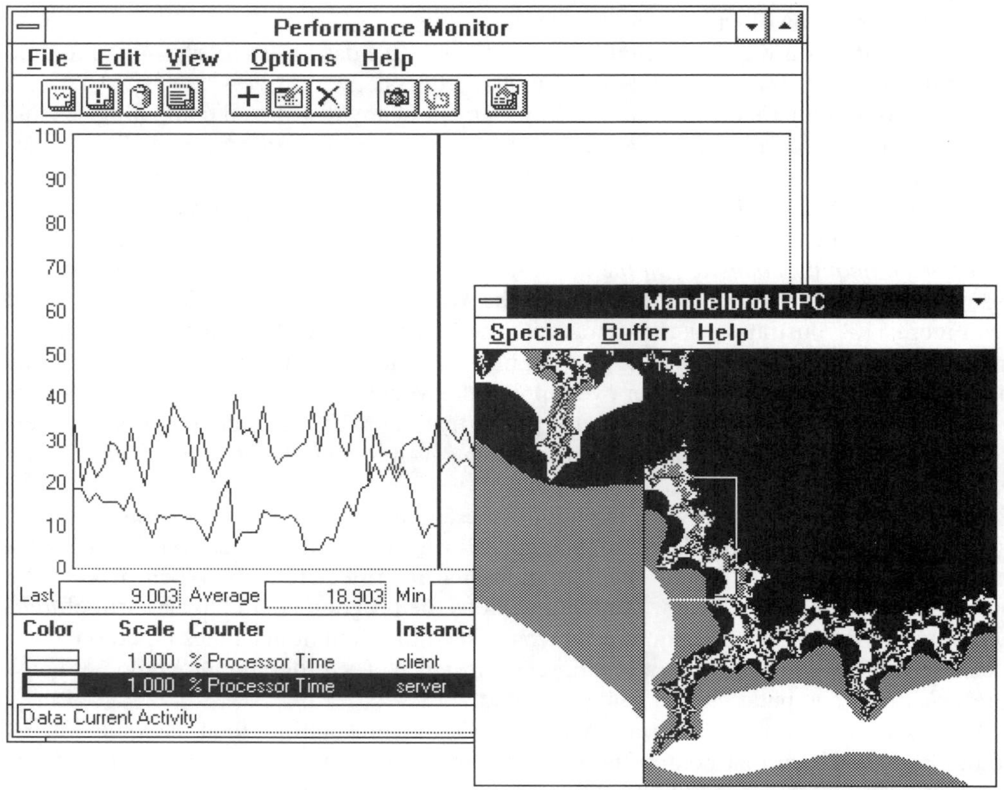

Figure 11.8 Mandelbrot RPC application.

Microsoft's 32-bit Windows System Development Kit (SDK) includes this example of a true client/server application. The client application, shown in the foreground, is responsible for all screen updates but does not perform the Mandelbrot fractal transform computations necessary to draw the Figure. Instead, it uses Remote Procedure Calls (RPCs) to execute the computations in a separate server program which need not execute on the same system. The Performance Monitor screen shows % CPU Time for both processes.

workstations on that same network with a total excess disk capacity far in excess of 100MB. Why couldn't we use the excess disk capacity on the other machines on the network?

With Windows NT (or Windows for Workgroups), this is in fact possible in an-ad hoc way. Each system can have a public shared directory, and by manually distributing files onto those public shared directories you could take advantage of the excess disk capacity. Yet this would create an administrative nightmare. If you're looking for a particular file do you look for it on \\johnspc, \\davespc, or \\main_server? What's needed, again, is a mechanism for adding a *level of indirection.* That is, one needs the ability to refer to a disk storage location, say \\DistributedDiskspace, *without being concerned about the physical location that's being referred to.*

Obviously, what's needed is some kind of mechanism for resolving those abstracted references into the precise physical references needed to locate the object in question. We say *object* because this concept need not apply only to disk files—it could as easily apply to named pipe addresses, for instance, or to compute services as mentioned above. The key to a fully effective form of distributed computing is *an object-oriented namespace.* This sounds like a big buzzword. It's not. What it really means is quite simple: We need a *database*—and that's exactly what lies hidden at the heart of Microsoft's OLE 2.0 programming model.

Chicago: OLE 2.0 and Windows 4.0

Now that we've looked at the large-scale *strategic* issue of distributed computing, let's discuss *tactics.* In particular, let's consider what distributed computing might look like from an end-user perspective.

As we've discussed, the central issue of distributed computing is the creation of an object-oriented name space. That is, you stop referring to physical disk drives as locations for files, and you stop referring to servers as locations for computations such as database queries. Instead, you refer to *network objects,* which may span many storage volumes or many servers. Clearly the Program Manager/File Manager user interface of Windows 3.1 (and the current version of Windows NT) is inadequate for this kind of situation.

Microsoft realized this some time ago and began creating the foundation for an entirely new type of user interface. This foundation is the second generation of the Object Linking and Embedding (OLE) specification. OLE 1.0 is familiar to most Windows users as the mechanism by which one can, for instance, embed a Paintbrush picture in the middle of a word processing document. Double-clicking on the picture then brings up the Paintbrush application with the picture loaded, so that it can be edited by the recipient. It's a cute feature that is *somewhat* more convenient than simple cut-and-paste.

OLE 2.0 is designed to go far beyond this capability—and it does so (pause for effect) by providing an object-oriented namespace (and thereby providing the all-important additional level of abstraction that we've determined is needed for the large-scale concept of distributed computing to become effective). In OLE 1.0 objects can either be *embedded in* or *linked to* a parent document. An object embedded in a parent document has its data embedded within the parent file. Among other things, this has the side effect that one can now receive relatively short word processor documents that take up megabytes of disk space because of an embedded Paintbrush picture.

A more sophisticated alternative to embedding the data is to link it. In a linked object, the only thing embedded in the parent document is a *reference* to the file that is linked to the document. Unfortunately OLE 1.0 only understood how to refer to direct physical addresses. These could, in fact, be network addresses—it's possible (using the OLE 1.0 object packager included with Windows NT, for instance), to provide a link to a network object—but you have to specify the precise address of the network object.

This gets away very nicely from the problem of multimegabyte word processing documents because of embedded pictures, but since it requires a precise physical address (even if it's a network address) for the location of the parent file, it still doesn't provide that all-important additional level of abstraction that's needed. This has rather severe consequences—for instance, what happens if a linked file is moved? The link "breaks." The next attempt to refer to the linked object within the parent document will result in an error, because OLE 1.0 does not provide the necessary level of abstraction.

OLE 2.0 *does* provide abstraction, in the form of a *moniker*. An OLE 2 moniker is just a name that refers to an object without being specific as to its location. The name can be resolved either to a physical address or to a relative address. Monikers that expand to absolute addresses work exactly the same way that the absolute addresses do in OLE 1.0. Monikers that expand to *relative* addresses begin to show us some new capabilities. For example, if you use relative addressing on an embedded Paintbrush object that refers to the same directory in which the parent word processing document is kept, then moving the contents of the directory will *not* break the link (because the new directory will still contain the Paintbrush picture). That may not sound like much of an improvement, but the fact that you now have a level of indirection through the moniker means that a number of extremely powerful capabilities can be provided.

OLE Automation

In addition to the capability of embedding foreign data types within a document, OLE 2.0 provides completely new features. Through OLE Automation it's possible for applications to expose their computational functions as OLE 2.0 objects. These objects can then be addressed by other OLE 2.0-compatible programs and documents in much the same manner as a Custom Control is accessed from Visual Basic. For example, it might be possible in future versions of Windows-compatible word processing documents to expose the functionality of the Spell Checker. You can then use the spell checking functions in other programs—perhaps in a Mail client or some other type of application. For that matter, it may also be possible to build *compound* applications by combining features of these objects—replacing the Spell Checker included in a word processor with another one provided as a separate OLE 2.0 object, for example.

This capability is very new and has generally been discussed only in terms of leveraging the power already provided in applications on end-user desktops. That is a mistake. OLE 2 Automation is not something that an end-user can easily do. The fact that an application exposes its spell checker as an object doesn't automatically mean that an end-user can make use of that feature. An end-user must find a way to access the features of that object and (to adjust its properties, for instance) determine whether it's case sensitive or not, which word or sentence or paragraph is being checked, whether the spell checking is interactive or batch mode, etc.

This will most probably require the services of a programmer—at least a script programmer. Properly using OLE 2.0 within an embedded application will require the use of some kind of application scripting capability. This is why Microsoft is now investing such heavy resources in their applications division developing Visual Basic for Applications (VBA) as a consistent scripting language for use between Microsoft applications. Doubtless other companies will follow suit in one way or another. But let's consider a more powerful possibility.

After all, OLE Automation deals with objects. The fact that the object contains code now rather than data isn't relevant. That's the whole point of an object.

This feature of object-oriented models is called *polymorphism*. It means that you don't distinguish between code and data. Both are just objects. So it *should*[19] be possible for the OLE Automation objects to be referred to using monikers *in exactly the same way that the data objects can*. Based on what we've discussed so far, this merely means that you can access the objects through link structures and that the links won't break when you move them from one directory to another. That's because at this point we're looking at OLE 2 minus one important element. We're looking at it without an all-important *Object Server*. We think that, logically, an Object Server will be provided with the next version of Windows NT—codenamed *Cairo*.

Windows 4.0: Chicago and Cairo

Now we enter the realm of speculation. Windows 4.0 and Windows NT 4.0 are not announced products as of this writing. Microsoft has made some limited public disclosure about prototypes of two new versions of Windows that are currently in an early stage of development. They're codenamed *Chicago* and *Cairo*. The former is a desktop program whose features generally parallel those of Windows for Workgroups[20] (with some significant additions). Specifically, Chicago is a full 32-bit system, and it provides preemptive multitasking—just as Windows NT does (in fact, it will run many Windows NT programs).

A more advanced product, codenamed *Cairo*, will be the next generation of Windows NT. Both Chicago and Cairo fully exploit OLE 2.0 in their user interfaces. The descriptions you're about to read are extremely speculative at this point. However, based on what information is publicly known about Chicago and Cairo, and some early hands-on experience with a Chicago pre-Beta prototype, we believe we can give you a useful preview of their general characteristics.

Chicago—the next major version of Windows—is, at the desktop level, a radical revision indeed. It does not look at all like Windows 3.1 or even Windows NT. In fact, it looks surprisingly like Macintosh System 7, and it *behaves* surprisingly like the OS/2 2.0 workplace shell.

The Chicago desktop has *folders*. Folders are containers that can hold other objects. Objects contained within the folders may be other folders—icons that can seamlessly represent programs or data files. If they represent programs they can represent programs that exist

---

[19] Be forewarned—we are speculating here. Just how far this capability works out in practice will depend on how good the *Chicago/Cairo* OLE 2.0 implementation is, something we can only guess at now.

[20] Whether the peer networking features will be included in the base-level product or provided in an add-on (currently being called the *Chicago Plus Pack*) is really immaterial for the purposes of this discussion—where peer services are required, we assume that Chicago will either provide them or may be upgraded to do so. We know for a fact that they are included in the current prototype.

either directly on the local machine or on the network. If they represent files, these files can be local files, network files, or compound OLE 2 documents where parts of the document may reside in one location and parts in another location.

All of these objects can be moved around by clicking and dragging—and extensive use is made of drag-and-drop. You can click on an icon representing a file in a folder that represents a directory, for example, and then drag that icon to another folder representing another directory; or you can drag it to the Print Manager to have it printed; or you could drag it to a word processor and have the word processor execute it, opening the file in question.

OLE 2.0 gives Chicago and Cairo a more powerful top-level interface than we've had in Windows (and Windows NT) 3.x. The range of *verb* actions we could use in the Windows or Windows NT Program Manager and File Manager was quite limited. The double-click verb meant "open me." The click-and-drag verb meant "move me." And the drag-and-drop verb meant "copy me" or "print me"—because the only applications that understood it were File Manager and Print Manager. Moreover, the only application that was reliably capable of serving that click-and-drag function was Windows or Windows NT File Manager.

Through OLE 2, *all* elements of the Chicago/Cairo desktop can function as drag-and-drop servers—and the richness of the point/click/drag/drop "language" becomes much greater. We can also hope (although this may not happen in the first release) that many of the functions of the top-level desktop interface will be exposed to programmers through OLE 2 Automation. This will allow you to use Visual Basic or Visual Basic for Applications to write custom software, allowing the automation of a wide variety of tasks that must be done manually today (or at best, in Windows 3.1 can be done with the Windows Recorder). It will be possible to actually write a BASIC language script, for example, to conduct a backup operation—moving files from one directory to another, say, or taking other actions on objects. This will become enormously significant once programmers learn to exploit it, particularly in that it will give Windows desktop capabilities comparable to those enjoyed in the typical UNIX or mainframe command-line environment through script or batch language.[21]

From a networking perspective, Chicago appears to represent an incremental improvement over Windows for Workgroups. The prototype provides features generally equivalent to those of Windows for Workgroups: share-level security (that is, no individual user logons for multiple users). It does provide simple resource sharing—and it does so through a dramatically improved user interface.

All network activity appears on the desktop through a single world-globe[22] icon called *Networks*. Double-clicking the globe opens a Networks folder, which exposes icons for all the networks to which one has connections—for instance, Novell NetWare, Microsoft Windows NT, NFS, etc. Double-clicking on one of those network icons in turn *drills down* to a folder

[21]A tantalizing question this raises is what becomes of the command-line scripts Windows NT inherited from LAN Manager. Does OLE automation replace these, or simply augment them? Inquiring programmers want to know!

[22]Symbolizing, we suppose, *worldwide networking*.

that exposes the various servers on the local segment or the local domain. Double-clicking on a server drills down to the resources available within that server, and on, and on, and on. This drill-down approach makes it visually much simpler to locate a particular resource—and largely eliminates the need to assign network shares and resources to a local drive letter.

It should no longer be necessary in this interface to limit us to twenty-six disk drive letters in representing shared network resources. Instead, you will simply drill down to the relevant shared directory icon, and double-click on it. To edit a file from that shared directory, just drag the relevant file icon onto a word processor. This is a dramatically simpler system for end-users to understand and use. Administering such a system may represent a challenge.

The conventional mechanisms administrators use to establish administrative control of networks typically involve the use of script files to preassign commonly used shared resources to common drive names. For instance, on any network using Microsoft Mail it is virtually certain that the \\MAILSERVER\MSMAIL\MSMAILDATA directory will be assigned the drive letter M:. The equivalent in the new interface would be to expose the mail data directory on the desktop and to create a *virtual link* between that mail directory and the MS-Mail application. The drive letter M: does not appear anywhere in this calculation (although in the interim, when we will be undoubtedly using products designed for both systems, there will continue to be drive assignments for some purposes).

If you're uncomfortable thinking in terms of the icons and graphics, think in terms of *environment variables*. It's quite common for an administrator to use assigned local environment variables to contain the actual network address of a resource. It's much simpler, for example, to assign %mail% to \\MAILSERVER\MSMAIL\MAILDATA and then carry out the necessary assignments to assign %mail% to M:. If you do this, then if the mail services are ever moved to another server it is only necessary to redefine what %mail% represents rather than reassigning M: to the new fixed address for every system. This level of indirection behaves much as an OLE 2 moniker—and it's this level of indirection that administrators will be manipulating on the OLE 2.0 desktop to manipulate network resources.

Aside from its network features, Chicago provides a full 32-bit operating system environment with preemptive multitasking. In this sense it can be thought of as *Windows NT Light.*[23] However, it lacks a number of the most critical Windows NT components. The most important of these appear to be the Security Subsystem, the Services Interface, and the Unicode Subsystem. Chicago is also not designed for portability to RISC architectures and does not exploit symmetric multiprocessors. Clearly, it is designed as a next-generation network *client*—but not as a network *server*, certainly not in high-powered environments.

Cairo: Windows NT 4.0

This is the most speculative section in this chapter, if not in this book. While the preceding section was written with some hands-on experience of a Chicago prototype, *this* section is

[23]Microsoft doesn't approve of this description, as it tends to obscure the need for Windows NT.

being written with no experience whatever of the Cairo operating system. There has been a limited amount of public information discussed and we are drawing conclusions based on that information as follows: It has been publicly stated that Cairo will share the same OLE 2.0–based user interface as Chicago. Therefore, we can safely assume that everything we've just said about the Chicago user interface and desktop probably applies to Cairo.

Thus, we expect that Windows NT 4.0 will look like Windows 4.0, much as Windows NT 3.1 looks like Windows 3.1. Of course, since Chicago does not provide security services, Unicode APIs, or fault tolerance, we can expect that these will be represented by some variant—presumably an OLE 2-compatible variant—of the present User Manager, Server Manager, Event Viewer, Performance Monitor, and Services Control Panel applets we see in Windows NT today.

It has also been publicly stated that Cairo will provide a new object-oriented file system. This has been the subject of a great deal of speculation in the press, much of it ill-informed. We would like to point out (again this is sheer speculation on our part) that you must be extremely careful when you hear the words *file system* used in respect to Windows NT. A Windows NT File System can refer to many things—it is, in effect, a *namespace*. The UNC names used by Windows NT's built-in networking are, in fact, a file system, as are Novell's NetWare services. Therefore, we think that it may be more useful to back up a step and think about an object-oriented *namespace* rather than an object-oriented *file system*.

An object-oriented namespace has great advantages—particularly if we think about the OLE 2.0 *moniker* discussed earlier—and assume that these monikers can refer to object-oriented Cairo namespace addresses as well as to conventional FAT or NTFS filenames. We believe that the object-oriented namespace provided by Windows NT will provide (through the OLE 2 moniker mechanism) a truly distributed environment with distributed object-oriented applications and documents.[24]

We've consistently referred to the simple example of embedding a Paintbrush picture within a word processing document. The implication—up to now—has been that *both* Microsoft Paintbrush *and* Microsoft Word (or another word processor) were present on the client machine of any client that needed to edit that compound document. We believe that Windows NT Cairo will change this relationship. It will become possible (by exploiting the OLE Automation features across the object-oriented namespace for applications and documents) to refer to components of objects located on other computers, particularly on Windows NT Cairo "Object Servers." Rather than having a local copy of the word processor on every machine—or certainly *all* components of the word processor on every machine—when spell checking a document, there will be client/server communication over the network with a spell

[24]We've heard rumors that this will be based on Microsoft's Access database technology, which leads us to a matter of some concern: Is Access relational? If not, Microsoft would appear to be betting its future on a *weaker* technology than that available in its flagship database product! Perhaps we've been misled? Or maybe Access really *is* relational, after all.

checking OLE 2 Automation object located in an Object Server.[25] The same logic applies to a wide variety of other applications.

In point of fact, the example given is probably not the most likely one to be applied first—business productivity applications may very well remain client-centric for the foreseeable future. But the ability to take the kind of client/server database model that we examined in the first half of this chapter and apply it in an object-oriented fashion with various components at varying locations across the network should supply substantial new capabilities. It's a natural extension if one considers the combination of OLE 2 Automation with the Services API provided in Windows NT 3.1.

As we said in Chapter 9, Windows NT services are the functional equivalent of NetWare Loadable Modules (NLMs) in NetWare 3.11 and NetWare 4.0. The combination of this with OLE 2 on the desktop provides the functional equivalent to Novell's *AppWare* approach to shrinkwrapping client/server. In fact, this leads to one of our most tantalizing speculations: By fully applying the capability to use Windows NT Services over NWLink IPX/SPX it *should* be possible for Windows Cairo servers to participate as AppWare servers in a NetWare network. If the server in question is running an appropriate Windows NT Cairo *service*, then that same server should be capable of providing similar services to the distributed OLE 2.0 equivalent to AppWare across the network. Thus, it may actually be possible for a single server to span *both* forms of distributed computing, with results illustrated in Figure 11.9.

Again, of course, everything that we're saying here is speculative. We are referring to what we *believe* will be the logical consequence of combining the OLE 2 API set with the existing Windows NT APIs. We do know that Microsoft has referred to fully utilizing Windows NT RPCs in the Windows NT implementation of OLE 2.0 for Cairo—and this makes it seem reasonable to assume that OLE 2 will be a networkwide capability for Cairo.

Microsoft has made one other interesting public statement with respect to Windows Cairo: It intends to replace the existing security object monitor subsystem with a system based on the Kerberos distributed security system invented at the Massachusetts Institute of Technology. Kerberos introduces the concept of a *security server* on a network that validates security requests against networked objects in much the same way that the Windows NT Security Object Monitor validates attempts to access internal objects in the system. The significance of this is that the physical location of an object becomes unimportant in determining its security context. The fact that a particular object exists in the local file system on your computer does not necessarily give you the right or the capability to access it.

This makes sense in the context of a truly distributed architecture like the one we've been describing. A compound document might wind up containing many linked objects from many directories, but the compounded document *as a unit* will have an owner—and will

[25]Again, note that this is sheer speculation. We know of no plans for such a spell-checker object at Microsoft or other vendors; but it certainly seems to make sense. A centralized spell-checker could have a much larger dictionary than that available on a client, and it could provide more sophisticated services—context-sensitive grammar checking, for instance.

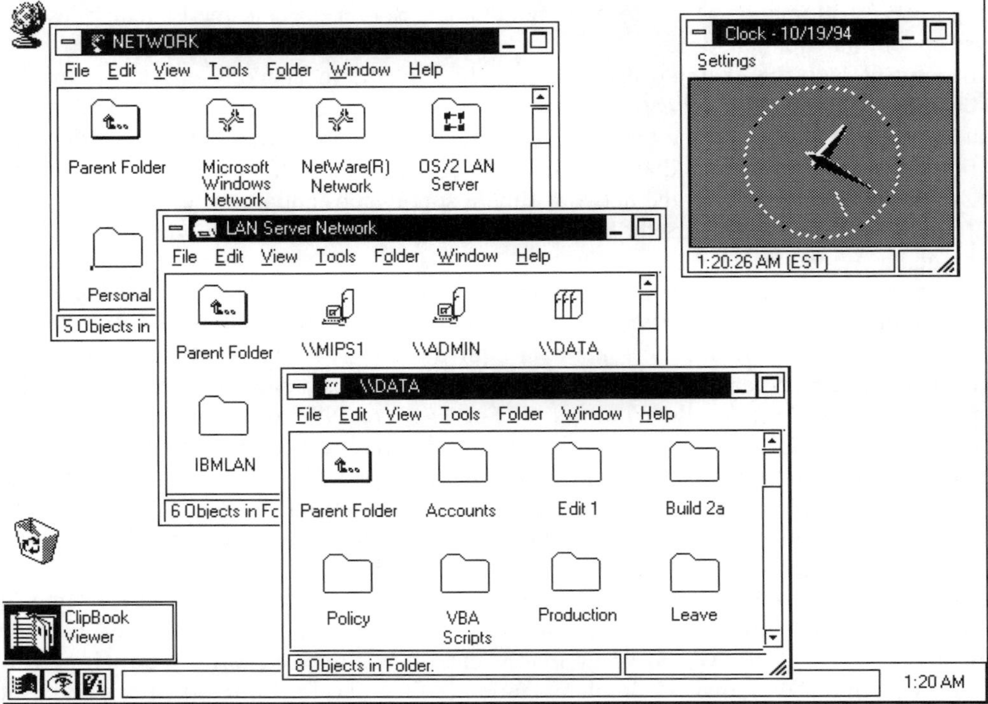

Figure 11.9 Notional view of Windows NT 4.0.

The Windows NT 4.0 ("Cairo") system will probably have a user interface similar to this—the world-globe icon opens to a folder of network icons, which open to show the servers within the network, etc. Applications and data files communicate seamlessly across the network through the facilies of an object-oriented namespace backed up by a database that maintains the linkage between objects. Even application functions may be distributed—the clock application shown might be drawing its time data from a timeserver *object* on the network.

inherit the highest security certification level of any component. (There may be embedded objects within it that are public but as an embedded portion of the total document they will be confidential if the overall container document is confidential.)

Moreover, a confidential document *owned* by one person may not be read by another person unless either the security administrator for the system or the owner has granted the right to read the document—*even though that person might have confidential level access*. This would be appropriate (indeed, essential) in upgrading Windows NT Cairo security to be compatible with the Department of Defense B-level security standards, which would permit it to handle information at the Secret classification level. It would also be extremely useful in secure operations such as banks or in the handling of financial information.

Finally, we want to draw attention to the fact that Microsoft's MS-Mail architecture is scheduled to be drastically revised, emerging with the Enterprise Messaging Services (EMS) architecture *at about the same time frame that Windows NT Cairo becomes available* (some information on this was given in Chapter 7). EMS will replace the current store-and-forward shared directory model used by MS-Mail with a true client/server model based on x.400 and x.500 standards.

Some months ago one of us was informed by a senior Microsoft executive[26] that Microsoft really means what it says about integrating Mail file system. Among other things, he said, *"In the Windows Cairo environment you may not be able to tell whether a File Manager operation involves physically copying the file between local directories or whether it involves mailing the file to another system."* Just how specifically he meant that is difficult to say, but in the object-oriented namespace we've been discussing, mail addresses would be a natural extension to the namespace. This might make it possible to provide *very* direct integration of mail with other components of the system on an ad-hoc basis, or for use by client/server applications.

Of course, everything that we've said in talking about the brave new Windows Cairo world has been concentrated on the new features. What we haven't pointed out is that in order for this to have any chance of actually happening Microsoft *must* (and undoubtedly *will*) find a way to present these new capabilities while maintaining backward compatibility with the existing Windows NT system. Windows NT 3.1 Services will probably work under Windows NT Cairo system environments. Windows NT 3.1 applications will undoubtedly run—although they may not fully exploit OLE 2 capabilities.

We can also reasonably anticipate that today's support for legacy applications will be maintained (perhaps even expanded) in the Windows NT Cairo environment. In all probability then, the resource requirements for Windows NT Cairo will likely come out even higher than the resource requirements for the present version of Windows NT. (Microsoft will direct those who cannot accept such high resource requirements to the Windows 4.0/Chicago product as an alternative.) We can certainly hope that along the way some of the problems we've examined in this book may be resolved to the advantage of users and administrators.

The advent of EMS, for example, should drastically reduce the problems with MS-Mail that were discussed in Chapter 7. We also hope that reliance upon NetBIOS and Browser broadcasts will be reduced in future generations of Microsoft's Windows NT built-in networking—and that Windows NT (and the other Windows networking products) will become more accommodating to other protocols. There is already evidence for this in the documentation for the Remote Access Server, which refers to RAS being designed to be protocol independent (although the present implementation of RAS on Windows NT is *very* closely tied to NetBIOS). Perhaps the next generation RAS in Windows NT Cairo and its sister products will provide services that might include the PPP networking for TCP/IP utilities and perhaps extension of IPX/SPX links across the WAN for NetWare clients. We can only hope.

[26] Cameron Mhyrvold, who was then in charge of developer relations at Microsoft.

Conclusion—*The Operating System Designed to Connect*

We began this book by defining Windows NT as the operating system designed to connect. We then examined a wide variety of the features and functions of Windows NT that indeed meet this specification. We've provided as much information as we think possible as of this writing on administration and maintenance features. We've provided as much information as was made available to us on connectivity to third-party products like NetWare, TCP/IP, Banyan VINES, and so forth, and we've now closed out with some speculative—but hopefully useful—information on where the Windows NT product is headed in the foreseeable future.

We hope you've found this book readable and interesting. Our greatest hope (of course) is that you'll find it *useful*. If you would like to write us about the book, either with suggestions for future editions or just with comments on the current one, please do so in care of:

John Wiley and Sons
605 Third Ave.
New York, NY 10158

The Windows NT world is an exciting (and *very* fast-moving) one. It's difficult to keep up with, as we discovered writing this book. Chapter 9 (on connecting NetWare and NT) was in its third and (we thought!) final revision the week that Microsoft announced its own NetWare Requester—and just two days later, Beame and Whiteside announced that they were going to provide network core protocol services for Windows NT. We were forced to rewrite Chapter 9 literally at the last minute (and, in fact, delayed putting the book to press) so that we could get the most recent information out to you. We'd like to hear from you. Besides physical mail, you can reach us electronically at:

John Ruley	564-8339@mcimail.com
Dave Methvin	312-2224@mcimail.com
Dave Dix	496-3891@mcimail.com
Arthur Germain	agermain@ mcimail.com
Jim Powell	531-4564@mcimail.com
Jeff Sloman	jsloman@bix.com
Eric Hall	519-1255@mcimail.com
Martin Heller	337-1828@mcimail.com

For More Information

Renaud, Paul. (1993), *Introduction to Client/Server Systems*. New York: John Wiley. ISBN: 0-471-57774-X. Excellent overview of client/server theory. Bit thick for the average reader, but worth working through if you really want to understand the topic.

Stephenson, Peter and Hartwig, G. (1992) *SQL Self-Teaching Guide*. New York: John Wiley. ISBN: 0-471-54544-9. Solid introduction to SQL, focusing on user (and programmer) issues rather than on theory. Invaluable in understanding the SQL Server manuals.

Sawyer, Tom (1993) *TPC Benchmark B Full Disclosure Report for Compaq ProLiant 2000 Model 5/66-4200A and Compaq ProLiant Model 486/50-4200A Systems using Microsoft*

SQL Server for Windows NT. Houston, TX: Compaq Computer Corp. This report gives the gory details on a full TCP-B evaluation of Windows NT on Compaq hardware, as done by Tom Sawyer of Performance Metrics, Inc.

Voth, Gary (1993) *Microsoft SQL Server Business and Product Update*. Redmond, WA: Microsoft Corp. This set of slides from the SQL Server for Windows NT press tour in September, 1993, largely duplicates the information in Microsoft's published white paper—in particular, including the stunning TPC-B results that are covered by Sawyer in more detail.

Microsoft Staff (1991-1992) *Using Microsoft SQL Server on a NetWare Network*. Redmond, WA: Microsoft Corp. A technical note (part number 098—32655) from the SQL Server for OS/2 days, but still useful in understanding SQL Server on NetWare issues.

Steele, Tammy (1993) *The Win32 Story: Targeting Windows 3.1, Windows NT, Chicago and Cairo with the Win32 API*. Article on page 1 of *Microsoft Developer Network News*, Volume 2 Number 5, Redmond, WA: Microsoft Developer's Network. Good (if limited) overview of the relationship between Chicago, Cairo, and OLE 2.0 for developers. Less accessible to the rest of us.

Strehlo, Kevin (1993) *Alpha Windows 4.0 Lacks Clear Blueprint*. Article on Page 1 of *InfoWorld*, Volume 15, Issue 43, San Mateo, CA: InfoWorld Publishing Co. Basically accurate article marred by slanted conclusions.

Ruley, John D., and Powell, Jim (1993) *Windows 4.0 Dispenses with DOS*. News story on Page 31 of *WINDOWS Magazine*, December 1993. Manhasset, NY: CMP Publications. Extremely brief, but accurate, article on Chicago. Followed by feature (cover story of February issue) that has not reached print as this is written.

Appendix 1

Programming NT Networks

In the rest of this book, we've concentrated on matters of concern to end-users and system administrators—but there are network issues for programmers as well. While it's not possible to cover network programming in depth (that's a topic for another book entirely!), we endeavor here to give a solid general overview.

Windows NT, and specifically its 32-Windows subsystem, Win32, contains a plethora of interprocess and networking mechanisms of varying degrees of complexity. The fledgling Win32 network programmer often feels like a kid in a candy store. Let's start by briefly tasting each networking, interprocess communication, and related mechanism: NetBIOS, WNet, mailslots, MAPI, pipes, RAS, sockets, RPCs, DDE, NetDDE, OLE, memory-mapped files, security, service control, event logging, and performance monitoring.

Sorting Out NT Interprocess Communications

The *NetBIOS function* supports raw IBM NetBIOS, a very low-level protocol controlled by network control blocks (NCBs). According to Microsoft, NetBIOS is in Win32 primarily for compatibility with existing systems written to NetBIOS that need to be ported to Windows and Windows NT. On the other hand, NetBIOS will work whether your Windows NT system is communicating via NetBEUI, TCP/IP, or IPX/SPX. Various NetBIOS commands allow the use of communication sessions with individual partners, as well as datagram broadcasts to specific recipients or entire networks. The Win32 NetBIOS function works in Win32s as well as Windows NT; other implementations of NetBIOS are available for DOS, OS/2, and 16-bit Windows.

The *WNet functions* allow you to enumerate, connect, and disconnect from network resources (shares). One of the WNet functions also gives you access to the current network user name.

A *mailslot* is a one-way interprocess communication (IPC) mechanism, amounting to a temporary pseudofile, which works over a network. Mailslot communications are not guaranteed to be reliable because they use the datagram, but they are convenient for broadcasting messages throughout a domain. Mailslots require a *universal thunk* to work in Win32s.

MAPI is the Messaging Application Program Interface. MAPI gives an application a simple way to send messages and files to network users via the Microsoft Mail application included with every copy of Windows NT and Windows for Workgroups. Don't confuse MAPI with mailslots: MAPI is really the programmatic interface to Microsoft Mail, while mailslots are a system-level interprocess communication mechanism. MAPI is supported in 16-bit Windows and in Windows NT, but not in Win32s.

A *pipe* is a communication conduit with two ends: a process with a handle to one end can communicate with a process having a handle to the other end. Win32 supports both named pipes and anonymous pipes; only named pipes can work over a network. Named pipes were the preferred IPC mechanism in OS/2, so applications ported from OS/2 to Windows NT often use named pipes. Pipes are inherently reliable—they use a protocol that lets you know that each message has been received—and are therefore preferable to mailslots when reliability is important. Named pipes can be a two-way mechanism, where mailslots are strictly a one-way mechanism. However, pipes cannot broadcast messages to multiple clients: for broadcasting, mailslots are preferable to pipes. Named pipe APIs are not supported in 16-bit Windows or in Win32s, although file-level access to named pipes may work, depending on the network redirector.

Remote Access Services (*RAS*) allow one Windows NT machine to connect to another over a serial line, modem, X.25 connection, or ISDN connection. While the Windows NT RAS applets probably will allow most people to use RAS well enough, it is possible to use the RAS API functions to control the process from within another program—which might make sense for applications involving remote reporting and wide-area networking. RAS services are not supported in Win32s.

Sockets are a standard networking mechanism that originated in Berkeley UNIX; more recently, the Windows Socket (WinSock) specification codified extensions to Berkeley Sockets for the Windows environment. Windows NT implements a 32-bit version of Windows Sockets. Sockets allow for a wide variety of network addressing schemes and protocols, although they were historically associated with TCP/IP. Sockets are supported in Win32s as well as in Windows NT and most UNIX implementations. Implementations of 16-bit Windows Sockets are available from several vendors.

The Windows NT Remote Procedure Call (*RPC*), a partial implementation of the OSF DCE (Open Software Foundation Distributed Computing Environment) specification, is conceptually a simple mechanism for distributed computing, but is by its nature complex to program and debug. The NT implementation of RPC includes a Microsoft implementation of the Interface Description Language (IDL) compiler, used for specifying the interface to remote procedures and generating the required local stub functions; RPC runtime libraries, which let the local stubs call the remote procedures; and the actual network transport used by the client and server runtime libraries.

RPC can use a variety of transports, network address formats, and protocols. Windows NT RPC 1.0 supports TCP/IP, named pipe, NetBIOS, and Local Procedure Call transports. Network addresses can be in IP, DECNet, or OSI formats as needed. The RPC protocol can be NCA connections or NCA datagrams. The exact combination of protocol, address format, and transport used by a given connection is specified by an ASCII *protocol sequence*, which is combined with the actual endpoints to form a *binding*. RPC *naming services* allow a client to find a server on the network.

NT RPCs are supposed to work with DOS and Windows clients and UNIX servers as well as other NT RPC clients and servers. The DOS/Windows client software ships with the NT SDK, although it needs to be installed separately from the native Windows NT tools. It is not clear whether NT RPC servers will work with all UNIX clients, as the UNIX clients might rely on DCE services not present in the NT RPC implementation. RPC is not supported in Win32s.

Dynamic Data Exchange (*DDE*) is an old local Windows interprocess communication protocol that is supported in Windows NT in both 16-bit and 32-bit form. NetDDE is an enhancement to DDE that allows it to work over networks. Object Linking and Embedding (OLE) is a different enhancement to DDE to support compound documents and application programmability. OLE is not completely network-enabled as of this writing, but should be in the near future. DDE works in Win32s and 16-bit Windows as well as in Windows NT. OLE does not seem to be supported in Win32s 1.1.

Memory-mapped files are Windows NT's answer to shared memory, which is not supported since each process in Windows NT has its own address space. Memory-mapped files are useful as a high-bandwidth interprocess communications method. File byte range locking and Flush View Of File must be used to synchronize access. For instance, memory-mapped files could be used to implement the high-bandwidth part of a database server involving several processes; one of these processes could then accept queries and send results over the network using named pipes or another network transport. Memory mapped files are supported in Win32s as well as in Windows NT.

Windows NT has *built-in security* designed to be certifiable at the US C2 level. While security functions are not specifically interprocess or networking functions, it is often in networking applications that the programmer must pay attention to security issues. Similarly, the Windows NT Service Control Manager, Event Logging, and Performance Monitoring services are not specifically for networks, but are often used when programming for networks.

Windows NT also includes the full *LAN Manager* API, although this is not considered part of the Win32 API. Existing LAN Manager code can be ported to Windows NT with little more than some code tweaks and a recompile. More information on the LAN Manager API under Win32 can be found in DOC\SDK\MISC\LMAPI.HLP on the Win32 SDK CD-ROM (however, use of the LM API is *not* recommended).

In the balance of this appendix, we will briefly examine the functions provided by each of the service groups mentioned above. When appropriate, we will go over simple examples of their use.

NetBIOS

There is only one function to support NetBIOS in Win32, **NetBIOS**. It takes one parameter: a pointer to a network-control block (NCB) structure, which holds all the semantic content for the service. The NCB contains a command, a return code, information about the network environment, and a pointer to a buffer that is used for messages or for further data about the network:[1]

```
typedef struct _NCB { /* ncb */
    UCHAR   ncb_command;  /* command code                 */
    UCHAR   ncb_retcode;  /* return code                  */
    UCHAR   ncb_lsn;      /* local session number         */
    UCHAR   ncb_num;      /* number of network name       */
    PUCHAR  ncb_buffer;   /* address of message buffer    */
    WORD    ncb_length;   /* size of message buffer       */
    UCHAR   ncb_callname[NCBNAMSZ];
                    /* blank-padded name of remote */
    UCHAR   ncb_name[NCBNAMSZ];
                    /* blank-padded name of local   */
    UCHAR   ncb_rto;      /* receive timeout/retry count */
    UCHAR   ncb_sto;      /* send timeout/system timeout */
    void (*ncb_post) (struct _NCB *);
                    /* POST routine address       */
    UCHAR   ncb_lana_num; /* lana (adapter) number        */
    UCHAR   ncb_cmd_cplt; /* 0xff => command pending     */
    UCHAR   ncb_reserve[10]; /* reserved, used by BIOS      */
    HANDLE  ncb_event;    /* signaled when ASYNCH completes */
} NCB, *PNCB;
```

The Win32 implementation of the NetBIOS function includes some enhancements that are not part of the IBM NetBIOS 3.0 specification, and a few differences in implementation from IBM NetBIOS 3.0. The enhancements allow POST routines to be called from C, and allow for completion notification using a Win32 event object. The differences are minor.

The **ncb_command** member of the **NCB** structure specifies the command code and a flag in the most significant bit (the ASYNCH constant) that indicates whether the NCB is processed asynchronously. The command codes have the actions given in Table A1.1. Note that the symbolic NCB command names used here, which match those in the NB30.H file supplied with the Win32 SDK, might be somewhat different from the symbolic names defined for DOS NetBIOS programming environments.

[1]This and succeeding reference materials in this appendix are based on information supplied by Microsoft in their Win32 documentation from the *Windows NT System Development Kit*.

NCB Command Code	*Action*
NCBACTION	Enables extensions to the transport interface. NCBACTION commands are mapped to TdiAction. When this value is specified, the ncb_buffer member points to a buffer to be filled with an ACTION_HEADER structure, which is optionally followed by data. NCBACTION commands cannot be canceled by using NCBCANCEL.
NCBADDGRNAME	Add a group name to the local name table.
NCBADDNAME	Add a unique name to the local name table.
NCBASTAT	Retrieve the status of the adapter. When this value is specified, the ncb_buffer member points to a buffer to be filled with an ADAPTER_STATUS structure, followed by an array of NAME_BUFFER structures.
NCBCALL	Open a session with another name.
NCBCANCEL	Cancel a previous command.
NCBCHAINSEND	Send the contents of two data buffers to the specified session partner. For Windows NT, this is equivalent to the NCBCHAINSENDNA command.
NCBCHAINSENDNA	Send the contents of two data buffers to the specified session part ner and do not wait for acknowledgment. For Windows NT, this is equivalent to the NCBCHAINSEND command.
NCBDELNAME	Delete a name from the local name table.
NCBDGRECV	Receive a datagram from any name.
NCBDGRECVBC	Receive broadcast datagram from any host.
NCBDGSEND	Send datagram to a specified name.
NCBDGSENDBC	Send a broadcast datagram to every host on the local area network (LAN).
NCBENUM	Enumerate LAN adapter (LANA) numbers. When this value is specified, the ncb_buffer member points to a buffer to be filled with a LANA_ENUM structure.
NCBFINDNAME	Determine the location of a name on the network. When this value is specified, the ncb_buffer member points to a buffer to be filled with a FIND_NAME_HEADER structure followed by one or more FIND_NAME_BUFFER structures.
NCBHANGUP	Close a specified session.
NCBLANSTALERT	Notify the user of LAN failures that last for more than one minute.
NCBLISTEN	Enable a session to be opened with another name.
NCBRECV	Receive data from the specified session partner.
NCBRECVANY	Receive data from any session corresponding to a specified name.
NCBRESET	Reset a LAN adapter. An adapter must be reset before any other NCB command that specifies the same number in the ncb_lana_num member will be accepted. The IBM NetBIOS 3.0 specification documents several NCB_RESET NCBs. Win32

Continued

Table A1.1 NetBIOS Commands

NCB Command Code	*Action*
	implements the "NCB.RESET Using the Dynamic Link Routine Interface." Particular values can be passed in specific bytes of the NCB. More specifically: If ncb_lsn is not 0x00, all resources associated with ncb_lana_num are to be freed. If ncb_lsn is 0x00, all resources associated with ncb_lana_num are to be freed, and new resources are to be allocated. The byte ncb_call name[0] specifies the maximum number of sessions, and the byte ncb_call name[2] specifies the maximum number of names. A nonzero value for the byte ncb_callname[3] requests that the application use NAME_NUMBER_1.
NCBSEND	Send data to the specified session partner. For Windows NT, this is equivalent to the NCBSENDNA command.
NCBSENDNA	Send data to specified session partner and do not wait for an acknowledgment. For Windows NT, this is equivalent to the NCB SEND command.
NCBSSTAT	Retrieve the status of the session. When this value is specified, the ncb_buffer member points to a buffer to be filled with a SESSION_HEADER structure, followed by one or more SESSION_BUFFER structures.
NCBTRACE	Activate or deactivate NCB tracing. Support for this command in the system is optional and system-specific.
NCBUNLINK	Unlink the adapter.

Table A1.1 NetBIOS Commands *(continued)*

The **ncb_retcode** member of **NCB** specifies the return code. This value is set to **NRC_PENDING** while an asynchronous operation is in progress. Once the operation is completed, the return code is set to one of the values listed in Table A1.2.

The **ncb_lsn** member of **NCB** specifies the local session number, **ncb_buffer** points to the message buffer, and **ncb_length** specifies the size, in bytes, of the message buffer. **ncb_callname** specifies the string that contains the remote name, and **ncb_name** specifies the string that contains the local name. Trailing space characters should be supplied in both names to pad the length of the strings out to the length specified by the **NCBNAMSZ** command.

ncb_rto sets the receive timeout period, in 500-millisecond units, for the session, and is used only for **NCBRECV** commands. Likewise, **ncb_sto** sets the send timeout period, in 500-millisecond units, for the session, and is used only for **NCBSEND** and **NCBCHAINSEND** commands. A value of 0 implies no timeout.

ncb_post specifies the address of the routine to call when an asynchronous NCB finishes. The completion routine is passed a pointer to the completed network-control block.

ncb_lana_num specifies the LAN adapter number. This zero-based number corresponds to a particular transport provider using a particular LAN adapter board. **ncb_cmd_**

Return Code	*Meaning*
NRC_GOODRET	The operation succeeded.
NRC_BUFLEN	An illegal buffer length was supplied.
NRC_ILLCMD	An illegal command was supplied.
NRC_CMDTMO	The command was timed out.
NRC_INCOMP	The message was incomplete. The application is to issue another command.
NRC_BADDR	The buffer address was illegal.
NRC_SNUMOUT	The session number was out of range.
NRC_NORES	No resource was available.
NRC_SCLOSED	The session was closed.
NRC_CMDCAN	The command was canceled.
NRC_DUPNAME	A duplicate name existed in the local name table.
NRC_NAMTFUL	The name table was full.
NRC_ACTSES	The command finished; the name has active sessions and is no longer registered.
NRC_LOCTFUL	The local session table was full.
NRC_REMTFUL	The remote session table was full. The request to open a session was rejected.
NRC_ILLNN	An illegal name number was specified.
NRC_NOCALL	The system did not find the name that was called.
NRC_NOWILD	Wildcards are not permitted in the ncb_name member.
NRC_INUSE	The name was already in use on the remote adapter.
NRC_NAMERR	The name was deleted.
NRC_SABORT	The session ended abnormally.
NRC_NAMCONF	A name conflict was detected.
NRC_IFBUSY	The interface was busy.
NRC_TOOMANY	Too many commands were outstanding; the application can retry the command later.
NRC_BRIDGE	The ncb_lana_num member did not specify a valid network number
NRC_CANOCCR	The command finished while a cancel operation was occurring.
NRC_CANCEL	The NCBCANCEL command was not valid; the command was not canceled.
NRC_DUPENV	The name was defined by another local process.
NRC_ENVNOTDEF	The environment was not defined. A reset command must be issued.
NRC_OSRESNOTAV	Operating system resources were exhausted. The application can retry the command later.
NRC_MAXAPPS	The maximum number of applications was exceeded.
NRC_NOSAPS	No SAPs available for NetBIOS.
NRC_NORESOURCES	The requested resources were not available.
NRC_INVADDRESS	The NCB address was not valid. This return code is not part of the IBM NetBIOS 3.0 specification. This return code is not returned in the NCB; instead, it is returned by the NetBIOS function.

Continued

Table A1.2 NCB Return Codes

Return Code	*Meaning*
NRC_INVDDID	The NCB DDID was invalid.
NRC_LOCKFAIL	The attempt to lock the user area failed.
NRC_OPENERR	An error occurred during an open operation being performed by the device driver. This return code is not part of the IBM NetBIOS 3.0 specification.
NRC_SYSTEM	A system error occurred.
NRC_PENDING	An asynchronous operation is not yet finished.

Table A1.2 NCB Return Codes *(continued)*

cplt specifies the command-complete flag, which has the same as the **ncb_retcode** member. **ncb_reserve** is reserved, and must be set to zero.

ncb_event specifies a handle to a Windows NT event to be set to the signaled state when an asynchronous network-control block finishes. The event is signaled if the **NetBIOS** function returns a nonzero value. The **ncb_event** member of **NCB** must be zero if the **ncb_command** member does not have the **ASYNCH** value set or if **ncb_post** is nonzero. Otherwise, **NRC_ILLCMD** is returned. In other words, you can't ask for more than one notification that a NCB request has completed: it is either synchronous, signals an event, or calls a completion routine.

The event specified by **ncb_event** is set to the nonsignaled state by the system when an asynchronous NetBIOS command is accepted, and is set to the signaled state when the asynchronous NetBIOS command finishes. Using ncb_event to submit asynchronous requests requires fewer system resources than using **ncb_post**. Also, when **ncb_event** is nonzero, the pending request is canceled if the thread terminates before the request is processed. This is not true for requests sent by using **ncb_post**.

Only manual reset events should be used with NetBIOS. A given event should not be associated with more than one active asynchronous NetBIOS command.

How can we use NetBIOS? Let's go through a *very* simple example, one that doesn't actually do anything, but does illustrate working successfully with NetBIOS from Win32. We'll start by initializing the session and adding a name. This is normally done from the server:

```
#define WIN32
#include <windows.h>
#include <nb30.h>
#include <stdlib.h>
#include <stdio.h>
#include <memory.h>

#define NSESSIONS 1
#define NNAMES    1
//...

char chNameBuffer [ NCBNAMSZ ];
```

```
unsigned char ucRc;
int i;
NCB ncb;
//...

// Code to initialize chNameBuffer should come here (not shown)

//....

/* reset NetBIOS session */

memset(&ncb,0,sizeof(ncb));
ncb.ncb_command = NCBRESET;
ncb.ncb_callname[0] = NSESSIONS;
ncb.ncb_callname[1] = NNAMES;
ucRc = NetBIOS (&ncb);

/* Add a Name */

memset(&ncb,0,sizeof(ncb));
ncb.ncb_command = NCBADDNAME;
memcpy (ncb.ncb_name, chNameBuffer, NCBNAMSZ);
ucRc = NetBIOS (&ncb);
if (ucRc )
  return (1);
```

The server would normally start a session and post a receive at this point, assuming it uses connections and not datagrams. Basically the server now has to wait for the client. The client first has to find the server by name:

```
struct {
  FIND_NAME_HEADER fnh;
  FIND_NAME_BUFFER fnb;
  } fn;

/* Find the Name  */

memset(&ncb,0,sizeof(ncb));
memset(&fn.fnh,0,sizeof(fn.fnh));
memset(&fn.fnb,0,sizeof(fn.fnb));
fn.fnh.node_count = 1;
fn.fnb.length = sizeof(fn.fnb);
ncb.ncb_command = NCBFINDNAME;
memcpy (ncb.ncb_callname, chNameBuffer, NCBNAMSZ);
ncb.ncb_buffer = (PUCHAR)&fn.fnh;
ncb.ncb_length =  sizeof(fn);
ucRc = NetBIOS (&ncb);
```

Now we can send a datagram, or establish a session and send messages. When the server is all done, it needs to delete the name:

```
/* Delete the Name */
```

```
memset(&ncb,0,sizeof(ncb));
ncb.ncb_command = NCBDELNAME;
memcpy (ncb.ncb_name, chNameBuffer,  NCBNAMSZ);
ucRc = NetBIOS (&ncb);
```

If you're already familiar with NetBIOS programming from DOS, Windows, or OS/2, you probably now understand the Win32 **NetBIOS** function well enough to use it. If you aren't familiar with NetBIOS programming and need to use it from Windows NT, you'll want to consult a good NetBIOS programming book—but expect to have to mentally translate between systems.

The Win32 **NetBIOS** function, unlike DOS, doesn't require you to issue interrupts. Unlike Windows, it doesn't require you to call it from assembly language, from a DLL, or with locked NCBs. Unlike OS/2, it doesn't require you to call additional functions. Like all of those, however, it requires NetBIOS names to be padded with blanks, so you'll want to use a function like **CopyToBuffer** to work with them:

```
void CopyToBuffer ( char *pchDest , char *pchSrc)
{
    register count;

    /* Check for null pointer */
    if ((!pchDest) || ( ! pchSrc))
        return ;

    /* set the name field with nulls */
    memset ( pchDest, 0x20, NCBNAMSZ);

    /* copy from source to destination */
    count =  NCBNAMSZ;
    while ((*pchSrc) && ( count))
    {
        *pchDest++ = *pchSrc++;
        count--;
    }
    return;
}
```

As you are probably aware, you can build entire client-server systems using only NetBIOS—although no one would call that a convenient way to develop new programs. Fortunately, Win32 supports a number of other network mechanisms.

WNet

The WNet group of functions allows you to explicitly manipulate network disk and printer connections and other network resources from your applications. As such, they allow you to add some of the functionality of File Manager, Print Manager, **net use**, and **net view** to your own programs. The WNet functions are listed in Table A1.3. To use any of these functions, you need to link to MPR.LIB, the multiple-provider router library.

Note that **WNetAddConnection** and **WNetCancelConnection** are already obsolete: they are present in Win32 for compatibility with Windows for Workgroups programs, and have been replaced with **WNetAddConnection2** and **WNetCancelConnection2**, respectively, which are considerably more flexible. **WNetAddConnection2** and the resource enumeration functions **WNetOpenEnum**, **WNetEnumResource**, and **WNetCloseEnum** use the **NETRESOURCE** structure to describe network resources:

```
typedef struct _NETRESOURCE {  /* nr */
    DWORD  dwScope;        //connected, global, or persistent
    DWORD  dwType;         //any, disk, or print
    DWORD  dwDisplayType; //domain, generic, server, or share
    DWORD  dwUsage;        //connectable or container
    LPTSTR lpLocalName;    //i.e. H: or LPT3:
    LPTSTR lpRemoteName;   //remote network name
    LPTSTR lpComment;      //provider-supplied comment
    LPTSTR lpProvider;     //provider name
} NETRESOURCE;
```

If you want to give control of network connections to the user, use the **WNetConnectionDialog** function to put up a dialog box, enumerate the network resources and display them, and allow the user to connect to resources:

```
DWORD dwResult;
dwResult = WNetConnectionDialog(hWnd, RESOURCETYPE_DISK);
if(dwResult != NO_ERROR) {
    MyErrorHandler(hWnd, dwResult, (LPSTR)"WNetConnectionDialog");
    return FALSE;
   }
```

In general, the alternatives to **RESOURCETYPE_DISK** are **RESOURCETYPE_PRINT** and **RESOURCETYPE_ANY**. **WNetConnectionDialog**, however, works

Function Name	*Action*
WNetAddConnection	Redirects a local device to a network resource
WNetAddConnection2	Redirects a local device to a network resource
WNetCancelConnection	Breaks an existing network connection
WNetCancelConnection2	Breaks an existing network connection
WNetCloseEnum	Ends a network resource list
WNetConnectionDialog	Starts a network connection dialog box
WNetDisconnectDialog	Starts a network disconnection dialog box
WNetEnumResource	Continues listing network resources
WNetGetConnection	Gets name of network resource
WNetGetLastError	Returns last error for network functions
WNetGetUser	Gets the current network user name
WNetOpenEnum	Starts listing network resources

Table A1.3 WNet Functions

only with **RESOURCETYPE_DISK**—it brings up the standard "Connect Network Drive" dialog (Figure A1.1). One wonders whether some future version of the function will implement printer browsing as well.

One more function in this group bears comment. **WNetGetUser** does more than meets the eye: it not only can find the current default user name, but it can also find the user name used to establish any given network connection:

```
DWORD WNetGetUser(lpszLocalName, lpszUserName, lpcchBuffer)

LPTSTR lpszLocalName;  /* address of local name to get user name for    */
LPTSTR lpszUserName; /* address of buffer for user name  */
LPDWORD lpcchBuffer; /* address of buffer-size variable  */
```

If you use **NULL** for the local name, you get the current user name for the process. If you specify a share name, you will get the user name used to connect to the share. If there are multiple connections with multiple names, you'll get one of the user names—but there's no telling which one.

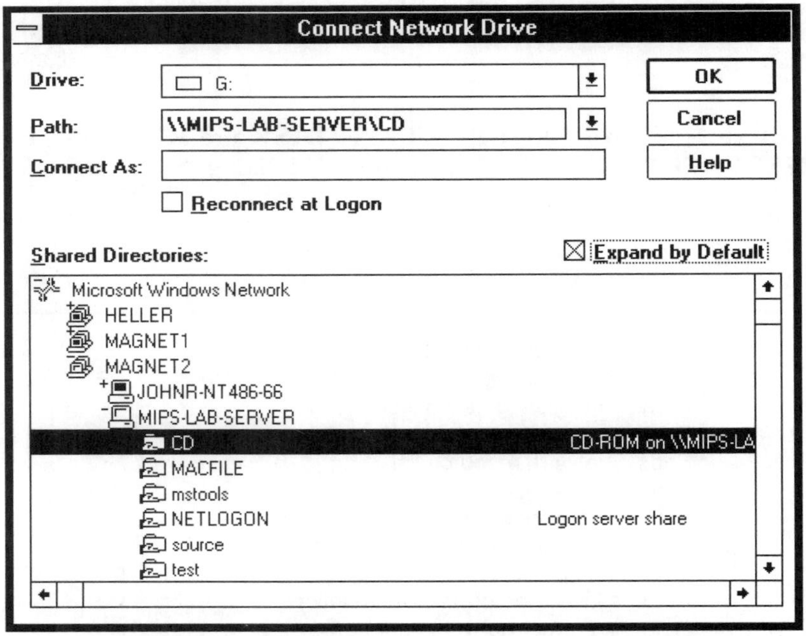

Figure A1.1 WNetConnectionDialog .

The WNetConnectionDialog Win32 API function generates the familiar Connect Network Drive dialog used to associate drive letters with network resources in Windows NT.

Mailslots

As we mentioned earlier, mailslots are convenient for broadcasting messages and other one-way communications tasks. Only three API functions are needed to support mailslots, as shown in Table A1.4; the rest of the mailslot functionality is performed with standard file functions, since mailslots act as pseudofiles.

Note that, unlike real files, mailslots are temporary. When every handle of a mailslot is closed or the process owning the last handle exits, the mailslot and all the data it contains are deleted. The data in a mailslot message can be in any form, within the length limit set when the mailslot was created.

A server process creates a mailslot with the **CreateMailslot** function, which returns a handle to the mailslot:

```
HANDLE CreateMailslot(lpszName, cbMaxMsg, dwReadTimeout, lpsa)

LPCTSTR lpszName;          /* address of string for mailslot name*/
DWORD cbMaxMsg;            /* maximum message size         */
DWORD dwReadTimeout;       /* milliseconds before read timeout    */
LPSECURITY_ATTRIBUTES lpsa;       /* address of security structure      */
```

The **lpszName** parameter to **CreateMailslot** is required to be of the form **\\.\mailslot\[path]name**, and must be unique. The name may include multiple levels of pseudodirectories separated by backslashes. For example, both **\\.\mailslot\example_mailslot_name** and **\\.\mailslot\abc\def\ghi** are valid names. The **cbMaxMsg** parameter specifies the maximum message size that can be written to the mailslot, in bytes; zero means that the size is unlimited.

dwReadTimeout specifies the amount of time, in milliseconds, a read operation can wait for a message to be written to the mailslot before a timeout occurs. A value of zero means that reads return immediately if no message is present; a value of **MAILSLOT_WAIT_FOREVER**, defined as -1, means that reads to the mailslot never time out.

lpsa is a security descriptor for the mailbox; we'll discuss security descriptors a little later on. Most of the time you can safely use **NULL** for the security descriptor, which causes the object to get default security attributes. You'll need a real security descriptor if you want to pass the mailbox handle to child processes or you actually want to restrict access to the mailbox to authorized processes.

To open a mailslot from a client process, use on the mailslot name, with **FILE_SHARE_READ** and **OPEN_EXISTING** specified as flags. If the mailslot is local to

Function	*Action*
CreateMailslot	Creates a mailslot
GetMailslotInfo	Retrieves mailslot information
SetMailslotInfo	Sets mailslot read timeout

Table A1.4 Mailslot API server functions

the client, its name is the same one used when it was created, for example, **\\.\mailslot\name**. If the mailslot is remote, you can specify **\\computername\mailslot\name**, **\\domainname\mailslot\name**, or ***\mailslot\name**. The last two forms are used for domainwide broadcasts: the * form broadcasts in the local system's primary domain, and the **\\domainname** form broadcasts in the specified domain. If you use either domainwide broadcast form, you cannot write more than 400 bytes at a time to the mailslot.

Note that opening a mailslot from the client side can return a valid handle even if the mailslot doesn't exist. And remember that mailslot communications use datagrams, which are not inherently reliable. Don't use a mailslot for a message that absolutely, positively has to get through.

Once you've opened the mailslot, you can write messages to it using **WriteFile** and the handle returned from **CreateFile**. The server reads messages with **ReadFile**. When you are done with the mailslot, release it with **CloseHandle**. The only other functions that can be used with mailslots are **GetMailSlotInfo**, **SetMailSlotInfo**, **GetFileTime**, **SetFileTime**, and **DuplicateHandle**. Mailslot clients should restrict themselves to **CreateFile**, **DuplicateHandle**, **WriteFile**, and **CloseHandle**.

MAPI

While mailslots are good for sending transient one-way interprocess messages and message broadcasts, they are inappropriate for persistent messages, reliable messages, and applications that require two-way communication. For persistent, reliable one-way messages, it might be better to use MAPI, the Messaging Application Program Interface. For transient, reliable two-way interprocess communications, named pipes might be a better choice. Let's address MAPI first.

MAPI is a set of high-level functions that applications use to create, manipulate, transfer, and store messages. MAPI provides a common interface, which application developers use to create mail-enabled and mail-aware applications independent of the underlying messaging system. In addition to a message store interface used to create and manage collections of messages, MAPI also includes an address book interface for access to mail recipients and distribution lists.

MAPI comes in two flavors, Simple MAPI and Extended MAPI. Simple MAPI is built into Windows NT and Windows for Workgroups, as Microsoft Mail comes with both systems. You can add Simple MAPI capabilities to a Windows 3.1 system by adding Microsoft Mail to the system. Extended MAPI will require a *Windows Messaging Subsystem*, expected in future releases of Windows, probably both "Chicago" and "Cairo."

Extended MAPI augments Simple MAPI with additional functions for advanced addressing, and folder and message management. Applications will be able to use Extended MAPI to create and deal with large and/or complex messages, to access portions of a directory service, and to organize and search a large store of messages.

The Simple MAPI functions are listed in Table A1.5. To use these functions, you will need to include MAPI.H and dynamically link to MAPI32.DLL (from a 32-bit application) or MAPI.DLL (from a 16-bit application).

The following code will allow you to dynamically link to the MAPI service DLL and get the address of the single function needed to mail-enable an application, **MAPISendDocuments**:

```
#ifdef WIN32
#define MAPIDLL "MAPI32.DLL"
#else
#define MAPIDLL "MAPI.DLL"
#define SZ_MAPISENDDOC "MAPISendDocuments"
extern ULONG (FAR PASCAL *lpfnMAPISendDocuments)(ULONG, LPSTR,
                                                 LPSTR, LPSTR, ULONG);
extern HANDLE hLibrary;

int FAR PASCAL InitMAPI() {
  if ((hLibrary = LoadLibrary(MAPIDLL)) < 32)
    return(ERR_LOAD_LIB);
  if ((lpfnMAPISendDocuments= GetProcAddress(hLibrary,
       SZ_MAPISENDDOC)) == NULL)
    return(ERR_LOAD_FUNC);
  return(0);
}
```

Function	*Description*
MAPIAddress	Addresses a Mail message
MAPIDeleteMail	Deletes a Mail message
MAPIDetails	Displays a recipient details dialog box
MAPIFindNext	Returns the ID of the next (or first) Mail message of a specified type
MAPIFreeBuffer	Frees memory allocated by the messaging system
MAPILogoff	Ends a session with the messaging system
MAPILogon	Begins a session with the messaging system
MAPIReadMail	Reads a Mail message
MAPIResolveName	Displays a dialog box to resolve an ambiguous recipient name
MAPISaveMail	Saves a Mail message
MAPISendDocuments	Sends a standard Mail message using a dialog box
MAPISendMail	Sends a Mail message, allowing greater flexibility in message generation

Table A1.5 Simple MAPI Functions

Once you've successfully linked to MAPI32.DLL or MAPI.DLL and retrieved a pointer to **MAPISendDocuments**, you should add a **Send** menu item to the File menu of your application. Enable the menu item when there is a current document in the application, and disable it when there is no current document.

When the menu item is picked, you'll need to process it. If yours is an MDI application, you might want to offer a choice between "Send current document" or "Send all documents." Whether you are sending a single document or multiple documents, the logic for each document is the same: save the current file as a temporary, call **MAPISendDocuments** for the temporary file, and finally delete the temporary file. The following code snippet calls **MAPISendDocuments**:

```
ulResult = (*lpfnMAPISendDocuments)(hWnd, ";",
 lpszFullPathToTemporaryFile, lpszTemporaryFileName, 0L);
```

Amazingly, that's all there is to mail-enabling an application. The user will see a login dialog if not already logged into Mail, and then will see a mail dialog with the file already listed, like the one shown in Figure A1.2. Where in the world did all *that* user interface come from? From MS-Mail. You're actually using MAPI to tap into MS-Mail, which is acting as the mail service provider.

That's quite a bit of application to get from one function call. If you want to send documents or mail messages without involving the user—or you simply want more control over the message—you can use an alternate function, **MAPISendMail**:

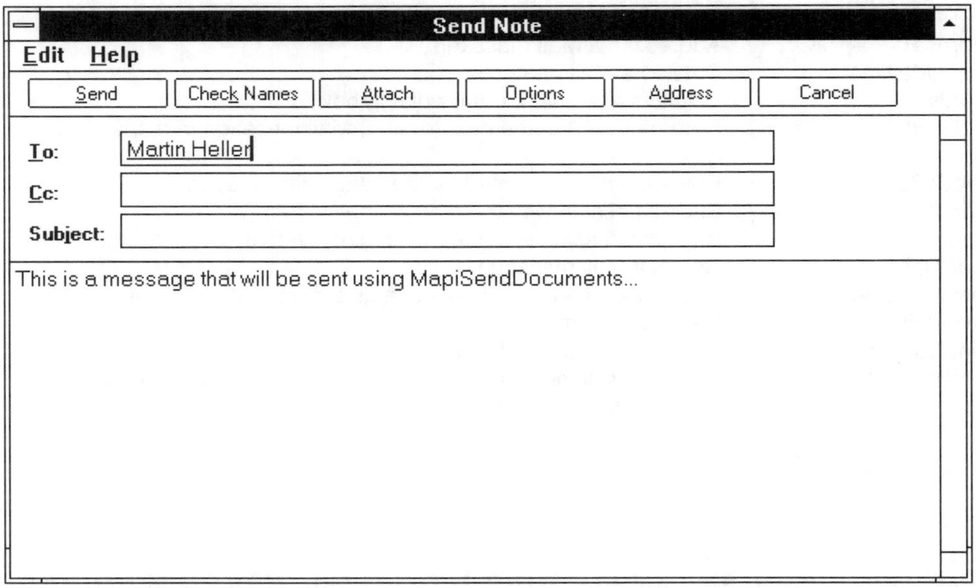

Figure A1.2 MAPISendDocuments.

The MAPISendDocuments Win32 API function generates the Send Mail dialog shown here. This allows applications to be mail-enabled with a minimum of programming.

```
ULONG MAPISendMail(lhSession, ulUIParam,  lpMessage, flFlags,
             ulReserved)
LHANDLE  lhSession; //session handle, 0 or as returned by MAPILogon
ULONG  ulUIParam; //parent window handle, or 0
lpMapiMessage  lpMessage; //pointer to MapiMessage structure
ULONG  flFlags; //specify whether or not to display login and send
             //message dialogs, and whether to use a default
             //MAPI session if it exists
ULONG  ulReserved;  //must be 0
```

You can use **MAPISendMail** to accomplish much the same end as **MAPISendDocuments**, if you wish:

```
long err;
MapiFileDesc file = {0, 0, "c:\tmp\tmp.wk3", "budget17.wk3", NULL};
MapiMessage note = {0,NULL,NULL,NULL,NULL,NULL,0,NULL,0,NULL,1,&file};

err = MAPISendMail (0L,0L,&note,MAPI_DIALOG,0L);
if (err != SUCCESS_SUCCESS )
  printf("Unable to send the message.\n");
```

Or, you can use **MAPISendMail** to send a completely automated message:

```
MapiRecipDesc recip[2];
MapiFileDesc file = {0, 0, "c:\budget17.wk3", "budget17.wk3",
               NULL};
MapiMessage note = {0,NULL,
  "Attached is the budget proposal.\r\nSee you Monday.\r\n",
  NULL,NULL,NULL,0,NULL,2,NULL,1,&file};

recip[0].ulReserved = 0;
recip[0].nRecipClass = MAPI_TO;
recip[0].lpszName = "Sally Jones";
recip[0].lpszAddress = NULL;
recip[0].ulEIDSize = 0;
recip[0].lpEntryID = NULL;

recip[1].ulReserved = 0;
recip[1].nRecipClass = MAPI_CC;
recip[1].lpszName = "Marketing";
recip[1].lpszAddress = NULL;
recip[1].ulEIDSize = 0;
recip[1].lpEntryID = NULL;

note.lpRecips = &recip;

err = MAPISendMail (0L,0L,&note,0L,0L);
if (err != SUCCESS_SUCCESS )
  printf("Unable to send the message.\n");
```

None of the other Simple MAPI functions are any trickier than this. You would use **MAPILogon** and **MAPILogoff** to control sessions; **MAPIFindNext**, **MAPIReadMail**, **MAPISaveMail**, and **MAPIDeleteMail** to read and dispose of incoming mail; and **MAPIAd-**

dress, **MAPIDetails**, and **MAPIResolveName** to assist the user in addressing outgoing mail. **MAPIFreeBuffer** is needed to release memory allocated by **MAPIAddress**, **MAPIReadMail**, and **MAPIResolveName**.

Pipes

A pipe is a communication conduit with two ends: a process with a handle to one end can communicate with a process having a handle to the other end. Pipes can be one-way—where one end is read-only and the other end is write-only, or two-way—where both ends of the pipe can read or write. Pipes are similar to mailslots in that they are written to and read from like files. Win32 supports both anonymous (unnamed) pipes and named pipes. The pipe functions are listed in Table A1.6.

Anonymous Pipes

Anonymous pipes are unnamed, one-way pipes intended to transfer data between a parent process and a child process, or between two child processes of the same parent process. Anonymous pipes are always local: they cannot be used over a network. The **CreatePipe** function creates an anonymous pipe and returns two handles: one to the read end and one to the write end of the pipe. The read handle has only read access to the pipe, and the write handle has only write access to the pipe. To communicate through the pipe, a handle to one of the ends must be passed to another process. Usually, this is done through inheritance, where a child process inherits a handle from its parent process.

To read from the pipe, a process uses the read handle in a call to the **ReadFile** function. To write to the pipe, a process uses the write handle in a call to the **WriteFile** function. Neither **ReadFile** nor **WriteFile** returns until the specified number of bytes has been read or written or an error occurs. Asynchronous I/O is not supported for anonymous pipes. An anonymous pipe

Function	*Action*
CallNamedPipe	Multiple pipe operations
ConnectNamedPipe	Waits for a client to connect
CreateNamedPipe	Creates an instance of a named pipe
CreatePipe	Creates an anonymous pipe
DisconnectNamedPipe	Disconnects server end of a named pipe
GetNamedPipeHandleState	Returns named-pipe handle information
GetNamedPipeInfo	Returns named-pipe handle information
PeekNamedPipe	Previews pipe-queue data
SetNamedPipeHandleState	Sets pipe read and blocking mode and controls local buffeing
TransactNamedPipe	Reads and writes a named pipe

Table A1.6 Pipe Functions

exists until all handles to both read and write ends of the pipe are closed by the **CloseHandle** function.

Named Pipes

Named pipes are considerably more flexible than anonymous pipes. Named pipes can be one-way or two-way, they can work over a network, and a server process can use a named pipe to communicate with one or more client processes.

The server process uses **CreateNamedPipe** to create one or more instances of a named pipe. All instances of a named pipe share the same pipe name, but each instance has its own buffers and handles and provides a separate conduit for client-server communication. When a client process specifies a pipe name in the **CreateFile** or **CallNamedPipe** functions, it connects to an instance of the pipe. This enables multiple client processes to use the same named pipe simultaneously. It is entirely possible for a single process to act as both a named pipe client and server.

The **CreateNamedPipe** function offers a number of options:

```
HANDLE CreateNamedPipe(lpName, dwOpenMode, dwPipeMode,
  nMaxInstances, nOutBufferSize, nInBufferSize, nDefaultTimeout,
  lpSecurityAttributes)

LPCTSTR lpName;                  /* address of pipe name        */
DWORD dwOpenMode;                /* pipe open mode      */
DWORD dwPipeMode;                /* pipe-specific modes */
DWORD nMaxInstances;             /* maximum number of instances */
DWORD nOutBufferSize;            /* out buffer size in bytes    */
DWORD nInBufferSize;             /* in buffer size in bytes     */
DWORD nDefaultTimeout;           /* timeout time in milliseconds */
LPSECURITY_ATTRIBUTES lpSecurityAttributes;/* security attributes       */
```

The pipe name at creation has the form:**\\.\pipe\pipename**. The pipename part of the name can include any character other than a backslash, including numbers and special characters. The entire pipe name string can be up to 256 characters long. Pipe names are not case sensitive. When a client connects to a named pipe over a network, it uses the name form **\\servername\pipe\pipename**. If the pipe is local, the **\\.\pipe\pipename** can be used by the client.

The pipe's open mode can be **PIPE_ACCESS_DUPLEX**, **PIPE_ACCESS_INBOUND**, or **PIPE_ACCESS_OUTBOUND**, corresponding to bidirectional data flow, flow from client to server, and flow from server to client, respectively. A named pipe can optionally use write-through and/or overlapped mode, which can vary for different instances of the same pipe.

FILE_FLAG_WRITE_THROUGH, which enables write-through mode, only affects write operations on byte-type pipes, which we'll explain shortly. Write-through mode keeps the system from buffering data written into the pipe: in write-through mode, any function that writes to the pipe returns only when the data is actually transmitted across the network to the remote computer. Write-through mode improves reliability at the expense of efficiency.

FILE_FLAG_OVERLAPPED, which enables overlapped mode, allows functions that perform read, write, and connect operations to return immediately. Overlapped mode allows one thread to service multiple instances of a pipe or perform simultaneous read and write operations on the same pipe handle. The alternative to overlapped mode, assuming that you want your named pipe server to handle multiple clients, is to spawn a thread per client.

In addition to directionality, write-through, and overlap, a named pipe's open mode can include any combination of security access flags, which can be different for different instances of the same pipe. The three possible security access flags are **WRITE_DAC**, which gives the caller write access to the named pipe's discretionary ACL, **WRITE_OWNER**, which gives the caller write access to the named pipe's owner, and **ACCESS_SYSTEM_SECURITY**, which gives the caller write access to the named pipe's system ACL. An ACL is an access control list, the basic security control structure in Windows NT. A discretionary ACL is controlled by the owner of the object; a system ACL is controlled by the system administrator.

All of the above options apply to the named pipe's *open* mode, specified in the second parameter to **CreateNamedPipe**. A named pipe's *pipe* mode, specified in the third parameter to **CreateNamedPipe**, determines the pipe's type, read mode, and wait mode.

We mentioned earlier that a pipe must be in byte mode for write-through mode to be effective. **PIPE_TYPE_BYTE** means that data is written to the pipe as a stream of bytes. The alternative, **PIPE_TYPE_MESSAGE**, means that data is written to the pipe as a stream of messages. A pipe's write mode has to be the same for all instances.

In addition to a type or write mode, a named pipe has a read mode and a wait mode, which can differ among instances. **PIPE_READMODE_BYTE** is valid no matter what write mode was specified for the pipe. **PIPE_READMODE_MESSAGE** works only for a message type pipe: the pipe data has to be written as messages to be read as messages, but messages can always be broken down into bytes.

PIPE_WAIT enables blocking mode, which means that transactions do not complete until there is data to read, all data is written, or a client is connected. Blocking pipes can in fact wait indefinitely. For nonblocking pipes, enabled by **PIPE_NOWAIT**, **ReadFile**, **WriteFile**, and **ConnectNamedPipe** always return immediately. Nonblocking mode is basically there for compatibility with LAN Manager: if you want to enable asynchronous pipe I/O, use **FILE_FLAG_OVERLAPPED** in the open mode.

The fourth parameter to **CreateNamedPipe** specifies the maximum number of instances that can be created for the pipe, in the range of 1 through **PIPE_UNLIMITED_INSTANCES**. The fifth and sixth parameters size the pipe's output and input buffers, in bytes: the system will actually round the suggested sizes to allocation boundaries and limit them to some range.

The seventh parameter assigns the pipe a default timeout value, in milliseconds. The final parameter points to a **SECURITY_ATTRIBUTES** structure; it can be **NULL** if you want the pipe to have a default security descriptor.

The server calls **CreateNamedPipe** the first time specifying the pipe's maximum number of simultaneous instances. To create additional instances, the server calls **CreateNamedPipe** again.

Once a pipe instance is created, a client process can connect to it by calling either **CreateFile** or **CallNamedPipe**. If a pipe instance is available, either function returns a handle to the client end of the pipe instance. If no instances of the pipe are available, a client process can use **WaitNamedPipe** to wait for one to become available, then try **CreateFile** again.

CallNamedPipe is a client function that combines connecting to a pipe instance (and waiting for one to be available, if necessary), writing a message, reading a message, and closing the pipe handle. **CallNamedPipe** can be used only with a message-type pipe.

The server process uses **ConnectNamedPipe** to determine when a client process is connected to a pipe handle. If the pipe handle is in blocking mode, **ConnectNamedPipe** does not return until a client is connected.

Both clients and servers can use **ReadFile** and **WriteFile** with pipes. Alternatively, **ReadFileEx** and **WriteFileEx** functions can be used if the pipe handle was opened for overlapped operations.

PeekNamedPipe performs a nondestructive read on a pipe, and also reports information about the pipe instance. **TransactNamedPipe**, which works only with message-type pipes in message-read mode, writes a request message and reads a reply message in a single operation.

DisconnectNamedPipe is a server function to close the connection to the client process: it makes the client's handle invalid (if it has not already been closed), and discards any unread data in the pipe. The server can avoid closing the connection before the client has read all the data by calling **FlushFileBuffers** prior to calling **DisconnectNamedPipe**. Once the client is disconnected, the server can either call **CloseHandle** to destroy the pipe instance, or call **ConnectNamedPipe** to let a new client connect to this instance.

GetNamedPipeInfo returns the type of the pipe, the size of the input and output buffers, and the maximum number of pipe instances that can be created. **GetNamedPipeHandleState** reports on the read and wait modes of a pipe handle, the current number of pipe instances, and so on. **SetNamedPipeHandleState** function sets the read mode and wait modes of a pipe handle, maximum number of bytes to collect (for a client), and/or the maximum time to wait before transmitting a message.

Let's recap the high points of named pipes. Named pipes are reliable network pseudo-files of the form **\\servername\pipe\pipename**. They can be unidirectional or bidirectional, buffered or unbuffered, overlapped or synchronous, and contain byte or message streams. For compatibility with LAN Manager, pipes can be nonblocking, but normally you should use blocking pipes and enable overlapping if you want asynchronous I/O. Servers can create multiple instances of a pipe, and vary some of the pipe's parameters on an instance-by-instance basis; they can spawn a thread per synchronous pipe instance, or use a single thread to service multiple asynchronous pipe instances. Clients connect to a single instance of a pipe at a time.

Named pipes are reliable and have good performance for communications across a network. Because a single named pipe server can optionally connect to multiple clients, named pipes can be the basis of any client-server application requiring 1 to 1 or 1 to *N* connections in which it is reasonable for each client to establish its own connection. Named pipes would be a reasonable choice of transport for a database server, a transaction-processing system, a multi-user chat application, or a multiplayer game. Named pipes would not be a reasonable way to implement a message broadcast facility—that would be better implemented with mailslots, which don't require each receiver to explictly connect to the sender.

Microsoft supplies code for a multithreaded server service (and associated client) in the MSTOOLS\SAMPLES\SERVICE directory of the SDK.

Function	Action
RasDial	Establishes a RAS connection
RasDialFunc	Callback function called by RasDial on state changes
RasEnumConnections	Lists active RAS connections
RasEnumEntries	Lists entries in a RAS phone book
RasGetConnectStatus	Reports current status of a RAS connection
RasGetErrorString	Converts RAS error code to error string
RasHangUp	Terminates a RAS connection

Table A1.7 Remote Access Functions

You might also want to examine the SDK example programs NPSERVER and NPCLIENT, which together implement a primitive multi-user chat system. In the Windows NT SDK, you'll find them under the \MSTOOLS\SAMPLES\NAMEPIPE directory; in Visual C++ for NT, you'll find them under \MSVCNT\SAMPLES.

Remote Access

The Remote Access Services (RAS) functions offer the opportunity to develop applications that log into physically distant networks over modems and phone lines, or over better connections like X.25, ISDN, or T1 links. The RAS functions are listed in Table A1.7. RAS is an attractive alternative to developing your own remote access protocols or setting up bulletin board systems for remote reporting.

As you can see, the RAS API exposes the high-level functions used by the Windows NT RAS applets: functions to dial to and hang up from remote networks, functions to list the active connections and the entries in a RAS phone book, and a function to report the status of a connection. This set of functions is simple, so we won't show you a code sample: you won't have any trouble figuring out how to use them yourself. Once you have a connection established, you can use the WNet services to connect to remote hard disks, and then use ordinary file services to transfer information to the remote server.

Sockets

Aside from being the standard network programming mechanism in Berkeley UNIX, sockets are quite flexible and simple to use. The Windows and Windows NT implementation of sockets includes some extensions to make sockets more efficient, but you only really have to use the initialization and termination routines (**WSAStartup** and **WSACleanup**) from the Windows extensions.

The basic Berkeley-style socket routines included in Windows Sockets are listed in Table A1.8; the so-called "database" or "getXbyY" functions are listed in Table A1.9; and the Windows extensions are listed in Table A1.10.

You initialize Windows Sockets by calling **WSAStartup**. You'll find the appropriate logic in the **WM_CREATE** section of **MainWndProc** in the WSOCK.C sample application Microsoft supplies with the Windows NT System Development Kit (SDK). A client can connect to a server by calling **socket** with the required socket type and the desired protocol, as shown in the **WM_COMMAND / IDM_CONNECT** case of **MainWndProc**; identifying the server, which is done in **FillAddr** in the example; and calling **connect**, shown in the **IDM_CONNECT** case.

A server waits for a connection with **socket**, **bind**, and **listen**, as shown in the **IDM_LISTEN** case. When a client connects, the server calls **accept**. The **WSAAsyncSelect**

Function	*Action*
accept()	An incoming connection is acknowledged and associated with an immediately created socket. The original socket is returned to the listening state.
bind()	Assign a local name to an unnamed socket.
closesocket()	Remove a socket descriptor from the per-process object reference table. Only blocks if SO_LINGER is set.
connect()	Initiate a connection on the specified socket.
getpeername()	Retrieve the name of the peer connected to the specified socket descriptor.
getsockname()	Retrieve the current name for the specified socket.
getsockopt()	Retrieve options associated with the specified socket descriptor.
htonl()	Convert a 32-bit quantity from host byte order to network byte order.
htons()	Convert a 16-bit quantity from host byte order to network byte order.
inet_addr()	Convert a character string representing a number in the Internet standard "." notation to an Internet address value.
inet_ntoa()	Convert an Internet address value to an ASCII string in "." notation, i.e., "a.b.c.d".
ioctlsocket()	Provide control for descriptors.
listen()	Listen for incoming connections on a specified socket.
ntohl()	Convert a 32-bit quantity from network byte order to host byte order.
ntohs()	Convert a 16-bit quantity from network byte order to host byte order.
recv()*	Receive data from a connected socket.
recvfrom()*	Receive data from either a connected or unconnected socket.
select()*	Perform synchronous I/O multiplexing.
send()*	Send data to a connected socket.
sendto()*	Send data to either a connected or unconnected socket.
setsockopt()	Store options associated with the specified socket descriptor.
shutdown()	Shut down part of a full-duplex connection.
socket()	Create an endpoint for communication and return a socket descriptor.

* The routine can block if acting on a blocking socket.

Table A1.8 Berkeley-Style Socket Routines

Function	Action
gethostbyaddr()*	Retrieve the name(s) and address corresponding to a network address.
gethostname()	Retrieve the name of the local host.
gethostbyname()*	Retrieve the name(s) and address corresponding to a host name.
getprotobyname()*	Retrieve the protocol name and number corresponding to a protocol name.
getprotobynumber()*	Retrieve the protocol name and number corresponding to a protocol number.
getservbyname()*	Retrieve the service name and port corresponding to a service name.
getservbyport()*	Retrieve the service name and port corresponding to a port.

* The routine can block under some circumstances.

Table A1.9 Socket "Database" Functions

function causes window messages to be sent when socket events, like incoming data, need to be handled. Alternatively—most appropriately in a threaded application—the server can use **select** to determine when a socket needs to be read, or simply use **recv** or **recvfrom** to read the

Function	Action
WSAAsyncGetHostByAddr() WSAAsyncGetHostByName() WSAAsyncGetProtoByName() WSAAsyncGetProtoByNumber() WSAAsyncGetServByName() WSAAsyncGetServByPort()	A set of functions that provide asynchronous versions of the standard Berkeley getXbyY() functions. For example, the WSAAsyncGetHostByName() function provides an asynchronous message-based implementation of the standard Berkeley gethostbyname() function.
WSAAsyncSelect()	Perform asynchronous version of select().
WSACancelAsyncRequest()	Cancel an outstanding instance of a WSAAsyncGetXByY() function.
WSACancelBlockingCall()	Cancel an outstanding "blocking" API call.
WSACleanup()	Sign off from the underlying Windows Sockets DLL.
WSAGetLastError()	Obtain details of last Windows Sockets API error.
WSAIsBlocking()	Determine if the underlying Windows Sockets DLL is already blocking an existing call for this thread.
WSASetBlockingHook()	"Hook" the blocking method used by the underlying Windows Sockets implementation.
WSASetLastError()	Set the error to be returned by a subsequent WSAGet LastError().
WSAStartup()	Initialize the underlying Windows Sockets DLL.
WSAUnhookBlockingHook()	Restore the original blocking function.

Table A1.10 Windows Asynchronous Socket Functions

next data packet. This is demonstrated in **AcceptThreadProc**. To send data, use **send** or **sendto**, as shown in case **IDM_SENDTCP**.

The functions **recv** and **send** work only with connected stream sockets—the rough equivalent of NetBIOS sessions or named pipes. The functions **recvfrom** and **sendto** can also work with datagrams—the unreliable protocol that also allows broadcasting. You can use datagram sockets in the same sort of applications as you would use NetBIOS datagrams or mailslots.

With the above summary in mind, you'll find WSOCK.C enlightening.

Remote Procedure Calls

Remote Procedure Calls (RPCs) are simultaneously the simplest and most complicated network programming mechanism supported by Windows NT. They are the simplest in concept: a program on one machine asks another program possibly running on another machine to perform some function on its behalf, in a way that looks a lot like an ordinary function call. But they are the most complicated in practice: defining the interface to a remote procedure requires a whole separate specification language, IDL, and implementing the call requires several layers of services.

The *RPC Programmer's Guide and Reference* is completely separate from the five-volume *Win32 Programmer's Reference*. The RPC manual and the MIDL compiler come with the Windows NT SDK; they do not come with Visual C++ for Windows NT. Obviously, we're not going to give you the contents of a 650-page manual here: all we want to do is give you a good feel for what RPCs can do and how to go about learning more. Table A1.11 lists the RPC API functions, but the API functions don't give you the whole picture.

RpcAbnormalTermination	RpcNetworkInqProtseqs	RpcNsProfileEltAdd
RpcBindingCopy	RpcNetworkIsProtseqValid	RpcNsProfileEltInqBegin
RpcBindingFree	RpcNsBindingExport	RpcNsProfileEltInqDone
RpcBindingFromStringBinding	RpcNsBindingImportBegin	RpcNsProfileEltInqNext
RpcBindingInqAuthClient	RpcNsProfileEltRemove	RpcObjectSetInqFn
RpcBindingInqAuthInfo	RpcNsBindingImportDone	RpcObjectSetType
RpcBindingInqObject	RpcNsBindingImportDone	RpcObjectInqType
RpcBindingReset	RpcNsBindingImportNext	RpcProtseqVectorFree
RpcBindingSetAuthInfo	RpcNsBindingInqEntryName	RpcRaiseException
RpcBindingSetObject	RpcNsBindingLookupBegin	RpcRevertToSelf
RpcBindingToStringBinding	RpcNsBindingLookupDone	RpcServerInqBindings
RpcBindingVectorFree	RpcNsBindingLookupNext	RpcServerInqIf
RpcEndExcept	RpcNsBindingSelect	RpcServerListen

Continued

Table A1.11 RPC API Functions (1.0)

RpcEndFinally	RpcNsBindingUnexport	RpcServerRegisterAuthInfo
RpcEpRegister	RpcNsEntryExpandName	RpcServerRegisterIf
RpcEpRegisterNoReplace	RpcNsEntryObjectInqBegin	RpcServerUnregisterIf
RpcEpResolveBinding	RpcNsEntryObjectInqBegin	RpcServerUseAllProtseqs
RpcEpUnregister	RpcNsEntryObjectInqDone	RpcServerUseAllProtseqsIf
RpcExcept	RpcNsEntryObjectInqNext	RpcServerUseProtseq
RpcExceptionCode	RpcNsGroupDelete	RpcServerUseProtseqIf
RpcFinally	RpcNsGroupMbrAdd	RpcServerUseProtseqEp
RpcIfIdVectorFree	RpcNsGroupMbrInqBegin	RpcStringBindingParse
RpcIfInqId	RpcNsGroupMbrInqDone	RpcStringFree
RpcImpersonateClient	RpcNsGroupMbrInqNext	RpcStringBindingCompose
RpcMgmtEnableIdleCleanup	RpcNsGroupMbrRemove	RpcTryExcept
RpcMgmtInqStats	RpcNsMgmtBindingUnexport	RpcTryFinally
RpcMgmtIsServerListening	RpcNsMgmtEntryCreate	RpcWinSetYieldInfo
RpcMgmtSetComTimeout	RpcNsMgmtEntryInqIfIds	YieldFunctionName
RpcMgmtSetServerStackSize	RpcNsMgmtHandleSetExpAge	UuidCreate
RpcMgmtStatsVectorFree	RpcNsMgmtInqExpAge	UuidFromString
RpcMgmtStopServerListening	RpcNsMgmtSetExpAge	UuidToString
RpcMgmtWaitServerListen	RpcNsProfileDelete	

Table A1.11 RPC API Functions (1.0) *(continued)*

In addition the the RPC API functions, you need to understand the Interface Definition Language (IDL), bindings, attributes, and transports. You can get all of this from the Microsoft RPC documentation, but you'll find it hard going unless you're already familiar with another implementation of RPCs, such as the Open System Foundation's Distributed Computing Environment (OSF DCE) standard for UNIX. What we'd like to do is walk you through "Hello, World" done with RPCs at the most basic level (as basic as Chapter 2 of the RPC manual, but more concise), so that you'll be ready to attack the Microsoft RPC materials on your own.

We won't bore you with the standard code for "Hello, World." The example we'll use first takes the small step of using a **HelloProc** function to write the string (we won't bore you with that, either); then it makes **HelloProc** a remote procedure.

The first step in setting up a remote procedure is to define the interface in IDL. An IDL file also needs a unique identification string, which you generate by running UUIDGEN, a tool that comes with the NT SDK. A minimal IDL file for HELLO might look like this:

```
[ uuid (6B29FC40-CA47-1067-B31D-00DD010662DA),  version(1.0) ]
interface hello
{
void HelloProc([in, string] unsigned char * pszString);
}
```

The top line of the file, the IDL header, contains the unique ID and the version number in square brackets. The last three lines of the file—the curly brackets and the declaration—constitute the IDL body. The non-C stuff in square brackets in the declaration gives additional information about the interface—in this case, **pszString** is an input string variable.

In addition to an IDL file, you need an ACF (Application Configuration File). A minimal ACF file for HELLO might look like the following:

```
[implicit_handle(handle_t hello_IfHandle)]
interface hello
{
}
```

While the IDL file contains the interface definition, the ACF contains RPC data and attributes that don't relate to the transmitted data. In this case, a binding handle is defined, which the RPC client uses to connect to the server. The interface name has to match the interface name given in the ACF file; the interface body is empty.

Compiling the IDL and ACF files with MIDL generates client and server C stub files and an include file. The stub files generated are actually pretty complicated—they're C programs to handle the client-server interaction over the network with RPC function calls. For instance, the client and server stubs for **HelloProc** look like this:

Hello_C.C (HelloProc client stub generated by MIDL)

```
#include <string.h>
#include "hello.h"
handle_t hello_IfHandle;
extern RPC_DISPATCH_TABLE hello_DispatchTable;
static RPC_CLIENT_INTERFACE ___RpcClientInterface =  {
  sizeof(RPC_CLIENT_INTERFACE),
  {{0x906B0CE0,0xC70B,0x1067,{0xB3,0x17,0x00,0xDD,0x01,0x06,0x62,
   0xDA}},  {1,0}},
  {{0x8A885D04L,0x1CEB,0x11C9,{0x9F,0xE8,0x08,0x00,0x2B,0x10,0x48,
   0x60}},  {2,0}}, 0,0,0,0 };
RPC_IF_HANDLE hello_ClientIfHandle =
   (RPC_IF_HANDLE) &___RpcClientInterface;
void HelloProc(unsigned char *pszString)
  {
  unsigned char * _packet;
  unsigned int    _length;
  RPC_STATUS _status;
  RPC_MESSAGE _message;
  PRPC_MESSAGE _prpcmsg = & _message;

  ((void)( _packet ));
  ((void)( _length ));
  _message.Handle = hello_IfHandle;
  _message.RpcInterfaceInformation =
     (void __RPC_FAR *) &___RpcClientInterface;
  _prpcmsg->BufferLength = 0;
  if (pszString == (void *)0)
   RpcRaiseException(RPC_X_NULL_REF_POINTER);
  tree_size_ndr(&(pszString), _prpcmsg, "s1", 1);
  _message.ProcNum = 0;
  _status = I_RpcGetBuffer(&_message);
  if (_status) RpcRaiseException(_status);
```

```
_packet = _message.Buffer;
_length = _message.BufferLength;
_message.BufferLength = 0;
tree_into_ndr(&(pszString), _prpcmsg, "s1", 1);
_message.Buffer = _packet;
_message.BufferLength = _length;
_status = I_RpcSendReceive(&_message);
if (_status) RpcRaiseException(_status);
_status = I_RpcFreeBuffer(&_message);
if (_status) RpcRaiseException(_status);
}
```

Hello_S.C (HelloProc server stub generated by MIDL)

```
#include <string.h>
#include "hello.h"
extern RPC_DISPATCH_TABLE hello_DispatchTable;
static RPC_SERVER_INTERFACE ___RpcServerInterface = {
  sizeof(RPC_SERVER_INTERFACE),
  {{0x906B0CE0,0xC70B,0x1067,{0xB3,0x17,0x00,0xDD,0x01,0x06,
   0x62,0xDA}}, {1,0}},
  {{0x8A885D04L,0x1CEB,0x11C9,{0x9F,0xE8,0x08,0x00,0x2B,0x10,
   0x48,0x60}}, {2,0}}, &hello_DispatchTable,0,0,0 };
RPC_IF_HANDLE hello_ServerIfHandle =
   (RPC_IF_HANDLE) &___RpcServerInterface;
void __RPC_STUB hello_HelloProc(PRPC_MESSAGE _prpcmsg)
  {
  unsigned char *pszString = (void *)0;
  unsigned long _alloc_total;
  unsigned long _valid_lower;
  unsigned long _valid_total;
  unsigned char * _packet;
  unsigned char * _tempbuf;
  unsigned char * _savebuf;
  RPC_STATUS _status;
  _packet = _prpcmsg->Buffer;
  ((void)( _alloc_total ));
  ((void)( _valid_total ));
  ((void)( _valid_lower ));
  ((void)( _packet ));
  ((void)( _tempbuf ));
  ((void)( _savebuf ));
  RpcTryExcept
    {
    _tempbuf = _prpcmsg->Buffer;
    // recv total number of elements
    long_from_ndr(_prpcmsg, &_alloc_total);
    if (pszString == (void *)0)
      {
      pszString = MIDL_user_allocate ((size_t)
     (_alloc_total * sizeof(char)));
      }
    data_from_ndr(_prpcmsg, (void __RPC_FAR *) (pszString),
```

```
        "s1", 1);
      }
    RpcExcept(1)
      {
          RpcRaiseException(RpcExceptionCode());
      }
    RpcEndExcept
    if (((unsigned int)(((unsigned char *)_prpcmsg->Buffer)
      - _packet)) > _prpcmsg->BufferLength)
      RpcRaiseException(RPC_X_BAD_STUB_DATA);
    RpcTryFinally
      {
      if (_prpcmsg->ManagerEpv)
        {
        ((hello_SERVER_EPV *)(_prpcmsg->ManagerEpv))
          ->HelloProc(pszString);
        }
      else
        {
       HelloProc(pszString);
        }
      _prpcmsg->BufferLength = 0;
      _prpcmsg->Buffer = _packet;
      _status = I_RpcGetBuffer(_prpcmsg);
      if (_status) RpcRaiseException(_status);
      }
    RpcFinally
      {
      MIDL_user_free ((void __RPC_FAR *)pszString);
      }
    RpcEndFinally
    }
```

You aren't spared from writing all the RPC code, however. In this application, the client is responsible for connecting to the server. You notice that the default protocol sequence used is for a named pipe, **\pipe\hello**:

From HELLOC.C (hand-written client code)

```
RPC_STATUS status;
unsigned char * pszUuid                        = NULL;
unsigned char * pszProtocolSequence = "ncacn_np";
unsigned char * pszNetworkAddress = NULL;
unsigned char * pszEndpoint                    = "\\pipe\\hello";
unsigned char * pszOptions                     = NULL;
unsigned char * pszStringBinding  = NULL;
unsigned char * pszString                      = "hello, world";
unsigned long ulCode;
int i;
//...
 status = RpcStringBindingCompose(pszUuid,
                       pszProtocolSequence,
```

```
                              pszNetworkAddress,
                              pszEndpoint,
                              pszOptions,
                              &pszStringBinding);
    printf("RpcStringBindingCompose returned 0x%x\n", status);
    printf("pszStringBinding = %s\n", pszStringBinding);
    if (status) {
       exit(status);
     }
    status = RpcBindingFromStringBinding(pszStringBinding,
                           &hello_IfHandle);
    printf("RpcBindingFromStringBinding returned 0x%x\n", status);
    if (status) {
       exit(status);
     }
    printf("Calling the remote procedure 'HelloProc'\n");
    printf("Print the string '%s' on the server\n", pszString);

    RpcTryExcept {
       HelloProc(pszString);  // make call with user message
      }
    RpcExcept(1) {
       ulCode = RpcExceptionCode();
       printf("Runtime reported exception 0x%lx = %ld\n", ulCode,
            ulCode);
      }
    RpcEndExcept

    status = RpcStringFree(&pszStringBinding);
    printf("RpcStringFree returned 0x%x\n", status);
    if (status) {
       exit(status);
     }

    status = RpcBindingFree(&hello_IfHandle);
    printf("RpcBindingFree returned 0x%x\n", status);
    if (status) {
       exit(status);
      }
```

Boiled down to its essentials, the above code amounts to composing the binding string, establishing the binding, calling the remote procedure through its stub, freeing the binding string, and freeing the binding.

In addition to establishing its own binding prior to calling the remote procedure, the client has to provide callback routines so that the RPC libraries can allocate and free memory. In this case, they are trivial:

```
void __RPC_FAR * __RPC_API midl_user_allocate(size_t len)
{
   return(malloc(len));
}
```

```
void __RPC_API midl_user_free(void __RPC_FAR * ptr)
{
    free(ptr);
}
```

On the server side, you need to write code to set the protocol sequence, register the interface, and listen for a client. The protocol used has to match on client and server:

```
RPC_STATUS status;
unsigned char * pszProtocolSequence = "ncacn_np";
unsigned char * pszSecurity                        = NULL;
unsigned char * pszEndpoint                        = "\\pipe\\hello";
unsigned int   cMinCalls                   = 1;
unsigned int   cMaxCalls                   = 20;
unsigned int   fDontWait                   = FALSE;
int i;
//...

 status = RpcServerUseProtseqEp(pszProtocolSequence,
                      cMaxCalls,
                      pszEndpoint,
                      pszSecurity);  // Security descriptor
 printf("RpcServerUseProtseqEp returned 0x%x\n", status);
 if (status) {
     exit(status);
    }

 status = RpcServerRegisterIf(hello_ServerIfHandle, //interface
                      NULL,    // MgrTypeUuid
                      NULL);   // MgrEpv
 printf("RpcServerRegisterIf returned 0x%x\n", status);
 if (status) {
     exit(status);
    }

 printf("Calling RpcServerListen\n");
 status = RpcServerListen(cMinCalls,
                    cMaxCalls,
                    fDontWait);
 printf("RpcServerListen returned: 0x%x\n", status);
 if (status) {
     exit(status);
    }

 if (fDontWait) {
     printf("Calling RpcMgmtWaitServerListen\n");
     status = RpcMgmtWaitServerListen(); // wait operation
     printf("RpcMgmtWaitServerListen returned: 0x%x\n", status);
     if (status) {
        exit(status);
       }
    }
```

You'll need to provide **midl_user_allocate** and **midl_user_free** callbacks on the server side: they're the same as on the client side. And finally, you'll need a way to tell the server to shut down, which we've omitted here for brevity. (You'll find it in the Microsoft MSTOOLS\SAMPLES\RPC\HELLO sample.)

If we build the client and server and run the server we'll see:

```
RpcServerUseProtseqEp returned 0x0
RpcServerRegisterIf returned 0x0
Calling RpcServerListen
```

Then the server will stop. If we run the client on another machine or in another CMD session on the same machine, the server will continue and display:

```
hello, world

Calling RpcMgmtStopServerListening
RpcMgmtStopServerListening returned: 0x0
Calling RpcServerUnregisterIf
RpcServerUnregisterIf returned 0x0
RpcServerListen returned: 0x0
```

What the client will display in its CMD session is:

```
RpcStringBindingCompose returned 0x0
pszStringBinding = ncacn_np:[\\pipe\\hello]
RpcBindingFromStringBinding returned 0x0
Calling the remote procedure 'HelloProc'
Print the string 'hello, world' on the server
Calling the remote procedure 'Shutdown'
RpcStringFree returned 0x0
RpcBindingFree returned 0x0
```

Obviously, that was an awful lot of work to make "Hello, World" display. On the other hand, a great deal of the work was done with a few lines of IDL and ACF code, and the resulting client-server application works not only on a single Windows NT machine, but between two NT machines linked by a network, and between a DOS or Windows client and a Windows NT server. In addition, it works on a variety of network transports: in addition to named pipes, the NT implementation of RPC supports NetBIOS and TCP/IP transports. The Windows implementation supports all three of these plus DECnet, and the DOS implementation supports all the aforementioned plus SPX. There is no Win32s implementation of RPCs, however, at least in version 1.1 of Win32s.

We have the sense that RPCs are, at least in the long term, *the* strategic way to write distributed applications. Learning the IDL and ACF languages shouldn't be much of a challenge for a C or C++ programmer: make the effort, and you won't regret it.

DDE and NetDDE

DDE is the principal mechanism for interprocess communication in 16-bit Windows. The Microsoft Windows Dynamic Data Exchange (DDE) protocol defines a method for communi-

Function	*Action*
DdeImpersonateClient	Impersonates a DDE client window
DdeSetQualityOfService	Specifies DDE quality of service
FreeDDElParam	Frees a DDE message lParam
ImpersonateDdeClientWindow	Impersonates a DDE client window
PackDDElParam	Packs data into a DDE message lParam
ReuseDDElParam	Reuses a DDE message lParam
UnpackDDElParam	Unpacks data from a DDE message lParam

Table A1.12 New DDE functions in Win32

cating among applications that takes place as applications send messages to each other to initiate conversations, to request and share data, and to terminate conversations.

In the *hot link* form of DDE transfer, the *server* application sends data to the *client* application whenever the data changes; this guarantees that the derived form of the data (perhaps a table in a word processing document) will always reflect the current state of the original data (perhaps a spreadsheet). A variation of this, the *warm link* notifies the client when the data has changed, but sends the data only if the client wants it; this enables the client to control the rate at which it receives data. A simpler mechanism, the *request,* is equivalent to a single copy operation from the server and a single paste operation to the client, without the need for the intermediate step of putting the data on the clipboard.

DDE also supports a back channel transfer, the *poke*. And *execute,* perhaps the most intriguing DDE mechanism of all, allows one application to control another.

DDE supports a *client-server* architecture in which both client and server programs carry on multiple *conversations* with other applications. Each conversation has a *topic* and may include multiple *advisories* each of which refers to an *item*. The application is responsible for keeping track of ongoing conversations and advisories; conversations are uniquely identified by the window handles of the client and server.

Windows NT and Windows for Workgroups continue to support DDE as an interprocess communication protocol, and additionally support NetDDE, a special form of DDE that allows it to work across the network. Because of NT's security requirements and change from 16-bit handles to 32-bit handles, a few new DDE functions have been added in Win32. They are listed in Table A1.12.

The functions **PackDDElParam** and **UnpackDDElParam** allow the 32-bit program to pack and unpack parameters in the DDE message's **lParam**: use them instead of **MAKELONG**, **LOWORD**, and **HIWORD**. **ReuseDDElParam** and **FreeDDElParam** allow you to manage the dynamic memory used for packing parameters. The two impersonation functions allow a DDE server to take on the security attributes of its client: this is useful when a server has a higher privilege than the client and needs to maintain security.

While you can still program DDE by sending messages, the preferred method for programming DDE is to use the Dynamic Data Exchange Management Library (DDEML). Both

Function	*Action*
DdeAbandonTransaction	Abandons an asynchronous transaction
DdeAccessData	Accesses a DDE data object
DdeAddData	Adds data to a DDE data object
DdeCallback	Processes DDEML transactions
DdeClientTransaction	Begins a DDE data transaction
DdeCmpStringHandles	Compares two DDE string handles
DdeConnect	Establishes a conversation with a server
DdeConnectList	Establishes multiple DDE conversations
DdeCreateDataHandle	Creates a DDE data handle
DdeCreateStringHandle	Creates a DDE string handle
DdeDisconnect	Terminates a DDE conversation
DdeDisconnectList	Destroys a DDE conversation list
DdeEnableCallback	Enables or disables one or more DDE conversations
DdeFreeDataHandle	Frees a DDE data object
DdeFreeStringHandle	Frees a DDE string handle
DdeGetData	Copies data from a DDE data object to a buffer
DdeGetLastError	Returns an error code set by a DDEML function
DdeInitialize	Registers an application with the DDEML
DdeKeepStringHandle	Increments the usage count for a string handle
DdeNameService	Registers or unregisters a service name
DdePostAdvise	Prompts a server to send advise data to a client
DdeQueryConvInfo	Retrieves information about a DDE conversation
DdeQueryNextServer	Obtains the next handle in a conversation list
DdeQueryString	Copies string-handle text to a buffer
DdeReconnect	Reestablishes a DDE conversation
DdeSetUserHandle	Associates a user-defined handle with a transaction
DdeUnaccessData	Frees a DDE data object
DdeUninitialize	Frees an application's DDEML resources

Table A1.13 DDEML Functions

methods are explained in Chapter 5 of *Advanced Windows Programming*. For your convenience, the DDEML functions are listed in Table A1.13.

NetDDE is a minor variation on DDE that can be used by all DDE-aware applications. Normally, you establish a DDE conversation with an application on a topic and specify items within the topic. With NetDDE, the true application and topic are maintained in a DDE share, which is kept in a database. You establish a DDE conversation indirectly, by connecting to the special application NDDE$ on the remote machine, using the share name as the topic. This is the way the ClipBook applet works: it establishes a DDE share for each ClipBook page on each machine.

NetDDE acts as a redirector for DDE, and communicates over the network using NetBIOS. In Windows NT, NetBIOS can work on any transport protocol. When NetDDE establishes the conversation, it retrieves the DDE share and connects to the real application and

Function	*Action*
NDdeGetErrorString	Converts net DDE error code to error string
NDdeGetShareSecurity	Obtains net DDE share's security descriptor
NDdeGetTrustedShare	Retrieves net DDE trusted share options
NDdeIsValidAppTopicList	Validates net DDE app and topic string syntax
NDdeIsValidShareName	Validates net DDE share name syntax
NDdeSetShareSecurity	Sets a net DDE share's security information
NDdeSetTrustedShare	Applies trust options to a net DDE share
NDdeShareAdd	Adds a net DDE share
NDdeShareDel	Deletes a net DDE share
NDdeShareEnum	Lists net DDE shares
NDdeShareGetInfo	Obtains information about a net DDE sharer
NDdeShareSetInfo	Modifies an existing net DDE share's info
NDdeTrustedShareEnum	Lists trusted shares in calling process's context

Table A1.14 Win32 Network DDE Functions

topic locally. Then the applications can exchange data on the actual items, and neither application needs to be explicitly aware of NetDDE.

On the other hand, a network application that is aware of NetDDE can browse for shares, establish its own shares, and delete its own shares. The Network DDE Functions are listed in Table A1.14.

With the exception of the functions that deal with trusted shares and security, the Win32 NetDDE functions are also supported in Windows for Workgroups. They are not, however, included in Win32s. Accessing them in Windows for Workgroups programs requires you to have a copy of NDDEAPI.H and NDDEAPI.LIB,[2] or dynamically link to the functions in NDDEAPI.DLL.

Should you build networked applications with NetDDE? If you want them to work on Windows for Workgroups and Windows NT machines, or they already support DDE, certainly. If you need to access other environments, no. And if you have a high-volume communications application and care about transfer rate, consider another mechanism.

If you're interested only in networked communications, you can skip the rest of this appendix. On the other hand, there's more to network programming than the core communications functions, so you might want to read on.

File Mapping (Memory-Mapped Files)

File mapping is often used for interprocess communications—partly because it allows high-rate local communications, and partly because it is very similar to a UNIX mechanism often

[2]Available on CompuServe—download the Windows for Workgroups SDK from the WinExt forum.

Function	*Action*
CreateFileMapping	Returns handle to a new file mapping object
FlushViewOfFile	Flushes a byte range within a mapped view
MapViewOfFile	Maps a view into an address space
MapViewOfFileEx	Maps a view into an address space
OpenFileMapping	Opens a named-file mapping object
UnmapViewOfFile	Unmaps a file view

Table A1.15 Win32 File Mapping Functions

used to implement databases. 16-bit Windows allows you to pass pieces of global shared memory among processes: file mapping is as close as Windows NT comes. The Win32 file mapping functions are listed in Table A1.15.

File mapping actually has two uses. The first is to let you treat a file like memory: mapping is the copying of a file's contents to a process's virtual address space. The copy of the-file's contents is called the file view, and the internal structure the operating system uses to maintain the copy is called the file-mapping object.

The second use is data sharing. Another process can create an identical file view in its own virtual address space by using the first process's file-mapping object to create the view. Any process that has the name or a handle of a file-mapping object can create a file view. Note that you can map named files, or simply ask for shared memory backed by the system paging file. The signal that you want shared memory backed by the page file is a file handle of **(HANDLE)FFFFFFFF**.

The following example demonstrates data sharing using file mapping. As you can see, the process creating the shared memory uses **CreateFileMapping** and **MapViewOfFile**, while the process sharing the memory uses **OpenFileMapping** and **MapViewOfFile**.

```
//-----------------------------------
// In creating process
//-----------------------------------
hFileMapping = CreateFileMapping(
          hFile,          //file handle to map
          NULL,        //security
          PAGE_READWRITE, //protection
          dwSizeHigh,     //high 32 bits of size
          dwSizeLow,   //low 32 bits of size
          "NameOfFileMappingObject");
assert(hFileMapping);
base = MapViewOfFile(
          hFileMapping,
          FILE_MAP_WRITE, //access mode
          dwOffsetHigh,   //high 32 bits of file offset
          dwOffsetLow,    //low 32 bits of file offset
```

```
          dwSizeToMap);   //size to map, 0 means whole file
// base points to mapped view of file
assert(base);
//...

//--------------------------------
// In sharing process
//--------------------------------
hFileMapping = OpenFileMapping(
          FILE_MAP_READ, //access mode
          FALSE,        //inherit handle?
          "NameOfFileMappingObject");
assert(hFileMapping);
base = MapViewOfFile(
          hFileMapping,
          FILE_MAP_READ, //access mode
          dwOffsetHigh,         //high 32 bits of file offset
          dwOffsetLow,   //low 32 bits of file offset
          dwSizeToMap);         //size to map, 0 means whole file
//
// base points to mapped view of file.
// Note that the value of base
// is not necessarily the same in both
// processes sharing the file
// mapping object.
//
assert(base);
```

When the processes are done with the mapped file, they should call **UnmapViewofFile** to remove the map from their address space and flush any dirty pages to the disk image of the file. Processes that need to commit portions of the shared file map to disk without unmapping the file can use **FlushViewOfFile** as needed.

Security

Windows NT has a centralized security facility in which all named objects (and some unnamed objects) have security descriptors (SDs), and all users and processes have access tokens and security identifiers (SIDs). Security descriptors include information about the owner of the object and an access-control list (ACL), which contains access-control entries (ACEs) that identify the users and groups allowed or denied access to the object.

When you program Windows NT, you access objects by getting handles to them, then using the handles. The security process applies when you try to get the handle: the system compares your access token with the object's access-control entries, and grants you a handle only if at least one ACE exists that allows your token access.

There can be two kinds of access control lists in a security descriptor. A system ACL is controlled by the system administrator, and is used to control *auditing*, among other things. A discretionary ACL is controlled by the owner of the object.

With sufficient privilege, you can manipulate access programmatically, often by adding a discretionary ACL to an object's security descriptor. The functions to manipulate SDs, ACLs, ACEs, tokens, SIDs, and related objects like audit alarms are listed in Table A1.16.

Function	*Action*
AccessCheck	Validates a client's access rights
AccessCheckAndAuditAlarm	Validates access, generates audit and alarm
AddAccessAllowedAce	Adds ACCESS_ALLOWED_ACE to ACL
AddAccessDeniedAce	Adds ACCESS_DENIED_ACE to ACL
AddAce	Adds an ACE to an existing ACL
AddAuditAccessAce	Adds SYSTEM_AUDIT_ACE to ACL
AdjustTokenGroups	Enables/disables groups in a token
AdjustTokenPrivileges	Enables/disables token privileges
AllocateAndInitializeSid	Allocates and initializes SID with subauthorities
AllocateLocallyUniqueId	Allocates an LUID
AreAllAccessesGranted	Checks for all desired access
AreAnyAccessesGranted	Checks for any desired access
CopySid	Copies an SID to a buffer
CreatePrivateObjectSecurity	Allocates and initializes a protected SD
DdeImpersonateClient	DDE server impersonates client
DeleteAce	Deletes an ACE from an existing ACL
DestroyPrivateObjectSecurity	Deletes a protected server object's SD
DuplicateToken	Duplicates an access token
EqualPrefixSid	Test two SID prefixes for equality
EqualSid	Tests two SID security IDs for equality
FindFirstFreeAce	Retrieves a pointer to first free ACL byte
FreeSid	Frees an allocated SID
GetAce	Retrieves a pointer to an ACE in an ACL
GetAclInformation	Retrieves access-control list information
GetFileSecurity	Gets file or directory security information
GetKernelObjectSecurity	Retrieves kernel object SD
GetLengthSid	Returns length of an SID
GetPrivateObjectSecurity	Retrieves protected server object SD
GetProcessWindowStation	Returns process window-station handle
GetSecurityDescriptorControl	Retrieves SD revision and control info
GetSecurityDescriptorDacl	Retrieves SD discretionary ACL
GetSecurityDescriptorGroup	Retrieves SD primary group information
GetSecurityDescriptorLength	Returns SD length
GetSecurityDescriptorOwner	Retrieves SD owner
GetSecurityDescriptorSacl	Retrieves SD system ACL
GetSidIdentifierAuthority	Returns ID authority field address
GetSidLengthRequired	Returns required length of SID
GetSidSubAuthority	Returns subauthority array address
GetSidSubAuthorityCount	Returns subauthority field address

Table A1.16 Win32 Security Functions

Function	*Action*
GetThreadDesktop	Returns thread desktop handle
GetTokenInformation	Retrieves specified token information
GetUserObjectSecurity	Retrieves server object SD information
ImpersonateNamedPipeClient	Pipe server acts as client
ImpersonateSelf	Gets impersonation for calling process
InitializeAcl	Creates a new access-control list
nitializeSecurityDescriptor	Initializes a security descriptor
InitializeSid	Initializes an SID
IsValidAcl	Validates an access-control list
IsValidSecurityDescriptor	Validates security descriptor
IsValidSid	Validates an SID
LookupAccountName	Translates account name to SID
LookupAccountSid	Translates SID to account name
LookupPrivilegeDisplayName	Retrieves a displayable privilege name
LookupPrivilegeName	Retrieves a programmatic privilege name
LookupPrivilegeValue	Retrieves LUID for privilege name
MakeAbsoluteSD	Creates absolute SD from self-relative
MakeSelfRelativeSD	Creates self-relative SD from absolute
MapGenericMask	Maps generic access to specific/standard
ObjectCloseAuditAlarm	Generates audit/alarm when object is deleted
ObjectOpenAuditAlarm	Generates audit/alarm when object is accessed
ObjectPrivilegeAuditAlarm	Generates audit/alarm on privileged operation
OpenProcessToken	Opens process token object
OpenThreadToken	Opens thread token object
PrivilegeCheck	Tests client security context for privileges
PrivilegedServiceAuditAlarm	Audit/alarm on privileged system service
RevertToSelf	Stops impersonation
SetAclInformation	Sets information in an ACL
SetFileSecurity	Sets file or directory security
SetKernelObjectSecurity	Sets kernel object security
SetPrivateObjectSecurity	Modifies existing SD
SetSecurityDescriptorDacl	Sets DACL information
SetSecurityDescriptorGroup	Sets SD primary group information
SetSecurityDescriptorOwner	Sets SD owner
SetSecurityDescriptorSacl	Sets SACL information
SetTokenInformation	Sets various token information
SetUserObjectSecurity	Sets security-descriptor values

Table A1.16 Win32 Security Functions *(continued)*

We won't give any security example programs here: you can find them readily in the Win32 SDK help files and in the CHECK_SD, EXITWIN, REGISTRY, SIDCLN, and TAKE-OWN samples. We will summarize the key points, though.

If you want to deny all access to an object, you can add an *empty* discretionary ACL to its security descriptor. If you want to allow all access to an object, you can give it a **NULL** discretionary ACL. Note the difference between empty and NULL here: empty means there is an ACL, but it has no entries; NULL means there is no ACL.

Both File Manager and REGEDT32 include security editors that use the above functions extensively. If you want the security editors to work on an object whose security you've set programmatically, follow the editors' conventions.

Service Control Manager

A *service* is an executable object that is installed in a registry database maintained by the service control manager. The services database determines whether each installed service is started on demand or is started automatically when the system starts up; it can also contain logon and security information for a service so that a service can run even though no user is logged on.

Win32 services conform to the interface rules of the service control manager. Driver services conform to the device driver protocols for Windows NT. The service control manager functions are listed in Table A1.17. Device drivers are beyond the scope of this work.

Function	*Action*
ChangeServiceConfig	Change service configuration parameters.
CloseServiceHandle	Close Service Control Manager object.
ControlService	Send a control to a service.
CreateService	Create a service object.
DeleteService	Remove service from SC Manager database.
EnumDependentServices	Enumerate services dependent on device.
EnumServicesStatus	Enumerate services in SC manager database.
Handler	Control handler function of a service.
LockServiceDatabase	Lock specified SC Manager database.
NotifyBootConfigStatus	Notify/respond to acceptability of boot configuration.
OpenService	Open an existing service.
OpenSCManager	Connect to service control manager.
QueryServiceConfig	Get service configuration parameters.
QueryServiceLockStatus	Get service database lock status.
QueryServiceObjectSecurity	Get service object security descriptor.
QueryServiceStatus	Get service status.
RegisterServiceCtrlHandler	Register service control request handler.
ServiceMain	Main function of a service.
SetServiceStatus	Update service status to SC Manager.
SetServiceObjectSecurity	Modify service object security descriptor.
StartService	Start running a service.
StartServiceCtrlDispatcher	Connect thread as dispatch thread.
UnlockServiceDatabase	Unlock specified database.

Table A1.17 Win32 Service Control Manager Functions

The service control manager is actually an RPC server, so you can control services on remote machines. You can write three kinds of programs that would use service control functions: a Win32 service process, which provides executable code for services and provides status information to the service control manager; a service configuration program, which manipulates the service control database; and a service control program, which starts a service and controls a running service.

The SDK SERVICE sample demonstrates a simple service process, a client for it, and a program to install and remove service processes. SIMPLE.C is a service process that echoes and mangles input it receives on a named pipe. CLIENT.C sends a string on the named pipe and displays the resulting echo. And INSTSRV.C demonstrates using **CreateService** and **DeleteService**.

A Win32 service process has to include a main function that immediately calls the **StartServiceCtrlDispatcher** function to connect the main thread of the process to the Service Control Manager. It also needs an entry point function, **ServiceMain** in Table A1.17, for each service that can run in the process, and a control handler function, **Handler** in Table A1.17, for each service that can run in the process. The actual names for the service entry points are determined by the dispatch table passed to **StartServiceCtrlDispatcher**:

```
VOID main() {
    SERVICE_TABLE_ENTRY dispatchTable[] = {
        { TEXT("SimpleService"), //first service in list
        (LPSERVICE_MAIN_FUNCTION)service_main },
        { NULL, NULL } //NULLs terminate list of services
    };

    if (!StartServiceCtrlDispatcher(dispatchTable)) {
        StopSimpleService("StartServiceCtrlDispatcher failed.");
    }
}
```

The actual name for the handler is determined by the main service entry point, and registered with the service control manager using the **RegisterServiceCtrlHandler** function:

```
VOID service_main(DWORD dwArgc, LPTSTR *lpszArgv) {
    DWORD                   dwWait;
    PSECURITY_DESCRIPTOR    pSD;
    SECURITY_ATTRIBUTES     sa;

    // register our service control handler:
    //
    sshStatusHandle = RegisterServiceCtrlHandler(
                            TEXT("SimpleService"),
                            service_ctrl);
    if (!sshStatusHandle)
        goto cleanup;
```

A simple service process might include all the code it needed to do its job in its own executable. A more complicated service process might well spawn additional daemon processes. For instance, you could write a service process that accepted an SQL query on named pipes, submitted the query to a separate database process through named shared memory, signaled the database that a query was pending using an event, and returned the query result to the originator via the named pipes.

It might also be possible to write a generic service process that did nothing but start and stop other processes. For instance, you might have a character-mode OS/2 server process that you want to run on your Windows NT system. You could make it look and act like a real NT server process, even though it runs in the OS/2 subsystem, by writing a small NT service process to start and control it. The OS/2 process would handle its own interprocess communications.

It's really fairly easy to turn a service application of any kind into a true Win32 service process. Consider doing this for any server application that should run independent of the current user—which applies to most network services.

You should also consider making your service configuration program a Control Panel applet. A Control Panel applet resides in a DLL, typically is given the CPL extension, and includes a standard callback entry-point function named **CPlApplet**, which must be exported. The application needs to include the CPL.H header file for the definition of the messages that Control Panel sends to the applet.

You can find all the information you need to write your own Control Panel applets in the Win32 SDK help by searching for "Control Panel Applications Overview." From there, you can browse through the successive help topics, or investigate the cross-references. There is a fairly complete example included in one of the help topics, as well—and a sample in \q_a\samples\cpl—although it won't make much sense until you've read the preceding topics. In any case, doing a control panel applet isn't difficult—once you have the information.

Event Logging

One issue many server applications face is how to display error conditions. Often, the server process has no user interface, and can't even be sure it is running on a machine with an active screen: even a standard message box might pop up on a screen that is powered down, or hidden in a closet.

Event logging provides a standard, centralized way for applications (and Windows NT) to record important software and hardware events—not only error conditions, but events that ought to leave an audit trail. The Windows NT Event Viewer offers a standard user interface for viewing the logs, and the event logging functions provide ways to examine and back up the logs as well as to report events. The Win32 event logging functions are listed in Table A1.18.

Events are classified as information, warnings, and errors. All event classifications have well-defined common data and can optionally include event-specific data. For example, information can assert that a service has started or is stopping, that a process connected or disconnected, or that some specific action was performed.

To give a somewhat trivial example, we might have a process that is controlling a soda machine. Information might record that the machine was filled, or that a column of cans was changed to a different kind of soda. Information might also record each transaction on the machine—what kind of soda was dispensed, what coins were tendered, and what coins were

Function	Action
BackupEventLog	Saves an event log in a backup file
ClearEventLog	Clears the event log
CloseEventLog	Closes an event-log handle
DeregisterEventSource	Closes a registered event handle
GetNumberOfEventLogRecords	Gets number of records in event log
GetOldestEventLogRecord	Retrieves number of oldest record
OpenBackupEventLog	Opens a handle to a backup event log
OpenEventLog	Opens an event-log handle
ReadEventLog	Reads entries from an event log
RegisterEventSource	Returns a registered event-log handle
ReportEvent	Writes an event-log entry

Table A1.18 Win32 Event Logging Functions

given in change. A viewing process for the soda machine's event log would be able to deduce the machine's exact status, plot historical usage, and predict future usage for ordering purposes.

Warnings are used for recoverable problems. For our soda machine, we might want to log a warning when any column drops below three cans, or when the machine gets low on change. Errors are used for nonrecoverable conditions that might cause an application to fail. For the soda machine, that might be running out of soda in any column, running out of change, or being unable to keep the soda cold.

Of course, you can use event logs for more serious purposes as well. Windows NT itself uses the event log for conditions like drivers failing to load, disk drive timeouts, and network errors. It also uses the event log to keep an audit trail (if the administrator enables it) of users logging in and out, security policy changes, system restarts, and so on.

Performance Monitoring

Network administrators often need to monitor network and disk server performance in order to maintain and tune their facilities. Windows NT has a useful Performance Monitor program in the Administrative Tools group. True to the open spirit of Win32, the key functions used by the Performance Monitor are exposed in the API and available for anyone to use. They are listed in Table A1.19.

Why would anyone want to reinvent the Performance Monitor? You might, for instance, want to write a statistics-gathering program, or an alarm panel. The statistics-gathering program might collect selected performance numbers from a list of machines on the network at predetermined intervals and save them in a database: a companion program would process the saved data on demand, computing means and standard deviations, displaying time series graphs, histograms and scatter plots, and otherwise making sense of the network's behavior over time. The alarm panel would scan the network at intervals and send a message to the des-

Function	Action
RegConnectRegistry	Connects to registry on a remote system
RegQueryValueEx	Retrieves the type and data for a specified value name associated with an open registry key
QueryPerformanceCounter	Obtains performance counter value
QueryPerformanceFrequency	Returns performance counter frequency

Table A1.19 Win32 Performance Monitoring Functions

ignated administrator when hard disks were full or performance figures fell outside their normal range.

NT's high-resolution performance counter functions allow you to access the system's high-speed timer. **QueryPerformanceFrequency** tells you the number of counts per second for the timer, and **QueryPerformanceCounter** tells you the current reading of the timer. These functions are similar to the C library function **clock** and the associated constant **CLOCKS_PER_SEC**, but might give you better time resolution.

NT's *system* performance numbers are accessed through the registry, although they are not actually stored in the persistent registry "hives." You can get system performance information by calling **RegQueryValueEx** with the key **HKEY_PERFORMANCE_DATA**. If you wish, use **RegOpenKey** to open the **HKEY_PERFORMANCE_DATA** handle, but remember to use **RegCloseKey** to close the handle when you're done with it.

Using **RegQueryValueEx** with **HKEY_PERFORMANCE_DATA** causes the system to collect the data from the appropriate system object managers. To collect data from a remote system, use **RegConnectRegistry** with the name of the remote system and the **HKEY_PERFORMANCE_DATA** key to retrieve a key usable with **RegQueryValueEx** to actually retrieve performance data from the remote system.

RegQueryValueEx returns a **PERF_DATA_BLOCK** structure followed by one **PERF_OBJECT_TYPE** structure and accompanying data for each type of object being monitored. The system being observed defines objects that can be monitored, typically processors, disks, and memory.

The performance data block describes the performance data returned by **RegQueryValueEx**:

```
typedef struct _PERF_DATA_BLOCK { /* pdb */
    WCHAR        Signature[4];
    DWORD        LittleEndian;
    DWORD        Version;
    DWORD        Revision;
    DWORD        TotalByteLength;
    DWORD        HeaderLength;
    DWORD        NumObjectTypes;
    DWORD        DefaultObject;
    SYSTEMTIME   SystemTime;         //time of measurement in UTC format
```

```
    LARGE_INTEGER PerfTime;            //actual data value counts
    LARGE_INTEGER PerfFreq;            //timer counts per second
    LARGE_INTEGER PerfTime100nSec;  //data value in 100 ns units
    DWORD         SystemNameLength;
    DWORD         SystemNameOffset;
} PERF_DATA_BLOCK;
```

The **PERF_OBJECT_TYPE** structure describes the object-specific performance information:

```
typedef struct _PERF_OBJECT_TYPE {  /* pot */
    DWORD  TotalByteLength;
    DWORD  DefinitionLength;
    DWORD  HeaderLength;
    DWORD  ObjectNameTitleIndex;
    LPWSTR ObjectNameTitle;
    DWORD  ObjectHelpTitleIndex;
    LPWSTR ObjectHelpTitle;
    DWORD  DetailLevel;
    DWORD  NumCounters;
    DWORD  DefaultCounter;
    DWORD  NumInstances;
    DWORD  CodePage;
    LARGE_INTEGER PerfTime;
    LARGE_INTEGER PerfFreq;
} PERF_OBJECT_TYPE;
```

The **PERF_OBJECT_TYPE** structure for an object is followed by a list of **PERF_COUNTER_DEFINITION** structures:

```
typedef struct _PERF_COUNTER_DEFINITION { /* pcd */
    DWORD  ByteLength;
    DWORD  CounterNameTitleIndex;
    LPWSTR CounterNameTitle;
    DWORD  CounterHelpTitleIndex;
    LPWSTR CounterHelpTitle;
    DWORD  DefaultScale;
    DWORD  DetailLevel;
    DWORD  CounterType;
    DWORD  CounterSize;
    DWORD  CounterOffset;
} PERF_COUNTER_DEFINITION;
```

The **PERF_INSTANCE_DEFINITION** is used to define each instance of a block of object-specific performance data. Not all counters have instances. For instance, memory objects don't have instances, since the system has only one memory. Disk objects do have instances, because the system can have more than one disk.

```
typedef struct _PERF_INSTANCE_DEFINITION { /* pid */
    DWORD ByteLength;
    DWORD ParentObjectTitleIndex;
    DWORD ParentObjectInstance;
    DWORD UniqueID;
```

```
    DWORD NameOffset;
    DWORD NameLength;
} PERF_INSTANCE_DEFINITION;
```

Finally, the object-specific data is held in a **PERF_COUNTER_BLOCK** structure:

```
typedef struct _PERF_COUNTER_BLOCK { /* pcd */
    DWORD ByteLength;
} PERF_COUNTER_BLOCK;
```

The names of the objects and counters, as well as the text that explains their meaning, are kept in the registry. To access them, open the registry node:

```
\SOFTWARE\Microsoft\Windows NT\CurrentVersion\Perflib\<langid>
```

The language node (langid) is the ASCII representation of the 3-digit hexadecimal language identifier. For example, the U.S. English node is "009." This node, once opened, can be queried for values of either 'Counters' or 'Help.' The names of object types are included in the 'Counters' data. The 'Help' data supplies the Explain text. The 'Counters' and 'Help' data are stored in MULTI_SZ strings, listed in index-name pairs; for example:

```
2     System
4     Memory
6     % Processor Time
10    Read Operations/sec
12    Write Operations/sec
```

Navigating the performance registry tree is somewhat complicated. You can find some working code samples, however, in the Win32 help file: search for "Performance Monitoring Overview," then select the item "Using Performance Monitoring." The next two sections of the help file give examples that display counters and their titles.

Summary

We've introduced a lot of material here. We started with a road map to the different Windows NT interprocess communication mechanisms, then went over the details of programming the individual mechanisms. In addition, we looked briefly at Windows NT security, services, event logging, and performance monitoring.

In a few cases, we've given enough information for you to actually write programs. In the rest of the cases, we only got you started. You'll find more information in the Win32 SDK help files, and in the references listed below. Complete source code for the performance monitor is in \mstools\samples\sdktools\perfmon on the Win32 SDK CD.

For More Information

Arick, M. (1993), *The TCP/IP Companion*. Wellesley, MA: QED Publishing Group, ISBN: 0-89435-466-3. Good end-user-oriented discussion of TCP/IP and utilities.

Heller, Martin (1993), *Advanced Win32 Programming*. New York: Wiley, ISBN:0-471-59245-5. Indispensable for NT programmers.

Heller, Martin (1992), *Advanced Windows Programming*. New York: Wiley, ISBN: 0-471-54711-5. Indispensable for Windows programmers.

Microsoft Windows NT Software Development Kit (1993), *Remote Procedure Call Programmer's Guide and Reference*. Redmond, WA; Microsoft Corporation.

Microsoft Windows NT Software Development Kit (1993), *Programmer's Reference Vols 1–5*. Redmond, WA; Microsoft Corporation.

Nance, Barry (1990), *Network Programming in C*. Carmel, IN; Que Corporation, ISBN: 0-88022-569-6. Good coverage of Windows network programming.

Sinha, Alok, and Patch, Raymond (1992), "An Introduction to Network Programming Using the NetBIOS Interface." *Microsoft Systems Journal*, March–April.

Sinha, Alok, and Patch, Raymond (1992), "Developing Network-Aware Programs Using Windows 3.1 and NetBIOS." *Microsoft Systems Journal*, July–August.

Appendix 2

Network Protocols

Different network protocols exist for a reason. A particular protocol that works best for one network might be completely unsuitable for another, seemingly similar network. However, a few key areas of concern do span all protocols. Memory consumption, bandwidth utilization, level of functionality (simple data transport versus application programming interface [API]), and scalability are all important.

For example, if your network only needs to read and write files on a small file server, you probably want fast transport performance and little else. To get that performance, you can pick a protocol that uses little memory and carries no application overhead. But if your users need to log into interactive hosts and transfer large amounts of data, you will probably choose a protocol offering functionality and features and be less concerned with size and performance.

On a Windows NT network, the protocols you'll most likely encounter are Microsoft's NetBEUI, Novell's IPX, and the worldwide standard TCP/IP. NetBEUI is the smallest, fastest, and easiest to use of the three, but it's also the least feature-rich, and the most limiting in large environments. Novell's IPX, while also small and fast, can run in complex networks that would break NetBEUI. Finally, TCP/IP is the most complex and scalable of the lot, but isn't very small, and most implementations of it aren't very fast.

NetBIOS and NetBEUI

NetBEUI, in its simplest terms, is Microsoft's favorite protocol. As such, it is a moving target: It has been redefined, rebuilt, and repackaged many times in many products, including LAN Manager, Windows for Workgroups, and now Windows NT. NetBEUI means different things to different people depending on when they bought it. In its earlier releases, NetBEUI was a large monolithic protocol, hardly distinguishable from IBM's NetBIOS, on which it was based.

When IBM started work on NetBIOS, the goal was to develop a network protocol that would work on small networks of PCs only. The key word in that sentence is "small." At the time, the practical limit for an ethernet segment was 30 nodes, while IBM's own vaunted and undelivered Token Ring was limited to 255 nodes. There was no need to build in capabilities for moving data between multiple network segments, since nobody was doing it, and the use of gateways to link networks was assumed. When IBM reworked NetBIOS into NetBEUI, they did include some capabilities for routing, but only on Token Ring networks that use Source Level Routing.

Thus, the design goal was to build a very small and fast protocol. The protocol would provide APIs for the development of network-specific applications that could communicate on a machine-to-machine, or application-to-application basis. Also, the network naming system would allow for human-assigned names of devices, like "MyServer," which is easier to remember and work with than a complex numbering scheme. This is actually pretty insightful, considering that this is the same company that gave us SNA. Unfortunately, like the PC itself, this simple yet limited design would prove to haunt users even up to now.

NetBIOS was (and continues to be) a broadcast-intensive protocol. Since the assumption was that there were only a few nodes on the network, and that devices would be appearing and disappearing at random (as PCs are apt to do), then it was best to be able to locate a device with a broadcast rather than with any sort of centralized registry. Unfortunately, broadcast packets don't work in today's router-based networks, since the routers don't pass packets that aren't specifically destined for another network segment. And since the NetBIOS naming structure is non-hierarchical, devices can't specify remote network segments. Thus, the only way to make NetBIOS work in large networks is to bridge the various segments into a large virtual network. Unfortunately, NetBIOS's reliance on broadcasting limits its use to relatively small networks, so large bridged networks don't work very well either.

When Microsoft chose NetBIOS as the basis for its MS-Net software they added another component specific to their software, called *Server Message Blocks* (SMBs). SMBs provide network-specific functionality beyond that provided by NetBIOS (SMBs are covered in more detail later in this appendix).

Today's NetBEUI doesn't look much like the original NetBEUI. While the old version was monolithic, the new one is segmented into three components: the NetBIOS API, SMBs,

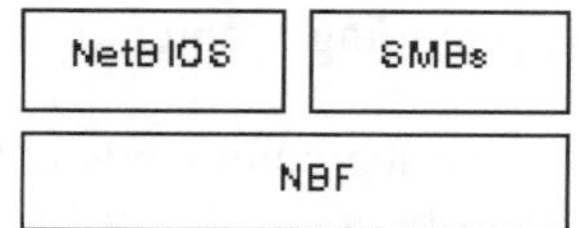

Figure A2.1 The three layers of the NetBEUI "protocol."

and the NetBIOS Frame (NBF) transport protocol. Figure A2.1 shows how these modules interrelate.

NetBIOS the API

NetBIOS-based applications, such as the Chat applet bundled with Windows NT, work with the NetBIOS APIs.[1] These high-level applications are not generally concerned with users or security, but function directly at the workstation level. When a NetBIOS-based application needs to communicate with a counterpart application, it locates the device and initiates the dialog. When the applications are finished, they disconnect, sometimes gracefully, sometimes not.

NetBIOS applications range from simple Chat-like applets to mainframe gateways and multi-user databases. Any application that needs to communicate with another can use the NetBIOS APIs to do so. Lotus's Notes server for Windows is a NetBIOS application. Microsoft Mail for Windows NT can support NetBIOS. This allows one NT mail client to notify another client that new mail has been sent, using a NetBIOS message. The normal method requires that the recipient routinely check the inbox for new messages.

People often confuse NetBEUI with NetBIOS. It's important to remember that the term *NetBIOS* generally refers to an API for network applications, and does not specify how data is moved between systems, but only how data is packaged and acquired by applications. *NetBEUI* is generally recognized as a transport protocol, an API, and an SMB processor.

Server Message Blocks (SMBs)

When two Windows NT (or LAN Manager, or Windows for Workgroups) nodes communicate, they use the X/Open standard Server Message Block (SMB) protocol. SMBs provide a standard and well-defined method for servers and nodes (called *consumers* in the SMB definition) to communicate with each other, similar to the way that NetBIOS-based applications do.

The SMB specification contains a dictionary, more or less, of commands specific to network I/O. For example, if a user wants to open a file residing on a server, then the SMB command "SMBopen" is passed between the two systems. This occurs at the redirector level, of course, since the user simply double-clicked on the file.

SMB commands exist for a wide range of functions, and provide a quick and cost-effective way to do the most common network functions. Commands exist for things like login security, printing, and working directly with files and directories. In other words, the

[1]Indirectly–through the NetDDE interface described in Appendix 1.

SMB protocol is the heart of the network, providing a common language for all the clients and servers.

Although these embedded, high-performance commands cover a good percent of the average network's activity, there also needs to be a capability for passing raw data between two nodes when needed. For example, if a large file is opened, then the capability to chain subsequent packets onto the lead packet allows for much greater throughput.

The commands that make up the SMB specification can be thought of as lowest common denominator commands. Since the SMB spec assumes different types of machines on the network, "extension protocols" are permitted, thereby streamlining operations significantly. For example, two DOS PCs would use the DOS extension when speaking with each other, while two NT systems would use the NT extension, and so on. This allows nodes to communicate most efficiently, while also guaranteeing compatibility between dissimilar devices.

NetBIOS Frames (NBF)

The lowest level of the NetBEUI protocol block is the NBF protocol. NBF provides both the transport- and network-layer functions, and provides the raw connectivity services between devices. When network I/O occurs, the upper layers (either NetBIOS applications or SMB transactions) pass data directly to NBF for processing. NBF then encapsulates the data into frames, locates the device(s) it needs to communicate with, and hands the data to the NIC for delivery.

NBF also handles the error correction services if needed, although through different mechanisms. Some services are established as connection-oriented, meaning a detailed and highly monitored conversation is held through a virtual circuit between two systems. Other services are established as *connectionless*, using datagrams. In this situation, packets are sent and then forgotten. This is generally used where repetitive broadcasts are sent frequently, such as status updates and the like.

NBF is another weak link in the NetBEUI stack. It is a non-routable protocol, meaning that it can only communicate with devices that it sees on the immediate subnet, or that are bridged into a virtual subnet. However, since none of the overhead is required for maintaining routing tables or the like, NBF is extremely small and fast, and is the ideal protocol for small networks of 20 to 200 devices. Also, since NetBEUI was designed by IBM with Token Ring in mind, the default frame size of the packets is 4,096 bytes, which allows for great throughput on networks that can handle it.

Another protocol that can be used instead of NBF is NBT, or NetBIOS-over-TCP/IP. This module replaces NBF directly, and SMBs and NetBIOS applications can communicate over TCP/IP directly, allowing them to function in large or complex networks. For information on implementing NBT refer to Chapter 6, which deals exclusively with Windows NT's TCP/IP capabilities.

IPX and Complementary Protocols

Novell's protocol set differs considerably from NetBEUI, mostly in that it is somewhat larger and much more usable in complex environments. Its design called for multiple network segments from the start, and numbers instead of names for both networks and resources. Devices still have names, but this is seen at the higher-level redirector, and not by the lower-level protocols themselves.

The heart of the NetWare protocol suite is based largely on Xerox's XNS (Xerox Network System). In fact, the two are almost identical, except for slight differences in some of the subprotocols. For example, Novell's IPX (or Internetwork Packet Exchange) is based on Xerox's IDP (or Internetwork Datagram Packet). Novell did not copy the entire stack however, since XNS includes subprotocols for things like mail handling. A lot of the secondary protocols were not needed in the PC environment, and others were not even published until after Novell did their initial development. Many other networking products are based on XNS, including VINES, Ungermann-Bass, and older 3Com software. Indeed, Microsoft's internal network has used XNS for years, only recently shifting toward TCP/IP. The NetWare protocol suite looks something like Figure A2.2.

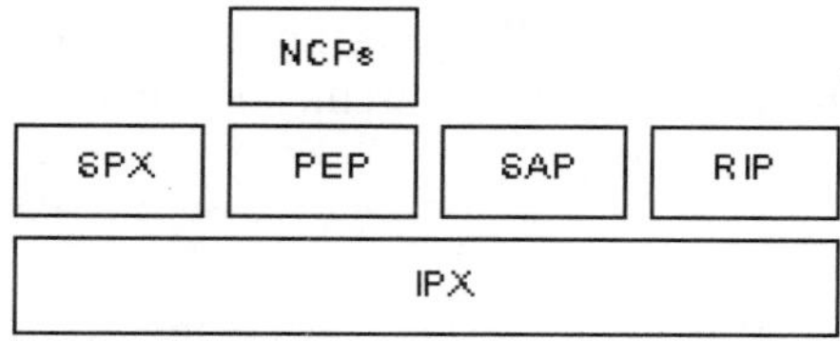

Figure A2.2 The NetWare protocol suite.

IPX

IPX, the protocol most generally associated with NetWare, resides at the bottom layer of the stack, and provides the "network" functions for the rest of the suite. In this instance, the term "network" refers to the network-layer of the OSI model (refer to Appendix 4 for more details about the OSI reference model).

IPX tracks the various network segments that are available, and directs the delivery of data accordingly. If a recipient node is local, the data is handed directly to it, and if remote, the data is handed to a router for delivery. IPX provides other network-layer functions, such as encapsulation of higher-level protocols, and is the single data-moving protocol for the NetWare environment. IPX does not guarantee delivery, or provide error-correction services, however. These functions are left to the transport protocols, SPX and PEP.

Another aspect of IPX is that it determines packet sizes based on the "strength" of the media that it is attached to. Although the minimum (and theoretical maximum) size of an IPX packet is 512 bytes, if two nodes are directly attached to an ethernet segment, they will use 1,024 byte packets. If they are both on Token Ring, they will use 4,096 byte packets. IPX routers, however, always convert the packets back to 512 bytes.

SPX, PEP, and NCPs

SPX (or Sequenced Packet Exchange) is an API similar to NetBIOS. Applications can use SPX to pass data directly between systems or applications. This is assisted by SPX's virtual circuit capabilities, which provide guaranteed delivery of data over IPX. SPX does not acknowledge all packets, but instead uses a "window" method, acknowledging all packets received within the window and conducting error-recovery based on that information.

Another higher-level transport protocol is PEP (Packet Exchange Protocol), used exclusively for the delivery of NCP (NetWare Core Protocol) commands. NCPs are similar to SMBs in that they provide a dictionary of I/O-related network commands. NCPs are the closely guarded heart of the NetWare server system. PEP is considered a part of the NCP subsystem, and is just as undocumented.

PEP provides error-correction services with the use of *timers*. When a packet is sent from PEP, an internal timer is started within NCP, and no other NCP packets are generated until a response is received. If the timer expires, PEP rebuilds the packet, and NCP restarts the timer. This handshaking and waiting consumes lots of NCP utilization bandwidth, but guarantees that the packets get delivered. On small LANs this goes unnoticed, but in large or exceedingly complex networks performance can suffer tremendously.

SAP

The advertisement of network devices and resources is managed by the Service Advertisement Protocol (SAP), naturally enough. SAP provides information about servers, routers, intelligent printers, and the like. Although SAP is really an application-level protocol, it uses IPX directly. Other subprotocols, such as NCP and SPX, rely on SAP for information as well.

Since NetWare is a number-based network, there must be a way to translate human-defined device names into the device's "real" numerical address. SAP provides this registry service. When a program or service becomes available, SAP picks up on it and creates an entry in its tables. Although this dynamic name-keeping registry makes life easy for users, the constant updating of information can consume network bandwidth very quickly, since every device has its own SAP tables. For users in a WAN environment, filtering SAP entries at your routers is a good way to get your bandwidth back.

RIP

Remember that IPX is a network-layer protocol—it doesn't know anything about other networks except that they exist. When IPX has a packet for a remote subnet, it passes it to the closest router and forgets about it. RIP (or Routing Information Protocol) provides the routing services for IPX packets. When a node first comes onto the network, it issues a RIP request to find out what network number it is on.

If the node is on multiple networks and configured as a router, then it will send out an RIP update to all the nodes on the network, advertising the routes it can offer. Routers send out

RIP updates every 60 seconds, telling other devices what networks it knows about. If a router doesn't send out an update within an allotted time, the router is assumed to be down, and the entry is removed.

IPX networks are nonhierarchical, meaning all routers must know how to get to every other network segment. As networks grow, this becomes an unmanageable and extremely overhead-expensive way to track remote networks. Novell has announced the development of a link-state routing protocol called NLSP (for NetWare Link State Protocol), which will work much better in extremely complex networks.

The TCP/IP Protocol Suite

First and foremost, TCP/IP is not a single protocol, but a term defining various protocols acting together to provide various connectivity functions. These protocols are all specific in function, ranging from the mundane task of providing transport services to more esoteric ones providing extended management functions.

Most network operating systems use a small set of proprietary protocols. For example, Microsoft's Windows NT uses NetBEUI and SMBs for almost all of its network services, and Novell uses IPX, SPX and NCP for its connections. These small, functional protocols allow the network operating system to streamline their operation, resulting in fast file and print sharing.

However, these protocols by themselves don't allow for much of anything else. Neither the LAN Manager or NetWare environments let a user log into the server and run an interactive application within the remote server's memory. You must run the applications from a client PC, perhaps running the program from the server's shared file system, but that's as far as it goes. Thus the LAN Manager and NetWare server platforms are contained and are optimized specifically for file and print sharing.

But TCP/IP offers an incredible breadth of services. Users can share files and printers, just as they can with LAN Manager or NetWare. They can also use terminal emulation services to execute applications on remote machines, letting them harness large system horsepower for specific applications. TCP/IP is a highly scalable set of protocols, and users can choose to implement any subset they wish, as either client or server services.

Another important aspect of TCP/IP is the issue of *openness*. While Microsoft's LAN Manager uses the publicly available SMB specification for communicating, it incorporates proprietary network services into other aspects of the product. You can't just put any SMB-based client into a Windows NT–based domain, and expect it to work. Novell is even worse, since they guard their proprietary NCPs as if they were the crown jewels.

Sure, both Microsoft and Novell license their server products to run on a variety of platforms, including minicomputers and mainframes. But you as a user must run that network service on each host and client in your organization, an exceedingly expensive and ungainly prospect at best. By comparison, TCP/IP is a fully public domain specification. Addenda to the specifications can be offered by anybody (even you), and the process is witnessed in full sight. Thus, many companies already offer TCP/IP protocols and services integrated with their platforms. This makes it easy for an end-user to connect resources together, without relying on any one vendor.

TCP/IP comprises a robust set of protocols that are highly efficient in wide area networks. NetBEUI and IPX were both designed for small LANs of 30 users or less. LAN Manager's NetBEUI is a *nonroutable* one, meaning that users on one network wire can't see servers on another unless the two segments are "bridged" into a single logical network wire. This doesn't work well in WAN environments by any measure. NetWare's NCP runs over IPX, which is a completely *routable* protocol. However, NCP relies on acknowledgments for all network packets sent, which is ungainly over slow WAN links. TCP/IP was originally written for connecting hosts over WANs, and as such it is both routable and efficient. These benefits apply to LANs just as well, making it a good choice for both small and large environments.

These three elements (scalability, openness, and robustness) make TCP/IP an attractive choice for users in mixed environments. They can run the same protocols and services on almost all of their host and client systems. For this reason, many customers have made TCP/IP a checkoff item for network purchases. No wonder Microsoft put TCP/IP into the basic Windows NT package! Of course, all is not rosy with TCP/IP, and we'll explore these limitations alongside its advantages.

A Brief History of TCP/IP

Back in the very early days of commercial computing (the late 1960s), most users bought a single large computer for their data processing needs. As their needs expanded, they rarely bought a different system from a different vendor. Instead, they added to their existing platform, or replaced it with a newer, larger model. Cross-platform connectivity was essentially unheard of, nor was it expected by customers. They were generally too busy just trying to keep these newfangled computers running.

These systems used proprietary networking architectures and protocols. For the most part, networking in those days consisted of plugging "dumb" line printers or terminals into a "smart" multiplexer or communications controller. And just as the networking protocols were proprietary, the network nodes were proprietary as well. To this day you still can't plug an IBM terminal into a DEC computer and expect it to work. The architectures and protocols are incompatible.

In an effort to help major research sites share resources, the Advanced Research Projects Agency (ARPA) of the Department of Defense (DOD) began coordinating the development of a vendor-independent network to tie the sites together. The logic behind this is clear: The cost and time to develop an application on one system was too much for each site to reengineer the application on other incompatible systems. Since each facility used different computers with proprietary networking technology, a vendor-independent network was the first priority. In 1968, work began on a private packet-switched network, using Honeywell-based communications hardware.

In the early 1970s, authority of the project was transferred to the Defense Advanced Research Projects Agency (DARPA). DARPA began developing and implementing protocols that would allow for the connection and use of the various systems. Although the original protocols were written for use with the ARPA network, they were designed to be usable on other systems as well. In 1981, DARPA placed the TCP/IP protocol suite into the public domain. Shortly thereafter, it was adopted by the University of California at Berkeley, which began bundling it with their freely distributed version of UNIX. In 1983, DARPA mandated that all new systems connecting to the ARPA network use TCP/IP, thus guaranteeing its long-term success.

During the same time period, other government agencies like the National Science Foundation (NSF) were building their own networks, as were private regional network service providers. These other networks also used TCP/IP as the native connection mechanism, since it was both a completely "open" protocol and readily available on a number of different platforms.

When these various regional and government networks began connecting to each other, the term *Internet* came into being. To "internet" (with a lowercase "i") means to interconnect networks. You can create an internet of Macintosh networks using AppleTalk and some routers, for example. "Internet" (with a capital "I") refers to the global network of TCP/IP-based systems, originally consisting of the ARPA and regional networks. Any organization (or any*one* for that matter) can join the Internet, and information on where to look is provided at the end of this appendix.

Connecting to the Internet

Getting connected to the Internet requires you to follow some very specific procedures. First of all, you must decide whether you will connect directly to the backbone, or go through a third-party service provider. Connecting directly requires you to be sponsored by a government agency, which carries its own sub-set of requirements. Most of you will choose to connect through a service provider such as PSI, AlterNet, or the like.

If you use a service provider, they will obtain formal address assignments for you, and depending on the class of service you subscribe to, may do other things for you as well, such as set up a DNS server, or provide and configure a router, or any other number of services beyond simple connectivity. An excellent starting point for finding these service providers is to get the book *Connecting to the Internet* by Susan Estrada (publisher information is listed at the end of this appendix). If you wish to bypass a third party, this book also gives the necessary information for doing it yourself.

TCP/IP's Architecture

This anarchic peer-to-peer structure is purposefully designed directly into TCP/IP's architecture. Consider the distributed nature of TCP/IP, in contrast with the classic security model of other host-based architectures of the time. Most systems had a hierarchical structure permeating the entire computing architecture. Everything was managed by the central host, including the network services themselves. Two nodes couldn't communicate without sending data through the host.

With TCP/IP, there is no central authority. Nodes communicate directly among themselves, and each maintains complete knowledge of the available network services. If any host fails, none of the others know or care (unless they need data from the down machine!). This is similar to Windows NT's basic server design, where servers are relatively independent of each other. (Windows NT Advanced Server domain management unifies many servers into a single logical entity, however, which eases management, but also breaks the independence of each system.)

Addressing

In order to identify themselves in this peer-to-peer environment, nodes are given explicit addresses that not only identify the computer, but the network segment that it is on as well. For example, the address 192.123.004.010 specifies node number 10 on network 192.123.004. Another node on the same network segment might be numbered 20, and so on. Networks and the nodes on them are separate entities, with separate numbers.

Host 10 from the example above might also be connected to network 192.123.005 on a different network adapter. This host could then act as a router between networks 192.123.004 and 192.123.005. Routers perform the task of moving traffic between networks. A node that needs to send data to another node on another network will send the data to the router, and the router will send the data to the destination node. If the destination isn't on an immediately connected network, the router will send the data to another router for delivery. This network-based routing scheme allows devices to keep their local overhead low. Otherwise, they'd have to remember how to get to each node, which would require a tremendous amount of processing and memory. Network-based routing requires much less in terms of end-node resources.

Each node's address is actually a 32-bit binary number (like 11000000 01111011 00000100 00001010). For convenience, this is broken into four 8-bit fields, called octets. TCP/IP represents these binary octets with their decimal equivalents (192.123.004.010 in this case). This makes life much easier for us humans. Although computers have no trouble dealing with 32-bit binary strings, we sure do!

The four octets signify different things in different networks. Some sites have only a single large network, but millions of nodes. They would use the first octet of the address to identify the network, and the remaining three octets would be used to identify the individual workstations. This is known as a "Class A" address. The most common users of Class A addresses are network service providers, who maintain extremely large and flat networks with thousands of endpoints.

Another site may have thousands of nodes split across many networks. They would use "Class B" addresses, where the first two octets (or 16 bits) are used to identify the network, and the remaining two octets are used to identify the individual nodes. Universities and large organizations are the most common users of Class B addresses.

Finally, the most common address is the "Class C" address, where the first three octets (or 24 bits) are used to identify the segment, and the last octet is used to identify the workstations. These are good for users with only a few dozen nodes on many separate networks. This is most often found in LAN environments, which average around 40 nodes per network segment.

When connecting a Class A network to a Class B network, there must be some way for the router to recognize the difference between the two. Otherwise, it would think that traffic originating from the Class C network and destined for a Class A node would be identifiable by the last octet. In truth, the Class A node is identified by the last three octets, a significant difference. Without this knowledge, the router would attempt to locate the three-octet network that the one-octet host is on. In actuality, it should be trying to send the data to the one-octet network that the three-octet host is on.

TCP/IP uses the first three bits of the first octet to identify the class of network, allowing devices to automatically recognize the appropriate address types. Class A addresses are identified by the first bit being set to "0." This leaves only 7 other bits for identifying the network portion of the address (remember that Class A addresses use the first octet to identify the network and the remaining three octets to identify the nodes). Since there are only 7 available bits, there can only be 128 possible networks. Network numbers 000 and 127 are reserved for use by software, so there are really only 126 possible networks (001 through 126). However, there are 24 bits available for identifying nodes, for a maximum of 16,777,124 possible node addresses for each of these networks.

Class B addresses are identified by having the first two bits set to "0." Since they use the first two octets to identify the network, this leaves 14 bits to identify each network segment. Thus, there are a possible 16,384 Class B addresses, ranging from 128.001 to 191.254 (numbers 000 and 255 are reserved).

Class C addresses are identified by having the first three bits in the first octet set to "0." Class C addresses use the first three octets to identify the network, so there are 21 bits available. The possible network numbers range from 192.001.001 through 254.254.254, a whopping 2,097,152 possible segments. However, since there is only one octet left to identify the nodes, there can be only 254 possible devices on each segment.

Out of Addresses

All told, there are over 4.7 billion possible host addresses. Now most of you are probably thinking that almost five billion possible addresses is plenty, but unfortunately, the four-octet structure causes some major restrictions. Every time a Class A address is assigned to an organization, almost 17 million host addresses go with it. If all 126 of the Class A addresses are assigned, then over three billion of the 4.7 billion possible addresses are gone. If all of the 16,000 Class B addresses are assigned, then another billion host addresses are gone as well. Whether or not all the workstation addresses are actually put to use or not is irrelevant; they have been assigned to a specific network and cannot be used again.

Class C addresses represent the biggest problem, however, for two reasons. First, there are fewer of them than with the other nodes (only about 500 million possible node addresses are available). Second, they are the most popular, since they reflect the size of the majority of the LANs. However, every time you assign a Class C address to a network segment, you take 254 possible node addresses with you. Remember that you need a new network number for every separate network. People who have three segments and only 60 nodes are therefore wasting over 700 possible workstation addresses (3 segments x 254 node addresses = 762 addresses – 60 active nodes = 702 inactive addresses). Clearly, at this rate, the available workstation numbers will run out soon (in fact, at the current rate of depletion the available addresses will be gone sometime in 1994).

To some readers, the logic for having different "classes" of addresses may seem vague at best. With the current design, there are only 2,113,662 possible networks. If all networks used the first 24 bits (without using "class bits") to identify the segment, there would be a possible 16,777,124 networks, with 254 nodes on each of them.

Remember however that TCP/IP networks are inherently router-based. It requires much less overhead on the part of nodes and routers to remember a few networks than many. Having to process 16 million networks would quickly overwhelm the router databases, and network traffic would slow down tremendously. Having network classes allows routers to deal with large networks easily, and performance is maintained.

Remember also that the original architecture of the Internet consisted mostly of large networks connecting to each other. It was easy to give one address to milnet (a network of unclassified military hosts) and another to NSFnet (the National Science Foundation's network). By doing this, routers only have to remember another router's address in order to pass data to literally millions of hosts.

For you and me, however, the potential for address depletion is frightening. No new organizations can connect to the Internet, and the existing networks can't expand. Several proposals for solutions are currently under development—most involve changing the address format somehow, or changing how routers communicate with each other.

Subnet Masks

There are ways to get more mileage from a single network number, however. Remember how the 32-bit binary address is divided into four logical 8-bit octets? Well, there's nothing to prevent you from changing this structure. Although you can't change the binary values of the address itself, you can change the way that your software interprets it. The interpretation of the address is called the *Subnet Mask.*

For clarification, let's look at the host address 192.123.004.010 from before. This is a Class C address. The first 24 bits identify the network number (3 bits for the Class C identifier, and 21 bits for addressing). The remaining 8 bits identify the host. You could just as easily set the subnet mask so that the first 30 bits identify the network and the remaining 2 bits identify the host.

Since the first 24 bits in a Class C address identify an organization, the remaining 8 bits can be used any way that organization sees fit. If they wish to use the bits for identifying hosts, they certainly can. However, another option would be to assign some of the remaining 8 bits to *subnetworks*. In essence, the network portion of the address gains another field, while the range of host numbers possible shrinks.

Let's show an example here to help clarify the discussion. Our imaginary company, Windows, Inc., has both an ethernet and token ring network. However, they only have a single Class C network address of 192.123.004. Rather than use the last octet to identify 254 hosts on a single network, they decide to add a subnet mask to their address, by "borrowing" the first bit of the last octet. This creates two subnets, with 128 possible hosts in each of them.

Now when they look at the network numbers, they see the following:

Segment	*Network Address*	*Node Addresses*[2]
Ethernet	192.123.004	001 - 127
Token Ring	192.123.004	128 - 254

Remember, however, that devices on the network don't see this logical breakdown automatically. Based on the Class C identifier in the head of the address, they still think that the last 8 bits of the address represent a host. All of the devices on a network segment have to be told about the mask.

The subnet mask uses a simple algorithm. If a bit mask is set to 1, it is part of the network number. If the bit mask is set to 0, it is part of the host number. Therefore, the subnet mask for our example above looks like 11111111 11111111 11111111 10000000. Shown below are the default subnet masks for the different network classes:

Class	*Subnet Mask*
A	11111111 00000000 00000000 00000000
B	11111111 11111111 00000000 00000000
C	11111111 11111111 11111111 00000000

The subnet mask for a node is appended to its binary address when processed by routers. Just as the router would look to see if network 192.123.004 were locally attached before forwarding the packet, it would now look to see if the subnet mask of the destination network matched as well. If the subnet mask doesn't match the local network, then the data is forwarded to another router that does match.

In order for subnet masking to work, all of the devices on a subnet must support it. Some older TCP/IP client programs don't support subnet masking, so make sure that they do before you try this at home. By the way, some software packages convert the binary subnet mask values into their decimal equivalents for ease of use. For example, Windows NT doesn't show the default Class C subnet mask, but rather shows it as 255.255.255.0 instead, the decimal equivalent of the binary octets. Again, this is to make life easier for us humans.

Subprotocols

Again, TCP/IP is a collection of protocols that span the OSI reference model from top to bottom. There are application-specific protocols such as Telnet and FTP, a collection of maintenance protocols, at least two major transport protocols, and one network-layer protocol. Figure A2.3 shows the major subprotocols in the TCP/IP suite.

---

[2]Numbers 000 and 255 are reserved.

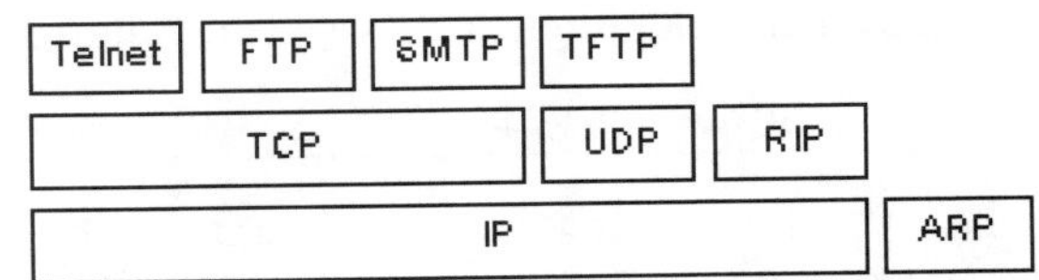

Figure A2.3 The TCP/IP protocol suite.

IP and ARP

IP, or the Internet Protocol, is the basic building block for all TCP/IP traffic, and works at the network-layer of the OSI reference model. It is where the internet address assignment is realized, and the layer of software responsible for determining how packets are passed to other networks. Other than that, IP is a pretty boring little protocol. All it does is get internet packets from one node to another, across the best route possible.

IP converts internet addresses into "real" network addresses, such as ethernet addresses, through the use of ARP (Address Resolution Protocol) and RARP (Reverse Address Resolution Protocol). An ARP packet will be sent with the destination IP address in the header, and if the receiving node is online, it will send back a response packet containing its real network address. RARP is used when a node needs to find out the IP address corresponding to a node's real address. Either way, when an ARP or RARP reply comes back, the node stores the address in a cache buffer for reuse.

TCP and UDP

The protocols that provide the transport-layer services are TCP (Transmission Control Protocol) and UDP (User Datagram Protocol). Since IP provides no error-recovery or control services, applications that need it go through TCP, and those that don't go through UDP. Almost all applications use TCP or UDP for the delivery of data, both of which pass packets to IP for delivery. Very few applications speak directly with IP.

TCP provides error-correction through the use of a connection-oriented transaction. A "start" packet is built and sent to the destination node (via IP), and when an "okay I'm ready" packet comes back, a monitored conversation between the hosts and/or applications begins. If a packet is lost or corrupted, TCP resends the data. The size, timeout interval, and other critical factors are determined by TCP, judging from the strength of the media that the node is connected to.

UDP, on the other hand, simply sends the data. If no error-correction or monitoring services are needed, then an application is best off using UDP, since it's much faster and requires less overhead than TCP. Like TCP, UDP makes decisions about packet sizes based on the strength of the underlying media, and passes the fully contained parcel to IP for delivery. This is what makes IP so boring; it just delivers the data, since all the big decisions have already been made for it.

RIP

If RIP looks familiar to you, it should. It is the same RIP (Routing Information Protocol) that NetWare uses with IPX, and is derived from the XNS source code. It was not originally a part of the TCP/IP suite, but Berkeley included it with their distribution, and it has since become one of the most popular routing protocols around. It also carries many of the same limitations that Novell's version has, and there are many alternatives available. If you use a non-RIP routing protocol on a router however, you need to make sure that you use it on *all* of them, since that's how they communicate with each other.

Locating Hosts

Once your system knows how to connect to the outside world, you are ready to start communicating with other systems. Although you can use the IP addresses of the hosts, this is undesirable for several reasons. First and foremost, IP addresses change. Hard-coding a host's address into an application is a sure way to break the app. Also, assigning "names" to hosts makes it easier for less-memory-talented users to work with different systems. Although a four-octet number is easier to remember than a 32-bit binary sequence, a *name* is better still—"Accounting" makes a lot more sense than 192.155.13.116!

You can assign names to hosts by editing the "HOSTS" file, located in winnt\system32\etc, or by using a DNS server on your network. NT offers no DNS server capabilities, so you'll only be able to use DNS if you have a UNIX host on your network already. Configuring the DNS client software on your NT systems is explained in Chapter 6, as is editing the HOSTS file.

For More Information

Malamud, C. (1990), *Analyzing Novell Networks.* New York: Van Nostrand Reinhold, ISBN: 0-442-00364-1. Great low-level peek at what goes on inside NetWare LANs.

Miller, M. (1991), *Internetworking.* Redwood City, CA: M&T Books, ISBN: 1-55851-143-1. Solid reference material on XNS, IPX, and TCP/IP protocols.

Arick, M. (1993), *The TCP/IP Companion.* Wellesley, MA: QED, ISBN: 0-89435-466-3. Good end-user-oriented discussion of TCP/IP and utilities.

Black, U. (1992), *TCP/IP and Related Protocols.* New York: McGraw-Hill, ISBN: 0-07-005553-X. Mandatory desktop reference for the TCP/IP administrator.

Albitz, P. and Liu, C (1992), *DNS and BIND.* Sebastopol, CA: O'Reilly & Associates, ISBN: 1-56592-010-4. Great book for learning Domain Name Service (DNS).

Estrada, S. (1993), *Connecting to the Internet.* Sebastopol, CA: O'Reilly & Associates, ISBN: 1-56592-061-9. Essential guide for getting yourself or your organization connected to the Internet.

Appendix 3

Legacy Applications

With some exceptions, Windows NT generally will run applications compiled to run in DOS, Windows 3.1, and (character-based only) OS/2 1.3. In addition, it supports the POSIX API (a generic subset of the UNIX API) so that application source code written to POSIX can be recompiled and run under Windows NT. These *legacy applications* will probably comprise the majority of software you run initially, at least until native Windows NT applications become available. This appendix details the operation and limits of compatibility for legacy applications.

Chapter 11 of the *Microsoft Windows NT System Guide* details the settings and operation of many aspects of legacy applications. This appendix supplements the information in that chapter.

Non-x86 (RISC) Limitations

If you plan to make heavy use of legacy applications, you should be aware of important limitations with Windows NT on non-x86 (e.g., MIPS R4000/4400, Intergraph Clipper, DEC Alpha, or other RISC-based) systems. (In this appendix, x86 refers to the Intel 386, 486, and Pentium, plus Intel hardware-compatible chips produced by Cyrix, AMD, and others.) Non-x86 systems use emulation software to interpretively execute the x86 instruction set. Two problems exist with this approach: performance and emulation level. Because the emulator must execute multiple non-x86 instructions to interpret one x86 instruction, it is slower by a factor of five-to-ten than a native application. So although the MIPS R4400 is about the equal of the Pentium for native Windows NT applications, it's only about as fast as a 386/25 when running a Windows 3.1 application.

What may be a more important limitation for many people is that the emulation software on the non-x86 versions of NT does *not* emulate 386 instructions. That means it runs Windows 3.1 applications in standard mode, not 386 enhanced mode.[1] Similarly, the emulator cannot run 386 DOS extended applications. Finally, native OS/2 1.3 applications are not supported at all on non-x86 platforms, despite the fact they generally do not use 386 instructions. If you have an EXE file compiled as an OS/2 family mode (bound) application (which combines both DOS and OS/2 executables in a single file), it will run on a non-x86 platform, but execute the DOS code in the EXE file, *not* the OS/2 code.

Finally, although DOS applications run on non-x86 systems, they can do so only in a window. The full-screen operation provided by x86 systems assumes VGA hardware compatibility that isn't present on non-x86 systems. (Conceivably, some x86 systems might not offer VGA compatibility either, but that's not true at present.)

DOS Support

Windows NT uses the virtual-86 feature of the 386 and 486 chip to provide a separate virtual machine for each DOS application you run. Most DOS applications will run under NT with no problem, but device drivers and low-level utilities may not. This was a conscious design decision by the NT designers to trade compatibility for security and system stability. If NT let DOS software access hardware directly, it could put hardware into an unstable state or corrupt the hard disk. So some "poorly behaved" DOS apps will not run under NT.

However, if the definition of a "poorly behaved" DOS app means that it accesses the hardware directly, then nearly all DOS apps are poorly behaved. Most of them write directly to VGA video buffers, reprogram the timer chip, or access the serial port hardware. Therefore, NT makes this most basic PC hardware available through Virtual Device Drivers (VDDs). A VDD virtualizes hardware so that each DOS application believes it is using the actual hardware when it really is not. This lets NT arbitrate access to the real hardware device when multiple DOS applications (or DOS and NT) try to access it.

There are two major problem areas in DOS support under NT:

1. *Specialized hardware that requires custom device drivers or TSRs.* This includes high-resolution DOS video drivers, the fax section of the Intel SatisFAXtion 400,

[1]Although some Windows 3.1 enhanced-mode memory management functions are supported, any application using 386 instructions will crash.

video capture boards, and many scanners. Vendors need to write VDDs for any hardware they want to be supported under NT, using the Windows NT Device Driver Kit.

You cannot install *DOS-based drivers for network cards, tape drives or CD-ROMs* in NT, since these typically interface to custom hardware. These devices should be installed under NT and accessed in DOS through the NT support. The SYSTEM32 directory includes special versions of the network redirector and MS CD-ROM extensions that are used with DOS and loaded in the AUTOEXEC.NT file (see below).

2. *Utilities that require low-level access to disk drives.* This includes disk-compression software like Stacker or DoubleSpace, or the disk doctor tools in Norton Utilities or PC Tools. These utilities present security and integrity risks, and assume things about the structure and layout of the disk that aren't necessarily true under NT. If you require these types of utilities, you will need to find NT equivalents. To perform an operation like disk defragmenting on a FAT disk volume, you should reboot into DOS and run the application from there.

The DOS compatibility built into NT is basically at the level of DOS 5.0, although the GetDOSVersion API call actually returns 5.32 as the version number. Since most applications aren't sensitive to DOS versions, this shouldn't be a problem. However, if you have your system set up to dual-boot between DOS 6.0 and NT, you will find that DOS 6.0 utilities fail with an "Incompatible DOS version" error if you try to run them in NT. Most of those utilities (like MORE or FIND) have equivalents in NT. You can overcome these version incompatibilities by using the SETVER.EXE utility that comes with DOS (version 5 and later). Load SETVER in the CONFIG.NT file as described below.

When you log on, NT reads the AUTOEXEC.BAT file from the boot drive and sets any environment variables it finds for later use by DOS or NT applications. It also adds directories from any PATH statement onto the end of the path that NT uses. NT sets the path so that its SYSTEM32 directory is searched before any other directory, so 32-bit equivalents to DOS commands will be found first.

Each time you start a command prompt window or launch a DOS application from Program Manager or File Manager, NT reads the CONFIG.NT and AUTOEXEC.NT files in the SYSTEM32 directory to configure the environment for the new application. These files are similar to their DOS analogs, and let you configure each DOS session for maximum memory, or to load a particular set of TSRs or device drivers. Chapter 11 of the *Windows NT System Guide* details the commands available in these two files. Each DOS session has its own environment, complete with high memory area. As with DOS, you can specify commands to load TSRs or device drivers into high memory. Since hardware devices aren't mapped into the high memory of these virtual DOS environments, you may be able to put much more into high memory than in a true DOS machine.

Like Windows 3.1, NT also supports Program Information Files (PIFs) for DOS applications (Figure A3.1). In fact, you can use the same PIFs you have been using under Windows 3.1, although NT ignores most of the DOS and Windows parameters. It does use the startup directory, EMS/XMS memory usage, priority, shortcut keys, and display usage (details are in

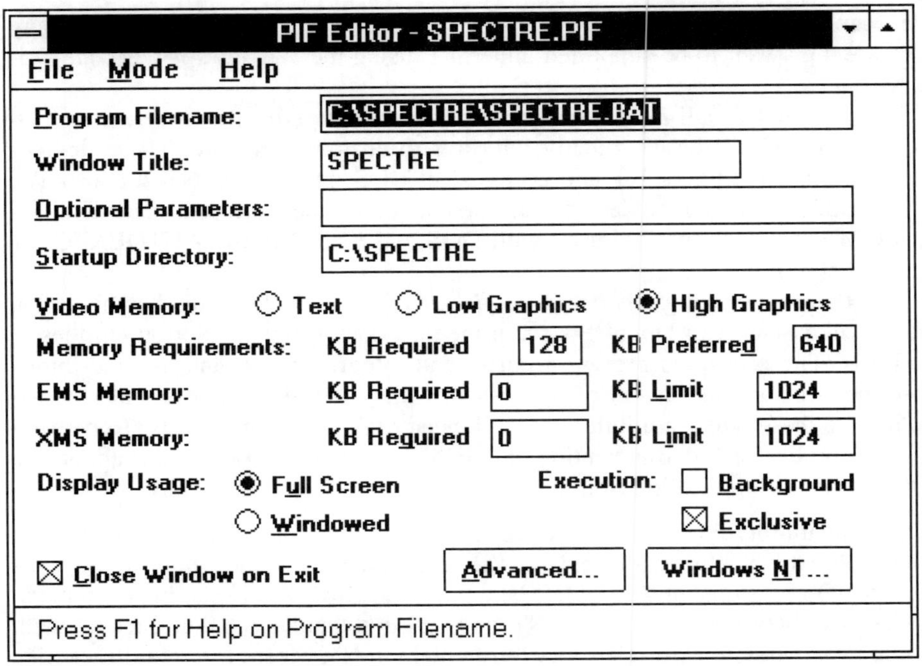

PIF Editor - SPECTRE.PIF
File Mode Help
Program Filename: C:\SPECTRE\SPECTRE.BAT
Window Title: SPECTRE
Optional Parameters:
Startup Directory: C:\SPECTRE
Video Memory: Text Low Graphics High Graphics
Memory Requirements: KB Required 128 KB Preferred 640
EMS Memory: KB Required 0 KB Limit 1024
XMS Memory: KB Required 0 KB Limit 1024
Display Usage: Full Screen Windowed
Execution: Background Exclusive
Close Window on Exit
Advanced... Windows NT...
Press F1 for Help on Program Filename.

Figure A3.1 PIF Editor.

The Windows NT Program Information File (PIF) editor allows you to customize settings for legacy applications, including 16-bit DOS, Windows, and OS/2 applications.

Chapter 11 of the *Windows NT System Guide*). You can also specify different AUTOEXEC and CONFIG files that can be used to initialize DOS before running this particular application, rather than the ones in SYSTEM32. For example, if you have a particularly memory-hungry DOS application, you could create a custom CONFIG.NT file to remove CD-ROM and/or network support to save memory.

If you are using an NTFS volume, NT creates DOS-compatible names for any files that violate the DOS 8.3 naming convention. When DOS applications access files on NTFS, they see only the DOS-compatible names. The following rules are used:

- Lowercase letters are converted to uppercase.
- Characters that aren't legal in DOS files are converted to underscores (_). (NTFS uses the 16-bit Unicode character set, whereas DOS uses 7-bit ASCII.)
- Spaces are removed.
- If the name has more than one period, all but the last (rightmost) are removed.
- The name is truncated to its first (leftmost) six characters before the period.
- The extension (after the period) is truncated to three characters.

- A tilde and sequence number (e.g., "~1") are added to the name to create a unique file name. If a single digit doesn't produce a unique name, the name is truncated to five characters and a two-digit sequence number is used.

Here are some examples, assuming that the files here are created in order (which affects the sequence numbering):

NTFS Name	*DOS Name*
This.Is.A.Very.Long.Name	THISIS~1.NAM
This Is A Very Long.Too	THISIS~1.TOO
This is a very_big.name	THISIS~2.NAM
Monthly Budget.DOC	MONTHL~1.DOC
Monthly Report.DOC	MONTHL~2.DOC

If you are not sure what DOS filename will be produced from the long name, you can select View/All File Details in File Manager or type DIR /X from the command prompt, to see both the long and short names (Figure A3.2).

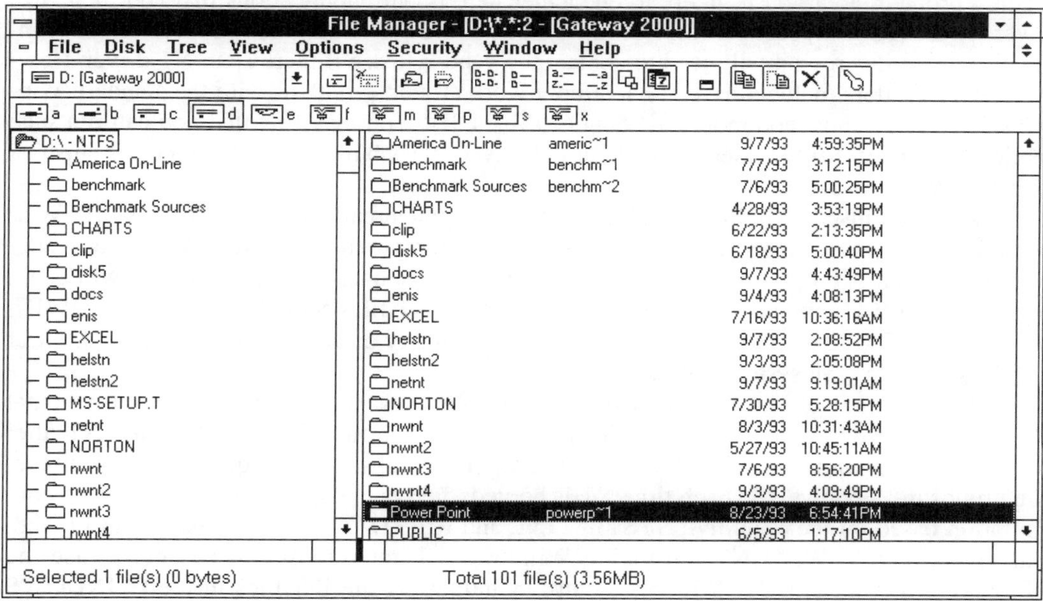

Figure A3.2 File Manager.

Windows NT supports legacy applications by automatically generating DOS-style "8.3" filename equivalents to long filenames in the New Technology File System. You can see both versions of the file's name using the View/All File Details option in File Manager.

In truth, though, much confusion will be saved in mixed (DOS and NT) environments if you stick to using DOS-style 8.3 names. This eliminates the need to remember that "Monthly Report.DOC" on the NT system is the same as "MONTHL~2.DOC" in DOS!

Windows 3.1 Support

Windows NT's support for Windows 3.1 is similar to Windows enhanced mode on x86 systems, but adds a significant improvement. (See the section on non-x86 system limitations at the beginning of this appendix.) Like Windows 3.1 enhanced mode, virtual memory is supported.

One major advantage with running Windows 3.1 applications under NT is that they are not limited to a tiny pool of system resources (128KB) as they are in Windows 3.1. This means that a Windows NT system can have more Windows 3.1 apps running simultaneously than Windows 3.1. It also means that a resource-hungry program like Microsoft Excel 4.0 can have *many* more worksheets open at once. For example, under Windows 3.1 you can open only about 30 empty Excel worksheets before running out of system resources; under NT we've opened more than 470 (yes, that's four hundred and seventy) before running out of paging file space. By increasing the paging file space (or adding more physical memory) we could go even higher!

As with DOS support, Windows 3.1 applications cannot access hardware directly. The primary problem area you're likely to encounter here is with applications that add their own drivers to the [386enh] section of SYSTEM.INI. Like the DOS emulation, if these drivers control custom hardware you will need to contact the vendor to see if there is an NT driver. However, some vendors include drivers that simply work around problems with the standard Windows drivers, the most common one being COMM.DRV. You may find that you can run such applications successfully under NT without the driver (NT's built-in comm support is superior to that in Windows 3.1).

When you install Windows NT, it looks to see if you already have Windows 3.1 (or Windows for Workgroups) installed on your system, for example in C:\WINDOWS. If so, it suggests you install NT in the same directory. There's little danger that installing NT will cause your Windows 3.1 setup to misbehave; nearly all of the NT files actually go into a new \WINDOWS\SYSTEM32 directory, and NT uses its own registry database (rather than WIN.INI or SYSTEM.INI) to save system settings.

The advantage of installing Windows NT and Windows 3.1 in the same directory is that NT will set up your Windows 3.1 applications for you. The first time you log onto NT after doing a same-directory install, NT will create program groups that are equivalent to your custom groups in Windows 3.1. Each time NT is booted, the system updates its Windows 3.1 configuration based on the WIN.INI, SYSTEM.INI, and REG.DAT (Object Linking and Embedding) information. When NT is running Windows 3.1 apps, they will be able to use the information in your existing Windows setup, including private INI files in the \WINDOWS directory and application-specific settings in WIN.INI. Whether you install an application in Windows 3.1 or NT, you will be able to run it in either environment.

If you choose to install NT in a location other than your Windows 3.1 directory (for example \WINNT), running 3.1 applications under NT can be a bit more complicated but still quite possible. One simple approach is to reinstall the application under NT but specify the same destination for the application files. This will usually recreate any changes required to INI files in the \WINNT directory without actually having a second copy of the application on disk. Remember that if you don't install NT and 3.1 in the same directory, the INI files can get out of sync. If you boot into 3.1, change some settings in an application, and later run that application in NT, you may find those settings are not changed.

OS/2 1.3 Support

On x86-compatible systems, Windows NT will run 16-bit OS/2 character-based applications. It won't run OS/2 applications that depend on Presentation Manager (even some character-based apps do), and it won't run 32-bit OS/2 2.0 applications. NT doesn't run OS/2 applications at all on non-x86 systems (see the first section in this appendix).

When you start Windows NT for the first time, it looks at the CONFIG.SYS file on the boot disk; if it detects OS/2 commands, NT will add entries for PROTSHELL, COMSPEC, and OS2LIBPATH to the registry based on the entries in this file. These go into the NT environment along with the NT and DOS environment settings; you can examine them all using the System applet in Control Panel. Nearly all other commands in the CONFIG.SYS file are ignored by NT; Chapter 11 of the *Windows NT System Guide* details how they are handled.

Most likely, you will need to deal with CONFIG.SYS changes when an OS/2 application installs itself and changes this file. To handle this situation, Microsoft created an unusual approach: An OS/2 application (it *must* be an OS/2 application) can edit the file named C:\CONFIG.SYS (Figure A3.3). In response, NT retrieves the OS/2 configuration data from

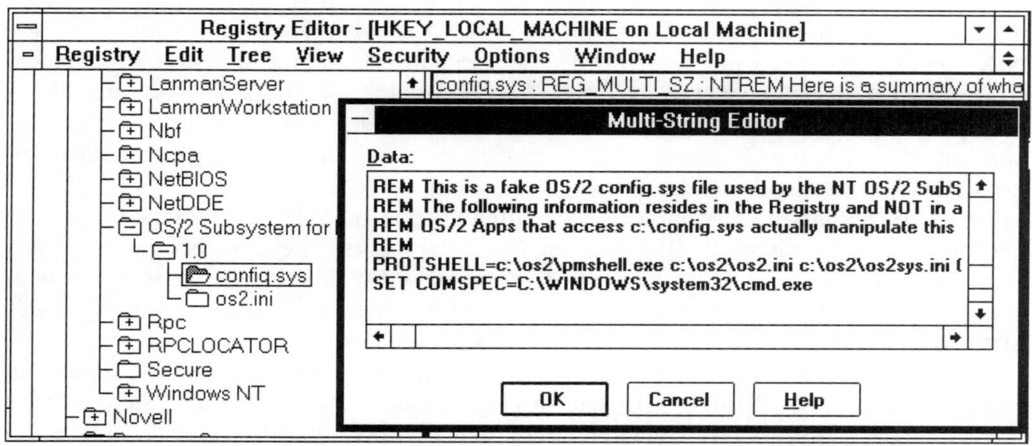

Figure A3.3 Registry Editor.

The Windows NT Registry includes a complete OS/2 CONFIG.SYS file, which can be edited either using an OS/2 text editor (the preferred method), or by opening the appropriate sub-key in the Registry Editor.

the registry and puts it into a temporary text file. When the file is closed, NT parses the file and updates the registry. If you don't have an OS/2 text editor, you can't get NT to perform this magic. However, you can examine the OS/2 CONFIG.SYS by using REGEDT32 to edit the key HKEY_LOCAL_MACHINE\SOFTWARE\Microsoft\OS/2 Subsystem for NT\1.0\config.sys. Be aware, however, that Microsoft does not recommend changing the file in this way.

Like NT, OS/2 generally insulates applications from the hardware through device drivers. However, OS/2 has a "trap-door" that allows applications to perform I/O directly to devices, called IO Privilege Level (IOPL). OS/2 applications that require IOPL will not run under NT. Although OS/2 device drivers are not supported under NT, you can map an NT device so that it appears as an OS/2 device using the DEVICENAME command in CONFIG.SYS. This approach should allow most OS/2 software to run correctly.

POSIX Support

Windows NT is likely to make inroads into areas where the UNIX operating system is currently used. To increase the attractiveness of Windows NT to the UNIX community, Microsoft has added a large degree of UNIX compatibility to the operating system. Another impetus for Microsoft is that the U.S. government favors the use of UNIX-compatible systems in many projects. Windows NT could not compete for many government projects without UNIX compatibility.

There are actually many different versions of UNIX, in addition to operating systems that are UNIX-like but not licensed to use the UNIX name. In the mid-1980s the Institute for Electrical and Electronics Engineers (IEEE) sponsored a committee to define the UNIX environment in a vendor-neutral way that would promote standardization. By 1990, that work progressed into International Standards Organization (ISO) standard IS-9945, commonly called POSIX. There is actually a family of POSIX standards that define the system API, graphical interface, command shell language, tools (like grep and awk), security, and networking. However, most of these are still being defined. One of the few parts of POSIX that is fully standardized is POSIX.1, the C-language API to system services. This is the part of POSIX that Windows NT currently addresses.

The POSIX support in Windows NT is different from other legacy application support because it is not at the binary (EXE-file) level, but at the source-code level. Source code must be recompiled on Windows NT using the POSIX compatibility libraries. For an end-user with shrink-wrapped applications this is not feasible, but it's standard procedure for the UNIX developers that Microsoft is targeting with POSIX compatibility.

UNIX developers are also familiar with another tradeoff created by POSIX: portability versus functionality. The POSIX.1 API standard is bare-bones, mostly providing access to the file system and the ability to start and communicate with other processes. There is simple tty-style (text only) I/O, but nothing like the event-driven graphical interface that is the basis of both Windows 3.1 and Windows NT. (UNIX systems often provide a graphical user interface called X Windows, but this is outside the scope of POSIX.1 and covered instead by the unfinished POSIX.12 standard.)

Generally, the POSIX libraries are just thin wrapper functions that translate POSIX API calls into their Windows NT equivalents. The operating systems use models that are similar enough that there are not major problems in most translating operations. Since POSIX applications are compiled using a Windows NT 32-bit compiler, their performance can be quite good compared with 16-bit DOS or Windows 3.1 applications.

POSIX applications generally expect a file system that behaves like a UNIX file system. NTFS has some features specifically designed for maximum compatibility with POSIX. For example, NTFS is normally case preserving when creating files, but not case sensitive when opening files. Thus, you can save a file to an NTFS partition as “DaveM.DOC” but open it later using the string “davem.doc”. However, when using the POSIX subsystem you must specify the capitalization exactly, because a POSIX application expects the file system to be both case sensitive and case preserving. Using POSIX you can, in fact, create a file named “DAVEM” and a different one called “DaveM” in the same directory. You can start POSIX applications like any other application, either by typing the application name from a command line, or through File Manager or Program Manager.

As this book went to press, Microsoft's *Windows NT Resource Kit* had just started shipping, which includes a wide range of POSIX utilities that can give NT a very UNIX-like “feel” at the command-line level. More information on the Resource Kit will be found in the "Late-breaking News" section of the Preface.

Appendix 4

The OSI Seven-Layer Model and Windows NT Network Architecture

Operating systems don't normally know much about networks. They understand I/O, but may not care exactly how the data got in or where it's going. Windows NT is different in this regard, as it *does* know about and understand issues pertinent to networking. Information stored in the Windows NT Registry tells the operating system about services that are available, and the Windows NT kernel monitors and acts upon network activity explicitly.

When a new product such as Windows NT comes to the marketplace, potential buyers want to be assured that the product will be compatible with the hardware and software they already have. One way to ensure compatibility is to develop the product in accordance with industry standards. This appendix explains, in basic terms, an important computer industry standard known as the OSI Model and shows you how Windows NT fits into the basic scheme followed by other computer industry vendors. If you already understand the seven-layer model, see Appendix 2 for an in-depth technical description.

The Need for Standards

The basic function of networking software is to move information between one device and another. This process usually consists of transmitting requests from one device to another, carrying out the request, and then returning the results to the original device. Sometimes these devices are on the same local area network (a small network, usually for a department or a workgroup); sometimes they are located on different segments of a wide area network (one that connects separate network sites, such as buildings or even cities). These devices are usually computers, but they can be printers or other networked machines.

To handle these requests, the network software has to determine how to reach the destination device. Then it has to put the request into a form that can travel across the network and be understood by the destination device. Once the request has arrived safely, it must be checked for errors, put into a form the device can use, and properly executed. Then it must be put back into proper transmission form and returned to the original sending device.

The networking industry is constantly searching for viable standards that the various members of the industry can use as they design new hardware, new operating systems, new protocols, or other new concepts. Once certain standards have been accepted within the industry, it becomes easier for manufacturers to create products that work well together. In this way, information can eventually be transmitted anywhere in the world, no matter whose equipment is being used to send, carry, or receive it. This ideal scenario has yet to be achieved, but Microsoft is working with other vendors (even competitors) to make this kind of easy communication possible.

One such attempt at creating a standard is the OSI seven-layer model.

The OSI Model

The OSI Model is a communications reference model defined by the International Standards Organization, or ISO. The ISO is a voluntary, international standards organization whose communications protocols are widely accepted. (A protocol is a set of rules that make it possible for all computers that know these rules to communicate with each other.) Founded in 1946, the ISO is comprised of standards bodies from more than seventy-five countries. Similar organizations include ANSI (American National Standards Institute), which represents the United States in the ISO; CCITT (Comite Consulatif International de Telegraphie et Telephonie), an international committee that sets communications standards; and IEEE (Institute of Electrical and Electronic Engineers), who have set many standards used in LANs.

In 1978, the ISO published the OSI (Open Systems Interconnection) Reference Model. This model, sometimes referred to as the "seven-layer model," has become the basis for designing and evaluating methods of communication between devices. The OSI Model has been helpful to the networking industry as manufacturers of networking products strive for compatibility between their products and those of other vendors. Official implementation of each layer as a standard, however, has been an ongoing process for many years. Top-down standards, burdened by bureaucracy, achieve popularity much more slowly than grass-roots de facto standards, usually created by vendors in leadership positions in their industry niches.

The OSI Model is similar to, but not identical to, IBM's seven-layer SNA model. The OSI model describes levels of communication that occur between client and server machines to ensure that data sent across a network arrives intact. The seven software layers of the OSI Model are numbered consecutively from the actual physical hardware connections (layer 1) up to the layer that services the applications, or programs, that run on the network (layer 7). Each layer communicates only with adjacent layers. The model is shown in Table A4.1.

The networking industry is constantly searching for viable standards that the various members of the industry can use as they design new hardware, new operating systems, new protocols, or whatever new concepts they bring to fruition. Once certain standards have been accepted within the industry, it becomes easier for manufacturers to create products that work well together. In this way, information can eventually be transmitted anywhere in the world, no matter whose equipment is being used to send, carry, or receive it.

The Seven Layers

- Level 1 (the physical layer) is concerned with the actual transmission of data over the local area network. This layer is comprised of the physical media used in interconnecting different network components. Examples of such media are fiber optics, twisted-pair cable, or coaxial cable.
- Level 2 (the data link layer) is concerned with the transmission techniques used to place the data on these different media. This layer is responsible for gaining access to the network and transmitting data packets from one device to another. (Computer systems divide a data transmission into small portions called packets or frames.) Examples of transmission techniques include tokens and error-detection codes. This layer retransmits data packets that fail to reach their destination.
- Level 3 (the network layer) is responsible for finding the workstation the data is addressed to. If there are several possible routes on the LAN the data could travel across, the network layer must choose the best one. Level 3 is the highest layer that understands the physical configuration of the network.
- Level 4 (the transport layer) provides reliable transportation of data. This layer is responsible for converting messages into the required formats for transmission over

Layer	*Client*		*Server*
7	Application	<—- virtual communication —->	Application
6	Presentation	<—- virtual communication —->	Presentation
5	Session	<—- virtual communication —->	Session
4	Transport	<—- virtual communication —->	Transport
3	Network	<—- virtual communication —->	Network
2	Data Link	<—- virtual communication —->	Data Link
1	Physical	<—- virtual communication —->	Physical

Table A4.1 The OSI Model

the network. If the transmission isn't successful, the transport layer may request a retransmission.

- Level 5 (the session layer) establishes a connection so one user can communicate with another. This layer also queues incoming messages and terminates connections. It also recovers from an abnormal termination. IBM's NetBIOS (Network Basic Input/Output System) is on this layer.
- Level 6 (the presentation layer) must make certain that the commands and the data of an application can be understood by other computers on the network. In other words, it converts one format to another—such as a word processor format to a database format—or it translates between two different codes, such as EBCDIC and ASCII. This layer can also make a communication device seem like something else for reasons of economy or security. That's why a user manual may tell you that a hard disk "looks like" a floppy disk to your program.
- Level 7 (the application layer) refers to direct interaction with application processes. This layer consists of the messages that applications use to request data and services from one another. This layer provides distributed processing services, including file transfer, database management, and network control. DOS (Disk Operating System) and NOS (Network Operating System) are on this level.

OSI and Windows NT

Windows NT emerged into a personal computer industry already rich in network operating system technology. File server-based networks, in which a central computer stores and manages the data that users generate, have been prevalent for about ten years; peer-to-peer networks, which let users share data between the personal computers in a workgroup, have been around for about half that long. In addition, networking sites use hardware and software from many different vendors. Windows NT must be able to communicate in a variety of computing environments.

Because of the multivendor environment in which many users must work, the standards laid down in the OSI Model have influenced Windows NT development. Windows NT offers what Microsoft calls "built-in networking." This means that Windows NT users can communicate with other personal computer users without the need for a separate network operating system. (The term *operating system*, or OS, refers to the software that controls a personal computer. The term *network operating system*, or NOS, refers to the software that manages an entire personal computer network.) You can share data with other users, send and receive messages, and use a remote printer without any of these machines having to become a server. In other words, Windows NT can function as a peer-to-peer network. In addition to communicating with other computer users in your own workgroup, you can communicate with servers on other types of networks, such as Novell's NetWare or Banyan's VINES.

When your Windows NT workstation communicates with another workstation, both machines use a seven-layer system based on the OSI Model. When you send a transmission over the network, it passes down each layer on your machine, travels across the network, then passes up each layer on the receiving machine until it reaches the layer that can properly handle your request.

Let's look at the relationship between the OSI Model and the Windows NT networking components. Note that the seven layers described above do not correspond precisely to actual software.

- At the physical layer, your data transmission must travel over a physical medium; this usually refers to a type of network cabling such as Ethernet, Arcnet, Token-Ring, or fiber optics.
- At the data link layer, your Windows NT workstation uses a Microsoft standard known as NDIS (Network Device Interface Specification). The NDIS 3.0 interface makes certain that your data gets onto the network so it can be transmitted.
- At the network and transport layers, Windows NT uses various transport protocols, whose job it is to move your data across the network. Windows NT uses a transport protocol known as NetBEUI. It also uses TCP/IP (Transmission Control Protocol/Internet Protocol), the most widely used transport protocol for enterprise networks (large internets that connect whole companies, including sites all over the city, the country, or the world).
- Above the transport layer resides the transport driver interface. An interface is simply a connection between two entities; a driver is software that controls the operation of a device.
- At the session layer, the Windows NT redirector provides your machine the ability to access resources on other computers on your peer-to-peer network. It uses the SMB (Server Message Block) protocol to format messages for transmission over the network. Actually, this protocol functions at the top three layers (session, presentation, and application).
- At the presentation layer, Windows NT makes certain your message can be read by the device to which you send it. It does this by converting your format to another one, if necessary.
- At the application layer, your Windows NT workstation interfaces with the programs, or applications, you use, such as your word processor or spreadsheet. The application layer interprets the commands issued by your application and passes them on to the processes that will carry them out. You might use named pipes, an interface that passes data between two processes, or a mailslot, an interface that provides one-to-many and many-to-one communication.

This basic explanation should give you an idea of the way Windows NT follows the standard provided by the OSI Model, at the same time using Microsoft technology to implement the functions the product promises to provide. Now let's look at some specifics of the Windows NT protocol implementation.

There are three distinct layers of activity within Windows NT's network subsystem. At the bottom, a set of device drivers provides hooks into network adapters. Above that, protocols bind to the network adapters to provide well-defined means to communicate with other systems. Finally, network redirectors provide user- and application-level interfaces to other systems using those protocols.

Any of these layers can act in a many-to-many relationship with the neighboring layer; that is, multiple adapters can service a single protocol, or multiple protocols can run over a single adapter. Likewise, multiple redirectors can run over a single protocol, or a single redirector can run over multiple protocols. However, redirectors and adapters can't speak to each other directly. They must use a common protocol in between them, and communicate directly with it. In effect, the protocol layer becomes a traffic cop, saying who can send data where and over what media.

Above each of the layers are "interfaces" that provide virtual portholes for layers to communicate through. The NDIS Interface maps network adapters to protocols, for example, while the TDI Interface maps redirectors to protocols. If multiple redirectors are in use, a Provider Interface maps incoming network requests to the appropriate redirector. For simplicity's sake, we'll examine the three layers and their interfaces separately. Appendix 2 examines some of the more popular protocols individually and in detail.

Network Adapters and Device Drivers

Just like a computer needs a video adapter to display output, it also needs a network adapter to communicate over a network. The network media may be coax cable, modems and phone lines, or even radio waves broadcast over the air. Regardless of the media, the operating system and the computer must have a way to communicate with the hardware that provides the network signaling.

This is handled through device drivers loaded at boot time. These drivers tell Windows NT what type of communications media are in use, the speed of the link, etc. Parameters stored in Windows NT's Registry tell Windows NT how to communicate directly with the adapter, so that it knows when the network needs servicing. A NIC (Network Interface Card) may use hardware interrupts (the same as a keyboard) to grab the CPU's attention. It may also use shared memory (like most SCSI cards) for the exchange of data between the system memory and the NIC's memory. It may also use port addresses (like serial ports) for data I/O. Information stored in the Registry tells Windows NT how the adapter is configured and how it communicates with the operating system.

To the user, this information is represented and configured in the "Network" control object within Control Panels. Network adapters are installed, adjusted, and removed here. For more information, refer to Chapter 2. Multiple adapters can be installed, up to a maximum of eight. As long as the adapters don't conflict with each other or any other peripherals within the computer, they can all be used. However, they are completely useless without protocols to take advantage of them.

Network Device Interface Specification (NDIS)

The NDIS Interface provides a way for protocols to bind to the underlying network adapters. Without this layer, each protocol would have to implicitly know about each adapter and the network media it used. By providing an interface between the NICs and protocols, the latter only has to send data to the interface for processing. It in turn has already registered information about the specific adapters, and can make changes to the data as needed.

Another benefit of using the NDIS Interface is that multiple adapters can be bound to a single protocol, or conversely, multiple protocols can use a single adapter. In the earlier days of networking, using multiple protocols meant you *had* to use multiple adapters, as each one would be locked to the other. The NDIS Interface provides a virtual network layer that protocols can address. The virtual layer then passes the data to the appropriate adapter.

Transport Protocols

Webster defines a protocol as "the code of ceremonial forms and courtesies ... accepted as proper and correct in official dealings." That about defines network protocols as well. A protocol is simply a well-defined method for computer systems to use when communicating with other devices. Two computers must use the same protocol in order to communicate.

Different protocols are suited to different kinds of network environments. For example, NetBEUI uses "names" for computers as the primary method of distinction between systems. Although this makes the network easy to use and diagnose, other problems are introduced that limit the protocol's effectiveness on large networks. In contrast, TCP/IP uses a 32-bit binary addressing scheme, which makes it quite effective, but is a nightmare for users to interact with (without help, anyway).

A protocol is generally implemented as a background process, such as a TSR under DOS, or as a daemon under UNIX. With Windows NT, protocols run as threads within the privileged subsystem, as a part of the executive. For information on specific protocols, refer to Appendix 2.

The TDI (Transport Driver Interface)

Some network software—like Windows NT's native LAN Manager stuff—lets users run multiple protocols. This makes it more effective in complex environments. Just as the NDIS Interface provides a single point of communication between NICs and protocols, the TDI Interface provides a link between redirectors and protocols. Without this interface, the redirector software would need to explicitly understand each of the protocols and their capabilities. Whenever a new protocol was introduced, the redirector would have to be rewritten.

For example, Windows NT's native network software can run over NetBEUI, TCP/IP, or even IPX. It doesn't have to know anything specifically about all of these protocols however. It simply needs to communicate with the TDI, which handles the necessary conversion and spoofing needed to make the network software work over the appropriate protocol.

The biggest problem with this design is that there must be a virtual protocol for the redirectors to address. In Windows NT's case, that protocol happens to be based on NetBEUI, which isn't very robust. In order for TCP/IP or IPX to act like NetBEUI, lots of trickery has to occur. You lose a lot of the features that came with the underlying protocols by using a lowest-common-denominator approach such as this.

Redirectors

Although the protocol does the majority of the grunt work in terms of finding and communicating with other systems, the network redirector is what handles the presentation of resources on the network, and also acts as the component that communicates directly with the Windows NT kernel.

Under Windows NT, network redirectors run as file system drivers, the same as FAT, NTFS and CD-ROM file system drivers. This allows the network resources to appear exactly the same as any device that is physically attached to the system. When an application makes a call for a file or device, the application doesn't need to know anything about the device, since the underlying file system management subsystem handles all the communications.

For example, File Manager doesn't understand network concepts explicitly, but instead relies on the redirector to handle requests for it. Since all filesystem requests are passed to the Windows NT kernel, when you open a folder, the kernel looks to see if the resource is local or remote. If remote, it passes the request to the redirector, which passes it to the remote system. That system processes the request, and returns some sort of data. The redirector then passes the data back to the kernel for presentation to the application that requested it. A redirector can communicate with remote systems using any protocol that both systems understand and have configured.

Provider Interface

Just as you can bind multiple protocols to multiple adapters, you can also bind multiple redirectors to multiple protocols. In order for Windows NT to present and understand these different networks cleanly, a method for making them all look the same had to be devised. The result is the Provider Interface.

This interface is really made up of several smaller modules, each of which provide specialized services. The Multiple Provider Router (MPR) tracks what network a request is for, and coordinates communication between the application and network.

Another module is the WNet APIs, which provide a consistent "look and feel" to different vendors' networks (see Appendix 1 for details). NetWare resources typically look like server/resource; NFS resources are represented by /server/resource; and LAN Manager resources look like \\server\resource. Part of the WNet subsystem maps all network resources into the Microsoft-favored and -built \\server\resource format called the *Universal Naming Convention* (UNC).

The WNet subsystem, in conjunction with the MPR and several other modules, combine to form the Provider Interface. This allows you to use Microsoft's LAN Manager software as well as Novell's NetWare, Banyan's VINES, or any other redirector, with almost any Windows NT application, without the developers having to code in support for all these networks directly. If you're using only one redirector, you won't need the Provider Interface layer, although portions of it may be in use anyway.

Appendix 5

Alternative Architectures

The microkernel (see Chapter 1) architecture of Windows NT makes it possible to use a variety of different types of computer with this advanced operating system. Selecting the right type of computer for a particular Windows NT application is a matter of cost versus performance and could dramatically affect the cost effectiveness of a Windows NT installation. Alternatives supported by the current release of Windows NT, over and above single-processor PC-compatible systems, include Symmetric Multiprocessor (SMP) and Reduced Instruction Set Computer (RISC) systems.

Why Not a Conventional PC System?

Before we examine the more exotic alternatives, it's worth considering just what might drive a decision to purchase a more exotic design. After all, the conventional PC architecture is well-understood, technically mature—and let's not ignore the most important feature—it is *cheap*. The basic reason to consider an unconventional architecture is performance. In the classic conventional PC-compatible, performance is limited because only a single central processor (CPU) can be used in each machine and the performance of that CPU is limited to the highest performance of the available Intel microprocessors, currently the 66MHz Pentium chip. In order to understand why we might wish to consider moving to an SMP or RISC architecture, we need to consider just what the performance limitations of the Intel chips are.

Integer Performance

The most commonly used measure of a CPU's performance is the figure of Millions of Instructions Per Second (MIPS). This is a direct measure of the computational performance of any microprocessor chip. It refers to the number of individual instructions (or steps) that can be executed in a single second. Such steps might include fetching a data word from memory, performing an addition or subtraction, comparing one data word to another, etc. Computer programs are nothing more than a collection of such steps and so any given program will execute twice as fast on a machine that performs at twice as many MIPS.

Intel microprocessors capable of running Windows NT span a considerable range of MIPS in their current configurations. The minimum system for running Windows NT currently is a 25MHz Intel 386 processor capable of somewhere in the vicinity of 15 MIPS. The highest performance processor currently available is a 66MHz Pentium processor, which employs an exotic dual unit of issue design to achieve nearly 120 MIPS. A particular characteristic of the Intel architectural design that affects its integer performance is the fact that Intel processors have, up to now, been designed according to a Complex Instruction Set Computer (CISC) architecture rather than a RISC design. In a CISC microprocessor the instruction set is very rich and single instructions can carry out quite complex tasks. For instance, it's possible to copy an entire character string from one location to another in an Intel 486 system with a single instruction. However, the availability of such a rich set of instructions enforces some limitations on the design such that individual instructions may take many clock cycles to execute. This is particularly apparent in the 386 design where it quite commonly takes two to four clock cycles to execute an instruction. Thus, although one is running a 25MHz 386 chip one cannot reasonably expect to achieve 25 MIPS performance. The 486 chip is much more nearly RISC-like in its performance. The Pentium chip actually exceeds this by a design that involves two parallel instruction pipelines and that can under certain circumstances execute two instructions at the same time, a process called *superscalar execution*. However, again the point is that other (RISC) designs can achieve throughputs as high as the clock rate. A 50MHz MIPS R4000 processor for instance, by definition, will achieve 50 MIPS.

Floating Point Performance

There is a second important figure of merit for CPU performance—Millions of Floating Point Operations Per Second (MFLOPS). Like the MIPS figure, MFLOPS refers to the number of simple floating point instructions (such as fetching a floating point operand into memory, performing a floating point multiplication or division, comparing two floating point operands, etc.) that can be performed per second. The significance of this figure by comparison with the MIPS figure of merit is that for certain operations, especially in technical applications, the floating point figure becomes overwhelmingly important. This is also significant because a major weakness of Intel microprocessors prior to the Pentium chip has been a substantially lower floating point performance than integer performance. For example, a 50MHz Intel 486DX chip will achieve somewhere in the vicinity of 40–45 MIPS throughput executing 32-bit code such as Windows NT. It's only capable, however, of less than 20 MFLOPS because of the limitations of its floating point unit design.

Typically, RISC processors have been designed with significantly more efficient, better optimized floating point units and can achieve floating point execution speeds approaching those of their integer execution speeds. For applications that are floating point intensive, such as Computer Aided Design/Computer Aided Engineering (CAD/CAE), scientific applications, and the like, this could be a significant advantage. With an understanding of these figures of merit, we can now take a look at the alternatives available for Windows NT.

Figure A5.1 summarizes the performance range covered by Windows NT systems, illustrating integer performance on the horizontal axis, and floating-point performance on the vertical axis.

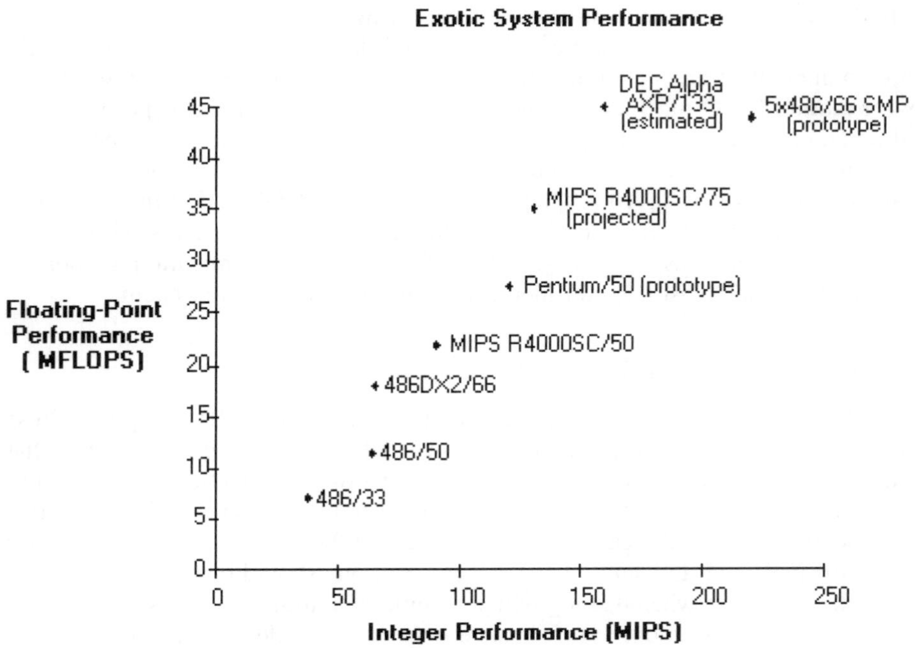

Figure A5.1 NT Performance chart.

The performance range covered by single-processor CPU designs currently running Windows NT extends over a 4:1 range in integer throughput—and nearly 10:1 in floating-point. Symmetric multiprocessor (SMP) systems can use multiple CPUs to achieve still higher speeds.

The First and Usually Best Alternative: The Classical Intel PC-Compatible Single Processor Machine

Lets begin by looking at what is possible with the conventional architecture. Currently available Intel CPUs span performance ranges as high as 120 MIPS and 80 MFLOPS in the 66MHz Intel Pentium chip. This performance compares very favorably with individual RISC processors and under a wide variety of conditions can compete quite effectively against the lower end of the symmetric multiprocessor machines. The classical single-processor PC-compatible has a number of significant advantages as a Windows NT platform. The first of these, of course, is price. The Intel PC compatible market is very much a commodity market. You can generally find a variety of manufacturers and assemblers providing machines at a given performance class. This competition tends to drive the price down. There is also a tremendous infrastructure of accessory cards, service, and support available for these machines and it should not be overlooked that these are the only machines that will run both Windows NT and other operating systems like DOS, OS/2, or NetWare. Therefore, an investment in such a machine is *safe*. If Windows NT for any reason fails to live up to your expectations, it's entirely possible to replace it with another operating system.

It's therefore always incumbent upon anyone considering a more exotic design to begin by examining the available Intel compatible machines and determining whether in fact it's necessary to use an alternative architecture. One rather subtle point of significance will come up again as we examine RISC machines. Windows NT can provide superior performance when executed on an exotic architecture machine by comparison with a classical architecture machine, *but only when executing 32-bit Windows applications written for Windows NT*. For a variety of reasons, when executing 16-bit legacy applications—DOS and Win16 applications—you cannot expect to see performance gains with the more exotic systems. This is particularly true in RISC systems, as we will see. Therefore, if legacy application support is important, this is another good reason to consider a conventional architecture system.

Symmetric Multiprocessors (SMP)

No feature of the Windows NT design has received more attention than its SMP support. Press reports treat this, to all intents and purposes, like science fiction—referring to machines that can deliver mainframe-class performance. And indeed the raw specifications can be quite impressive. As of this writing, Sequent Systems has demonstrated Windows NT on a thirty-processor SMP machine theoretically capable of somewhere in the vicinity of 1500 MIPS, far in excess of the performance of any single CPU system. Yet, one should beware when seeing these kinds of numbers because when dealing with a symmetric multiprocessor issues become extremely complicated and raw integer performance does *not* provide an adequate guide to overall system capabilities.

Problem of Contention

The basic idea of a symmetric multiprocessing system is quite simple. The system operates a number of CPUs in parallel. Each executes a copy of the Windows NT microkernel and each can execute either kernel or application code at any given time. This allows the system to have throughput that can theoretically be N times as fast as a single processor computer (where N is the number of processors). If one considers, for instance, an SMP containing four 50MHz Intel 486 processors one would expect to achieve a performance four times as high as a single 50MHz Intel 486 CPU. And, under certain circumstances, this can be correct. However, this *linear scaling* assumption breaks down whenever any two or more processes *contend* for a single resource. This contention problem represents the ultimate limit on SMP performance.

Contention can occur when any two or more processors attempt to access a shared resource. A shared resource can be an I/O device (such as the video display, or a network card), or it can be a memory location in the system, or it can be a component of the operating system. For instance, while Windows NT can execute multiple copies of its microkernel there are certain shared resources within the kernel. The most critical of these is the task switcher database which determines when each task in the system may be scheduled for execution. It should be obvious that only a single copy of that database can be maintained, and so each processor will at various times have to access that database. When any one processor is accessing it, the other processors cannot. In the event that they attempt to, they will "spin lock" waiting on that database until the other processor or processors release it.

Designing an SMP architecture to minimize contention is something of an art form. It most critically demands careful attention to the memory architecture of the system. Consider again the aforementioned four-way 486 SMP. Such a system is capable of four times the performance of a 50MHz 486, theoretically on the order of 160 MIPS. Since all four processors will be attempting to access memory simultaneously, in order to achieve full throughput it will be necessary for this system to have a memory architecture capable of supporting up to 160 million memory fetches per second. That is a very complex task and results in an extremely expensive memory system.

This problem can be mitigated to some extent by providing a large secondary memory cache for each central processor. Thus, in most existing SMP designs it's typical to see each processor buffered with 256KB of fast cache RAM. The assumption is that the majority of memory fetches will occur from the cache. With each CPU having its own cache there will be no contention for data fetched from cache. The only contention will occur when a fetch is made to load the cache from the main system memory. This can safely occur at a lower data rate. Still, it's clear that this provides a severe impact on the cost of the system and in extreme cases it can provide a severe limitation on performance.

Consider, for example, a database application written to exploit Windows NT memory mapped file architecture. We can foresee a situation in which a large number of cache fetches need to occur simultaneously—with the result that the system slows down to the speed of the non-cached memory architecture, typically 25MHz. If the memory architecture is capable of only 25MHz then the maximum total throughput the system will achieve under these conditions is 25 million instructions per second *no matter how many processors are built into the system.* Even on a system that has been designed with an optimal memory architecture contention can become a severe problem for I/O. For example, during test procedures at *Windows Magazine* in May 1993, we experimented with an early two-processor machine based on the Intel Pentium CPU and we saw very impressive performance (up to 120 MIPS) from it. However, in an effort to determine the real-world performance of this system, we experimented with running multiple graphical applications simultaneously—and got something of a shock. As we added many graphical applications to the system we found that, with both processors operating, the system would actually run more slowly with two processors than with one.

The reason for this turned out to be contention for the screen as a shared resource. Consider two applications attempting to access the screen at the same time, where each issues operating system calls to its own copy of the Windows NT kernel. One copy of the Windows NT kernel then accesses the screen. The other "spin locks" waiting on the screen. The data rate then becomes limited to the performance of the video subsystem. In the particular case in question this was a Super VGA system that had a fairly limited overall throughput. And so for graphic-intense applications we found that the SMP, far from offering an advantage, actually produced lower overall performance.

It's highly unlikely that this particular kind of situation will arise in practice. Systems designed for graphic-intense applications will surely use highly optimized graphic display subsystems that are unlikely to be fully loaded by the processors. But we still need to make the point very clear. *SMP is not a panacea.* It will produce very fast results on computationally intensive tasks where the maximum advantage can be taken of multiple simultaneous computations exploiting local cache memory. However, if a large percentage of the computations require fetches from outside the cache or contend for external I/O, system performance can be expected to slow down dramatically. The assumption that one will achieve five times the performance with five processors in an SMP machine is naive.

Finally, we should reinforce the cost issues. One can ask (for example, for a server application), whether a single-CPU RISC-based machine operating at 150 MIPS or a three-processor Intel machine with three 50 MIPS processors would be preferable. Thinking about this naively one can assume that the three-processor machine will give some advantage because, after all, one can indeed have three tasks executing at the same time. This logic is incorrect. Regardless of the architecture of a system, it has an upper limit enforced by the total number of MIPS it can execute. If you have three 50 MIPS processors the most computational work you can *ever* get done is 150 million instructions per second. There is no way you will achieve any higher figure of merit than that. That identical figure can be achieved by a single-processor machine operating at 150 MIPS. But the single-processor machine needs to have only a single cache. It will not require the additional system board complexity. It will almost certainly be cheaper. It will also be more reliable because in general, the reliability of a system is inversely proportional to its parts count and an SMP system is invariably more complex than a single-CPU system.

Therefore, use of an SMP system should *never* be considered unless all possible CPU alternatives have been exhausted. There can be one exception to this rule. Some of the SMP designs currently being offered for Windows NT are *scalable*. That is, you may purchase them with a single processor and then add more processors as your needs grow. This can be a very attractive approach, especially in a situation where you are uncertain of your needs for ultimate system performance but expect them to grow with time. In such a case, an SMP is worth considering. However, you should be careful to carry out a cost analysis. The reason for this is that you may find that the cost of upgrading your SMP system to add more processors exceeds the cost of replacing a single processor system with a more powerful single-processor system when the time comes. If the cost is higher then there is no advantage to the SMP.

You should also very carefully examine the contention issue. In a server application, is the system supplied with enough network bandwidth to support the kind of loads you will see as you add multiple processor cards? There is no sense in providing a system with an additional processor card when that processor will spend most of its time waiting for access to the network card. In a desktop application, is the application principally bound by graphic speed? And what is the graphic performance? If a graphic card is in use in a system that is capable of only 100 million graphical operations per second, then adding processors to push performance above 100 MIPS will not produce a significant performance improvement in graphic-intense applications. Evaluate these facts very carefully.

For large-scale client/server use, however, particularly for mainframe replacement in downsizing applications, the SMP may very well offer the best alternative.

Alternative Three: RISC

It's an odd coincidence that the acronym for Reduced Instruction Set Computing should sound "risky" to so many people. But it's a peculiar fact that RISC solutions *do* represent a risky alternative, one that can potentially offer a great payback but one that is fraught with uncertainty. The promise of the RISC approach is significantly higher performance from a given set of components. The classical Intel processors in the 386 and 486 series generally offer about half the number of MIPS as the number of MHz. That is, in general, it takes two clock cycles for them to complete an average instruction. Thus a 50MHz Intel 486 generally delivers about 25 MIPS. Floating point performance of these systems tends to be even less, generally on the order of four clock cycles per instruction. This can be compensated to a certain extent by the mechanism of clock doubling (in which a CPU runs internally at twice the external clock rate). For instance, in the 486DX2/66 chip, a 33MHz external clock is doubled internally to 66MHz. Since the 486 on the average requires two clock cycles to accomplish an instruction, the 66MHz internal clock is well matched to an effective throughput of 33 MIPS.

The problem with this approach is that access to external devices and memory has to be mediated at the external clock rate of 33MHz. Thus the chip cannot be serviced at any more than a 33 million memory-fetch-per-second rate. Since the chip generally accomplishes 33 million instructions per second this tends to work out reasonably well, and the 486's 8KB on-chip cache provides sufficient buffer capacity to make up the difference. But it can become a problem at higher rates and the anticipated 99MHz clock tripled 486 chip will probably have a severe problem in this regard.

As discussed earlier, RISC processors, by limiting the number of instructions and optimizing these instructions for speed, attempt to achieve an overall throughput of one instruction per clock. Thus a 50MHz RISC processor should, theoretically, achieve 50 MIPS. They also attempt to do the same thing for floating point instructions, although they are generally less successful with this. But the overall result is approximately twice the performance provided by an equivalent x86 chip at a given clock rate. That is, you can anticipate that at a given clock rate in MHz, you will see twice as much integer and floating point performance with a RISC processor. Since the cost of a computer tends to be governed by the number of components and the clock rate (particularly the clock rate at which memory is accessed), a computer that can accomplish twice as much at a given clock rate has an obvious advantage. Against this is the cost of additional RAM—since each RISC instruction does less work, there have to be more of them—so RISC programs tend to be larger than their Intel equivalents.

One need only look at the relative costs today of 33 and 66MHz 486 computers to see the point. All things being equal then, the world would long since have converted from CISC processors such as the Intel processors to one of the various RISC processors. Of course, this has not happened and in order to understand why RISC is in fact "risky" we need to examine the reasons why it hasn't happened.

No Single Standard

While Intel is not viewed with love by vendors in the computer industry, the fact that a single company has dominated the microprocessor market for the last ten years has had a number of notable advantages. It's possible to order computers from any of hundreds of vendors, even to order them by mail, and be reasonably certain they will all execute the hundreds of PC-compatible applications on the market without being seriously concerned about the possibility that some applications will prove to be incompatible. The reason for this is that all of these computers use the Intel x86 family of microprocessors and are thus inherently compatible. No such single family compatibility exists in the RISC market. Indeed, Intel itself has made several different varieties of RISC chips, the *i*860 chip among them.[1] Other major players in the RISC business have at various times included SUN Microsystems, Data General Corporation, IBM, Hewlett-Packard, Fairchild, and virtually every maker of microprocessors in the United States and many other places.

This situation has produced what might be called a *RISC anarchy*. There are dozens of different families of RISC processors today, each more or less incompatible, each running their own operating system. The operating systems have this in common—they are all *called* UNIX. The resemblance begins and ends right there. Windows NT, of course, hopes to change this. As we noted in Chapter 1, the Windows NT microkernel is portable. Providing Windows NT for a new architecture requires only that the portable C-based NT source code be recompiled for that architecture and that a new Hardware Abstraction Layer for that architecture be written. However, it's worth noting that when one moves to RISC one leaves behind all that vast legacy of compatibility; one cannot expect to run DOS, OS/2, SCO UNIX, or any other Intel-based operating system on a RISC machine. When you buy into RISC, you have locked yourself into Windows NT.

The 16-Bit Legacy Application Issue

Windows NT endeavors to overcome the problem of RISC anarchy in a second way. Beyond the portability of Windows NT itself to the new architecture, a high degree of legacy application support is provided for DOS, Windows, and OS/2 1.x applications. Windows NT accomplishes this by providing a special version of Insignia Systems' *Soft PC* emulation software optimized for each version of Windows NT. On RISC processors, Soft PC provides

[1]This was, in fact, the first CPU on which NT was implemented.

a software environment that appears to legacy programs as though it were in fact a PC, specifically a very fast 286 (AT-compatible) PC. The effectiveness of Soft PC is generally quite good. One of us routinely runs Visual Basic, Word for Windows, Microsoft Project, Microsoft Excel, and various other applications on a MIPS R4000 machine.[2] All of these are 16-bit programs and all, for the most part, perform on the MIPS machine just as happily as though they were sitting on the 486 machine on the other side of the office.

Unfortunately, they do not perform as well (that is, as fast) as they do on the 486. The reason for this is the inherent inefficiency in the Soft PC emulation approach. The way the emulator works is to examine each Intel instruction in the legacy application that is executing. This instruction (for instance, the single 486 instruction that copies strings), is then *emulated* by a number of RISC instructions. Ideally, in the string copy this might be no more than one instruction per byte. But that is significantly less efficient than the 486 implementation. In general, our experience is that the Soft PC emulation on NT RISC machines tends to require approximately five RISC instructions per Intel instruction. Thus it has the effect of slowing down the machine by a factor of five and our clock-doubled 100MHz R4000 machine thus runs about as fast as a 20MHz 386SX. The R4000 (MIPS Magnum SC) in question costs over $10,000; this is hardly a cost-effective approach.

You might wonder at this point then why in fact we use Visual Basic (and Word for Windows and Excel and Power Point) on a RISC machine when it gives only 20MHz performance. The reason is that we have been oversimplifying a bit. The raw integer performance is equivalent to a 20MHz machine. The other performance parameters, however, are somewhat improved. We get an average of about 1.5 megabytes per second of disk access speed out of the machine. That is three to five times what you would get on a 386SX. Similarly we get significantly better video performance and somewhat better floating point performance than on a 386SX. The overall result has a throughput that feels like a 486SX—and it's quite acceptable for most tasks. You would not wish to use it for a performance-intensive application—it's irritating to wait while Excel recalculates large spreadsheets. But for most purposes it's fine.

32-Bit Windows Applications—The Holy Grail

Of course, running largely 16-bit applications on a 32-bit RISC machine is ridiculous. This effectively cuts the clock rate of the machine by a factor of five, so you've bought 386 performance at a Pentium price. However, as soon as 32-bit applications compiled for the RISC processor in question become available the situation changes, because this machine's overall performance with a 100MHz internal clock rate (and generally achieving one instruction per clock) is in the vicinity of twice the performance of a 486/66 and compares very well with a Pentium machine. The R4400 processor machines now becoming available at 150MHz will give even better results. Moreover, since the advantage in floating point performance even exceeds the advantage in integer performance, you could conceive that, for example, a 32-bit version of Excel would suddenly reverse your experience. Rather than wishing to switch to a 486 machine when recalculating large spreadsheets, you might very well find yourself prefer-

[2] John D. Ruley, who has used a MIPS R4000 for day-to-day work throughout the NT Beta program.

ring to run them on the R4000, which is likely in a 32-bit implementation to perform spreadsheets somewhere between two and four times as fast as they are performed on the 486. Unfortunately, as with everything else, nothing in life is quite so simple—and this is equally true of 32-bit Windows applications.

The principal problem with 32-bit Windows applications is simply this: they have to be compiled separately for *each version of Windows NT*. This is a great complication and a great burden for software developers. It means that the developer of a Windows NT utility, for instance, cannot simply compile one Windows NT-executable file and ship this blindly assuming that it will work on every machine in sight. If she or he has designed the application properly, it will run on all Intel machines including symmetric multiprocessor (SMP) machines without modification. But to provide a version for an R4000 or other RISC platform the developer must compile it for that specific platform. To support another platform the developer must compile it again.

As this is written the announced platforms for Windows NT include the x86 platform, the MIPS R4x00 platform, the DEC Alpha AXP platform, and the Intergraph Clipper platform. There are a variety of other platforms that are widely rumored but have not been officially announced.[3] An application developer wishing to cover the entire market then must, as of today, supply four separate executable versions of each application. Moreover, the developer must keep a close eye on the news and plan to provide versions for the other architectures as they become available. This problem is accentuated by the fact that as of this writing the development tools for each of these platforms are different. It is therefore necessary to have physical access to each of these machines in order to compile the application for it. There is (as of yet) no cross compiler, no way that you can sit at an Intel machine and compile a MIPS executable. That, to coin a phrase, is *bad*. Fortunately there are vendors planning to fill this gap, but when their products will ship is not clear at this writing.

Pentium: RISC in a CISC Box?

As if things were not already confusing enough, in 1993 Intel introduced its long-awaited fifth-generation Pentium chip. The Pentium turns out to be something extremely interesting in that it combines most of the generally accepted advanced features of RISC architectures with full x86 compatibility. That is, in effect, the Pentium is an x86-compatible RISC chip. This would appear to offer the best of all possible capabilities. At 60MHz external clock rate the Pentium (with a dual pipeline architecture) is capable of internal throughputs of 120 MIPS. It has an eight-stage floating point pipeline that can achieve floating point execution rates of over 60 megaflops. This compares very favorably with the R4000/R4400 processors. Exactly how it compares to the DEC Alpha chip is hard to say at this moment but it will likely compete very well with the Alpha once clock rates are increased. It suffers none of the 16-bit difficulties of other RISC processors, and it executes x86 code right out of the box, although there are rumored to be some special optimizations that will benefit coders who wish to get the max-

[3]Between the time this was written and final editing, NT support was also announced for Apple/IBM/Motorola Power-PC and Sun SPARC-II architectures.

imum performance from the Pentium. Thus it would appear that those who are interested in RISC performance have an easy solution. Buy a Pentium: get the RISC performance without taking any "risks."

Again, matters are not so simple. Pentium is, to all intents and purposes, a RISC chip. It is x86-compatible. It works just fine. However, it has three tiny little problems. One is extraordinarily high cost. The other is heat, and the third is cache design. Pentium chips are being shipped in quantity pricing currently rumored to be about $1,500 in thousand-unit lots. Moreover, they are in short supply so that price is not likely to come down any time soon. That makes the Pentium by far the most expensive of the chips we have discussed. And it means that while the Pentium can give you performance comparable to an R4400 it does so at a premium price that will tend to be about $1,000 higher than the R4400 in an otherwise equivalent system configuration.

Pentium also suffers a thermal problem. Indeed, all high-speed chips suffer a thermal problem and with the 486DX2 chips many of us became familiar with the unusual design feature of planting a cooling fan directly on top of the processor. In the Pentium, however, this becomes considerably heightened. Pentium processors operating at full speed can dissipate some sixteen watts of power—comparable to a small light bulb. In the Pentium's case this heat will wind up being dissipated through the pins that connect the chip to the motherboard if one doesn't get rid of the heat by other means. This means that it is entirely possible for a Pentium chip to *literally* melt its own solder connections. Other RISC chips have this problem as well. However, the Pentium, for reasons that are not entirely clear at this writing, appears to have the problem to a greater degree than its competitors.

As to cache, the Pentium interfaces to the outside world at 60 (or 66) MHZ, while internally it operates at up to 120MHZ. Yet it has only 32KB of internal cache. This means that it's relatively easy for the memory system in a Pentium computer to be overstressed by the processor—a problem that's exacerbated by inefficient memory design in many first-generation Pentium computers.

It's worth noting that the Pentium is a very new chip while the various RISC architectures we've been discussing are now in their second, third, and fourth generations and it is likely, over time, the Pentium situation will improve. But again, what this points to is the fact that the Pentium system is not quite as RISC-free as Intel would have you believe.

Exotic Alternatives

Virtually all press attention about Windows NT and exotic architectures has focused on the SMP and RISC approaches and to a lesser extent on the trade-offs between these approaches. There's been less attention paid to the likelihood that NT will be applied to more exotic architectures. In particular, one can think of the IBM/Parallan hyperserver design and the Compaq SystemPro, both of which are asymmetrical multiprocessors. One can also think of various fault-tolerant machines from NetFrame Systems[4] and others. The exotic architectures tend to be special purpose. They also tend to be optimized for large-scale network applications.

[4]Makers of fault-tolerant super-server systems, located in Milpitas, CA.

The Parallan[5] hyperserver was originally designed to accelerate OS/2 operations and large-scale server applications. The system includes no less than five CPUs, only one of which is a general purpose CPU. The others are dedicated to accelerating one or another I/O task. The machine is coupled with a custom version of the OS/2 operating system that exploits these processors to speed up I/O. Such a system violates the NT "religion" in that NT expects all processors to have equal access to the bus and to interrupts. Thus the NT microkernel can dispatch *any* task whether it be a system or user task to any CPU without being concerned about what resources a CPU does or does not have access to. However, don't be misled into thinking that Windows NT cannot be used in the other architecture. Any "bus master" advanced I/O card used in an EISA or microchannel bus environment is in effect a microprocessor or at least is microprocessor based.

The microprocessor does not communicate with the operating system in the direct sense. Rather the microprocessor is controlled by its driver software. The operating system communicates with its driver. This approach is entirely amenable with Windows NT. It just means that an intelligent driver architecture will be used and it means that Windows NT can dispatch tasks to the I/O processor by communicating with the driver and then go on and get some other work done. It seems certain that this approach will then ultimately be applied with Windows NT. It will almost certainly be applied by Parallan in the very near future. These kinds of systems can offer unique advantages. In particular, the Parallan and some of the other ultra-high reliability systems provide hot-swap capability. That is, components of the system including but not limited to disk drives and even accessory cards can be pulled from the system and new ones placed in the system without turning the computer off. This capability would go perfectly hand-in-hand with Windows NT's built-in warm boot driver functionality discussed in Chapter 1.

The disadvantage of these systems in Windows NT (or any other operating system) is that they are very much custom systems and they very much require custom software. The off-the-shelf Windows NT package is never going to run properly on a Parallan server. Parallan users will need a custom version of NT and a series of special device drivers. And they will be tied just as tightly to that hardware and that particular implementation of NT as they are today to the special version of OS/2 on which the Parallan system depends. However, such machines can offer significant advantages. And in situations that require these advantages these may outweigh any disadvantages these systems represent.

Given All That, How Do You Choose?

The ultimate decision in selecting a CPU architecture for Windows NT needs to be subjected to the kind of rigorous bottom-line cost justification analysis we recommend in examining the selection of a Window NT Advanced Server versus a standalone conventional Windows NT

[5]A fault-tolerant asymmetric multiprocessor (AMP) server, made by Parallan systems of San Jose, CA, and also sold by IBM as the Model 295 system.

system in a midrange network. However, there are some rules of thumb that can prove useful. We will build a simple decision tree to take you through the process of elimination that will enable you to make a rough decision as to the types of system you should examine.

Step 1, examine your requirements.

Step 2, decide whether these requirements can be met by a classic 386/486 system. (No cheating! This is not the place to worry about whether you have adequate growing room or whether this system will scale. Can your needs today be addressed by this kind of system?) Yes—stop here. The cost advantages of a classical 386/486 system and their known reliability and their ability to run other software outweigh any other consideration. If you spend $2,000 or $3,000 today on a 486 system and you outgrow your need for it then you can recycle that system to another application, which need not be Windows NT-based, while you spend money to upgrade to the next larger system. If a 386/486 architecture is adequate for the job then the decision process stops right here.

Step 3, consider whether 16-bit legacy application performance is a major issue. Yes—then don't bother with the RISC machines. The thing to bear in mind here is that the RISC machines are always going to be a bad deal for 16-bit application support. It is true that higher-performance RISC machines will show higher 16-bit performance. The 150MHz R4400, for instance, would probably give 486DX performance rather than the 486SX performance you'd see from an R4000. The DEC Alpha would give even better performance but it still would not be performance anywhere near the limits of the machine. Nor will it be performance that will justify the cost of the machine. Compare the $15,000 to $20,000 one pays for a RISC machine today to the few thousand dollars one pays for a 486. This is no issue. However, it is worth stepping back and considering this simple fact: 16-bit applications are never run on the server. They are always run on the client. This being the case, it's worth noting that there is nothing to prevent you from running classic x86 machines in connection with a RISC-based server. And indeed, this combination can be cost effective. If 16-bit legacy application performance is a nonissue take a close look at RISC. Why? Because dollar-per-MIPS, RISC is always a better deal than SMP. The reason for this is a simple one. The cost of any computer system is largely a function of the number of components in the system. Take the lid off the system and count the chips. You'll find you can get a very close correlation between the number of chips on the motherboard and the cost of the system. Indeed, the decreasing cost-per-performance of systems over the years is attributable to the fact that the density with which electronic components can be incorporated into a chip doubles approximately every eighteen months. If you've ever wondered why you never quite seem to get two years' use out of your system before it becomes obsolete, that's your answer.

A single-processor RISC machine at any given performance level has approximately the same number of components as a single-processor classic x86 machine. The SMP machine, on the other hand, has to have a second processor, support chips to support that processor (mostly custom AISC chips), cache RAM to support the second processor, and a more sophisticated memory controller architecture. Therefore, at a given performance level, the number of chips, and therefore the cost, increases. So the minute classic performance becomes an issue, if the 16-bit problem doesn't bother you then you need to look at RISC.

In particular, if you are looking for a high performance file and print server it is virtually incumbent upon you that you look at RISC. The RISC machines generally provide extraordinarily high performance, not only in their internal CPU architecture but also in their file and I/O performance. These machines quite commonly have 64-bit data busses. While Windows NT is a 32-bit system and cannot fully exploit that bus bandwidth, it's a completely safe assumption that you will not fully load such a system with the current generation of software. You can achieve very high disk performance at a significantly lower cost than you can achieve it in a multiprocessor system using RISC CPUs. The only situation where you should have any concern about RISC in a server environment is if you are concerned about application services rather than file and print services.

Example: as of this writing, Microsoft has delivered Beta versions of its SQL Server database and SNA Server mainframe connectivity. It has provided them on the x86 platform including support for SMP on the x86 and it has provided them on the MIPS platform. It has not as yet provided them for the Alpha or any other platform. If you are dependent upon applications services or particularly interested in these services it would be wise to check which platforms are supported before selecting a platform for your server. But again, for basic file and print services any RISC architecture is a good bet.

Step 4: If there is no other way to achieve acceptable performance look at SMP. That's the basic rule of thumb. The SMP is an extreme situation. It is complex. Because it is complex, it is expensive. Also, because it is complex, it is unreliable. But as mentioned earlier, Sequent can deliver machines providing up to thirty 486 processors and some 1,500 MIPS—performance that boggles the mind. There is no way you can achieve this performance with single processor systems. DEC with its Alpha CPU is predicting that they will achieve performance in the region of 10,000 MIPS by the turn of the century, but even they are speaking of achieving part of that by using an SMP configuration. Windows NT does work well in an SMP configuration, albeit with the limitations discussed earlier.

For More Information

Custer, Helen (1993), *Inside Windows NT.* Redmond, WA: Microsoft Press, ISBN: 1-55615-481-X. Good detail on how SMP and RISC systems are supported.

Patterson, David, and Hennessy, John (1988), *Computer Architecture—A Quantitative Approach.* San Mateo, CA: Morgan Kaufmann, ISBN: 1-55880-069-8. Covers Amdahl's Law, which governs system performance in both single-processor and multiprocessor cases.

Van Zandt, John (1992), *Parallel Processing in Information Systems.* New York: Wiley, ISBN: 0-471-54822-7. Good general work on multiprocessor systems.

Kane, Gerry and Heinrich, Joe (1992), *MIPS RISC Architecture.* Englewood Cliffs, NJ: Prentice-Hall, ISBN: 0-13-590472-2. Aside from details of the R4000/4400 architecture, Chapter 1 gives an outstanding overview of basic RISC theory, and was extremely helpful in formulating this chapter.

Sites, Richard (1992), *Alpha Architecture Reference Manual.* Burlington, MA: Digital Press, ISBN: 1-55558-098-X. Not for the faint of heart, this is an engineering text on the Alpha CPU design. Interesting, but far too technical for general readers.

Appendix 6

Principles of Preventative Maintenance

Chapter 5 gives all the details available to us on the specific steps you can take to tune Windows NT system performance and correct faults when they happen—but a larger question is how to prevent the faults from happening in the first place. As we saw in Chapter 5, the main approach to this is called *Preventative Maintenance (PM)*, and in this appendix we explore PM concepts in some detail.

In principle, unlike hardware, computer *software* does not wear out (indeed, it tends to become *more* reliable with age), and should not normally require adjustment. However, examination of one simple fact should show you that this nice theory breaks down when it's applied to a Windows NT network or any other network.

Why Does Software (and Hardware) Fail?

First of all, the probability of a piece of software malfunctioning is roughly proportional to the number of lines of code that make up that software—simply because the more code programmers write, the more likely they are to make a mistake. There's been a good deal written about

Windows NT, much of it misinformation, but many writers seem to agree on one point: Windows NT, as of this writing, (it's just reaching production) contains some *two million* lines of code. Would anyone care to place a bet with me on the odds that all two million lines of code are bug free?[1]

Beyond this we have to bear in mind that even though the probability of failure of any single component, software or hardware, in a modern PC system may be infinitesimally small, that infinitesimal smallness has to be multiplied by the number of connections in a network. The basic microcomputer we know today can be described as a "state machine"—a very large table that says when the input state is *X*, the output state is *Y*. At the time I went to technical school, state machines were the basic mechanism used to describe all sorts of interesting things ranging from simple switches to microprocessors. The state machine for a modern microprocessor is slightly large—the size of one's office, perhaps. But the state machine that you'd need to describe a modern microprocessor, disk controller, video controller, several dozen megabytes of RAM, and the rest of a Windows NT PC would be *appallingly* large.[2]

It gets worse—connect two of those machines together on a network and I defy anyone to write a state table that completely describes the resulting (very simple) network. No one can write that state table—*the state of one machine may depend on the state of another*. In a Windows NT network the size of each state machine is multiplied by the number of machines connected on the local segment, perhaps also by the state of the gateway that connects one segment to another, perhaps by the state of the server.

Such a system can't be described by the use of a state table. If you'll forgive me for dragging in some modern mathematics, such a system is, by definition, *chaotic*. It is describable only in probabilistic terms. Take heart, this doesn't mean that the operational status of your network is a crap shoot! *You can load the dice.*

The way you can load the dice is to employ a technique that people in the insurance business have been using since time immemorial. It's called *actuarial statistics*, and we're now going to examine it in detail. Let's begin with one of the most overused terms in computing today, *mean time between failure* (MTBF). MTBF is the statistical number that's used to describe hardware reliability, and the MTBF numbers that are quoted are typically pretty huge. It's not uncommon, for instance, to find a hard disk with an MTBF quoted at 30,000 hours. Since there are just 8,760 hours in a calendar year it is not surprising that most people look at a 30,000-hour MTBF disk drive and assume that they don't have to worry about it for three years or so.

Such an attitude is naive. The MTBF refers to the *mean* time to failure—that is, the *average*. While a disk drive may have a mean time to failure of 30,000 hours it, in fact, may fail at 15,000 hours or it may run perfectly up to 45,000 hours. You can't make a precise prediction

---

[1]It's amusing to note that between the time this sentence was written and the time it was sent to production, Microsoft released the first bug-fix disks for Windows NT—so it really *wasn't* bug-free after all (and I win the bet!)—JDR.

[2] Maybe, if you write very small, the size of the state of New York... then again, given the permutations introduced by the state of the RAM, a Windows NT state table *might* be larger than the size of the known universe!

of exactly how long a disk drive will operate, but on average, it will operate for 30,000 hours. This becomes significant if you have an installation with a large number of disk drives. Let's say, for instance, that your organization bought ten drives with a mean time to failure of 30,000 hours. Since each disk drive has a mean time to failure of over three years, the naive approach would be to assume you could run them all for three years and then buy ten new disk drives. But let's look at the statistics.

With ten drives operating the probability of failure is multiplied. It is now *ten* chances in 30,000, or *one chance in 3,000 hours*. Guess what? 3,000 is a good bit less than one year! So the probability that one of the ten drives will fail within the first year is very high. The way you approach this problem is to buy insurance—in the form of buying spare disk drives. If you have ten of these drives you can be reasonably certain that one is going to fail the first year. So don't buy ten, buy eleven. Then you have the hardware in position and can respond as quickly as possible once the failure occurs.

The second thing you can do is monitor the performance of all ten disk drives—because disk drives, being electromechanical devices, very often will give some indication of failure before they fail completely. You may begin to notice a high error rate, low data transfer rate, continuing detection of soft errors, any of a variety of things that will give you early warning of an impending failure *if you take the time to look for the warning.*

Therefore, by maintaining a maintenance history of all ten disk drives and comparing them, you *may* be able to determine a drive is going to fail before it does[3]—but you can never be certain of predicting that, so you can't wait and buy a spare disk drive when the maintenance history begins to indicate that a drive failure is likely. You may get no warning at all.

You also can't wait and assume that you're going to be able to transfer data from a drive after it has given indications that it's going to fail onto a new disk drive. For this reason it's essential to run backups of mission-critical information so that you're in a safe position, in the worst case. If the drive has failed without giving any prior indication, you're in a position to pop in a new disk drive and restore the backup data and lose no more than the last twenty-four hours of work or so. This consideration should be looked at very carefully in establishing the backup procedures for your organization. If you can't afford to lose twenty-four hours of work then you had better do backups more frequently than once every twenty-four hours!

The Mathematics of Fault Prediction

As we've seen in the preceding section, probably the most critical number one deals with in setting up a maintenance system for Windows NT (or any other hardware/software environment) is the mean time between failures (MTBF). This number is generally part of the specifications for any hardware device. When you're quoted a price on a system, if you look closely at the specifications, you will see an MTBF listing. You will also see MTBF listings for disk drives, memory components, etc.

For software, of course, MTBFs are never stated—because the software industry persists in a naive belief that they can produce things that never fail (hah!); and also, one suspects that

[3]Depending on the nature of the failure—some failures give no warnings at all.

the software industry would be unwilling to publish its MTBF numbers because they are likely to be so poor. However, it is possible to achieve a statistically valid set of MTBF information over time simply by recording how frequently errors occur and building your own database. In any case, with MTBF information available to you, it becomes possible to get quite elaborate in predicting the availability of a system and when problems are likely to occur—and then to fix them *before* they occur.

Availability and Reliability

Of course the goal of any system maintenance project should be to maintain the highest possible availability of the overall end-to-end system. Achieving a 100 percent availability is impossible, frankly, but you can get quite close to it if you pay sufficiently close attention to the reliability of individual components.

We'll have to begin with some definitions and a little mathematics. (Trust us, the mathematics isn't that difficult—and if you pay attention you will achieve some considerable insight into what's going on). Let's begin with the **reliability** of a system: Assuming a constant failure rate (that is, that on average failures occur at a fairly constant interval), it can be shown that the reliability over time will follow the equation:[4]

$$\mathbf{r(t) = e^{-at}}$$

where:

r is the reliability at any given time

t is time the component has been in operation

a is a constant characteristic of the component in question

Given that you know these figures for the reliability you can then predict the mean time between failure (MTBF) which is equal to **1/a** (and obviously, this means you can get **a** if you have the MTBF—it's just

a = 1/MTBF).

(See Figure A6.1.)

This model is generally accurate for hardware components. Software, however, tends to be very different. The reason for this should be obvious. Hardware tends to wear out. After an initial burn-in period (which isn't covered by this equation), hardware will be at its most reliable when it is new and then it wears out over a period of time at a generally constant rate. So reliability falls off with time—as shown by the above equation.

[4]This and other equations in this appendix are taken from *Introduction to Client/Server Systems* by Paul Renaud (details in *For More Information* at the end of this appendix). While the author disagrees with Mr. Renaud's centralized approach to systems management, his book is very, very good!

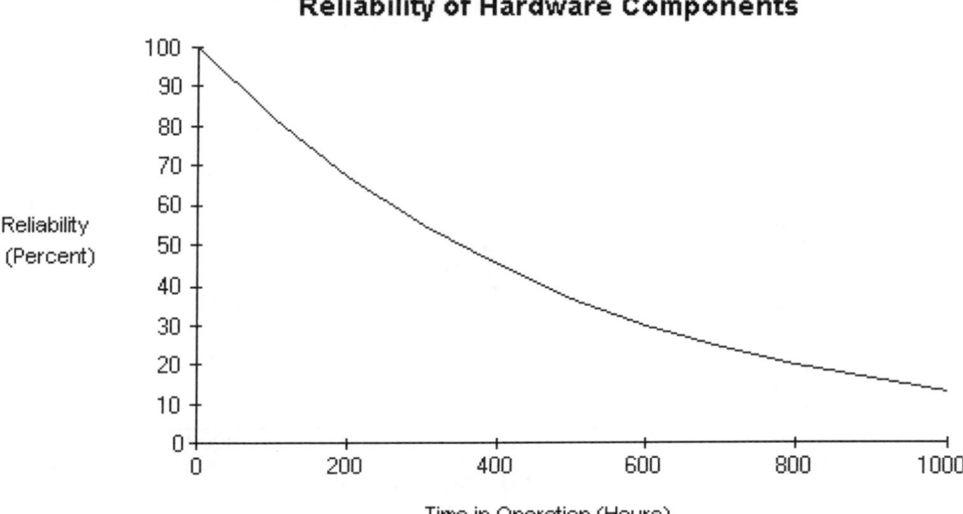

Figure A6.1 MTBF for hardware.

Reliability of hardware components falls off over time after an initial burn-in period; thus as components become old they are certain to fail.

The equation for software tends to be exactly the opposite. A new piece of software is apt to be buggy, but it will tend to become less buggy over time as bugs are found and fixed. There is no simple equation that can describe this adequately for all cases. One that is widely used will have the unavailability over time go as:

$$\mathbf{u(t) = a(1-e^{-bt/a})}$$

where **a** is the total number of defects, and **b** is a system-dependent constant.

The *mean time between defects* then is:

$$\mathbf{MTBD = (1/b)e^{at/b}}$$

Since a failure is by definition a defect, this equation also covers MTBF. The best way to find the **a** and **b** constants is by collecting data on a software system over time and then fitting the equation to the data— the fit will tend to improve with time as the amount of data increases. For instance, if you're running a piece of database software, the appropriate thing to do is to maintain a log of the bugs that are discovered in the software, the frequency with which they are discovered, and how long it takes to get a repair or a bug fix in place. It's then possible over time to fit the equation to the statistics. Please note that this equation will essentially start again when you upgrade to a new piece of software. New versions, while they will never be as unreliable as the first version (have you ever wondered where the hackneyed old

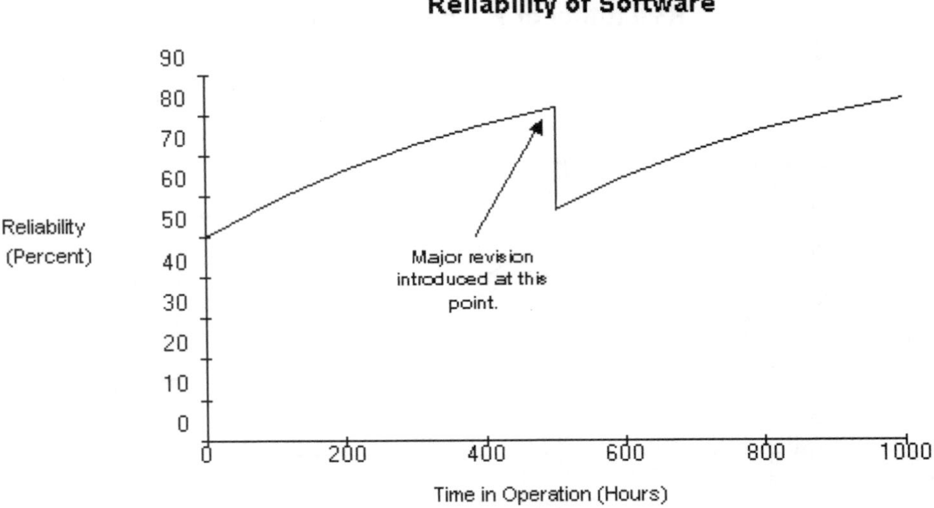

Figure A6.2 MTBD for software.

In contrast to hardware, the reliability of software *improves* over time—except for temporary unreliability introduced by new versions.

expression "never buy version one of anything" came from?) will represent a new start to the equation and so the curve will not be a simple downward slope as one might expect (see Figure A6.2).

Similarly, the MTBF equation given earlier does not cover the burn-in period for hardware—and for this reason it is highly desirable. For instance in our "buy eleven disk drives" example, you might burn in all eleven disk drives for some time before they're actually used. A general rule of thumb is that the burn-in period should be on the order of one tenth of one percent of the total life of the drive—for a 30,000-hour MTBF disk drive, the burn in period should be on the order of 30 hours. This can be conveniently accomplished by having a laboratory or maintenance shop set up with a test stand so that individual pieces of equipment can be subjected to continuous testing. A relatively simple program written in BASIC that will cycle the disk drive continuously writing data and reading it back is sufficient. One can then run it for a 30-hour burn-in period and once this is complete (assuming that the disk hasn't had any problems), format the disk and store it. A disk can then be taken out and applied as necessary. The odds are quite high that any burn-in defects will be detected during the burn-in period. That is, the drive will fail—at which point you can conveniently send it back to the manufacturer for replacement, since this will happen within the warranty period.

Given that the MTBF (or MTBD) is known, the one remaining factor that affects availability is the *mean time to repair*, or MTTR. This will be the time that it takes to correct the defect—the time to replace a failed disk drive, or to find and fix a bug in the software (or provide a workaround—like reindexing a corrupted database, for instance). Given this number, the availability of any component is then given by:

$$\mathbf{A} = \text{MTBF}/(\text{MTBF} + \text{MTTR})$$

Components in Series

The availability of a system that depends on a number of components connected together in series can be computed by multiplying the availability of the individual components. As an example, suppose you have a network backup system that's used to back up data on three file servers. If we ignore the issue of software reliability, the availability of the total backup will be equal to:

$$\mathbf{a}_{\mathbf{Total}} = \mathbf{a}_1 \times \mathbf{a}_2 \times \mathbf{a}_3 \times \mathbf{a}_{\mathbf{BS}} \times \mathbf{a}_{\mathbf{Net}}$$

where:

$\mathbf{a}_1,\mathbf{a}_2,\mathbf{a}_3$ = availability for file servers 1-3, respectively

$\mathbf{a}_{\mathbf{BS}}$ = availability of the back-up system

$\mathbf{a}_{\mathbf{Net}}$ = availability of the network

If the backup system and file servers each have an availability 99% and the network has an availability of 90% the total availability will be a total of:

$$\mathbf{a}_{\mathbf{Total}} = .99 \times .99 \times .99 \times .99 \times .90 = \mathbf{.87}$$

That is, the total reliability is just 87%. Notice that the governing factor is always the *least* reliable component, which will tend to reduce the reliability of the entire system, something that should be obvious from common sense in any case.

Redundancy

If you have a system with a certain number **n** of redundant components in which the operation of the system depends only on the correct functioning of one, then the overall availability will be:

$$\mathbf{a}_{\mathbf{Overall}} = \mathbf{1\text{-}((1\text{–}a_1) \times (1\text{–}a_2) \ldots (1\text{–}a_n))}$$

where **n** is the number of components in parallel

Suppose, for example, that you have a server that contains two mirrored disk drives, each of which has an MTBF of 10,000 hours and a mean time to repair of two hours. Availability of each drive will be over 99.98% but the availability of the mirrored pair will be:

$$\mathbf{a}_{\mathbf{Overall}} = \mathbf{1\text{–}((1\text{–}.9998)} \times \mathbf{(1\text{–}.9998))} = .9999999$$

or 99.99999%

The overall availability in this case is actually *higher* than the availability of any single component—exactly the opposite of the series case discussed above. This is the reason that the highest reliability systems are achieved by the maximum use of redundant components. Indeed, in the ultimate case, where one has to deal with systems that cannot be permitted to crash, one will typically run actual backup servers and employ mechanisms like the Windows NT Advanced Server's *directory replication*[5] feature to see that the data on one server is always duplicated on the second server.

All These Numbers Are Great—So What Do We Do with Them?

As we saw in Chapter 3, Windows NT includes some extremely sophisticated built-in system performance monitoring and event logging features. What we wish to suggest is that you maintain a continuous maintenance history on your system based on the information from the event log and the performance monitor. If you maintain this information over the life of your system you can apply to it the mathematics we have just described—and you will find that you then know a great deal more about the systems behavior than you would otherwise.

For example, you can, on a regular basis, conduct some simple performance tests on a system. First of all, examine event logs to note whether there have been any disk errors. If there have been any disk errors, these should be entered into a statistical log and the cause of the errors should be investigated. If you graph these disk errors over time, you are likely to find that they will fit the hardware reliability equation given earlier. As these errors begin to arise, you'll see that the reliability is decreasing with time—and at some point it's going to become apparent to you that if this trend continues, the component will fail. This is the time to replace the disk drive—*before* it fails.

Similarly you can maintain a record of overall system performance for a variety of components: the CPU, disks, network, and so on. This can be particularly valuable in two ways. First of all, just as with maintaining a record of information on the disk drive, it'll let you predict failures before they occur. But it also has another important advantage—the record can help you detect system bottlenecks and maximize throughput.

This is particularly important as networks grow. Initially, you may be able to simply stick network cards in PCs, link them together into an Ethernet, and assume that everything's going to work. But as the network becomes larger and larger, some inherent limitations of the hardware are going to start to show up. Ethernet has a maximum throughput (on conventional 10-base-2 or 10-base-T cabling) of ten million bits per second. It should be obvious, for instance, that if one continues to add machines to an Ethernet segment, you are eventually going to find that you are trying to push more than ten million bits down the wire each second. You can't do that. And you are going to find that your overall system performance will degrade. This is because of something called a queuing effect.

[5]See Chapter 7 for details on replication.

Queuing Effect and Performance Tuning

Queuing refers to the fact that in any kind of a shared service environment (such as a network) multiple simultaneous requests for access to the service will have to be *queued* —that is, suspended while they await a response. There will then be some average response time each request will experience before it can be responded to. The relationship between these factors is covered by the equation:

$$\mathbf{r} = \mathbf{n_s}/\mathbf{t}$$

where **r** is the response time, $\mathbf{n_s}$ is the average number of requests competing for service, and **t** is the overall throughput (responses per second) of the service. Obviously the response time increases as the number of requests increases.

This equation, for instance, governs the response time of a server with multiple clients competing for a response, say from a database server with multiple clients attempting to access it simultaneously. Response time will increase as the load on the server increases. If simple queuing effects apply (actual queuing models can become quite complex and while the mathematics involved are fascinating, they are far beyond the realm of this book), one can estimate the utilization of the system and the delay due to queuing according to a very simple model:

$$\mathbf{U} = \mathbf{r}/\mathbf{x}$$

where:

r is the rate of requests per second

x is the maximum throughput in transactions per second

Thus, if the number of requests per second is equal to the transactions per second, you have a utilization of 1.0 or 100%. The delay due to queuing will then be:

$$\mathbf{d} = (\mathbf{U}/\mathbf{x})/(1-\mathbf{U})$$

Total response time for the system will be the sum of the delay due to queuing plus the amount of time needed to process the request:

$$\mathbf{R} = \mathbf{d} + 1/\mathbf{x}$$

The *perceived* throughput at any workstation will then be equal to **1/R** (that is, users will see the system as slow because they see a slow response) although the actual system throughput is always going to be equal to the arrival rate (**r**). If you think about it this should be obvious: The system becomes fully loaded, then each workstation will experience a slowdown and will perceive the system as being slow when, in fact, the system is working at full capacity. That by itself is the single most important implication of the overall queuing equation for our purposes.

The other thing that's important to understand is that queuing effects occur for networks just as they do for servers. In effect, you can treat the LAN or WAN in a system as being a sort of server from the point of view of queuing delays. Again, bear in mind that the maximum throughput of an Ethernet is ten million bits per second. It should be obvious that the perceived response degrades as the number of requests on the system begins to approach ten million bits per second.

An example: if clients on a system generate fifty packets per second over a 1,000,000-bit-per-second network, and the packets have a mean size of 8192 bits (1 KB, standard for NetBEUI) the throughput will be:

$$\mathbf{x} = 1{,}000{,}000 / 8192$$

or 122.1 packets per second. Utilization will be:

$$\mathbf{U} = 50 / 122.1 = .41 \text{ or } 41\%$$

Then **d** will equal 6 milliseconds, and perceived throughput will be 71 packets per second. The significance of this is that although the total throughput to the network experiences is 122.1 packets per second, *perceived* throughput at any station is only 71 packets per second. This is key to understanding how low data rate lines in a WAN environment can become a bottleneck.

The Throughput Chain

Any network is inherently an end-to-end system. There is a "chain" of throughputs involved that extends from the client to the server. Consider a system in which each client CPU can process 1,000 transactions per second, the network interface cards can handle 1,000 packets per second, the LAN can carry 10,000 packets per second before saturating, routers can forward 5,000 packets per second, the WAN can handle 500 packets per second, and the server CPU can handle 5,000 transactions per second—but the server's only disk can perform just 50 I/O accesses per second. Then you have a chain extending from the client through the network interface to the LAN to the router to the WAN to the server to the disk—but the fastest that this overall system can work is only 50 transactions per second, assuming that a transaction requires one disk operation.

The server's disk drive is now the bottleneck for this system. If we upgrade the server's disk drive to something that can handle 3,000 I/O operations per second then the governing factor will be the next slowest link in the chain—the WAN which can only handle 500 packets per second. You get the point? It's important in examining the operation of an end-to-end system to examine the throughput of each component, looking for the slowest one, which is called a *bottleneck*.

The issue of Performance Tuning then is simply to find, and eliminate all bottlenecks—a subject covered in detail in the *Performance Tuning* section of Chapter 5.

For More Information

Renaud, Paul. (1993), *Introduction to Client / Server Systems*. New York: Wiley. ISBN: 0-471-57774-X. This is an *outstanding* text on maintenance and performance, as well as general LAN issues—in addition to providing good client / server coverage.

Jain, Raj. (1991), *The Art of Computer Systems Performance Analysis.* New York: Wiley. ISBN: 0-471-50336-3. A much deeper treatment of performance issues than Renaud, Jain gets deep into queing theory, simulation and modelling.

Fortier, Paul. (1992), *Handbook of LAN Technology (2nd Ed.).* New York: McGraw-Hill ISBN: 0-07-021625-8. Good modelling and simulation coverage, along with excellent general coverage of LANs from an engineering perspective.

Index

A

B

C

D

E

F

G

H

I

K

L

M

N

Q

R

S

T

U

V

W

X

Z